Lucy S. Dawidowicz was educated at Hunter College and
Columbia University in New York and studied East
European Jewish life at first hand at the Yivo Institute for
Jewish Research, formerly in Vilna, Poland. She now
teaches modern Jewish history at Yeshiva University.
Among her other publications are *The Golden Tradition:
Jewish Life and Thought in Eastern Europe, Holocaust
Reader, The Jewish Presence: Essays on Identity and History,
Politics in a Pluralist Democracy* (with Leon J. Goldstein),
and *For Max Weinreich on His Seventieth Birthday:
Studies in Jewish Language, Literature, and Society* (co-editor).

Lucy Dawidowicz

The War
against the Jews
1933-45

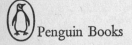 Penguin Books

Penguin Books Ltd, Harmondsworth,
Middlesex, England
Penguin Books, 625 Madison Avenue,
New York, New York 10022, U.S.A.
Penguin Books Australia Ltd, Ringwood,
Victoria, Australia
Penguin Books Canada Ltd, 2801 John Street,
Markham, Ontario, Canada L3R 1B4
Penguin Books (N.Z.) Ltd, 182–190 Wairau Road,
Auckland 10, New Zealand

First published in the U.S.A. 1975
Published in Great Britain by Weidenfeld & Nicolson 1975
Published in Pelican Books 1977

Copyright © Lucy S. Dawidowicz, 1975

Made and printed in Great Britain by
Hazell Watson & Viney Ltd, Aylesbury, Bucks
Set in Monotype Bembo

In memory of

Tuba (Tobtshe) Dawidowicz
Warsaw 1924–Warsaw Ghetto 1943

and

Zarek Dawidowicz
Warsaw 1927–Treblinka 1942 (?)

Two of six million

Contents

MAPS

Europe Under German Rule,
December 1942

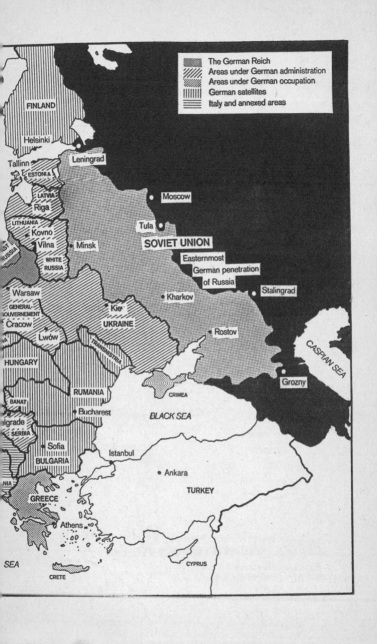

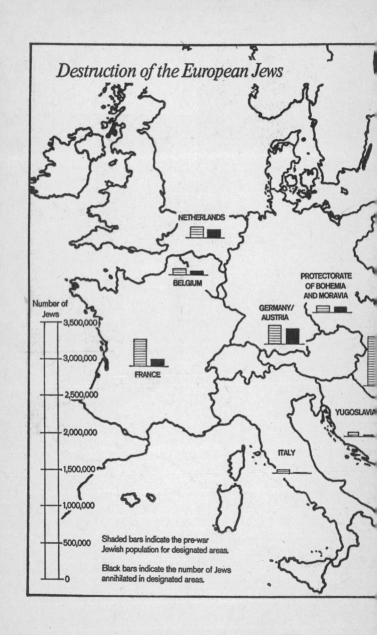

Destruction of the European Jews

Number of Jews

3,500,000
3,000,000
2,500,000
2,000,000
1,500,000
1,000,000
500,000
0

NETHERLANDS

BELGIUM

FRANCE

GERMANY/
AUSTRIA

PROTECTORATE
OF BOHEMIA
AND MORAVIA

YUGOSLAVIA

ITALY

Shaded bars indicate the pre-war
Jewish population for designated areas.

Black bars indicate the number of Jews
annihilated in designated areas.

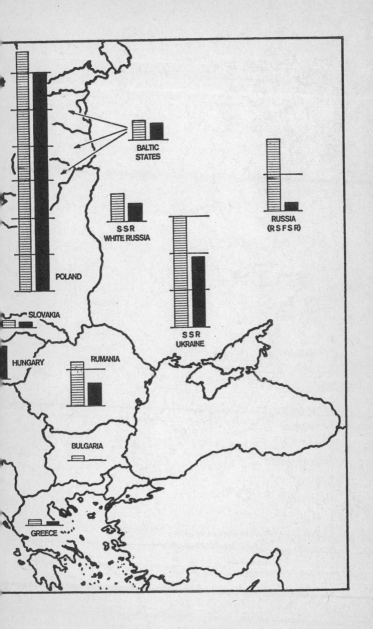

BALTIC
STATES

RUSSIA
(RSFSR)

S S R
WHITE RUSSIA

POLAND

S S R
UKRAINE

SLOVAKIA

RUMANIA

HUNGARY

BULGARIA

GREECE

Acknowledgements

This book had its genesis in a course I developed at the suggestion of Rabbi David Mirsky, Dean of Stern College for Women, Yeshiva University. I am grateful to Dean Mirsky for facilitating this undertaking and for his confidence in its successful completion.

The immense scope of the subject required assistance in research and translation. I am grateful to the following foundations whose grants during the last five years enabled me to obtain that assistance: Atran Foundation, Inc., and its vice-president, Mr Isaiah M. Minkoff; The Gustav Wurzweiler Foundation, Inc., and its president Dr Max Gruenewald; the John Slawson Fund for Research, Training and Education and Dr John Slawson; The Lucius N. Littauer Foundation and its president, Mr Harry Starr; the Memorial Foundation for Jewish Culture and its assistant executive director, Dr Jerry Hochbaum.

I am indebted to Miss Dina Abramowicz, librarian of the YIVO Institute for Jewish Research, and to Mr Harry J. Alderman, head of the Blaustein Library of the American Jewish Committee, for their unstinting helpfulness and expert advice. Mr Ezekiel Lifschutz, archivist of the YIVO Institute for Jewish Research, now retired, was courteous and accommodating. Mr Samuel L. Haber, executive vice-chairman of the American Jewish Joint Distribution Committee, kindly gave me permission to use that institution's archives and Mrs Rose Klepfisz, JDC's archivist, cheerfully and knowledgeably guided me through these massive records. Mr Milton Himmelfarb, director of the Information and Research Service of the American Jewish Committee, gave me permission to use the AJC's Records Center, and Mrs Ruth Rauch, in charge of those records, gave me every assistance. Dr Fred Grubel, secretary of the Leo Baeck Institute, was unfailingly helpful by giving me access to the Institute's unpublished collections and by sharing his wide store of knowledge in response to my many questions. Mr Hillel Kempinski, in charge of the Franz Kursky

Archives of the Jewish Labour Bund, and Mrs Sylvia Landress, head of the Zionist Library and Archives, were generous in helping me locate various unpublished materials in their collections.

Dr Hildegard von Kotze, archivist at the Institut für Zeitgeschichte in Munich, was most helpful in answering my inquiries and in providing me with copies of documents not available elsewhere. Mr Robert Wolfe, specialist for modern European history, and Mr John E. Taylor, assistant director of the modern military branch, both of the National Archives, were helpful in locating and providing me with copies of unpublished German documents which I requested. Mrs H. Czarnocka, honorary secretary of the Studium Polski Podziemnej in London, helped to trace documents of interest to me. I am indebted also for valuable data to Mr M. Mazor, director of the archives of the Centre de Documentation Juive Contemporaine in Paris; to Dr Eloisa Ravenna, secretary of the Centro di Documentazione Ebraica Contemporanea in Milan; and to Mme Luci Petrović, secretary of the Federation of Jewish Communities in Yugoslavia in Belgrade.

Dr Isaiah Trunk and Dr Lucjan Dobroszycki, both at the YIVO Institute, gave generously of their time and their vast fund of knowledge. Dr Friedrich Brodnitz, Mrs Chana Fryszdorf, Mr Milton Himmelfarb, Dr Ismar Schorsch and Dr Trunk read portions of the manuscript and I benefited from their corrections and advice. For intellectual stimulation of a high order I thank Dr Mortimer Ostow and the members of the ongoing Seminar on Jewish Response to Crisis, which he has conducted under the auspices of the Jewish Theological Seminary of America. My friend Rose Grundstein has encouraged me by her enthusiasm and dedication.

Above all, I owe this book to my husband Szymon, who gave me the courage to begin the work and the strength to complete it.

L.S.D.

The Subject:
Definitions and Contours

The annihilation of six million Jews, carried out by the German state under Adolf Hitler during the Second World War, has resisted understanding. The question persists: how could it have happened? That question embraces several questions, each charged with passion and moral judgement. They are:

1. How was it possible for a modern state to carry out the systematic murder of a whole people for no reason other than that they were Jews?
2. How was it possible for a whole people to allow itself to be destroyed?
3. How was it possible for the world to stand by without halting this destruction?

Part I of this book, 'The Final Solution', attempts to answer the first question. Part II, 'The Holocaust', attempts to answer the second. A partial answer or partial answers to the third question can be found in Appendix A, 'The Fate of the Jews in Hitler's Europe'.

'The Final Solution of the Jewish Question' was the code name assigned by the German bureaucracy to the annihilation of the Jews. The very composition of the code name, when analysed, reveals its fundamental character and meaning to the Germans who invented and used it. The term 'Jewish question', as first used during the early Enlightenment/Emancipation period in Western Europe, referred to the 'question' or 'problem' that the anomalous persistence of the Jews as a people posed to the new nation-states and the rising political nationalisms. The 'Jewish question' was, at bottom, a euphemism whose verbal neutrality concealed the user's impatience with the singularity of this people that did not appear to conform to the new political demands of the state.

Since a question demands an answer and a problem a solution, various answers and solutions were propounded to the 'Jewish question', by foes and even friends, that entailed the disappearance of the Jews as such – abandonment of the Jewish religion or its essential elements, of the Jewish language, Yiddish, of Jewish culture, Jewish uniqueness and separatism. The histories of Jewish emancipation and of European anti-Semitism are replete with proffered 'solutions to the Jewish question'. The classic illustration is the 'solution' offered by Constantine Pobyedonostsev, chief adviser to Tsar Alexander III, in 1881: one third of the Jews were to emigrate, one third to convert and one third to die of hunger.

To this concept that the National Socialists adopted they added one new element, embodied in the word 'final'. 'Final' means definitive, completed, perfected, ultimate. 'Final' reverberates with apocalyptic promise, bespeaking the Last Judgement, the End of Days, the last destruction before salvation, Armageddon. 'The Final Solution of the Jewish Question' in the National Socialist conception was not just another anti-Semitic undertaking, but a metahistorical programme devised with an eschatological perspective. It was part of a salvational ideology that envisaged the attainment of Heaven by bringing Hell on earth. 'The Devil is loose', Friedrich Reck-Malleczewen noted in his diary on 30 October 1942. The most important event of our time, André Malraux said, was *'le retour de Satan'*, citing the German system of terror.

To attain its heavenly Hell on earth the German dictatorship launched a war that engulfed the whole world. Over 35 million people were killed, more than half of them civilians. On the battlefields 1 out of every 22 Russians was killed, 1 out of every 25 Germans, 1 out of every 150 Italians and Englishmen, and 1 out of every 200 Frenchmen. The human cost of 2,191 days of war surpassed the losses of any previous war in the world. That war brought death to nearly 6 million Jews, to 2 out of every 3 European Jews. Though one third of them managed to survive, though the Jewish people and Judaism have outlived the Third Reich, the Germans nevertheless succeeded in irrecoverably destroying the life and culture of East European Jewry.

The Final Solution transcended the bounds of modern historical experience. Never before in modern history had one people made the killing of another the fulfilment of an ideology, in whose pursuit means were identical with ends. History has, to be sure, recorded terrible massacres and destruction that one people perpetrated against another, but all – however cruel and unjustifiable – were intended to achieve instrumental ends, being means to ends, not ends in themselves.

The German state, deciding that the Jews should not live, arrogated to itself the judgement as to whether a whole people had the right to existence, a judgement that no man and no state have the right to make. 'Anyone who on the basis of such a judgement', said Karl Jaspers, 'plans the organized slaughter of a people and participates in it, does something that is fundamentally different from all crimes that have existed in the past.'

To carry out this judgement, designated as the Final Solution, the German dictatorship involved and engaged the entire bureaucratic and functional apparatus of the German state and the National Socialist movement and employed the best available technological means. The Final Solution destroyed the East European Jews. In doing so, it subverted fundamental moral principles and every system of law that had governed, however imperfectly, human society for millennia.

In writing the history of the Final Solution, I approached the subject from the inside as best I could. Here the Germans are the actors and their acts are viewed through the lenses of German documents. In dwelling on Hitler's ideas about the Jews and on the development of modern German anti-Semitism, I have tried to show the intellectual and historical origins of the Final Solution. Throughout I tried to demonstrate the mutual influences and interplay of ideology and action, belief and programme, national character and political behaviour.

Part II, 'The Holocaust', describes the Jewish reponse to the Final Solution. 'The Holocaust' is the term that Jews themselves have chosen to describe their fate during the Second World War. At the most superficial level, the word 'holocaust' means a great destruction and devastation, but its etymological substratum interposes a specifically Jewish interpretation. The word derives from the Greek *holokauston*, the Septuagint's translation for the Hebrew *olah*, literally 'what is brought up', rendered in English as 'an offering made by fire unto the Lord', 'burnt offering', or 'whole burnt offering'. The implication is unmistakable: once again in their history the Jews are victims, sacrifices.

The Holocaust, then, becomes another link in the historic chain of Jewish suffering. The very word summons up the remembrance of the Jews in 1096 during the First Crusade. The chronicles and liturgical poetry of those days, in a striking concurrence, evoke the image of the Akedah, the Binding – or sacrifice – of Isaac, as the prefiguration of their own ordeals. For the Jews the Holocaust did not transcend history, but was part of the recurrent pattern of persecution that has been the Jewish historic experience. Still, within the perspective of Jewish history, the Holocaust is the most massive and disastrous catastrophe since the earliest days of that history. Even at the time of the greatest Jewish national trauma, the destruction of the Second Temple, the physical survival of the Jews was not in such jeopardy as during the Holocaust. In 70 C.E. only about one fourth of the Jews lived in Palestine, while the rest lived in the Diaspora. More Jews lived in Alexandria then than in Jerusalem. In 1939, in contrast, two thirds of the world's Jews lived in Europe and three fourths of them – half of all world Jewry – were concentrated in Eastern Europe.

The destruction of East European Jewry brought to an end the thousand-year-old culture of Ashkenazic Jewry that had originated in the Rhine Basin and that by 1939 was concentrated in Eastern Europe. It was a culture whose religious teachings and traditions defined its secular character and values. It was a culture whose language was Yiddish, the language in which Jewish males studied the Talmud, in which mothers sang lullabies and little children played games, in which merchants conducted business and preachers delivered sermons, in which shrews scolded and roughnecks cursed, in which young men courted their girls. Yiddish was a vehicle for a great religious and secular culture, and it generated a rich literature.

East European Jewry created a culture that venerated the *sefer*, the book of religious learning, but whose people laughed at themselves. It was a culture that put its people, familiar with poverty and hardship, on speaking terms with God. It was a culture unique in all Jewish history, and East European Ashkenazic Jewry, which fashioned that culture, was the wellspring of Jewish creativity for Jewish communities throughout the world.

Part II, 'The Holocaust', opens with a chapter about the German Jews in their encounter with National Socialism in the first stage of its rule. Thereafter, Part II focuses on the experiences of the East European Jews, mainly in Poland and Lithuania, because they were the most numerous of all European Jews, because they constituted a unique civilization and because Eastern Europe was the central locus of the Final Solution.

The primary task I set myself was to describe the responses of the organized Jewish community to the Final Solution in its several stages. I have stressed the role and functions of Jewish communal institutions and communal leadership at various levels in the re-ordered Jewish society under German occupation. To the best of my ability and within the limits set by the availability of sources, I have tried to delineate the varieties of Jewish communal policy as formulated and carried out in different communities and by different communal leaders at various levels, sometimes in harmony and sometimes at variance with each other, and to show wherever possible the responses of the masses to these policies. Consistently, I have used Jewish sources as the lenses through which to view the Jewish community and to analyse Jewish behaviour.

One impediment was the inadequacy of Jewish documentation, despite its enormous quantity. Holocaust documents were composed under extreme persecution, and they are the quintessential products of external censorship and self-imposed restraints. Jewish official documents that have survived reflect the writers' awareness of the omnipresent Germans and their all-seeing eyes. The absence of vital subjects from the records may be explained by the predicament of terror and censorship; yet, lacking evidence to corroborate or disprove, the historian will never know with certainty whether that absence is a consequence of an institutional decision not to deal with such matters or whether it was merely a consequence of prudential policy not to mention them. The terror was so great that even private personal diaries, composed in Yiddish or Hebrew, were written circumspectly, with recourse to Scripture and the Talmud as a form of esoteric expression and self-imposed reticence.

Survivor documentation, on the other hand, frequently suffers from subjectivity, bitterness and partisanship – commonplace and habitual defects of most historical records. These documents have a further shortcoming. For the most part, the experiences recounted by survivors bring to mind the adventures of Stendhal's Fabrizio del

Dongo at the Battle of Waterloo. Like him, they are never quite certain what great events they are witness to. Like him, they have just missed seeing the Emperor – in their case, they have been too distant from communal responsibility to be able to describe with any authority those critical situations at which significant decisions were made and policies framed for the Jewish community.

With the liquidation of the ghettos, Jewish communal existence came to an end. Some 5, perhaps 10, per cent of East European Jews lived a brief while longer in closed concentration/labour camps, but no formal Jewish communal institutions existed any more. A minuscule number of Jews, atomized individuals, managed to survive even the death camps, but their story is not the history of the Jewish community. For this reason this book closes with the liquidation of the ghettos.

Appendix A, 'The Fate of the Jews in Hitler's Europe', is an attempt to put on record the essential bare facts about the Jews in each European country. Each country is considered individually and its wartime status described. A sketch of that country's pre-war Jewish population follows, and then the course of the Final Solution in the country is briefly recounted. It was my intention here to provide, in a kind of historical shorthand, a summary account of the fate of the European Jews during the Second World War and, at the same time, within the limits of the presentation, to enable the reader to distinguish those political, historical, social and geographic factors that accounted for the different treatment accorded to the Jews in various countries.

This is not a value-free book. The very subject matter of the Final Solution precludes neutrality. In writing about a nation that transgressed the commandment 'Thou shalt not murder,' it is impossible to be what Charles Beard characterized as 'a neutral mirror'.

Whereas the Germans, in planning and executing the Final Solution, played the role of the Devil and his hosts, the Jews during the Holocaust were, alas, merely human, saints and sinners, imperfect earthlings. In writing about the Holocaust I have tried to avoid moral judgements, though I have not hesitated to describe demoralization. In discussing the deeds of the handful of Jewish leaders who have been charged by survivors and scholars with criminal behaviour, I have been persuaded by Professor Herbert Butterfield's view that the historian can never quite know men from the inside, because he can never carry his investigation into the interiority of their minds and hearts, where 'the final play of motive and the point of responsibility' are decided.

As best I could I have tried to present what actually happened. I strove to follow the two methods that Wilhelm von Humboldt perceived to be the historian's task in the approach to the historical truth: 'The first is the exact, impartial, critical investigation of events; the second is the connecting of the events explored and the intuitive understanding of them which could not be reached by the first means.'

Part 1
The Final Solution

1 The Jews in Hitler's Mental World

'If at the beginning of the War and during the War', Hitler wrote in the last chapter of *Mein Kampf*, 'twelve or fifteen thousand of these Hebrew corrupters of the people had been held under poison gas, as happened to hundreds of thousands of our very best German workers in the field, the sacrifice of millions at the front would not have been in vain.'[1]

Did the idea of the Final Solution originate in this passage, germinating in Hitler's subconscious for some fifteen years before it was to sprout into practical reality? The idea of a mass annihilation of the Jews had already been adumbrated by apocalyptic-minded anti-Semites during the nineteenth century. Yet even the most fanatic and uncompromising anti-Semites, when confronted with political actualities and social realities, invariably settled for an aggregation of exclusionary measures. Hitler did not. He succeeded in transforming the apocalyptic idea into concrete political action. The mass murder of the Jews was the consummation of his fundamental beliefs and ideological conviction.

The nexus between idea and act has seldom been as evident in human history with such manifest consistency as in the history of anti-Semitism. Jew-hatred is one of those 'unit-ideas', to use Arthur Lovejoy's phrase, with 'long life-histories of their own'. Yet not until Hitler's accession to power in Germany and his dominion over Europe had the abstract idea of Jew-hatred assumed so terrible a concrete and visible reality. Nor had anti-Semitism ever before been so obviously a product of a system of beliefs. For Hitler's ideas about the Jews were the starting place for the elaboration of a monstrous racial ideology that would justify mass murder whose like history had not seen before.

Only Hitler's followers took his ideas about the Jews seriously. His opponents found them too preposterous for serious consideration, too irrational and lunatic to merit reasonable analysis and rebuttal. Today, looking at his photographs, it seems easy to understand how Hitler could have been underestimated, disparaged. He was of medium height, with beady eyes and a comic moustache. The unmanageable cowlick of his pomaded hair became the burlesque symbol of unrestrained passion. He was a strutter and a posturer, 'one of those men without qualities', wrote Konrad Heiden, his face 'without radiance'.[2] Hermann Rauschning too characterized his look as lacking 'the brilliance and sparkle of genuine animation'. An authority on 'racial' biology described Hitler as he saw him in 1923: 'Face and head: bad race, mongrel. Low, receding forehead, ugly nose, broad cheekbones, small eyes, dark hair; facial expression, not of a man commanding with full self-control, but betraying insane excitement. Finally, an expression of blissful egotism.'[3]

'A raw-vegetable Genghis Khan', wrote Friedrich Percyval Reck-Malleczewen, observing Hitler without his usual bodyguard in a Munich restaurant in 1932. It would have been easy then, in the almost deserted restaurant, to shoot Hitler. 'If I had had an inkling of the role this piece of filth was to play, and of the years of suffering he was to make us endure, I would have done it without a second thought. But I took him for a character out of a comic strip and did not shoot.'[4]

A raving lunatic, a comic-strip character, a political absurdity. Yet his voice mesmerized millions, 'a guttural thunder', according to Heiden, 'the very epitome of power, firmness, command and will'. Was it the sheer physical quality of the voice that hypnotized them? Or was the charisma in the dark message of racial mastery and the rule of blood? Serious people, responsible people thought that Hitler's notions about the Jews were, at best, merely political bait for disgruntled masses, no more than ideological window-dressing to cloak a naked drive for power. Yet precisely the reverse was true. Racial imperialism and the fanatic plan to destroy the Jews were the dominant passions behind the drive for power.

Hitler's ideas about the Jews were at the centre of his mental world. They shaped his world view and his political ambitions, forming the matrix of his ideology and the ineradicable core of National Socialist doctrine. They determined the anti-Jewish policies of the German dictatorship from 1933 to 1945, and they furnished the authority for the murder of the Jews in Europe during the Second World War.

Few ideas in world history achieved such fatal potency. If only because these ideas had such consequences, they deserve serious analysis despite their irrationality, historical falsehood, scientific sham and moral loathsomeness.

Mein Kampf provides much of our knowledge about Hitler and his ideas. He wrote it in the prison at Landsberg, while serving a highly abbreviated term (11 November 1923–20 December 1924) of a five-year sentence for high treason in organizing the unsuccessful Munich Putsch. Graceless, prolix, disorganized, incoherent in parts, repetitious, *Mein Kampf* was written in the tradition of confessional biography, in which the hand of Destiny is clearly seen to be shaping the course of the writer's life. It is, above all, a self-aggrandizing document, in which the author is presented as intellectual nonpareil and political saviour. Nothing was to detract from this image of Hitler, and consequently he suppressed mention of persons or events that moulded and influenced him. As for his ideas, we can never really be confident that his descriptions in 1924 of the ideas he held in 1904 or 1908 or 1912 are honest, or whether he re-created his intellectual development swathed in legends. During his lifetime Hitler's champions and enemies furnished additional bits and pieces to the sketchy information about his early life. Subsequent scholarship has yielded a few more details to the portrait of the authentic Hitler. Still, much mystery surrounds his origins and early life.

Adolf Hitler was born on 20 April 1889, in the town of Braunau, on the Inn river, at the Austro–German border, the fourth child of Alois Hitler and Klara, his third wife, twenty-three years his junior.[5] Alois (1837–1903) was the illegitimate son of Maria Anna Schickelgruber (1795–1847), in whose name he had been christened. The identity of Adolf Hitler's paternal grandfather has remained an unravelled historical mystery of more than passing interest, since it raised doubts about Adolf Hitler's pure 'racial' ancestry. Nearly all the evidence is in dispute.

In 1842, when Alois was five years old, his mother married Johann Georg Hiedler (the family name variously spelled Hüttler, Hütler, Hitler). Alois, however, seems to have been brought up by Georg's younger brother, Johann Nepomuk, who, according to another version, was his real father. In 1876, when Georg was eighty-four years old, he formally acknowledged Alois, then thirty-nine, as his son, who, legitimated, took the name of his father, real or putative. Another version has it that with Georg long dead, Nepomuk managed to get the parish records changed, by bringing three witnesses to testify that they knew Georg had accepted Alois as his son.

A more fanciful version of Adolf Hitler's origins exists: the allegation that his paternal grandfather was Jewish. Its source was the confession by Hans Frank, governor general of German-occupied Poland, written while awaiting execution at Nuremberg. According to Frank, William Patrick Hitler, the son of Alois, Jr, Hitler's half-brother (by his father's second wife), had threatened in a letter to divulge Hitler's Jewish ancestry. Hitler asked Frank, then legal adviser to the NSDAP, confidentially to investigate the charge, which Frank claimed to have substantiated, that Maria Schickelgruber's child had been fathered by the nineteen-year-old son in a household, presumably Jewish, where she had been employed as a domestic. Post 1945 investigations of the local records indicate, however, that no Jews lived in that area at the time, and the story was probably groundless. Still, uncertainties about his own ancestry must have obsessed the man who made ancestry the measure of the Aryan man.

Adolf's father was a customs official in the Austrian civil service, and the family moved whenever his assignments were changed. Three years after Adolf's birth they moved to Passau, another border town. In 1894, when Adolf was five years old, they moved to Leonding, a suburb of Linz, where they finally stayed. Alois retired the next year and spent his time buying and selling farms, strolling about the neighbourhood, and socializing at the local tavern. His relations with his son Adolf were stormy and tense. An indifferent and indolent pupil, Adolf was, at his father's insistence, enrolled in the *Realschule* in Linz, a secondary school whose training would lead to a technical or business career. In sharp conflict with his father, Adolf wanted instead to become a painter, an artist. When Alois died in 1903, the pressure on Adolf ceased. Klara continued to draw her late husband's pension and Adolf continued his schooling.

The next year he was transferred out of the *Realschule* because of his poor scholastic record. He was enrolled in the *Staatsrealschule* at Steyr, where he boarded and which he left in 1905, with indifferent success, after completing four years of secondary school. The only two subjects in which he excelled were freehand drawing and gymnastics. He failed to take the final examinations and never received a diploma. Years later one of his teachers described him as lacking self-discipline, 'being notoriously cantankerous, willful, arrogant and bad-tempered'. When he returned home from Steyr, his mother sold the house at Leonding and moved with Adolf to Linz proper. Living on her monthly widow's pension and the proceeds of the sale of the house, she supported Adolf, who seemed to have no thought of settling down or looking for work.

In *Mein Kampf*, Hitler minimized the influences on him of his family, friends and general milieu in Linz. He said he did not remember having heard the word 'Jew' during his father's lifetime, characterizing Alois's views as 'more or less cosmopolitan'. There were just a few Jews in Linz, whom, Adolf said, he regarded merely as Germans of a different religion. He claimed that he 'did not so much as suspect the existence of an organized opposition to the Jews'. His boyhood friend August Kubizek remembered otherwise. Alois Hitler, he said, was a supporter of Georg von Schönerer, Pan-German nationalist and anti-Semite. One of Hitler's elementary school teachers was said to have been an open anti-Semite, and the *Realschule* had several teachers 'with decided anti-Semitic views'. According to Kubizek, Hitler himself was a confirmed anti-Semite as early as 1904. While attending the *Realschule* at Linz, he was reading the local anti-Semitic paper, *Linzer Fliegenden Blätter*. Furthermore, Linz was where Hitler discovered Wagner as composer and ideologue. He went to the theatre to hear Wagner, and in Linz he discovered Wagner's prose writings and no doubt read *Jews in Music* and the grandiloquent *Decay and Regeneration*. Wagner, Hitler would later write, stands besides Frederick the Great and Martin Luther: 'Whoever wants to understand National Socialist Germany must know Wagner.'

He visited Vienna briefly in 1906 and then managed to convince his doting mother to finance a lengthier trip there to fulfil his ambition of entering the Academy of Fine Arts. In October 1907 he submitted his drawings to the academy, but they were rejected as unsatisfactory. He stayed in Vienna, living on money sent by his mother, and applied again the following year to the academy. This time he was not even admitted to the test. Meanwhile his mother had developed breast cancer and was rapidly succumbing to the disease. On 21 December

1908 she died and Hitler came home for the funeral. A few weeks later he left Linz for good and returned to Vienna, where he would live in anonymity for four cheerless years.

These years in Vienna are the most obscure in Hitler's life. After he spent his modest inheritance and orphan's pension, he had to move into a doss-house. He joined forces with a Reinhold Hanisch, a tramp in the same lodgings. Hitler painted postcards, copying views of Vienna, which Hanisch peddled about town. In 1910 Hitler thought he was being cheated by Hanisch and brought a suit against him. Hanisch was put in jail and that broke up the partnership. Very little is known of Hitler's life during the next three years in Vienna, except that he continued to live the same miserable marginal existence that he later described as the unhappiest years of his life.

In *Mein Kampf* he set down the record of how he wanted the development of his intellectual life to appear. Vienna, Hitler said, transformed him into an anti-Semite. 'For me this was the time of the greatest spiritual upheaval I have ever had to go through. I had ceased to be a weak-kneed cosmopolitan and became an anti-Semite.' The apprenticeship in anti-Semitism that he had served in Linz was glossed over. Hitler wanted his discovery of the 'truth' to be wholly his own, untainted by any influence, especially a paternal one. Still, Vienna was far more decisive than Linz as the place where his ideas about Jews took shape and where he began to give serious attention to thoughts of race and racial biology.

Hitler dramatized his first confrontation with East European Jews: 'Once, as I was strolling through the Inner City, I suddenly encountered an apparition in a black caftan and black hair locks. Is this a Jew? was my first thought.' Observing the man, his next question was: 'Is this a German?' To find an answer, he turned, 'as always', to books: 'I bought the first anti-Semitic pamphlets of my life.' But he found the literature unsatisfying, for, he said, it presupposed knowledge or understanding of the Jewish question. Besides, the 'dull and amazingly unscientific arguments' were unconvincing. Only his own study, his own experience, his own 'slowly rising insights' brought him to an understanding of what the Jews were and of the need to combat them. That is, Hitler was saying, without the reinforcement of the then existent anti-Semitic movement, without prior influences from home, without benefiting from the plenitude of anti-

Semitic literature then in the public domain, he himself mastered the 'Jewish question' in the solitary genius of his mind. Vienna was for him, he wrote, 'the hardest, though most thorough school' of his life, where he obtained the foundations for 'a philosophy in general and a political view in particular', which remained with him for the rest of his life.

But outside influences were plainly at work upon him. In Vienna, in Hitler's time, anti-Semitic politics flourished, anti-Semitic organizations proliferated, anti-Semitic writing and propaganda poured forth in an unending stream. Despite his down-and-out doss-house existence, he was aware of much of the anti-Semitic doings. He was, for one, an avid, if unsystematic, reader. He tells us that he read the 'so-called world press', the *Neue Freie Presse* and the *Wiener Tageblatt*. Impressed at first, he soon came to see in them, he claimed, the ugly manipulation by the Jews. The hostile attitude the Viennese press took toward Germany particularly vexed him. On this subject, he admitted, 'I was forced to recognize that one of the anti-Semitic papers, the *Deutsches Volksblatt*, behaved more decently.' The *Deutsches Volksblatt* was a popular Viennese paper whose appeal was derived from its anti-Semitism, anti-capitalism, and anti-liberalism. Hitler was familiar, then, with the anti-Semitic press. Perhaps he read it regularly. In fact, by his own admission, he bought and read anti-Semitic pamphlets.

Which ones? Of the superabundance of such writings in those days in Vienna he probably sampled a variety. We know that he was for a time fascinated by the publications of Lanz von Liebenfels, an eccentric occultist-racist.[6] Between 1907 and 1910 Lanz published a series of pamphlets called *Ostara: Briefbücherei der blonden Mannesrechtler* (*Newsletters of the Blond Champions of Man's Rights*), in which he depicted the struggle between the blond Aryan heroes and the dark, hairy ape-men representing the lower races. All human existence revolved around this struggle, whose central burden was to preserve the purity of Aryan women from the demonic sexuality of the ape-men. *Ostara* was available at many newsstands, and Hitler had picked up a copy at the corner tobacconist's and then began to buy it regularly. In 1909 he sought out Lanz to get back issues, which Lanz, flattered, provided free of charge.

The ape-men in *Ostara* were not always explicitly identified as

Jews, perhaps because Lanz thought that the racial conflict as he depicted it was sufficiently lurid to gratify the erotic fantasies of his rootless, unemployed, down-and-out readers, most of whom, like Hitler, were unattached men. With regard to the Jews, Lanz wrote in an issue of *Ostara*: 'We would never dream of preaching pogroms, because they will come without encouragement.' Sterilization, the 'castration knife', would, Lanz held, solve the Jewish problem. The swastika was regarded as a symbol of racial purity, and *Ostara* dwelt tirelessly on the swastika's origins and secret meanings. Practising what he preached, Lanz hoisted the swastika over his castle, Burg Werfenstein, in 1907.

Besides *Ostara*, Lanz wrote pamphlets on race occultism, at least one of which was found in Hitler's private library: *Das Buch der Psalmen teutsch: Das Gebetbuch der Arisophen Rassenmystiker und Antisemiten* (*The Book of Germanic Psalms: Prayerbook of Ariosophic Race Mystics and Anti-Semites*). Another, *Das Gesetzbuch der Manu und die Rassenpflege* (*Manu's Book of Law and Race Cultivation*), published in 1908 and hence available to Hitler in those days, advocated that the 'mongrelized breed' of Jews and other inferior beings be wiped from the face of the earth. These horror tales of race defilement and the lurid depiction of the perils confronting Aryan womanhood obviously gratified the young Hitler, feeding his fears and obsessions – personal, sexual, racial.* *Ostara*'s influence – or its function as reinforcement – is evident in a much-quoted passage from *Mein Kampf*: 'With satanic joy in his face, the black-haired Jewish youth lurks in wait for the unsuspecting girl whom he defiles with his blood, thus stealing her from her people.'

Another racist pamphleteer whom Hitler read and perhaps also encountered was Guido von List, an indefatigable pseudo-scholarly occultist. During the years that Hitler lived in Vienna, List published several works, in which he glorified the ancient Germanic past and

* Some psychoanalysts have suggested that Hitler's hatred of the Jews was a projection of his self-hate and a consequence of guilt feelings for his dark and evil fantasies, and perhaps also for his putative Jewish ancestry. Still, not all self-haters became savage anti-Semites. People living in an anti-Semitic *milieu* – as Hitler did – already viewed Jews as diseased and filthy creatures, degenerate and corrupting, outsiders beyond fraternity or compassion. Since the society had already branded the Jews as loathsome pariahs, the Jews could then serve the symbolic and pathological needs of the obsessed and guilt-ridden.

extolled the Germanic wisdom in pagan nature which Christianity, regrettably, had enfeebled. The way to restore the true Germanic life force, List believed, was through the deciphering of ancient runic script and symbols. Like Lanz, List also regarded the swastika as one of the Teutonic mystic symbols. But, unlike Lanz, List gave political expression to his racial and ritual occultism. He was associated with Georg von Schönerer's anti-Semitic Pan-German movement and wrote for its publication. His political mysticism envisaged a leader who would be reincarnated from the Teutonic warrior heroes. When that leader came, List promised, the Reich would be divided into *Gaue* (districts), each with its own *Gauleiter* – archaic terminology that the Nazis revived when they came to power.

Hitler's Vienna was the locus of two major political movements – Schönerer's Pan-Germans and Karl Lueger's Christian Socials. By the time Hitler came to Vienna, Schönerer (1842–1921) was played out, but two decades earlier he had built the Pan-German movement into a significant force in and beyond Vienna, introducing anti-Semitism as a basic component in the ideology of Pan-Germanism.

Lueger was something else. For him, anti-Semitism had become the most successful of all political expedients, and his Christian Social party showed the greatest political viability of any anti-Semitic movement formed in Germany and Austria after the 1880s. The Viennese adored him and in election after election after 1895 returned him to the mayoralty (he did not take office till 1897 because both the Church and the Emperor refused to confirm his election).

In *Mein Kampf* Hitler discussed both Schönerer and Lueger at length and dismissed them both. Yet he confessed: 'When I came to Vienna, my sympathies were fully and wholly on the side of the Pan-German tendency.' Those sympathies had been formed in Linz, for when Hitler came to Vienna, Schönerer was then past sixty-five, a has-been, his movement torn by ideological differences and divided over tactics and strategy, impotent before Lueger's irresistible personality and pragmatic politics. But Schönerer had pioneered in legitimating anti-Semitism in Austrian politics. Still, Hitler is silent about any involvement on his part with the Pan-Germans. He devotes over twenty pages in *Mein Kampf* to the errors and misjudgements committed by the Pan-Germans. But he concedes, in one paltry sentence, that they were right on one point: the anti-Semitism of the

Pan-German movement 'was based on a correct understanding of the importance of the racial problem, and not on religious ideas'. The laconism is understandable. Any elaboration on the 'correct' anti-Semitic doctrines of the Pan-German movement would expose Hitler's intellectual and ideological borrowings.

As for Karl Lueger's Christian Social movement, Hitler praised its tactics but condemned its 'wrong' approach to anti-Semitism and its disinterest in German nationalism. Lueger, he believed, did not properly understand the 'Jewish danger', and his anti-Semitism was flawed because it 'was based on religious ideas instead of racial knowledge'. That, Hitler thought, was no way to combat the Jews: 'If the worst came to the worst, a splash of baptismal water could always save the business and the Jew at the same time.' The Christian Socials, Hitler asserted, engaged in 'sham anti-Semitism'. Hitler had a point. Lueger, the master of pragmatic politics, regarded anti-Semitism primarily as a political tactic rather than an evangelistic doctrine. His classic statement that must have been familiar to Hitler was *'Wer Jude ist, das bestimme ich'* ('Who is a Jew, that I decide').

Hitler never mentions that he belonged to any political party or organization in Vienna. Yet, given his ideas, it seems strange that he did not seek out some kindred group, or even stumble upon one of the numerous societies that made anti-Semitism the centre of their activity. As a matter of fact, Kubizek asserted that 'one day in 1908' Hitler came into their room with the announcement: 'Hey! Today I became a member of the anti-Semitic Bund and I enrolled you too.' Perhaps indeed Hitler did drift into some small anti-Semitic group, composed of down-and-outers like himself, misfits and malcontents who gathered to talk about the vile conspiracies afoot in Vienna for which the Jews were responsible. Perhaps it was a group that failed to recognize or acknowledge Hitler's abilities. 'In my little circle', Hitler writes in *Mein Kampf*, 'I talked my tongue sore and my throat hoarse', but to no avail. But, he confesses, 'speaking in the narrowest circles', he gained experience: 'I learned to orate less.'

But perhaps Hitler deliberately failed to mention any organizational affiliations he may have had because he wanted to preserve the classic legend of the man in the making, the political leader who reaches political maturity, while having protected his political virginity. 'Today it is my conviction that in general ... a man should not engage in public political activity before his thirtieth year,' he wrote in *Mein Kampf*. 'Otherwise he runs the risk of either having to change his former position on essential questions, or . . . of clinging to a view which reason and conviction have long since discarded.' Hitler was exactly thirty when he joined the Deutsche Arbeiterpartei in Munich in 1919.

What he 'learned' about Jews in the Vienna period, as recorded in a brief span of ten pages of *Mein Kampf* ('Years of Study and Suffering in Vienna'), is a mere foreshadowing of the ideas to come. Images of the Jew as unclean predominate: 'unclean dress', 'physical uncleanness'. Jews were at the heart of everything that was diseased. They were to blame for prostitution in Vienna and the white-slave traffic. (Psycho-analysts suggest here a projection of his guilt feelings about his sexual fantasies.) He had 'discovered' that Jews dominated the liberal press in Vienna and the city's cultural and artistic life, that they were behind the Social Democratic movement – Marxism. Triumphantly he had at last found an answer to the original question he had posed about the Jew: 'The Jew was no German.'

With this intellectual baggage, the claptrap of the conventional anti-Semitism of the time, and deep fears of political democracy, Hitler left Vienna in May 1913 and came to Munich, the Mecca of Germandom.

He arrived in Munich, a rootless young man of twenty-four, without friends, without family, without career or occupation, in a restless search for his identity or, as he would have put it, his Destiny.

He found a room with a tailor's family in a working-class quarter of Munich and continued the same hand-to-mouth existence he had led in Vienna, peddling sketches and drawings. He continued the anti-Semitic racist 'studies' he had begun in Vienna, reading the papers and pamphlets, 'observing'. He seems to have become more aggressive, more confident, speaking publicly in taverns and beer cellars. He had already cast himself as prophet: 'In the years 1913 and 1914, I, for the first time in various circles which today in part faithfully support the National Socialist movement, expressed the conviction that the question of the future of the German nation was the question of destroying Marxism.'

What various circles? Hitler makes them appear to have been more than a casual congregation of beer drinkers in a tavern. Did he perhaps belong to a National Socialist forerunner group? Of the various nationalist and anti-Semitic groups in Munich there were at least two proto-Nazi organizations he might have belonged to or frequented. The Germanen- und Wälsungsorden (Order of Teutons and Volsungs), founded in 1912 as a Masonic-style racist society, is a possibility. One of its offshoots or branches was called Armanenorden, and the inscription to Hitler found in a book in his private library supports the idea of such membership. It regarded its central function to be the struggle against the 'secret Jewish conspiracy'. The Germanenorden was replete with Teutonic vocabulary and symbols; its journal *Runen* was decorated with swastikas.

Another group that Hitler could have joined would have been the local Munich branch of Theodor Fritsch's Reichshammerbund, a minuscule network of nineteen discussion and propaganda groups throughout Germany, closely associated with the Germanenorden. As for Fritsch, he was the grand old man of anti-Semitic propaganda and it is inconceivable that Hitler could have failed to have read his classic work, *Antisemiten-Katechismus* (*Anti-Semites' Catechism*), later entitled *Handbuch der Judenfrage*, which went through innumerable editions.

Still, if Hitler actually ever belonged to any group, he made no lasting associations. In later years no one came forward with reminiscenes that could locate him in any specific anti-Semitic organization. Though *Mein Kampf* indicates that he had become more confident of himself, and had found places to frequent that were attuned to his ideas, he still appeared to have retained the characteristics of an eccentric loner.

The assassination of Ferdinand at Sarajevo unleashed the First World War, and the war unleashed the pent-up nihilistic impulses that were raging within Hitler: 'The sense of approaching catastrophe turned at last to longing: let Heaven at last give free rein to the fate which could no longer be thwarted.'

On 1 August 1914, the declaration proclaiming war was read in Munich's Odeons Platz before a flag-waving, anthem-singing assembled mass. A photograph that later came to light showed Hitler in the crowd, eyes popping, mouth open, wildly exultant. Two days later, he submitted a petition to Ludwig III, the last king of Bavaria, to join a Bavarian regiment. The request was approved. 'For me, as for every German, there now began the greatest and most unforgettable time of my earthly existence.'*

He fought in France, was wounded, received the Iron Cross, Second Class, returned to the front, was wounded a second time. Then, fighting at the front again, he was promoted to lance corporal, and fought again in France. In October 1918, blinded in a British gas attack, he was sent to a military hospital. That last year he received the Iron Cross, First Class, a decoration seldom given to a soldier of his low rank, though no one knows for what act of bravery it was presented. While at the hospital, he witnessed the Bavarian revolution of November 1918, led by Kurt Eisner, the overthrow of the monarchy, the armistice and the creation, in weakness and indecision, of the Weimar Republic – in his mind, all the work of the Jews.

It was then, Hitler recollected, that he decided to go into politics. He returned to Munich, where the following April he saw the establishment of a Soviet republic, and then, within a month, its suppression in blood by the Reichswehr. He got a job as educational officer, the first real job he ever had, in the Press and Propaganda Office of the Political Department of the District Army Command in Munich. The department's function was to indoctrinate Reichswehr recruits on the dangers of radicalism. Hitler had become an employee in the very centre of the military apparatus that would help undermine the new republic. He was called on to submit reports on various political organizations active in the Munich area. In 1919 he was assigned to cover a newly formed group called the Deutsche Arbeiterpartei (German Workers' Party). He joined the group. On 24 February 1920, its name was changed to Nationalsozialistische Deutsche Arbeiterpartei (NSDAP), when the new twenty-five-point programme that Hitler had drafted was adopted.

In the immediate post-war years in Munich Hitler's social life changed drastically from his pre-war solitariness. He was in contact with several circles of like-minded people and those associations gave him certitude and reassurance. Under a variety of influences – people, books and pamphlets – his ideas about race and about Jews

*cf. Friedrich Meinecke, *The German Catastrophe*: 'The exaltation of spirit experienced during the August days of 1914 . . . is one of the most precious, unforgettable memories of the highest sort' (p. 25).

crystallized. He had come to Munich with much of his anti-Jewish racist ideology already formed. He had emerged from the war still more politically paranoid, wildly blaming the Jews for the *Dolchstoss*, for that treacherous stab-in-the-back that made the Germans lose the war. Still, the influences in Munich were decisive, for they would make it possible for him to cast his ideas into one coherent system. One group with which he early came into contact was the Thule Society, a conspiratorial front for the post-war incarnation of the Germanenorden, which was involved in assassination attempts on Eisner and the leaders of the Munich Soviet. Besides counter-revolutionary violence, the Thule Society engaged in Volkist racist propaganda. Its members included Rudolf Hess, who was to become Hitler's most slavish follower; Karl Harrer, a co-founder of the Deutsche Arbeiterpartei; and Dietrich Eckart, an important influence on Hitler in those early Munich days.

Eckart (1868–1923) was the one man whom Hitler acknowledged as mentor and teacher, closing the second volume of *Mein Kampf* with a tribute to him: 'That man, one of the best, who devoted his life to the awakening of his, our people, in his writings and his thoughts and finally in his deeds.' Eckart, in his rootlessness and agitated mental state, was an elder version of Hitler, but was more Bohemian, addicted to alcohol and drugs. An unsuccessful playwright, he blamed the Jews for his failure. During the war he moved to Munich, barely managed to control his addictions, and became the bard of the Volkist movement. In 1919 he began publishing *Auf gut Deutsch*, a weekly replete with Volkist anti-Semitism, continuing until early 1921, when Hitler appointed him editor of the *Völkischer Beobachter*. One of Eckart's pamphlets, *Der Bolschewismus von Moses bis Lenin – Zwiegespräch zwischen Adolf Hitler und mir* (*Bolshevism from Moses to Lenin – Dialogue Between Adolf Hitler and Me*), published posthumously, has been adduced as an example of Eckart's influence on Hitler's ideas prior to *Mein Kampf*.

Eckart took Hitler under his wing, showed him the ropes, introduced him to influential and wealthy nationalists and proto-Nazis. In 1920 Eckart took Hitler with him on a flight to Berlin to join up with the right-wing Kapp *Putsch*, just before it collapsed. But Eckart's most lasting contribution to Hitler's intellectual development was merely coincidental. It was he who introduced Alfred Rosenberg to Hitler.

Rosenberg, the Baltic German whom Hitler would later ridicule and despise, enlarged Hitler's intellectual horizons, stretching his concepts beyond the borders of Germany. Rosenberg was one of those many Russian émigrés from the Bolshevik Revolution who imported into Western Europe the anti-Semitic notions of Tsarist Russia's Black Hundreds ('beat the Jews and save Russia') and commingled the anti-Semitism of Russia's darkest reaction with the anti-Semitism of Germany's paranoid nationalism. Rosenberg was born into a family of middle-class German Balts in 1893, in Reval (Tallinn), a Hanseatic city that since the early eighteenth century had been part of the Russian empire. In 1910 he was admitted to the Institute of Technology in Riga, where he studied architecture. In 1915, when the German front advanced, the institute was evacuated to Moscow, and Rosenberg went along with the complement of faculty and students. In January 1918 he received his diploma and returned home. His world collapsed when the revolution erupted. He started his peregrinations and finally left Russia with the retreating German army that had been in occupation.

When Rosenberg came to Munich, his interests were no longer cultural, but political – the politics of reaction and counter-revolution. Like many another Russian émigré, he had brought with him a booklet that utterly possessed him: the *Protocols of the Elders of Zion*. An implausible forgery concocted by the Tsarist secret police at the turn of the century, it purported to disclose the secret plans of the so-called international Jewish conspiracy for world domination. (It was 'incomparably' done, Hitler was to write in *Mein Kampf*.) The *Protocols* first appeared in German in 1920 and was constantly being reprinted thereafter. Rosenberg made something of a name for himself as a German commentator on the *Protocols*, writing innumerable articles and pamphlets on the subject.

His higher education, his penchant for wide-ranging philosophic schemas and the scope of his philosophic reading admirably equipped Rosenberg for the role of Hitler's intellectual mentor. From nineteenth-century West European thought – Fichte, Schopenhauer, Nietzsche, Gobineau and Houston Stewart Chamberlain – Rosenberg took those ideas of nation, Volk, nationalism, race, the rise and fall of civilizations, and conjoined them all with the crude and superstitious anti-Semitic and anti-Bolshevik ideas that the Russian émigrés had been nurtured on in their mother country. Chamberlain, Rosenberg confessed years later, was 'the strongest positive impulse in my youth', and it is no surprise that Rosenberg was said to have prepared, for Hitler's easy study, excerpts from Chamberlain's *Die Grundlagen des neunzehnten Jahrhunderts (Foundations of the Nineteenth Century)*.

Russian-speaking and authoritative about Russian culture and politics, Rosenberg became Hitler's mentor also on Russia and Bolshevism. He inducted Hitler into the domain of international relations and prepared him for the geopolitical concepts he would pick up from Rudolf Hess and Hess's teacher and friend, Karl Haushofer. Haushofer, general turned professor, probably introduced Hitler to the concept of 'space as a factor of power', but Rosenberg elaborated the idea of *Lebensraum* (living space) which was to become a cornerstone of National Socialist ideology and one of the chief objectives of Germany's foreign policy. Those early days in Munich were no doubt Rosenberg's finest. Hitler would never again regard him so seriously.

While the international aspects of National Socialist ideology were still germinating within him, Hitler's general ideas about the Jews were fixed by 1920. In a letter, dated 16 September 1919 and written at the request of his military superior in the Press and Propaganda Office, in reply to one Adolf Gemlich, who asked for enlightenment on the Jewish question, Hitler set forth some of the ideas that in *Mein Kampf* he claimed to have already discovered in Vienna.[7] 'Anti-Semitism as a political movement', he wrote, 'cannot and should not be determined by emotional factors, but on the contrary by an understanding of the facts.' The 'facts', he continued, are that 'in the first instance, Jewry is without question a race and not a religious fellowship'. He then expatiated on the alleged Jewish single-minded pursuit of money and power, touching on the already classic anti-Semitic notion that Jews dominate, falsify and exploit the press. 'The effect of Jewry will be racial tuberculosis of nations.' (In *Mein Kampf*, in the same context, he wrote: 'It was no accident that man mastered the plague more easily than tuberculosis.')

From his analysis, Hitler concluded that anti-Semitism grounded merely in emotion would find its ultimate outlet in pogroms. That was not enough.

Rational anti-Semitism, however, must lead to a systematic legal opposition and elimination of the special privileges which Jews hold, in contrast to the other aliens living among us (aliens' legislation). Its final objective must unswervingly be the removal [*Entfernung*] of the Jews altogether.

That paragraph carries, in the post-Auschwitz world, a staggering freight. It prefigures the political realities of the German dictatorship under Hitler, when the Jews were deprived of all rights systematically and 'legally', and then 'removed altogether', the ambiguity of the word 'removal' now more apparent than it was in 1919.

Hitler made his first public speech at a meeting of the Deutsche Arbeiterpartei on 13 November 1919, in a Munich beer cellar, and soon began to attract large audiences. Invariably he held forth on Germany's defeat in the war, which he blamed on Jewish treachery. On 29 April 1920 the subject of his address was 'Jewry', and according to the summary in an army political report, he concluded with a promise: 'We will carry on the struggle until the last Jew is removed from the German Reich.'

On 13 August 1920 he spoke at an NSDAP public meeting in a large hall on the topic 'Why Are We Anti-Semites?', the text of which has recently been published.[8] That speech differed in one respect from *Mein Kampf* in that it was directed towards working people and stressed the need for social and economic reform. Exalting labour, Hitler followed an old anti-Semitic tradition, asserting that Jews degraded and exploited labour. His evidence was the Pentateuchal injunction: 'In the sweat of thy face shalt thou eat bread,' which he interpreted to mean that the Jews regarded labour as 'a curse from God'. But in addressing himself to the subject of race and of Jews, the speech laid out the basic concepts that he was to develop in *Mein Kampf*.

He emphasized the need for a political organization to combat the Jews. It was not enough, he claimed, to deprive them of their economic power. The campaign for social reform must be accompanied by a struggle against 'the opponents of any social measures: Jewry'. The solution to the Jewish question must be 'removal

[*Entfernung*] of the Jews from our nation, not because we would begrudge them their existence – we congratulate the rest of the world on their company – but because the existence of our own nation is a thousand times more important to us than that of an alien race'.

During his enforced political inactivity in Landsberg prison, Hitler undertook to put his ideas together in *Mein Kampf,* which was autobiography, ideological doctrine and party manual all in one. In *Mein Kampf* he expounded on race as the central principle of human existence and explicated the relationship, since the start of time, between the two world adversaries – the Aryans and the Jews. 'The racial question', he wrote, 'gives the key not only to world history, but to all human culture,' for, he believed, 'in the blood alone resides the strength as well as the weakness of man'. All 'great questions of the day' he held to be momentary and derivative: only 'the question of racial preservation of the nation' was determinative, only that was significant as a causal factor in the rise and fall of civilization. An understanding of the 'Jewish problem' was a prerequisite for an understanding of the racial problem. The 'resurrection of Germany' would never be achieved 'without the clearest knowledge of the racial problem and hence of the Jewish problem'.

The 'Aryan' race was the 'bearer of human cultural development' and, consequently, 'human culture and civilization' are inseparably bound up with the presence of the 'Aryan'. The 'Aryans', therefore, by their nature, their 'blood', were chosen to rule the world. The very existence of world civilization depended on maintaining and safeguarding the purity of the 'Aryan' race:

What we must fight for is to safeguard the existence and reproduction of our race and our people, the sustenance of our children and the purity of our blood, the freedom and independence of the fatherland, so that our people may mature for the fulfilment of the mission allotted it by the creator of the universe.

The state, according to Hitler, existed merely as a means to an end – the preservation of the racial community. States that did not serve that purpose were 'misbegotten, monstrosities'. The Volkist state 'must set race in the centre of all life', for it is thus acting as 'the guardian of a millennial future'. The mission of the German people is the formation of such a Volkist state, which will have *"the task, not only of assembling and preserving the most valuable stocks of basic racial elements in this people, but slowly and surely of raising them to a dominant position"*.

But the obstacle, or threat, to the fulfilment of this racial millennium is the Jew: 'The mightiest counterpart to the Aryan is represented by the Jew.' In Hitler's system, the 'Aryans' represented the perfection of human existence, whereas the Jews were the embodiment of evil. *"Wer kennt den Jude, kennt den Teufel,"* the saying went ('Whoever knows the Jew, knows the Devil'). Indeed, Hitler wrote, the 'vileness' of the Jew is so gigantic 'that no one need be surprised if among our people the personification of the Devil as the symbol of all evil assumes the living shape of the Jews'. The Jew as outsider, as the Other, had been transformed into the ultimate evil.

The vileness of the Jew, he claimed, resided in the blood of the race and was evident in the Jew's physical, mental, cultural being. This vileness, Hitler declared, had permeated nearly every aspect of modern society. Over and over again he kept describing the Jews in terms of filth and disease. 'If the Jews were alone in this world, they would stifle in filth and offal.' Jews, he asserted, were at the centre of every abscess, were 'germ-carriers', poisoning the blood of others but preserving their own. The Jews were, Hitler said, 'a ferment of decomposition', quoting a phrase used by Theodor Mommsen which, out of context, had become an anti-Semitic platitude. The depiction of the Jews as the carriers of filth and disease and, hence, of death and destruction, goes back in the history of anti-Semitism to the Middle Ages, when Jews were accused of spreading the plague and poisoning the wells. As late as the seventeenth century, a pestilence in Vienna was readily explained: 'It is well known that such pestilential epidemics are caused by evil spirits, by Jews, by gravediggers and by witches.' Hitler accused the Jews particularly of sexual defilement and even blamed them for the presence of syphilis in post-war Germany. Nor did Hitler disregard cultural pollution: 'Was there any form of filth or profligacy, particularly in cultural life, without at least one Jew involved in it?' The 'poison' of the press allegedly controlled by the Jews 'was able to penetrate the bloodstream of our people'.

From the concept of the Jew as parasite, vampire, bloodsucker, contaminating the Aryan race, it was but a small step to the Jew as figurative bloodsucker in the financial and economic spheres: 'The spider was slowly beginning to suck the blood out of the people's pores' through the war corporations. That image had its source in the leftist anti-Semitic stereotype of the mid- and late-nineteenth century.

How had the Jews succeeded in insinuating themselves into the body of the Aryan race? By gigantic fraud and deception, Hitler said, by 'the first and greatest lie', that the Jews are 'a religious community while actually they are a race – and what a race!' As Hitler saw it, 'the Mosaic religion is nothing other than a doctrine for the preservation of the Jewish race'. He believed that the Jews had no language or culture of their own, that they sapped and drained other cultures and races so as ultimately to destroy them. That way, Hitler maintained, the Jews would achieve dominion over the world: "*It is the inexorable Jew who struggles for his domination over the nations.*"

The Jews had many conspiratorial techniques and vehicles for achieving world mastery, Hitler said, and in modern society these were Freemasonry, the press, democracy, parliamentarianism, the trade union movement, Marxism and Social Democracy. As for democracy, he held that 'only the Jew can praise an institution which is as dirty and false as he himself'. 'The Jewish doctrine of Marxism', Hitler contended, rejects 'the aristocratic principle of Nature'. The goal of Marxism 'is and remains the destruction of all non-Jewish national states'. Marxism itself, Hitler believed, 'systematically plans to hand the world over to the Jews'.

He did not have to scour long for evidence. The best proof for his argument was what had happened in Russia, or rather to Russia. Hitler's association of the Jews with Russian Bolshevism – an idea fostered and insisted on by Rosenberg – was, in its delusional conclusion, more original than his other ideas about Jews and race that derived from the ample sources of European anti-Semitism and racial doctrine. That the Jews were the revolutionaries *par excellence*, the masterminds of the Bolshevik Revolution – that was nothing new. The reality of Leon Trotsky and the forgery of the *Protocols* documented that charge to the satisfaction of most anti-Semites. But Hitler went beyond this and 'penetrated' beneath the surface of the conspiracy:

'*In Russian Bolshevism we must see the attempt undertaken by the Jews in the twentieth century to achieve world domination*.'' All Russia, he believed, had somehow become captive of the Jews. Schooled by Rosenberg, Hitler had concluded that the Slavs were an inferior race, incapable of building a state. For centuries, Hitler explained, 'Russia drew nourishment' from the 'Germanic nucleus of its upper leading strata'. But those strata, 'exterminated and extinguished', were then replaced by the Jews. (A similar fate, he warned, faced Germany, unless it would show sufficient national will to resist.) Since the Russians, according to Hitler's view, could never by themselves shake off Jewish domination, the Russian empire must necessarily collapse. Having reached this point in the development of his ideas about Russia, Hitler then elaborated his doctrines of race and space that culminated in his foreign-policy programme for a National Socialist Germany. Spurning with contempt the suggestion that Germany ought to conclude an alliance with the Soviet Union, Hitler solemnly declared: '*The fight against Jewish world Bolshevization requires a clear attitude towards Soviet Russia. You cannot drive out the Devil with Beelzebub*.'' (That metaphor was one of Hitler's favourites all his life, but he used it expediently. In a speech on 6 April 1920 he was reported to have said that in order to achieve the National Socialist goal of extirpating the evil – the Jews, that is – root and branch, 'every means is justified, even when we must ally ourselves with the Devil'.9)

Mein Kampf is a vision of the apocalyptic conflict between the Aryans and the Jews, of the two world systems struggling for dominion. It was his own Manichaean version of the conflict between good and evil, between God and the Devil, Christ and the Antichrist. He saw himself as the Messiah who would bring deliverance from the Devil: 'Hence today I believe that I am acting in accordance with the will of the Almighty Creator: *by defending myself against the Jew, I am fighting for the work of the Lord*.'' Some years later Hitler told Rauschning: 'We are God's people.' He repeated what he had written in *Mein Kampf*: 'Two worlds face one another – the men of God and men of Satan! The Jew is the anti-man, the creature of another god. He must have come from another root of the human race. I set the Aryan and the Jew over and against each other.'10

The Jews inhabited Hitler's mind. He believed that they were the source of all evil, misfortune and tragedy, the single factor that, like some inexorable law of nature, explained the workings of the universe. The irregularities of war and famine, financial distress and sudden death, defeat and sinfulness – all could be explained by the presence of that single factor in the universe, a miscreation that disturbed the world's steady ascent towards well-being, affluence, success, victory. A saviour was needed to come forth and slay the loathsome monster. In Hitler's obsessed mind, as in the delusive imaginings of the medieval millenarian sectarians, the Jews were the demonic hosts whom he had been given a divine mission to destroy.

All his life Hitler was seized by this obsession with the Jews. Even after he had murdered the Jews, he had still not exorcized his Jewish demons. At 4.00 a.m. on 29 April 1945, the last day of his life in the Berlin bunker, he finished dictating his political testament. His last words to the German people were: 'Above all I charge the leaders of the nation and those under them to scrupulous observance of the laws of race and to merciless opposition to the universal poisoner of all peoples, international Jewry.'[11]

The question continues to oppress us: how could a man with this poor baggage of deranged ideas and prejudices become Chancellor of Germany?* How was it possible that a state whose people and culture ranked high in the world's civilization should have entrusted its fate to this deluded man who believed that he had been chosen to lead a holy war against the Jews?

Many answers have been given and perhaps many are needed, for no single theory can satisfactorily explain Hitler's phenomenal success with the German people. They were mesmerized by his voice, and they responded to his message. Was it because their moral sense, at

---

*Historians interested in Hitler's psychobiography put another question: what made Hitler an anti-Semite? Their search to establish the motivation for Hitler's anti-Semitism (which they look for in his personal life and psychology) may have a clinical interest for the psychoanalyst and titillate the general reader, but it seems to me irrelevant, by-passing more important historical and political questions. Thousands of Hitler's contemporaries in Central Europe were being shaped and developed as anti-Semites. Their psychological motivations are of relatively little interest to the historian, for they did not effect the course of history. Hitler's motivations – e.g., his putative Jewish origin – was not nearly as significant as his ideology and his programme, that is, his beliefs and intentions.

least with regard to the Jews, had become atrophied under the effect of generations of virulent anti-Semitism? Had the German people already become mithridatized by anti-Semitic poison, so that they had become immune even to Hitler's deadly brand? Was it because he spoke for them?

2 Anti-Semitism
in Modern Germany

A line of anti-Semitic descent from Martin Luther to Adolf Hitler is easy to draw. Both Luther and Hitler were obsessed by a demonologized universe inhabited by Jews. 'Know, Christian,' wrote Luther, 'that next to the devil thou hast no enemy more cruel, more venomous and violent than a true Jew.' Hitler himself, in that early dialogue with Dietrich Eckart, asserted that the later Luther – that is, the violently anti-Semitic Luther – was the genuine Luther. Luther's protective authority was invoked by the Nazis when they came to power, and his anti-Semitic writings enjoyed a revival of popularity. To be sure, the similarities of Luther's anti-Jewish exhortations with modern racial anti-Semitism and even with Hitler's racial policies are not merely coincidental. They all derive from a common historic tradition of Jew-hatred, whose provenance can be traced back to Haman's advice to Ahasuerus. But modern German anti-Semitism had more recent roots than Luther and grew out of a different soil – not that German anti-Semitism was new; it drew part of its sustenance from Christian anti-Semitism, whose foundation had been laid by the Catholic Church and upon which Luther built. It was equally a product of German nationalism. Modern German anti-Semitism was the bastard child of the union of Christian anti-Semitism with German nationalism.

German nationalism arose out of the ashes of German defeat in the Napoleonic wars. Fragmented, without nationhood, without political definition, lacking military power and economic vitality, the Germans searched for a shared identity that would restore the self-esteem that the defeats by the French had shattered. Since the real world, in its materiality, its politics, economics and the force of arms, could give them no solace, they turned inwards for self-definition, in search of psychic and metaphysical values, qualities of feeling and spirit. And they turned backwards – to a remote past of glory and mastery, to a past deep in the womb of historic time, where they had once been secure.

This German backward-lookingness had emerged even before the Napoleonic wars, in the last quarter of the eighteenth century as a reaction against the Enlightenment, especially its French and English protagonists. The enlightenment represented the break with the medieval world and its concepts of man's innate sinfulness, whose only hope of salvation was through divine providence. For this world view the Enlightenment substituted the idea of progress, of man's perfectibility through the attainment of knowledge, and the theory that the universe was governed by reason. This idea of progress was to catch hold particularly among the French and the English, not only among the philosophers and sociologists, but in political circles as well.

In Germany these ideas spread too, but they were soon aborted by Germany's dominant conservative forces. The Holy Roman Empire, a paralytic, sclerotic, thousand-year survival, managed to exist, propped up by the strength of tradition and the inertia of apathy.[1] The Germans preferred to retain their loyalties to the past and resisted accommodation of their customs and folkways to the enormous changes of modernity. Instead they romanticized the values and ideals of their remote past. This commitment to the past explains the German preference for *Kultur* over *Zivilisation*. Culture was for them something innate, intrinsic, inherited, a tradition handed down from the past. Civilization was external, an artificial product of modernity, lacking the essence of a specific people, race or culture.

Progress and enlightenment were associated not only with the French and English, but also with Jews. Invoking the universality of these concepts, Jews asked for emancipation, political equality. All France was astir over the pros and cons. The Alsatian Jews asked Moses Mendelssohn, then Europe's most eminent Jew, to help them. Believing that a plea for Jewish emancipation would have a better reception if presented by a Christian, Mendelssohn asked his friend Christian Wilhelm von Dohm (1751–1820), historian, political writer and Prussian diplomat, to undertake the task. Dohm decided to extend his plea also on behalf of the German Jews. His work *Über die bürgerliche Verbesserung der Juden (On the Civic Betterment of the Jews)*, Berlin, 1781, presented the case for granting Jews political equality. Its basic argument was the extraordinary notion that 'the Jew is a human being even before he is a Jew'. But the idea was too radical for the Germans.

Most participants in the ensuing public discussion disagreed with Dohm's belief that the Jews would become better citizens if the conditions under which they lived were improved. Adducing traditional medieval objections and citing Scripture or the Devil as evidence, some maintained that the Jews were unfit for emancipation and that there was no reason to think that things would change in the future. Others presented the argument of 'Asiatic temperament': certain basic racial qualities inhered in Jews that were at variance with those of Germans. This fundamental difference between German and Jew was cited also, to the astonishment of Moses Mendelssohn, by Johann David Michaelis (1717–91), an aged, prestigious scholar of biblical ('Old Testament') and Mosaic law at the University of Göttingen. Mendelssohn replied to Michaelis and other opponents of Jewish emancipation in classical terms.

Instead of using the expression 'Christians and Jews', Herr Michaelis is continually served by 'Germans and Jews'. He refuses to recognize that the difference is in religion only and prefers to have us regarded as foreigners who must accept the conditions laid down to them by the owners of the land.

Being himself a man of progress and enlightenment, he could not then, in 1783, foretell that the Germans could and would indeed choose another road.

The German response to the Enlightenment was an intimation of the future. From 1789 to 1815, the quarter-century between the French Revolution and the Congress of Vienna, the ethos of modern Germany took shape. The doctrines of the revolution were anathema to the princely, priestly and knightly rulers of the German states and principalities. But the ideas had begun to infiltrate Germany, and within a few short years, as Napoleon's military success spread French influence across the face of Europe, French political domination of the German lands converted those ideas into political realities. German discomfiture with the new ideas of emancipation and equality turned into a deadly rancour both for the French and for the ideas and policies they had unleashed in Europe.

Wherever the French occupied German lands, Jews were the bene-ficiaries of the Rights of Man, winning emancipation in most of south-ern and western Germany. In some places under French command, the obligatory extension of equality to Jews enraged the Germans even more than French domination. Nevertheless, the trend towards emancipation reached even into the stronghold of Prussia. In 1812, as part of a sweeping programme of legislative and economic reform, Minister Karl August von Hardenberg, himself under the influence of the ideas of 1789, persuaded the reluctant Frederick William III to grant the Jews citizenship and political rights.

Napoleon destroyed the Holy Roman Empire, that is, the shadow of it that had persisted. After Jena, in 1806, he reorganized the German lands, secularizing the ecclesiastical states and incorporating most of the free cities into territorial states. He hastened the demise of the medieval order of Free Imperial Knights, reorganized the 600 myriad political units in a manageable number of middle-sized states, and formed a confederation of German states under French protection. (Ironically, that confederation would later provide a basis for German unification.) The formal bonds of historic empire that had linked the Germans to their Teutonic past had been destroyed. To compensate for the loss, for the humiliations at the hands of the French, for the fragmentation, the Germans began to forge a new nationalism that transcended the boundaries of the German states and the realities of their contemporary political life. That quarter century, inaugurated by the French Revolution and closed by the Congress of Vienna, was the formative period in shaping German national character. From it emerged a national ethos that was to animate German cultural, social and political life for well over a century.

To begin with, at the simplest and most obvious level, the Germans defined themselves in contrast to the French. What was French was un-German. Ernst Moritz Arndt (1769–1860), poet and pamphleteer, wrote of the war winter of 1812 that the German fatherland was located 'where every Frenchman is called foe, and every German is called friend'.[2] The great liberal ideas of the time – liberty, equality, frater-nity – were French ideas, and Germans of that generation denounced liberal ideas as un-German. That outlook proved to be a durable one.

The philosopher Johann Gottlieb Fichte (1762–1814), in his *Reden an die deutsche Nation* (1808), admonished Germans to 'have character and be German' ('*Charakter haben und Deutsch sein*'). His Gallophobia was equal to that of his contemporaries, but he excelled in his exaltation of Germanness. At a time when the Germans had been abjectly defeated, he consoled them with a messianic future:

> Among all modern peoples it is you in whom the seed of human perfection most decidedly lies, and you who are charged with progress in human development. If you perish in this your essential nature, then there perishes together with you every hope of the whole human race for salvation from the depths of its miseries.[3]

Called the father of German nationalism, Fichte has also been called the father of modern German anti-Semitism. His celebration of German nationalism was matched by his denigration of Jews. In 1793 he had argued against Jewish emancipation, characterizing the Jews as a state within a state that would undermine the German nation. Jewish ideas were as obnoxious as French ideas. The only way in which he could concede giving rights to Jews, he said, would be 'to cut off all their heads in one night, and to set new ones on their shoulders, which should contain not a single Jewish idea'.

Similarly, Arndt, who had defined German specificity by distinguishing the Germans from their external enemy, the French, refined that uniqueness by further distinguishing the Germans from an internal enemy – the Jews. The Jews, beneficiaries of political emancipation that the French had thrust upon the unprepared and unwilling Germans, became identified in the German mind with the ideas and values of revolutionary France. They were not seen as true insiders. In Christian feudal Germany, the Jews had been outsiders, and in the newly emergent idea of an ethnic, national Germany, the Jews continued to be outsiders.

Arndt and his disciple, Friedrich Ludwig Jahn (1778–1852), are credited with developing that particular concept of German nationalism associated with the word '*Volk*'. It is a word that has come to mean more than simply 'a people', more than the usual idea of a people united by common traditions and cultural heritage, language, territory, values and morality. '*Volk*', according to George Mosse, signified the union of a group of people with a transcendental 'essence', never specified, sometimes called 'nature', 'cosmos', 'mythos'. This essence, Mosse says, 'was fused to man's innermost nature, and represented the source of his creativity, his depth of feeling, his individuality, and his unity with other members of the *Volk*'.[4]

Jahn, a fiery German patriot who fought in the wars of liberation against Napoleon, in his book *Deutsches Volkstum (German Volkdom)*, published in 1810, elaborated on the concept of *Volk*: 'A state without *Volk* is nothing, a soulless artifice; a *Volk* without a state is nothing, a bodiless airy phantom, like the Gypsies and the Jews. Only state and *Volk* together can form a Reich, and such a Reich cannot be preserved without Volkdom.'[5] (Is it mere coincidence that the two wandering peoples, Gypsies and Jews, against whom Jahn contrasted the 'rooted' Germans, were precisely the two ethnic groups that Hitler consigned to the gas chambers?) In this work Jahn used the word *Volksthümlichkeit* (literally, 'quality of Volkdom') to express his glorification of the simple people, the little folk, and the qualities associated with them – simplicity, naturalness, homespunness unspoiled by education and civilization.

According to Jahn, the *Volk* needed a state to house its soul and provide the means for its preservation. The German state was to serve some 'larger' purpose – the preservation of the *Volk* and vehicle through which it could exercise its will. It was a Volkist idea that was to persist in Germany down to Hitler, who incorporated it into his ideology. The state was conceived as a kind of metahistorical entity that was identical with national spirit.

The 'Christian' state had once been meant to serve 'Christian' purposes, that is, the expansion of Christianity. The Volkist state appropriated that purpose. The Jew, by definition an outsider in the 'Christian' state, remained an outsider in the Volkist conception of the state. Indeed, the idea of a 'Christian' country in which Jews were outsiders served as a transition to the idea of the Volkist state. Thus Christian Friedrich Rühs (1781–1820), who held the chair for history at the University of Berlin, denied the claims of the Jews to the rights of German citizenship, because 'a foreign people cannot obtain the rights which Germans enjoy partly through being Christians ... Everything should be done to induce [the Jews] ... to accept Christianity and through it to be led to a true acquisition of German ethnic characteristics and thus to effect the destruction of the Jewish people.'[6]

Because Jews were loyal to their own 'state within the state', Rühs said they could not be loyal to the Christian state. They could, therefore, be only its subjects, but not its citizens. (That distinction was to be made by Hitler – at first, with regard to the Jews, but later, when in his scheme of things they were not even entitled to the status of subjects, it was a distinction made between the Czechs in the Protectorate, who were subjects, in contrast to the Sudeten Germans, who were citizens.) The Jews, Rühs believed, as a tolerated alien group, should be excluded from holding public office, from the army and from the guilds and corporations, that is, from institutions representing the economic as well as public and national life of the country. To identify this alien and hostile group within the German midst, Rühs proposed reviving the medieval yellow patch.

Emancipation was the consequence of revolution and of the political realization that all men, even Jews, were equal, but the concept of *Volk* was the consequence of counter-revolution and of a belief in superiority and inferiority among peoples, of difference and inequality. Out of the defeat inflicted upon them by the French, the Germans devised a notion of national, Volkist superiority to redeem their self-image. That self-image could not have been drawn without the Jew as antagonist.

The glorification of the natural man, the simple life, uncontaminated by the artificialities of civilization and the fetters of organized society, was a Romantic Rousseauist idea. The romanticization of the peasant as the natural man turned him into a receptacle of certain mystic qualities in his relationship to the land. The Volkist conception turned these universal qualities into specifically German ones. The peasant, by virtue of his descent from Germanic–Teutonic stock and by virtue of the mysterious qualities of Germanness in the very soil he worked, became the embodiment not merely of natural man, but of Germanic man. The antagonist of Germanic man became the Jew, the embodiment of the urban man, the man of civilization. A money economy, for example, as the product of disintegrative civilization, was associated with Jews, who were buyers, sellers and lenders. Whereas rootedness was an essential element of *Volk*, the Wandering Jew became the symbol of the flesh-and-blood Jews, condemned to eternal homelessness for having rejected the Messiah, whose fathers or forefathers had lived outside Germany, in other lands.

After Napoleon's defeat and the Congress of Vienna, the Germans took their revenge on the French and the Jews. The Congress of Vienna had provided for full civil and political rights 'to differing parties of the Christian religion', but the 'civil betterment' of the Jews was put off for further study. The Congress stated that Jews could retain such rights as they already had, but nearly everywhere in Germany the rights that the Jews had won were disavowed and rescinded. (Prussia was an exception: only some Jewish rights were abolished; most were retained.) A period of reaction set in, in which anti-Semitism was a major component.

A cyclical pattern in German political life began to emerge. The Congress of Vienna marked the first of four such cycles in subsequent German history that were to appear with startling regularity every two decades – long periods of reaction, repression, conservatism and anti-Semitism following brief spells of liberalism and the expansion of rights. In all cycles the position of the Jews gradually improved, economically and educationally, even if their political rights were curtailed or denied. The changes in Jewish occupational or educational status did not appreciably decrease the deep hostility to them. The changes merely served to alter the specific arguments of anti-Semitic agitation.

The second cycle was defined by the short-lived revolution of 1848 and the subsequent decade of reaction. The third cycle opened with the unification of Germany as a triumph of German liberalism that began to turn conservative, reactionary and anti-Semitic in 1873. The fourth cycle, beginning after the First World War, was marked by the simultaneity of both its liberal and its reactionary phases.

Not only did the German states abrogate Jewish rights from 1813 on, but the *furor teutonicus* that had found no satisfaction in the Congress of Vienna expressed itself in violent attacks and pogroms against the Jews. Peasants and burghers demonstrated and rioted in Bavaria, Württemberg, and elsewhere against Jewish rights. Some cities even attempted to banish the Jews altogether. But the most violent pogroms, whose like had not been witnessed in Europe since the Middle Ages, came with the 'Hep! Hep!' movement, first erupting in Würzburg in 1819 and rapidly spreading throughout Germany. The origin of this movement was obscure, but it is generally conceded to have been an outburst of resentment against Metternich's repression of German nationalistic propaganda and activities. The movement called for 'revenge' against the Jews, 'who are living among us and who are increasing like locusts ... Our battle-cry will be "Hep! Hep! Hep! Death and destruction to all the Jews!"' It was the first major chapter in the history of German nationalism in which the Jews were marked as the enemy.

Meanwhile, hostility to the Jews began to emerge from the newly developing socialist movement. That anti-Jewish outlook had two sources: first, the atheist, anti-Christian bias condemning Judaism as the antecedent of Christianity, and second, the anti-capitalist ideology that depicted the Jew as the embodiment of capitalism, the banker, the middle-man, the parasitic profiteer. First to articulate this leftist anti-Semitism was Bruno Bauer (1809–82), who in 1842 published an article on the Jewish question, which he supplemented and issued the following year as a separate book, *Die Judenfrage*. In this work he argued against political equality for the Jews. Orthodox Judaism was, in his view, an anachronistic phenomenon, whereas Reform Judaism was worthless; the Jews had never contributed to the civilization of the world – arguments that were later to become the stock-in-trade of the anti-Semitic right. Marx disputed Bauer's ideas on the ground that his view of the Jews as a religious group was distorted. The true Jewish religion, Marx argued, was *Schacher* (haggling, huckstering) and their god was money. Jews would first have to emancipate themselves from this 'religion' of theirs; then their religious consciousness would disappear and human emancipation would be possible.

But despite the opposition to Jewish emancipation and the antipathy to Jews, the oncoming revolution of 1848 heralded a growing liberalization in public opinion. When the National Assembly convened in Frankfurt and formulated a constitution, it included a section on 'the fundamental rights of the German people', which declared that 'the enjoyment of civil and political rights is neither dependent upon, nor restricted by, religious creed'.[7] There was no question here of a bountiful bestowal of rights upon Jews by a graciously consenting ruler. The Jews were here equal beneficiaries of rights granted to all. The accomplishment was due to the overwhelmingly liberal character of the body. It was also the achievement of Gabriel Riesser (1806–63), the notable advocate of Jewish emancipation during the previous two decades, who had been elected to the Frankfurt parliament. But within a year reaction set in. Bismarck was later to say that the great mistake of 1848–9 was to think that the great questions of the day would be settled 'by resolutions and majorities' rather than by 'blood and iron'. It was a judgement that bespoke the spirit that would later dominate German politics, where blood would erase resolutions and iron crush majorities.

For Jews 1848 was two-faced. The liberal constitution enacted a great principle that remained barely fulfilled, for its implementation depended on the individual states. In the very heat of revolutionary ardour counter-emancipatory trends came alive, and their pressure on the state governments was irresistible. When news of the revolution in Paris reached the peasants in the Rhineland, they too revolted, seizing land, destroying tax and tithe records, burning castles and pogromizing Jews. Revolutionary propaganda called for wiping out the nobility, assassinating the officials, establishing a republic and expelling the Jews from Germany. The popular agitation in many states brought about restrictions of Jewish rights or failure even to grant them. In Bavaria, for example, petitions with 80,000 signatures submitted to the Chamber of Reich Counsellors opposing Jewish emancipation succeeded in their purpose.

The liberals were too weak and too indecisive to withstand the reaction of the next decade. (Weakness and indecisiveness became hallmarks of German liberal polics – in the late 1870s *vis-à-vis* Bismarck and, still later, in the Weimar régime.) The Conservative party was founded in 1848 as a vehicle for the counter-revolution, and the 1850s witnessed the expansion and elaboration of an anti-Semitism that was not only political, but also Volkist and racist. Then Wilhelm Heinrich Riehl (1823–97), historian and novelist, began publishing his massive *Naturgeschichte des Volkes als Grundlage einer deutschen Sozial-Politik (The Natural History of the* Volk *as the Foundation of a Germanic Socio-Political System)*, idealizing pre-capitalist German society, condemning contemporary commercial and industrial developments. Then Paul de Lagarde (1827–91), later the Volkist patron saint of the anti-Semitic movement, began his career with an attack on Christianity and contemporary theology. Eventually Lagarde would call for an expurgation of the Jewish elements from Christianity and for its transformation into a Christian–Germanic faith.[8] The Germans, he believed, were too soft for the Jews to be allowed to live together with them: 'Every Jew is proof of the enfeeblement of our national life and of the worthlessness of what we call the Christian religion.'[9]

Lagarde, in another essay, was to write of Jews as vermin:

One would need a heart as hard as crocodile hide not to feel sorry for the poor exploited Germans and – which is identical – not to hate the Jews and despise those who – out of humanity! – defend these Jews or who are too cowardly to trample this usurious vermin to death. With trichinae and bacilli one does not negotiate, nor are trichinae and bacilli to be educated; they are exterminated as quickly and thoroughly as possible.[10]

That imagery was to be repeated time and again until Hitler appropriated it and applied it with terrible literalness.

Meanwhile, the new 'science' of race was developing, under the impetus of advances in anthropology and philology. Christian Lassen (1802–71), a learned professor of ancient civilizations at the University of Bonn, in his *Indische Altertumskunde (Indian Antiquities)*, argued that among the Caucasians, only Semites and Aryans built up human civilizations. He counterposed one against the other: 'History proves that Semites do not possess the harmony of psychical forces that distinguishes the Aryans.' But the Semite has other qualities: he is 'selfish and exclusive'.

Then Arthur de Gobineau (1816–82) became convinced that 'the racial question overshadows all other problems of history, that it holds the key to them all, and that the inequality of the races from whose fusion a people is formed is enough to explain the whole course of its destiny.' Though Gobineau's *Essai sur l'inégalité des races*, published in Paris 1853–5, was not to be translated into German for another forty years, the idea of race as the determinant of the rise and fall of civilizations appeared among the German philologists and ethnologists and philosophers. Social degeneration, they believed, was caused by racial degeneration. Racial mixture, the dissipation of the pure racial blood, brought mediocrity and decline. Gobineau's basic scheme was to serve as a framework for the refinements of Chamberlain and other epigoni who saw the rise and fall of civilization as dependent on the preservation of the racial purity of the Germanic or Aryan race.

Richard Wagner (1813–83), in his specifically Teutonic racialism and ferocious hatred of Jews, surpassed earlier Volkist anti-Semites. 'Emancipation from the yoke of Judaism appears to us the foremost necessity,' he wrote. He was to develop, in his music and journalism, the idea of a de-Judaized, hence de-Christianized, Germanic religion, in which the pagan Teutonic elements merged with, or displaced, the Christian ones.

The third cycle of liberalism/reaction came with the unification of Germany. Unification in itself represented a liberal turn in German history, if only in the modest sense that it abolished the particularism of the various states, introduced administrative uniformity and erased the internal trade and tariff barriers. Bismarck needed liberals' support to achieve his ambitions, and in exchange he conceded universal political and civic rights. (In 1847, as a member of the Prussian Diet, he had opposed political rights for Jews.) The Reichstag of the North German Federation on 3 July 1869 voted such rights into law, abolishing all restrictions of civil and political rights because of religious creed and making participation in local, state and federal government independent of religious creed.[11]

The unification of Germany introduced new facets to German anti-Semitism. The leaders of the liberals were Jews (Eduard Lasker and Ludwig Bamberger); both liberal parties (the National Liberal party and its split-off, the Progress party) and liberalism in general became the target of Volkist hostility and anti-Semitism. The unification of Germany and the creation of the nation-state forced the Germans into modernity. The nation-state was a concomitant of a new industrial, commercial, financial way of life that was changing the old bases of society and overturning that antiquated hierarchical order which, in Volkist minds, had become identified with the German Volkist past.

The expansive role of capital in the new state intensified charges that the Jews were using their newly acquired rights to exploit the Germans and manipulate their interests. The economic crisis of 1873 was adduced by the anti-Semites as further evidence that the Jews engaged in financial manipulations to undermine the country. Feverish and unchecked speculation had boomed in the wake of the spectacular growth of industry, railway expansion, foreign trade and banking that unification had stimulated and that the successful war against France had emboldened. Then, with the onset of a worldwide depression in 1873, came financial collapse in Germany. The crash was blamed on the Jews and the liberals, who were identified as Jews anyway.

In the next six years, the period of economic depression, a complete reorientation took place in German politics, with an authoritarian right turn by Bismarck. He no longer needed his liberal supporters; his Prussian conservatism and absolutism made him the natural enemy of the rising working class and its political spokesman, the Social Democratic party. The attack on both Jews and liberals began to gather momentum, from both right-wing Conservative sources and from populist agitators representing the 'little people' in Germany who had indeed been severely affected by the financial disaster. The stereotype of the Jew as international financier became more common. Catholics joined in using the Jews and the liberals as the sticks with which to beat Bismarck and the government.

The first assault came from Wilhelm Marr, an unsuccessful journalist who blamed the Jews for his professional failure, and who is credited with having invented the word 'anti-Semitism' (whose use in this context developed out of racial theories about the 'Semitic' and 'Aryan' races). His pamphlet *Der Sieg des Judentums über das Germanentum (The Victory of Jewry over Germandom)*, published in 1873, became his first success, going through twelve editions in six years. Drawing on the ideas of race and Volkist nationalism, Marr argued that their 'racial qualities' had enabled Jews not only to survive through the ages, but to become 'the first major power in the West' in the nineteenth century. The Germanic state, he pessimistically concluded, had degenerated too far to withstand Jewish superiority.

Political anti-Semitism began in Berlin with Adolf Stöcker, though Stöcker did not actually begin with overt, explicit anti-Semitism. In 1878, in Berlin, where he was court preacher, he founded the Christian Social Workers' party. The name itself suggested the party's implicit anti-Semitic bias.★ His purposes were to provide a political counter-vehicle to the Social Democratic party and to combat what he regarded as the dangerous and debilitating secularization and de-

★The word 'Christian' in a European organization's name indicated its anti-Semitic character. The classic illustration is Admiral Horthy's joyous embrace of the secretary of the American YMCA as the head of 'such an important anti-Semitic organization'.

moralization of society in the capital city. But the workers who came to Christian Social political rallies came only to mock and heckle.

The Progressives continued to hold their strength in Berlin in the election of 1878, but elsewhere in Germany they and the National Liberals lost about half their seats. Gains were made by the Conservatives and the Catholic Centre party. That Reichstag gave Bismarck what he had previously been denied: passage of the 'law against the pernicious pursuits of Social Democracy', which declared the Social Democratic party illegal and abolished freedom of speech, press and assembly. (The law was extended four times, with the support of the National Liberals, and remained in force until 1890, when Bismarck resigned. It inaugurated a pattern that would be repeated in Germany's later history and showed how fragile was the new nation's commitment to political liberalism.)

Stöcker's failure to win support at a time when the whole country was making a right turn indicated to him that he was appealing to the wrong group. Indeed, the people at his meetings who shared his discontent with state and society were not workers, but members of the *Mittelstand*, which was then beginning to emerge as a political force in German society. Consisting of diverse elements whose economic interests and status drives were not necessarily common or consistent with each other – small farmers and peasants, artisans, small businessmen, lower echelons of officialdom and lower levels of professionals – the *Mittelstand* shared a hostility to the rapidly burgeoning industrial urban society and to its political arrangements.

Farmers and peasants feared that industrialism would bring urbanization and destroy their land and way of life. Artisans feared that the factory system and mass production would render them and their crafts obsolete. Small businessmen were apprehensive that the national expansion of trade and a more rational organization of business would make them economically uncompetitive. The lower professionals, white-collar workers and petty officials felt that their status was being lowered and that the old values they defended were being eroded, if not actually destroyed, by the emergent modern society. Only the workers and the industrialists, it appeared, were in harmony with contemporary economic and industrial developments.

In the next forty years the *Mittelstand* turned increasingly to the right. Its constituent groups shared an incredible susceptibility to political propaganda that blamed the Jews for the changes that were undermining their traditional ways of life. The 'Jewish conspiracy' became the single and simple explanation for whatever had gone wrong in their world. To this audience, consequently, on 19 September 1879, at a Christian Social meeting, Stöcker made his first anti-Semitic speech: 'What We Demand of Modern Jewry'.[12]

He began, as he put it, 'in the spirit of Christian love'. Modern Jewry, he declared, was 'a great danger to German national life'. He did not mean the Jewish religion as such, he claimed, though he characterized Orthodox Judaism as 'a form of religion which is dead at its very core' and Reform Judaism as nothing more than 'a pitiful remnant of the Age of Enlightenment'. But modern Jews were 'most certainly a force against religion', a destructive, secularizing, anti-Christian force who, themselves not believing in Judaism, persisted in remaining Jewish. Using the platitudes of Volkist/racial anti-Semitism, Stöcker described the Jews as 'a people within a people, a state within a state, a separate tribe within a foreign race', who pitted 'their unbroken Semitic character against Teutonic nature, their rigid cult of law or their hatred of Christians against Christianity'. Germans must protect themselves against the Jews. That protection could come only through 'wise legislation'. Stöcker's 'wise' legislation included a number of general proposals and three explicitly anti-Semitic ones: (1) reintroduction of the denominational census 'so as to find out the disproportion between Jewish capital and Christian labour'; (2) limiting the number of appointments of Jewish judges in proportion to the Jews in the population; (3) removing Jewish teachers from the elementary schools, while strengthening the schools' 'Christian–Germanic spirit'.

Stöcker's legislation originated out of both populist/leftist and rightist sources. The leftist proposals were those directed towards control of the credit system, the regulation of the stock exchange, easements (or complete abolition) of the mortgage system – measures designed to protect the peasant or small landholder, the small businessman and the small investor from the manipulative power of big capital. They were implicitly anti-Semitic, since in the popular mind big capital was Jewish. The rightist proposals were explicitly anti-Semitic. With these proposals Stöcker, like many after him, succeeded in attracting followers from both the left and the right.

1880 was a watershed year, the start of a torrent of anti-Semitism that did not abate for nearly twenty years. It was as if all the quiet streams of prejudice conjoined in a massive flow of anti-Semitic hate, inundating the whole country. It began at the end of 1879, when Heinrich von Treitschke, National Liberal and prestigious professor of history at the University of Berlin, started a series of articles on the Jewish question in the *Preussische Jahrbücher*, which he edited. 'Even in circles of the most highly educated, among men who would reject with disgust any ideas of ecclesiastical intolerance or national arrogance, there resounds as if from one mouth: *Die Juden sind unser Unglück!*'[13]

'The Jews are our misfortune' – the phrase was to ring down through later German generations. Heinrich Class, a leading anti-Semite a generation later, wrote that the phrase 'became a part of my body and soul when I was twenty years old; it essentially influenced my later political work'. Issued in pamphlet form, Treitschke's articles gave reinforcement and professorial authoritativeness to the anti-Semitic movement. Treitschke spoke, the anti-Semites said, 'for thousands, perhaps millions of his countrymen'.

In the autumn of 1880 the 'Anti-Semites' Petition' began to be circulated. Initiated by two schoolteachers (Ernst Henrici and Bernhard Förster, Nietzsche's brother-in-law) and a minor aristocrat (Max Liebermann von Sonnenberg), it was distributed with the help of a newly organized association of German students, explicitly organized as an anti-Semitic group. In the preamble, addressed to Bismarck, the petitioners asked for 'the emancipation of the German people from a form of alien domination which it cannot endure for any length of time'.[14] The Jew was depicted as the exploitative 'master' of the labouring German people, who was gaining control of German urban and rural property and who would destroy the German fatherland. Jews were an alien people, whose very feeling and thinking were completely alien to the German *Volk*. If the ideals of the Germanic *Volk* were not to be destroyed, if the German people were not to fall into the economic slavery of the Jews, steps would have to be taken to liberate the German people from this Jewish danger.

The following steps were proposed: (1) the immigration of foreign Jews was to be restricted at the least, if not entirely prevented; (2)

Jews were to be excluded from all government positions, and their appointment to the judiciary was to be subject to appropriate limitation; (3) the Christian character of the grammar school, even if attended by Jewish pupils, was to be strictly maintained and only Christian teachers admitted; in all higher schools the appointment of Jewish teachers could be made only in exceptional cases; (4) the census of the Jewish population was to be resumed.

While the petition was circulating (its centre of strength was in Prussia, and especially Berlin), a Progressive deputy asked the Minister of the Interior what the Prussian government intended to do about it. The interpellation was intended to elicit a condemnation, but the minister's *pro forma* reply that the government did not intend to abrogate Jewish rights was seen by the petitioners as an encouraging sign. When finally presented to Bismarck, in April 1881, the 'Anti-Semites' Petition' had 225,000 signatures, mostly from Prussia, with 9,000 from Bavaria. Some 4,000 university students had signed it. (A counter-petition circulated by liberal students, did poorly. At the University of Göttingen, for instance, the liberals received 180 signatures, compared with 400 for the 'Anti-Semites' Petition'.)

At the time of the interpellation, Berthold Auerbach, the Jewish novelist who had been an ardent German nationalist and whose most successful work was the romantic idealization of the German peasant life of his *Schwarzwälder Dorfgeschichten* (*Black Forest Village Tales*, 1848), was in despair. In a letter from Berlin on 23 November 1880, he wrote: 'Living and working in vain! That is the crushing impression I have of this two-day debate in the House of Deputies. And if I tell myself again that it is perhaps not so bad, the horrible fact remains that such coarseness, such deceit and such hatred are still possible.'[15] A few months later, Leopold Zunz, then nearly eighty-seven years old, took another view, in a letter to a friend: 'Thus I live, unconcerned about the anti-Jewish agitating swine-eaters: their din is a childish imitation of the Crusades, no longer in style. World literature today and in the newspaper press are more powerful than all the blockheads aping the Middle Ages.'[16]

In 1880 Ernst Henrici, one of the organizers of the 'Anti-Semites' Petition', founded a new anti-Semitic party, the Soziale Reichspartei (the Reich Social party), which, in contrast to Stöcker's Christian conservative anti-Semitism, disseminated a radical racist spirit: 'If it is a question of racial characteristics, then both body and spirit must be kept in mind ... The religion of the Jews is a racial religion.' Wherever Henrici spoke, he aroused masses to anti-Semitic violence. In Berlin his agitation at mass meetings around the 'Anti-Semites' Petition' led to street brawls, attacks on Jews, window smashing, the hoodlums shouting *'Juden raus!'* In July 1881 he came to Neustettin, where he harangued the population with his anti-Semitic views. Serious anti-Jewish riots followed, and right after he left the Neustettin synagogue was burned down. Henrici's party lasted barely two years, but he had succeeded in setting up a model for a radicalized political anti-Semitism.

In 1881 the Deutsche Reformpartei,* patterned after Stöcker's party in Berlin, was founded in Dresden. Unsuccessful as a political party, it took on new life as a parapolitical organization, with the formation of Reformvereine (reform unions) throughout Germany, groups in which anti-Semitism in all varieties flourished. By 1885 there were fifty-two such unions; by 1890, 136. The Reformvereine attracted members of the *Mittelstand* and provided an organizational framework of sorts for the burgeoning anti-Semitic movement. (The various leaders of the anti-Semitic movement tried, from time to time, to form a united organization, but their ideological differences, personal rivalries and psychological instabilities conspired against them.)

The Vereine came under different intellectual influences in the anti-Semitic movement, from both the left and the right. In Westphalia, for instance, the branches were largely affected by the ideas of Eugen Karl Dühring, an anarchist with a strong following among the Social Democrats. A philosopher and an economist, he taught at the University of Berlin until his inability to get along with the university authorities forced his retirement in 1877. Like Marr and other malcontents, he attributed his failures to Jewish plotting. He had first propagated a proto-national type of socialism, but by 1881 the Jewish question had moved to the centre of his mental universe, when he published *Die Judenfrage als Rassen- Sitten- und Kulturfrage (The Jewish Question as a Racial, Moral and Cultural Question)*. In this

---

*'Reform' was a word appropriated largely by the right and usually meant restrictions on free-trade policies. 'Reform' movements often took on a populist, anti-Semitic coloration.

work he argued that the German spirit had sold itself to Judaism, that Germany's 'social corruption' was the consequence of the parasitic Jews' settling in Germany and bringing about Germany's complete deterioration. Developing the crudest and most vicious racism, Dühring looked upon the Jews as a 'counter-race' separated from all humanity, whom neither conversion nor assimilation could affect because their basic nature was evil and unchangeable. He shared the Wagnerian thesis that Christianity was a product of a 'Hebraic orientalism', and that those who clung to the 'entire' Christian tradition could not truly oppose Judaism or defend the 'Nordic tradition'. His influence among university students was substantial, beginning with his economic ideas and ending with his anti-Semitic racism.

The Leipzig branch of the Reformvereine was headed by Theodor Fritsch (1844–1933), a linchpin in the anti-Semitic movement, holding it together as political organizer, publisher, editor, author from its early political/nationalist stirrings in the 1880s until Hitler's accession to power. He bought up an unsuccessful anti-Semitic publishing house and in 1882 began to issue the *Antisemitische Correspondenz*. He was less interested in forming an anti-Semitic political party than in infusing all political parties with anti-Semitism.

Political anti-Semitism began also in Austria at this time. In Germany, the concomitants to anti-Semitism were German nationalism and anti-modernity. In Austria the key element was Pan-Germanism, union with Germany and the preservation of the 'German' character of 'German' territory. The Austrian Germans stressed their German-ness to distinguish themselves from the East European nationalities in the Hapsburg Empire and to separate Cisleithan Austria from Transleithan Hungary. The doctrine of Pan-Germanism was first formulated by Georg von Schönerer and the university intellectuals who had supported him. Schönerer, in turn, acknowledged Dühring as teacher and master. Thus is tradition transmitted: Schönerer learned from Dühring, and Hitler learned from Schönerer.

Schönerer began his political career as a liberal in the Reichsrat in 1873, but he soon opted for a more radical economic programme (his leftist heritage from Dühring) and a preference for German national-ism. In 1882 Schönerer and his followers formulated the so-called 'Linz Programme', which combined Pan-Germanism with a reform programme that was part socialist and part romantically anti-industrialist. Anti-Semitism was scarcely apparent. But like Stöcker, Schönerer learned that anti-Semitism was the mainstay of the *Mittelstand* elements who supported him. He took his cue from the farmers and the craftsmen who saw the Jew as their enemy and regarded industrialism and urbanism as Jewish machinations. In 1885 Schönerer added one more point to the Linz Programme that became the central one: 'The removal of Jewish influence from all sections of public life is indispensable for carrying out the reforms aimed at.' He introduced anti-Semitic motions in the Reichsrat, and in 1887 he sponsored a bill to restrict East European Jewish immigration into Austria. Anti-Semitism was to become the obverse side of Schönerer's German nationalism, the negative definition of his position and, as he lost his political footing and influence, both his nationalism and his anti-Semitism were to become, in the long years ahead, irrational obsessions coloured by freakishness. His hatred of Jews and Catholics constituted also a rejection of Christianity; the pagan practices he adopted were no mere bizarre oddities, but reflected the longing for an idealized primitive world of German tribesmen in dark Teutonic forests. Though Hitler had much empathy for these hallucinated visions that Schönerer was propagating to his coteries of cultists, he despised Schönerer for abandoning himself to these arcane notions and failing to make political capital of such precious assets as German nationalism and anti-Semitism.

If Schönerer turned out to be a discredit to anti-Semitic politics in Austria, Karl Lueger (1844–1910) was its shining success. He made anti-Semitism politically viable, acceptable and, finally, respectable. A master of pragmatic politics, an anti-nationalist and anti-Prussian, devoted to Emperor and Empire, Lueger saw anti-Semitism mainly as a political expedient. In a few years Lueger's Christian Social party attained the political success that Schönerer had dreamed of, but never achieved.

Perhaps it was a matter of timing, for in Germany, too, that was the time when the anti-Semitic parties began to amass electoral strength. Within a decade they had succeeded in infecting all the major political parties, except the Social Democrats, with the poison of anti-Semitism. It began in 1887 when Otto Böckel was elected to the Reichstag as a deputy from a poor peasant constituency in Hesse, winning a long-held Conservative seat. A librarian who had made the collection of German folklore his hobby and had thus become familiar with peasant life, Böckel had a year earlier helped found a branch of the Reform-vereine in Kassel and joined with Fritsch in an attempt to form an anti-Semitic alliance. He campaigned on a populist economic pro-gramme, stirring the peasants with his fiery slogan: 'Liberate your-selves from the Jewish middlemen!' Böckel believed that Jews were a racial group whose racial essence could not be affected by conversion or intermarriage and that Jews in Germany should never be allowed to have more than the rights of aliens, because they were by nature aliens. He argued that the Conservatives failed in their treatment of the Jewish question, which he regarded as the central 'national question' in Germany. This 'political' approach, with its unexpected success, threatened, above all, the Conservatives, who, then in a temporary alliance with the National Liberals, had soft-pedalled anti-Semitism. For the 1890 election Böckel organized the Anti-semitische Volkspartei (Anti-Semitic People's party), whose pro-gramme demanded 'the repeal, by legal means, of Jewish emancipa-tion' and 'placing the Jews under alien legislation'. His party won five seats in Hesse, his Conservative and other anti-Semitic rivals having withdrawn lest they split the vote.

Böckel was not an isolated phenomenon. In a by-election in 1892, in a rural district in eastern Germany, similarly without party backing or organization funds, Hermann Ahlwardt defeated his Conservative opponent. A schoolteacher who had advanced to school principal, his financial peccadilloes had entangled him in debts and scandals – though, using an ancient staple of anti-Semitic propaganda, he attri-buted these entirely to Jewish usurers. He was fired when found dipping into the school till. Then, in 1890, he published a book called *Der Verzweiflungskampf der arischen Völker mit den Judentum (The Despairing Struggle of the Aryan Peoples with Jewry)*, in which he depicted the Jews as an octopus with claws in every sphere in German life. Two nasty anti-Semitic pamphlets followed, which brought him sentences of imprisonment for false charges, but having been mean-while elected to the Reichstag he enjoyed parliamentary immunity. His reckless rantings and his paranoia did not ensure his success in the Reichstag (eventually the anti-Semites came to regard him as a liability), but for years his constituency returned him to office, believing that he was a victim of nefarious Jewish power.

His racial anti-Semitism contained the familiar arguments drawn from the leftist, Volkist and racist repertoire. In a Reichstag address in 1895, supporting a bill to halt Jewish immigration into Germany, he analysed Jewish 'racial' qualities. The Jews were 'beasts of prey' and 'cholera bacilli'. The only chance the Germans had to defend them-selves was to 'exterminate those beasts of prey', and the best way to start would be to keep them out of the country.[17]

After Ahlwardt's stunning success in 1892, the Conservatives drew what they thought was the appropriate conclusion: anti-Semitism was a legitimate political weapon to be used to attain political power. At their party convention at the end of that year, the Conservatives revised their party programme to include not only implicitly anti-Semitic planks (for instance, 'We demand Christian authority and Christian teachers for Christian pupils'), but also the explicit anti-Semitic statement, 'We fight the multifarious and obtrusive Jewish influence that decomposes our people's life.' No greater gain could have been made, no greater respectability could have accrued to political anti-Semitism. No longer the possession of small splinter and sometimes crackpot parties, anti-Semitism had become the property of the most prestigious party of Imperial Germany.

The 1890s brought new vitality and organizational support to the anti-Semitic movement. The successes of populist racial anti-Semites had pushed the reluctant anti-Semitic 'moderates' into the extremist camp, but even more significant for the solidification of political anti-Semitism was the anxiety engendered by the tremendous expansion of the Social Democratic movement. In 1890, the first election after the expiration of Bismarck's anti-Socialist law, the Social Democrats amassed over 1·4 million votes, winning thirty-five seats (they had previously held eleven). Indeed, the only signific-ant opposition to the rising tide of political anti-Semitism that was inundating Germany's political institutions came from industrial labour and from the Social Democratic party. 'Anti-Semitism is the socialism of fools,' August Bebel, the party's leader, had said when leftist, populist anti-Semitism threatened to infect the Socialist movement. The party continued firmly to resist anti-Semitism and succeeded in immunizing its members and supporters against it.

How did the Social Democrats succeed in warding off anti-Semitism, when everyone else, it seemed, succumbed so easily? For one thing, the party leadership early set a model for the ranks by its aggressive articulated opposition. In a generally authoritarian society, that authoritative denunciation of anti-Semitism must have had some effect. For another, the ideology of the Social Democratic movement interpreted all economic, social and political phenomena in terms of an all-encompassing Marxist theory. Social Democrats did not need anti-Semitism, another all-embracing theory, to explain the great events of their lives. Finally, the Social Democrats, as industrial workers, had a stake in industrial urban society. With fewer romantic illusions about the primitive past, they had greater ambitions for a share in the comfort, convenience and wealth that their labour was helping to produce. This modernist outlook, then, helped to render them impervious to anti-Semitism.

The *Mittelstand*, in contrast, viewed much of this expanding restless urban society through Volkist eyes and increasingly gave its support not only to conservative centrist parties (Conservative and Catholic Centre parties), to Germany's expanding imperialism, but also to candidates representing a gamut of anti-Semitic opinion. From 1887, with Böckel's election, until the outbreak of the First World War, about ninety anti-Semitic deputies were elected to the Reichstag. The various parties grouped and regrouped, for a while united, sometimes sponsored jointly by the Conservatives. In 1893, for example, candidates of anti-Semitic parties polled 263,000 votes, but if those who ran jointly on the Conservative line are added, the anti-Semitic vote was as high as 400,000. As for the anti-Semitic deputies, they were themselves the essence of the *Mittelstand*. Nearly all were Protestants, none were of the aristocracy (except for two chronic anti-Semites) and none from labour. Mostly they were small entrepreneurs and craftsmen who had experienced economic hardships, teachers, lower civil servants, white-collar employees and lawyers – the same occupational groups that were also to provide support for the NSDAP after the First World War. They all shared a sense of frustration, deep resentments – seldom rationally articulable – against 'outside' forces that prevented their attainment of appropriate status or professional success. Cultists turned up in these movements, back-to-nature advocates, food faddists, occultists; all found a place in the anti-Semitic movement.

The year 1893 was the organizational highpoint for the *Mittelstand*. The Alldeutscher Verband (Pan-German League) was founded as a vehicle for the expression of middle-class nationalist imperialism and militarism, to cultivate 'German national values all over the world'. Under its first president, Professor Ernst Hasse, anti-Semitism was latent and secondary. In 1908, when Heinrich Class became president, the league became overtly anti-Semitic and closed its membership to Jews. At the turn of the century, its membership reached 20,000, with professors and university lecturers (over 5,000), small businessmen (4,900), teachers and civil servants (3,760) as the largest occupational groups.

Also founded in 1893 was the Deutschnationaler Handlungsgehilfen-verband (National Germanic League of Clerks), which started modestly with a group of thirty clerks in Hamburg; by 1913 it had nearly 150,000 members. The organization's constitution specified that 'Jews or persons whose character is not blameless' could not become members. (The league was not only anti-Jewish, it was also anti-feminist, in an attempt to maintain white-collar employment as a male preserve.) Both the Alldeutscher Verband and the clerks' league functioned as political pressure groups, throwing their strength behind candidates of the various right-wing and anti-Semitic parties and raising funds for their candidates and organizations.

The third parapolitical *Mittelstand* organization founded in 1893, and probably the most influential, was the Bund der Landwirte (Agrarian League), which was to become a major force in right-wing politics and to transform the Conservative party. Though its leadership remained in the hands of relatively few big landowners, its rank-and-file members were small farmers. By the end of the decade, the Agrarian League had nearly 250,000 members. What held the diverse and sometimes divergent economic and social interests of the large-scale and small-scale farmers together was a German nationalism defined by anti-Semitism. At its first general assembly in 1894, the Agrarian League restricted its membership to Christians and announced itself as 'an opponent of Jewry, which has become altogether too mighty in our country and has acquired a decisive say in the press, in trade and on the exchanges'. A year later the league's organ declared: 'Agriculture and Jewry must fight to the death, until one or the other lies lifeless – or at least powerless – on the ground.' It advocated boycotting Jewish stores, prohibiting social relations between Germans and Jews, and expelling Jews from Germany. In the Agrarian League, as in increasing numbers of German organizations and institutions, German nationalism and racist, Volkist anti-Semitism combined to form an effective, powerful political pressure group that radicalized German conservatism and made anti-Semitism a commonplace staple of any right-of-centre political body.

The student organizations, the gymnastic and sports organizations (the Deutsche Turnerschaft, whose ancestry went back to Father Jahn, was not only Volkist nationalist but explicitly anti-Semitic), the youth and back-to-nature movements, though apolitical, added variety and density to political anti-Semitism, thriving as they did on irrationality, anti-intellectualism, race superiority and race hate.

Anti-Semitic propaganda proliferated luxuriantly in the 1890s in the rich soil of political success and organizational abundance and grew into the twentieth century. In 1894 a society was formed by Gobineau's German translator, a disciple of Lagarde, to honour Gobineau and revive his work. The Wagner family circle gave the society its primary support, but when the Alldeutscher Verband became a supporting member of the Gobineau Society, a new union of racist Volkism and the *Mittelstand* was formed. Gobineau's work, as well as Houston Stewart Chamberlain's, became required reading for rightist German students. Julius Langbehn (1815–1907), a new Volkist prophet of discontent, having been exhorted by the tireless Fritsch to a hard anti-Semitic line, emerged with his dyspeptic version of cultural anti-Semitism. Langbehn saw to it that Lagarde's work was revived (a new edition appeared in 1891). Heinrich Class, whose pseudonymous book *Wenn Ich der Kaiser wär' (If I Were Kaiser)*, in which he expounded his anti-Semitic theories, first published in 1912, went into five editions before war broke out, wrote of the impact on him of the works of Lagarde, Count Gobineau and Houston Stewart Chamberlain: 'At the end of the century, I plunged into them, and I do not know from which of these three great men I derived the most profit.'[18]

At the turn of the century anti-Semitism had infected Germany. A book dealer found vast quantities of anti-Semitic literature in the libraries that he bought for resale. 'Every year', he wrote, 'tens of thousands of anti-Semitic pamphlets are sent free to all officials of the state and members of the upper ten thousand.'[19]

The next cycle of anti-Semitism came with the First World War. The elections of 1912 to the Reichstag had given a massive majority to the Progressives and Social Democrats. Political anti-Semitism, it seemed, was on the decline. But it erupted in the midst of the war, following the euphoria of patriotism at the outbreak of war, when even Jews had been included within the circle of national brotherhood.

By mid-1916 the war had begun to go badly. There were no military victories to compensate for the food shortages, the hardships, the wounded and the dead in battle. The Jews became the 'explanation' for whatever was going wrong. The Jews, the accusations went, were not fighting for Germany. Those in the army had cushy jobs behind the front; Jews were profiteering out of the war, getting rich from the war corporations. Popular anti-Semitism once again rose to the surface. Just as this grumbling discontent was turning into a massive rumble, and under pressure of the officer corps, the war hero Field Marshal Paul von Hindenburg was appointed to replace the chief of the General Staff, who had been charged with the army's military failures. Another war hero, Erich Ludendorff, was appointed Hindenburg's aide (Ludendorff in reality exercised the authority and made Hindenburg's decisions). A few days after Ludendorff's appointment, the War Ministry ordered a religious census of the members of the armed forces, according to service at the front, in garrisons or behind desks, and of the employees in the war corporations (war industry). In October, as if ignorant of these administrative measures, an anti-Semitic member of the Reichstag proposed that such a survey be made of the armed forces and a member of the Catholic Centre party moved the same for the war corporations. The National Liberals, some forty years earlier accused of being the party of Jewry, went along with the proposal. Only the Progressives and Social Democrats were opposed. This coalition of authoritarian military leaders, anti-Semites, Catholic conservatives and the components of the *Mittelstand* succeeded, without difficulty, in undermining the guarantee of equal rights of the Reichstag Act of 1869. The next two years of the war were marked by a crescendo of anti-Semitism, which Hitler epitomized in *Mein Kampf:* 'In the year 1916–17 nearly the whole production was under the control of Jewish finance . . . The spider was slowly beginning to suck the blood out of the people's pores.'

The Weimar Republic, born out of defeat and revolution, despair and hope, emerged with a new constitution that at long last gave the Jews complete equality. But at the very time that Jews had just begun to enjoy those political and civic rights for which they had been striving for a century, anti-Semitism burst forth in its most extravagant form. The Weimar Republic and its constitution had become an extreme example of the difference between the *pays légal* and the *pays réel*. The Jews now had the right to hold high public office (a few actually did), but they were also, in the minds of vast numbers of Germans, to blame for Germany's defeat, for the revolution, for the Munich Soviet, for the loss of the monarchy, for the passing of the past. They were the internal enemy. On 24 February 1920, just six months after the Weimar Constitution was enacted, the NSDAP issued its twenty-five-point programme, which asserted that no Jew could ever be a member of the German *Volk*, that only persons of German blood could be regarded as members of the *Volk* and citizens of the German state. The Deutschnationale Volkspartei (DNVP; German National People's party), the post-war incarnation of the German right, was at its founding at the end of 1918 conservative, Christian, nationalist, though not yet anti-Semitic. But soon it was seized by the anti-Semitic madness, and in 1920 its party programme took a stand 'against the predominance of Jewry in government and public life'. Parliamentary democracy survived in Germany for barely one decade, which witnessed the seemingly irresistible rise of the Nazis, the proliferation of anti-Semitic associations and societies – as many as 430 – and of anti-Semitic periodicals – as many as 700. Anti-Semitic bills were introduced with shameless regularity into state and national legislatures. The youth of the country, especially the students at the universities, were overwhelmingly anti-Semitic (in Berlin student elections in 1921, two thirds of the votes were cast for anti-Semitic candidates). Violence often ruled the streets, though Jews were not its only victims. After the assassination of Catholic leftist leader Matthias Erzberger, the war veterans, the members of the Free Corps, roaming the streets for victims and action, used to sing:

> *Knallt ab den Walter Rathenau*
> *Die gottverdammte Judensau.*
> (Mow down Walter Rathenau,
> The goddamned Jewish sow.)

And they did. By 1926 even the strictest law-abiding German Jews began to talk of learning how to develop their bodies and defend themselves.[20]

There was no dearth of anti-Semitic propaganda. Before the end of 1920 the *Protocols of the Elders of Zion*, translated into German that year, had sold 120,000 copies. A Jewish reporter at that time wrote:

In Berlin I attended several meetings which were entirely devoted to the Protocols. The speaker was usually a professor, a teacher, an editor, a lawyer or someone of that kind. The audience consisted of members of the educated class, civil servants, tradesmen, former officers, ladies, above all students, students of all faculties and years of seniority . . . Passions were whipped up to the boiling point.[21]

It was a world intoxicated with hate, driven by paranoia, enemies everywhere, the Jew lurking behind each one. The Germans were in search of a mysterious wholeness that would restore them to primeval happiness, destroying the hostile milieu of urban industrial civilization that the Jewish conspiracy had foisted on them.[22]

'*Deutschland erwache, Juda verrecke*' became a commonplace slogan. In 1923 the National Socialists had won 800,000 votes. In 1930 they had 6·5 million. In 1932 nearly 14 million voters out of 45 million voted for the NSDAP, in the last free election of the Weimar Republic.

National Socialism was the consummation towards which the omnifarious anti-Semitic movements had striven for 150 years.

3   Phase One:
Anti-Jewish Legislation, 1933–5

On 30 January 1933, shortly before noon, Paul von Hindenburg, President of the German Republic, administered the oath of office to Adolf Hitler, whom he had decided just the day before to make Chancellor. Hitler swore the oath: 'I will employ my strength for the welfare of the German people, protect the Constitution and laws of the German people, conscientiously discharge the duties imposed on me and conduct my affairs of office impartially and with justice to everyone.' When Hitler uttered those words he had already laid his plans to destroy the constitution and the laws he was swearing to protect. Exercising neither impartiality nor justice, he was about to conduct relentless war on his enemies – democracy, freedom, parliamentarianism, political pluralism and, above all, the Jews, the embodiment of everything he hated.

In the elections of 6 November 1932 the NSDAP had received over 33 per cent of the vote, a decrease from its high in 1930 of 37 per cent. Still, the National Socialists did better than any other party. The left had fared worse, the Socialists getting 20 per cent of the vote and the Communists 17 per cent. The Catholic parties had 15 per cent. The DNVP, the right-wing nationalist party that competed for votes with the NSDAP, got 9 per cent. That election deepened the parliamentary crisis; the government was paralysed. After months of political manoeuvring, Hindenburg decided to form a government based on a coalition of conglomerate right-wing nationalist organizations whose common opposition to the principles of the Weimar Republic occasionally transcended their political and tactical differences – the NSDAP, DNVP, the Stalhelm (a right-wing uniformed veterans' organization), right-wing Catholics and miscellaneous right-wing independents. Hitler was awarded the chancellorship (this, Meinecke said at the time, 'was not necessary') and the National Socialists were given two other seats in the cabinet – Wilhelm Frick

became Minister of the Interior and Hermann Göring minister without portfolio (simultaneously Prussian Minister of the Interior).

Hitler had been appointed Chancellor under Article 48 of the Weimar Constitution, which granted the President the authority to invoke dictatorial power to protect the democratic order from overthrow, a clause originally inserted to ensure against a feared Communist revolution. Yet Hitler himself had repeatedly threatened to overthrow the Weimar Republic. His first official act was to convince Hindenburg and the Cabinet to dissolve the recalcitrant Reichstag and to order new elections on 5 March. Hitler hoped by then to arrange to win a majority and have an incontestable 'legal' mandate from the German people. In his first official proclamation he promised the Germans a 'national awakening' and an end to the 'shameful past' of Weimar. His direction was clear. He persuaded Hindenburg on 4 February to sign a decree that, under Article 48, authorized the Minister of the Interior and the police to prohibit public meetings and to suppress publications that they believed would endanger public security. Providing for prolonged periods of police detention, the decree was used right away against the Socialists, Communists and other opponents of the NSDAP in the upcoming election campaign.

Hitler came to power legally, exploiting the letter of the law to subvert the law. Sensible people were sure that Hitler could not last long, that decency, rationality and political order would – must – reassert themselves. No civilized nation, no rational people, it was held, could endure mass hysteria as a substitute for parliamentarianism, the rule of terror instead of the rule of law. But the Germans had entered upon a macabre era in which evil and irrationality would reign for twelve endless years, in which the whole nation would be suborned. The frenzy of mass meetings would replace the decision in the voting booth, the fluttering of flags would supplant political discussion. The rhythm of the goose-step and the resonance of the Horst Wessel song, the crackling of terror in the streets and the bloodlust of massacres would define the political character of the Third Reich and describe its ambience. The Germans would live by two principles alone: rule by Führership and the dominion of race. They repudiated the Sixth Commandment.

On 27 February the Reichstag building was set afire. Marinus van der Lubbe, a deranged pyromaniacal Dutch Communist, was found on the spot. Even today no one knows for sure if van der Lubbe set the fire on his own initiative, whether he was a tool of the Communists or of the National Socialists conspiring to scapegoat the Communists. Whether by accident or by design, the fire gave Hitler the opportunity he needed. The very next day, over Hindenburg's signature, he issued a series of emergency decrees, the first phase in the process that would shortly undermine the constitution and destroy its guarantees of basic liberties. Described as measures to ward off 'Communist acts of violence endangering the state', these decrees suspended all fundamental freedoms of speech, press, assembly, freedom from invasion of privacy (post, telephone, telegram) and from house search without warrant. They gave the federal government the power to take over the state governments as needed to restore public security, and they imposed the death penalty – in place of life imprisonment – for treason, arson, railway sabotage and the like. Another set of decrees dealt with high treason, in a manner so deliberately ill-defined as to cover every possible form of dissidence, including the publication and dissemination of certain forms of printed matter.

In the next few days before the election, the NSDAP inundated the voters with propaganda about the imminent Communist revolution from which it had rescued Germany, but which still threatened. The terror had succeeded, but not quite enough. The National Socialists increased their vote to nearly 44 per cent, but without a majority Hitler was forced to reaffirm a nationalist coalition with the DNVP, which had won a mere 8 per cent of the votes.

Thereafter the Nazis began diligently to carry through their two-pronged assault of terror and pseudo-legality against their opponents. The SA (Sturmabteilung – Storm Troops), the NSDAP'S private army that had grown to 400,000 – four times larger than the German army permitted under the Treaty of Versailles – accelerated its terror against Communists, Socialists, trade unionists, Jews. At the same time, Hitler began to lay plans to obtain the two-thirds vote at the first session of the newly elected Reichstag needed to pass an Enabling Act – a measure giving the government, without recourse to the Reichstag, the power to promulgate emergency legislation for a specific period of time. The session was set to open on 21 March, marking the sixty-second anniversary of Bismarck's first Reichstag in a unified Germany. While Hitler was negotiating with the DNVP and the Catholic Centrists to get their support for the Enabling Act, his Storm Troopers and police were wrecking, burning and looting Socialist and Communist party offices, assaulting, beating and arresting Socialist municipal officials and Socialist deputies. The Socialist newspaper *Reichsbanner* was suppressed in many German states.

The day before the Reichstag opened, the Cabinet approved the text of the Enabling Act as drafted by Frick. That same day, Heinrich Himmler Reichsführer-SS (Schutzstaffel – Defence Corps, the most sinister of Nazi formations), then provisional police president of Munich, announced that arrangements had been completed for setting up the first concentration camp on the grounds of a former gunpowder factory in the area of Dachau, near Munich. It would serve, according to the *Völkischer Beobachter* to concentrate 'all Communist and, where necessary, *Reichsbanner* and Social Democrat officials . . . [who] cannot be allowed to remain free as they continue to agitate and to cause unrest'.[1]

On the evening of 21 March 1933 the Reichstag opened with an elaborate ceremonial at the Potsdam Garrison Church, where Frederick the Great was enshrined. Hitler, in cutaway and top hat, with unaccustomed tact and modesty, paid formal homage to the aged President in his field marshal regalia. That very day the first prisoners were brought under SA guard to the Oranienburg concentration camp outside Berlin. In the next ten days some 15,000 persons were taken into 'protective custody' in Prussia.

On 23 March the first working session of the Reichstag began, with all Communist deputies and twenty-six of the Socialist deputies missing – arrested or fled. Hitler had not yet convinced the Catholic Centre to support the Enabling Act, and in his introductory address he tried to allay their anxieties over how he would use that authority. In the ensuing three-hour recess, the Centrists bitterly debated the question among themselves and decided finally to support the act. The vote was 441 for the bill, with all ninety-four Socialist deputies against. Standing in the chamber with outstretched arms in their party salute, the National Socialist deputies sang the Horst Wessel song.

The Enabling Act provided Hitler with the legal authority for dictatorship. It gave the government the power for four years to promulgate legislation, even if it deviated from the Constitution. (Under this authority, Hitler himself renewed the act in later years.) In less than eight weeks, Hitler had accomplished his 'legal' revolution, having terrorized the Communists, as he soon would also the Socialists, and with cynical deceit, having promised the rightists and Centrists that he would restore legality and share power with them. But by early July the NSDAP alone remained in existence. The Communists and Social Democrats had been suppressed. Under Hitler's prodding, the DNVP, followed by the smaller parties and the Catholic Centre, proclaimed their own suicide by self-dissolution. 'The party has now become the state,' Hitler declared on 8 July 1933. On 14 July a government degree legally solemnized the *fait accompli* and declared the NSDAP to be the only political party in Germany. Any attempt to maintain another party or form a new one would be punishable by three years of imprisonment, 'if the action is not subject to a greater penalty according to other regulations' – those dealing with high treason, unmistakably.

After obtaining the Enabling Act, Hitler retired to Berchtesgaden. The question now uppermost in his mind concerned the Jews. On 26 March he summoned Goebbels, who had meanwhile become a member of the Cabinet as Minister of Public Enlightenment and Propaganda, and gave him instructions. Goebbels recorded that meeting in his diary:

We shall only be able to combat the falsehoods abroad if we get at those who originated them or at those Jews living in Germany who have thus far remained unmolested. We must, therefore, proceed to a large-scale boycott of all Jewish business in Germany. Perhaps the foreign Jews will think better of the matter when their racial comrades in Germany begin to get it in the neck.[2]

The organization of the anti-Jewish boycott showed Hitler's talent for rationalizing and politicizing raw anti-Semitism, channelling the passion for pogrom on the part of the rank-and-file anti-Semites into 'meaningful' political action. Actually the boycott originated in the spontaneous violence of SA and Nazi hooligans against Jewish businesses and Jews in public life. Department stores, by Nazi definition 'Jewish', were a particular target. (Back in 1920 the NSDAP programme demanded 'that the large stores shall be immediately communalized and rented cheaply to small tradespeople'.) Police protection for Jewish stores was not available. On 11 March, in a speech

at Essen, Göring gave official sanction to the violence: 'I will ruthlessly set the police at work wherever harm is being done to the German people. But I refuse to make the police the guardians of Jewish
department stores.' That same day in Breslau, after the SA had invaded a department store, the police came to stop them. The SA then
broke into the courts, seizing Jewish judges and lawyers and dragging
them through the streets. Again the police intervened, but local
officials were in a quandary, not sure what they should do. Similar
violence occurred in Braunschweig, Göttingen, Leipzig, Dresden,
Chemnitz. In parts of Upper Hesse and Prussia, the SA had organized
a series of boycotts against Jewish businesses and Jewish professionals.
The German propaganda machine implicitly communicated the
message: 'German Jews are our hostages. We will hold on to
them.'³

The crescendo of violence and atrocities had meanwhile aroused
world criticism. The strongest protests were being made on behalf of
the Jews. There was talk, especially in the United States, of a boycott
of German goods. In his characteristically improvisatory and oppor-
tunistic manner, Hitler had decided to exploit SA violence by brand-
ing the Jews as the enemies of Germany and the instigators of a worldwide campaign of lies and calumny to discredit the Reich. Even before
Hitler had summoned Goebbels, he had already instructed his friend
Julius Streicher, the notorious publisher of *Der Stürmer*, a perverted,
vicious anti-Semitic paper, to organize a boycott committee.

Göring too, had had his instructions. On 26 March he summoned
the leaders of the Jewish organizations to his office. Clear, direct and
hostile, Göring told them that they would have to inform the Jews
abroad to stop spreading atrocity stories about Germany and to halt
the anti-German boycott campaign. Otherwise – as one communal
leader later wrote – 'otherwise pogrom'.

The German Jews talked back. They called attention to the dangerous anti-Jewish agitation being carried on by the Nazi press, showing Göring a Nazi paper of Chemnitz, with a photograph of Jews
being forced to wash streets under armed Nazi escort. They wanted
to show other documents in their possession, but Göring impatiently
replied that he had already punished all those guilty. (Not one, of
course, had been punished.) Finally, however, they had to promise,
under threat, to contact Jewish organizations abroad and deny the

atrocity reports. A plethora of cables, telegrams and letters was issued by each Jewish institution in Germany to every contact abroad. Typical of the messages was a telegram of 30 March 1933 from the presidium of the Berlin *Gemeinde* (Jewish community) to the American Jewish Committee.

According to newspaper reports, atrocity and boycott propaganda against Germany is continuing overseas, apparently in part also by Jewish organizations. As Germans and Jews we must enter a decisive protest against this. The dissemination of untrue reports can only bring harm, affecting the reputation of our German fatherland, endangering the relations of the German Jews with their fellow citizens. Please try urgently to see to it that every atrocity and boycott propaganda report is halted.[4]

(The American Jewish oganizations realized that these telegrams were sent under duress.)

On 28 March, two days after Hitler's instructions, it was announced that a boycott of Jewish businesses was being called for 1 April by NSDAP leaders, who had organized a Central Committee for Defence Against Jewish Atrocity and Boycott Propaganda. The NSDAP issued instructions for the conduct of the boycott, whose enforcement became the responsibility of the SA, under supervision of the SS. All party units were to form local boycott committees – as a matter of fact, many had done this spontaneously weeks earlier. In one German town the Nazis placed an advertisement in the local paper, declaring that 'international Jewry' was spreading 'atrocity propaganda' against the Germans and that was why the boycott was being called. Three days later, a second advertisement appeared, with a list of specific businesses and individuals to be boycotted.[5] Party instructions were that teams of two SA and SS 'protective guards' were to be stationed in front of Jewish stores to 'inform' the public that these were Jewish establishments.

At his Cabinet meeting on 29 March Hitler explained that an organized boycott was necessary to control popular anti-Semitic out-breaks, but in an effort to calm the anxieties of the non-Nazis in the Cabinet who feared foreign repercussions, he promised that the boycott would last only one day. Formally, the boycott lasted three days, from Saturday 1 April to Monday 3 April. Though the party instruc-tions were to avoid violence, the police were advised not to interfere, and violence was activated all through Germany. A Jewish lawyer was said to have been lynched by a mob in Kiel.

On 4 April Goebbels announced that the boycott was over. He declared, with a regard for truth characteristic of a Minister of Propaganda, that it was a success since 'with only a few exceptions . . . [the] outrageous foreign propaganda has been stopped'.

Mass violence against Jewish business, in its prematurity, turned out to be politically and economically touchy. But the violence against Jews in public life – which Hans Kerrl, a National Socialist who had become Prussian Minister of Justice, characterized as the 'self-help actions' of the people – offered few risks. Weeks before the boycott, a combination of violence and administrative action had already forced hundreds of Jews from their positions as judges and lawyers in the courts, journalists on newspapers, conductors and musicians in orchestras, professors in universities. In Breslau, for example, in the wake of the disorders of 11 March, the Department of Justice responded within five days to the 'wishes of the people' to 'limit the influence' of Jews in the administration of justice, by reducing the number of Jewish lawyers attached to the Breslau courts.

The dismissals of Jews from positions in government and the professions accelerated through the month. On 25 March the Bavarian Ministry of Justice ordered that Jewish judges be replaced in criminal and disciplinary cases and that Jews be prohibited from serving as prosecutors. On 31 March Kerrl issued a statement to the effect that all persons in authority should ask their Jewish judges to retire the following morning, the day of the boycott. In case the Jews failed to retire, they would be prevented by other means from entering the courthouses. Similarly, Jewish state prosecutors should be retired and the number of Jewish lawyers henceforth admitted to practise in the courts would be limited to the proportion of Jews in the population. Jews would no longer be eligible to serve on juries. (A day earlier, Kerrl had sent one of his legal assistants to Frankfurt to enlighten the judges there about the upcoming Berlin procedures.)

The extent of these dismissals and forced resignations agitated even Hindenburg, whose compliance with Hitler's wishes had hitherto been unhesitating. What prompted Hindenburg to write to Hitler on 4 April was neither conscience over legal niceties nor compassion for Jews, but the honour of the German army:

In the last few days a whole series of cases have been reported to me in which war-wounded judges, lawyers and civil servants in the judiciary, with unblemished records of service, have been forcibly furloughed and will later be dismissed simply because they are of Jewish origin.

For me personally, revering those who died in the war and grateful to those who survived and to the wounded who suffered, such treatment of Jewish war veterans in the civil service is altogether intolerable. I am convinced that you, Herr Chancellor, share these human feelings and therefore I most sincerely urge you to concern yourself with this matter and to see to it that an honourable solution for the entire civil service is found. I believe that civil servants, judges, teachers and lawyers who were wounded in the war or fought at the front, or are sons of those who died or had sons who died in battle must – insofar as they have not given cause to be treated otherwise – be allowed to continue in their professions. If they were worthy to fight and bleed for Germany, then they should also be considered worthy to continue serving the fatherland in their professions.[6]

Hitler replied the next day, expatiating on the harmful effects of the Jewish presence in public life and the professions, and particularly on the deprivations suffered by German war veterans whom the Jews had displaced in the civil service. Nevertheless, taking into consideration the Marshal's 'generous and humane' approach and his 'noble motives', Hitler promised that Hindenburg's suggestions would be incorporated in a law on this question that was being prepared: 'The solution of this problem will be carried out legally, and not by capricious acts.'[7]

Anti-Jewish legislation was a familiar idea to the Nazis. From the earliest days of their parliamentary activity they had introduced anti-Jewish bills into the Reichstag and the state parliaments. In 1924, while Hitler was writing his memoirs in Landsberg, his party comrades had joined with like-minded groups in an election bloc and won thirty-two seats in the Reichstag. Frick held one, remaining in the Reichstag until he joined the Cabinet in 1933. On 27 May 1924 the Nazis introduced a motion 'to place all members of the Jewish race under special legislation [*Sonderrecht*]'. A few months later they proposed a bill to 'exclude members of the Jewish race from all public offices in the Reich' and to 'bring about their immediate removal from office'. Frick, on 17 July 1925, addressed himself especially to the question of civil servants and proposed a bill, 'Reduction of Personnel', which would dismiss from the civil service 'the so-called officials of the revolution' and 'members of the Jewish race'. In explaining the motivation of his bill to the members of the Reichstag, Frick declared: 'We deem it below our dignity to be governed by people of that race.'[8]

In 1930, with 107 Nazis in the Reichstag, there was a spate of Nazi-initiated legislation, including a 'socialist' measure to expropriate without indemnification the 'bank and stock-exchange princes' for 'the welfare of the German people as a whole'. The same was to be done with the property of all East European Jews in Germany and of 'persons of foreign race'. That particular bill, introduced on 14 October 1930, turned the National Socialists into a national laughing stock. Hitler's financial backers, industrialists and bankers, were incensed at such radicalism. On their protest, Hitler then ordered his deputies to withdraw the bill. The Communists promptly reintroduced it, in its original Nazi wording; on Hitler's orders, the NSDAP deputies voted against their own bill.[9] But only the National Socialists laughed when, in 1938, Jewish property, private and communal, was expropriated without indemnification for 'the welfare of the German people as a whole'.

Some legislative proposals that the National Socialists sponsored were incorporated in the twenty-five-point programme that Hitler had introduced at that memorable meeting of the Deutsche Arbeiterpartei on 24 February 1920. According to that programme, Jews could not be citizens of Germany and hence could not hold public office. But the NSDAP programme was itself derivative, drawing on a reservoir of anti-Semitic legislative proposals that had preceded it. The most influential, no doubt, was Heinrich Class's famous work, *Wenn Ich der Kaiser wär'*, in which these specific measures were enumerated:

All public offices, whether national, state or municipal, salaried or honorary, are closed to Jews.

Jews are not admitted to serve in the army or navy.

Jews have neither an active nor a passive right to vote. The occupation of lawyer and teacher is forbidden to them, also the direction of theatres.

Newspapers on which Jews work must make that known; newspapers that may be called 'German' are not permitted to be owned by Jews or to have Jewish managers or co-workers.

Banks that are not purely personal enterprises are not permitted to have any Jewish directors.

In the future rural property may not be owned by Jews or mortgaged by them.

As compensation for the protection that Jews enjoy as aliens, they must pay double the taxes that Germans pay.[10]

German anti-Semites regarded Class's book as 'trail-blazing', and his influence on the National Socialists was decisive. Paul Bang, in the early days a leading member of Class's Alldeutscher Verband and in 1933 State Secretary in the Ministry of Economy, regarded Class's book, which he called an 'excellent treatise', as a 'gold mine' of ideas.[11] On 6 March 1933 Bang sent a 'personal' and unofficial letter to Hans Heinrich Lammers, secretary of the Reich Chancellery, suggesting that the time was ripe for 'consciously Volkist' legislation. He proposed a law halting further East European Jewish immigration and another nullifying all name changes that had taken place since 1 November 1918. Lammers passed these recommendations on to Frick. He, for his part, had his own experts and thick files of draft bills on the 'Jewish question'.

In 1928, when the NSDAP was rapidly expanding, the party organization was divided into two sections: one whose task was to attack and undermine the Weimar régime, the second whose function was to plan for eventual takeover and the new state. Helmut Nicolai (1895–1951), a former official in the Prussian state government, was assigned to plan for the Ministry of the Interior. In the two years before the accession to power, he and his staff prepared memoranda and legislative proposals. An NSDAP memorandum of that time indicated the party's intentions: 'If the NSDAP will receive an absolute majority, Jews will be deprived of their rights by legal means. If however, the NSDAP will attain power only through a coalition, the rights of German Jews will be undermined through administrative means.'[12]

As a matter of fact, Nicolai had declared openly in 1932 that the NSDAP wanted to attain power legally and that it would respect the legal constitution: 'But that does not mean that the NSDAP defends the spirit of equal law, like the present power-holders, whose "system", that is, Jewish-Roman legal ideas, we oppose.'[13] Indeed, he went on to predict that the naturalization of Jews and 'other people of alien race' would be rescinded when the 'legitimate representation of the German *Volk*' came to power. All name changes, too, would be nullified, to prevent further racial contamination. The administration of justice would see to it that the courts and all government administration (civil service) would be 'cleansed' of Jews.

Hitler's 1920 party programme had demanded 'that the Roman law which serves as a materialist ordering of the world shall be replaced by German Common Law'. According to Nicolai, who was closely following party doctrine, 'Jewish–Roman law' derived from the idea of a world state, which erased and eliminated national differences. In contraposition stood 'Nordic, Teutonic, Germanic law', based on *Volk* and race. 'When we utter the word "race",' said Nicolai, addressing German lawyers on 2 October 1933, 'we are sounding the *leitmotiv* of National Socialism and of the National Socialist state. There is absolutely nothing that we, that the new state, do not consider or appraise under the aspect of race.'[14]

The legislation that Hitler's government began to enact sanctioned what violence had already accomplished to a considerable extent – the elimination of Jews from government service and public life. On 7 April, two days after Hitler's letter to Hindenburg promising a 'legal' solution to the 'Jewish problem', the first anti-Jewish law in the Third Reich was promulgated. Eventually, some 400 laws and decrees were enacted, inexorably leading to the destruction of the European Jews. The first decree, entitled 'Law for the Restoration of the Professional Civil Service', authorized the elimination from civil service of Jews and political opponents of the Nazi régime.[15] 'Civil servants of non-Aryan descent must retire', and honorary officials 'must be discharged'. Hindenburg's objections were met in a paragraph exempting 'officials who were already employed as civil servants on or before 1 August 1914, or who, during the World War, fought at the front for Germany or her allies, or whose fathers or sons were killed in action in the World War'.

A companion law, promulgated at the same time, cancelled the admission to the bar of lawyers of 'non-Aryan' descent and denied permission to those already admitted to practise law, with the Hindenburg exemptions. In rapid succession came similar laws excluding Jews from posts as lay assessors, jurors and commercial judges (7 April), patent lawyers (22 April), panel physicians in state social-insurance institutions (22 April), dentists and dental technicians associated with those institutions (2 June). On 25 April the Law Against the Over-crowding of German Schools and Institutions of Higher Learning was promulgated, limiting the attendance of 'non-Aryan' Germans to a proportion to be 'determined uniformly for the entire Reich ter-ritory'. An accompanying executive decree set that ratio for the ad-mission of new pupils at 1·5 per cent until the proportion of 'non-Aryans' would be reduced to a maximum of 5 per cent. On 6 May the Law for the Restoration of the Professional Civil Service was ex-tended to effect honorary professors, university lecturers and notaries. With the promulgation of three more laws – the first forbidding the employment by government authorities of 'non-Aryans' or of per-sons married to them (28 September 1933); the second establishing a Reich Chamber of Culture (29 September 1933), which saw to the exclusion of Jews from cultural and entertainment enterprises (art, literature, theatre, cinema); and the third, the National Press Law (4 October 1933), placing political newspapers under state super-vision and applying to so-called Aryan paragraph to newspapermen – the Nazi régime had accomplished a cardinal objective towards which German professionals and academicians had striven as far back as 1847: the exclusion of Jews from public life, government, culture and the professions.[16]

To simplify and clarify this procedure, a decree defining a 'non-Aryan' was promulgated on 11 April. A 'non-Aryan' was anyone 'descended from non-Aryan, especially Jewish, parents or grand-parents'. Descent was 'non-Aryan' even if only one parent or grand-parent was 'non-Aryan': 'This is to be assumed especially if one parent or grandparent was of Jewish faith.' Thus, in cases of 'racial' ambi-guity, the religious affiliation would be decisive. Every civil servant had to prove 'Aryan' descent, through submission of the appropriate documents – birth certificates and parents' marriage certificate. (Even-tually, elaborate genealogical questionnaires had to be answered.) Finally, to deal with ambiguous or exceptional cases, the decree pro-vided that 'if Aryan descent is doubtful, an opinion must be obtained from the expert on racial research attached by the Reich Minister of the Interior'.

The Nazi definition was simple: a Jew is a Jew is a Jew – that is, down to the third generation.* The files of the Ministry of the Interior probably bulged with legal formulas defining who was a Jew. Precedents in the anti-Semitic literature were abundant. Rudolf Jung, an Austrian Nazi, in his book *Der nationale Sozialismus*, first published in 1919, declared that proof of 'German blood' must be furnished down to the third generation, meaning that all grandparents must be of 'German blood'. At about the same time, Gottfried zur Beek (Ludwig Müller) published, as a supplement to the German translation of the *Protocols of the Elders of Zion*, a *Deutsche Judenordnung (German Regulations for Jews)*, with a somewhat more cumbersome definition: 'All persons are considered as Jews whose ancestors belonged to a community of Mosaic faith until the issuance of the Edict on Jews of 11 March 1812 in Prussia,† or the equivalent laws in other states of the German Federation.'[17]

Class had a more manageable definition: 'A Jew is one who on 18 January 1871‡ belonged to the Jewish religious community, as well as all offspring of persons who were then Jews, even if only one parent was or is Jewish.' In practice, Class's definition worked out to three generations, according to his own illustration: 'The grandchild, for example, of a Jewish convert to Protestantism in 1875, whose daughter married a non-Jew, for example, an officer, would be considered as a Jew.'[18]

Three other laws were promulgated in 1933 that were taken from the standard anti-Semitic and Volkist treasury of legislative proposals. On 21 April a law was promulgated banning *shehitah*, Jewish ritual slaughtering of animals for food. Anti-*shehitah* agitation long predated the Nazis and was a staple of all anti-Semitic propaganda that depicted the procedure of *shehitah* as brutal and inhumane. The Nazis pre-

---

*Hilberg cites a passage from Hellmut von Gerlach's *Von Rechts nach Links* (Zurich, 1937), which states that the anti-Semites in the Wilhelminian Reichstag did not propose any anti-Semitic legislation because they could not agree on a definition of who was a Jew. But Gerlach was wrong. Those deputies proposed many bills. The stumbling block was not in the definition of a Jew, but in the fact that such anti-Jewish draft legislation was transparently illegal under the North German Federation Reichstag Act of 1869 and the Weimar Constitution. The legislators of the Third Reich had no such problem.

† The reference is to Hardenberg's edict emancipating the Prussian Jews.

‡ The date of the founding of the German Empire, when Wilhelm I was inaugurated.

empted the issue. During the 1920s they sponsored an anti-*shehitah* campaign in the state parliaments, and under their influence Bavaria enacted an anti-*shehitah* law in 1930. (No other legislation affecting the practice of Judaism was enacted.)

The Law on the Revocation of Naturalization and Annulment of German Citizenship, promulgated on 14 July, cancelled, on Volkist grounds, naturalization of 'undesirables', which had been granted during the lifetime of the Weimar Republic. The law's executive order (26 July) specified East European Jews as political undesirables, even if they had committed no offence. On 29 September the Hereditary Farm Law was issued, stipulating that only those farmers could inherit farm property who could prove that their ancestors had no Jewish blood as far back as 1800. This was evocative of the 'Anti-Semites' Petition' of 1880, which had complained that rural land, 'the most significant preservative basis of our political structure', was falling increasingly into Jewish hands.

By October 1933, a little more than six months since the Enabling Act had been passed, the National Socialists had succeeded in establishing a 'uniquely German legal system', a phrase taken from a joyful pledge of support given to Hitler by the German Federation of Judges. With German thoroughness, the laws had seen to it that the Jews were dismissed from all positions in public life – government, professions and all of Germany's social, educational and cultural institutions. Both instrumental and affective purposes were served by the enactment of this legislation. For one thing, thousands of jobs became available. Furthermore, the ouster of the Jews brought high elation, solidified party loyalty and augmented party strength. What had begun as popular anti-Semitism, when the taste of victory had stimulated the taste for blood, now received complete legal sanction.

Hitler was consolidating his power. His will was transmitted through decrees; through the courts, whose judges had slavishly prostrated themselves before National Socialism; through the terror of the swaggering SA on the streets and the élitist SS in the concentration camps; and in the relentless flow of propaganda, in print, on the radio and at the mass meetings. All sources of opposition had been crushed or had collapsed. Socialist and Communist leaders had been arrested or had fled. The Protestant clergy assented and gave their blessing. The Catholics were kept in line by the Concordat with the Vatican, ratified on 10 September 1933; their religious rights and institutions were paid for by yielding political rights. Most professors and intellectuals, like most lawyers and judges, in an unparalleled abdication of mind and honour, submitted to the National Socialist state and enhanced it with their prestige. The army, scenting that it would be restored to grandeur and fully reactivated, climbed on the bandwagon.

The only dissatisfaction, it seemed, came from the SA, which had by the end of 1933 become a behemoth of four million, but whose leader, Ernst Röhm, felt unrewarded in the National Socialist state. Hitler began to regard the SA as a threat to his authority. Even though Röhm had been one of his old comrades from the Reichswehr days in Munich of 1919, Hitler did not hesitate to move against him. Over a period of months the SS and the army were readied, at Hitler's orders, to attack the SA. It was then that the SS emerged as the 'élite' party military organization that would eventually dominate all Europe; it was then that the army smelled its great opportunity. On 30 June 1934 about 200 SA men, including Röhm himself, were murdered with unspeakable brutality. The SA was finished as a major force in the German dictatorship and would henceforth exist under the shadow of the SS.

The ugly massacre was misunderstood within Germany and outside. Instead of seeing that Germany was being run, in Gerhart Ritter's characterization, by 'a gang of criminals' who did not hesitate to shoot each other down with the vilest cruelty, many Germans believed that the purge of the SA represented Hitler's wish to halt the arbitrary terror of the SA in the streets and to restore a measure of legality to the country. After Hindenburg's death on 2 August and Hitler's 'legal' merger of the chancellorship and the presidency, people hoped that things would somehow settle down. No significant anti-Jewish legislation was enacted during 1934, and that fact, too, reinforced the illusion that Jews might remain in Germany, albeit with limited rights.

1935 brought Hitler new triumphs that had repercussions on the Jews. The year opened with a plebiscite in the Saar, for which the Nazis had launched a propaganda campaign as far back as 1933. It paid off, when 90 per cent of the voters supported reunion with Germany. That victory released some of Germany's restraints in international politics. On 16 March Hitler publicly repudiated those clauses of the Versailles Treaty that had disarmed Germany, and he announced the inauguration of compulsory universal military service in Germany. The European powers were dismayed, but using a formula that he would apply time and again with repeated success despite repeated deception, Hitler allayed their fears. In a major foreign-policy address on 21 May 1935 he offered to conclude bilateral non-aggression pacts with all Germany's neighbours and solemnly assured the world that he wanted only peace.

The mood in Germany was exuberant. German rearming and re-militarization had restored what the National Socialists liked to call German national honour. With an abundance of boisterous aggression to spend, in the absence of an external enemy, the Germans turned with renewed fervour against the internal enemy. Just as the Crusaders, who could not contain their passion for deliverance until they reached the Holy Land, struck the infidel in their midst, so too did the Germans. At the end of March 1935 acts of terror and boycotts of Jewish businesses were renewed. All local and national NSDAP party organizations and their associated institutions joined in a massive discharge of hate and violence. During the summer of 1935 Jews were prevented from going into cinemas, theatres, swimming pools, resorts. Small businesses were paralysed by boycott and by violence, particularly in Berlin's main shopping street. Jewish newspapers were forced to suspend publication for periods of two or three months. But, precipitously, the party called a halt. The *Schwarze Korps*, organ of the SS, then editorialized: 'The Jewish question is one of our people's most burning problems; it will not be solved by terror in the streets.'

The records are not clear, but we can surmise that the violence against businesses was held to be premature. Besides, Hitler and most of his Cabinet increasingly showed a dislike of authentically spontaneous mob violence that was unpredictable and ungovernable. Though the party had become the state, the view of party leaders and Cabinet ministers differed sharply. At a conference called by Reichsbank President Hjalmar Schacht on 20 August 1935 of the heads of departments of the Ministry of Economy, the disagreement was overt and acrimonious.[19] Schacht condemned the 'irresponsible Jew-baitings' because they diminished his ability to perform his duties effectively. He especially referred to repercussions abroad. Frick, who was present, had even drafted an order to the state governments demanding ruthless police intervention in 'illegal actions' against the Jews. (The order was never issued because it was feared that it would be construed as capitulation to 'international Jewry' and tantamount to admission of the extent of the terror, which had hitherto been officially minimized.) Despite the general tenor of the meeting, which favoured legal measures to exclude the Jews from economic life, the NSDAP continued to justify 'radical action' against them for 'politico-emotional and abstract ideological considerations'.

As once before in 1933, so now in 1935 the violence of anti-Semitism was channelled into law. On the occasion of the annual NSDAP congress in Nuremberg, new anti-Jewish laws, the so-called 'Nuremberg Laws', were adopted unanimously by the Reichstag on 15 September 1935. These laws legitmated racist anti-Semitism and turned the 'purity of German blood' into a legal category. They forbade marriage and extra-marital relations between Germans and Jews and disenfranchised those 'subjects' or 'nationals' of Germany who were not of German blood.

As with previous legislation, the Nuremburg Laws validated practices already in effect through administrative order or NSDAP pressure. As early as October 1933 the mayor of Mainz had instructed the Mainz Registry Office to inform him of every announcement of an impending marriage between a 'person of German origin' and a 'racial Jew'. The information was to be transmitted to the regional NSDAP, which would then 'suggest' that the German partner reconsider the marriage in view of the problems that would arise as a consequence. The Registry Office was also to point out to the German partner the difficulties that might ensue from such a marriage, with regard to employment and offspring.[20] The Mainz directives were not an isolated instance in Germany. The combined pressure of state and party, as delineated in the Mainz order, was being exerted wherever an impending 'mixed' marriage became known in Germany. Mob law was not uncommon in forcing a halt to such marriages.

Nicolai, in his speech of 2 October 1933, had characterized the regulation of marriage for the purpose of maintaining the racial purity of Nordic stock as the 'first legally creative act of the Nordic people'. Even earlier, in June 1932, Göring, in a campaign speech, promised that not only would all Jews be removed from government offices and public life, but he specifically pledged also that the Nazis would not allow marriages between Germans and Jews. For years this racial/sexual prohibition had been a staple of Streicher's *Stürmer* and it can no doubt be traced back to racist pornographers like Lanz von Liebenfels whose writings had titillated Hitler in his early days. Fritsch's 'Ten German Commandments of Lawful Self-Defence', in his *Antisemiten-Katechismus*, contained two 'commandments' for maintaining racial purity, whose spirit the Nuremberg Laws later captured:

Thou shalt keep thy blood pure. Consider it a crime to soil the noble Aryan breed of thy people by mingling it with the Jewish breed. For thou must know that Jewish blood is everlasting, putting the Jewish stamp on body and soul unto the farthest generations.

Thou shalt have no social intercourse with the Jew. Avoid all contact and community with the Jew and keep him away from thyself and thy family, especially thy daughters, lest they suffer injury of body and soul.[21]

Nicolai had tried to legitimate Volkist racial legislation through tradition and claimed to base himself on the *Sachsenspiegel*, an authoritative legal code in northern Germany, *circa* 1230, which was allegedly purely Germanic, uninfluenced by Roman law. But the centrality of *Volk* and race in Nazi legal thought actually derived not from the *Sachsenspiegel*, but from *Mein Kampf*. There was one specific passage in which Hitler rambled on about racial purity and its importance in the light of the 'syphilization' of the German people. This provided the rationale for National Socialist racial legislation: '*Blood sin and desecration of the race are the original sin in this world and the end of a humanity which surrenders to it.*' In Hitler's mind, the 'fight against syphilis' was associated with a campaign against prostitution and the restoration of the true purpose of marriage – offspring. Marriage, Hitler wrote, cannot be an end in itself, but 'must serve the one higher goal, the increase and preservation of the species and race'. Indeed, Hitler had already conceived of the state's regulating marriage for racial purposes in *Mein Kampf*: '*A folkish state must therefore begin by raising marriage from the level of continuous defilement of the race, and give it the consecration of an institution which is called upon to produce images of the Lord and not monstrosities half-way between man and ape.*' The ape-men of Lanz von Liebenfels's *Ostara* were apparently still vivid in Hitler's mind. Within a very short time after their accession to power, the Nazis began to promulgate laws whose purpose was to 'increase and preserve' the German people biologically. On 1 June 1933 a Law for the Reduction of Unemployment was issued, whose Section 5, 'Encouragement of Marriages', offered financial aid to needy young couples wishing to marry, with remittances of the loan for each child born. Candidates for such state aid had to submit certificates attesting to personal and 'racial' health and also pass a test of political health, that is, loyalty to the Nazi state. This dual qualification of racial purity and political loyalty foreshadowed the qualifications for Reich citizenship as defined in the Nuremberg Laws.

On 28 June 1933 Frick spoke at the first meeting of the Council of Experts on Population and Race Policy: 'Only when the State and the public-health authorities will strive to make the core of their responsibilities the provision for the yet unborn, then we can speak of a new era and of a reconstructed population and race policy.' As a first step, he concentrated on the necessity of preventing those afflicted with serious hereditary diseases from reproducing themselves. A law to this effect was promulgated on 14 July, legalizing sterilization for nine categories of people afflicted with hereditary disease. The law empowered so-called Hereditary Health Courts to carry out sterilization even against the will of the individual concerned.

Soon a host of institutions would come into being for racial breeding and purification. The preservation of German racial purity – 'positive' eugenics – was as important an aspect of racial policy in National Socialist legislation as the exclusion of Jewish 'impurity'. The 'euthanasia' programme eventually followed as a logical consequence.

The disenfranchisement of the Jews embodied the most fundamental demand of every anti-Semitic movement from the start of the Emancipation. The NSDAP programme of 1920 clearly related citizenship to race:

Only those who are our fellow Germans [*Volksgenosse*] shall be citizens of our state. Only those who are of German blood can be considered as our fellow Germans regardless of creed. Hence no Jew can be regarded as a fellow German.

Those who are not citizens of the state must live in Germany as foreigners and must be subject to the law of aliens. ◦

Early in January 1934 Nicolai, now president of Madgeburg, published his ideas of appropriate draft legislation for citizenship in the
National Socialist state. There were to be four categories: (1) full-
blooded 'Aryan' citizens, (2) foreigners residing in Germany, (3)
Germans residing abroad, (4) Germans of alien blood, specifically Jews,
Poles and Gypsies. (The categories, except for Germans residing
abroad, were all taken from Hitler's discussion of 'Subjects and
Citizens' in *Mein Kampf*.) The fourth category would have the protection of the state, but would not be allowed to hold public office,
marry or have sexual relations with 'Aryans'.[22] That proposal was
likely a product of Nicolai's apprentice years, before his accession to
power, and similar draft bills must have bulked in the files of the
Ministry of the Interior.

On 27 July 1935, just seven weeks before the promulgation of the
Nuremberg Laws, Frick sent a memorandum to all states informing
them that marriages between Aryans and non-Aryans would shortly
be regulated by law. He instructed all registry offices to postpone not
only such marriages, but even their announcement.[23] Still, nothing
was done until Hitler decided, suddenly and unexpectedly, on 13
September, that he wanted such legislation for the special ceremonial
session of the Reichstag on 15 September, to mark the festive closing
of the party congress. The only law in preparation for that occasion
was one forbidding the Jews to display the Nazi flag, which Hitler had
thought of as a response to a demonstration in New York on 26 July
1935, when the swastika flag was ripped off the SS *Bremen*. Hitler now
wanted something more spectacular and told Frick to prepare legislation regulating German–Jewish 'blood' relationships.

Frick put Hans Pfundtner and Wilhelm Stuckart, his two top men in
the Ministry, both then in Nuremberg, on the assignment. Needing
the various draft bills in the files in Berlin, Stuckart telephoned
Bernhard Lösener, the expert on 'racial law' in the Ministry, and instructed him to fly to Nuremberg with the files.[24] Lösener arrived on
Saturday morning, 14 September, and from then until about 3.00 a.m.
on 15 September they composed drafts of bills that Frick then brought
to Hitler for his consideration. Before long the Law for the Protection
of German Blood and German Honour, whose basic provisions Hitler
had outlined to Frick, was completed. Its preamble declared:

Imbued with the insight that the purity of German blood is pre-requisite for the continued existence of the German people, and inspired by the inflexible will to ensure the existence of the German nation for all times, the Reichstag has unanimously adopted the following law, which is hereby promulgated.

The provisions were simplicity itself: marriage between Jews and 'nationals of German kindred blood' was forbidden; extramarital relations between the two groups were forbidden. Jews were forbidden to employ female domestic help under forty-five years of age who were of 'German or kindred blood'.* Finally, Jews were forbidden to fly the German national colours, but could display 'Jewish' colours.

Then Hitler asked them to prepare a basic Reich citizenship law. This took about an hour to prepare, and Hitler accepted the first draft. In line with Hitler's views in *Mein Kampf* and with the NSDAP programme of 1920, this law gave the Jews a special status as subjects in Germany, reminiscent of a medieval Teutonic 'law of aliens'. The Reich Citizenship Law distinguished between a subject (*Staatsange-hörige*) and a citizen of the Reich (*Reichsbürger*). A subject was anyone who enjoyed the protection of the Reich and was therefore obligated to it. A Reich citizen was a subject with 'German or cognate blood' and acquired a 'Reich certificate of citizenship', a reward that Hitler had already conceived in *Mein Kampf*.

The Reich Citizenship Law, as State Secretary Stuckart and his assistant, Hans Globke, explained in their commentary on German racial legislation, represented a revolutionary break from past concepts of individual rights and freedoms.[25] National Socialism, confronting the doctrines of the past on the equality of men, discovered that these doctrines did not take cognizance of the inequality of men, of their racial and national differences. Differences in rights and obligations should derive from racial differences, and that was the achievement of the Reich Citizenship Law. National Socialism conceived the state as the political instrument of the *Volk*. Consequently, citizenship was not a matter of individual rights but derived from membership in

*Psychoanalysts see in this a projection of Hitler's anxieties about his own origins, but the idea was commonplace in National Socialist ideology. A demand that Jews be forbidden to employ 'Aryan' women as servants appeared, for instance, in Streicher's *Stürmer* on 2 January 1934.

the *Volk*. 'The recognition of the significance of blood and race for *Volk* and State', they wrote, 'is one of the principal bases of the National Socialist world view.' Yet even race did not suffice as a criterion for citizenship in this racial state. Additionally, the Reich subject of German or cognate blood also had to prove by his conduct that he was 'willing and able loyally to serve the German people and the Reich'. Thus Reich citizenship was bestowed upon those both racially pure and politically subservient. *Kadavergehorsam* (slavish obedience) had long been regarded as an unfortunate German trait. Now it had its political reward. Yet the Reich Citizenship Law perpetrated a fantastic hoax upon the Germans. The Reich citizen was declared to be the 'sole bearer of full political rights'. But rights no longer existed in Germany. There were no political parties, no elections, no freedoms, no protection. The only right a citizen had was to give his assent – by shouting himself hoarse at mass rallies or by voting '*Ja*' in one of the five plebiscites that Hitler had substituted for political democracy. For unless the Reich citizen was *kadavergehorsam*, he would more likely be cadaver than citizen.

The Jews, however, were not hoaxed. The law and its thirteen supplementary decrees (the last published on 1 July 1943) set the Jews apart from the Germans legally, politically, socially. Henceforth, they would be outside the protection of the state. Eventually, they would be completely at the mercy of the secret police, without access to law or courts. Indeed, the *Sachsenspiegel* had been far more humane in the protection it afforded the Jew as alien.

The centrality of 'blood and race' that obsessed National Socialism was transformed with bureaucratic fastidiousness into legal racial categories. While drafting the Law for the Protection of German Blood and German Honour, the legal experts proposed certain distinctions among different categories of *Mischlinge*, the 'mixed' offspring of Germans and Jews. Hitler had rejected these at the time, but left their legal clarification for supplementary decrees. After week-long conferences of legal and racial experts (Hitler had himself called a meeting on this subject), the Ministry of the Interior finally arrived at a set of definitions of the different categories of *Mischlinge*. The basic definition of a Jew, supplanting the defintion of 11 April 1933, was published on 14 November 1935 in the first supplementary decree to the

Reich Citizenship Law. Later regulations defined categories of *Mischlinge* that did not come under the rubric of 'Jew'.

Briefly, the categories were: (1) Jew, (2) *Mischling*, first degree, and (3) *Mischling*, second degree. A Jew was anyone with at least three full Jewish grandparents. Also legally to be regarded as a Jew was someone who had two full Jewish grandparents and who belonged to the Jewish religious community when the law was promulgated on 15 September 1935, or who joined later, or who was married to a Jew then or later, or (looking to the future) who was the offspring of a marriage contracted with a Jew after 15 September 1935, or who was born out of wedlock after 31 July 1936, the offspring of extra-marital relations with a Jew. Anyone who was one-eighth or one-sixteenth Jewish – with one Jewish great-grandparent or great-great-grandparent – would be considered as of German blood.

More complicated was the status of the 'part-Jews'. A person with two Jewish grandparents, who did not otherwise fit into the group defined as Jews, that is, who was not affiliated with the Jewish religious community, who was not married to a Jew, etc., was designated as '*Mischling,* first degree'. A person with only one Jewish grandparent was designated as '*Mischling*, second degree'. For the time being, these distinctions affected marriage and offspring of that marriage. Within a few short years they were to decide between life or death.

The Nuremberg Laws completed the disenfranchisements of the Jews of Germany. The first stage of the National Socialist programme had been achieved. Hitler himself, in introducing the laws to the Reichstag assembled at Nuremberg, hinted at a forthcoming change in anti-Jewish policy. The Law for the Protection of German Blood and German Honour, he said, was 'an attempt to regulate by law a problem that, in the event of repeated failure, would have to be transferred by law to the National Socialist Party for final solution'.[26]

During the next few years no substantial anti-Jewish legislation was enacted. Instead the SS, the most prestigious and dreaded branch of the National Socialist movement, increasingly began to assert its hegemony with regard to the Jews over all state and party institutions.

4 The SS: Instrument of
the Final Solution

In 1936 a standard lecture for SS units contained the following passage: 'The Jew is a parasite. Wherever he flourishes, the people die ... Elimination of the Jew from our community is to be regarded as an emergency defence measure.'[1] The 'right of emergency defence' was the title Hitler used for the last chapter of *Mein Kampf*, in which he had advocated the gassing of 'twelve or fifteen thousand' Jews. The SS text reveals the emerging role of the SS as an expression of Hitler's will and as the central executing arm in the Final Solution of the Jewish Question.

The SS came into being early in 1925, by Hitler's order, as a select corps drawn from SA membership to serve as an efficient, élite and completely dependable bodyguard for the party's leadership. The emphasis from the start was on loyalty, obedience and discipline, but the SS remained insignificant in size and undistinguished in function until Hitler appointed Heinrich Himmler to head it and conferred upon him, in January 1929, the grandiose title of Reichsführer-SS. Himmler soon transformed the SS into an organization guided solely by the will of the Führer and that became, in Hans Buchheim's words, 'the real and essential instrument of the Führer's authority'.[2] Indeed, Himmler came to regard himself as an instrument of Hitler's will.

Himmler's name and title have come to evoke images of a demonic evil contained within a frame of steely iciness, rigour and discipline, unloosed not in the passion of rage or hate, but on calculation. Yet his early life, shaped by familial authoritarianism, seemed ordinary and dull, never suggestive of the sinister role he would later assume.

Born in 1900 in Munich, the second son of middle-class Catholic parents, Himmler had an unexceptional youth. The diary that he started to keep in 1914 shows him as pedantic, pedestrian and unimaginative, already moulded according to the parental tradition of rigid self-discipline. When war broke out, he was stricken with patriotic passion. At seventeen, when he reached the age of eligibility, he applied to an officer training programme and was eventually admitted, but while he was still in training the armistice was signed. However, the cadets in training were not discharged until after the military had suppressed the revolution, dissolved its institutions, and regained political control. Here the young Himmler may have had his first lessons in the uses of the military for political suppression.

1919 was the critical year for Himmler as it had been for Hitler. During his military training, Himmler was no doubt indoctrinated in rightist–nationalist politics. Surely there was talk about the Dolchstoss, betrayal by the Jews, and the 'Jewish' role in the abortive Communist revolution that he witnessed. It must have been an extraordinary revelation. In mid-1919, while recuperating from an illness – he was always sickly and ailing – he read twenty-eight books, some of which showed his newly developing interest in politics and war as well as in anti-Semitism and anti-Masonry.[3] Of a tract replete with anti-Semitic anecdotes, which drew lavishly from the *Protocols of the Elders of Zion* and which depicted Jews, Freemasons and Democrats as fomenters of revolution, Himmler noted in his diary: 'A book that explains everything and tells us whom we must fight against next time.' He was to continue reading this kind of literature for the next few years.

Early in 1920 Himmler joined the Einwohnerwehr, a home-guard force, one of the many military and paramilitary groups formed by ex-soldiers reluctant to abandon military pursuits, whose nationalist bias intensified their discontent with Germany's new democratic government. Later that year, having decided that he would be a farmer, he enrolled in an agricultural training school and undertook to do his practical training on a farm. During this period, living in relative isolation, his nationalist political passion seemed to have been stilled, but shortly after his return to Munich at the end of 1921 he renewed his interest in rightist politics. He resumed his anti-Semitic reading, which now included Houston Stewart Chamberlain's booklet *Rasse und Nation*, of which he wrote in his diary: 'It is true and one has the impression that it is objective, not just hate-filled anti-Semitism. Because of this it has more effect. These terrible Jews.'

German racial notions began to absorb him. He had apparently renewed his contacts with the paramilitary and clandestine nationalist

organizations then flourishing in Munich, and seemed eager to participate in their activities. When he completed agricultural school, he got
a job just outside Munich with a nitrogen fertilizer company, reflecting, no doubt, a streak of coprophilia. While there, in the autumn of
1922, he joined the Reichsflagge, one of the military groups under Ernst
Röhm's leadership, and in August 1923, following Röhm, Himmler
joined the NSDAP. The next month he quit his job and joined the
Bavarian Reichswehr, fulfilling his boyhood warrior ambitions. In
Hitler's attempted putsch that November, Himmler was the ensign
bearer for Röhm's military formations. Although the ignominious
failure of the putsch and the subsequent suppression of the rightist
nationalist organizations (including the NSDAP) depressed Himmler,
they did not weaken the magnetism that drew him to rightist politics.

Early in 1924 he joined the Nationalsozialistische Freiheitsbewegung
(NSFB; National Socialist Freedom Movement), headed by General
Ludendorff and Gregor Strasser, one of the new Volkist organizations
set up as a substitute for the banned NSDAP. He threw himself in-
tensively into work for Volkist causes, speaking and writing. He
stopped looking for work, lost touch with his old friends and his old
way of life. But his reading habits and his literary taste persisted without change. About half the books he read were anti-Semitic or Volkist,
or at the very least elicited anti-Semitic comments that he set down in
his diary. He discovered Fritsch's *Handbuch der Judenfrage*, in which
'one can find all the relevant material . . . If only some of the eternally
blind could have it put before their eyes.' He read avidly about Hitler
and was deeply impressed by Eckart's *Der Bolschewismus von Moses bis
Lenin*, which he promised himself to re-read often. In 1924 Himmler
wrote of Hitler that he 'is truly a great man, and above all a genuine
and pure one. His speeches are splendid works of Germandom and
Aryanism.'

About this time, too, Himmler discovered that his interest in agriculture could be brought into a racial context. He is believed to have
come under the influence of the Artamanen Bund, a racialist utopian
group that held that a nation could be kept vital and creative only
through the existence of peasant communities of racial and national
purity. This pseudo-mystical and occultist doctrine of 'blood and soil'
deeply affected him, but would not find an outlet until after he had

attained sufficient confidence in himself and high rank in the Nazi party to indulge in such exercises. (Hitler, though himself attracted to occultist Volkism, had learned the lesson of Schönerer's failure and tried to discourage these tendencies within the party.)

In June 1924 Himmler finally found a job he wanted, one that would satisfy him ideologically and provide him with the political environment he had come to need. He became secretary and general assistant to Strasser, who was the NSFB Gauleiter for Lower Bavaria. Early in May 1925 the whole Strasser organization, lock, stock and barrel, went over to the NSDAP, which Hitler had begun to rebuild after his release fron Landsberg. Thus Himmler automatically became the NSDAP Deputy Gauleiter of Lower Bavaria. A year later, when Strasser became the party's propaganda leader, Himmler was once again made his deputy. In 1927 Himmler was appointed deputy leader of the SS, and finally, in 1929, at the age of twenty-nine, with the appointment as Reichsführer-SS, he emerged at the top of the field in his chosen career – the professional Nazi.

As Reichsführer-SS Himmler was able to integrate his diverse compulsions and obsessions – with the military, the occult, racial nationalism and anti-Semitism – and give them form and substance. The SS became a proving ground for Himmler's romantic, grandiose and sinister ideas and offered scope for him to exercise his pedantry and his proclivities for spying and informing. It became the vehicle through which his meanness, hardness and vindictiveness found deadly expression. His rigid sense of duty and obedience turned him into a zealot carrying out Hitler's murderous ideology with fanatical 'idealism'. No wonder the SS's most distinctive insignia was to become the death's-head.

The SS began, as its name, Schutzstaffel (Defence Corps), indicates, as an armed formation within the SA to protect the Führer, top party leaders and party meetings. It also gathered confidential information about suspect party members. When Himmler took it over, the SS had 280 members, while the SA, its parent body and the party's paramilitary organization, had some 60,000 members. Himmler decided not just to expand the SS, but to convert it into an élite brotherhood selected according to racial criteria, permeated with a racial mystique, imbued with medieval, chivalric concepts (loyalty, honour, bravery and the like), using the symbols and practising the rituals of Teutonism.

The appeal to 'élitism' succeeded in recruiting into the SS a broader variety of men than the down-and-outers who had joined the SA. By the end of 1930 the SS had nearly 3,000 members. The enmity between the SS and SA had then become so intense that Hitler had to step in. Fearing that the SA was or might become disloyal to him, Hitler threw his support to the SS, making it independent of the SA and even giving permission for an SS black uniform to distinguish it from the SA's brown shirts. More important, Hitler expanded the SS's functions: 'The task of the SS is primarily to carry out police duties within the party.'[4] The SS was thenceforth to be Hitler's vigilant force, blindly dedicated to him, unflinching in its loyalty. On induction, the SS man swore an oath: 'I swear to you, Adolf Hitler, as Führer and Chancellor of the German Reich, loyalty and valour. I pledge to you and to the superiors whom you will appoint obedience unto death, so help me God.'

To ensure the high racial quality of SS recruits and also to lay the groundwork for Germany's future racial policy as he saw it, Himmler set up in 1931 a Rasse- und Siedlungsamt (RuSA; Race and Settlement Office), later Rasse- und Siedlungshauptamt (RuSHA; Race and Settlement Main Office). To head it he appointed Richard Walther Darré, the author of the 'blood and soil' doctrine, who had strongly influenced Himmler some years before. The RuSA had as its primary function the physical and racial screening of prospective SS candidates. After Himmler's Betrothal and Marriage Order of 31 December 1931 the RuSA also investigated the racial genealogy of the prospective brides of SS members. SS members who married without permission of Himmler and the RuSA were expelled from the organization. The ultimate goal of this procedure was to form a racially superior stock from which Germany's future leadership would come. (To encourage the bearing of racially valuable children, Himmler established within the SS in 1935 an organization called Lebensborn – Well of Life.)[5] This racial élite would have to return to the soil for its vitality. The RuSA conducted an intensive racial and ideological indoctrination programme along these lines and Darré tried to encourage SS families to settle in rural areas. Although this rural settlement programme was of no practical consequence, it prefigures the more fanatical programme, on a wholesale scale, that Himmler embarked on during the war, involving population transfers and rural resettlement on a racial basis, carried out in characteristic SS fashion.

Himmler's SS grew rapidly. When the Nazis came to power, it had 50,000 members. On the eve of the war, it had nearly a quarter of a million. Most of these men belonged to the Allgemeine SS (General SS), which, as it expanded, came to be organized in about thirty regional divisions. The Allgemeine SS spun off two other formations: the Verfügungstruppe (Reserve or Special Troops) and the Totenkopfverbände (Death's-Head Units).

The Verfügungstruppe originated out of political stand-by squads, which served as an auxiliary police force ready to go into action at any threat to Hitler, at any order from Himmler. (The most famous unit was the Leibstandarte Adolf Hitler, set up in March 1933.) Aware of the advantages of having his own military force, Himmler united these squads into the Verfügungstruppe, a sort of National Socialist army to be relied on in the event of treachery on the part of the regular army. In September 1934 it was accorded official status by a decree of the Defence Minister, permitting the SS to maintain 'a standing armed force for such special internal political tasks as may be allotted to the SS by the Führer'. By 1936 the Verfügungstruppe numbered 10,000 and even had its own cadet schools. Though service in the Verfügungstruppe under Nazi law counted as military service, the regular army resented it and until the outbreak of war refused to legitimate it as part of Germany's armed forces. On 17 August 1938 Hitler issued a secret directive clarifying the relationship between the Verfügungstruppe and the Wehrmacht in peacetime and in the event of war. The directive reaffirmed the military character of the Verfügungstruppe. In peacetime, under Himmler's command, its units – which belonged neither to the Wehrmacht nor the police, but were a permanent armed formation of the NSDAP exclusively at Hitler's disposal – were to be available for 'internal political tasks'. But in the event of mobilization, the Verfügungstruppe could be used by the commander-in-chief of the army and, though remaining a branch of the NSDAP, its units would then be subject to army instructions and military law.

The Totenkopfverbände originated from the guard unit at Dachau, the first concentration camp in National Socialist Germany. When the Nazis came to power, 'deprivation of freedom in the form of protective custody' became the order of the day, and by March 1933 the prisons could no longer hold the thousands arrested in 'preventive' measures to eliminate 'threats from subversive elements'.[6] Camps then were set up throughout Germany by Himmler in his capacity as head of the Bavarian police, the first at Dachau. By the summer of 1933 there were ten or more camps and detention centres, organized and operated by the SS, the SA or the police, with over 25,000 inmates – Social Democrats, Communists, members of other opposition parties, journalists and writers (especially Jews) and various other 'unpopular' categories.

In this early period, 'wild improvisation', to use Martin Broszat's phrase, characterized the operation of the camps, but soon they came under Himmler's exclusive authority and were thenceforth removed from the control of the state's administrative and legal jurisdiction and operated outside the ordinary processes of law.

To reorganize the camps Himmler chose Theodor Eicke, an SS Oberführer (brigadier general), whom he had once committed to a psychiatric clinic, then released in June 1933 for appointment as commandant at Dachau. Eicke's hardness, ruthlessness, ideological commitment and his exemplary organization of the camp, especially his systematization of 'disciplinary camp regulations', won him advancement in May 1934 to reorganize the other camps and standardize their procedures. Eicke distinguished himself a month later by personally shooting Röhm, an act for which he was rewarded on 4 July 1934 with a new title of Inspekteur der Konzentrationslager und Führer der SS-Wachverbände (Inspector of Concentration Camps and Commander of SS Guard Units) and, a week later, with a promotion in rank.

Eicke's reorganization led to consolidation of the smaller camps into larger ones with uniform procedures and administration. By March 1935 there were seven camps, with a prison population under 10,000 (Dachau, the largest, had 2,500 inmates). The guard units were enlarged, organized in battalions and given their chilling designation as Totenkopfverbände. Thereafter, funds for the operation of the concentration camps and for Eicke's armed-guard units came from the budget of the Ministry of the Interior. Though the number of prisoners in protective custody in the next two years declined and the small camps were closed down, two new camps were built with a capacity as large as Dachau's – Buchenwald and Sachsenhausen.

By the end of 1937 the Totenkopfverbände numbered 5,000 men, in three formations that Himmler hoped to bring into his military establishment. But although the military had been forced to yield in some areas with regard to the Verfügungstruppe, they drew the line at the Totenkopfverbände, clearly an ideological organization that had no aspirations to acquire a spit-and-polish military character. After the war began, however, Himmler managed to bring some of Eicke's units into his SS army, and along with the Verfügungstruppe, these also took part in the military campaign in Poland. In mid-1940 the Verfügungstruppe, augmented by Totenkopfverbände units and police reinforcements, were redesignated as the Waffen-SS (Armed SS).

High in the hierarchy of terror was the SS's Sicherheitsdienst (SD; Security Service). It grew into a surveillance system that encompassed all Germany and then all occupied Europe, an evil organizational eye whose vigilance no one could escape. The SD was originally established in accordance with Hitler's directive, in 1930, when the spy mania in the NSDAP was rampant. A security service was wanted not just to sniff out disloyalty and treachery in the tangle of intra-party intrigue that threatened Hitler's leadership, but also because the NSDAP was being infiltrated by spies from opposition parties and by police agents of the Weimar government. Himmler gave this new intelligence-gathering agency a modest name – Unterabteilung Ic (Ic Subdivision), 'Ic' being army code for a section dealing with enemy intelligence. To head this subdivision he appointed Reinhard Heydrich.

Heydrich, barely four years younger than Himmler, had, like him, been too young for service in the First World War, but his patriotic military fervour found an outlet in his imagination. Years later he claimed he had been a runner in the Freikorps at fifteen.[7] But it is not unlikely that at sixteen he did belong to some military or paramilitary group, perhaps a home-guard troop. During the war he is said to have developed 'extreme Volkist' ideas and turned into a 'fanatic about pure race'. He joined, or tried to join, various Volkist, nationalist organizations in the immediate post-war years. He is said to have told a fellow cadet in the German navy some years later that he had once been a member of the Deutsch-Völkische Schutz- und Trutzbund (German-Volkist Protective and Offensive Alliance), an aggressively anti-Semitic, rightist, nationalist group. He joined, he said, because in his home town of Halle his father was considered a Jew and called 'Jew Süss'. This injured his pride and honour; the only way to silence such talk, he thought, was to be active in anti-Semitic circles. That was why he joined the Schutz- und Trutzbund. The talk in Halle then took a different tack: the elder Heydrich could surely not be a Jew since his son was such a furious anti-Semite.

The story of Heydrich's alleged Jewish ancestry persisted during his lifetime and after. The genealogical facts are these: Heydrich's paternal grandmother was married twice. By her first husband, Reinhold Heydrich, she had many children, including Richard Bruno Heydrich, Reinhard's father. After Reinhold's death, she married a locksmith called Süss, an Evangelical-Lutheran with impeccable 'Aryan' credentials. In later years 'Süss' was sometimes appended to Bruno Heydrich's name. The Jewish attribution came about because Süss was commonly regarded as a Jewish surname (for example, in Lion Feuchtwanger's novel *Jud Süss*, published in 1926). Whatever his motivating impulse, Heydrich spent a good part of his adolescent years in anti-Semitic and Volkist, nationalist circles where his identity as an uncompromising anti-Semite and Nazi was shaped.

He became a naval cadet in 1922 and in a few years had a promising career ahead of him. But early in 1931 he was cashiered from the navy because of scandals involving a woman. He then joined the Naval SA, not that it offered the possibility of a career, but presumably because of ideological compatibility and the opportunity to continue to wear a military uniform. Since he was without a job or the possibility of one, his sister cast about among friends and family for useful contacts and found a leading SA officer, who brought Heydrich to Himmler's attention.

In appearance Heydrich was the Nordic dream, the 'Blond Beast', once described as a 'young evil god of death'. He was the embodiment of the SS ethos of 'hardness', a man of action, whose deeds were intended to refute the gossip that he was of Jewish origin.* Hitler, in a eulogy at Heydrich's funeral, called him 'the man with the iron heart'. Ambitious, calculating, with an élan that the pedantic and cranky Himmler lacked, Heydrich was eventually to wield nearly as much power as Himmler himself. Indeed, within a year of his appointment, Heydrich rose rapidly to the rank of Standartenführer (Colonel) and the Ic Subdividion emerged as the Sicherheitsdienst (SD) des Reichs-führers-SS (Security Service of the Reichsführer-SS), foreshadowing the dreaded power it would exercise all over Europe.

The SD started out modestly. From Himmler's files and with a staff of three working in his own small apartment in Munich, Heydrich began to organize a card index of NSDAP opponents – those in the opposition parties, suspected spies within the Nazi party, antagonists in government posts, Jews and Catholics whose overt activities marked them as anti-Nazis. To combat these enemies (as well as to document and verify their enmity) Heydrich fashioned a network of espionage and counter-espionage that in a short time enabled the SD to out-distance parallel and competing apparatus in the NSDAP and in the SA.

After the Nazi accession to power, the demarcation between state and party became blurred and even erased. In a few years the SS and SD usurped most police functions and entangled them in their own networks. The process began on 9 March 1933 when Himmler was appointed acting police president of Munich and Heydrich was put in charge of political security. A week later the entire Bavarian political police came under Himmler's charge. Within the year Himmler had managed to become head of the political police in all the states except Prussia, where Göring maintained his authority over the Gestapo (Gchcime Staatspolizeiamt – Secret State Police Office), established in April 1933. For some time Himmler tried to capture control of the Gestapo, and finally, in April 1934, the coveted Prussian police came into his hands. He then appointed Heydrich chief of the Gestapo. Now in control of all the police apparatus of the various German states,

---

*In mid-1932 the rumours of Heydrich's putative Jewish ancestry led to a party investigation that finally validated his 'Aryan' origins. Himmler is be-lieved even to have discussed the matter with Hitler. They held that Heydrich's fear of being branded a Jew was so excessive that he would be everlastingly grateful to them for letting him hold his high position in the party.

Himmler and Heydrich moved to consolidate their enhanced position in both party and state by undertaking to integrate the police organizations into the all-embracing network of the SS.[8]

On 9 June 1934 Hitler formalized the transfer of all NSDAP intelligence services to the SD, declaring that there was to be no other party intelligence or counter-espionage service. The following month Hitler further rewarded the SS for 'the great services' it had rendered in connection with the purge of the SA: 'I hereby promote the SS to the status of independent organization within the framework of the NSDAP.' Having attained primacy and autonomy within the party, Himmler and Heydrich moved to attain similar status in the government. After two years of a power struggle in which Frick, Göring and the civil administrators of the Gestapo were engaged, Hitler settled the matter by issuing a decree on 17 June 1936,[9] which gave Himmler and Heydrich the authority they aspired to and which they had in fact in large measure already usurped. Himmler became, by decree, Reichsführer-SS and Chief of the German Police and could now operate autonomously, for it became impossible to disentangle his power as Reichsführer-SS from his authority as Chief of the German Police. The whole police apparatus was now centralized, nationalized and Nazified, a part of the SS and an instrument of the Führer's will.

A few days later Himmler undertook a basic reorganization of the police, setting up two main departments: the Main Office of the Ordnungspolizei (Orpo; Regular Police), under Police General Kurt Daluege, and the Main Office of the Sicherheitspolizei (Sipo; Security Police), under Heydrich. Orpo comprised the uniformed urban and rural constabulary and the municipal police. Sipo consisted of the political police (Gestapo) and criminal police (Kripo). Thus the Gestapo, dealing with 'enemies of the state', became separated from the regular police and was brought even closer to the party apparatus. The culmination of this process came with Himmler's decree of 27 September 1939, amalgamating Sipo and the SD into one organization under Heydrich, to be known as the Reichssicherheitshauptamt (RSHA; Reich Security Main Office). The merger of the state and party apparatuses was now 'legally' complete, with Heydrich designated as Chief of Sipo and the SD (CSSD), a title paralleling Himmler's as Reichsführer-SS and Chief of the German Police. From a minuscule body of 280 men in 1929, Himmler had built the

SS into a mammoth organization of nearly a quarter of a million men, whose myriad institutions operated even beyond the pseudo-legality of the National Socialist state. In a few years this complex SS network would become the instrument for the annihilation of the Jews.

When the National Socialists came to power, the state took over the Jewish question and the SS remained satisfied for the time being to have its interest in the Jewish question lodged in Heydrich's card file in SD headquarters in Munich. Slowly the SD expanded in 1933, when two 'specialists' were brought in, one for Catholic matters and one – a Major Walter Ilges – for 'Jews and Freemasons'. But in the first eighteen months after the accession to power the main thrust of SD activity was towards institutional expansion and consolidation of power. The SD's primary functions during that period were to assist Himmler in his drive to gain control of the police apparatuses in all the German states and to support, in the name of NSDAP security, the attack on the SA.

After June 1934, when the SA was eliminated as a contender for political power within the National Socialist movement, Heydrich began in earnest to expand the SD bureaucracy and simultaneously to penetrate the political police with SD personnel. The SD Main Office in Munich was enlarged to three departments. Within the department known as SD-Inland (domestic affairs), a separate desk for Jewish affairs (coded II-112) was set up with SS-Untersturmführer Leopold von Mildenstein in charge. Mildenstein hired Adolf Eichmann at the end of 1934 as his expert on Zionism, that niche in the bureaucracy coded II-1123. About a year later an ambitious research programme got under way, with the gathering of data about prominent Jews in Germany and abroad.[10] The Jewish press was monitored. Studies were prepared about the ORT, a worldwide Jewish organization promoting vocational education and training, and the Agudat Israel, a worldwide organization of Orthodox Jews. Other studies were under way and additional experts were put on. Besides Eichmann, who specialized in Zionism, there were desks for 'assimilationists' and for 'Orthodoxy and philanthropy'. (According to Eichmann, his colleagues were Dieter Wisliceny and Theodore Dannecker, both of whom were to become his dedicated troubleshooters in organizing the deportation of the European Jews.)

A somewhat similar set-up existed in the Gestapo in Berlin. In January 1934, when Göring still controlled the Gestapo, a desk for matters concerning 'émigrés, Jews, Freemasons' was established in its Legal Department (coded II-F-2). It was directed by Karl Hasselbacher, a young lawyer whose experience in 'Jewish' affairs had been obtained in the Ministry of the Interior, working on the Law for the Restoration of the Professional Civil Service.[11] After the Gestapo came under SS jurisdiction in April 1934 it underwent many changes, taking on, for one, a pseudo-military character with all the military titles and uniforms brought in by the new staff from the SD and SS. A thoroughgoing transformation was effected in the next few months when the previous five departments were consolidated into three, their staffs increased and their scope enlarged. Its new Main Office, coded II, would become the keystone of the Gestapo. Its sub-division II-1 dealt with 'enemies of the state' and was headed jointly by two officials whom Heydrich had brought in from the Bavarian political police. (One Heinrich Müller, made a big career in the Gestapo and later played a key role in the annihilation of the Jews. To distinguish him from other Heinrich Müllers in the Nazi galaxies, he became known as 'Gestapo Müller'.) Subsection II-1-B handled religious associations, Jews, Freemasons and émigrés, with Hasselbacher retaining charge of Jews, Masonic lodges and émigrés (expatriation and revocation of citizenship), and enjoying the services of two assistants.

As soon as he could, Heydrich tried to turn his card files and bureaucratic paper work to practical effect. Once he took over the Bavarian political police, he began to exploit its apparatus for ideological purposes. With regard to the Jews, his first act in this capacity was his order of 19 July 1933 affecting all Jewish organizations in Bavaria that were not purely religious or did not serve purely charitable purposes. He forbade them to continue their activities and ordered their property to be confiscated. Presumably he regarded such organizations as political and therefore actually or potentially hostile to the National Socialist state. Moreover, he may have felt that synagogues and Jewish charitable agencies were useful inasmuch as they segregated Jews from Germans. But the ban on other organizations did not continue very long. Heydrich had apparently concluded that police surveillance might serve his purposes better than suppression. Accordingly, in a decree dated 20 March 1934 he lifted the ban on the Reichsbund jüdischer Frontsoldaten (Federal Union of Jewish War Veterans) and various Jewish student and sports organizations, allowing them to meet and conduct business.[12] Now, however, they were forbidden to pursue any political objectives and were subject to close police supervision. The police were to be given a list of members, including the place and date of their birth and their present residence (data that no doubt then found their way into the SD files); new members had to be cleared by the police; police were to be informed of the resignation or expulsion of members. Orders by the police authorities about administration, activity and sports exercises were to be strictly obeyed. All meetings were monitored. Thus Heydrich began to draw a tight net of police supervision over the Jewish community.

Police surveillance of Jewish organizations soon became a standard procedure all over Germany. In Prussia, before Heydrich's time, Gestapo surveillance over the Jews had been limited to 'legal' and economic matters, but it did not take long before the system that Heydrich had innovated in Bavaria was introduced there. Agreements were worked out between the Gestapo and the SD arranging for joint activities as well as separate jurisdictions. Spying on the Jewish organizations was one such cooperative undertaking.

Surveillance was useful since it provided jobs for otherwise unemployed NSDAP members and it increased the activity of the SD bureaucracy. Although it fulfilled an expressive purpose through its exercise of terror over the Jewish community, surveillance in itself served no instrumental purpose for the National Socialists. It provided no 'solution' to the Jewish question.

After the spate of violence, the boycott and the enactment of the exclusionary legislation in 1933, neither the German state nor the NSDAP appeared to have a clear-cut policy with regard to the Jews. In fact, some government agencies continued to deal with Jews in a correct, even courteous manner, according to the rules and regulations that had prevailed in Weimar. Emigration, for example, was handled by the Reichswanderungsamt (Reich Office of Migration) within the Ministry of the Interior. It was staffed mostly by officials who were not National Socialists, but had, before 1933, been members of the Catholic Centre and other non-leftist parties. These bureaucrats continued to operate up to 1938 not only according to Weimar legality, but also with sympathetic understanding for the problems and priorities of the Jewish organizations in trying to foster a systematic programme of emigration.[13]

Matters affecting Jews that were within the competence of the Ministry of Economy, also largely staffed with old-line government officials, were handled according to the habitual bureaucratic routine. A paradoxical example was the successful appeal, after initial prohibitions, by Jewish textile and clothing factories to obtain government contracts to produce goods for the armed services. The most significant instance of normal official procedures was the negotiations between the Ministry of Economy and the Jewish Agency for Palestine, concluding in the so-called 'Haavara agreements' of August 1933. These were, in essence, a compromise on the issue of emigrants' blocked accounts. Under this arrangement Jews emigrating to Palestine deposited their assets in special blocked accounts in Germany, held by a Jewish trust company. Once in Palestine the emigrant would be paid off half the amount in Palestine pounds. The other half was credited towards the purchase of finished German goods by the Jewish Agency, which paid half the cost in Palestine pounds. The Foreign Office, too, was involved in the implementation of the agreements over the years, and the officials there manifested similar courtesy and correctness, and sometimes even more.[14]

The Haavara agreements were not regarded as an ideological matter related to the Jewish question, but rather as a matter of the German economy. The arrangement was seen as boosting German production and German exports and discouraging a worldwide Jewish boycott of German goods. Hitler appeared to have no objections to the agreement, for he made a neutral passing reference to it in a speech on 24 October 1933. As evidence that England was bad and Germany good, Hitler said that while England was hindering Jewish settlement in Palestine, Germany was aiding it, even to the extent of letting the emigrant take out of the country the currency required for the landing fee in Palestine.[15]

In 1934 it was widely held in Germany that the Jewish question had already been settled, though few people in the NSDAP leadership thought so. In the absence of clear-cut directives or guidelines, various ideas began to be bruited about in National Socialist circles about how to deal with the Jews. Goebbels, for one, seemed to be thinking along the lines of extending formal recognition of a ghettoized Jewish community. The idea no doubt derived from his experience with the Kulturbund deutscher Juden, an organization of Jewish actors, musicians, singers and entertainers set up in 1933, after they had lost their jobs. The Kulturbund was formed to provide a means of livelihood for its members by arranging concerts, plays and entertainment exclusively for the Jewish community. It was permitted to function under the supervision of a cultural commissar in Goebbels's Propaganda Ministry, who evolved a policy that Goebbels pridefully called 'Jewish cultural autonomy'. The Kulturbund was not only encouraged to perform the works of Jewish writers and composers, but was forbidden to perform works by Germans and 'Aryans'. This *de facto* situation may have given rise to the thought of formalizing it in a *de jure* arrangement applying to the entire Jewish community. At the end of 1934, another official in Goebbels's ministry, Hans Friedrich Blunck, then president of the Reichsschrifttumskammer (Reich Board of Literature), in an article in *Europäische Revue*, introduced that notion in a backhanded way. 'The efforts of German literature', he wrote, 'to achieve a concordat between the remaining Jewish population in the Reich and the government have been impeded again and again at the decisive moment by attacks from abroad.'[16] Presumably that sentence was a sort of trial balloon. Though the response in the Jewish press indicated cautious interest in the proposal, nothing further came of the idea. It may have been suppressed at a higher level in the National Socialist hierarchy, perhaps even by an angered reaction from Hitler.

The SS, for its part, continued to cast about for ideas that would provide a long-range solution to the Jewish question. In mid-1934 an SS report on this very subject remarked, with disappointment, that the 'armchair anti-Semites' were satisfied now that the Jews had been pulled down a peg or two. It was consequently the responsibility of the party to devise an anti-Jewish policy that would 'keep alive an awareness of the Jewish problem within the German people'.[17] The unknown writer of the report rejected the exercise of further economic pressures on the Jews on the ground that that might arouse a foreign boycott of German goods. Next he explored the idea of mass Jewish emigration as an alternative, calling attention to the fact that among German Jews only the Zionists advocated emigration and only they acknowledged that Jews could not truly be Germans. The reporter then proposed, as a desirable programme, that the National Socialists give official preference to those Jewish organizations that promoted Jewish nationalism and separatism, while also encouraging those activities that prepared Jews for emigration.

Precisely such official encouragement was extended by the Bavarian political police, when Heydrich issued a directive to all police offices in the state on 28 January 1935: 'The activity of the Zionist-oriented youth organizations that are engaged in the occupational restructuring of the Jews for agriculture and manual trades prior to their emigration to Palestine lies in the interest of the National Socialist state's leadership'. These organizations, therefore, 'are not to be treated with that strictness that it is necessary to apply to the members of the so-called German-Jewish organizations (assimilationists)'.[18]

By spring, this approach had been legitimated, according to a directive of April 1935 that asserted that 'the attempts of German-Jewish organizations to persuade Jews to remain in Germany' directly contradicted National Socialist principles and were to be prevented. The Jewish press, too, was to be monitored 'to see that the more subtle forms of this propaganda are not disseminated'.[19] One way the policy was executed was to deny permission to speakers to address public Jewish gatherings if they were known to advocate a Jewish presence in Germany. Persons who did express such views were often brought to the Gestapo for interrogation and threatened with detention in a concentration camp.

On 15 May 1935 the *Schwarze Korps*, official organ of the SS, supported this policy as the correct ideological posture for National Socialists. The Jews, it was argued, had to be separated into two categories – Zionists and assimilationists: 'The Zionists adhere to a strict racial position and by emigrating to Palestine they are helping to build their own Jewish state.' But the assimilationists were objectionably tenacious: 'The assimilation-minded Jews deny their race and insist on their loyalty to Germany or claim to be Christians, because they have been baptised, in order to subvert National Socialist principles.'[20]

The enactment of the Nuremberg Laws encouraged this approach. The Zionists and proponents of emigration to Palestine were less badgered in their activities by the police and the SD than the non-Zionists. Pressure was constantly exerted on Jewish communal leaders to pursue a policy of emigration, especially to Palestine. Removal of the Jews from Germany, *Entjudung* (de-Jewification) of Germany, seemed to have become the SS policy in the period between 1935 and 1938. Nevertheless, it was in no way official National Socialist policy and did not affect the routine bureaucratic procedures of the Reichs-wanderungsamt. The Haavara agreements were regarded with favour in SD circles as an incentive to Jewish emigration, but the Auslands-organisation, the NSDAP branch dealing with Germans living abroad, strongly opposed it because it gave 'valuable support for the formation of a Jewish national state with the help of German capital'.[21]

Hitler issued no definitive statement in support of the SS policy of encouraging the Zionists and emigration to Palestine, apart from that reference in his speech in October 1933. Yet if Eichmann had read *Mein Kampf* (at his trial he admitted he never had), he would have seen that making a distinction between Zionists and assimilationists was not likely to win Hitler's approval. For Hitler had asserted that there was no difference when he had studied them in Vienna: 'This apparent struggle between Zionistic and liberal Jews disgusted me; for it was false through and through, founded on lies.' Furthermore, Hitler had little regard for Palestine as a Jewish state. He referred to Palestine only once in *Mein Kampf*, expressing the view that the Jews never intended to build a state for the purpose of living there: 'All they want is a central organization for their international world swindle, endowed with its own sovereign rights and removed from the intervention of other states: a haven for convicted scoundrels and a university for budding crooks.'

The international complications of Jewish settlement in Palestine and of Arab opposition do not seem to have become apparent to Hitler until 1937, when Palestinian Arabs first turned to the Germans for help against the Jewish settlement. In mid-1937 Foreign Minister Konstantin von Neurath began to formulate a policy on Palestine along the lines of *Mein Kampf*, asserting that the creation of a Jewish state was not in Germany's interest, because it would create a position of power for 'international Jewry somewhat like the Vatican State for political Catholicism or Moscow for the Comintern'. Hitler was apparently undecided, trying to reconcile the conflicting interests of his ministries with his own ideological views. Though he himself did not put anything down on paper, a government official reported in July 1937 that

Hitler had concluded that Jewish emigration should be concentrated on Palestine, because this would create 'only *one* centre of Jewish trouble in the world', which Germany could oppose by concerted counter-measures.[22] It may be no more than mere coincidence that about this time a Gestapo official who supervised Jewish organizations told a Jewish leader that the Gestapo did not like to have the Jews emigrate to America, but preferred Palestine, because 'there we will catch up with you'.[23]

By 1937 Eichmann had developed the idea that all matters relating to Jewish emigration should be centralized in one agency, and he adumbrated the idea of forced emigration, in actuality a policy of expulsion, as an expression of the German people's wrath against the Jews. That idea appealed to Heydrich, and in a short time it would become official policy.

The SD meanwhile still searched for an ideological or theoretical basis for an ongoing anti-Jewish policy for the National Socialist state. In a report of 28 August 1936 SS-Oberscharführer Schröder, Eichmann's superior at that time, described the work of his section with regard to the problem of arriving at an encompassing National Socialist definition of the concept of 'Jewry as an enemy of the State and Party'.[24] Schröder elaborated:

The Jew already as a person is a 100 per cent enemy of National Socialism, as proven by the difference in his race and nationality. Wherever he tries to transmit his work, his influence, and his world outlook to the non-Jewish world, he discharges it in hostile ideologies, as we find it in Liberalism, especially in Freemasonry, in Marxism, and not least also in Christianity. These ideologies then accord with a broader concept of Jewish mentality.

He concluded that the correct method of combating Jewry demanded sober judgement rather than the 'fantastic notions of well-known, so-called anti-Semites', an idea reminiscent of Hitler's earliest statement on anti-Semitism, his letter to Gemlich in September 1919. Here, then, was the germ of the idea that the Jew, simply by being a Jew and thereby an enemy of the 'Aryan' and hence of the National Socialist movement, would automatically become an enemy of the National Socialist state. The ideological concept was being transformed into a legal one.

Himmler, too, was developing the idea of the Jew as an enemy of the state, less in a legal sense than in a combative sense. Early in 1937, in a lecture to the Wehrmacht on the nature and purpose of the S S, he spelled out the idea that the 'enemy in a war is an enemy not only in the military sense, but also an ideological enemy'.[25] A few months earlier he described the methods with which the S S would defend Germany against this enemy:

> We shall unremittingly fulfil our task, to be the guarantors of the internal security of Germany, just as the Wehrmacht guarantees the safety of the honour, the greatness and the peace of the Reich from the outside. We shall take care that never more in Germany, the heart of Europe, can the Jewish–Bolshevistic revolution of sub-humans be kindled internally or by emissaries from abroad. Pitilessly we shall be a merciless executioner's sword for all these forces whose existence and doings we know . . . whether it be today, or in decades, or in centuries.[26]

Thus, at a time when talk of war was becoming the everyday rhetoric of National Socialist Germany, the S S, too, despite the careful paperwork of the S D, began increasingly to talk of war against the ideological enemy.

5 Foreign Policy, Race and War

The task of German foreign policy, Hitler stated in *Mein Kampf*, was to 'preserve, promote, and sustain our people for the future'. Because of the Dolchstoss, the sapping of Germany's virility through betrayal, that task had to be executed in two stages; the first, domestic policy, was 'to restore', in Hitler's words, 'to the nation its strength in the form of a free power state'. The second stage entailed war and expansion into foreign territory. In Hitler's view there was no division between domestic and foreign policy. Domestic policy, he wrote, 'must furnish the Volkist instrument of strength' for the exercise of foreign policy, and that foreign policy, in turn, would protect and sustain the Volkist instrument.

Hitler had spelled out his foreign-policy ideas and plans in repetitive detail first in *Mein Kampf* and later, in 1928, even more elaborately in a second manuscript, unpublished during his lifetime.* These ideological objectives as well as his broad strategical plans remained essentially unchanged in the decade between the writing of *Mein Kampf* and his accession to power. When Hitler became dictator of Germany, his ideology and strategy both became the ends and means of German foreign policy. 'In political life there are no principles of foreign policy,' Hitler declared early in 1930. 'The programmatic principle of our party is its position on the racial problem, on pacifism and internationalism. Foreign policy is only a means to an end. In matters of foreign policy, I shall not permit myself to be bound.'[1] This was a cardinal principle in his outlook. In *Mein Kampf* he argued that since the goal of a state's diplomacy was to preserve its people, '*every road that leads to this is then expedient . . .*' Here were embodied the two integral elements of policies he would pursue – unwavering commit-

---

*Found after the war, the manuscript was identified by Professor Gerhard L. Weinberg and published, with his annotations, as *Hitlers zweites Buch*. An English version is called *Hitler's Secret Book*.

ment to National Socialist ideology, and a strategy combining opportunism, expediency and improvisation.

The first stage of German foreign policy, Germany's internal restoration, was to accomplish two ends. Germany first had to purge itself of its internal enemies, and second, make itself strong. 'Whoever wants to act in the name of German honour today must first launch a merciless war against the infernal defilers of German honour,' he wrote in his second book. He used the language of war often in speaking of the Jews. The National Socialist movement, he wrote in *Mein Kampf*, 'must call eternal wrath upon the head of the foul enemy of mankind', the 'inexorable Jew' seeking domination over all nations. Only the sword, he held, could stave off the enemy, in a process that 'is and remains a bloody one'.

The application of the sword against the Jews would come later, but the first step in this process was purgation, which had been achieved with the promulgation of the laws of 1933 and the Nuremberg Laws.

The second means of restoring German virility was re-militarization. The German people, now racially purified, would have the will to war, but it needed the means to make war, which the hated Versailles Treaty had denied them. In his second book, Hitler declared that 'the first task of German domestic policy ought to be that of giving the German people a military organization suitable to its national strength'. From his very accession to power, Hitler began to build according to this blueprint. On 4 April 1933 a National Defence Council was set up and began, in secret, the process of military planning and German rearmament. Six months later, Germany withdrew from both the international disarmament conference at Geneva and from the League of Nations. In November the German people enthusiastically affirmed that policy in a plebiscite, while the nations participating in the disarmament negotiations, despite deep misgivings about Germany's course, took no action that would discourage or halt German re-militarization. That passivity continued. Indeed, though the major European powers protested Germany's restoration of universal compulsory military service in 1935, Great Britain – one of the protesters – rewarded Germany with a naval agreement on 18 June, establishing naval parity between England and Germany. It was the first of a long series of diplomatic and military acts of appeasement that raised Germany's international prestige and succeeded in strengthening the dictatorship at home.

German rearmament accelerated, though not yet too openly lest France claim violations of the Locarno Pact of 1925, which had re-affirmed the conditions of the Versailles Treaty, stating that the Rhine-land was to remain de-militarized. But having prepared his ground diplomatically as well as militarily, Hitler sent German troops into the Rhineland on 7 March 1936, while denouncing the Locarno Pact. Within a week the flurry of crises was over. The British fear of risking war had prevailed over French indecisiveness. Germany had achieved a stunning triumph without cost. Hitler's gambles and his strategy of wile, bluff and outright deceit had succeeded, within three years, in setting Germany on the path to war. In August 1936 Hitler drafted a memorandum, which became known as the Four Year Plan, that was to put Germany on a war footing economically and militarily. Hitler felt that Germany was ready for 'the reconquest of freedom for to-morrow'.

In his scheme, war was inevitable. 'War is life,' Hitler said in 1932. 'War is the origin of all things.'[2] War would be the means to realize his quest for *Lebensraum*, a word that incorporated Hitler's ideas of racial supremacy into a pretentious geopolitical scheme. War, invasion, expansion, in National Socialist ideology, were not merely the expression of an imperialist drive for natural resources, exploitable markets in underdeveloped countries, or power over vast territories and numerous peoples (though they were that also); primarily they were instruments to serve national/racial survival. In *Mein Kampf* Hitler first expounded his theory of *Lebensraum*:

> The foreign policy of the Volkist state must safeguard the existence on this planet of the race embodied in the state, by creating a healthy, viable natural relation between the nation's population and growth on the one hand and the quantity and quality of its soil on the other.

Hitler's concepts about the basis of a state's physical existence and about population growth in relation to available agricultural land and food supply were derived from geopolitical ideas with which he be-came familiar in Landsberg. The basic idea was that of population pres-sure. While population grows, the amount of soil remains constant. Increasing soil productivity is not a satisfactory or long-range solution to relieve the pressure of population growth, Hitler believed. Nor could population control be a solution, for that would contravene the very purpose of the Volkist racial state. (Indeed, shortly after the Nazis came to power, birth-control centres were shut down, advertising for contraceptives was halted and abortions became difficult to obtain.) The only satisfactory and fundamental way of eliminating the 'intolerable' relation between population and territory was war: 'The bread of freedom grows from the hardships of war.'

Germany was entitled to more land, not only because its people would have 'the courage to take possession of it, the strength to preserve it and the industry to put it to the plough', but because Germany was the 'mother of life', not just 'some little nigger nation or other'. Furthermore, Germany's leaders were justified in shedding even German blood to attain that goal:

> ... we National Socialists must hold unflinchingly to our aim in foreign policy, namely, *to secure for the German people the land and soil to which they are entitled on this earth.* And this action is the only one which, before God and our German posterity, would make any sacrifice of blood seem justified ... The soil on which some day German generations of peasants can beget powerful sons will sanction the investment of the sons of today, and will some day acquit the responsible statesmen of blood-guilt and sacrifice of the people, even if they are persecuted by their contemporaries.

Where would the soil come from? There were, in Hitler's plan, two sources – the 'lost territories' and 'new soil'. The 'lost territories' were the lands that would soon become part of Greater Germany – Austria and western Czechoslovakia – and which would have to be won back by war, *"back to the bosom of a common Reich, not by flaming protests, but by a mighty sword"*. But these territories would not solve Germany's problems. Only new soil would give Germany 'a path to life'.

The new soil that would give Germany its *Lebensraum* could be 'only in the East'. Hitler spelled it out in *Mein Kampf*: 'If we speak of soil in Europe today, we can primarily have in mind only *Russia* and her vassal border states.' The rationale for a German conquest of Russia was twofold. Using Rosenberg's ideas, he advanced a historical claim of centuries-old German colonization in Russia. But even more important was the notion, assimilated also from Rosenberg, that the

Jews had taken control of Russia by means of revolution and Bolshevism.

War for *Lebensraum* was thus associated in Hitler's mind with war against the Jews, not alone in an apocalyptic sense of a final struggle between Gog and Magog, between Aryans and Jews, but also in a conventional sense. Back in 1927, Rudolf Hess wrote to a friend that 'in Hitler's opinion [world peace would] . . . be realizable only when one power, the racially best one, has attained complete and uncontested supremacy'.[3] That such supremacy could be achieved only by war Hess did not spell out, but he clearly articulated Hitler's view that this 'great step' towards world understanding was possible only 'upon the solution of the Jewish question'. War, the Jews and racial utopia were all inter-related in Hitler's mind. In 1935 he referred to war as a cover for planned murder, when he told Gerhardt Wagner, the NSDAP's top medical officer, 'that if war came, he would pick up and carry out this question of euthanasia', for then 'such a programme could be put into effect more smoothly and readily' and in the general upheaval public opposition would be less likely.[4]

Often in discussing foreign-policy matters, Hitler shuttled back and forth between a real world of nations and armies and a phantasmagoric universe ruled by the Jews. For instance, in 1935, shortly after the Nuremberg party congress, Hitler had several occasions to speak to small groups of party and government people. Consul General Fritz Wiedemann, Hitler's adjutant, later recorded Hitler's plans at that time with regard to the Jews: 'Out of all the professions, ghetto, imprisoned in a territory where they can disport themselves according to their nature, while the German people looks on as one watches wild beasts.'[5] Though Wiedemann mentions no talk of war, Hitler was already fantasizing of a time during or after the war, when some territory, not precious German soil, would be available for the internment of the Jews.

On 24 September 1935, nine days after the Nuremberg congress at which the Law for the Protection of German Blood and German Honour had been promulgated, Hitler called a closed meeting of party leaders, Reich officials and Gauleiters to share his decisions with regard to racial determinations of the 'half-Jews'. Hitler spoke with considerable expertness, Bernhard Lösener noted, but then flabbergasted his listeners by breaking off, remarking that he needed to obtain further clarification on some points. He then turned to other subjects, alluding quite unmistakably to his war plans, saying that he still needed about four years to be ready.[6] Lösener thought he was rambling incoherently, but there could be no misunderstanding the associations in Hitler's mind between making fine racial distinctions among different categories of 'half-Jews' and his plans for war.

At the end of August 1936, after the Olympic Games, Hitler went to Berchtesgaden, where he prepared his memorandum on the Four Year Plan. The body of the memorandum dealt with practical matters like saving foreign exchange, stepping up fuel production, mass-producing synthetic rubber and increasing iron ore production so as to make Germany self-sufficient and ready for war within four years, but the ideological preamble on the need for war read like a chapter from *Mein Kampf*. The world, he stated, had been moving towards a new conflict, 'the most extreme solution of which is called Bolshevism, whose essence and aim, however, is solely the elimination of those strata of mankind which have hitherto provided the leadership and their replacement by worldwide Jewry'.[7] Since the victory of Bolshevism over Germany would lead to the annihilation of the German people, Hitler concluded: *"In face of the necessity of defence against this danger, all other considerations must recede into the background as being completely irrelevant.'* Ideology had clearly superseded rational political and economic calculations. Hitler had decided on war against Bolshevism, which he had long regarded as a contrivance through which the Jews manipulated world power. Thus this holy war against Jewish Bolshevism would defeat the prime and ultimate enemy and win for the German people their *Lebensraum*.

The Four Year Plan also provided for the expropriation of all Jews when Germany went to war. The Reichstag was to pass a law 'making the whole of Jewry liable for all damage inflicted by individual specimens of this community of criminals upon the German economy, and thus upon the German people'. With this authority, Göring, as Plenipotentiary for the Four Year Plan, would, after the Kristallnacht (see p. 137 below), levy a billion-mark contribution on the Jews.

Hitler had the craft to plan and the patience to wait for the opportunity to carry out that plan. Even before he had come to power, he

had devised his strategy. 'We must be strong first,' he said in Rauschning's company. 'Everything else will follow in due course. I shall
advance step by step. Never two steps at once.'[8] Five years later, he
made precisely the same point with regard to the Jews. On 29 April
1937, in a long speech before a regional NSDAP meeting, in which
he addressed himself to the Jewish question, among others, he referred
contemptuously to the insistent demands within the party for more
action against the Jews. He reminded his listeners that he did not need
pressure on this matter, being the original expert. Everything would
be done in due time, within a total context, and at the opportune
moment:

> Then: the final aim of our whole policy is quite clear for all of us.
> Always I am concerned only that I do not take any step from which I
> will perhaps have to retreat, and not to take any step that will harm us.
> I tell you that I always go to the outermost limits of risk, but never
> beyond. For this you need to have a nose more or less to smell out:
> 'What can I still do?' Also in a struggle against an enemy. I do not
> summon an enemy with force to fight, I don't say: 'Fight!' because I
> want to fight. Instead I say, 'I will destroy you! And now, Wisdom,
> help me, to manoeuvre you into the corner that you cannot fight back,
> and then you get the blow right in the heart.' That's it.[9]

Preparations for war proceeded apace. In August 1936, about the
time he was working on the Four Year Plan, the term of compulsory
military service was extended from one year to two years. In October
and November 1936 the Berlin–Rome–Tokyo Axis was forged. At
the same time the Germans recognized the insurgent government of
General Franco in Spain, openly supplying Franco's forces with
matériel, experts and even men. Germany and Japan also formed an
explicitly anti-Soviet alliance, the Anti-Comintern Pact, and anti-
Bolshevism thereafter became the central theme of the Nazi pro-
pagandists in and out of Germany. The whole Nazi apparatus became
engaged in producing enormous quantities of deceitful and deliberately falsified propaganda describing Russia as the centre of operations
of the Elders of Zion. Goebbels and Rosenberg had major organizations devoted to anti-Communist propaganda and activities.

Yet none achieved Hitler's terrible potency. His speech at the
NSDAP congress, on 13 September 1937, dwelled on the worldwide Bolshevik menace, using the themes he had developed in *Mein*

Kampf: the preparation for world insurrection 'without doubt originates from the authorities of Jewish Bolshevism in Moscow'.[10] Having gained a foothold in Russia, the Jews would use it as the bridgehead in their quest for world domination. 'I confirm only what is!' Hitler cried out with pathos. National Socialism had already 'banished the Bolshevik world peril from the inner heart of Germany'. Now it would protect the 'community of European-culture nations' from 'Jewish world Bolshevism'. In a crescendo of hatred, the National Socialists depicted the 'Jewish–Bolshevik world conspirators' as the primary enemy of mankind in a campaign that intended not only to justify the launching of the war, but to provide a continuous warrant in defence of both the conduct of the war and the execution of the Final Solution.

Hitler's plans for war were quite definite, when, on 5 November 1937, he called a select conference in the Reich Chancellery. His guests were Foreign Minister Konstantin von Neurath, a hold-over from Hindenburg's Cabinet; War Minister Field Marshal Werner von Blomberg, another Hindenburg appointee; commander-in-chief of the army General Werner von Fritsch; commander-in-chief of the navy Admiral Erich Raeder; and Göring, in his capacity as commander-in-chief of the air force. All five were engaged in the business of war and/or foreign relations. Also present was Colonel Friedrich Hossbach, Hitler's army adjutant, who took minutes of the meeting.[11] Hitler began by stressing the high-level importance of the meeting and that in the event of his demise his statements were to be regarded as his 'testamentary legacy'. He then expatiated on German foreign policy as the means of racial preservation of the *Volk* through *Lebensraum*, just as he had set it forth in *Mein Kampf* and in his second book. The agenda for this meeting was Hitler's timetable for the conquest of Austria and Czechoslovakia. Of the possibilities for earlier or later deadlines that he presented, he obviously wanted the nearest, 'even as early as 1938', asserting that the attack on Czechoslovakia must occur 'with lightning speed'.

The minutes are almost exclusively devoted to Hitler's presentation. The last three paragraphs barely reveal the shock of some of those present and the brief and hesitant discussion that followed. Blomberg, Fritsch and Neurath, one reads between Hossbach's lines, disagreed with Hitler's political calculations and with his military assessments,

cautiously wording their dissent. Their objections determined their
fate, for Hitler had definitely made up his mind to go ahead in 1938.
In less than three months Blomberg, Fritsch and Neurath were removed from their positions (Blomberg and Fritsch by the most sordid
and underhanded machinations).

Under the all-embracing cover of the Four Year Plan, Hitler
planned 1938 as the decisive year to go ahead with the annexation of
Austria and the invasion of Czechoslovakia – 'Operation Green',
whose military planning he ordered early in December 1937. His first
spectacular success came on 12 March 1938, when he annexed Austria
in an unresisted invasion. A month later, after an unprecedented show
of terror and violence, the National Socialists held a plebiscite in
which 99·75 per cent of the voters supported union with Germany.
The war fever then began to be fanned around the manufactured
crisis of the Sudeten Germans in Czechoslovakia. The implications
for the Jews in Germany grew more sinister, for their total expropriation and ultimate disposition had been awaiting the maturation
of Hitler's war plans.

After the Four Year Plan had gone into operation, Hjalmar Schacht,
Minister of Economy, had come into constant and bitter conflict with
Göring. Schacht resigned late in 1937 and Göring, as Plenipotentiary for the Four Year Plan, assumed total control over all economic
policies. When Walter Funk took over the Economy Ministry in
February 1938, it had already been thoroughly reorganized by Göring, who continued to retain most of its authority. Freed from
Schacht's legalisms and anxieties about unfavourable repercussions
from abroad, and certainly acting under Hitler's orders, Göring
turned his attention to the expropriation of the Jews.

The economic situation of the Jews had been continually deteriorating. By the end of 1937, Jewish professionals and civil servants,
actors, musicians and journalists, numbering tens of thousands, had
lost their livelihood. Many Jews, workers and employees, had
been dismissed from their jobs under pressure from rabid party and S A
members. Shortly after Schacht's resignation, an 'Aryan' organization was created whose purpose was to hasten the ouster of some
20,000 Jews still employed in the clothing and leather industries.
Innumerable small Jewish businesses were liquidated in the first two

years of the régime, after experiencing boycotts and violence. 'Voluntary' transfers of Jewish firms to 'Aryan' purchasers usually involved smaller businesses; larger ones, especially those that brought large sums of foreign exchange into Germany, managed to continue to operate, partly because of Germany's pressing need for foreign currency and partly because of Schacht's resistance to taking formal action. According to official statistics, as of April 1938 nearly 40,000 Jewish firms were still doing business in Germany, many of them fulfilling crucial roles either in rearmament or in the import–export trade.

Early in January 1938 Göring initiated systematic planning for expropriation, declaring that first of all 'it was necessary to have a legal definition of what constitutes a Jewish firm'.[12] On 26 March, speaking in Vienna (having not Austria, but Germany, in mind), Göring declared that 'Aryanization' should not be impaired by wrong or stupid measures, but must be carried out 'quite systematically, with full deliberation'.[13]

The first decree, issued on 22 April 1938, provided that any German engaged in an effort to camouflage the Jewish 'character' – that is, ownership – of a business enterprise would be imprisoned or fined. (As a matter of fact, the district Gestapo office in Düsseldorf had concerned itself with such 'camouflage' back in November 1936.) The next decree, issued on 26 April over Göring and Frick's signatures, was the fundamental Decree Regarding the Reporting of Jewish Property. It provided that no later than 30 June 1938 every Jew had to report and assess his entire domestic and foreign property, except for personal and household goods, or if the total value of the property did not exceed 5,000 Reichsmarks. A hint of things to come was contained in paragraph 7: 'The Plenipotentiary for the Four Year Plan may take measures necessary to ensure that the use made of property subject to reporting will be in keeping with the interests of the German economy.'[14]

The Third Decree to the Reich Citizenship Law, issued on 14 June 1938, defined a Jewish business enterprise: 'A business enterprise is considered Jewish if its owner is a Jew' by the standards of the Reich Citizenship Law. The 'Jewish' character of large corporations or branch businesses was determined by fixed percentages of number of Jews or the amount of their capital in them. To make sure that no enterprise the government wanted to seize would escape the net, an enterprise was regarded as Jewish even 'when it is under the dominant influence of Jews'. In mid-June Frick began circulating drafts of a decree providing for compulsory 'Aryanization' of Jewish businesses. On 6 July a decree was issued requiring the termination, no later than 30 December 1938, of Jewish businesses that rendered a variety of commercial services. On 25 July a decree forbade Jewish physicians (there were still about 4,000) from practising as of 30 September. (With permission from the Minister of the Interior, Jewish doctors could treat Jewish patients not as doctors, but as orderlies.) On 27 September 1938 Jewish lawyers (still about 1,700) were forbidden to practise law as of 30 November.

'Voluntary' transfers of Jewish businesses to non-Jews continued in 1938 at a moderate pace of about fifty per month, despite an intensification of grass-roots street anti-Semitism by restless elements in the Nazi party and the SA. In August, at a meeting of party Gauleiters, Martin Bormann promised that Göring would make a 'fundamental settlement of the Jewish question' which would fully satisfy the party's demands. In September, under the impact of both arbitrary and systematic violence, the number of 'Aryanisations' rose to 235, and the same pace continued into October. In mid-October, at a meeting of German and Austrian senior civil servants, Göring spoke on the need of mobilizing all German armed forces and increasing military production for the coming war. The time had come for an energetic handling of the Jewish question, he said, and the Jews 'must be removed from the economy'. But what must be prevented, Göring said, was that 'wild commissar economy' that was developing in Austria, where over 3,500 party members, most of them without qualification, had become 'commissars' over 'Aryanized' Jewish businesses. The solution of the Jewish question, Göring emphasized, was not intended as a 'charitable scheme for incompetent party members'. It was his firm conviction that Jewish property belonged to the Reich and not to individual party members who wanted to enrich themselves. (Göring, of course, was permitted to enrich himself in the style of an Eastern potentate, not only with industrial property that had belonged to Jews, but also with European art treasures.)

The war plans were synchronized also with plans to put the Jews under the complete control of the police. On 5 January 1938 a Law

Regarding Changes of Family Names and Given Names was promulgated, which authorized the Minister of the Interior to issue regulations about names and to order changes of names that did not conform to those regulations. The ominous character of the law became apparent only on 23 July, in a decree requiring all Jews to apply for identification cards, which they would have to carry with them at all times. On 17 August 1938 the Law Regarding Changes of Family Names and Given Names was issued, providing that as of 1 January 1939 all male Jews must assume the given name of Israel and all female Jews the name of Sarah. Furthermore, Jews were forbidden to take as given names any other than specifically designated 'Jewish' given names, as listed in an appendix to the decree. (More than a hundred years before, the Prussian government prohibited Jews from using 'Christian' given names. Leopold Zunz, the founder of *Wissenschaft des Judentums*, then wrote a scholarly paper, *Die Namen der Juden*, showing that Christian and Jewish given names had a common source in the Bible. His scholarship was so persuasive that the Prussian government revised its restrictions to apply only to names associated with traditions of the New Testament.)

On 5 October 1938 a Law on Passports of Jews, signed by Werner Best, then head of the Sipo administrative office, required Jews to hand in their passports for foreign travel within two weeks; these would be reissued designating the holder as a Jew.

Other disquieting developments occurred. At the very outset of the year Himmler ordered the expulsion within ten days of all Jews in Germany who were Russian nationals, many of whom had been living in Germany since the Bolshevik Revolution.[15] On 28 March a decree was issued, signed by the Führer himself together with the Minister for Church Affairs and the Minister of the Interior, withdrawing from the Jewish religious communities and their central organizations (*Gemeinden*) their status as public legal bodies and subjecting them to government control. Following the decree a year earlier dissolving the B'nai B'rith, the Law Regarding the Legal Status of the Jewish Religious Communities was to prepare for the eventual centralization of all Jewish affairs in one organization that would be under the total control of the police.

Violence, too, had exploded again in the streets, no doubt a concomitant to the Austrian Anschluss and the war hysteria against

Czechoslovakia. Attacks on the Jews and Jewish stores intensified. A Jewish journalist described the SA violence and havoc on Berlin's main shopping street: 'A gang of ten youngsters in Hitler Youth uniforms smashed the shop window and stormed into the shop, brandishing butcher's knives and yelling: "To hell with the Jewish rabble! Room for the Sudeten Germans!"'[16]

But far worse and more terrifying than the sporadic violence of the mobs and hoodlums was the expanding activity of the Gestapo and SS. On 25 January 1938 the Minister of the Interior issued a new order that extended the definition of 'protective custody' to apply to 'persons whose behaviour endangers the existence and security of the *Volk* and the State'. Under the guidelines of another order the concentration camps were being given new functions, besides detention of political opponents, as state reformatories and labour camps for criminals and anti-socials. Mass Jewish arrests began late in May, and most of those arrested were sent to Dachau. On 1 June Heydrich issued instructions that between 13 and 18 June each criminal police district was to take into 'preventive police detention at least two hundred male able-bodied persons (anti-socials) as well as all male Jews with previous criminal records'. They were to be sent to Buchenwald.[17] The action was in implementation of the Four Year Plan and the demands of the war economy to put every able-bodied person to work. This would provide the rationale for turning the concentration camps into forced-labour and then slave-labour camps. The idea had a history going back to the 1923 *Putsch*. According to the draft constitution prepared then for the eventuality of takeover, concentration camps were to be established for 'all persons dangerous to security and useless eaters'.[18]

The seizure of some 1,500 Jewish 'anti-socials' served a different purpose. The police records of many consisted of a parking violation or two. The Gestapo was willing to release them only upon completion of arrangements for their immediate emigration.[19] The Gestapo had begun to coerce emigration along lines that Eichmann had advocated a short while before. After the Anschluss he had the opportunity to carry out his ideas in real life in Vienna.

During the summer of 1938 Buchenwald, Dachau and Sachsenhausen began to be enlarged and provisions made for the exploitation of their prisoners' labour. Prisoners at Dachau were ordered to sew

Stars of David on uniforms in preparation for a mass influx of Jewish prisoners.[20]

The plans for war and for the expropriation of the Jews, the directives providing for their identification, the rash of police arrests and the explosion of violence all converged that summer of 1938 in a tidal wave of terror. On 12 September, at the Nuremberg party congress, Hitler was still sure that Operation Green would come off as planned on 1 October, for he continued to promise the Sudeten Germans military assistance. But British Prime Minister Neville Chamberlain, the architect of appeasement, thwarted Hitler's bid for war with the Munich Conference of 29 September 1938. By awarding Hitler the Sudetenland, Chamberlain removed the pretext for Hitler's threatened invasion. Operation Green was called off. Instead, German troops marched only into the Sudetenland on 1 October, in accordance with the Munich agreement. But Hitler did not abandon his original plans. Just three weeks later, in violation of that agreement, a new directive was issued to the armed forces for the dismemberment of Czechoslovakia.

The plan for war had, for the time being, misfired and with it the opportunity for taking drastic, but less visible, action against the Jews. But an unexpected opportunity for dealing with the Jews opened up with the assassination on 7 November 1938 of Ernst vom Rath, a third secretary in the German embassy in Paris, by a seventeen-year-old Polish Jewish student, Hershl Grynszpan. Grynszpan's parents, Polish Jews who had lived in Hanover since 1914, had just been expelled from Germany. In March 1938 the Polish government, fearful that the Germans would soon expel Jews who were Polish nationals and return them to Poland, promulgated a denaturalization decree designed to annul the citizenship of Poles living abroad for more than five years unless they received a special stamp by Polish consular officials by 31 October. Lacking that, they would be refused re-entry to Poland. About 50,000 Polish Jews were then resident in Germany. Overnight they became stateless when Polish officials refused to issue the requisite stamp. The German government soon learned that the Polish government was firm in its intention of barring the re-entry of Jews. On 28 October the Gestapo, on orders from the Foreign Office, began rounding up Polish Jews to transport them to the Polish border. Prevented from entering Poland, they were kept in appalling conditions in a no-man's-land on the Polish side at Zbąszyń, near Posen.* Grynszpan's parents had been among the first rounded up, and the son had become unsettled by their fate.

Hitler himself never uttered a word publicly on vom Rath's assassination or on the events of the Kristallnacht (night of glass). Yet those events could not have occurred without his approval. The incitement against the Jews began on 8 November with the first news report that vom Rath had been seriously wounded (he died two days later of his wounds) and an accompanying incendiary editorial in the *Völkischer Beobachter*. Goebbels called the signals, which were picked up by party and SA leaders all over Germany. In many small towns, meetings were called on 8 or 9 November, at which the party leader and the local mayor agitated the assembled mob, which then went into action, setting fire to the local synagogues, destroying Jewish businesses and homes and manhandling Jews.[21] At that moment in German history, with war fever running high and the Jews already clearly identified as enemies, the rank-and-file National Socialist was eager for a little action on his own. Many times in the past the NSDAP had bridled these anti-Semitic enthusiasms in the interests of broader goals. Now Goebbels became the advocate of mob violence and the architect of a mob-action programme.

Early in the evening of 9 November it was learned that vom Rath had died of his wounds. That very evening the NSDAP's leaders were congregating in the Old Town Hall in Munich for the anniversary celebration of the Munich *Putsch*. Hitler had dinner there with his old comrades and was seen in prolonged conversation with Goebbels. Hitler usually delivered the main speech on this occasion, but this evening he left early. He had been overheard to say that 'the SA should be allowed to have a fling'.[22] Hitler had presumably decided, at Goebbels's suggestion, that 'spontaneous' demonstrations, manifestly not initiated or organized by the party, were not to be discouraged.[23] His absence from the festivities was planned to exculpate him – and the government – from responsibility for the subsequent events. After Hitler left, Goebbels delivered an inflammatory exhortation to the assemblage, calling for 'spontaneous' demon-

*Eventually, under international pressure, Poland admitted its Jewish nationals.

strations. NSDAP members were used to such instructions from the party's earliest days, when it expediently served as the anonymous organizer of violent demonstrations. Now, the party members and SA men took Goebbels's hints as he intended them to be taken: Jewish blood was to flow for the death of vom Rath.

Three of Goebbels's colleagues in Hitler's cabinet were absent from the Munich celebration – Himmler, Heydrich and Göring. Göring was then on a train to Berlin and learned only in the morning what had happened during the night. Himmler and Heydrich were both in Munich that evening, but not at the Old Town Hall, and were informed shortly before midnight about what was being planned. Long hostile to Goebbels, Himmler charged that his 'lust for power' was behind this planned action. Himmler immediately checked with Hitler and then passed the word on to Heydrich: 'The headquarters offices of the State Police are to conform to the wishes of the Propaganda offices.' In the early hours of 10 November Heydrich issued a series of orders to all state police stations with instructions to deal ruthlessly with all looters, to guard against the spread of fires from burning Jewish buildings to non-Jewish property, and to see to it that foreigners, including Jews, not be molested. These orders also included instructions for the arrest in all districts of as many able-bodied male Jews, 'especially rich ones', as could be accommodated in the space available for protective custody.[24] Thus the SS exploited Goebbels's plan for the sake of their own. These concentration-camp internees would have to buy their freedom by emigrating from Germany immediately upon release.

That night fires were ignited all over Germany, and the shattered plate glass that was to give the pogrom its name littered the streets of German towns and cities. (It was later estimated that the amount of plate glass destroyed equalled half the annual production of the plate-glass industry of Belgium, from which it had been imported.) Synagogues and Jewish institutions were burned to the ground. Over 7,000 Jewish businesses were destroyed. Nearly 100 Jews were killed, and thousands more subjected to wanton violence and sadistic torments. David H. Buffum, American Consul General in Leipzig, in a report on 21 November 1938 to the State Department, described one of these sadistic amusements: 'Having demolished dwellings and hurled most of the moveable effects to the streets, the insatiable perpetrators threw many of the trembling inmates into a small stream that flows through the Zoological Park, commanding horrified spectators to spit at them, defile them with mud and jeer at their plight.' About 30,000 Jewish men were arrested and incarcerated in Buchenwald, Dachau and Sachsenhausen.

If the death of vom Rath had triggered Goebbels's progrom, the pogrom itself provided the National Socialist government with the opportunity, short of actual war, to proceed with the total expropriation of the Jews and the complete removal of their freedom. Göring, in his capacity as Plenipotentiary for the Four Year Plan, took the initiative. In the next two days he conferred extensively with Hitler; he instructed Heydrich to prepare a report on the extent of the damage to Jewish property and to estimate the losses from looting of that property. On 12 November at 11.00 a.m. he convened a large meeting in his offices at the Reich Air Ministry, attended by top government and party people.[25] He opened the meeting by announcing that he had received a letter written on orders of the Führer, requesting that 'the Jewish question be now, once and for all, coordinated and solved one way or another'. Furthermore, the Führer had asked him the day before by phone 'to take coordinated action in the matter'.

The business at hand was primarily an economic matter, and Göring deplored the demonstrations: 'They don't harm the Jew but me, who is the final authority for coordinating the German economy.' The purpose of the meeting was to involve all the competent agencies in taking the necessary measures 'for the elimination of the Jew from the German economy'. The measures, it appeared, had already been decided on. The meeting was to coordinate the procedures for confiscating Jewish businesses and factories. 'We must agree', said Göring, 'on a clear action that shall be profitable to the Reich.' The elimination of the Jews altogether from the German economy was the chief topic of discussion. At one point Funk asked whether the Jewish stores should be re-opened and Göring responded: 'That is up to us to decide.' Within a week Funk issued a circular letter to appropriate authorities declaring that Jewish businesses should not be re-opened unless their management by non-Jews was assured.[26]

Goebbels asked about further legislation barring Jews from all public places – theatres, cinemas, beaches, resorts and Pullman sleeping-car compartments – and expelling Jewish children still in German schools. Three days later, on 15 November, the Ministry of Education issued an ordinance barring all Jewish children from the schools; two weeks later, on 28 November, Heydrich issued a decree signed by the Minister of Interior giving various state and district authorities the right to impose curfew restrictions on the Jews. A month later the Führer himself approved Göring's proposal to forbid Jews access to most of the public places specified by Goebbels.[27]

A representative of the German insurance companies was then invited to report on compensation for damages caused by the demonstrations. After a lengthy discussion it was decided that the insurance companies had to pay the damages to retain their credibility. Where compensation was paid to Jews, the German government would arrange to confiscate those payments. Jews would also be made liable to repair the damages.

Heydrich then commented that even if Jews were eliminated from the economy, 'the main problem, namely, to kick the Jew out of Germany, remains'. He proposed forced emigration as successfully developed by his staff in Vienna. He also suggested making the Jews wear identifying insignia. Göring raised the question of ghettos, to which Heydrich objected; a ghetto 'would remain the permanent hideout for criminals and also for epidemics and the like'. But Göring favoured the idea of the ghetto. (Hitler had mentioned the ghetto as a possibility back in 1935, and he may have spoken of it to Göring.) But the discussion trailed off into details of how to isolate Jews from 'Aryans' in hospitals and public conveyances.

Göring had one more item on the agenda: what would the gentlemen present think if he would announce that Jewry should have to contribute one billion marks as a penalty? There were no objections and Göring remarked, 'Incidentally, I'd like to say again that I would not like to be a Jew in Germany.' Then, parroting his Führer's style, he closed the meeting with an ominous threat: 'If in the near future the German Reich should come into conflict with foreign powers, it goes without saying that we in Germany should first of all let it come to a showdown with the Jews.'

That same afternoon Göring issued the Decree on Eliminating the Jews from German Economic Life, which excluded Jews from retail stores, export mail-order firms, the calling of independent craftsman;

from selling any goods or services anywhere; from serving as executives or managers of any firms; and from being a member of a cooperative.[28] At the same time he issued the Decree on the Penalty Payment by Jews Who Are German Subjects, imposing the one-billion-mark contribution, because, according to the decree's preamble, the 'hostile attitude of Jewry towards the German *Volk* and *Reich*, which does not shrink even from committing cowardly murder, necessitates determined resistance and harsh penalty'.[29]

In his testimony at Nuremberg, Göring, trying to evade responsibility, claimed that the idea for the levy had been Goebbels's, even though the idea for it had come from Hitler's Four Year Plan. The one-billion-mark payment had been intended, in Hitler's original memorandum and in Göring's decree to relieve Germany's critical financial situation, particularly at that stage of its war preparations. Indeed, at a meeting of the Reich Defence Council, just six days later, with Göring in the chair, all ministers and state secretaries, all commanders-in-chief of the armed forces and chiefs of the General Staff present, Göring mentioned the 'very critical situation of the Reich Exchequer' and said that relief had been attained 'initially through the billion imposed on Jewry and through profits accruing to the Reich in the Aryanization of Jewish enterprises'.[30]

On 14 December Göring sent a memorandum to the highest officials of the Reich, informing them that henceforth all decrees and other important directives touching on the Jewish question would have to go through his office and receive his approval, to assure the necessary centralization in dealing with the Jewish question, especially with regard to economic matters. All independent actions on the Jewish question, Göring emphasized, were to cease.[31]

Everything relating to the Jewish question, it seemed, had been disposed of, except the Jews themselves. On 24 January 1939 Göring gave Heydrich the power to take all measures for a stepped-up forced emigration of the German Jews, along the lines that Eichmann had pioneered in Vienna after the Anschluss. SS terror was rampant there, and the Jews were its primary target; thousands were rounded up and incarcerated in Dachau, Buchenwald and a new camp at Mauthausen; other thousands were forced to clean streets and public latrines. Eichmann then offered 'emigration' as an alternative to the terror. He set up the central organization that he had first proposed in 1937, a

Zentralstelle für jüdische Auswanderung (Central Office for Jewish Emigration). For its successful operation, he demanded the re-establishment of the Jüdische Kultusgemeinde (Jewish Religious Community), which had been dissolved, and the release from detention of some Jewish communal leaders. With their cooperation, procured by terror, Eichmann began to process the forcible exit of Jews from Austria. The application of apposite doses of terror and blackmail, coupled with the centralization of bureaucratic procedures, so success-fully speeded up 'emigration' that in about six months after the Anschluss, 45,000 Jews had left Austria. Over 100,000 more would leave before war broke out.

Eichmann's activities were closely observed in Germany. The most serious drawback, from Göring's point of view, was the depletion of Jewish accounts abroad to finance emigration. All this was discussed at Göring's conference on 12 November 1938, at which Heydrich proposed to set up a similar procedure for the Reich, but without the 'mistakes' to which Göring had alluded. To this Göring agreed on the spot. The directive, issued on 24 January 1939, provided for the establishment of a Reichszentrale für die jüdische Auswanderung (Reich Central Office for Jewish Emigration), operating under Hey-drich's direction. Its object was to promote the 'emigration' of Jews from Germany 'by every possible means'. The directive further re-quired that an 'appropriate Jewish organization for the uniform pre-paration of emigration applications' be created. The 'appropriate Jewish organization' was to be used in the same way that Eichmann had exploited the Jüdische Kultusgemeinde in Vienna.

Since the Jews were now deprived of all means of livelihood and all state benefits, and their children were barred from German schools, it was decided that the 'appropriate Jewish organization' should also take over the tasks of welfare and education for the Jewish population. To this end, the Germans made use of the framework of the Reichs-svertretung der Juden in Deutschland (Federal Representation of the Jews in Germany), a loose coordinating body representing the major German Jewish organizations that had been set up autonomously by the Jews in 1933. It was reconstituted, in the aftermath of the Kristall-nacht, under a new name, Reichsvereiningung der Juden in Deutsch-land (Federal Union of the Jews in Germany) with three functions – emigration, education and social welfare. The decree, formalizing the new organization, stipulated that it would be under the surveillance of the Ministry of the Interior, which meant the police.[32] (The decree was issued on 4 July 1939 but the Reichsvereinigung was actually in operation under its new name and under Gestapo supervision as early as February.)[33]

The first working session of the Reichszentrale, under Heydrich's chairmanship, was held 11 February 1939, and began the process of concentrating all matters concerning Jewish emigration that had been handled by various ministries, in the hands of the police.[34] But the Reichszentrale did not have much of a life, for the outbreak of the war ended the possibilities of emigration, an eventuality that had surely not escaped Göring's attention. Gestapo Müller, whom Heydrich had first appointed to head the agency, gave up the post in October 1939, recommending Eichmann to succeed him. When Sipo and the SD were merged in October 1939 to become the RSHA, Eichmann was shifted from the SD bureaucracy to the political police (RSHA *Amt* IV), under Müller. He took over the desk for Emigration and Evacuation, coded IV-D-4, which in a later reorganization became Jewish Affairs and Evacuation Affairs, coded IV-B-4, From this office he would schedule, organize and manage the deportation of the European Jews to the death camps. In 1938 'emigration' was a euphemism for 'expulsion'. Once war began, 'evacuation' became a euphemism for 'deportation', which, in turn, signified transportation to a place of death.

On 21 January 1939 Hitler told the Czech Foreign Minister Chvalkovsky: 'We are going to destroy the Jews. They are not going to get away with what they did on 9 November 1918. The day of reckoning has come.'[35] That was confidential, but on 30 January 1939 Hitler dilated on this theme when he addressed the Reichstag on the anniversary of his accession to power. The most salient passage of that long speech was two paragraphs to which Hitler himself would refer often during the war. They constituted his declaration of war against the Jews:

And one more thing I would like now to state on this day memorable perhaps not only for us Germans. I have often been a prophet in my life and was generally laughed at. During my struggle for power, the Jews primarily received with laughter my prophecies that I would someday assume the leadership of the state and thereby of the entire *Volk* and then, among many other things, achieve a solution of the Jewish problem. I suppose that meanwhile the then resounding laughter of Jewry in Germany is now choking in their throats.

Today I will be a prophet again: If international finance Jewry within Europe and abroad should succeed once more in plunging the peoples into a world war, then the consequence will be not the Bolshevization of the world and therewith a victory of Jewry, but on the contrary, the destruction of the Jewish race in Europe.[36]

Hitler's early invasions had been greeted with flowers, not guns. The entry of the German army into the Rhineland, then into Austria and thereafter into the Sudetenland were adventures in diplomatic and military brinksmanship that had attained Hitler's goals without war. So, too, Germany's destruction of the Czech republic in mid-March 1939 proceeded without impediment. Hitler annexed Czechoslovakia's western provinces of Bohemia and Moravia as a German protectorate; the eastern province of Slovakia became a puppet state under the rule of Father Jozef Tiso, a right-wing Catholic priest and Slovak nationalist.

On 15 March Prime Minister Chamberlain, addressing the House of Commons, explained that in the light of Slovakia's self-proclaimed independence Britain did not have to honour its treaty obligations to Czechoslovakia by coming to its assistance in the event of an act of unprovoked aggression. That was the kind of reaction that Hitler had contemptuously expected of the English, and it appeared to vindicate his strategy. But now Hitler miscalculated. Two days later, Chamberlain publicly admitted he had been deceived and disappointed, that the assurances that Hitler had given in Munich in September 1938 had been worthless. (The annexation of the Sudetenland, Hitler had said then, would be 'the last territorial claim' he would make in Europe.) Just two weeks later, on 31 March 1939, Chamberlain informed Parliament that the British government would come at once to Poland's aid 'in the event of any action which clearly threatened Polish independence and which the Polish Government accordingly considered it vital to resist with their national forces'. The French government, too, had authorized him to make it plain that on this question they took the same position as the British.

Hitler's rage at the Anglo-French stand and their agreement with

Poland signed on 6 April still did not deter him from the course on which he had already embarked towards Poland's destruction. In March he had begun to make excessive demands of Poland – Danzig became the symbolic issue – and brash diplomatic manoeuvres accompanied outrageous propaganda. On 3 April Hitler gave Field Marshal Wilhelm Keitel, Chief of the High Command of the armed forces, instructions to prepare Operation White, the invasion of Poland. In mid-April, addressing top military officers, Hitler argued that since Germany could not count on Poland's neutrality in case of a war with the Western powers, Germany must therefore first eliminate Poland through a lightning campaign (*Blitzkrieg*). He assured the officers that such an undertaking would not lead to another war.[1]

Just about this time a new diplomatic possibility unfolded that showed Hitler's capacity for opportunism, expediency and deceit and that would, in addition, give impetus to Operation White. On 17 April, for the first time since he had presented his credentials nearly a year before, the Russian ambassador visited Ernst von Weizsäcker, then state secretary in the German Foreign Office. The Russians, it appeared, had contracted with the Czech Skoda Works for munitions and were now concerned about their delivery. The conversation then turned from trade to politics, and Weizsäcker recorded the position of the Soviet ambassador: 'There exists for Russia no reason why she should not live with us on a normal footing. And from normal, the relations might become better and better.'[2]

Though the Soviet Union appears to have taken the initiative for a German–Soviet rapprochement, it was Germany that more eagerly pursued the undercover negotiations. On 28 April Hitler denounced his 1934 agreement with Poland. That may have been intended to demonstrate to the Russians the German interest in coming to an understanding. The Russians then signified their interest on 3 May by suddenly dismissing Foreign Minister Maxim Litvinov. Litvinov embodied all that the Germans detested about Bolshevism – he was a Jew, a peace advocate, a supporter of the League of Nations, a friend of the Western democracies and an opponent of Nazi Germany and its anti-Comintern Axis. Litvinov was replaced by Vyacheslav V. M. Molotov, the complete antithesis to Litvinov: a non-Jew, a close associate of Stalin's, a hard, ruthless man said to favour accommoda-

tion with Germany. With remarkable prescience the French ambassador in Berlin noted on 7 May that a fourth partition of Poland would
surely be the basis of the German–Russian rapprochement.[3]

At a meeting on 23 May 1939 of his highest-ranking military officers
to brief them on 'the situation and political objectives', Hitler dilated,
as usual, on racial and ideological matters as the basis for Germany's
politics and then set forth his military strategy to attain both the
racial and the political goals.[4] He said that while 'the ideological
problems' of the German people had been already solved, the question
of German self-sufficiency still awaited solution. That was a question,
he told them, not of Danzig but of *Lebensraum*: 'If fate forces us into a
showdown with the West it is good to possess a largish area in the
East.' The decision had to be to attack Poland at the first suitable opportunity. Possible accommodation with Russia was barely hinted at:
'Economic relations with Russia are only possible if and when political relations have improved.'

On 30 May the German Foreign Office instructed their ambassador
in Moscow: 'Contrary to the policy previously planned, we have now
decided to undertake definite negotiations with the Soviet Union.'
Hitler had decided that in the event of Anglo-French intervention on
behalf of Poland, it was the wiser strategy to protect his eastern flank.
Once again, in the most backhanded way, he resorted to expediency
and opportunism to advance his ideological and political goals. In
fact, on the very eve of the invasion he admitted as much. General
Franz Halder recorded Hitler's remarks at a meeting with top party
people on 28 August: 'Soviet pact in many ways misunderstood by
party. Pact with Satan so as to drive out the Devil.'[5] (The metaphor
was one he had used in the past, positively or negatively, as it suited
his purpose.)

Everything was 'go' for the Polish invasion. On 23 June Göring, as
Plenipotentiary for the Four Year Plan, called a meeting of the Reich
Defence Council to discuss manpower problems that war would impose on Germany. Funk was given the responsibility of deciding what
kind of work could be assigned to war prisoners and to inmates of
penitentiaries and concentration camps. Himmler promised that
greater use would be made of the concentration camps during wartime, and Göring talked of employing foreign workers in Germany.

The most extensive and inhumane network of forced and slave labour began to be organized.

The summer passed rapidly in the din of German threats against Poland, while official conversations with allies-soon-to-be-enemies concealed the simultaneous pursuit of secret negotiations with the Russians. Hitler had set 26 August as the start of Operation White (the Polish campaign was to be completed before the autumn rains) and therefore pressed vigorously to conclude an agreement with Russia before then. On 19 August Stalin informed the Politburo that he would sign a pact with Germany, and that same day a trade agreement between both countries was brought off. On 23 August Foreign Minister Ribbentrop arrived in Moscow and in the afternoon conferred with Stalin. In an extraordinary burst of energy, agreement on the text was reached later that day and the pact was signed after midnight. The pact, in its secret protocol, defined the spheres of influence of each signatory (Lithuania was in the German sphere; Latvia, Estonia and Finland were in the Russian) and drew a demarcation line for the partition of Poland. Both parties obligated 'themselves to desist from any act of violence, any aggressive action and any attack on each other, either individually or jointly with other Powers'.

On 25 August Britain signed a formal treaty with Poland, confirming the guarantees given on 6 April. That day Hitler postponed Operation White to 1 September, in the hope of eliminating British intervention, but he failed to detach the British from their commitment to Poland. Operation White was nonetheless ordered, and by 6.30 a.m. on 1 September 1939 German troops invaded Poland all along the frontier.

Later that morning Hitler addressed the Reichstag with self-justifying and belligerent rhetoric. Projecting upon the enemy his own intentions, he threatened: 'Whoever fights with poison will be fought back with poison gas. Whoever deviates from the rules for the humane conduct of war can expect nothing else from us, but that we will take the same steps.'[6] It was one of the few speeches in which he failed to mention Jews. (Was the passage just quoted an esoteric reference?) Yet later Hitler fixedly and repeatedly referred to *this* speech on *this* day as the speech in which he had threatened the Jews with destruction in the event of a war, though he had made *that* speech on

30 January 1939.* In his mind he associated his declaration of war on 1 September 1939 with his promise to destroy the Jews.

War and the annihilation of the Jews were interdependent. The disorder of war would provide Hitler with the cover for the unchecked commission of murder. He needed an arena for his operations where the restraints of common codes of morality and accepted rules of warfare would not extend. He had set into motion a twofold war – one that was traditional in its striving for resources and empire and that would be fought in traditional military style, and one that was unconventional inasmuch as its primary political objective was to attain

---

*There were, to my knowledge, four such 'slips.'⁷.

1. **30 January 1941:** 'And I should not like to forget the indication that I had already given once, on 1 September 1939, in the German Reichstag. The indication I gave then was that if the rest of the world were plunged into a general war by Jewry, then the whole of Jewry would have finished playing its role in Europe!

'They may still laugh today at that, exactly as they laughed at my prophecies. The coming months and years will prove that I also saw correctly here.'

2. **30 January 1942:** 'We see our way clearly on the point that the war can end only in that either the Aryan peoples are annihilated or Jewry will disappear from Europe. On 1 September 1939 I declared in the German Reichstag – and I guard myself against premature prophecies – that this war would not end as the Jews imagine, namely, that the European-Aryan peoples will be annihilated, but on the contrary that the consequence of this war will be the destruction of Jewry.'

3. **30 September 1942:** 'On 1 September 1939 I stated two things at the meeting then of the Reichstag:

'First, that after this war was already forced upon us, no force of arms and also no term would ever force us down, and second, that if Jewry would plot an international world war for the annihilation of the Aryan peoples of Europe, then not the Aryan peoples would be annihilated, but on the contrary Jewry... The Jews laughed once also in Germany at my prophecies. I do not know if they are still laughing also today, or if their laughter has not already subsided. But I can also now only assert: Their laughter everywhere will subside. And I will be right also with these prophecies in the end.'

4. **8 November 1942:** 'You will recall still that meeting of the Reichstag in which I declared: If Jewry perchance imagines that it can bring about an international world war for the annihilation of the European races, then the consequence will be not the annihilation of the European races, but on the contrary, it will be the annihilation of Jewry in Europe. I was always laughed at as a prophet. Of those who laughed then, countless ones no longer laugh today, and those who still laugh now will perhaps in a while also no longer do so.'

National Socialist ideology and that would be conducted in an innovative style of mass murder.

On 3 September Britain declared war on Germany, and a few hours later France followed suit. That same day Prime Minister Chamberlain broadcast the news. 'It is evil things', he said, 'we shall be fighting against, brute force, bad faith, injustice, oppression and persecution. But against them I am certain that the right will prevail.'

Poland was in no way a match for the Germans in the number of its fighting troops or in their equipment. Within a few days German air superiority had rendered Polish resistance ineffective. The German ground invasion moved so swiftly that the Russians, for their part, could barely keep up with them. On 17 September, when the western half of Poland was in German hands except for Warsaw, which was holding out heroically against German besiegement, the Russians overran eastern Poland and occupied those areas agreed upon in the German–Soviet pact. On 27 September, when Warsaw capitulated, the Polish campaign was over. The following day Ribbentrop and Molotov signed a German-Soviet Boundary and Friendship Treaty and a number of secret protocols adjusting the boundaries of the spheres of influence that had been defined in the agreement of 23 August. They also issued a public declaration to the effect that they had now created 'a firm foundation for a lasting peace in Eastern Europe', and called on England and France to end the state of war against Germany.[8]

The partition of Poland and its occupation* at last gave Hitler the opportunity to effect the racial programmes that had obsessed him for two decades. On 12 October 1939 he issued a decree establishing a civil administration in Poland, called Generalgouvernement, with Hans Frank as Governor General. Frank would later describe himself to Curzio Malaparte as 'the German King of Poland', a claim based more on vanity than on reality. Just three days before, on 9 October 1939, by secret decree Hitler had appointed Himmler Reich Commissar for the Strengthening of German Folkdom (RKFDV), a position that augmented his already vast authority as head of the SS with all its

* See Appendix A for a brief account of the occupation and fate of the Jews in Poland.

divisions and enterprises and that made him the *de facto* master and chthonian monarch of occupied Poland, in effect Hitler's plenipotentiary for racial empire. In the welter of conflicting jurisdictions in Poland – among the military, civil administration, labour supply, economic undertakings and the SS – ideological interests, above all, the war against the Jews, became the province of the SS.

Racial policies to be pursued in Poland, according to Hitler's decree, were designed to eliminate the 'harmful influence' of 'alien' populations and to create new German colonies by resettlement. All non-Germans were to be expelled from those areas of Poland that would be integrated into Germany proper. As Hitler put it to Keitel on 17 October, 'the old and new Reich area' was to be 'cleansed of Jews, Polacks and company'. 9 A German racial 'reclamation' project was put into operation, racially screening persons who claimed to be Germans or had Germanic features. Such persons were regarded as 'racially valuable' and hence eligible for 're-Germanization'. (Blond, Teutonic-looking Polish children were especially desirable.) These were sent to Germany to undergo the proper ideological indoctrination, while nearly half a million racially pure Germans from the Reich were brought in to establish German peasant colonies in the areas from which the Poles had been expelled.

In the Generalgouvernement, however, as Hitler told Keitel, a 'tough struggle for national existence [*Volkstumskampf*]' that 'permits no legal restraints' would have to be conducted. The Generalgouvernement was to serve as a dumping ground for the Poles and Jews expelled from the parts of Poland that Germany annexed. The total number involved in this population transfer has been estimated at one million. The Polish leadership élite was to be killed, the Polish population to serve only as a source of labour for the Germans. The Jews were to be concentrated in a few large centres and then segregated from the non-Jewish population as a first step in a long-range plan that would end in their annihilation. The responsibility for this programme was lodged with Himmler, and its execution entrusted to Heydrich and his SD striking force – Einsatzgruppen (special-duty groups).*

---

*   *Einsatz* is a word with many meanings, most of them vague. In some usages it carries an overtone of self-sacrifice or dedication to duty, in the sense of 'stake' (one stakes one's life for a meaningful outcome). 'Special-duty groups'

The German Partition of Poland 1939/41-45

The Einsatzgruppen, as a paramilitary police force, were conceived of by Heydrich to provide a striking force for the political police and security intelligence. They were first used during the invasion of Austria, hunting down persons suspected of opposition to National Socialism. In connection with the planned invasion of Czechoslovakia, they were to follow, wherever possible, directly behind the advancing troops and take over all security, including also the security 'of all enterprises necessary to the national economy and so, also, to the war economy'.[10] Their role was to become increasingly important as the war accelerated.

Six Einsatzgruppen were attached to the army during the military campaign in Poland. Their wholesale murder of Poles and their sadistic atrocities against Jews shocked some army generals. The generals' recoil from the sanguinary acts of the SS may be ascribed not to moral objections but instead to the Einsatzgruppen's deviations from army regulations and army discipline, and to the generals' desire to preserve the hegemony of the army. By September 1939 the army had been thoroughly ideologized, its men and officers indoctrinated in the teachings of National Socialism through the spoken and printed word. (Top-ranking officers usually got their ideological briefings directly from Hitler.) An army indoctrination booklet on 'The Jew in German History', published early in 1939, shows how thoroughly the army had adopted Nazi doctrine and, concomitantly, a double standard in combat.

We Germans fight a twofold fight today. With regard to the non-Jewish peoples we want only to accomplish our vital interests. We respect them and conduct a chivalrous argument with them. But we fight world Jewry as one has to fight a poisonous parasite; we encounter in him not only the enemy of our people, but a plague of all peoples. The fight against Jewry is a moral fight for the purity and health of God-created humanity and for a new more just order in the world.[11]

The army's hostile reactions to the Einsatzgruppen served notice on Himmler and Heydrich that they had to convince the army of the top priority of their 'political' tasks. On 19 September Heydrich conferred with army Quartermaster General Eduard Wagner, explaining

---

perhaps best renders the meaning; 'striking force' too conveys some flavour of the German.

that though the Einsatzgruppen chiefs were subordinated to army HQ, they received their instructions directly from him as Chief of the Security Police. Heydrich regarded the discussion as a 'favourable outcome' in SD collaboration with the army.[12] Wagner passed on details of the conference to his superior, General Franz Halder, who recorded some laconic notes of the meeting in his diary:

a. Missions [of the SD] must be known to the army. Liaison officers: Himmler army CC [General Walter von Brauchitsch].

b. Cleaning out: Jewry, intelligentsia, clergy, nobility.

c. Army demands: Clean-up after the withdrawal of the army and after the transfer to stable civil administration . . .[13]

The SD did indeed get the better of the army, for the army had to be satisfied simply with knowing in advance about the special missions assigned to the SD. Furthermore, these 'clean-up' missions against the Jews and Polish élite groups would proceed as planned. The army asked Heydrich not to start these missions until after the General-gouvernement was transferred to a civil adminstration, but this was of no avail. Two days after his meeting with Wagner, Heydrich, at a conference in Berlin, issued to his Einsatzgruppen chiefs his first major directive affecting the Polish Jews and that same day sent it out as an express letter.[14]

At that conference, a luncheon meeting, with fifteen SS officers present (including Eichmann, representing the Reichszentrale für die jüdische Auswanderung), Heydrich outlined the racial policies planned for Poland and the tasks of the Einsatzgruppen. They were instructed to prepare lists of top Polish leaders and also of those on the middle level of leadership – teachers, clergy, nobility, legionnaires. Those listed were clearly foredoomed. As for the Jews, the policy was to concentrate them in city ghettos 'for a better possibility of control and later possibility of deportation'. Jewish smallholders were to disappear. Jewish retailers could remain in rural areas only if they provided the army with supplies it required. A directive, Heydrich informed them, would be issued covering four points: (1) moving Jews as fast as possible into the cities; (2) transferring Jews out of the Reich into Poland; (3) moving the remaining 30,000 Gypsies also into Poland; (4) systematically ejecting the Jews from the German territories in freight cars.

Heydrich's directive, 'The Jewish Question in the Occupied Territory', issued later that day, is a guidepost in the chronology of the Final Solution. It testifies that a master plan for annihilating the Jews had already been conceived, though only the preliminary stages were now to be implemented. Heydrich 'once more' reminded the Einsatzgruppen chiefs that 'the *planned overall measures* (i.e., the final aim) are to be kept strictly secret'. He distinguished between 'the final aim', requiring an extended period of time, and 'the stages leading to the fulfilment of this final aim'. The 'final aim' is not mentioned further. (Eichmann, when confronted with the document at his trial, said right away that it could mean only 'physical extermination'.)[15] First, Heydrich described the task of expelling the Jews from the areas that were to be incorporated into the German Reich (Danzig, West Prussia, Posen and Eastern Upper Silesia) and then of concentrating all the Polish Jews in a few urban areas. The aim should be, Heydrich emphasized, to establish as few concentration points as possible, and, 'so as to facilitate subsequent measures', these concentration points should be at rail junctions or places located along railway lines. At his conference Heydrich thought that this process would take three to four weeks. Actually, it took much longer, partly because of a temporary halt to meet army objections, but mainly because of the complexities involved in moving such vast numbers of people.

The second section, titled 'Jüdische Ältestenräte' ('Councils of Jewish Elders'), prescribed that a Jewish council be established in each community to carry out the instructions of the Einsatzgruppen.* It was to consist of available 'influential personalities and rabbis'. The idea of a Jewish council headed by an 'Eldest' (*Älteste*) probably derived from the practice in medieval Germany, when the internal affairs of the Jewish community were regulated by a so-called *Judenbischof*, 'bishop of the Jews', in fact, chief rabbi. He was assisted by an advisory council of twelve *dayanim*, composing a Judenrat, all usually chosen or elected by the tax-paying members of the community and

---

*The creation of a Jewish council, called 'Judenrat', was proposed back in April 1933 in a draft Law to Regulate the Status of Jews (*Judengesetz*).[16] It was prepared by several persons, including Rudolf Diels, the first Gestapo chief, and by Dr Johannes von Leers, a professor of history and 'expert' on the Jews. The draft was submitted to Frick at that time, but never used. There is no evidence that Göring, then Diel's superior, or Heydrich ever knew of it.

approved by the Emperor. Members of the council were called 'Elders', and the chairman was designated the 'Eldest'. The practice persisted until the Reformation.

The term *'Judenrat'* eventually became more common than *'Ältestenrat'*, while *'Älteste'* was reserved for the council's chairman. This council, Heydrich stressed, was to be made *'fully responsible, in the literal sense of the word, for the exact and punctual execution of all directives issued or yet to be issued'*, and failure to do so would entail the 'severest measures'.

The functions assigned to the Jewish councils, though few, were onerous beyond the capacity of any non-governmental agency: they were charged with the responsibility for carrying out the evacuation of the Jews from the countryside, for providing food supplies en route and housing in the cities of concentration. The Jewish councils were also to prepare censuses of the Jewish population in their jurisdiction, by age and principal occupational groups, which were intended, in time, to eliminate the non-working populations – children and the old – and to indicate which occupations were needed by the army or the wartime economy.

Once the Jews were concentrated in a few large cities, Heydrich foresaw that for general reasons of security, it would probably be necessary to bar 'Jews from certain sections of cities, or, for example, forbid them to leave the ghetto or go out after a designated evening hour'.

Back on 12 November 1938, at Göring's conference, Heydrich had objected to Göring's proposal for ghettos on the grounds that they would harbour Jewish resistance, but now ghettos, which Hitler had already alluded to in 1935, were the obvious 'solution' for concentrating the Jews during the preparations for the 'final aim'.

The third section of the directive, concerning the Jews in their economic and industrial capacities, indicated that these functions should be transferred to 'Aryans' without impairing the 'economic security' of the occupied territories. The army's needs were essential, Heydrich stressed, and Jewish-owned or Jewish-operated enterprises meeting the needs of the army were to be tolerated only until 'prompt Aryanization' could be accomplished.

The chiefs of the Einsatzgruppen were instructed to report to Heydrich, with statistics, on their accomplishments in evacuating and concentrating the Jews and in gathering the economic and industrial data required. To attain these goals Heydrich stated that he expected 'total deployment of all forces of the Security Police and the Security Service', and to make sure that all areas were covered he advised the Einsatzgruppen chiefs in adjoining territories to consult each other. Copies of the directive were sent to the army, the Plenipotentiary for the Four Year Plan, the departments of Interior, Food, Economy as well as the heads of the civil administration of the occupied territory. The whole wartime German bureaucracy was thus informed and involved in the SS's plan to deal with the 'Jewish question in the occupied territory'.

Some analysts have suggested that 'the final aim' to which Heydrich had alluded in his directive was, at this time, not the planned annihilation of the Jews, but the establishment of a vast Jewish reservation. Hitler himself had mentioned that as a possibility back in 1935: the Jews would be 'imprisoned in a territory where they can disport themselves according to their nature'. From the start of the war, the Germans spread reports that a 'Jewish reservation' would be set up in the Lublin district,[17] and indeed tens of thousands of Jews from the newly annexed territories and from Germany proper were sent there, beginning in October 1939. The plan seemed even to have been approved by Göring, Himmler and Frank in early February 1940, but it was cancelled a month later, without explanation. Meanwhile, another site for a reservation had been bruited about – the French island of Madagascar. Certain Foreign Office and SS bureaucrats were enthusiastic about the idea, indefatigably drafting memoranda on various aspects of the plan, ranging from problems in international law to transportation. Even Himmler, in a memorandum, 'Some Thoughts on the Treatment of Foreign Nationals in the East', that he submitted to Hitler in May 1940, wrote: 'I hope to see the concept of Jews completely obliterated with the possibility of a large migration of all the Jews to Africa or else in a colony.'[18]

Yet everything we know of National Socialist ideology precludes our accepting the idea of a Jewish reservation as the last stage of the Final Solution. In the hierarchy of Nazi racial values, the Jews were bottommost, slated for a crueller fate than the Slavs, a layer higher. The Slavs were *Untermenschen*, sub-humans who, Himmler said, were to learn that to obey the Germans was a divine command. Hitler's 'final' racial policy for the Slavs was 'depopulation', which would prevent them from propagating, except to provide a continuous supply of slaves to serve the Germans. Hence, if justice was to be rendered according to the scale of National Socialist racial values, then clearly a more sanguineous fate than that of the Slavs was intended for the Jews. A reservation, whether in Lublin or Madagascar, could have been conceived of only as a transitional stage, comparable to ghettos as a means of concentration. Perhaps it was no mere coincidence that the first ghetto in Poland was established in Lodz in the spring of 1940, right after the Lublin plan was dropped.[19] Another enlightening datum on the purpose of a reservation can be derived from the report – surely a sick joke – that Philipp Bouhler, the head of Hitler's private chancellery, was slated to become governor of the Madagascar reservation. Bouhler headed the so-called 'Euthanasia Programme' (see below, p. 171), the first mass murder by gassing, experience that doubtless qualified him to run a reservation for Jews that would become truly their final destination. (Madagascar would have afforded the privacy that the Germans wanted for the Final Solution.)

By 21 September 1939, when Heydrich issued his instructions to his Einsatzgruppen chiefs, it seemed that the 'final aim' was already envisaged, although the precise steps leading to its implementation were still to be formulated, planned and executed. Poland was the launching area and testing laboratory not only for the execution of the Final Solution, but for all of Hitler's racial and imperial ambitions, but Russia would become the arena for the first encounter in the final struggle, the prelude to the millennium.

The plans to wage war against Russia were always in Hitler's thoughts. He told Keitel on 17 October 1939 that the area of Poland had military significance as an 'advanced glacis' and could be used for troop deloyment. Consequently, trains, highways and communication lines were to be kept in order.[20] But first Hitler prepared the invasions of Western Europe as part of a grand strategy to consolidate the West under German dominion and thus free him for that decisive struggle in the East.

On 9 October 1939, just days after the end of the Polish campaign, he issued the first directive for Operation Yellow, the invasion of the Low Countries, but that plan had to be postponed, perhaps because of an attempt to assassinate him. Spring invasions instead were set in motion – in April into Denmark and Norway, in May into the Netherlands, Belgium and France.* With the surrender of the French on 21 June 1940, Hitler stood triumphant at the English Channel. On his agenda now was Operation Sea Lion, the invasion of Britain. All through the summer he issued directives for an invasion that was scheduled to take place on 15 September, conditional on Germany's gaining air supremacy over England.

Meanwhile, Hitler vigilantly monitored Russia's moves in the East – its incorporation of the Baltic states into the Soviet Union, its threats against Finland and Bessarabia, its heavy troop concentrations in eastern Poland. Early in July he told the General Staff to draw up plans for an offensive in the East, and the following month he ordered that Poland be readied as an assembly platform for an Eastern campaign and that the necessary roads, railway lines, airfields and military quarters be constructed.[21]

On 15 September the air battle for Britain reached its dramatic climax when the British air force succeeded in repelling Germany's massive and concentrated air attack over the Kent promontory. Two days later Hitler ordered Operation Sea Lion postponed indefinitely. But the plans for an Eastern campaign continued, and a war game was ordered in September to test campaign possibilities. Hitler proceeded, impelled more by ideology than strategy. On 18 December 1940, barely fifteen months after the conclusion of the German–Soviet Boundary and Friendship Treaty, Hitler issued the first directive for a German invasion of Russia: 'The German armed forces must be prepared, even before the conclusion of the war against England, *to crush Soviet Russia in a rapid campaign* ("Operation Barbarossa").' According to this plan, preparations were to be concluded by mid-May, in time for an early summer invasion. (Fighting was expected to be over before the Russian winter set in). Hitler's only other strategic plan, meanwhile, was to keep the British out of the Mediterranean, lest they interfere with his military movements in the East.

Preparations continued according to schedule, and in the middle of March German troops began to move eastwards in readiness for the attack, then set for 12 May.[22] On 13 March 1941 Field Marshal Keitel

*For the fate of the Jews in these countries, see Appendix A.

issued a top secret directive, in five copies, containing a series of 'orders for special areas', in connection with Operation Barbarossa. Its main purpose was to define jurisdiction of competence and lines of authority in the areas of operation as they affected the armed forces, the SS and the civil administration. One paragraph defined the role and function of the SS:

In the area of army operations the Reichsführer-SS will be entrusted, on behalf of the Führer, with *special tasks* for the preparation of the *political administration* – tasks entailed by the final struggle that will have to be carried out between two opposing political systems. Within the framework of these tasks, the Reichsführer-SS will act independently and on his own responsibility. However, the executive power vested in the Supreme Commander of the army and in agencies acting under his orders will not be affected by this. The Reichsführer-SS is to see that operations are not disturbed by the execution of his tasks. Details are to be worked out directly between the High Command of the army and the Reichsführer-SS.[23]

The rhetoric about 'tasks entailed by the final struggle that will have to be carried out between two opposing political systems' was one seldom encountered in military directives. It was the rhetoric of Hitler's racial eschatology, of the final struggle between the Aryan hosts and their Jewish–Bolshevik opponents. The whole paragraph was said to have been dictated by Hitler himself.[24] It was the authorization for Einsatzgruppen to kill the Jews in the territory that the army would first wrest from the enemy.

Keitel later claimed that he 'had so stubbornly contested' the clause giving Himmler authority in the rear operational areas, but that his opposition was useless and he was overruled.[25] By clarifying the area of authority assigned to the SS and from the start obtaining Keitel's assent to the presence and activity of the SS Einsatzgruppen, both Hitler and Himmler assured themselves that the earlier conflicts between the army and the SS in Poland would not recur and that no impediment would arise to obstruct the programme laid out for Einsatzgruppen.*

* Similar arrangements defining the relationships between the SS and the civil administration of the Eastern occupied territories were also provided for. On 17 July 1941 Hitler issued a decree establishing a civil administration upon completion of military operations. He appointed Alfred Rosenberg to the post of Reich Minister for the Occupied Eastern Territories. That decree – as well as

One more decision had been taken in the relentless course towards the annihilation of the Jews. Though the abundant documents of the German dictatorship have yielded no written order by Hitler to murder the Jews, it appears from the events as we know them now that the decision for the practical implementation of the plan to kill the Jews was probably reached after 18 December 1940 – when Hitler issued the first directive for Operation Barbarossa – and before 1 March 1941.

At about the same time that Operation Barbarossa was being planned to include procedures for the murder of the Jews in synchronization with the conquest of Russia, Himmler was initiating an even more sinister undertaking that would encompass the rest of Europe's Jews. On 1 March 1941 he visited Auschwitz, where he gave orders to Rudolf Höss, the camp commandant, for a tremendous expansion of the camp to accommodate 100,000 prisoners of war and 30,000 'peacetime' prisoners, 10,000 of whom would be assigned to the I. G. Farben synthetic-rubber factory.[26] The 'prisoners of war' then in custody at Auschwitz, which served as a transit camp of sorts, had been arrested by the Security Police and could by no accepted standard be regarded as military prisoners. When Himmler spoke of providing accommodation for prisoners of war, he likely did not mean POWs in the traditional sense of captured men and officers of an enemy army, but rather ideological enemies, Jews and 'Bolsheviks'. Indeed, shortly after the invasion, on 17 July 1941, Heydrich issued a directive, in agreement with the army, giving his Einsatzkommandos authority to remove from prisoner-of-war camps in Russia 'politically intolerable elements', including Soviet state officials, Communist party functionaries and all Jews. That was one more example of the army's agreeableness to the SS's conducting ideological war in a military framework.

On 30 March 1941 Hitler met with his generals and top commanding officers assigned to the eastern front. After discussing at length the

another issued the same day signed by Hitler, Keitel and Lammers – gave Himmler jurisdiction in that area over 'police security' and within that sphere also the authority to give orders to the Reich commissioners who were subordinate to Rosenberg. Three-way conflicts among SS, army and civil administration, as well as conflicts between Rosenberg and his staff, persisted throughout the occupation of Russia, as they did in the Generalgouvernement.

military and political situation, he then expatiated on his thesis about the inevitability of war with the Soviet Union. The slogan for his Russian policy, he told them, was 'Destruction of Fighting Forces – Dissolution of State', in effect spelling out the strategy behind the 13 March order. Halder's elliptical diary entry conveys the brutal tone of Hitler's words:

Struggle between two opposing world outlooks. Destructive decisions on Bolshevism; is equal to social criminaldom. Communism extraordinary danger for future. We must disavow the point of view of soldierly comradeship. The Communist is not a comrade before and not a comrade after. It is a question of a war of destruction. If we don't conceive of it that way, then we will indeed beat the enemy, but in thirty years the Communist enemy will again confront us. We do not conduct war to conserve the enemy.

Future political picture: Northern Russia will belong to Finland. Protectorates in the Baltic lands, the Ukraine, White Russia.

Struggle against Russia: Destruction of the Bolshevik Commissars and the Communist intelligentsia . . . The struggle must be conducted against the poison of decomposition. This is not a question of courts martial. The leaders of the troops must know what is at stake . . . In the East hardness is gentle for the future.[27]

According to Keitel, everyone appeared shocked, but no one protested. Hitler concluded: 'I do not expect my generals to understand me, but I shall expect them to obey my orders.'[28]

At that time – 30 March 1941 – Operation Barbarossa was probably still scheduled for mid-May, but on 26 March 1941 a military coup had taken place in Yugoslavia, overthrowing the government that had just formally joined the Tripartite Pact of Germany, Italy and Japan. Fearing that the new government, supported by the revolutionary partisan movement, would jeopardize the success of Operation Barbarossa, Hitler had issued a directive on 27 March to invade Yugoslavia. To ensure Hungary's and Bulgaria's cooperation in that invasion, he offered them portions of Yugoslav territory to which they had revanchist claims, and he directed the German military to encourage internal tensions in Yugoslavia by dangling before the Croats the prospect of independence. Operation Barbarossa had to be postponed. After the capitulation of Yugoslavia on 17 April, the Germans proceeded into Greece to bolster the collapsing Italian armed forces there. By the end of May all of Greece, including Crete, where British and Greek forces had offered resistance, was effectively under German control.*

Despite the Balkan military interlude, planning for Operation Barbarossa continued, especially with regard to the upcoming tasks of the SS and the Security Police and the efforts to legitimate them. On 13 May Hitler issued a decree that gave members of the armed forces a free hand in summary execution or 'relentlessly' shooting down enemy civilians and which authorized 'collective measures' to be taken against whole communities when individual culprits could not be identified. It promised protection to members of the armed forces and their 'ancillary services' who engaged in such activities against enemy civilians, by guaranteeing that they 'would not be subject to the constraint of prosecution even if the action is also a military crime or misdemeanour'. A court martial would be instituted only when required by military discipline or security.[29]

This unprecedented issuance of pre-packaged immunity for acts normally subject to severe military discipline was followed up on 6 June 1941 by the heinous Kommissarbefehl (Commissar Order), signed by General Walter Warlimont, for the High Command of the armed forces, 'on the treatment of political commissars'.[30] The covering memorandum, thirty copies of which were prepared, asked that the decree be distributed only to the commanders of armies or air force territorial command and that 'its further communication to lower commands follow by word of mouth'. The decree was an ideological justification of Hitler's directive of 13 May, specifically singling out 'political commissars' as symbols of the Bolshevik régime. Its language indicated the extent to which the German army had become indoctrinated with National Socialist ideology and how far the war itself had become ideologized.

In the struggle against Bolshevism, we must *not* assume that the enemy's conduct will be based on principles of humanity or of international law. In particular, hateful, cruel and inhuman treatment of our prisoners is to be expected from *political commissars of all kinds* as the real carriers of resistance.

The troops must be advised:

1. In this struggle consideration and respect for international law with

*For the fate of the Jews in these countries, see Appendix A.

regard to these elements are wrong. They are a danger for our own security and for the rapid pacification of conquered territory.

2. The originators of barbaric Asiatic methods of warfare are the political commissars. Accordingly measures must be taken against them *inmediately* and with full severity. Accordingly, whether captured *in battle or offering resistance*, they are in principle to be disposed of by arms.

The regulations that followed specified that commissars were not to be treated as soldiers and that the protection provided by international law for prisoners of war would not apply to them. They would be segregated from other prisoners and 'disposed of'.

The Commissar Order was distributed only to top officers, while ideological guidelines were prepared for the troops. Thus an army HQ directive, 'Guidelines for the Conduct of the Troops in Russia', issued on 4 June 1941, instructed the troops in National Socialist thinking and conduct:

1. *Bolshevism is the mortal enemy of the National Socialist German people. Germany's struggle is directed against this destructive ideology and its carriers.*
2. This struggle demands ruthless and energetic measures against *Bolshevik agitators, guerrillas, saboteurs, Jews,* and the complete elimination of every active or passive resistance.[31]

Once the German army had invaded Russia, the generals found it necessary to repeat these directives lest the men on the front forget their ideology on encountering the human reality of the enemy. On 12 September 1941 Keitel drafted a directive regarding 'Jews in the newly occupied eastern territories', which repeated the language of the earlier guidelines: 'The struggle against Bolshevism demands ruthless and energetic measures, above all against the Jews, the main carriers of Bolshevism.'[32] Field Marshal Walter von Reichenau, commander-in-chief of the Sixth Army, issued a directive on 10 October 1941 whose ideological wording Hitler described as 'excellent' and which Keitel ordered distributed as a model for all commanding generals. Reichenau's directive began:

With respect to the conduct of troops towards the Bolshevist system, vague ideas are still widely ~~prevalent.
The most essential aim of the campaign against the Jewish-Bolshevist system is the complete crushing of its means of power and the extermination of Asiatic influence in the European region.

This poses tasks for the troops that go beyond the one-sided routine of conventional soldiering. In the Eastern region, the soldier is not merely a fighter according to the rules of the art of war, but also the bearer of an inexorable national idea and the avenger of all bestialities inflicted upon the German people and its racial kin.

Therefore the soldier must have *full* understanding for the necessity of a severe but just atonement on Jewish sub-humanity.* An additional aim in this is to nip in the bud any revolts in the rear of the army, which, as experience proves, have always been instigated by Jews.[33]

Given this extensive exposure of the regular troops to National Socialist propaganda, the ideological indoctrination of the newly organized Einsatzgruppen must have been even more intensive. Their special task, transmitted orally, was to kill the Jews, to perform the mission entrusted to Himmler by the Führer, according to Keitel's directive of 13 March 1941. The Einsatzgruppen training programme began in May 1941 at the recruitment centres in Pretzsch and Düben, in Saxony, where the 3,000 men who were to form the four groups were assembled. The officers were recruited from the SS, the SD, the Gestapo and Sipo. Men were drawn from these bodies too, but also from Kripo, the State Police (Stapo), Orpo and the Waffen-SS. (Later, while at work, the Einsatzgruppen procured the services of Ukrainians, White Russians, Letts and Lithuanians.) The size of the groups ranged from 800 to 1,200 men. Besides basic military exercises, they were frequently briefed on their mission and exhorted to maintain the SS ethos of toughness. They learned from Heydrich, for example, that 'Judaism in the East is the source of Bolshevism and must therefore be wiped out in accordance with the Führer's aims'.[34]

The men who joined the Einsatzgruppen, in contrast to the ordinary Wehrmacht recruits, were already committed to National Socialist ideology and thoroughly imbued with the notion that Jews were Bolsheviks, and vice versa, and that the Jew-Bolshevik was the 'mortal enemy' of the German people and the German state. Yet even so,

---

*German original: '*Sühne am jüdischen Untermenschentum*'. A strange use of the word '*Sühne*', which seems to be applied in the sense of revenge or reprisal. The sense may be that the Jews are being made to atone for their 'crimes', though atonement is normally an internal, subjective process and not performed by an outsider.

every effort was made to indoctrinate the members of the Einsatzgruppen so that they could perform their 'special tasks' with requisite zeal and efficiency. The reports of the Einsatzgruppen chiefs attest to the internalization of the ideology. There the platitudes of National Socialist doctrine are cited to support the statistics of killing: 'The fight against vermin – that is, mainly the Jews and Communists', 'the population of the Baltic countries had suffered very heavily under the government of Bolshevism and Jewry', 'the terror of Jewish–Bolshevik dominion'.[35]

The Einsatzgruppen performed their special tasks with staggering competence. When the German armed forces drove into Russia on 22 June 1941, in a line of attack extending from the Baltic to the Black Sea, with them, or right behind them, came the four Einsatzgruppen.*[36] Einsatzgruppe A, assigned to Army Group North, operated in the Baltic countries; Einsatzgruppe B, assigned to Army Group Central, in White Russia and the territory farther east towards Moscow; Einsatzgruppe C, assigned to Army Group South, in the Ukraine, except for the southern portion, which, together with the Crimea, came under the jurisdiction of Einsatzgruppe D, assigned to the Eleventh Army. Their operational directives came from Heydrich's RSHA.

Russian resistance crumbled. In a brief span Hitler had won his *Lebensraum* and the unhindered possibility of creating his racial utopia. The Einsatzgruppen went to work. Their methods, combining guile, terror and systematic savagery, must have been worked out at Pretzsch and Düben, for they are remarkably alike in widely separated geographic areas. Otto Ohlendorf, head of the RSHA Amt III (originally SD-Inland) and chief of Einsatzgruppe D, explained at Nuremberg how it was accomplished. Each Einsatzgruppe was divided into smaller units, commandos, led by a member of the SD, the Gestapo or Kripo. The unit assigned to killing the Jews of a given place

would enter a village or city and order the prominent Jewish citizens to call together all Jews for the purpose of resettlement. They were requested to hand over their valuables to the leaders of the unit, and shortly before the execution to surrender their outer clothing. The men, women

*For an account of the occupation of the Soviet Union and the Baltic countries and the fate of the Jews, see Appendix A.

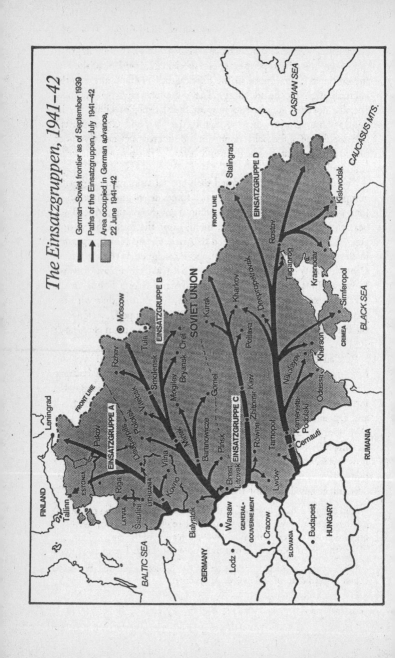

The Einsatzgruppen, 1941–42

▮ German–Soviet frontier as of September 1939

↑ Paths of the Einsatzgruppen, July 1941–42

░ Area occupied in German advance,
22 June 1941–42

EINSATZGRUPPE A

EINSATZGRUPPE B

EINSATZGRUPPE C

EINSATZGRUPPE D

SOVIET UNION

◉ Moscow

FRONT LINE

CASPIAN SEA

CAUCASUS MTS.

BLACK SEA

CRIMEA

FINLAND

ESTONIA

LATVIA

LITHUANIA

GERMANY

GENERAL-GOUVERNEMENT

SLOVAKIA

HUNGARY

RUMANIA

BALTIC SEA

Leningrad

Tallinn

Pskov

Riga

Siauliai

Vilna

Kovno

Brest-Litovsk

Białystok

Warsaw

Lodz

Cracow

Budapest

Dvinsk

Polotsk

Vitebsk

Minsk

Baranowicze

Pińsk

Mogilev

Gomel

Smolensk

Bryansk

Orel

Rzhev

Tula

Kursk

Kharkov

Dnepropetrovsk

Poltava

Kiev

Zhitomir

Rowne

Tarnopol

Lwów

Kamenets-Podolski

Cernauti

Odessa

Nikolayev

Kherson

Simferopol

Krasnodar

Taganrog

Rostov

Kislovodsk

Stalingrad

FRONT LINE

and children were led to a place of execution which in most cases was located next to a more deeply excavated anti-tank ditch. Then they were shot, kneeling or standing, and the corpses thrown into the ditch.[37]

A report of 1 December 1941 by SS Colonel Jäger, who headed a commando in Einsatzgruppe *A*, described his procedures:

The decision to free each district of Jews necessitated thorough preparation of each action as well as acquisition of information about local conditions. The Jews had to be collected in one or more towns and a ditch had to be dug at the right site for the right number. The marching distance from collecting points to the ditches averaged about three miles. The Jews were brought in groups of 500, separated by at least 1·2 miles, to the place of execution. The sort of difficulties and nerve-scraping work involved in all this is shown by an arbitrarily chosen example:

In Rokiskis 3,208 people had to be transported three miles before they could be liquidated . . .

Vehicles are seldom available. Escapes, which were attempted here and there, were frustrated solely by my men at the risk of their lives. For example, three men of the Commando at Mariampole shot thirty-eight escaping Jews and communist functionaries on a path in the woods, so that no one got away. Distances to and from actions were never less than 90–120 miles. Only careful planning enabled the Commandos to carry out up to five actions a week and at the same time continue the work in Kovno without interruption.

Kovno itself, where trained Lithuanian [volunteers] . . . are available in sufficient numbers, was comparatively speaking a shooting paradise.[38]

A report sent out from Warsaw in May 1942 by the Jewish Labour Bund, then underground, to the Polish government-in-exile in London was the first documentation to reach the West of the work of the Einsatzgruppen. Concerned primarily with the fate of the Jews in pre-1939 Poland, the report began:

From the day the Russo-German war broke out, the Germans undertook the physical extermination of the Jewish population on Polish territory, using for that purpose Ukrainians and Lithuanian Šiauliai.* It began first of all in Eastern Galicia in the summer months of 1941. Their method everywhere was as follows: Men from fourteen to sixty were rounded up in one place – a square or cemetery – where they were slaughtered, machine-gunned or killed by hand grenades. They had to

*Members of a paramilitary fascist police organization.

dig their own graves. Children in orphanages, inmates of old-age homes and the hospitalized sick were shot, women were killed on the streets. In many towns Jews were taken away to an 'unknown destination' and executed in the near-by woods. 30,000 Jews were murdered in Lwów, 15,000 in Stanisławów, 5,000 in Tarnopol, 2,000 in Złoczów, 4,000 in Brzeżany (the town had 18,000 Jews, now has 1,700). The same happened in Zborów, Kołomyja, Stryj, Sambor, Drohobycz, Zbaraż, Przemyślany, Kuty, Śniatyn, Zaleszczyki, Brody, Przemyśl, Rawa Ruska and other places . . . According to various estimates, the number of Jews bestially murdered in the Vilna regions and Lithuanian Kaunas is put at 300,000.[39]

At Nuremberg the International Military Tribunal concluded that of the approximately six million Jews murdered, two million were killed by the Einsatzgruppen and other units of the security police.

7 The Annihilation Camps: Kingdom of Death

Some time during that eventful summer of 1941, perhaps even as early as May, Himmler summoned Höss to Berlin and, in privacy, told him 'that the Führer had given the order for a Final Solution of the Jewish Question', and that 'we, the SS, must carry out that order'.[1] Himmler had become the chief receiver and transmitter of Hitler's orders for the Final Solution and its operational principal, a role that he assumed with confidence and authority. In the late summer of 1941, addressing the assembled men of the Einsatzkommandos at Nikolayev, he 'repeated to them the liquidation order, and pointed out that the leaders and men who were taking part in the liquidation bore no personal responsibility for the execution of this order. The responsibility was his alone, and the Führer's.'[2] A year later, in a letter to one of his top SS officials who had just become liaison officer to Alfred Rosenberg, Himmler wrote: 'The occupied Eastern territories are to become free of Jews. The execution of this very grave order has been placed on my shoulders by the Führer. No one can deny me the responsibility anyway.'[3]

The murder of the Jews was clearly a 'political/ideological' task that fell within the purview of the NSDAP apparatus and especially its combat arm, the SS. But the success of the task depended on the cooperation of various state bureaucracies with mutually impinging jurisdictions. Consequently, Hitler transmitted his orders for the annihilation of the Jews not only to Himmler but also to Göring, who, as Plenipotentiary for the Four Year Plan, headed the state apparatus. Whereas Himmler was the responsible agent in carrying out the Final Solution, Göring served in effect mainly as an administrative conduit. It was he who authorized the involvement of the state apparatus in the Final Solution and legitimated it as a state undertaking. He did so by assigning the task of co-ordinating state and party agencies to Heydrich, who, as Chief of the Security Police and

SD and head of the RSHA, represented the nexus of state and party. On 31 July 1941 Göring sent Heydrich the following directive:

As supplement to the task that was entrusted to you in the decree dated 24 January 1939, namely, to solve the Jewish question by emigration and evacuation in the most favourable way possible, given present conditions, I herewith commission you to carry out all necessary preparations with regard to organizational, substantive and financial viewpoints for a total solution of the Jewish question in the German sphere of influence in Europe.

Insofar as the competencies of other central organizations are hereby affected, these are to be involved.*[4]

As a result, administrative responsibility for co-ordinating the Final Solution was given to Heydrich and was lodged in the RSHA's office IV-B-4, where Eichmann supervised 'Jewish Affairs and Evacuation Affairs'. Operational responsibility remained Himmler's. Back in March he had already instructed Höss to enlarge Auschwitz. Now, in the summer of 1941, when Himmler transmitted Hitler's order for the Final Solution, he told Höss that Auschwitz had been selected for that purpose because of its easy rail access, its isolation from populated areas and the physical possibilities its location afforded for concealment and camouflage of its installations. Himmler said that Höss would get further instructions from Eichmann. At about the same time Himmler passed on similar instructions, specifically on the construction of Majdanek, to Odilo Globocnik, then SS and police leader in Lublin. Globocnik would soon become the head of a vast kingdom of death encompassing three annihilation camps – Bełżec, Majdanek and Sobibór – and countless labour camps.

Some weeks later Eichmann came to Auschwitz and discussed with Höss various matters, such as scheduling the murder of the Jews and the techniques of killing to be used – some form of gassing.

---

*According to Eichmann's associate, Dieter Wisliceny, Himmler had written to Heydrich and to the Inspector of Concentration Camps, informing them that 'the Führer had ordered the Final Solution of the Jewish Question' and that both 'were entrusted with carrying out this so-called final solution' (*TMWC* 4: 358–9). Wisliceny said that Eichmann showed him this order, dated April 1942, at the end of July 1942. But the Final Solution was long under way by then. Wisliceny may have been mistaken about the date or that order may have been an implementing rather than an initiating directive.

According to Höss, Eichmann mentioned 'killing with showers of carbon monoxide while bathing, as was done with mental patients in some places in the Reich'. Eichmann also told Höss 'about the methods of killing people with exhaust gases in trucks, which had previously been used in the East'. In September 1941 such a truck had been put at the disposal of Einsatzgruppe C, according to an affidavit by Paul Blobel who headed one of its units.

There was then no need for innovation, since the techniques of mass killing by gas had already been developed, under Hitler's close supervision, to carry out what was euphemistically entitled the 'Euthanasia Programme'. That programme, like the Final Solution, evolved from National Socialist ideology and from Hitler's fanatical ideas about racial health and racial eugenics, which he first spelled out in *Mein Kampf*.

Besides 'positive eugenics', encouraging 'racially healthy' elements in the German population to breed, Hitler also fostered a programme to destroy life and to prevent 'the physically degenerate and mentally sick' from procreating. In *Mein Kampf* Hitler insisted that the Volkist state, using 'the most modern medical means' at its disposal, *'must declare unfit for propagation all who are in any way visibly sick or who have inherited a disease and can therefore pass it on . . .'* These notions of racial health that had become the stock of the National Socialist movement were incorporated into legislation in the National Socialist state. The actual programme for killing was lodged in Hitler's private chancellery, from which its top staff was recruited. Its head, SS–Obergruppenführer Philipp Bouhler, an old party member, was appointed by Hitler to run the Euthanasia Programme. SS–Oberführer Victor Brack, who served in Hitler's chancellery as liaison with the Health Department in the Ministry of the Interior, became Bouhler's deputy. Sharing the top responsibility with Bouhler was Karl Brandt, Hitler's personal physician since 1934. (Brandt's experience gained in killing the sick by gas apparently qualified him for appointment in 1942 as Plenipotentiary for Health and Medical Services.)

Hitler's chancellery had a department to handle various petitions for mercy. In late 1938 or early 1939 a request was received from the father of a deformed child, asking that the child be killed. Hitler turned the matter over to Brandt, instructing him to investigate. If the father's statement was true, Brandt was authorized to inform the physicians, in Hitler's name, to 'carry out euthanasia'. He was also to tell them that should they become involved in legal procedures as a consequence, these would be quashed on Hitler's orders. In fact, Hitler expressly informed the parents that he alone, not they, bore the responsibility for this action. He furthermore authorized Bouhler and Brandt to do the same in similar cases.[5]

In spring 1939 Hitler regularized this procedure of killing mentally deficient and physically deformed children through the establishment of the Reichsausschuss zur wissenschaftlichen Erfassung von erb- und anlagebedingten schweren Leiden (Reich Committee for Scientific Research into Hereditary and Severe Constitutional Diseases).*

In compliance with a secret decree of the Ministry of the Interior, health departments, heads of children's clinics and hospitals, doctors and midwives were to submit reports to the experts on the Reich committee regarding the presence of such children in their institutions. The experts then decided, case by case, whether to perform 'euthanasia'. To facilitate this programme, twenty-one special children's departments were set up in as many hospitals. An estimated 5,000 children were killed in this programme, in operation until November 1944.

Having set in motion the official destruction of 'racially valueless' children, Hitler next turned to the murder of the adult insane. In July 1939 he conferred on this with Hans Lammers, head of the Reich Chancellery, and with SS–Obergruppenführer Dr Leonardo Conti, head of the Health Department in the Ministry of the Interior. At Nuremberg Lammers testified that Hitler had originally appointed Conti as head of the Euthanasia Programme, but after learning that Conti had asked Lammers for official legitimation, something in writing, Hitler, enraged, replaced Conti with Bouhler, who willingly accepted oral orders. Also involved in the discussions was Dr Herbert Linden, of the Health Department, who was commissioner of all the insane asylums in Germany. This programme to kill the adult insane

* The names given to these institutions for killing, as well as the words used later to designate the killing of the Jews, were originally intended as camouflage to conceal from the general public these systematic programmes of murder. This neutral bureaucratic terminology for various methods of murder no doubt later reinforced schizoid and delusional traits among the killers.

began to operate out of Bouhler's office in Hitler's chancellery at Tiergartenstrasse 4 – hence its code name T-4.

After the occupation of Poland, Hitler discussed with his people the matter of a written authorization for these programmes of 'medical' murder, and at the end of October issued such an authorization, written on his personal stationery and pre-dated 1 September 1939. (The association between war and other forms of killing was fixed in his mind.) The authorization read:

> Reichsleiter Bouhler and Dr Brandt, M.D., are charged with the responsibility of enlarging the authority of certain physicians to be designated by name in such a manner that persons who, according to human judgement, are incurably sick may, upon the most serious evaluation of their medical condition, be accorded a mercy death.[6]

Of greater scope than the programme to murder the deformed children, T-4 was an enterprise with more complex institutional arrangements. Three camouflaged front organizations were set up: (1) Allgemeine Stiftung für Anstaltwesen (General Foundation for Affairs of Insane Asylums), which employed the staff in the killing institutions; (2) Reichsarbeitsgemeinschaft Heil- und Pflegeanstalten (Reich Operative Team of Asylums and Nursing Homes), which distributed questionnaires to institutions regarding patients eligible for T 4 and obtained the appropriate judgements; and (3) Gemeinnützige Krankentransportgesellschaft (Public-Benefit Patient Transportation Society), which transported patients from their institutions to the killing centres. A significant portion of the personnel, medical and non-medical, was drawn from the SS. Himmler himself was familiar with all these operations and apprised of problems.

Patients slated for killing were transferred first to a transit facility, called an 'observation institution', of which there were five. They were then transferred to one of six 'euthanasia' installations (at Bernburg, Brandenburg, Grafeneck, Hadamar, Hartheim and Sonnenstein). Whereas the deformed children were put to death individually, usually by injection, these six installations became the mass German dictatorship's first laboratories for mass murder.[7]

A committee of physicians and medical experts, headed by Brandt, were looking for a means of mass killing that would disguise to the victims the fate in store for them and deceive their families. Various gases were experimented with.* At first carbon monoxide was used, but cyanide gas – known by its German trade name as Zyklon B – proved to be most effective. Late in 1939 the first gas installation was set up at Brandenburg, where Brandt, Bouhler, Brack and company observed a test experiment, gassing four insane male patients. Hitler was informed of the results and was said to have decided then that only carbon monoxide was to be used.[8] Then the five other installations were similarly equipped. The procedure was pragmatically simple and convincingly deceptive. In groups of twenty to thirty, the patients were ushered into a chamber camouflaged as a shower room. It was an ordinary room, fitted with sealproof doors and windows, into which gas piping had been laid. The compressed gas container and the regulating equipment were located outside. Led into the chamber on the pretext that they were to take showers, the patients were gassed by the doctor on duty.

It did not take long before people learned what was going on and watched for the heavy smoke to rise from the crematory building, said to be visible over Hadamar every day. In Grafeneck people began to recognize the SS vans carrying the patients to the gas chambers. Children seeing the bus in Hadamar would shout: 'There goes the murder-box again.'[9] After more than a year of rising public clamour in Germany, Hitler, reluctant to 'legalize' this operation, instructed Brandt in August 1941 to 'stall' this killing of mental patients. It has been estimated that between 80,000 and 100,000 people were murdered under the auspices of T-4. But before T-4 ground to a halt, it visibly demonstrated the continuity between killing 'racially valueless' elements within the Germany community proper and killing the racial enemy.

The T-4 experts also fathered the killings of 'non-Aryans' in the German concentration camps, known under the code name 'Sonderbehandlung [special treatment] 14 f 13'. Bouhler supplied Himmler with 'experts' to examine camp inmates – Jews and non-Aryan Germans – who became too sick to work. In practice, the 'race' or the political records of the victims sufficed for a murder decision. At first the victims were transferred to the 'euthanasia' stations to be killed, but as the waiting lines grew very long, every concentration

---

*A historical curiosity, perhaps more than coincidental: Germany was the first country to use poison gas in the First World War.

camp installed a gas chamber of its own. Before the Final Solution became operative, thousands of Jews were murdered under the auspices of 14 f 13.

Most of the manpower and even some of the apparatus of T-4 were transferred to the Final Solution in a time sequence of such exquisite precision as to suggest that Hitler yielded T-4 in preference to the Final Solution. Globocnik, in charge of the annihilation of the Jews in the Generalgouvernement (code name: Operation Reinhard), reported that Hitler's private chancellery had provided ninety-two men to staff Operation Reinhard.[10] One of these was Christian Wirth, formerly chief of criminal police in Stuttgart, who was transferred from Brandenburg to become Globocnik's top aide. Another was SA-Oberführer Oldenburg, who went from Hitler's chancellery to the T-4 programme to Globocnik.[11] Treblinka's first director was Dr Irmfried Eberl, also from Brandenburg, and the nucleus of the first operative death camp at Chełmno was formed from a 'Euthanasia Commando' in Prussia.[12] Finally, in a burst of frugality, some of the gas chambers in the T-4 programme were dismantled, shipped to, and reassembled at Bełżec, Majdanek and Treblinka.[13] In October 1941 Brack consulted Eichmann and members of Rosenberg's staff regarding the construction of gassing facilities in the Russian occupied territory.[14] Clearly, when Eichmann conferred with Höss in the summer of 1941, he was already familiar with the technical aspects of the T-4 programme.

That summer of 1941 a new enterprise was launched – the construction of the Vernichtungslager – the annihilation camp. Two civilians from Hamburg came to Auschwitz that summer to teach the staff how to handle Zyklon B, and in September, in the notorious Block 11, the first gassings were carried out on 250 patients from the hospital and on 600 Russian prisoners of war, probably 'Communists' and Jews whom Heydrich's Einsatzkommandos had taken out of the army's prisoner-of-war camps. Construction of Birkenau, which would become Auschwitz's killing centre, got under way.

The first death camp to be completed was at Chełmno (Kulmhof in German), sixty kilometres from Lodz, intended for the Jews from the ghetto of Lodz. Chełmno began functioning on 8 December 1941, with mobile vans, using engine exhaust gases. (Gas trucks turned up at the same time to kill the Jews assembled in a makeshift camp in Semlin, Serbia, where the occupying German army had been embarrassingly efficient in rounding up the Jews for slaughter before annihilation facilities were ready.)

The next death camp to be completed was at Bełżec, near Lublin, at the end of 1941; it became operational in February 1942. Construction at Sobibór began in March 1942. The labour concentration camp Majdanek, near Lublin, which had been set up at the end of 1940, was transformed into an annihilation camp. Similarly, Treblinka, fifty miles from Warsaw, a labour camp since 1941, was turned into a death camp. In the second half of 1941, the technicians of death took over, building camouflaged gassing facilities. Different methods of gassing were experimented with – in mobile or permanent installations, using exhaust engine gases or Zyklon B. In the first half of 1942 both Majdanek and Treblinka joined the roster of functioning killing camps.

The mass killers by gas and the mass killers by shooting exchanged information, and in early autumn 1941 the experts at Chełmno who had been schooled in the T-4 programme dispatched a gas van to an Einsatzkommando in the Ukraine. In spring 1942 gas vans became more available to Einsatzgruppen, but whether or not they were used was a matter of individual taste. Höss, a man of schizophrenic sensibility, preferred gassing to shooting because he was 'spared all these bloodbaths'.[15] In contrast, an Einsatzkommando chief held that an execution by shooting was 'more honourable for both parties than killing by means of a gas truck'.[16]

These trials and experiments with mass-killing techniques were the subject of Heydrich's classic understatement, when he reported at the Wannsee Conference that 'even now practical experience is being gathered that is of major significance in view of the coming Final Solution of the Jewish Question'. The Wannsee Conference was held in a villa located in Am Grossen Wannsee in suburban Berlin, affording more privacy than RSHA headquarters, at which drinks and lunch were provided. It was originally called for 9 December 1941, but had to be postponed to 20 January 1942, after the Japanese attack on Pearl Harbor and America's declaration of war against Germany's Axis partner Japan. Heydrich called the conference for the purpose of effecting co-ordination among the various agencies with regard to the

Final Solution, in accordance with Göring's directive of 31 July 1941, copies of which went out with the letters of invitation.

Heydrich chaired the meeting and did most of the talking to the thirteen persons present, representing both state and party apparatus.[17] The state agencies sent second-echelon men, deputies and State Secretaries, representing the civil administrations of the Occupied Eastern Territories and of the Generalgouvernement, the ministries of Interior, Justice, the Foreign Office, the Plenipotentiary for the Four Year Plan, the Reich Chancellery and the Gestapo (Müller). The party apparatus was represented by delegates from the NSDAP Chancellery, Himmler's RuSHA and two Sipo/SD commanders, one representing the Generalgouvernement, the other both Latvia and Ostland (the Eastern occupied territories), the last already with extensive practical experience in mass killing, having just completed massacres in Riga affecting some 27,000 Jews. Eichmann, who had prepared the conference and done the administrative work connected with it, took the minutes.

Heydrich began with a lengthy review of Germany's policy towards the Jews, referring to the Reichszentrale under his direction, and the subsequent change in policy from 'emigration' to 'evacuation', in view of 'the possibilities in the East'. (In writing the minutes, Eichmann had obviously mastered the National Socialist technique of euphemism. With so much actual blood-letting, no wonder the vocabulary of murder was so bloodless.) Heydrich then presented a statistical review of the Jews in Europe – far from accurate, but so thorough that it included England, Ireland, Sweden, Switzerland and Turkey – as an introduction to the first item on the agenda: how to proceed with the Final Solution in various foreign states. Some states posed difficulties, for they did not have adequate racial definitions, thus creating problems about eligibility for annihilation, while other states – Rumania was cited – were ready to sell citizenship protection to Jews. Heydrich outlined the general procedure in the Final Solution's 'practical implementation', in which Europe was 'to be combed through from west to east' for Jews, who would be evacuated 'group by group, into so-called transit ghettos, to be transported from there farther to the East'.

There would be a few exceptions – German Jews over sixty-five and those who had been seriously wounded in the First World War or who had been distinguished for war service (reminiscent of Hindenburg's plea to Hitler in April 1933 on behalf of Jewish war veterans who were being thrown out of their civil-service positions). Heydrich had an 'efficient solution'. Jews in these categories were to be assigned to a ghetto for the aged. The site under consideration, he reported at Wannsee, was Theresienstadt, an old fortress town in Bohemia. In a few months Theresienstadt did indeed become a 'model camp', the only one into which the Germans ever allowed foreign observers. It was a Potemkin village, purporting to be an autonomous Jewish community. Among its inmates were many prominent German Jews whose disappearance would prove embarrassing to the Germans in case of international inquiries about their welfare. In reality Theresienstadt was, for most of its inmates, just a stopping place before their final destination at Auschwitz.

In carrying out the Final Solution in countries occupied by the Germans or under German influence, Heydrich proposed that 'the appropriate specialists in the Foreign Office confer with the competent official of the Security Police and the SD'. He then remarked that 'in Slovakia and Croatia the undertaking is no longer too difficult'. (Most of the Jews had already been murdered by local initiative.) The appointment in Rumania of a Commissioner for Jewish Affairs would help, Heydrich thought, and in the near future the Germans should 'impose an adviser on Jewish problems on the Hungarian government'. In France, too, Heydrich foresaw no special difficulties. In this connection, the Foreign Office representative with the unlikely name of Martin Luther – like Eichmann, an eager-beaver fanatic on the 'Jewish question' – cautioned that 'thorough handling of this problem' would cause difficulties in a few countries, 'such as the Nordic states', but that the Foreign Office saw 'no great difficulties with respect to the South-east and West of Europe'.

The second, and final, item on the short agenda concerned the application of the Nuremberg Laws to various categories of partners in mixed marriages and of *Mischlinge*. For the time being, Heydrich said, the discussion was theoretical, but the basic problem was where to draw the line as to which categories of *Mischlinge* could be exempted from the Final Solution. For example, a second-degree *Mischling*, a category normally classed with 'persons of German blood', who had an 'especially unfavourable appearance in racial terms' would now be classified as Jewish 'on the strength of his exterior alone'. Sterilization was proposed as an alternative, in some instances, to 'evacuation'.*

In the concluding discussion, the representative from Göring's Office for the Four Year Plan categorically stated that the Jews in essential war industries should not be evacuated as long as replacements for them were not available. Heydrich responded that they would not be evacuated anyway, according to instructions that he had already issued. But as a matter of fact, there had already been conflicts over killing Jews needed for the war economy and there would be more, the outcome usually favouring the SS point of view. State Secretary Dr Bühler, representing Governor General Hans Frank of the Generalgouvernement, pressed for the solution of the 'Jewish question' in his territory as speedily as possible.

The Wannsee Conference, like other high-level meetings involving the Final Solution, began with an ideological lecture, labelled in the minutes as a 'brief review of the struggle conducted up to now against this enemy'. But actually a spirit of administrative efficiency informed the proceedings at Wannsee, for the annihilation of the Jews had by now moved beyond ideology. The technical machinery for murder had been tested and was now under construction. A smooth functioning of the bureaucratic machinery had also to be assured. As a matter of fact, many basic administrative arrangements had already been worked out, for example, agreements between the Foreign Office and the RSHA, not unlike those between the SS and the army. In October 1939 Ribbentrop had given the RSHA the right to attach its intelligence agents to German diplomatic missions abroad, with the understanding that these agents were to be 'solely devoted to serving the interests of the Reich'. The Foreign Office soon discovered, as the army had in its case, that the RSHA was intruding on its jurisdiction, that the police attachés were interfering in the internal politics of the states in which they operated. A new Himmler-Ribbentrop agreement was drawn up on 9 August 1941, which specifically prohibited such interference unless covered by a special agreement. By October 1943 more than seventy police attachés or 'experts' of one kind or another were attached to German

---

*Two more conferences were held, on 6 March and 27 October 1942, to discuss administrative practices with regard to forced sterilization and dissolution of mixed marriages. Both were under Eichmann's chairmanship.

missions in countries allied to Germany and in neutral countries.[18] In this way, the Foreign Office became an auxiliary to the SS in the murder of the Jews. Indeed, the functions performed by the Foreign Office in assisting the SS took precedence over the conventional Foreign Office operations. In all European countries the Foreign Office gave shelter and support to RSHA bureaucrats and SS agents whose business was the Final Solution, who intervened with the governments to enact anti-Jewish legislation, helped accelerate the concentration of the Jews and arrange the expropriation of their property, arranged for the exploitation of their labour and, finally, expedited their deportation to the death camps.

Its technical problems having been mastered and its administrative matters arranged, the Final Solution entered its second operative stage – mass murder by gassing. Though the Einsatzgruppen were to continue to perform their 'special tasks' in the East, most SS energies were now directed to bringing the Jews from all over Europe to the killing camps. Everywhere the deportations were accomplished by stratagem, terror and force. 'Resettlement for work in the East' was the fundamental lie used to deceive the Jews concerning their fate. To bolster the deception, the Germans usually permitted the Jews to take personal belongings with them. In the ghettos of Poland, where hunger ravaged its inmates, offers of bread and marmalade induced thousands of Jews to turn up voluntarily for 'resettlement'. 'Resettlement' became the euphemism for the process of transporting Jews to the gas chambers.

The schedule prepared in the RSHA's IV-B-4 was put in motion in March 1942, when the first party of Slovakian Jews arrived at Auschwitz and when Jews from the ghetto of Lublin began to be deported to Bełżec. On 27 March 1942 Goebbels noted in his diary: 'Beginning with Lublin, the Jews in the Generalgouvernement are now being evacuated eastwards. The procedure is a pretty barbaric one and not to be described here more definitely. Not much will remain of the Jews.'

On 19 July Himmler ordered that the 'resettlement' of all the Jews of the Generalgouvernement be completed by the end of the year. Only those Jews still employed in five assembly camps (tightly closed forced-labour installations) would be allowed to remain, though not for very long. These measures, Himmler explained, were 'necessary for the ethnic separation of races and peoples required in the context of the New Order of Europe, as well as in the interest of the security and purity of the German Reich and the spheres of its interest'.[19]

Three days later, deportations began from the Warsaw ghetto to Treblinka, whose gas chambers had just been completed. In August the Jews from the ghetto of Lwów were sent to Bełżec. During the summer the Einsatzgruppen renewed their activity in White Russia, while Jews from France, Belgium and Holland began to be deported to Auschwitz. In late summer the Jews from Croatia arrived in Auschwitz, followed by Dutch Jews. In November Norwegian Jews arrived in Auschwitz.

In February 1943 deportations began from the Bialystok ghetto, and that same month the remaining Jews in Berlin were deported. In March the Greek Jews began to arrive at Auschwitz. They were followed by the Jews from Macedonia and Thrace. The ghetto in Cracow was liquidated. Jews from Holland, Luxembourg, Vienna and Prague were sent to the death camps.

On 16 February 1943 Himmler ordered the destruction of the Warsaw ghetto. The liquidation began on 19 April, setting off an uprising, which SS troops quelled after about six weeks. In June the ghetto in Lwów was liquidated. During the summer the Jews from Upper Silesia and elsewhere in Poland were sent to Auschwitz, and the ghetto in Bialystok was liquidated.

On 21 June 1943 Himmler ordered the liquidation of the ghettos in the Ostland, allowing the survival only of Jewish workers in a few labour concentration camps. All others were to be destroyed. In September the ghettos in Minsk, Lida and Vilna were liquidated; in the next two months the remainder of the White Russian ghettos were liquidated and also the Riga ghetto. In September and October Jews from southern France and Rome were deported. In October the Germans scheduled the deportation of the Danish Jews, actually netting about 400. At the end of the year about 7,000 Jews from northern Italy were deported.

The deportation of Jews from Athens began in the spring of 1944. In May and June the Hungarian Jews began to be sent to Auschwitz. The Lodz ghetto was liquidated in August and its 70,000 inhabitants sent to Auschwitz. Deportations from Slovakia were renewed in

September 1944; at the same time the last transport of French Jews left for Auschwitz. In the last two months of 1944 the Jews from Budapest were deported to concentration camps near Vienna.

The Final Solution had top priority, even at a time of military exigencies. The need for railways to transport Jews to their death often competed with the need for railways to transport soldiers and military supplies to the front. Both received equal consideration. At a meeting called by Governor General Frank with the SS police in Cracow on 18 June 1942 the question of transportation to remove the Jews was discussed. According to Frank's summary of the proceedings, Friedrich Wilhelm Krüger, higher SS and police leader* for the Generalgouvernement, Himmler's top agent in Poland, said:

For the carrying out of such an action, the provision of adequate numbers of transport trains was necessary. Although a total railway ban had been ordered for the next 14 days, he had managed in negotiations with President Gerteis [of Ostbahn] to see to it that trains would be provided now and again for the deportation of the Jews. At the conclusion of the ban, the Jewish action would have to be carried out on an increased scale.[20]

At that time the Germans were preparing to launch a new summer offensive in southern Russia. They had committed 266 divisions – all their reserves – on the Eastern front. In preparation for the offensive, scheduled for early July, Gerteis, head of the Ostbahn, the Generalgouvernement's railway system, declared a two-week embargo on all civilian traffic. Though Gerteis had been amenable to Krüger's persuasion to provide some transportation, this was not good enough for Himmler, who then moved the negotiations to a higher level. SS-Obergruppenführer Karl Wolff, the head of Himmler's personal staff, contacted Theodor Ganzenmüller, the new State Secretary for Transportation. On 28 July Wolff received a satisfactory report. 'Since 22 July', according to information that Ganzenmüller had received from the responsible people in Cracow, 'a train with 5,000 Jews apiece has been leaving Warsaw via Malkinia for Treblinka

*Höhere SS und Polizeiführer (HSSPF; higher SS and police commanders), according to a decree promulgated on 13 November 1937, were appointed by Himmler for wartime supervision of all SS forces operating in each military district. They were regarded as Himmler's plenipotentiaries in their districts.

every day; in addition, twice weekly a train with 5,000 Jews from Przemyśl to Bełżec.'[21]

The following winter, Germany's military position had begun to deteriorate, but the top priority of the Final Solution remained unchanged. German troops, besieging Stalingrad, had been encircled by the Red Army. In mid-December 1942, the Germans sent in a fresh Panzer division in an effort to break up the Russian encirclement, and consequently a railway embargo on civilian traffic had been imposed for one month beginning on 15 December. On 4 December Krüger asked Himmler to negotiate with the top people of the armed forces High Command and the Transport Ministry for trains to move the Jews. Because of the railway embargo, Krüger wrote, 'our master plan for Jewish resettlement is severely jeopardized'.[22]

Himmler may have delegated Wolff to negotiate, or he may have decided to wait out the embargo. Finally, he appealed to Ganzenmüller on 20 January 1943, when the disaster at Stalingrad still necessitated extensive rail transport:

> One necessary condition for the pacification of the Generalgouvernement, of Bialystok and of Russian territories is the removal of all helpers of partisan bands and of persons suspected of partisan activities. In particular, the removal of Jews belongs under this head. So does the removal of Jews from the West, since we would otherwise have to reckon with an intensification of ambushes in those regions too.
>
> For this I need your help and your support. If I am to wind things up quickly, I must have more trains for transports. I know very well how taxing the situation is for the railways and what demands are constantly made of you. Just the same, I must make this request of you: Help me get more trains.[23]

His plea succeeded, for in February 1943 trains were available to deport Jews from the Bialystok ghetto to Treblinka and from Berlin to Auschwitz. By March the trains were carrying Jews from all over Europe to the death camps.

According to Dieter Wisliceny, transports of Jews from Greece to Auschwitz 'commanded a sufficiently high priority to take precedence over other freight movements'. Even when the Germans began evacuating Greece in July 1944 and rail transport was critically needed, the deportation of Jews continued on schedule.[24]

Hitler had embarked on an ideological war to achieve ideological/racial goals, but to win that war he needed also to fight a conventional war. Yet the rational interests of the latter often were sacrificed to the racial imperatives of the ideological war. This was especially evident in the treatment the Germans accorded the Poles, Russians and Ukrainians, who, in Hitler's scheme of things, were *Untermenschen*. The Germans alienated large numbers of them, especially the Ukrainians, many of whom subscribed to National Socialist philosophy in other respects and who would willingly have fought on the German side for the prize of national autonomy and independence from the Soviet Union. In the end, that manpower might have affected the outcome of the war. (For want of a nail was a kingdom lost?) The military constantly urged the use of Slavic formations, but Hitler opposed the idea on ideological grounds. Still, in a last-ditch effort to save the conventional war, he agreed to the presence of Slavs with the German fighting troops.[25]

No such concessions were ever made with regard to the Final Solution. Its categorical execution was accelerated at the very time when Hitler himself called a halt, because of wartime exigencies, to Himmler's grandiose racial plans. On 12 January 1943 Himmler ordered the expansion of Generalplan Ost (General Plan for the East), a fantastic plan to colonize Russia proper and the Ukraine with German settlements, written up at the end of 1941 in the RSHA. Himmler now wanted the Baltic countries, White Russia and Crimea included as well. But in the wake of the calamities that had befallen the Germans since the previous November – the entrapment of Paulus's Sixth Army at Stalingrad, the defeat inflicted by the British Eighth Army on Rommel's army in North Africa, and, the worst yet, the Anglo-American landings in French Algeria and Morocco – Hitler became the realist. On 13 January he grounded Himmler's schemes by issuing an order for the complete suspension thenceforth of all 'preparations and plans for future peacetime projects'.[26] But the Final Solution did not fall into this category. Its completion was urgent and delays were tolerated only on the few occasions when short-term opportunities could be won.

The top war priority given to the Final Solution is most evident in the handling of the acute wartime shortage of labour. Rational considerations with regard to the war economy demanded the use of all available hands to produce armaments and provide essential services to the army. In occupied areas where in pre-war times Jews had dominated industry and trade, a conflict erupted between the army, pursuing rational interests, and the SS, unflinching in its commitment to the Final Solution.

The conflict broke out first in the areas where the Einsatzgruppen operated:

Since a large part of the trades in Lithuania and Latvia are in Jewish hands and others carried on nearly exclusively by Jews (especially those of glaziers, plumbers, stove-builders, cobblers), many Jewish partisans are indispensable at present for repairing installations of vital importance for the reconstruction of towns destroyed and for work of military importance. Although the employers aim at replacing Jewish labour with Lithuanian or Latvian labour, it is not yet possible to displace all employed Jews, especially not in the larger towns.[27]

The civil administration opposed the 'larger executions' in view of the labour problem, but the Einsatzgruppe chief responded 'that it was a matter of carrying out basic orders'.

According to a later report of the same Einsatzgruppe, the 'definitive and fundamental elimination of the Jews' caused difficulties, because the Jews included 'an extraordinarily high percentage of skilled workers', who were 'indispensable because of the lack of replacements from other quarters in that area'.[28] But a decision in principle had already been rendered, in response to an inquiry from a top official in the office of Heinrich Lohse, Reich Commissioner for Ostland. He had turned to the Reich Minister for the Occupied Eastern Territories for guidance regarding the liquidation of the Jews. Was it to take place 'without regard to age and sex and economic interests (e.g., the Wehrmacht's in skilled workers in armament plants)'? The elimination of the Jews, he argued, 'must be harmonized with the necessities of the war economy'. The reply from Berlin on 18 December 1941 was succinct: 'As a matter of principle, economic considerations should be overlooked in the solution of the problem.'[29]

In Galicia, too, the deportation of the Jews had crippled the local war economy. The writer of a weekly situation report took it in his stride. Since 'the fundamental question, whether in the elimination of the Jews priority was to be given to political considerations over those of the war economy, was clearly decided at the highest level in favour of the political factor', the lowering of economic achievement in the affected areas had to be accepted.[30] In Przemyśl, the Galician town from which Ganzenmüller was running trains twice weekly to Bełżec, the conflict between the ideological aim and economic considerations actually came to a physical clash. On 27 July 1942, when Jews began to be rounded up for deportation, the town's military commandant demanded exemptions for those Jews employed by the Wehrmacht. Upon the Gestapo's refusal, the army seized the bridges over the San river that connected both parts of the town, and even threatened to halt the departure of the deportation train. The local Gestapo called headquarters in Cracow, which then gave the Wehrmacht its exemptions.[31]

Another short-term postponement occurred in October 1942, when the RSHA had ordered the liquidation of the ghetto in Bialystok and of all other ghettos in the district. The head of the local Armaments Inspectorate, aware of the difficulty of obtaining replacements for the Jewish workers, appealed to the High Command in Berlin. He was supported by the local civil administrator, who adduced the deleterious effect that the elimination of the ghetto would have at the front. That intercession, too, succeeded – for a time.[32] All the ghettos in the area were liquidated, but the Bialystok ghetto remained unharmed for another four months, when part of its inmates were deported. A half year later, in August 1943, it was totally liquidated.

The ideological decision to kill the Jews, it would appear, was occasionally susceptible to rational argument on behalf of the war economy. But the concessions seem to have been decided by the opportunism of geography and the confidence of the SS that their quarry was secure, regardless of the military situation. According to the geographic pattern that emerges, the exemption of certain groups of Jews from deportation or a halt in liquidating an entire ghetto within the Polish and Russian occupied territories lasted from three to six months, depending on the position of the westward-moving front. The longest deferment occurred in Lodz, in the so-called 'Wartheland', which the Germans had incorporated into Germany proper.

In the Generalgouvernement the conflict between the army and the SS over the Jews sharpened after 19 July 1942, when Himmler ordered the 'resettlement' of all the Jews in the Generalgouvernement by the end of the year. The officials of the High Command's Armaments Inspectorates attempted to get some concessions from Krüger, but he told them on 14 August that they could not expect to hold on to their Jewish workers until the end of the war. The orders were quite definite and valid for all of occupied Europe, and he presumed that 'the reasons for them must be of a quite exceptional nature'.³³ Although the SS made certain small concessions, such as separating the Jews employed in war industries from the rest of the ghetto, the basic order remained in effect. On 5 September 1942 Keitel added his authority to that of the SS and issued an order that all Jewish workers were to be replaced. General Curt Ludwig Freiherr von Gienanth, commander of the military district of the Generalgouvernement, knew that getting replacements for Jewish workers was an unrealistic possibility. On 18 September 1942 he sent a memorandum to General Jodl, head of the High Command army operations, in which he pointed to the disastrous labour-supply situation in the Generalgouvernement, where Fritz Sauckel, Plenipotentiary for Labour Allocation, was siphoning off whatever Polish labour was still available for work in the Reich. Of the more than one million workers in war industries, over 300,000 were Jews, one third of them skilled workers. Their immediate removal, Gienanth asserted, 'would cause the Reich's war potential to be considerably reduced, and supplies to the front as well as to the troops in the Generalgouvernement to be at least momentarily halted'. Gienanth asked that the removal of the Jews be postponed until certain essential war production was completed, since he was prepared to accept the principle that the Jews were to be eliminated 'as promptly as possible without impairing essential war work'.³⁴

There was no reply from Jodl, but Himmler issued a blistering memorandum on 9 October. It was addressed to top members of his staff, with copies to the appropriate army officers, reiterating that portion of his decree of 19 July 1942 that ordered Jews still employed in war-industry shops (clothing, fur, shoes) to be assembled in concentration camps. The army was to submit its requisitions for clothing to the SS, which would guarantee uninterrupted delivery. Furthermore, Himmler had issued instructions 'that steps be ruthlessly taken against all those who think it their business to intervene in the alleged interests of war industry, and who in reality want only to support the Jews and their businesses'. (On 30 September Gienanth had been relieved of his command.) The consolidation of Jewish munitions workers into 'a few large Jewish concentration-camp enterprises' was the next step, but, Himmler concluded, 'even from there the Jews are some day to disappear, in accordance with the Führer's wishes'.[35]

The next day the army High Command sent out teletype instructions that 'in agreement with the Reichsführer-SS' it supported 'the principle that the Jews who are employed by the Wehrmacht for auxiliary military service and by the armament industry are to be replaced by Aryan labour at once'. The full text of Himmler's directive was attached.[36] Once again the German army's High Command had capitulated to National Socialism and to the SS. Once again, rationality was abandoned for the pursuit of ideology.

Lodz was just some seventy-five miles west of Warsaw, located in Wartheland, which was incorporated in the Reich. It was governed by Gauleiter Arthur Greiser, a man who could always spot the main chance and who knew how to get on with Himmler. Before the war Lodz had been Poland's major industrial centre, with the Jews preponderant as workers and manufacturers. The ghetto perpetuated that tradition. According to a report of the regional Armaments Commission for February 1944, the largest armaments establishment in the region was 'the ghetto in which 80,000 Jews do 95 per cent of the armaments work and two thirds of the textile production'. The Jews were 'in the meantime' not being deported, the report averred, because of 'consideration for the importance of armaments'. That conclusion was only partly justified. From late autumn 1943 until spring 1944, Greiser, the SS and the army were engaged in a struggle for the ghetto. As a major war producer the ghetto was a lucrative enterprise, and one that Greiser wanted to retain. The SS wanted to turn the ghetto into one of its closed labour camps and reap the profits. The army wanted to protect its own interests. This tug-of-war continued until the beginning of June 1944, when Himmler ordered the liquidation of the Lodz ghetto. Even at that late hour, the army mustered effort to counter the order. On 5 June Speer asked the regional Armaments Inspectorate for data on the ghetto as a productive enterprise, 'to report, in the light of these figures, to the Führer'. (On 9 June Greiser 'dutifully' passed this information on to Himmler and, at the same time, sycophantically called attention to his completion of preparations to clear the ghetto.)[37] Meanwhile Anglo-American forces had landed on the Normandy beaches, and the Germans were now engaged in a two-front war. But the drastic change in their military situation permitted no accommodation with regard to the Final Solution. On 23 June the deportations from Lodz began, and by August 1944 the last 70,000 Jews in the Lodz ghetto had been sent to Auschwitz.

As long as the Jews were permitted to live, their labour was extracted without reward or mercy. After their deportation, the Germans expropriated their remaining goods. 'The wealth they had we have taken from them,' said Himmler in his talk to SS leaders at Posen on 4 October 1943. Operation Reinhard systematized the disposition of the loot and the flow of proceeds from its sale into German hands. All cash proceeds in German notes were to be deposited to the Reichsbank account of the SS's Wirtschafts- und Verwaltungshauptampt (WVHA; Economic and Administrative Main Office), which managed the SS's economic enterprises and administered the concentration camps. Foreign currency (specie or paper), precious metals, jewellery, precious or semi-precious stones, pearls, dental gold and scrap gold were to be delivered to the WVHA for immediate transmittal to the Reichsbank. All timepieces, alarm clocks, fountain pens, mechanical pencils, hand- or electric-operated shavers, pocket knives scissors, flashlights, wallets and purses were to be sent to a WVHA installation for cleaning and price estimation, and then forwarded for sale to the combat troops. Men's underwear, men's clothing, including footwear, were first to fill staff needs at the concentration camps and then to be sent for sale to the troops as an undertaking of the Volksdeutsche Mittelstelle (VOMI; Ethnic German Welfare Office). The proceeds were to go to the Reich. Women's clothing, underwear and footwear and also children's clothing and underwear were to go to VOMI for cash. Pure silk underwear was assigned to the Ministry of Economy. Eiderdowns, quilts, blankets, dress materials, scarves, umbrellas, canes, thermos bottles, ear mufflers, baby carriages, combs, handbags, leather belts, shopping bags, tobacco pipes, sunglasses, mirrors, cutlery, knapsacks, leather and synthetic-material suitcases were to go to VOMI, with specific provisions for payment. Bed linen, sheets, pillowcases, handkerchiefs, facecloths, tablecloths were delivered to VOMI for cash. All kinds of eyeglasses and spectacles were assigned to the Public Health Office for sale. High-class furs, dressed or undressed, were to be delivered to WVHA; cheaper fur goods (neckpieces, hare and rabbit furs) were to be delivered to the Clothing Works of the Waffen-SS at Ravensbrück.

A provisional balance sheet of Operation Reinhard for the period 1 April 1942–15 December 1943 showed that Reich income was augmented by about 180 million Reichsmarks from moneys and values in kind. On 4 November 1943, Globocnik, then on assignment in Trieste, submitted his final report to Himmler, closing out Operation Reinhard. The Generalgouvernement, he wrote, had been a special centre of contagion that he tried to arrest. As justification for future history, Globocnik unctuously advised Himmler to call attention 'to the elimination of this danger'. He asked for some Iron Crosses to be awarded to members of his staff for their 'special achievements in this difficult task'. Himmler replied on 30 November: 'I express to you my thanks and my recognition for the great and unique merits that you acquired for the whole German people in the execution of Operation Reinhard.'[38]

Arriving at Auschwitz, Bełżec, Chełmno, Majdanek, Sobibór and Treblinka, the Jews encountered a standard procedure. At camps maintaining labour installations, like Auschwitz, 10 per cent of the arrivals – those who looked fittest – were selected for work. The remainder were consigned to the gas chambers. They were instructed to undress; the women and girls had their hair cut. They were then marched between files of auxiliary police (Ukrainians usually) who hurried them along with whips, sticks or guns to the gas chambers. As in Operation T-4, these were identified as shower rooms. The Jews were rammed in, one person per square foot. The gassing lasted from ten to thirty minutes, depending on the facilities and techniques used. In Bełżec, according to an eyewitness, it took thirty-two minutes and 'finally, all were dead', he wrote, 'like pillars of basalt, still erect, not having any space to fall'.[39] To make room for the next load, the bodies were right away tossed out, 'blue, wet with sweat and urine, the legs covered with faeces and menstrual blood'. Later the bodies were burned, either in the open air or in crematoria. Himmler complained about the slowness of the proceedings. But no quicker or more secret method could be found. A worker at Auschwitz said that 'the stench given off by the pyres contaminated the surrounding countryside. At night the red sky over Auschwitz could be seen for miles.'[40]

The statistics of the death camps are only approximate. At Auschwitz, the largest mass-killing installation, many transports of deportees went directly from the detraining ramps to the gas chambers and were never statistically registered. On 16 March 1946 Höss made the following statement to two officers of the War Crimes Investigation Unit of the British Army of the Rhine: 'I personally arranged on orders received from Himmler in May 1941 the gassing of two million persons between June–July 1941 and the end of 1943, during which time I was commandant of Auschwitz.' Most victims at the death camps were Jews, but also all Gypsies and thousands of non-Jews – selected for particular reasons – were gassed.

Auschwitz	2,000,000
Bełżec	600,000
Chełmno	340,000
Majdanek	1,380,000
Sobibór	250,000
Treblinka	800,000
TOTAL	5,370,000

On 4 October 1943, Himmler addressed a body of SS-Gruppenführer (lieutenant-generals), in a long rambling speech about the SS. He spoke also about the annihilation of the Jews:

I also want to refer before you here, in complete frankness, to a really grave matter. Among ourselves, this once, it shall be uttered quite frankly; but in public we will never speak of it . . .

I am referring to the evacuation of the Jews, the annihilation of the Jewish people. This is one of those things that are easily said. 'The Jewish people is going to be annihilated,' says every party member. 'Sure, it's in our programme, elimination of the Jews, annihilation – we'll take care of it.' And then they all come trudging, eighty million worthy Germans, and each one has his one decent Jew. Sure, the others are swine, but this one is an A-1 Jew. Of all those who talk this way, not one has seen it happen, not one has been through it. Most of you must know what it means to see a hundred corpses lie side by side, or five hundred, or a thousand. To have stuck this out and – excepting cases of human weakness – to have kept our integrity, this is what has made us hard. In our history, this is an unwritten and never-to-be written page of glory . . .[41]

8 A Retrospective View

The Final Solution had its origins in Hitler's mind. In *Mein Kampf* he tells us that he decided on his war against the Jews in November 1918, when, at the military hospital in Pasewalk, he learned, in rapid succession, of the naval mutiny at Kiel, the revolution that forced the abdication of the Emperor, and finally the armistice. 'Everything went black before my eyes,' he wrote. In the ensuing 'terrible days and even worse nights', while he pondered the meaning of ·these cataclysmic events, 'my own fate became known to me'. It was then that he made his decision:

There is no making pacts with Jews; there can be only the hard: either – or. I, for my part, decided to go into politics.

Did Hitler really decide then, in November 1918, on the destruction of the Jews as his political goal? Or did the idea remain buried in his mind until it took shape in *Mein Kampf*, which he wrote in 1924? *Mein Kampf* was the basic treatise of Hitler's ideas, where he brought together the three essential components that formed the embryonic concept of the Final Solution. Each component originated in a politically commonplace notion that Hitler transformed into an inordinately radical one. First, he turned political anti-Semitism into a racial doctrine whose purpose was the destruction of the Jews. Second, having defined Bolshevism as a Jewish conspiracy for world rule, he transformed anti-Bolshevism into a holy crusade to liberate Russia from its allegedly Jewish masters. Third, using race as a rationale, he transformed the imperialist drive for autarky and world power into the concept of *Lebensraum*. These three notions were consolidated into a unified concept that became the theoretical, ideational foundation of the Final Solution. In *Mein Kampf* that concept appeared in its matured form and remained a central tenet in Hitler's ideology from which he never deviated. It was already then a fixed idea, in both the everyday and psychiatric meaning of the term, awaiting only the political opportunities for its implementation.

If *Mein Kampf* is the *terminus ad quem* for the conception of the Final Solution, does its beginning indeed go back to November 1918, as Hitler himself claimed? It is a hazardous task to construct a chronology of the evolution of this idea in Hitler's mind. The historical evidence is sparse and no doubt would be inadmissible as courtroom evidence. The very idea of the destruction of the Jews as a political goal demanded, when Hitler first began to advocate it, camouflage and concealment. Its later consummation demanded, within limits, secrecy. Consequently there is a paucity of documents, and even those we have handicap the search for definitive evidence because of the problem of esoteric language.

How does one advocate publicly an idea or a programme whose novelty lies in its utter radicalism? No matter how anti-Semitic the Munich of 1919 and 1920 was, the explicit transformation of a slogan like '*Juda verrecke*' into a practical political programme would have brought on the censorship of the local authorities and discredited the incipient National Socialist movement even among conventional anti-Semites. In this situation Hitler availed himself of a time-honoured device – the use of esoteric language. In all periods of history, when government or society has put limits on public discussion, those who wish to circumvent censorship resort to the use of esoteric language. Exoterically understood, the text is unexceptionable, but to the insiders who know how to interpret the words, the message is revolutionary and dangerous to the *status quo*.

Hitler complained in *Mein Kampf* that in the early days it was hard to get a hearing for the anti-Semitic point of view. 'Our first attempts', he wrote, 'to show the public the real enemy then seemed almost hopeless.' He exaggerated, as usual, but the problem was that the National Socialists did not want to be dismissed 'merely' as anti-Semites, single-minded crackpots without political solutions to contemporary problems. In the Reichswehr, where Hitler's oratorical talents and anti-Semitic presentations to the recruits were much admired by his superiors, there was anxiety that these speeches would be characterized as 'anti-Jewish agitation'. Instructions were consequently given for a cautious treatment and the avoidance of 'plain references' to the Jews.[1]

The National Socialists in their public meetings seldom exercised such caution, for the word 'Jew' occurs with obsessive repetitiveness. Still, according to the earliest reports of Hitler's speeches, the code words he used for Jews outnumbered the plain references: usury (usurers), profiteering (profiteerers), exploiters, big capitalism (big capitalists), international big and/or loan capital, international money power, Communists, Social Democrats, November criminals, revolution criminals, aliens, foreigners. References to the press unmistakably were meant and interpreted as 'Jewish' press. In one circumlocution, Hitler spoke of the fight 'against the races [*sic*] who are the money representatives'.[2]

The code words served to invest the crude anti-Semitic agitation of the National Socialists with the dignity of political argument and economic analysis. Simultaneously they served to depict for the insiders the vast ramifications of the 'Jewish conspiracy' and to document the multifarious roles of the mythic Jew. From the use of these code words, the insiders came to learn that all of Germany's enemies were Jews or tools of Jews.

Having defined the enemy exoterically and esoterically, Hitler in his speeches began to indicate how he would deal with that enemy. In those early days his favourite words were '*Entfernung*' and '*Aufräumung*', both meaning 'removal', 'elimination', 'cleaning up'. (In *Mein Kampf* he preferred to use '*Beseitigung*', also meaning 'removal', 'elimination', but less ambiguous about its finality.) According to a Reichswehr report of a meeting of 27 April 1920, Hitler in his closing remarks said: 'We will carry on the struggle until the last Jew is removed [*entfernt ist*] from the German Reich.' According to the Bavarian police report, Hitler's conclusion that the NSDAP would make a revolution that would 'thoroughly clean out [*aufräumen*] the Jew-rabble' received 'protracted, stormy applause'.[3]

Whether he used both words interchangeably or whether the several reporters 'interpreted' what they heard, Hitler had resorted to language whose meaning he intentionally made ambiguous, to be understood both exoterically and esoterically. 'Removal' or 'elimination' could be understood to mean 'expulsion', and no doubt some of Hitler's listeners thought, if they thought at all about specifics, that he planned to drive the Jews out of Germany.

In this very early period only two documents are extant that are authentically Hitler's, the direct product of his hand and mind. These lend themselves better to a probing of his meaning than the second-hand reports of Reichswehr and police. The first document is his letter to Gemlich, written while he was still working for the Reichswehr. Here, once more, is that key passage:

Rational anti-Semitism, however, must lead to a systematic legal op-position and elimination [*Beseitigung*] of the special privileges that Jews hold, in contrast to the other aliens living among us (aliens' legislation). Its final objective must unswervingly be the removal [*Entfernung*] of the Jews altogether.

What Hitler is saying here is that a systematic programme of anti-Semitism consists of two stages: a preliminary stage in which Jews are deprived of all rights, and then the accomplishment of a 'final ob-jective' – 'removal of the Jews altogether'. The phrase is obviously open to two interpretations. It was not that Hitler was unable to ex-press himself clearly and unequivocally. Rather he deliberately used a word that could be interpreted two ways – one, vague and con-ventional; the other, specific and radical.

Such ambiguous usage persisted in the National Socialist move-ment until the end, though its function became somewhat different. Himmler, in his speech to the S S-Gruppenführer on 4 October 1943, used the word '*Ausschaltung*', meaning 'elimination', as synonymous with '*Ausrottung*', meaning 'annihilation'. There was no reason to invoke esoteric language to that particular audience on that occasion at that late date, but by then the political need for esoteric language had given way to the psychological need for euphemistic language.

In the second Hitler document, the text of his speech of 13 August 1920, a typescript apparently made from a stenographic record, with editorial emendations in Hitler's own hand, '*Entfernung*' reappears as a solution to the 'Jewish question':

Removal of the Jews from our nation, not because we would begrudge them their existence – we congratulate the rest of the whole world on their company [great merriment], but because the existence of our own nation is a thousand times more important to us than that of an alien race.

Here Hitler has introduced the very question of whether the Jews are to live or die. The irony is heavy. But precisely where does it begin? How did the inflections of his voice, his pauses and emphases communicate his message? Does the irony begin with the phrase 'not because we would begrudge them their existence'? Perhaps the party members are already responding to an inside joke, whereas the outsiders get the joke only at the next clause, which itself compounds the original ambiguity of the word 'removal'. Are the Jews to be expelled from Germany and thus forced upon other countries, or is Hitler referring to the Jews already living in other countries? The ambiguity is calculated. Nevertheless, Hitler posited an incontrovertible dichotomy: 'their existence' versus 'our existence'.

The 'either – or' that he had predicated in *Mein Kampf* was already evolving. In a speech on 12 April 1922 he said, referring to the 'Jewish question': 'Here, too, there can be no compromise – there are only two possibilities: either victory of the Aryan or annihilation of the Aryan and the victory of the Jew.'[4] Hitler frequently used the rhetorical device of paired antitheses. Strictly, the construction should have read:

> *either victory of the Aryan [and annihilation of the Jew]*
> or
> *annihilation of the Aryan and the victory of the Jew.*

The ellipsis of half of one pair was a signal to the cognoscenti of what he meant to say. Today we can appreciate a similar ellipsis in his famous prophecy of 30 January 1939:

> *Bolshevization of the world and a victory of the Jews*
> or
> *[Aryanization of the world and] destruction of the Jewish race.*

In 1922 Hitler had to propagate the annihilation of the Jews in esoteric language. In 1939 he used the same technique to express his ambition for world dominion.

In the summer of 1922 a young man named Kurt Ludecke joined the National Socialist party and first met Hitler. Overwhelmed by both, he described his feelings at that time about the goals the movement had set for itself. These were his perceptions:

The hugeness of the task and the absurdity of the hope swept over me. Its execution meant the liquidation of Jewry, of Rome, of liberalism with its tangled capitalistic connections; of Marxism, Bolshevism, Toryism –

in short, an abrupt and complete break with the past and an assault on all existing world political forces.[5]

Hitler's goals had unmistakably been communicated, despite the handicaps of esoteric language. Within the movement, the destruction of the Jews seemed to have been accepted as a basic programmatic task, though the average National Socialist probably still thought of pogrom, despite Hitler's frequently expressed opposition to such 'emotional' outbursts of anti-Semitism. Still, even in those early days of the movement, when plans were being laid for the *Putsch* and the takeover of political power the Jews figured importantly in Nazi strategy. The destruction of the Jews was not just a matter of words, in esoteric language even then, but a deathly reality. Hermann Esser, one of Hitler's earliest party comrades, at an NSDAP meeting held in December 1922, at which plans for a forthcoming *Putsch* were discussed, mentioned the possibilities of foreign intervention on behalf of the Weimar Republic. That would not work, he said, for there would be '500,000 Jews as hostages carefully guarded, who will be ruthlessly dispatched, if even a single enemy crosses the German frontier'. At the time of the *Putsch*, one battalion was assigned to keep the Jews from fleeing Munich, presumably to ensure their remaining as hostages.[6]

A draft constitution prepared by one of Hitler's associates in readiness for the NSDAP takeover provided, as a start, for the expropriation of 'all movable and immovable property of the members of the Jewish people'.[7] Any attempt to circumvent expropriation was punishable by death. Concentration camps (*Sammellager*) were to be set up to 'cleanse' the 'cities, spas, and resort towns', especially 'for the removal of all persons dangerous to security and useless eaters'. Since these were to be the first steps during the transitional period while the NSDAP would be consolidating its power, it does not appear unlikely that still more draconian measures were in store for the Jews.

In restrospect, it seems likely that Hitler had settled on his radical 'either – or' anti-Semitism, as he formulated it in the Gemlich letter of 1919, already back in November 1918, as he claims in *Mein Kampf*. During the next few years Hitler's thinking remained geographically limited to Germany, albeit a 'greater Germany'. In his mind, the destruction of the Jews was the way to restore Germany to its virile Germandom. But once he encountered Alfred Rosenberg, Hitler's political horizons expanded; he began to see the Jews primarily as an international group whose destruction demanded an international policy.

This new approach is distinctly evident in his speech of 28 July 1922, delivered a month after Rathenau's assassination and upon Hitler's emergence from prison where he had served one month for breaking up an opposition meeting. The enforced leisure of prison had given him time to think, as later in Landsberg. Hitler now viewed his struggle against 'Jewish world domination' in global terms:

Today we all of us feel that two worlds are struggling with one another, and not alone in our country, but everywhere we look, in oppressed Russia, in Italy, in France and England, etc. An inexorable struggle between the ideals of those who believe in a national people and the ideals of the intangible, supra-national international . . .[8]

The content of this speech was a mostly familiar attack on the Jews and the 'Jewish' conspiracy in which 'the stock-exchange Jew and the labour leader' together 'pursue a single direction and a single aim'. The new factor was Hitler's global perspective: 'How long will it be before the whole world falls to ruin . . . ?'

Rosenberg further showed Hitler the possibilities of exploiting Russia as the political locus of international Jewry, thus providing him with the eventual major theatre of operations for his war against world Jewry. Under the influence of Rosenberg and the other Russian and Ukrainian émigrés with whom he associated and with whom the National Socialist movement collaborated, Russia became a key element in Hitler's thinking. The émigrés spoke constantly of the imperative need to invade Russia so as to liberate it from the bondage of the 'Jew-Bolsheviks'. In the very first issue of the *Völkischer Beobachter*, Rosenberg speculated that the Soviet Union would shortly invade Poland and argued that Germany should then intervene in what he called 'the eastern marches of Germany'. (Hitler was to use this idea in *Mein Kampf*.) Here, in Rosenberg's mind, is the justification for Germany's 'liberation' of the Eastern territories from the 'Jewish

Bolsheviks', which would simultaneously restore the land to its original German owner. It was an idea that Hitler and Himmler were to hold tenaciously for the next twenty years. Thus, fitting piece by piece into a large scheme, Hitler combined the annihilation of the Jews with the destruction of Bolshevism, both of which could be accomplished by an invasion of Russia. The whole was supported in racial terms: the innate racial perniciousness of the Jews and the innate racial superiority of the Aryans whose culture justified their need for *Lebensraum*.

Hitler probably derived the components for the idea of *Lebensraum* from the impositions of the Versailles Treaty. His earliest speeches all dwell, in one way or another, on the treaty, for which, as he saw it, the Jews were responsible. He often referred to Germany's lost colonies, the forfeiture of her merchant and fishing fleets, the obligatory deliveries of coal to France and the Low Countries, and the burdensome monetary payments. According to the Reichswehr report of a speech of 10 December 1919 on the 'shame of the Versailles Treaty', Hitler spoke of Germany's need to import raw materials; according to the Bavarian police report, he complained that there was eighteen times more land for every Russian than for every German. (In that speech, he expressed the view that the Russian had a right to his land, a position he did not long hold.) In a speech on 20 September 1920 the racial justification for *Lebensraum* had already emerged. According to the Reichswehr report, Hitler said that Germany had a right to live, not only on the basis of its population, but also 'on the basis of its culture'. Thus, with the help of Rosenberg and eventually Haushofer, Hitler shaped his concept of *Lebensraum*, in which racial ideology became as vital as the imperialist drive.

Hitler wrote the first volume of *Mein Kampf* in Landsberg prison in 1924 and the second volume in 1925, when he was forbidden to engage in public speaking. The tone of the second is more aggressive and outspoken than that of the first;[9] Volume 2 is said to have benefited also from professional editorial assistance. The writing of *Mein Kampf* forced Hitler into a process of organizing his ideas in one all-embracing schema, however unsystematic and inchoate the final product. At its centre was the war against the Jews that would culminate in their annihilation and the world supremacy of the Germans. The language, especially in the second volume, is no longer esoteric, but plain-spoken.

Though Hitler's hysteria and chiliastic rhetoric made the prose appear deceptively metaphorical, the words were meant to be taken literally. The destruction of the Jews is advocated time and again (all italics in original):

> *Only the elimination of the causes of our collapse, as well as the destruction of its beneficiaries, can create the premise for our outward fight for freedom.*

> ... *It is the inexorable Jew who struggles for his domination over the nations.* No nation can remove this hand from its throat except by the sword. Only the assembled and concentrated might of a national passion rearing up in its strength can defy the international enslavement of peoples. Such a process is and remains a bloody one.

Writing about the failure of the 1923 *Putsch*, Hitler accused the Weimar government of lacking sufficient nationalism. 'And in my opinion, it was then the very first task of a truly national government to seek and find the forces which were resolved to declare a war of annihilation on Marxism and then to give these forces a free road ...' Not only was the government derelict in its task, Hitler argued, but so were all the political parties, which 'continued to bicker with the Marxists only out of competitors' envy, without any serious desire to annihilate them.'

At the same time, Hitler kept projecting on the Jews the very destructive ideas he held about them: 'The Jew would really devour the people of the earth, would become their master', 'the international world Jew slowly but surely strangles us', 'the Jew destroys the racial foundations of our existence and thus destroys our people for all time'.

He even argued retroactively for a 'preventive' war against the Jew in 1914–18, which could have saved Germany from defeat:

> It would have been the duty of a serious government, now that the German worker had found his way back to his nation [in August 1914], to exterminate mercilessly the agitators who were misleading the nation.

> If the best men were dying at the front, the least we could do was to wipe out the vermin.

> If at the beginning of the War and during the War twelve or fifteen thousand of these Hebrew corrupters of the people had been held under poison gas ... the sacrifice of millions at the front would not have been

in vain. On the contrary: twelve thousand scoundrels eliminated in time might have saved the lives of a million real Germans, valuable for the future.

In the years between 1919 and 1925, the political climate had changed and Hitler now openly espoused his programme of annihilation, without having to resort to concealment or camouflage. But only his followers took his words literally. Others, when they listened to Hitler or read *Mein Kampf*, dismissed his words as lunatic ravings. Yet these words were to become the blueprint for his policies when he came to power and would become, astonishingly, political and miltary reality.

Once Hitler adopted an ideological position, even a strategic one, he adhered to it with limpet-like fixity, fearful lest he be accused, if he changed his mind, of incertitude or capriciousness on 'essential questions'. He had long-range plans to realize his ideological goals, and the destruction of the Jews was at their centre.

The grand design was in his head. He did not spell it out in concrete strategy. Nothing was written down. (On 29 April 1937 he advised NSDAP leaders: 'Everything that can be discussed should *never* be put in writing, never!')[10] He even elevated his tactics of secrecy into a strategic principle: as few people as possible to know as little as possible as late as possible.[11]

The implementation of his plans was contingent on the opportunism of the moment or the expediency of delay. As head of both the German state and the National Socialist movement, he had to weigh the urgent passions of the little man in the party against the foreign-policy interests of the state, and to balance his own desire for surprise attack with the state's readiness to mount one. Often he decided suddenly that the opportune occasion had arrived to carry out a specific aspect of his programme, and then the practical work had quickly to be improvised.

In Hitler's schema, the removal of the Jews from posts in the state apparatus and from society's cultural and educational institutions represented, along with the re-militarization of Germany, the first phase of his programme, the internal cleansing and healing of Germany. Whereas the anti-Jewish legislation of 1933 was for him merely the prerequisite for later stages of his programme that would culminate in the Final Solution, this undoing of the emancipation of the German Jews represented for the conventional anti-Semites the attainment of their political ambitions. That was the time when the widest consensus existed in Germany with regard to anti-Semitism, when the values and goals of the conventional anti-Semites were identical and undistinguishable from those of the radical anti-Semites. That particular convergence made it easier for the conventional anti-Semites subsequently to acquiesce to the radical anti-Semitic programme.

At the National Socialist party congress in Nuremberg in September 1935 Hitler introduced new anti-Jewish legislation, describing these laws as a repayment of a debt of gratitude to the National Socialist party, under whose aegis Germany had regained her freedom, and as the fulfilment of an important plank of the movement's programme.[12] The Reich Citizenship Law, depriving the German Jews of the rights and protections of citizenship, marked the goal of conventional anti-Semitism – the total disenfranchisement of the Jews.

The Law for the Protection of German Blood and German Honour, on the other hand, even though it drew heavily upon a half-century's tradition of racist anti-Semitism, was a new departure. With its implementing decrees and with those of the Reich Citizenship Law, it initiated Hitler's programme of radical anti-Semitism, with the process of identifying and isolating the Jews from the non-Jews, readying them, as it were, for their later fate.

The Nuremberg Laws were a watershed also in another respect, to which Hitler alluded ominously. In introducing the Law for the Protection of German Blood and German Honour, he said that it was 'an attempt to regulate by law a problem which, in the event of repeated failure, would have to be transferred by law to the National Socialist party for final solution'.* He was, it now appears, indicating that the state had come to the end of its competency in handling the Jewish question and that thenceforth all anti-Jewish measures would be carried out by the party. In this period, too, he spoke of sweeping plans for the Jews, involving ghettos and possibly a reservation, and on another occasion he talked of carrying out the 'euthanasia' murder programme once war came.

*In his speech of 27 April 1920 Hitler was reported to have said, with regard to carrying out his planned anti-Jewish programme: 'First we try to carry it out kindly, and then, when that does not work, with ruthless violence.'

By the summer of 1936, Hitler believed that the first phase of his programme – the internal domestic stage – was virtually completed and in August, having composed a memorandum on the Four Year Plan, he entered into preparations for the second phase – aggression and war. That memorandum, with its ideological justification for a war against 'Jewish Bolshevism', transformed *Mein Kampf* into state policy. The doctrine of the party leader now became the plan for the state. The annihilation of the Jews, who are explicitly referred to as the power behind Bolshevism, is implicit in Hitler's familiar rhetorical construction (italicized in the original): '*For a victory of Bolshevism over Germany would not lead to a Versailles Treaty but to the final destruction, indeed to the annihilation, of the German people.*'[13] As further clarification, Hitler specified that the Reichstag would have to pass a law expropriating the Jews. Thus the expropriation of the Jews had become, in Hitler's thinking, correlated with the advancement of his war plans. That decision explains why Hitler rejected the insistent demands of the National Socialist movement between 1935 and 1938 to plunder Jewish property and possessions.

That decision explains also Hitler's apparent indifference to the unregulated pluralism with regard to the Jews that then flourished within in state and party – the use of National Socialist law, arbitrary violence, normal bureaucratic procedures for normal migration coexisting with the SD's ideas of forced emigration. Hitler's toleration for such assorted 'solutions' extended only until he was ready to put his war plans into operation.

Hitler appointed Göring to be his Plenipotentiary for the Four Year Plan and gave him a copy of that memorandum. They surely discussed aspects of this programme, and Hitler must have shared his plans concerning the Jews. At least one other person also shared Hitler's confidences in this respect at this time – Heinrich Himmler. In the early summer of 1936 Himmler had, with Hitler's support, become Reichsführer-SS and Chief of the German Police, directly subordinate to Hitler and only to him. Hitler had by then already decided to hand over to the National Socialist movement the authority to 'solve' the Jewish question. Himmler, then one of the most powerful figures in the party, had probably been inducted into the inmost circle and told of Hitler's plans for war and the destruction of the Jews – a task that would fall, at the proper time, within his jurisdiction.

How often and how specifically Hitler discussed his plans with Göring and Himmler no one knows. Yet they spoke, for instance, about ghettos as an interim measure, because Göring, at his post-Kristallnacht inter-ministerial conference of 12 November 1938, proposed ghettos as a possible means of concentrating the Jews. (Heydrich's objections at that time indicate that he had not yet become privy to these plans.)

If the plans for dealing with the Jews were vague and non-specific, so were the plans for military invasion, as the Hossbach protocol reveals. Hitler's military and diplomatic staffs were appalled to learn in November 1937 of Hitler's intentions to invade Austria and Czechoslovakia in 1938, not so much because of the suddenness with which they had to confront these plans, but because of lack of preparation. Their demurral, however, cost them their posts and careers, for Hitler remained inflexible, committed to his timetable. The Austrian invasion advanced smoothly, but Chamberlain's intervention in Czechoslovakia frustrated Hitler's plans. It appears that he had intended, under cover of the seizure of Czechoslovakia, to carry out the expropriation of the Jews, for the first National Socialist legislation in this area was issued early in 1938. Hitler no doubt counted on the general public upheaval over Czechoslovakia to muffle protests about robbing the Jews.

Thwarted by Chamberlain, but impatient to move ahead according to his schedule, Hitler took the first opportunity that would give him apparent justification to expropriate the Jews: the assassination of vom Rath. That opportunism proved doubly useful, for it gave the little Nazi a last chance for a fling. The pogrom and the expropriation were not really part of Hitler's new, radical anti-Semitism, but rather a reversion to medievalism, when Jews were subjected not only to violence, but to all sorts of taxes, fines, levies, exactions, amercements and confiscations. In the Middle Ages complete expropriation went hand in hand with expulsion, and for the brief period that National Socialist pressure for Jewish emigration intensified following the Kristallnacht, Hitler seemed to be emulating Edward I and Philip the Fair. But pressure for emigration was, in Hitler's plans, only by-play. After the Kristallnacht the Jews in Germany became little more than hostages, perhaps no different from the way Hitler and Esser had envisaged the situation in 1923. The Reichszentrale, which Göring had instructed Heydrich to set up on 24 January 1939, effectively put the Jews at the mercy of the police and SD. (Probably then, Heydrich was made a party to the plan to destroy the Jews.)

On 30 January 1939 Hitler made his declaration of war against the Jews, promising 'the destruction of the Jewish race in Europe'. The decision to proceed with this irreversible mission had already been taken. Thenceforth the Final Solution entered the stage of practical planning for implementation. Hitler's first opportunity to put into practice his ideas about killing the crippled and insane presented itself at this time, and shortly thereafter, on 3 April 1939, he instructed Keitel to start planning the invasion of Poland.

Hitler's gamble, then, was on a quick military victory in Poland, to be completed before Russia could gather wits or force to act. Afterwards he would consolidate his position, using Poland as the launching pad for his invasion of Russia. (The rapprochement with Russia, ideologically embarrassing but tactically expedient, did not at all affect his long-range plans, but merely eased his short-range military risks.) While planning the Polish invasion, Hitler, Himmler and Heydrich worked out the first stage of the Final Solution, concentrating the Jews while consolidating the Polish gains. Heydrich's instructions to the chiefs of the Einsatzgruppen on 21 September 1939 are clear enough about present programme and future intentions. The second, ultimate stage of the Final Solution was to be synchronized with the attack on Russia, when 'Jewish Bolshevism' would be destroyed.

While the Jews in Poland were concentrated in ghettos and began to expire slowly of 'natural' causes like hunger, disease, cold, exhaustion, the idea of systematically killing the Jews began to appear as an inevitable and even desirable development to a number of Germans not privy to the still-secret plans for the Final Solution. Thus SS-Brigadeführer Friedrich Übelhör, Regierungspräsident of Lodz (the top official in the civil administration of the district of Lodz), on 10 December 1939, in planning to establish a ghetto, already thought of its destruction:

> The establishment of the ghetto is of course only a provisional measure. I reserve for myself the points in time and the means with which the ghetto and thereby the city of Lodz will be cleansed of Jews. The end goal [*Endziel*] in any case must be that we burn out this pest-hole without a remainder.[14]

Übelhör's hubris reveals that he knew nothing of the plans for the Final Solution, otherwise he would hardly have arrogated to himself a decision of the highest state and party priority.

A year later, on 20 December 1940, Governor Hans Frank addressed a Wehrmacht battalion stationed in Cracow. Remarking, as he often did, that their families must commiserate with them for having to serve in Poland, where there were so many lice and Jews, Frank said it would indeed be nice if they could write home and say that things with regard to lice and Jews had improved: 'To be sure, in one year I can do away with neither all the lice nor all the Jews [merriment]. But in the course of time and, above all, if you help me, that will be made attainable.'[15]

Still later, in July 1941, an official by the name of Höppner, in the city administration of Posen, sent Eichmann the official minutes of a discussion regarding the 'Solution of the Jewish Question' in the Wartheland. One proposal read:

There is an imminent danger that not all the Jews can be supplied with food in the coming winter. We must seriously consider if it would not be more humane to finish off the Jews, insofar as they are not fit for labour mobilization, with some quick-acting means. In any case this would be more agreeable [*angenehmer*] than to let them die of hunger.

In his covering letter asking for Eichmann's comments, Höppner was optimistically categorical: 'These things sound to some extent fantastic, but in my view absolutely practicable.'[16] Eichmann, for his part, at precisely that time was working on the practicability of such fantastic ideas.

In December 1940 Operation Barbarossa entered the formal planning stage, and Hitler then no doubt explored with Himmler, and perhaps Heydrich, various practical possibilities for the last stage of the Final Solution. By February 1941 they had decided on a two-pronged attack against the Jews. In the active war zone, the Einsatzgruppen would coordinate their murder attack on the Jews with the military invasion. The rest of the European Jews in countries under German occupation or governed by rulers sympathetic to Germany would be brought to annihilation camps in or near the Generalgouvernement of Poland. (Himmler's visit to Auschwitz on 1 March 1941 was obviously exploratory, for he did not inform Höss then why Auschwitz was to be expanded.) All the decisions had been taken. The rest was a matter of technology, administrative clearance, and efficient operation. Through a maze of time Hitler's decision of November 1918 led to Operation Barbarossa. There never had been any ideological deviation or wavering determination. In the end only the question of opportunity mattered.

The Final Solution grew out of a matrix formed by traditional anti-Semitism, the paranoid delusions that seized Germany after the First World War, and the emergence of Hitler and the National Socialist movement. Without Hitler, the charismatic political leader who believed he had a mission to annihilate the Jews, the Final Solution would not have occurred. Without that assertive and enduring tradition of anti-Semitism by which the Germans sought self-definition, Hitler would not have had the fecund soil in which to grow his organization and spread its propaganda. Without the paranoid delusion of the Dolschstoss that masses of Germans shared in the wake of Germany's military defeat, political upheavals, economic distress and humiliations of the Versailles Treaty, Hitler could not have transformed the German brand of conventional anti-Semitism into a radical doctrine of mass murder.

Anti-Semitism was the core of Hitler's system of beliefs and the central motivation for his policies. He believed himself to be the saviour who would bring redemption to the German people through the annihilation of the Jews, that people who embodied, in his eyes, the Satanic hosts. When he spoke or wrote about his 'holy mission', he used words associated with chiliastic prophecy (not only in the millennial concept literally rendered as the 'Thousand Year Reich'), like 'consecration', 'salvation', 'redemption', 'resurrection', 'God's will'. The murder of the Jews, in his fantasies, was commanded by divine providence, and he was the chosen instrument for that task. He referred often to his 'mission', but nowhere so explicitly as in *Mein Kampf*: 'Hence today I believe that I am acting in accordance with the will of the Almighty Creator: *by defending myself against the Jew, I am fighting for the work of the Lord.*' From the moment he made his entrance on the historical stage until his death in a Berlin bunker, this sense of messianic mission never departed from him, nor could any appeal to reason deflect him from pursuing his murderous purpose.

Generations of anti-Semitism had prepared the Germans to accept Hitler as their redeemer. Layer upon layer of anti-Semitism of all kinds – Christian church teachings about the Jews, Volkist anti-Semitism, doctrines of racial superiority, economic theories about the role of Jews in capitalism and commerce, and a half century of political anti-Semitism – were joined with the solder of German nationalism, providing the structural foundation upon which Hitler and the National Socialist movement built. Of the conglomerate social, economic and political appeals that the NSDAP directed at the German people, its racial doctrine was most attractive. Yet for the average National Socialist, and still more for the party's fellow travellers, out of the whole corpus of racial teachings, the anti-Jewish doctrine had the greatest dynamic potency. The reports of early NSDAP meetings reveal, from the record of audience responses, that violent attacks on the Jews provided orgasmic outbursts and that Hitler was most adept at getting the blood to tingle with his threats against the Jews.[17] For the audience, the convolutions of Hitler's ideology were, in the end, reduced in significance to the time-worn slogan of German anti-Semitism: '*Juda verrecke*.'[18]

The insecurities of post–First World War Germany and the anxieties they produced provided an emotional milieu in which irrationality and hysteria became routine and illusions became transformed into delusions. The delusional disorder assumed mass proportions. Germans, otherwise individually rational, yielded themselves to pathological fantasies about the Jews.[19] In that climate, where masses of Germans had lost the ability to distinguish between the real Jew and the mythic Jew of anti-Semitic invention, the chiliastic system of National Socialist beliefs could further influence their already distorted sense of reality, Belief in National Socialism was like belief in magic and witchcraft during the Middle Ages, similarly ruling and inflaming the minds of men.[20] In the Middle Ages private misfortunes and public calamities were attributed to witches and demons, whereas in modern Germany the Jews were regarded as the source of evil and disaster. A popular children's book of the time made it plain:

> *Ohne Lösung der Judenfrage*
> *Kein Erlösung der menschheit.*[21]
> (Without solution of the Jewish question
> No salvation of mankind.)

In medieval days entire communities were seized with witchcraft hysteria, and in modern Germany the mass psychosis of anti-Semitism deranged a whole people. According to their system of beliefs, elimination of the Jews resembled medieval exorcism of the Devil. The accomplishment of both, it was variously held, would restore grace to the world.

German hysteria was rooted in fear. 'That which drives the German to cruelty,' wrote Curzio Malaparte, 'to deeds most coldly, methodically and scientifically cruel, is fear.'[22] That fear, which assumed pandemic proportions, operated through projection. What the Germans hated and feared most in themselves they projected onto the Jews, endowing the Jews with those terrible and terrifying attributes they tried to repress in themselves. The farther the image of the Jew receded from reality, taking on the fantastic distortions of primeval hatred, the more abhorrent it became.

There were, fundamentally, two totally disparate and mutually contradictory images of the Jew that collided with each other in the paranoid propaganda of National Socialist anti-Semitism, both inherited from the recent and medieval treasury of anti-Semitism. One was the image of the Jew as vermin, to be rubbed out by the heel of the boot, to be exterminated. The other was the image of the Jew as the mythic omnipotent super-adversary, against whom war on the greatest scale had to be conducted. The Jew was, on the one hand, a germ, a bacillus, to be killed without conscience. On the other hand, he was, in the phrase Hitler repeatedly used from *Mein Kampf* until the end of the war, the 'mortal enemy' (*Todfeind*), to be killed in self-defence.

Also the counter-images that the Germans held of themselves were dual and inconsistent. In one scenario, the 'Aryan' German was the wholesome, vigorous superman, invulnerable to 'Jewish' poison, who was destined by innate racial superiority to rule the world. According to the other scenario, however, the Germans saw themselves as latter-day Laocoöns in the grip of a death struggle. In a paranoid vision, they believed themselves to be innocent and aggrieved victims, outwitted by the machinations of a supercunning and all-powerful antagonist, engaged in a struggle for their very existence. It was a struggle, as Hitler put it, of 'either – or'.

Once the illusory notions about 'Jewish' power had been transformed into delusions about a Jewish conspiracy to rule the world, the Germans became possessed by the belief that mythic world Jewry was committed to their destruction. Consequently, in the deluded German mind, every Jewish man, woman and child became a panoplied warrior of a vast Satanic fighting machine. The most concrete illustration of this delusion is the now familiar photograph taken from the collection attached to Stroop's report of the Warsaw ghetto uprising. It shows uniformed German SS men holding guns to a group of women and children; in the foreground is a frightened boy of about six, his hand up. This was the face of the enemy.

Hitler skilfully translated this mythic warfare into a real war in which the Germans engaged the real enemy along with the mythic enemy. On 15 April 1945, when six million Jews were already murdered, Hitler issued his last military order. He exhorted his soldiers to perform their utmost: 'For the last time our mortal enemies the Jewish Bolsheviks have launched their massive forces to the attack. Their aim is to reduce Germany to ruins and to exterminate our people.'[23]

In one sense the German war against the Jews fitted into Clausewitz's classical definition of war as a political act, the continuation of politics by other means. This was National Socialism's innovation, having transformed conventional anti-Semitism with its metaphoric imagery of combat into a literal war of annihilation. 'True wars', said Himmler, 'wars between races, are merciless and fought to the last man, until one side or the other is eliminated without trace.'[24] But only the truly mad could have believed that it was war that they were waging against the Jews. For the Jews were a civilian population, dispersed among the European nations, having no country and no political power, and consequently none of the resources that even small nations could muster for war.

Part 11
The Holocaust

9 Between Freedom and Ghetto: The Jews in Germany, 1933–8

Presiding over a meeting of Jewish communal organizations soon after the National Socialists had come to power, Leo Baeck, teacher, scholar and rabbi extraordinary of Liberal Judaism, uttered prophetic words: 'The thousand-year history of the German Jews has come to an end.'[1] But most German Jews rejected his visionary judgement as a political verdict. They lived with a historical perspective that, like the tangle of all history, taught contradictory lessons. In the long perspective of Jewish history, in which anti-Semitism was a constant factor, National Socialist anti-Semitism seemed just a contemporary manifestation of the persecution that afflicted the Jews in all ages. In the shortened range of German Jewish history, however, National Socialism appeared as the latest passing cycle of reaction in the wake of dramatic progress. The German Jews had had to learn to live with anti-Semitism in the long run and to combat it in the short run.

Combat anti-Semitism they did as best they knew how. The Centralverein deutscher Staatsbürger jüdischen Glaubens (CV; Central Association of German Citizens of Jewish Faith), founded in 1893 to defend German Jewry, had been indefatigable in anti-defamation, refutation of anti-Semitic canards, apologetic recitals of Jewish contributions to German culture and civilization. But these tactics, which we, having learned from their failures, belittle today, were not their only strategy. Beginning in 1929, when National Socialist victories threatened the republic, the CV made alliances with the political parties of the centre and the left. It set up front organizations, some of which used unorthodox methods not characteristic of the staid Jewish organization. In 1930 the CV and the Zionist Federation formed a joint committee for the election campaign (that year about 65 per cent of the Jews voted for the Deutsche Demokratische Partei, or DDP, and 30 per cent for the left parties). The following year both organizations jointly mustered their political influence, publicly appealing to Heinrich Brüning, then Chancellor, to condemn anti-Semitism and violence and, with the prestige of his office, to reassure the Jews as to their rights and place in Germany. That he refused to do so testifies not to a Jewish failure to resist National Socialism, but to National Socialism's irresistibility to the Germans. In 1932, when the DDP had collapsed, about two thirds of the Jews voted for the Social Democrats. Every democratic party received electoral and financial support from the Jews, the Social Democrats getting the greatest share.[2]

The Jews were the one group in Germany that invested most of their talents and resources in the defence of the Weimar Republic. True, there were Jews whose dazzling success in business or a profession blinded them to the encroaching blackness. True, there were Jews in the leftist movements whose total alienation from Judaism and the Jewish community enabled them to see Nazism only as the last gasp of a moribund imperialist capitalism. But the organized Jewish community – and the Jews who were their constituency – knew that National Socialism in power would threaten their status and rights as citizens of Germany. But, impotent in halting the National Socialist rise to power, the Jews in Germany evolved a basic strategy of survival that had served Jews in the past: a policy of holding on and holding out, of bargaining and negotiating. It was a strategy that appealed to most Jews during the first two years of the National Socialist régime.

The 500,000 Jews of Germany formed a remarkably homogeneous community. Well over 80 per cent were natives and about as many were affiliated with the Liberal wing of Judaism, a modified form of Orthodoxy similar to Conservative Judaism in America. About one third lived in Berlin, and nearly 40 per cent more in other big cities. Over 60 per cent were engaged in trade and commerce, about one quarter in industry and manual trades and one eighth in public service and the professions, primarily law and medicine. Nearly half of the gainfully occupied were self-employed.[3] The Jews of each city were members of a *Gemeinde*, a communal organization based on religious association, in which each Jew was registered at birth. (There were over 1,300 Gemeinden.) The Gemeinde was a public body for whose upkeep the state was authorized to tax the affiliated Jewish members. The functions of the Gemeinde were to maintain religious institutions, promote religious education, and dispense philanthropy. The Gemeinden of each state (*Land*) belonged to an association.

The most representative secular organization of German Jewry was the CV, whose membership in 1933 of 70,000 probably comprised 60 per cent of all Jewish families. The Zionistische Vereinigung für Deutschland (ZVfD; Zionist Federation of Germany), in contrast, had 10,000 members. The CV stood for the belongingness of the German Jews in Germany, not only in the civil polity, but also in German culture and society. The CV was ideologically anti-Zionist, but in the early 1920s some of its leaders joined the non-Zionist component of the Jewish Agency for Palestine. The CV generally supported practical, pragmatic Zionism (Palestine as a place of refuge) rather than ideological Zionism (Palestine as the Jewish national home). Somewhat to the right of the CV stood the Reichsbund jüdischer Frontsoldaten (RjF; Federal Union of Jewish War Veterans), which shared the simple-minded patriotism of all veterans' groups. Its membership of 30,000 was consistently and vociferously anti-Zionist.

The modal German Jew, then, was native, metropolitan, a businessman or professional, Liberal in his practice of Judaism, centrist in his politics, with a more passionate attachment to Germany than to Jewishness. In contrast to this modal type, three minority groups stood out within the Jewish community: the Orthodox, the Zionists and the *Ostjuden* (East European Jews). The Orthodox were about 15 per cent of all German Jews. (An even smaller segment belonged to the Conservative movement, close to Orthodoxy in its religious observance, but nearer to Liberalism in its anti-Zionism.) The organization that spoke for them was the Agudat Israel. German Orthodox Jews were unique among European Orthodox Jews in that they shared with all German Jews a profound sense of German identity. Most had deep roots in Germany and grew up in the unique tradition of Samson Raphael Hirsch's neo-Orthodoxy: *Torah im derekh eretz*, the preservation of Torah within the world of modern secular culture. Their primary attachment was to Judaism, yet their German patriotism was sincere and meaningful.

The Zionists and the *Ostjuden* – to some extent congruent – were the more conspicuous minorities among German Jews, for they challenged the central tenet of German Jewish existence – Jewish belongingness to Germany. During the life of the Weimar Republic most German Jews regarded Zionism as an alien doctrine: the son who left Judaism for Communism was less likely to be rejected than the one who chose Zionism. The ZVfD had originally consisted of a small circle of intellectuals and academicians, reinforced by the influx of Russian Zionists after the Bolshevik Revolution. *Ostjuden* – some 20 per cent of Jews in Germany – predominated among the Zionist rank and file, their presence aggravating the reputation of the Zionists as alien to the German Jewish community. To be sure, by 1933 the acrimonious animosity that had characterized the relations of the German and East European Jews a decade earlier had evaporated, but social distance still prevailed and political differences were marked.

On the very margins of the Jewish community, beyond discourse with the modal or oppositional groups within German Jewry, were the rightists and the leftists. The Verband nationaldeutscher Juden (Society of German Nationalist Jews), a minuscule group founded in 1920, was dedicated to the basic idea that Jews were indissolubly German except for a formal tie to Judaism. On the left was the 'red assimilation', which attracted some 10 per cent of German Jewish youth. They were the cultural *avant-garde*, the Weimar intellectuals, the Communists, the 'homeless left' who congregated around *Die Weltbühne*, the iconoclastic weekly Kurt Tucholsky edited in Berlin.

The National Socialist accession to power sent tremors throughout this Jewish population from right to left. On the one hand, panic and flight, despair and suicide. On the other, steadfastness and solidarity, courage and a stubborn will to resist. Immediately after Hitler was appointed Chancellor, the CV issued a statement, published on 2 February 1933, in its organ *C-V Zeitung*, defiantly challenging the National Socialists: 'We are convinced that no one will dare to violate our constitutional rights. Every adverse attempt will find us at our post ready for resolute defence.' The CV advised its constituents: 'Stand by calmly.'

In a matter of days and weeks, the shadowy nightmares of National Socialism became daylight realities. Thousands upon thousands of Jews lost their livelihood; typists, clerks and judges alike were ousted from positions in the government; writers, actors, musicians, teachers and professors, men who had earned the rewards of position and prestige, overnight became outcasts. Hundreds of small Jewish communities throughout Germany became exposed to the full fury of rank-and-file Nazism. The dissolution of the Jewish settlement in Germany began in those small, vulnerable communities, as their residents fled to the larger cities. By October 1938, just before Kristallnacht, over 400 Jewish communities – 25 per cent of all Jewish communities in Germany – had been dissolved or were in the process of liquidation.[4]

Among some Jews who had staked their whole existence on identity with Germany, despair led to suicide. Between 1932 and 1934, nearly 350 Jews committed suicide, a rate 50 per cent higher than in the rest of the population. So sweeping was the epidemic in the Rhineland in mid-1933 that the Gemeinde and rabbinate of Cologne issued a public appeal:

Under the shattering impact of the events of recent weeks, during which suicide claimed victim upon victim within our community, we turn to you, men and women of the Jewish community, with the appeal:
Maintain your courage and will to live, preserve your confidence in God and in yourself!
The fate which has befallen each one of us is a part of the great universal Jewish suffering: Let us bear it together and help one another fraternally! Advisory boards of our Gemeinde as well as the homes of all members of the undersigned bodies are open to you – come to us with your spiritual and material needs; we will advise and help you as much as we can.
Do not take the path into darkness from which there is no return. Think of those whom you must leave behind in all their sorrow and affliction; think of human and Jewish destiny; do not lose hope for a better future![5]

That first year the flight of panic was most marked. Some 37,000 Jews fled Germany, the highest annual figure in the subsequent record of Jewish emigration.[6] First to flee were the leftists, for whom the only alternative in Germany was the concentration camp. Government and professional men whose accomplishments had won them international renown were also quick to leave, and some of the well-to-do businessmen calculated on the wisdom of leaving sooner rather than later. That the movement was flight rather than emigration is evident in the fact that three fourths of the migrants fled not overseas, but elsewhere in Europe, about half returning to their native Poland or Czechoslovakia. Many fled unthinkingly, hoping to return soon with the anticipated collapse of the National Socialist régime. They were unprepared for life in a strange country, with a strange language and an alien culture, whether England, France, Italy or Holland. Many returned after the *Putsch* in June 1934, thinking that legality had been restored to Germany. The emigration to America that year was small; as for the fewer than seven thousand who emigrated to Palestine in 1933, nearly all had been preparing for *aliya* years earlier.

Emigration was a traditional Jewish response to persecution, but in 1933 in Germany emigration – or flight – was an individual decision, not communal policy. Within the Jewish community, every organized group replied to National Socialism with resounding affirmations of the right of Jews to be German, to live in and love Germany. *Daseinrecht*, the right to maintain a Jewish presence in Germany, was construed as a legal right, a moral necessity and a religious imperative by all Jewish organizations from Orthodox to Reform, right to left, Zionist and non-Zionist.

The *C-V Zeitung* on 9 March 1933 transmitted editorially the encouragement of 'our countless friends in town and country'. Their message was: 'Germany will remain Germany and no one can rob us of our homeland and of our fatherland.' Alfred Hirschberg, a veteran CV leader, exhorted the readers of the *C-V Zeitung* on 13 April 1933 that 'it is our aim to preserve within Germany a German-Jewish community, unbroken financially, physically and spiritually'. Bruno Weil, CV vice-president, in one of his early speeches to the organization, transmitted a message of faith and hope in a German future for the Jews:

Fear? We have shown by a thousand martyrs that we have no fear of the deeds of human beings. Desperation? Even in the most trying times Jewry has never been desperate but was always strengthened by its faith in God and by the consciousness of its right. Faith? Yes. Faith in the inner strength which is born of the knowledge of events, and a clear conscience. Hope? Yes. The hope that coexistence through centuries with the German people will prove itself stronger than all prejudices.[7]

A youth leader, granting that the era that he defined as the 'external Emancipation' had come to an end, argued that this had not affected 'internal emancipation' which he defined as cultural sensibility and love for homeland. The time now required a renewal of the synthesis of Germandom and Jewry: holding on to one's German identity and acquiring also a Jewish one.[8]

The Zionists did not differ from the anti-Zionists or non-Zionists in respect to their deep attachment to Germany. An editorial, 'Jüdische Zwischenbilanz' ('Jewish Trial Balance'), in the Zionist organ, *Jüdische Rundschau*, on 13 April 1933 addressed itself to the profound identity of Jews with Germany: 'The historical tie of centuries is not so easy to dissolve. Our avowal of Jewish peoplehood has never signified that we discarded, or could discard, anything that the German spirit bestowed upon us.' Indeed, German culture had moulded Zionist-minded Jews: 'National Jewry, after its Jewish sources and values, learned from German writings what character and freedom are.' Furthermore, even those thousands of German Jews who fled Germany would in their emigration continue to nurture German culture for years and decades: 'Generations will remain faithful to what they received from the German spirit.'

After the German army instituted the 'Aryan' paragraph for officers and men on 23 March 1934 the Reichsbund jüdischer Frontsoldaten tried to assert its *Daseinrecht* by appealing to Hindenburg that no community should be deprived of the right and duty to defend the homeland. The Reichsbund declared that the Jews would remain in Germany and that just as they had fought for Germany before, so they would do again.[9]

Joseph Lehmann, rabbi of the Reformgemeinde in Berlin, denied that the political changes of the spring of 1933 had affected 'our position as Germans of the Jewish faith nor do they demand a change of our philosophy'. Emigration could be a solution for some people, but most German Jews would struggle to retain their position and the 'heritage of their German homeland'.[10] *Dasein*, for Heinrich Stern, head of the Liberal Jews, was seen as a religious commandment, essential if the Jews were to achieve their universal mission to the world. Furthermore, he argued that fleeing from Germany was cowardly, just 'because five painful months lie behind us and probably painful years of misjudgement, hate and need lie ahead of us'. Practically speaking, 'we, as Jews, reaffirm a life in Germany and for Germany'.[11]

Hans Joachim Schoeps, a young intellectual who organized the Deutsche Vortrupp (German Vanguard) in the spring of 1933, after the Jews were ejected from the 'Aryan' youth movement, articulating a religious philosophy compounded of anti-Zionism, traditionalism and messianic hope, believed that the Jew remaining in Germany fulfilled himself as Jew and German. Germany, wrote Schoeps, was more than merely a community of blood and race; it was also a community of fate and history. Consequently, 'we are enclosed for all time as Prussian, Bavarian, Hessian and Franconian Germans of Jewish faith and Jewish origin, because through acknowledgement of fate and history, we are actually and consciously German'.[12] (In his memoirs written after the war, Schoeps describes his nightmarish remorse for not having advised those hundreds of thousands who were later murdered to flee right away at all costs.)

In all life and especially in times of crisis, as Freud teaches us, the patterns of the past re-emerge in a person's confrontation with the present and the future. For most German Jews the first response to National Socialism – insistence on their rootedness in Germany and on their German identity – represented a recurrence of the Enlightenment/Emancipation syndrome. The Jews once again ritually dredged up the nineteenth-century arguments, hoping these would serve also in the twentieth century. As for the Orthodox, they reverted to a far more ancient response to persecution and oppression: *mipnei chatoenu*, 'because of our sins', we have been punished. An editorial in *Der Israelit*, organ of the Agudat Israel, on 7 April 1933 saw in National Socialism 'the admonition of God to all German Jews' to return to traditional Judaism. Two weeks later another editorial declared that the present 'completely hopeless' political situation of the Jews illuminated the 'brittle condition of internal decay', exemplified by mixed marriages, conversions, birth control. Only *teshuva* – repentance, religious return – and adherence to the Torah could restore the Jews.

The Zionists too responded according to pattern. In the now celebrated editorial 'Wear the Yellow Badge with Pride', written on the occasion of the anti-Jewish boycott of 1 April 1933, Robert

Weltsch, editor-in-chief of the *Jüdische Rundschau*, directed his animosity against the Zionists' internal antagonists – assimilationists and self-haters. If today, wrote Weltsch, the Shield of David 'is stained, it has not been entirely the work of our enemies', for many were the 'Jews whose undignified self-mockery knew no bounds'. The Jews were themselves to blame:

> Jewry bears a great guilt because it failed to heed Theodor Herzl's call and even mocked it in some instances. The Jews refused to acknowledge that 'the Jewish question still exists'. They thought the only important thing was not to be recognized as Jews. Today we are being reproached with having betrayed the German people; the National Socialist press calls us the 'enemies of the nation', and there is nothing we can do about it. It is not true that the Jews have betrayed Germany. If they have betrayed anything, they have betrayed themselves and Judaism.
>
> Because the Jews did not display their Jewishness with pride, because they wanted to shirk the Jewish question, they must share the blame for the degradation of Jewry.[13]

Hardly an adequate response to National Socialism, the editorial nevertheless heartened the Jews, Zionist or not, with its message of self-affirmation and self-esteem. (Like Schoeps in this respect, Weltsch was later remorseful. On several occasions, he told friends that he deeply regretted having written that editorial, that instead of calling for Jewish pride, he should have exhorted the Jews to flee for their lives.) That Zionist effort to restore Jewish self-respect, coupled with the recurring shocks of the boycott and the anti-Jewish legislation, brought thousands of Jews into the Zionist movement, replacing those who had gone on *aliya* or returned to Poland. Most of the Zionist gains were registered by the fall of 1933. Thereafter, the early shock of National Socialism began to wear off, and Zionist membership growth slackened to a slow pace. By the end of 1935 membership stood at 22,500. The Zionist youth organization Hehalutz, numerically insignificant before 1933, within months turned into a mass movement with a membership of 15,000. Before 1933, the Zionists in Germany had over the years sent out about 2,000 Jews on *aliya*, a token of the movement's micro-dimensions. Sadly the ZVfD acknowledged in its report of 1936 that its new adherents joined not out of inner ideological conviction, but 'under pressure of external circumstances'.[14]

Most Jews looked to their religion and their community for comfort in their distress. In March 1933 the Rabbinical Union in Germany issued a statement declaring that Judaism required no defence against the attacks being made on it, for 'the authentic spirit of our religion speaks to whosoever will listen'. The Jews were exhorted to hold fast to their faith and conviction, to preserve their pride and keep up their courage.[15] Appeals for Jewish return that were intellectually more challenging and Jewishly more profound were issued by Baeck and Martin Buber. Responding to the self-denigration of Jewish youth who complained that the Jews had become mere objects in history, Baeck expounded the idea that Jewry was a living, effective subject of history and that the Jew was, above all, the subject of his own history. Each Jew, Baeck reasoned, had to discover himself and thus renew his history.[16]

The most persuasive summoner to Jewish return and Jewish self-awareness was Martin Buber, whose lectures and writings in the first years of the German dictatorship struck his Jewish audiences with the impact of revelation. 'German Jews', he wrote in April 1933, 'are confronted with Jewish world fate.' How were they to confront this crucial test, this ordeal by fire? First, Buber said, the German Jew had to re-order his system of personal existential values. Paramount was the return to authenticity of self in all aspects and relations, but above all in relation to God. In all his work, Buber called for the diffusion of the Jewish spirit and Jewish values throughout the whole person and the whole community, not merely in one segmented part of the individual's life or the community's programme.[17]

The synagogues became full to overflowing. They were not only houses of prayer, but the locus of solidarity and solace, the place that recompensed for the loneliness outside. Jews felt secure and at home in the company of other Jews in a Jewish setting. People who had never been in a synagogue before came to pray or, at the very least, to be with other Jews.[18] Judaism flowered during those early years of National Socialism in a spontaneous response to persecution.

The ritual of Judaism remained undisturbed, except for the prohibition of *shehita*, which went into effect on 7 December 1933. The provision of ritually slaughtered meat became the chief concern of the Reichszentrale für Schächtangelegenheiten (Federal Central Agency for Matters of Ritual Slaughtering), which arranged for the purchase and importation, primarily from Denmark, of *kosher* beef and its distribution throughout Germany. Illegal *shehita* of poultry, which did not require public abattoirs, was commonly practised despite threats of severe punishment. Eventually, as the Jewish community grew more impoverished and controls on the export of currency became tighter, the importation of *kosher* meat became a hardship. At one time two rabbis were sent to Holland to try to raise the necessary funds to import *kosher* meat for the Jewish sick in hospitals in Germany, whose medical recovery depended on meat diets.[19]

The vehicle through which the rabbi comforted his congregation, strengthened their self-esteem in the face of the external onslaught, was the sermon, which, according to Rabbi Joachim Prinz, then a young rabbi in Berlin, was 'an attempt at collective therapy'. Yet the watchful Gestapo was everywhere. (Police attended religious services and reported on the sermons.) The merest hint of criticism of the National Socialist régime could provoke a summons to the Gestapo. Thus, under censorship and persecution, an old means of discourse was revived, which Ernst Simon called the 'New Midrash'.[20] Haggadic Midrash – imaginative exegesis of the Bible with a moral or devotional purpose – had been, at least in part, a response to oppression, the exercise by a persecuted minority of an internal esoteric language that was not understood by the persecuting enemy. 'Thus a sort of cryptic style developed which was interchanged with a smile between speaker and audience, presupposing and nourishing an intimate conspiratorial understanding.' In Germany after 1933, the New Midrash sometimes created new parables on biblical, Talmudic, or even secular themes, but mostly it drew on the old sources, infusing them with contemporary meaning and topical allusion. The Psalms especially proved immediately relevant in their timelessness. In 1936 Buber issued a selection of twenty-three Psalms entitled 'Out of the Depths Have I Called Thee', published in a sequence that provided not only comfort and consolation, but also an outlet for otherwise impotent rage:

> Be Thou my judge, O God, and plead my cause
>   against an ungodly nation;
> O deliver me from the deceitful and unjust man.

As always in times of persecution, the cycle of Jewish festivals assumed freshness and relevance. Passover, the festival of freedom marking the liberation from Egypt, became a living reality. At Purim, during the reading of the Scroll of Esther, Haman became Hitler and the din of the noise-makers, the stomping and booing traditionally accorded each mention of Haman's name, surged through the synagogue. The celebration of Hanukkah, which in Weimar Germany had become a consolatory surrogate for Christmas, was restored to commemoration of the Maccabean struggle against the powerful armies of pagan Rome. The Hanukkah Haftorah afforded rich opportunities for the New Midrash: 'Not by might, nor by power, but by My spirit, saith the Lord of hosts.'

The religious return was matched by a swelling interest in Jewish learning and in Jewish secular culture. Buber's summons for renewal and authenticity elicited a mass response. The desire for immersion in Jewish living was both nurtured and satisfied by the Kulturbund deutscher Juden, founded on the initiative of Kurt Singer, a physician with more than amateur standing as musicologist, critic, choir director. The idea for the Kulturbund was first broached in April 1933 as a vehicle to provide employment for the thousands of Jewish actors and musicians who were prevented from performing on the German stage and in German concert halls.[21] Theatrical troupes, an orchestra and choir, and ensembles were organized from the membership of 19,000. Hundreds of artistes and technicians were given full-time employment. In the first years of its existence, about 8,500 presentations were offered – operas, plays, concerts (orchestra, chamber music, choir and soloists), lectures, recitations, cabaret performances, ballets, film showings and art exhibitions. Similar cultural associations began to be formed in other large communities. Jewish artistes performed exclusively for Jewish audiences, and the content of the work performed was mostly Jewish. The walls of an invisible ghetto were beginning to rise around the German Jews.

When the news came on 30 January 1933, during a meeting discussing Jewish handicrafts, that Hitler had been named Chancellor, the chairman addressed the mixed conference of Liberals and Zionists: 'A historical turning point has been reached. All differences among Jews have now become meaningless. We are all in the same danger.'[22]

Actually, the search for communal unity had begun long before, on the part of both the Gemeinden and the national organizations. Early in 1932 the association of Gemeinden in Prussia called an extraordinary conference to deal with the defence of Jewish rights. The Berlin Gemeinde independently convened a closed meeting of its delegates to discuss the political situation as it affected the Jews. By June 1932 a national association of all Gemeinden was approved provisionally, subject to ratification by the *Land* associations. Simultaneously, the national Jewish organizations (CV, ZVfD, B'nai B'rith and welfare agencies) decided to form a joint committee for concerted action in defence of Jewish rights and for the eventuality of negotiating with government authorities 'to ensure the honour, life and economic existence of the Jewish population'.

Yet neither the Gemeinden nor the national organizations managed to put together a central body before 30 January 1933. In view of the urgency of the Jewish situation, the provisional national Gemeinde association on 12 February set up a five-man Präsidium der Reichsvertretung der jüdischen Landesverbände Deutschlands (Executive Board of the Federal Representation of the Jewish Land Associations of Germany), to function on an emergency basis. Representatives of the national organizations were soon co-opted to the board, while negotiations continued to create a permanent representative body of men whose leadership would be accepted by the diverse movements among the German Jews.²³ Foundering on regional rivalries, the Reichsvertretung der jüdischen Landesverbände succeeded only in establishing the Zentralausschuss der deutschen Juden für Hilfe und Aufbau (Central Committee of German Jews for Relief and Reconstruction) on 13 April 1933. Intended to serve as a central conduit for funds from abroad for the mammoth tasks of welfare facing the Jewish community, it would become a major bolstering force at a time of precipitous decline.²⁴

The idea of strong central leadership became ever more urgent. There was a general feeling that the Jews needed one single organization that could represent them *vis-à-vis* the government, a role that demanded 'dictatorial leadership'.²⁵ At the initiative of three leaders of the Essen Gemeinde, a new try for communal unity began. Integral to this effort was the plan to put Leo Baeck at the head of the organization. He was the most prestigious Jew in Germany, whose

Essence of Judaism, published in 1923 in answer to Adolf Harnack's *Essence of Christianity*, had elevated him to the role of spokesman for the Jews. A Liberal rabbi, a CV board member, and chairman of the Keren Hayesod, he was probably the only Jewish leader who could reconcile the internal differences within the community. Conducting their preliminary negotiations with tact and patience, the Essen Gemeinde leaders managed to subdue most of the regional animosities among the Gemeinden, especially the distrust the Southerners felt for the Northerners and the antipathy of all towards the Berliners. (Berlin, with a third of Germany's Jews, regarded itself as a super-Gemeinde. Its cultural big-town snobbishness further exacerbated relations with the Gemeinden of southern and eastern Germany.) At a preliminary meeting convened in Essen on 23 July 1933 all the regional Gemeinde associations were represented along with the Berlin Gemeinde and all national organizations except the Zionists. The ZVfD had refused to participate because its demand for two delegates had been refused. Negotiations continued; the Zionists were promised more representation on the executive committee. The Berlin Gemeinde reluctantly relinquished its bid for control. Finally, on 17 September 1933, with Leo Baeck as its chairman, the Reichsvertretung der deutschen Juden (Federal Representation of German Jews) came into being. Co-chairman was Otto Hirsch, a former government official in Württemberg and a deeply committed Jew.

Communal unity on an intellectual level was pursued also by Martin Buber, who early in 1933 called together a group of ranking Jewish communal and intellectual leaders to discuss informally the problems confronting German Jewry. The group was designated as the Homburg Circle (the meeting was held at Bad Homburg, near Frankfurt). A second meeting was held on 10 September 1933. The extant minutes indicate a high level of intellectuality and abstraction.[26] Plans for a third meeting never materialized.

The creation of the Reichsvertretung, nearly eight months after the Nazis came to power, at last provided an instrument of Jewish solidarity. Yet the solidarity was fragile and superficial, a valiant attempt to cement a politically divided community. Though everyone paid lip service to the idea of unity and the need for it, conflicts over ideology and policy persisted. Few organizations were prepared to yield their institutional sovereignty for the chimera of unity. The CV appeared most sincere in its assiduous pursuit of unity – perhaps because, speaking for the majority of German Jews, it was under less pressure to compromise, or perhaps, being more pragmatic and less ideological than other segments in the Jewish community, it was more willing to compromise.

Other organizations held fast to their basic commitments. The Reichsbund jüdischer Frontsoldaten sought to preserve its autonomy in matters affecting its constituency, even attempting independent negotiations with the National Socialist régime to obtain special status for Jewish war veterans. The Agudat Israel recognized only the 'unity around the Torah'. Rabbi Jacob Rosenheim, head of the Aguda, granted that cooperation in practical matters was possible, though he held that each political or religious grouping should approach its problems on its own, somewhat in the spirit of Lessing's words:

> Let each man zealously pursue where love,
> From prejudice and from corruption free,
> Shall lead him.[27]

In March 1934 the Aguda withdrew from the Reichsvertretung over differences in education policy. In 1936 another Orthodox group, the Vertretung der unabhängigen jüdische Orthodoxie Deutschlands (VUO, Representation of Independent Jewish Orthodoxy in Germany), concluded an agreement with the Reichsvertretung, which provided that it would speak for the VUO in all areas except religious–cultural matters.[28]

The Reichsvertretung was also used as a combat area by some of its constituents. The most serious disturbers of communal peace were the Berlin Gemeinde and the Zionists, each antagonistic to the other and both assaulting the Reichsvertretung in their bids for control. The Berlin leadership continued to argue from the strength of numbers, prestige and experience. As for the Zionists, they were now, paradoxically, in the communal saddle. Each Nazi turn of the screw vindicated their ideological diagnosis of the Jewish predicament in the Diaspora. On that ground alone, besides an increasing membership, they felt that they deserved the decisive role in communal leadership.

The Reichsvertretung set itself the goal of representing all the Jews in Germany, and its primary aim – at least for the public record – was 'a vigorous and honourable Jewish life on German soil within the German state'.[29] This was to be accomplished by providing the Jews with possibilities for economic existence, by systematically planning and organizing emigration from Germany for those who had to or wanted to leave, and by defending the Jews against defamation. Education and culture, relief and welfare would soon become major functions.

From the start, the Reichsvertretung had conceived that its chief task would be to represent the Jews *vis-à-vis* the National Socialist régime, though no one knew how to do so or if it could be done at all. In the early months of its existence, the Reichsvertretung began to explore these possibilities, making new contacts or renewing old ones in various government ministries. That was a time of memoranda, submissions, petitions to the National Socialist government, attempts to establish a legal basis for Reichsvertretung activity, efforts to release Jews from 'protective custody', and to protect them from violence and brutality.[30]

One of the earliest perilous diemmas confronting the Jews involved the upcoming plebiscite of 12 November 1933. The plebiscite demanded a vote of approval for Hitler's domestic and foreign policies. What should Jews do? In the German dictatorship, absence from the polls would be regarded as opposition, treason. In small communities, where the Jews were visible and exposed, whether and how they voted would become a matter of local Nazi party or police interest. Yet how could they vote '*Ja*' for Germany's anti-Jewish policies? The Reichsvertretung inquiries at last yielded clarification. On 3 November the Reichsvertretung issued a statement:

With the entire German people also we Jews as citizens are summoned to cast our votes on the foreign policy of the Reich government. They are required for Germany's equality among the nations, for the conciliation of the nations, and for the peace of the world. Despite all that we have had to undergo,

The vote of the German Jews can be only Yes.[31]

The idea of approaching the régime for clarification as to the situation of the Jews was not exclusively the Reichsvertretung's.

In the anarchy of autonomy that prevailed in the Jewish community, it was no surprise that about twelve different proposals were submitted to various government agencies by various Jewish organizations with a view to defining the position of the Jews in Germany.

On 21 June 1933 the ZVfD submitted a memorandum to the National Socialist government.[32] That memorandum proposed that the 'new German state' recognize the Zionist movement as the most suitable Jewish group in the new Germany with which to deal, that Jewish status in Germany thenceforth be regulated on the basis of group status rather than individual rights,* and finally, that since emigration would provide a solution to the Jewish question, it should therefore receive government assistance.

In presenting their proposals, the Zionists said that they were not concerned with the interests of individual Jews who had lost their economic and social positions, but rather with creating an opportunity for the existence of the whole group:

> On the foundation of the new state, which has established the principle of race, we wish so to fit in our community into the total structure that for us too, in the sphere assigned to us, fruitful activity for the Fatherland is possible.

This vague proposal for an apparent ghetto autonomy within the racial National Socialist state was followed by an exposition of

---

*Minority rights for some Jews in Germany were under discussion in the League of Nations at just that time. A petition claiming deprivation of his rights had been presented to the League of Nations by one Franz Bernheim, from Upper Silesia, who had lost his job after the National Socialists came to power. In 1922, after part of Upper Silesia had been awarded to Germany in accordance with a plebiscite, Germany signed the Geneva Convention, thus placing national minorities in Upper Silesia under a system of international protection for a period of fifteen years. Under these terms the League of Nations discussed the Bernheim petition in May and June 1933; by September 1933 the German dictatorship formally agreed to fulfil its obligations under the convention. (Until the convention expired, in 1937, the Jews in Upper Silesia could hold office and work in the professions; *shehita* was permitted.) In September 1933 the League of Nations opened a general debate on minorities, which focused on the plight of the German Jews. The international Jewish organizations submitted a memorandum asking, among other things, for the restoration of the rights of the Jews in Germany. But Germany refused to acknowledge the Jews as a national minority. The question became academic when Germany left the League of Nations in late October.[33]

emigration as a means of reducing the 'pressure on the Jewish position in Germany', and thus as being in the interests of the German people. For this reason the Zionist movement hoped to win 'the collaboration even of a government fundamentally hostile to Jews', and held out bait – in the event the Germans cooperated – that the Zionists would try to get the Jews abroad to call off the anti-German boycott. Finally, the memorandum argued that recognition of the Jews as a 'national minority' might also benefit those Germans living abroad who wished to maintain their German identity.

The régime never responded to this memorandum, but the Zionists continued to pursue the idea of group rights for the Jews in Germany, from the start conceding individual rights and the achievements of the Emancipation.

The Reichsvertretung, for its part, refused to waive these rights. The Reichsvertretung wanted to discuss with, negotiate with or petition the government for alleviation of the present situation of the Jews. Proceeding slowly and cautiously, the Reichsvertretung on 23 January 1934 submitted a memorandum to that effect to each member of the Reich Cabinet. The submission was regarded as a trial balloon, to see whether it would elicit a response and thus provide a basis on which further discussions could be conducted.[34]

The Reichsvertretung memorandum first addressed itself to the ouster of Jews from employment in government, the professions and business. The impoverishment and eventual pauperization of the Jews in Germany would, the argument went, affect their status as taxpayers. Consequently, the Reichsvertretung petitioned 'that differential treatment as between Aryan and Jewish employed be discontinued in the future; that any pressure to displace or oust Jewish employees be checked'.*

* An ambitious programme had been elaborated on 15 August 1933 by Werner Senator, then head of the Zentralausschuss, for negotiations to be conducted with the government by the Riechsvertretung-to-be and the Zentralausschuss.[35] Senator believed that the economic problems confronting the Jews were too massive to be dealt with by voluntary organizations through infusions of relief and welfare. His draft guidelines included such points as the protection of the rights of Jews as citizens and taxpayers, the integral relationship between the economic life of the Jews and that of the whole country, the development of Jewish self-help through the development of a 'buy Jewish' market, the development of a credit policy to help the middle class, occupational restructuring

The second item concerned Jewish occupational structure, which the Reichsvertretung conceded was presently 'unhealthy'. To remedy that situation, the community was engaged in a programme of vocational retraining. Consequently, the Reichsvertretung expressed the hope 'that as a matter of principle no occupation be closed to Jews; that within the corporate state's reconstruction of manual trade and labour, agriculture and forestry, Jews, too, be afforded training and admission'.

Occupational restructuring was then one of the few ideas on which Zionists and non-Zionists agreed.[36] According to Zionist dogma, Jewish occupational structure in the Diaspora was 'abnormal', top-heavy in trade, commerce and the professions, instead of widely based in agriculture and industry. The notion derived from the Enlightenment era, when it was argued by Jewish friend and foe alike that Jews had to engage in 'useful' occupations before they deserved to be emancipated. Thereafter, criticism of the 'abnormal' Jewish occupational structure became a staple of anti-Semitic propaganda. In 1933 German Jewish leadership, themselves professionals and businessmen, began advocating occupational restructuring as Jewish public policy to appease the National Socialists and at the same time to obtain new economic opportunities for Jews.

The third item in the Reichsvertretung memorandum dealt with emigration. It described the proportional decline in the past century of the Jewish population in Germany, thus drawing attention to the small space Jews occupied in the nation. Nevertheless, the memorandum continued, since many German Jews would have to emigrate, a systematically prepared and regulated emigration would be in German interests. Under conditions of a properly planned emigration, the emigrant would retain an attachment to his home country; his family and cultural ties would create 'valuable economic connections with the old homeland'. To that end, the Reichsvertretung requested the government to 'support the work that we and competent organizations are doing for emigration to Palestine and other countries'.

The final subject of the memorandum dealt with anti-Semitic

---

and emigration. He also suggested that if quotas were being set, then 'quota rights' should obtain, especially in the lower ranks of the civil service. Senator returned to Israel in September, before the Reichsvertretung's work got far under way.

agitation, prudently defined as 'spiritual oppression', and substantially documented with appended materials. In deference to the racial premises of the state, the Reichsvertretung did not dispute 'the alienness of its Jewish component'. That much – but no more – was conceded. The charge of inferiority was repudiated, unacceptable to a 'Community that values its honour and dignity'. The influence of world Jewish opinion and the implications for Germany were raised, as if to suggest that the Jews had a bargaining point. The government was urged that 'in the future every defamation of Jewish group association and origin be discontinued'.

No response to this submission was ever received from any quarter of the régime. Yet from time to time the Reichsvertretung continued to submit appeals or protests. The most quixotic no doubt was the two-sentence telegram sent to Hitler himself, on 3 May 1934, protesting a special issue of *Der Strürmer* that 'with monstrous insults and horrifying statements' accused the Jews of ritual murder. The Reichsvertretung solemnly swore: 'Before God and man we raise our voice in solemn protest against this unparalleled desecration of our faith.'[37]

While it soon became apparent that the role of the Reichsvertretung as spokesman for the Jewish community *vis-à-vis* the régime was severely limited, it became just as apparent that its role within the Jewish community was growing to unprecedented responsibility and magnitude. The Reichsvertretung was becoming the community's primary instrument for support and sustenance, a Jewish self-government whose functions far surpassed those of the medieval *kehilla*.

The existence of the Reichsvertretung was distinguished by paradoxes. It had been organized for unity, yet it was beset by divisiveness from its origin to its demise. Its public face was compliant and law-abiding, yet it engaged in conspiratorial activities. It supplied the press worldwide with documentation about the plight of the Jews; it salvaged Jewish property and funds from the rapacious state. It even provided clandestine services and facilities that the German dictatorship had officially denied to Jews. The Hochschule für die Wissenschaft des Judentums, for instance, was transformed in 1935 into a Jewish university after Jews had been banned from attending German universities. Nazi authorities were told that the Hochschule was, and they believed it to be, an institution to train rabbis and teachers of Jewish religion.[38] While undertaking the systematic liquidation of the Jewish settlement in Germany, the Reichsvertretung found itself strengthening, even building, Jewish communal and cultural life. It tried resolutely to hold on to the achievements of the Emancipation, while in effect concurring in the ghettoization of the Jews. That paradox was especially evident in the area of general education.

After the Law Against the Overcrowding of German Schools was enacted on 25 April 1933, schooling had to be provided for thousands of Jewish youths who had been ousted from their schools and for thousands more in the elementary schools, where prejudice, hate and hysteria had made their attendance untenable. The responsibility fell to the Reichsvertretung.

Before 1933 Jewish all-day schools had attracted a small proportion of Jewish children, mostly from Orthodox and/or East European backgrounds. In 1933 about 10,000 children – one sixth of all Jewish children – attended thirty-five private Jewish schools, mostly on the elementary level.[39] Now, not by choice, most Jewish children began to attend all-Jewish schools.

As early as May 1933 Martin Buber had submitted a proposal to the Reichsvertretung for a programme of Jewish education whose central postulate was that such an educational undertaking should be 'not only formally but intrinsically Jewish', that it should 'not merely remedy an external state of distress, but should also fill a great internal void in German Jewry by providing our youth with the firm stability of being united with the eternity of Judaism'.[40] But Buber's educational philosophy was rejected. The guidelines for Jewish schools that the Reichsvertretung issued early in 1934 stipulated that the educational basis for the Jewish school was to be the dual Jewish/German experience to which each child living in Germany had been exposed. The coexistence of Jews and Germans as well as the tension between them was to be demonstrated in the classroom. Furthermore, the German subjects were 'intended to demonstrate what Jewish being and Jewish thought owe to the German mind' and, reciprocally, 'what Jewish minds and Jewish work have contributed to the fashioning of German culture'.[41] The individual schools were free to work out the details of their curricula; eventually each school reflected the outlook of its teaching staff and of its pupils rather than the guidelines of the Reichsvertretung. In secondary schools, where students developed a consuming passion for Palestine, Frederick the Great and Goethe lost relevance. Zionist-oriented schools abandoned German history for Palestinian studies. Modern Hebrew was a required subject for those planning to emigrate to Palestine. Some schools stressed Judaism, Jewish history and literature; others concentrated on vocational studies.

Tensions developed between teachers and pupils, between classroom and home. Many teachers in the newly organized Reichsvertretung schools who had taught in German secondary schools were poorly equipped in Jewish matters and retained a stubborn passion for things German. But others, jolted by the collapse of their German world, plunged into Jewish studies with the intensity of converts. That nationalist or religious intensity sometimes came into headlong conflict with children from assimilated homes, where Jewishness was lukewarm at best. But despite its tensions, inadequacies and problems, the Jewish school offered the Jewish child shelter from the storm outside, warmth and love instead of rejection and hostility, simultaneously strengthening self-esteem.

Though Buber failed to influence the course of Jewish education, his success in Jewish adult education was spectacular. In November 1933, four years after Franz Rosenzweig's death had closed the Frankfurt Lehrhaus, the remarkable centre of adult Jewish studies that he had founded in 1920, Buber re-opened it, with a lecture on the tasks of Jewish adult education. A half-year later, the Mittelstelle für jüdische Erwachsenenbildung (Central Office for Jewish Adult Education), with Buber at its head, was set up within the Reichsvertretung. In an address at the founding conference in May 1934 Buber expatiated on the purpose of Jewish adult education: 'No longer the equipment with knowledge, but the mobilization for existence'. Through its grooming of individuals, Jewish adult education would, he said, 'groom a community that will stand firm, that will prevail, that will guard the spark'.[42]

A broad programme evolved – lectures, discussions, courses and community singing – which encompassed the gamut of religious and ideological thought. Subject matter included the Bible (Buber's own special field), Semitic languages, medieval history, the philosophy of Plato, Kant and Hume, general economic history, contemporary sociology, and study of the languages of emigration – English, Spanish, Hebrew.[43] The Mittelstelle trained the teachers from the German school system in Jewish subjects and the teachers in the Jewish school system in general and methodological matters.

The Mittelstelle and all its works constituted, in Ernst Simon's phrase, a bulwark of spiritual resistance. Yet some German Jews, in hindsight came to regard this chapter of exaltation with self-reproach, because it had slowed down the process of dissolution. 'A joint historic guilt', wrote a survivor of those times, rests on those who believed 'that we had very, very much time'.[44]

Vocational training and retraining, to accomplish the 'occupational restructuring' of German Jews, consumed a major portion of Reichsvertretung resources, though probably no more than 25,000 persons benefited from the programme. Not merely ideological appeasement of the Nazis, it was intended to provide a means of livelihood in the manual trades for the civil servants, professionals and business people who had lost their jobs. To that end, training schools and workshops were set up to teach manual occupations, gardening and agriculture. By 1937 there were sixteen training workshops for locksmiths, blacksmiths, tinsmiths, electricians, carpenters, etc., six in Berlin and the rest in other large cities, each with some hundred to two hundred young people enrolled. At thirty training centres, girls were prepared for work in Jewish hospitals, orphanages, homes for the aged and public kitchens, and were taught cooking, laundering, housekeeping, sewing, dressmaking, tailoring. Thirty training centres for agriculture and gardening, mostly Zionist-operated, prepared young emigrants for Palestine. (One was non-Zionist; its trainees eventually settled as colonists in Argentina). With each passing year it became clearer that the programme benefited prospective emigrants more than unemployed civil servants.

Individual German Jews and the Jewish community were coming to the recognition that emigration was a more viable response to National Socialism than occupational restructuring. Emigration reflected the fluctuations of Nazi policies. In the first reaction of panic in 1933, some 37,000 Jews fled. With the apparent cessation of anti-Jewish legislation and the *Putsch* against the SA, emigration dropped to 23,000 in 1934 and to 21,000 in 1935. After the enactment of the Nuremberg Laws in September 1935, the figures rose to 25,000 in

1936, but fell once more in 1937 to 23,000, following the quiet that enveloped the 1936 Olympic Games.[45] Everyone scanned the political horizon for signs of change; an unexpected mildness in anti-Jewish policy or an inexplicable inconsistency was interpreted as a herald of change. Even Leo Baeck, who in 1933 had predicted the end of the thousand-year history of the German Jews, in 1934 dreamed that a military coup would soon overthrow Hitler. Once he remarked: 'My idea is still this: I wake up one day and find on the billboards posters with the imprint: "I have taken over executive power – General von…"'[46]

Other factors, too, practical and psychological, determined the statistics of emigration. In 1933 some 14,000 persons (besides the 37,000 who actually emigrated) applied for information about migration possibilities to the Hilfsverein der deutschen Juden (Welfare Association of the German Jews), the agency specializing in migrant assistance. The following quarter however, the number of inquiries dropped, because, in the words of one communal official, 'many have lost the courage and determination to leave because of the negative answers with reference to immigration, length of stay, and work possibilities in continental countries as well as overseas countries'.[47]

The scarcity of visas for any country was the major obstacle. Not only was the number of visas insufficient for those who wanted to leave Germany, but many available visas were to countries where settlement was hazardous for the middle-aged, middle-class urban Jews of Germany, as for instance in some Central and South American countries, where hardy pioneers were called for. Altogether, emigration entailed a total transformation of one's life and culture. Observant Jews faced a particularly poignant dilemma if they received visas to Latin American countries, where few, if any, facilities existed for religious observance, burial, ritual slaughter and ritual baths.[48] The alternative of remaining in Germany may have appeared less perilous.

Emigration to Palestine too was tightly controlled. Not only did the British limit the number of certificates, but the Zionist movement itself set up rigid standards for prospective immigrants. The Eighteenth Zionist Congress in 1933 established, within the Jewish Agency for Palestine, a Central Bureau for the Settlement of German Jews, which, to begin with, excluded anti-Zionists as applicants for certificates.[49] Young people in good health, with some training for agricultural work or manual trades, and persons with capital were the preferred candidates for *aliya*, in a process where the needs and interests of Palestine took precedence over the strategy of rescue.[50] Systematic training and careful selection of candidates remained the chief characteristics of the migration until 1938. Indeed, the ZVfD opposed a plan of illegal migration to Palestine, approving it only after Kristallnacht.[51]

The search for places of refuge consumed the Reichsvertretung and its subsidiary agencies. When the Evian Conference was convened in July 1938, the Reichsvertretung obtained permission from the German authorities to send a delegation.* They submitted to the conference and its individual delegations a memorandum that presented a grand plan for systematic emigration.[52]

For some Jews, lack of means hindered emigration, though the Hilfsverein could usually help. But there were some Jews for whom making money or protecting it had higher priority. Either business was too good to abandon or the estimated loss, around 1935, of 30 to 40 per cent of property in transferring assets abroad was too great to endure. 'Only business', wrote Kurt Tucholsky in a letter to Arnold Zweig, with bitter contempt because few Jewish businessmen had left Germany in 1933, reluctant to lose their profits. But now, in 1935, he wrote, 'they slink out, gloomy, soundly thrashed, in shit up to their ears, bankrupt, their money robbed – and *without honour*'.[53]

Finally, age was the central and determining factor in emigration. From the start all emigration programmes – Reichsvertretung and Zionist – stressed the communal obligation to help the young people leave first of all. In late August 1934 a leading English Zionist who visited Berlin reported that Dr Baeck had told him definitely that there was no place in Germany for the young Jews: 'The only thing to do is to get them out.'[54] Already in 1933 the German Jewish community was an ageing community, which, in a century-old process of attrition through intermarriage, conversion and a low birth rate, had

---

*The Austrian Jews too sent a delegation, even though they were then already under closer Gestapo/SD surveillance than the German Jews. They worked closely with the Reichsvertretung delegation. Hans Habe's novel *The Mission*, written after the Eichmann trial, whose plot about a Gestapo plan to 'sell' Jews which the Austrian Jews were to transmit at the Evian Conference, is pure fantasy, suggested no doubt by the negotiations between Eichmann and the Hungarian Jews in 1944. But in 1938 no such negotiations were undertaken, and no historical evidence exists for such speculation.

twice as many persons over the age of sixty as a population of normal growth. This demographic characteristic affected the selection of migrants, for emigration was determined not only by necessity, but by the ability to build a new life and the availability of time for a fresh start. The selective process of emigration each year left the remaining German Jewish population successively older. In June 1933, not quite half of German Jews were over forty; by September 1939 three fourths were. In 1933 nearly 30 per cent were under twenty-four; in 1939, only 13 per cent were. Over 80 per cent of the Jews under forty left Germany between 1933 and 1939, compared to half of those aged forty to sixty and a fourth of those over sixty.[55] By 1936 American Jewish philanthropic leaders worried that the Jewish community in Germany would become a gigantic old-age home whose inmates would have to be maintained by Jews abroad.[56]

Between January 1933 and November 1938, some 150,000 Jews – 30 per cent of the original population – left Germany. After Kristallnacht, under Gestapo pressure, nearly another 150,000 left.*

The year 1935 brought new misfortunes to the Jewish community as National Socialist anti-Jewish policy shifted into a higher gear. The isolation of the Jews became more confining, responsibilities of the Reichsvertretung multiplied, and internal dissension was aggravated, expressing the rage of impotence towards the outside foe. That January Heydrich issued a directive to the Bavarian political police stating that 'the activity of the Zionist-oriented youth organizations that are engaged in the occupational restructuring of the Jews for agriculture and manual trades prior to their emigration to Palestine lies in the interest of the National Socialist state's leadership'.† By early March Jewish organizations learned about that directive as well as about another that forbade propaganda urging Jews to remain in Germany.

On 31 March the ZVfD Executive Committee prepared a declaration that was adopted at the ZVfD annual meeting on 5 May 1935. The declaration demanded a reorganization of the entire Jewish community at national and local levels, which would ensure recognition of the 'due' influence of the Zionists.[57] Shortly thereafter the ZVfD

---

*For the fate of those who remained, see Appendix A.
†See Chapter 4, p. 118, for context and sources.

turned the policy statement into a demand for Zionist parity with non-Zionists on the boards of the Reichsvertretung, its institutions and the Berlin Gemeinde. Officially the Zionists justified their power bid with the argument that history had vindicated the correctness of their philosophy and that 'the programme which has been accepted by the overwhelming majority of the Jews residing in Germany can be realized only when it is conducted by men who are inspired by Zionist ideals'.

Publicly no one attributed the Zionist power bid to the Heydrich directive and to then current National Socialist policy favouring the Zionists, but the connection did not pass unnoticed. The non-Zionists were convinced that there was a connection and that the Zionists themselves believed that the Gestapo favoured them over the non-Zionists.[58]

The Zionist demand for parity stunned the non-Zionists. The *C-V Zeitung* of 9 May 1935 branded it 'unjustified, disruptive, and astonishing', an attempt to turn present events in Germany to Zionist profit. Nonetheless, the Zionists did eventually win parity, perhaps because the Reichsvertretung feared Gestapo intervention, perhaps because it had yielded to fatigue and a sense of defeat.

The heaviest blow to the non-Zionists came with the promulgation of the Nuremberg Laws. It then became clear as it had not been before that the Jewish community had no future in Germany, that the pursuit of *Daseinrecht* was illusory. In 1933 the key ideological difference between the Zionists and non-Zionists was that the latter regarded emigration as 'a' solution and the former as 'the' solution, though in actual practice no real difference existed. But in 1935 the non-Zionists realized that emigration had become 'the' solution. (Only extreme anti-Zionists continued, deep into 1937, to hold stubbornly to the conviction that a Jewish future in Germany was still possible.) After 1935 the ideological quarrel hinged on the destination of emigration, the Zionists insisting on Palestine exclusively and the non-Zionists searching the globe for any haven. The Zionist/non-Zionist difference became one of rigid ideology versus flexible pragmatism.

After the promulgation of the Nuremberg Laws, the Reichsvertretung reformulated its programme in an attempt 'to create a basis on which a tolerable relationship between the German and the Jewish people is possible', citing Hitler's words at Nuremberg as their frame of reference. The prerequisite for that tolerable relationship, the Reichsvertretung declared, was that a moral and economic existence be allowed the Jews and the Jewish communities in Germany through a halt of the defamation and the boycott against them.[59] Furthermore, in a courageous bid to retain control of the community and stave off increasing Gestapo intervention, the Reichsvertretung declared that any regulation of the life of the German Jews required 'governmental recognition of an autonomous Jewish management'.

The new programme redefined the Reichsvertretung's most urgent tasks. First came Jewish education, to train the young 'to become religiously secure, upright Jews, who will draw strength for meeting the heavy demands life will make of them from a conscious belonging-ness to the Jewish community'. The second task was to further emi-gration to 'Palestine above all' but also to other countries. The third task was care of the needy, the sick and the aged. The fourth task en-tailed safeguarding the existing means of Jewish livelihood and pro-viding aid to those without employment. The fifth item explicitly expressed the emotional identification of the Jewish community with Palestine, and the readiness on the part of the Reichsvertretung to establish institutional ties with the Jewish National Fund in Palestine. The heavy hand of the German distatorship was evident: there were no longer any declarations of love or loyalty to Germany, its language or culture. The Jews had become completely isolated.

After the enactment of the Nuremberg Laws, Jews were no longer allowed to call themselves Germans. The Jewish organizations had to change their names so that they spoke for 'Jews in Germany' rather than 'German Jews'. The Central Verein report, issued at the end of 1935, recorded its defeat. 'Our relations with the German world around us have changed,' the document commented drily. The new realities 'have redefined our thoughts, feelings and behaviour. It would be undignified and foolish if we were not to comprehend this experience in its full significance.'[60] The CV report was an institutional swan song, a melancholy statement of the defeat of its ideology not by Zionism, but by the victory of National Socialism. It attempted to draw up a balance sheet of the Emancipation, weighing the loss in Jewish content against the gains in individual achievement and creati-vity. It soberly recognized Palestine as a place of refuge, but adhered to its 'historical Diaspora line'.

The intrusion of the Gestapo in the Jewish community became ever more oppressive. Every public Jewish gathering was aware of the Gestapo's listening ear and watchful eye. Jewish organizations had to conduct their business in the presence of Gestapo agents. Documents were scrutinized or subject to scrutiny. For privacy, communal leaders resorted to meetings in each other's homes, at tea, lunch, dinner. They did not record all their transactions. For their constituencies, rabbis used to arrange local visiting, with small groups meeting periodically in one another's homes for religious study and discussion of current events.[61]

Any hint or suspicion of criticism of National Socialism and the German dictatorship brought immediate reprisals. Rabbis and communal leaders were summoned to the Gestapo for having spoken, or on suspicion of having spoken, forbidden words. If they were not arrested, they were prohibited from speaking publicly, preaching or lecturing. Buber was banned from public speaking. Baeck was arrested again and again. In 1935, after the enactment of the Nuremberg Laws, he composed a prayer to be read from the pulpit as part of the Kol Nidre service. The Gestapo discovered the text, arrested him and forbade the prayer to be used. The Nazis regarded the prayer as a revolutionary document, though it was written in the language of faith and tradition. It began in this way:

> In this hour every man in Israel stands erect before his Lord, the God of justice and mercy, to open his heart in prayer. Before God we will question our ways and search our deeds, the acts we have done and those we have left undone. We will publicly confess the sins we have committed and beg the Lord to pardon and forgive. Acknowledging our trespasses, individual and communal, let us despise the slanders and calumnies directed against us and our faith. Let us declare them lies, too mean and senseless for our reckoning.
>
> God is our refuge. Let us trust Him, our source of dignity and pride. Thank the Lord and praise Him for our destiny, for the honour and persistence with which we have endured and survived persecution.[62]

Censorship of the Jewish press went to extraordinary lengths. Subject to vague or nonsensical regulations, Jewish journals were given lists of prohibited subjects. (The German landscape was one.) Words and phrases were scanned for transgressive meanings. The word 'blond' was banned in oral and written use, because it had become a code word for 'Nazi'. Periodicals were suspended arbitrarily for days or weeks, their licences revoked, their writers and editors arrested. German censorship of Jewish cultural activities tightened and Jews were forbidden to perform works by 'Aryan' writers and composers. Musicians who had once played Bach, Beethoven and Wagner now played, often to their personal distaste, East European Jewish folk-songs.[63]

Above all, the Gestapo wanted to gain control of the Reichsvertretung or, failing that, other communal Jewish organizations. In pre-1938 days the Jewish community had not yet fallen wholly under the 'legal' jurisdiction of the Gestapo as it would in post-1939 days. In their ambition to capture the Jews, the Gestapo tried to place a man they could trust on the Reichsvertretung Executive. Their man was Georg Kareski, a General Zionist suddenly turned Revisionist in the spring of 1933. To this day no one knows what hold the Gestapo had over Kareski or why he lent himself to the ugly drama.[64] Yet in spite of several forceful efforts by the Gestapo beginning in 1935, Kareski was rebuffed, partly by happenstance, but mainly because Jewish communal leaders resisted Gestapo pressure. (Later, in Eastern Europe, similar resistance brought certain death.) In June 1937, for the last time, the Gestapo tried to put Kareski on the Reichsvertretung Executive, but the rejection was unequivocal: in Max Gruenewald's lapidary phrase, 'borrowed authority' had no place in Jewish life. Leo Baeck told the Gestapo: 'You can force me to appoint Kareski as a member of the Executive of the Reichsvertretung. But you cannot force me to continue as president of the Reichsvertretung.'

The National Socialist victory in 1933 had shaken the Jewish community, but within a few short months it had rallied, summoning an energy and will for organizational unity and fraternal solidarity and stimulating a powerful resurgence of Jewish identity. The wellsprings of this energy were the hope, faith and belief that the German dictatorship would be short-lived or, at the very least, that a tolerable *modus vivendi* would be established. But after the Nuremberg Laws no such sanguine faith could be held. Morale began to decline, as the community became ever more impoverished by Nazi oppression, ever more enfeebled by emigration.

German Jewry had once been a prosperous community, contributing generously towards the needs of other Jewish communities less favourably situated, but with the growing Jewish impoverishment, the income of the Gemeinden from taxes – about 10 to 12 per cent of income taxes – kept declining. (Actually not all Jews became impoverished: Jews in a host of businesses and industries, paradoxically, shared in the increasing prosperity of the National Socialist state.) Still, the sense of self-help was strong. To meet the costs of their communal programmes, a system of voluntary monthly contributions was instituted under the name Blaue Beitragskarte (Blue Contribution Card), operated by volunteers on behalf of the Zentralausschuss. Though the contributions, scaled according to income, were small, the Blaue Beitragskarten raised respectable sums – in 1936, for instance, two million Reichsmarks. Still, that fell far short of the enormous needs. To close the gap, the American Jewish Joint Distribution Committee (JDC), the chief philanthropic organization of American Jews for overseas aid, and the Central British Fund, a comparable organization of British Jews, provided large amounts of money and goods. (On 1 April 1935 the Reichsvertretung took over most communal institutions in the field of relief and welfare, including the Zentralausschuss, and incorporated them into its structure.)

In 1936 about 20 per cent of the Jewish population – 83,761 persons out of 409,000 – were in need. That year Jewish public kitchens dispensed 2,357,000 free meals. More than 75,000 persons, one third of them in Berlin, received free *matzot* during Passover, the largest number of applicants for Passover relief in the history of Germany.[65] In 1937 the Reichsvertretung used most of its funds for emigration and preparation for emigration – 5 million Reichsmarks out of a total of 7 million (about $1·7 million). Relief and economic aid were next in importance. The morale-building functions – schools, culture, religious life – were shrinking.

By January 1938 the Jewish situation had so deteriorated, the outlook had become so bleak, that even Heinrich Stahl, president of the Berlin Gemeinde, the most persistent advocate of *Dasein*, publicly declared: 'To those among our youth who have not yet decided to emigrate, I say, there is no future for Jews in this country. Whatever changes may be forthcoming for us will probably not be for the better.'[66]

1938 was the last year that any communal autonomy was exercised.

The accelerated confiscation of Jewish property and the final expulsion of Jews from the economy began. The mass arrests of June were followed by the mass expulsion of the *Ostjuden* in October. A few days later, on Kristallnacht, the Jewish community of Germany went up in flames. For months thereafter suicides accounted for more than half the Jewish burials. All Jewish institutions were burned down or banned by order of the Gestapo. The Jewish press was suppressed. The Reichsvertretung was turned into the Reichsvereinigung with tasks of emigration, welfare and education assigned by the Gestapo. Its real function was to preside over the final liquidation of German Jewry.

In March 1939 the *Jüdische Rundschau* reappeared in Paris as the *Jüdische Welt Rundschau*, a new name that bespoke the exile of German Jewry. Its first issue contained an article by Martin Buber, 'The End of the German–Jewish Symbiosis', both eulogy and elegy for that era:

I testify: it was the most extraordinary and meaningful circumstance. For the symbiosis of German and Jewish existence as I experienced it in the four decades that I spent in Germany, was the first and the only one since the Spanish Era to receive the highest confirmation that history can bestow, confirmation through creativity . . . But this symbiosis is at an end and it is not likely to return.

With the German invasion of Poland on 1 September 1939 some two million Jews came under German rule. Two years later, when the Germans attacked the Soviet Union, some three million more Jews came under German dominion – the rest of the Jews of pre-war Poland, all the Jews of Lithuania, Latvia, Estonia and Soviet White Russia, and most of the Jews in the Ukraine, the Crimea and Russia proper. These five million Jews lived in metropolitan industrial centres like Lodz and Warsaw, Kiev and Kharkov; in ancient historic cities like Cracow, Vilna, Lublin and Riga; in provincial capitals like Kovno (Kaunas), Bialystok, Radom, Odessa and Minsk. They lived in hundreds of county seats and market towns and were dispersed in thousands of villages. In pre-war Poland, Jews had resided in over 16,000 localities.[1]

The East European Jewish settlement was massive and concentrated. The 350,000 Jews of pre-war Warsaw equalled the whole Jewish population of pre-war France. The 200,000 Jews of Lodz matched the number of Jews in all of Czechoslovakia. Kiev's Jewish population of 150,000 was nearly the size of the Netherlands' Jewish population. The 100,000 Jews of Lwów (Lemberg) exceeded in number the combined Jewish populations of Belgium, Luxembourg, Denmark and Norway. Cracow's 56,000 Jews equalled all of Italy's Jews; Vilna's pre-war Jewish population of 55,000 was greater than the Jewish population of Bulgaria. The very numbers and density of East European Jewry determined their fate. In the past their concentration had enriched their creativity. Under the Germans it would hasten their doom.

The Jews of Eastern Europe remembered the last war, its havoc and hunger, and the pogroms that had drenched a wide swath of eastern Poland and the Ukraine in Jewish blood. In 1939 Jews knew that they would suffer the hardships that were the common lot of war. They knew also that as Jews they would endure still other afflictions at the hands of the Germans and even of the Poles among whom they had lived for centuries more in tension than comradeship.

When German bombs rained down on Poland – on Warsaw, Lwów, Piotrków, Bialystok, Radom and countless other non-military targets in Poland – Jews suffered along with everyone else, sharing in the devastation of Polish cities. Warsaw underwent the most massive destruction, as torrents of bombs turned the city into a mass of craters, ruins and ashes. On 16 September, the eve of Rosh Hashana, the Jewish New Year, German planes bombed the dense Jewish quarter, flying so low that there could be no mistaking the deliberate intent.

When Warsaw came under siege, the Germans exploded some ten to thirty thousand shells daily on the city.[2] Warsaw became a battle zone, with civilians digging trenches to halt the advance of the German tanks. Some 20,000 Polish Jews lost their lives during the invasion and bombardments; Jewish homes, stores, buildings, workshops, factories and other installations were destroyed, the losses estimated at 50,000 to 100,000 units. In Warsaw alone, about one third of Jewish-owned buildings were demolished and the main centres of Jewish trade were reduced to rubble.[3]

All over Poland, the first response among Jews to the German invasion was flight. Thousands upon thousands of Jews set out on foot, in carts, in wagons, seeking refuge. Jews in small towns fled to the big cities; Jews in the metropolises fled to towns and villages. They moved eastwards, towards Russia and Russian-held territory. Along the German-Russian demarcation line, territory passed back and forth between the Germans and Russians as border adjustments were made, the population surging forwards and back, finally subsiding on the Russian side.

Jews, to be sure, were not the only people in flight. Thousands of Poles had taken to the roads and highways. On 7 September, during the siege of Warsaw, the military, fearing that Warsaw would fall the next day, issued an order for all able-bodied men to leave the city. In the next few days, as many as 100,000 men set out eastwards, large numbers of Jews and Jewish communal leaders among them. Since Hitler, in his declaration of war on 1 September, had promised that he would 'not war against women and children', the men, Poles and Jews alike, calculated that no harm would come to the womenfolk, whereas they, especially political and communal leaders, were endangered.

As soon as the Germans occupied Poland, their Einsatzgruppen began to direct a flow of human traffic that soon radically altered the age-old patterns of Jewish settlement in Poland. The Jews were driven from hundreds of localities in the Wartheland. They were expelled from thousands of small towns and villages throughout Poland and sent to near-by big cities. In Cracow, the ancient residence of the kings of Poland, the pre-war Jewish population of 56,000 swelled to 68,000, as Jews in the neighbouring small towns and villages fled to the big city. When Cracow was designated as the capital of the Generalgouvernement, Governor Frank ordered the 'voluntary departure' of all Jews, except for those 'economically indispensable'. But only a few thousand – refugees from elsewhere – complied. After three months, the Germans took matters into their own hands: in one day they expelled 32,000 Jews.

In hundreds of small towns ancient Jewish communities were uprooted. The fate of the Jews of Aleksandrów, seven miles west of Lodz, was typical. Aleksandrów, one fourth of whose 12,000 residents were Jews, was the hosiery centre of Poland. It was also the seat of the Aleksanderer *rebbe*, one of the most distinguished hasidic dynasties in all Poland, and the *hasidim* gave a special Jewish character to the town. The Germans entered Alexsandrów on 7 September and the next day burned down its synagogues. After three months of terror, arrests, shootings, expropriations, impressments into forced labour, the Jews were expelled on 27 December 1939. In the depths of the Polish winter they were marched out on the highway, men, women, children and infants, the hale and the halt, with the few belongings they were permitted to take in sacks and baby carriages, wheelbarrows and pushcarts, bicyles and sleds. The nearest town was Głowno, on the border of the incorporated area and the Generalgouvernement, which most managed to reach. Wayworn, some eventually arrived in Lodz, others in Warsaw.[4]

Within a few months of the German occupation, thousands of Jewish settlements were erased from the map of Poland, their inhabitants ejected without notice, forbidden to take bare necessities, condemned to exposure, hunger and homelessness. By the end of 1940, Warsaw had taken in 78,000 refugees from Lodz, Kalisz, and some 700 other places in the Wartheland. Piotrków's Jewish population swelled from 8,000 to nearly 12,000, with the accretion of refugees. Some 330,000 Jews – one tenth of the Jews in Poland – became homeless refugees, beggars of bread and shelter, candidates for disease and death.

The very moment the Germans entered a town or city, they turned the Jews into outcasts of society. On entering Warsaw, the Germans agreed to distribute soup to the hungry population, having extracted one million zlotys from the municipal adminstration for that purpose. The agreement stipulated that all the hungry in the city, without exception, were to benefit. Yet immediately the Germans began to eject the Jews from the soup lines, calling upon the Poles on the line to do the same, 'because the Jews deprive the Poles of their spoonful of soup'.[5] It was interesting to observe, wrote an eye-witness, how quickly the brotherhood born under the continuous danger of death disappeared and how quickly the difference between rich and poor, Christian and Jew once again became apparent.[6]

Right away the Germans started to confiscate Jewish businesses and industry and to seal off Jewish retail stores for the disposal of either the military occupation or the SS. Sometimes Jewish shops were ordered to be opened only so that they could be plundered and robbed. In large manufacturing centres military trucks carried off the goods of Jewish factories and stores. In small communities Jews were ordered to bring in all their gold and jewellery under threat of death. Hostages were taken to enforce the extortion of large sums of money from the Jewish community, but were seldom released even after the contribution had been delivered.

Terror enveloped the Jews. The Germans re-enacted the Kristallnacht in every town and city they invaded and occupied.[7] All over Poland synagogues went up in flames. (Those spared the fire were desecrated, turned into stables, garages and public latrines.) Everywhere the Germans organized pogroms, rounding up the non-Jewish population to witness and learn how to mock, abuse, injure and murder Jews. Unbridled killing and senseless violence became daily commonplaces for the Jews; the fear of sudden death became normal and habitual.

German terror in the Generalgouvernement in 1939 was wild and wanton. In the territory wrested from Russia in 1941, terror became systematic and massive. Within days of the German invasion, thousands upon thousands of Jews in Vilna, Kovno, Riga, Bialystok, Minsk and hundreds of other towns disappeared in raids carried out by Lithuanians, White Russians and Ukrainians under German orders. It was said that the Jews were taken away for work. By mid-July a survivor here or there staggered back, physically maimed, psychically scarred, to report the mass executions of the Jews. In Bialystok some 7,000 Jews were killed by the Einsatzgruppen in July; in Kovno, some 6,000 to 7,000; in Vilna, 20,000 or more – nearly half the city's Jewish population – were swallowed up in the death pits at Ponary, a desolate village ten kilometres from Vilna. 'How can one write about this? How can one assemble one's thoughts?' Herman Kruk asked in his diary on 4 September 1941, recording the eye-witness reports.[8] The reports were hard to believe; once believed, they were still harder to assimilate. They stunned the mind: they numbed sensibility. The Jews underwent a mass psychic occlusion, the normal flow of their emotions and energies shut off by shock and withdrawal, the business of their daily existence managed with a stringent economy of thought and feeling.

Everywhere the terror was aggravated by the sadism of the SS. In Częstochowa, on a frosty night in January 1940, the police surrounded a densely populated Jewish area, shouting *'Juden raus!'* Thousands of half-naked men and women were assembled in a large square and beaten to bleeding. Then they were kept standing for hours in the biting frost. Others – especially young girls – were taken into the synagogue now transformed into police headquarters, forced to undress, sexually shamed and tortured.[9] In Kowel, which the Germans occupied a few days after the attack on Russia, they arrested a beloved hasidic *rebbe*, tortured him and, in an act of mythic Chinese savagery, displayed his head for several days in the window of a high-street store.[10]

The refinements of cruelty were reserved especially for pious Jews and rabbis, whose traditional Jewish garb – hat and long coat – and whose beard and sidelocks identified them as quintessentially Jewish. (In Germany the National Socialists had often failed to distinguish Jews from 'Aryans' by 'racial' features. During the High Holy Days of 1932, a Nazi gang, bent on anti-Jewish violence, mistakenly beat up 'Aryans'.)[11] The Germans deliberately chose observant Jews to force them to desecrate and destroy the sacred articles of Judaism, even to set fire to synagogues. In some places the Germans piled the Torah scrolls in the market-place, compelling the Jews to set fire to the pile, dance around it, singing, 'We rejoice that the shit is burning.' Another German pleasure was 'feeding' pork to pious Jews, usually in the presence of an invited audience. The most popular German game, played in countless variations, was 'beards'. In its simplest versions Germans seized bearded Jews and beat them. A more sophisticated entertainment involved plucking beards, hair by hair or in clumps. Sometimes Germans herded bearded Jews into barber shops, ordering them to be shaved and making them pay for the service. Sometimes the Germans themselves hacked off Jewish beards with bayonets, often along with parts of cheeks, chins, faces. In some places, Jews were assembled in the town square and shorn in a ceremony of mass mockery; elsewhere, beards were set afire.[12]

German terror was not exercised just in play, it was used also to extract work. Random seizures of Jews off the streets and even from their homes for forced labour began spontaneously, as it were, long before 26 October 1939, when Frank issued a decree making forced labour compulsory for all Jews aged fourteen to sixty.[13] Jews were seized to clean the streets of rubble, to scrub the floors in German residences, to haul and move, load and unload, to labour beyond fatigue. Sometimes they were released at the day's end and allowed to return home, but more likely they were kept for a week or two, incommunicado, unable to inform their families of their whereabouts or even of their very existence.[14]

As the Germans consolidated their position in Poland, they set up labour camps outside the big cities, some of which – Treblinka and Majdanek – eventually became annihilation camps. Teams of forced labourers were assigned for periods of weeks and even months to construct these camps. After a stint of forest clearing, marsh draining, ditch digging, quarrying at these forced-labour installations, a normally robust man returned home sick, aged and wasted. 'Cursed Nazism now brings us physical slavery as well,' observed Chaim Kaplan in his diary on 14 September 1940.[15]

In time, the SS was operating some 125 forced-labour camps in the Generalgouvernement just for Jews, where terror, violence and sadism ruled. Workers were wantonly shot or beaten to death. Those who tried to escape were shot. Some expired of exhaustion or hunger. Nearly all contracted disabilities or diseases endemic to their work. Underclothed and underfed, they became frostbitten, even to necrosis of parts of the face, fingers and feet.[16] In the summer they suffered sunburn and severe blistering. Tendons, ligaments, muscles became swollen and inflamed under stress of unaccustomed labour. Heart muscles were seriously affected and coronary damage was a frequent affliction. Sites under construction had no dormitories. In one place the labourers used to march about ten kilometres to their place of work, where they toiled fourteen hours. Afterwards, they trudged back those ten kilometres to the base camp, where they were rewarded with ten ounces of bread, some jam and a plate of soup.[17]

Forced labour produced a new chapter in Yiddish folklore as dozens of songs, often plaintive and lachrymose, some bitter and ironic, were created to discharge the bitter accumulation of woe. Workers from Radom taken to the labour camp at Cieszanów used to lament:

> Work, brothers, work fast,
> If you don't, they'll lash your hide,
> Not many of us will manage to last –
> Before long we'll all have died.

Marching slave-labour brigades in the Libau ghetto used to sing:

> We are the ghetto Jews,
> The loneliest people on earth.
> Everything we had we lost,
> We have nothing left of worth.

To boost morale, the slave-labour brigades in the Kovno ghetto sang:

> We don't weep or grieve
> Even when you beat and lash us,
> But never for a moment believe
> That you will discourage and dash us.

> Jewish brigades,
> With rags for clothes
> March day in, day out
> And bravely bear their woes.[18]

On 23 November 1939 Frank issued an ordinance prescribing arm-bands for all Jewish men and women in the Generalgouvernement over ten years of age – a white band, at least ten centimetres wide, with the Star of David, to be worn on the right sleeve of both inner and outer clothing. Jews were being concentrated and identified, so that none would escape the ever-tightening meshes of German control. On 28 November 1939 Frank issued a decree ordering the formation in each city of a *Judenrat*, whose membership roster was to be submitted to German officials for approval. In many places the decree came after the fact, for Heydrich's instructions to the chiefs of the Einsatzgruppen on 21 September 1939 had already been put in force. Frank's order specified that the Judenrat was obliged to accept German orders and was answerable for their conscientious execution. Furthermore, it stipulated that all Jews had to obey the directives that the Judenrat issued to implement German orders.

The next step was *de facto* ghettoization, soon to become *de jure*. One of the first ventures to establish a twentieth-century ghetto occurred in Warsaw, where a Judenrat had already been set up on Gestapo instructions since early October. A month later, on Saturday noon of 4 November 1939, the SS ordered Adam Czerniaków, chairman of the Warsaw Judenrat, to summon all twenty-four members to an emergency meeting at 4.00 p.m. At the appointed time, sixteen or seventeen had arrived and were waiting apprehensively. At 4.15, eight armed Gestapo officers burst in. After a roll call, the commanding officer gave those present half an hour to assemble all twenty-four members and all twenty-four alternates. People randomly available in the building and passers-by were impressed to join the meeting. When the Gestapo officer returned, this time with some fifty men, he did not check credentials, but simply lined up the Judenrat members in one row and the putative 'alternates' in another. He then read a decree supposedly issued by the army Command that ordered all Jews of Warsaw to move within three days into an area that was to be designated as a Jewish ghetto. The twenty-four alternates were then removed as hostages with the warning that they would be shot if the Judenrat failed to comply with the order as specified.[19]

The Germans having left shortly before 7.00 p.m., the hour of curfew, the Judenrat decided to reconvene early next morning. Few slept that night and they returned the next morning tense and fatigued. Shmuel (Artur) Zygelboym, the representative of the socialist Jewish Labour Bund, held that the Judenrat had to refuse to carry out the order. How could they otherwise acquit themselves before the community and their children? But he received little support, for the majority feared that if they refused, the Germans would themselves forcibly carry out the ghettoization. What then of their women and children? A sense of their tragic destiny possessed them. Men wept.

Still, agreeing that they must try to halt the establishment of a ghetto, they sent a delegation to General Neumann, the top military officer in Warsaw. Neumann, astonished at this information, denied that he had issued any such order and asked the Judenrat to withhold action until he had investigated the matter. A few hours later, the Gestapo summoned Czerniaków. Dr Henryk Shoshkes, a member of the Judenrat, went along to give him moral support. The Gestapo officer was enraged because, by appealing to General Neumann, the Judenrat had circumvented his authority and disobeyed his warnings to deal only with the Gestapo. He savagely beat both men, while armed Gestapo men looked on. After Czerniaków apologized, the Gestapo officer, thus appeased, calmed down, even relenting sufficiently to negotiate minor expansions of the ghetto and concede a few streets to the Jews.

Meanwhile, though Warsaw had no newspapers and no radio,* news about the impending disaster swept through the Jewish community. Panic and terror seized the population. People with money and means started to look for apartments within the designated area. Thousands upon thousands of Jews besieged the offices of the kehilla, now Judenrat, pleading, weeping, clamouring for protection, for guidance, for instructions. Inside, the debate over the Judenrat's course of action continued. The Germans had not yet officially promulgated the order. On Monday, the day before the ghetto deadline, the crowds beleaguering the kehilla swelled to some 10,000. Zygelboym decided to address them. First, Shoshkes described the situation as it then stood. Zygelboym thereupon exhorted his listeners to courage and dignity, calling on them to remain in their homes, to

---

* The Germans confiscated all presses and radios; their possession was punishable by death.

resist until they were forcibly moved. No one, he said, should go voluntarily into a ghetto. Some in the crowd, probably a following of Bundists, responded warmly, but the record is silent about the reaction of the whole populace.

Immediately thereafter, the Judenrat reconvened its session, while some 400 young men, assembled as couriers to inform and instruct the Jewish population about the move into the ghetto, awaited orders. Zygelboym once again advocated resistance, but the majority held that failure to comply would bring both ghettoization and reprisals. Zygelboym then submitted his resignation. (Zygelboym's appeal for passive resistance spelled the end of his career in Warsaw. The Gestapo began to hunt for him. Two months later, he fled Poland.)

Suddenly the ghetto order was withdrawn. No one knows why – perhaps as the result of a confrontation between the German army and the SS. But the SS retreat was only *de jure*, because they had started actually to circumscribe a ghetto. As early as October barbed wire had enclosed the main streets of dense Jewish population. In December 1939 the Judenrat was compelled to set up large wooden signs, reading 'Danger: Epidemic Zone', at thirty-four street corners leading into the heart of the Jewish quarter. In the spring of 1940 these entries were walled up, restricting and hindering movement between the Jewish quarter and the rest of Warsaw. The world of the Warsaw Jews was becoming a prison.

Throughout Poland the Germans began to experiment with ghettos. The first try was in Piotrków in October 1939, but the plan was abandoned then and a ghetto was not established until as late as March 1942.[20] Detailed plans for a ghetto in Lodz were ready in December 1939, approved in February 1940, confirmed by Berlin in April; on 1 May 1940 the Lodz ghetto, with over 160,000 Jews, was sealed off. In Warsaw the ghetto walls began to be constructed in the summer of 1940, and by November 1940 nearly half a million Jews were enclosed and locked within its walls and guarded gates. Warsaw and Lodz, with the largest Jewish populations, were the most tightly, almost hermetically, sealed ghettos. Some ghettos had stone or brick walls; others had wooden fences with barbed wire entanglements. The Cracow ghetto was enclosed within walls in the form of Jewish tombstones, symbols of a terrifyingly literal character. Some ghettos, like Radom, Chełm, Kielce, with populations ranging from 15,000 to 25,000, were 'open' ghettos, with access to other parts of town.

All ghettos eventually became 'closed', rigidly circumscribed. On 10 November 1941 the governor for the district of Warsaw issued a proclamation instituting the death penalty for Jews illegally leaving the 'Jewish residential districts' and also for those aiding such Jews or harbouring them. Similar decrees were issued elsewhere in the Generalgouvernement. In the Eastern areas, ghettos were established soon after the first sweep of the Einsatzgruppen and were subject to the same regulations that obtained in the Generalgouvernement. In most communities there were actually two ghettos – the main ghetto and a so-called small or second ghetto, which served the Germans as a transit area.

The ghetto was an evil decree. Like sinners and criminals, Chaim Kaplan noted on 13 November 1940, 'we are segregated and separated from the world and the fullness thereof, driven out of the society of the human race'. Moving into the ghetto was everywhere a day of lamentation, a nightmare experience. Endless processions of weary men and women, babies in their arms, children at their sides, with bags, sacks, bedrolls on their backs and around their necks, the miserable remnants of their belongings loaded on carts, wheelbarrows or makeshift conveyances, left-overs of their past life, artifacts of a vanishing civilization, pushing, shoving, screaming, groaning, shuffled into the ghettos.

Jewish historian Emanuel Ringelblum observed in his diary on 8 November 1940: 'We are returning to the Middle Ages.'[21] But his history was imprecise. The medieval ghetto had originated as a strategy for Jewish existence and survival. During the Crusades Jews petitioned for separate quarters within whose walls they might better defend themselves. That ghetto met the need for common protection as well as for accessibility to Judaism's central institutions. Later, when the church advocated the ghetto as a means of separating Christians from Jews, the voluntary Jewish quarter was transformed into an obligatory ghetto, walled, its two gates guarded by Christian gatekeepers who locked the inhabitants in at night and during Christian festivals. Identifying badges were then imposed on the Jews and their pursuit of certain occupations and professions was restricted, but the medieval ghetto, however crowded and unsanitary, was not a prison. Every day Jews left the ghetto to conduct their business outside; every day Gentiles came into the ghetto to conduct their business. Social and economic intercourse between Jews and Gentiles was unobstructed.

The only institution comparable to the Nazi ghetto was the Nazi concentration camp, that 'concentrationary universe', where, in David Rousset's words, 'death lived among the concentrationees at every hour of their existence'.* Death bestrode the Nazi ghetto and was its true master, exercising its dominion through hunger, forced labour and disease.

In August 1943, Zelig Kalmanovich (1881–1944), scholar and writer, drafted a talk that was to have been delivered on 6 September, the second anniversary of the Vilna ghetto.[22] The agglomeration of people in the ghetto, he wrote, could not be classified as a human collective that generates a sense of cohesion among its members. No one cherishes the ghetto, no one wants it to continue to exist: 'On the contrary, the only desire that unites all the inhabitants of the ghetto from first to last is for the ghetto to disappear as rapidly as possible.' Only one social institution, Kalmanovich wrote, was to a degree comparable to the ghetto – the prison. (Dostoyevsky, in *The House of the Dead*, noted that besides the loss of freedom, besides the forced labour, there is another torture in prison life – 'compulsory life in common'.) Yet even that comparison, Kalmanovich noted, was inadequate, because the prisoners, no matter how much they detest the prison, know they are there as punishment for having deviated from society's norms. This is not the situation of the Jew

* Clear distinction must be made between the Nazi ghettos and the relocation centres established in the United States in 1942 to intern the Japanese Americans who were evacuated from their homes after Japan's attack on Pearl Harbor. The Japanese Americans were housed in prison-like barracks with primitive physical conditions, lacking the ordinary amenities of civilized life. Yet however severe the physical hardships and however humiliating the stigma of disloyalty, the internees never suffered hunger or epidemic disease, were not impressed into forced labour, were never tortured, nor were any ever deliberately killed by the authorities in sport or in earnest.

Even prisoner-of-war camps, with certain notable exceptions, fulfil their international legal obligations to feed their inmates and provide them with adequate medical care.

in the ghetto, who is incarcerated though innocent of any crime and, having broken no rules of human conduct, cannot fathom why he has been incarcerated.

The deprivation of freedom was universally felt. A thirteen-year-old boy in Vilna recorded in his diary the events of 6 September 1941, moving-day into the Vilna ghetto: 'I feel that I have been robbed, my freedom is being robbed from me, and my home, and the familiar Vilna streets I love so much.'[23]

The isolation was compounded by the removal of telephones from private homes. (Radios had long since been confiscated.) Mail within the Generalgouvernement and outside was erratic, undependable and censored (letters had to be written in either Polish or German). Once the Jews were inside the ghetto, the Judenrat had to assume postal functions. Telegrams and cables could be sent only through the Judenrat and required Gestapo approval. Parcels of food and clothing were more often than not confiscated by the Germans before they ever reached the ghetto post office.[24]

The ghetto's landscape sharpened the sense of isolation and imprisonment. The buildings huddled in a sombre grey mass. In Warsaw the park in the former Jewish area had been excised from the ghetto, and just a few trees remained. The only other greenery were flower-pots and boxes on windowsills and balconies. Only one tree grew in the Vilna ghetto. A popular song sentimentalized:

> For them the square and boulevards,
> For me a place of misery.[25]

The ghettos were located in the oldest, most run-down parts of town, sometimes in outlying areas that lacked the basic facilities of the city proper – paved streets, lighting, adequate sewage, sanitation facilities. Ghetto dwellings were the most dilapidated, often in ruined and devastated condition because of bombings and shellings, looting and wanton vandalism. The ghetto was congested, beggaring Baudelaire's vision of an ant-heap city. The air was foetid; the streets were filthy. A doctor in Vilna recorded some ghetto statistics: 'About 25,000 perons live in our ghetto, in 72 buildings on 5 street sections. Comes to $1\frac{1}{2}$–2 metres per person, narrow as the grave.'[26] People lived so crowded together that they could no longer observe the normal conventions of privacy and modesty. The sense of shame vanished. Congestion bred noise. From the Warsaw ghetto a girl wrote: 'My ears are filled with the deafening clamour of crowded streets and cries of people dying on the sidewalks. Even the quiet hours of the night are filled with the snoring and coughing of those who share the same apartment or, only too often, with the shots and screams coming from the streets!'[27]

In such congestion, keeping one's body and household clean posed Herculean tasks. In Vilna a young housewife, married to a doctor, vowed that she would never repeat 'the idiotic words' that to be clean one needed only to want to be clean.[28] If you have never been poor, she wrote, you don't know that to be clean you need soap and fuel to heat water. If you get the fuel, then you must decide whether to wash yourself or cook the family's main meal, for in the communal kitchen you can't have privacy for long. Moreover, after ten hours of hard work, you don't have energy to spare. As for keeping the room clean, if seven people sleep on the floor at night, and cook and eat there during the day, you have to keep scrubbing the floor to keep it half-way clean.

Overcrowding precipitated the breakdown of sanitation. Three and four families lived in space adequate for one. Toilets, running water, all plumbing and sewage facilities were taxed beyond capacity and beyond repair. The mephitic exhalations of latrines and broken toilets poisoned the air. In the long winters of bitter Polish cold, the water in the pipes froze.

Staying warm took priority over cleanliness. Fuel was as scarce as disinfectants, and dearer. In Warsaw coal was called 'black pearls'. In Lodz in January 1941 the Judenrat undertook a systematic programme of dismantling uninhabited places – stores, shops, fences – to provide wood for fuel. Flocks of freezing ghetto residents swarmed over the area, each with some small saw or hammer. They descended on a building, noted an observer, 'like crows on a cadaver, like jackals on a carcass. They demolished, they axed, they sawed, walls collapsed, beams flew, plaster buried people alive, but no one yielded his position.'[29] In the Lodz ghetto a man was arrested because he was found to have concealed from the official housing register the existence of another room in his apartment, which he had been dismantling for fuel.[30] In Warsaw, Ringelblum wrote in his diary in mid-November 1941, 'the most fearful sight is that of freezing children', standing 'dumbly weeping in the street with bare feet, bare knees and torn clothing'.

In December 1941 the Germans confiscated whatever furs could be taken from the Polish Jews. They took men's and women's fur coats and fur linings, neck pieces, fur collars, fur cuffs, skins and sheepskins.[31] The German army's troubles with the Red Army and the Russian winter made the cold in the ghetto tolerable. 'I'd rather have Hitler in my furs', went a ghetto joke, 'than for me to be in his skin.'

Hunger subjugated the ghetto. German policy was to starve the Jews and starvation stalked the great ghettos of the Generalgouvernement. Special instructions issued on 4 November 1941 by the German occupation authorities for feeding the civilian population in the Occupied Eastern Territories[32] prescribed that Jews were to receive half of the weekly maximum, in grammes, for a 'population which does no work worth mentioning', as follows:

Meat/meat products	none
Fat	70 [2½ oz.]
Bread	1,500 [3·3 lbs.]
Potatoes	2,000 [4·4 lbs.]

The average daily food ration provided about 1,100 calories per person – if it was all actually available. Even that wretched pittance of food was sometimes spoiled, stolen or sold on the black market.

Bread and potatoes were basic subsistence. The bread was, at best, rough and coarse, often stale, sometimes mouldy or compounded of foreign bodies, like sand. 'The bread is black and tastes like sawdust,' Mary Berg wrote in her diary on 28 February 1941.[33] Its price rose and fell, according to supply and demand. In pre-war days it cost just groszy. In 1940 the price of a kilogramme of bread hovered around 4 zlotys. In 1941 it fluctuated between 11 and 14·50 zlotys; by May 1942 it reached 15 zlotys.[34] Potatoes, Chaim Kaplan noted, are 'our whole life. When I am alone in my room for a few moments of quiet, the echo of that word continues in my ears. Even in my dreams it visits me.' Before the war, 100 kilogrammes of potatoes had cost 30 zlotys. On 27 November 1940 it had risen to 100 zlotys; a year later it reached 150 zlotys. In bad times, potato peelings substituted. In Lodz, in May 1942, a person with a medical certificate could get 3 free kilogrammes of potato peelings daily from the public-kitchen division of the food department. The queues grew so long that the demand outran the supply.[35]

Horsemeat was sometimes available and fish on occasion, as Mary Berg noted on 21 May 1941: 'Wagons full of stinking fish – tiny little fish in a state of decay.' Also cabbage, beets, carrots, kohlrabi, turnips, radishes, horseradishes and parsley could be had, usually in poor condition. In the big-city ghettos communal leaders instituted a campaign for home gardening under the auspices of Toporol (Towarzystwo Popierania Rolnictwa – Society for the Promotion of Agriculture), which gave courses in gardening and sold seeds. On 30 March 1942 Mary Berg observed that the seeds bought from Toporol were sprouting: 'The little green radish leaves were the first to appear in the black ground. We have also planted onions, carrots, turnips and other things.' In Warsaw, Toporol planted flowers and vegetables in some 200 yards. In the Lodz ghetto, small sections of a tenement yard were allocated as garden plots.

Hunger obsessed everyone. 'A *dybbuk* has entered my belly. My belly talks, shouts, even has complaints and drives me mad,' wrote Yehuda Elberg in his Warsaw ghetto diary.[36] 'The gnawing devils of hunger' of Conrad's *Heart of Darkness* attacked all ghetto residents, tormented their every waking moment. Everyone talked about food, at work, on the bread lines or in the soup kitchen, exchanging recipes for concoctions that could be prepared from one or another item on the ration. 'All became chemists, mixing this with that – just to turn out something.'[37] Turnips sliced, cooked, mashed, mixed with mashed potatoes, flour and seasoning became dumplings. Meat patties were made from ground horsemeat mixed with potatoes, rye flakes, a bit of flour and seasonings, and fried in a drop of oil. In Vilna a factory produced 'flour' and 'starch' from potato peels, syrup and sweets from potatoes.

The apportionment of one's bread ration required skill and art, for it had to last a week or ten days. How one managed depended not only on the tormenting pangs of hunger, but on strength of character, ability to postpone immediate gratification, and family responsibility. Elberg scored the loaf of his weekly ration to mark off each portion, for otherwise, 'with the glutton that my belly is, the whole bread could disappear in a moment'. Mary Berg told about an eleven-year-old girl who posed as a model in her art class, for whom the art students collected some small pieces of bread. She ate only a tiny piece, wrapping the rest in a bit of newspaper: 'This will be for my little brother.'

Hunger not only affected the belly, but injured the mind. People became coarsened, their manners less fastidious, their tastes less squeamish, their disgust for certain foods overcome by the intensity of their hunger. Hunger drove some to rapacity. To walk in the ghetto with an uncovered loaf of bread was neither prudent nor safe, for in a wink the bread could be snatched out of hand and whisked away.

Beggars lined the streets of the large ghettos, ubiquitous and commonplace, their doleful songs and plaintive laments filling the air. Children predominated among them, but also whole families begged, huddled together in rags, moaning and wailing. Some beggars in their desperation ignored the curfew and went out at night, crying for bread. 'In the surrounding silence of night', Ringelblum observed, 'the cries of the hungry beggar children are terribly insistent.'

Offsetting the German policy of starving the Jews far exceeded the capacity of any welfare organization on the spot or even in wealthy America. Reporting on 24 September 1940 on the hunger and disease in the ghetto of Lodz, a JDC official declared that it was imperative to set up soup kitchens to provide 100,000 warm midday meals, to prevent a complete castastrophe. The cost, estimated at 8 pfennig per person, would come to 8,000 Reichsmarks per day, or 240,000 Reichsmarks per month, which he said was then equivalent to $100,000 at the official rate of exchange. In the Warsaw ghetto a communal leader put the minimum budgetary needs for one person to survive at 5 zlotys per day, which, for a population of 400,000, would amount to 60 million zlotys per month. He did not count on charity, but calculated that to provide that amount of money the ghetto would require a labour force of some 300,000 persons earning 8 zlotys per day – a utopian vision under those conditions.[38]

Only the illegal importation of food into the ghettos kept most Jews from dying of hunger. To be sure, the Germans prohibited the sale or gift of any type of food to Jews from outside the ghettos, such sale or gift punishable by heavy fines and impressment into forced-labour brigades, but the ghetto police often showed leniency in permitting contraband food to come in. If they were strict, or if German police were at hand, bribery helped induce leniency The workers in labour brigades employed outside the ghetto used to bring in food, obtained by bartering clothing and household goods. In partly open ghettos peasants sometimes sold food at exorbitant prices. Children were the most numerous class of smugglers, small, spry and, if caught, an object of pity for the policeman. A popular ghetto song eulogized the child smugglers:

> Over the wall, through holes, and past the guard,
> Through the wires, ruins, and fences,
> Plucky, hungry, and determined,
> I sneak through, dart like a cat.[39]

Smuggling was also big business, especially in the Warsaw ghetto, with half a million mouths to feed. Thousands of Jews made a living from smuggling, from the big operators who took big risks for big profits, down to the little peddler whose small supplies came from middlemen. Whole cows were smuggled into the Jewish cemetery adjoining the Catholic cemetery and later transported into the ghetto in hearses that had come from the ghetto with corpses for burial. Buildings bordering the ghetto, with entrances on the 'Aryan' side and windows opening on the ghetto, became smugglers' nerve centres, operational headquarters for hoisting and lowering; small cranes, makeshift lifts, troughs and pipes delivered grain, milk, cereal, vegetables and even luxury products.[40]

But for the smugglers, the Germans would have succeeded in starving the ghetto to death. The ghetto's ingenuity and daring, the toughness of its brawling wagoners staved off massive hunger deaths. The greatest tribute to the smuggler appeared in a preface to a medical study on hunger in the Warsaw ghetto, prepared under the direction of Dr Israel Milejkowski, who headed the Judenrat's Department of Hospitals. Writing in October 1942, when some 300,000 Warsaw Jews had already been deported to Treblinka, Milejkowski declared that because the smuggler had penetrated the ghetto walls, the ghetto's isolation had not succeeded in destroying the Jews. The smuggler played a paradoxical role in the ghetto: though smuggling demoralized the ghetto, the smuggler, 'with his blood and sweat, gave us the possibility of existence and work in the ghetto'.[41]

The smugglers became the *arrivistes* of the ghettos, as the old social structure collapsed. Rubinstein, the Warsaw ghetto's madman, incessantly shouted, 'All are equal,' but he was wrong. The ghetto was a great leveller, but it also created a new class of the well-to-do, whose means were acquired by illegal or unscrupulous means. (Many arose out of the pre-war criminal ranks.) Smugglers, wheeler-dealers, swindlers, blackmailers, informers, rascals, bribe-takers and knaves thrived in the cankered milieu of the ghetto, battening on its misery. Every ghetto had underworld operators who preyed on the populace, blackmailing because of furs withheld, secret radios, contraband goods, evasion of labour duty, forbidden activities. Their financial rewards were great and their risks of punishment few. Some strutted because of their riches or authority borrowed from the Gestapo, yet they were despised and ostracized by the Jewish community. A few even tried to buy status through charity and good deeds for the poor and pious.

This new class – smugglers, underworld, *nouveaux riches* – became the clientele for dozens of cafés, restaurants and nightclubs that mushroomed in the ghetto. (Providentially, these gave a livelihood to actors, singers, musicians and entertainers.) A shrill mood of *khaye sho* (the fleeting moment) and *carpe diem* spread in these circles, even reaching some segments of the respectable population, whose response to the deprivations of their ghetto prison was the pursuit of pleasure.[42] They passed their time dining, drinking, dancing. Yet even so stern a moralist as Chaim Kaplan defended frivolity. 'It is almost a *mitzvah* to dance,' he wrote on 20 February 1941. 'Every dance is a protest against our oppressors.'

In normal societies class and status derive from wealth, occupation, education and family. In the ghetto, class was determined by occupation and personal property, both of which could buy food and provide security. (Status remained relatively stable: rabbis, scholars, doctors, political and communal leaders retained prestige and respect despite the precipitous decline in their material fortune.) Excluding illegal or criminal occupations, the top-ranking occupational categories in terms of food and security were officials and employees of the Judenräte, members of the Jewish police, foremen of labour brigades working outside the ghetto, and skilled workers. These people received larger food rations than the general public and higher wages; they were more secure from seizure for forced labour and for a while were exempt from deportation.

Personal property – furniture, household goods, clothing, cash, jewellery and other valuables – determined class. Wealth from real property, industrial investments and bank holdings had been wiped out. The more personal property one had, the greater opportunities for sale or barter – to buy food or guarantee protection. The declassed well-to-do habituated the used-merchandise street markets near the entrances to the ghetto, selling their belongings. The sale of a dress could provide a kilo of bread; a carpet, a month's ration. During summer 1941, several thousand non-Jews daily used to come to buy in the street markets of the Warsaw ghetto; total sales were estimated at nearly a million zlotys daily.[43]

Some fifty thousand Central European Jews – from Germany, Austria and Czechoslovakia – who were deported to ghettos in the Wartherland, the Generalgouvernement and the Ostland (in especially large numbers to Lodz and Riga) added to the social differentiation. They arrived with good clothes and much personal property. In Lodz they cornered the black-market supply of bread, thus exacerbating their already tense relations in the ghetto with the resident Polish Jews, who also depended on that bread supply to stave off hunger.[44]

Hunger killed, but first it wrought disabling change – mental, psychological and physical. Loss of weight and the disappearance of subcutaneous fat aged and withered its victims. Hunger destroyed the normal rhythm of existence, affected the physical capacity to work and the mental ability to think. Nutritional deficiencies caused anemia, suppressed the menses. Fatigue and dizziness, apathy and depression were part of the general sense of malaise. Nausea, vomiting and diarrhoea were the daily complaints of the hungry.

From September to December 1939, four Jews in Warsaw died of hunger; in 1940, ninety-one died; and in 1941, nearly 11,000.[45] Yet if hunger itself was not the big killer, it weakened and debilitated its victims so as to make them fall prey to countless other diseases.

> When we had nothing to eat,
> They gave us a turnip, they gave us a beet.
> Here, have some grub, have some fleas,
> Have some typhus, die of disease.

Breeding on human misery, typhus is associated with times of war, famine and disaster, when people are crowded together in abnormal conditions of filth, cold and hunger. The range of fatality varies from 5 to 25 per cent. In the Warsaw ghetto the death toll from typhus was estimated at 15 per cent, even though the Germans prevented proper treatment – basically, maintenance of nutrition – and refused to allow the necessary preventive measures to be taken and enforced. The relatively moderate death rate testifies to the physical, indeed moral, stamina of the ghetto inhabitants. In the Warsaw ghetto alone, epidemic typhus was believed to have affected between 100,000 and 150,000 persons, though the official figures were barely over 15,000. The spread of disease was concealed from the Germans. Hospital cases of typhus were recorded as 'elevated fever' or pneumonia. Mainly, the stricken were treated in their homes in a massive clandestine operation, covering up the presence of the disease from German inspection teams who periodically threatened to seal off the affected areas.[46]

The most prevalent ghetto disease, typhus was nevertheless not the most deadly. According to data from the Lodz ghetto for 1940, 1941 and 1942, heart disease alone accounted for about 30 per cent of all deaths, suggesting that the tensions and hardships of life in a Nazi ghetto were more deadly than typhus. Dysentery, tuberculosis, hunger and diseases of the digestive tract ranked next. Typhus as a cause of death ranked eleventh or twelfth in a field of thirteen.[47]

Infants, the elderly and, above all, the refugees succumbed with least resistance to hunger and disease. Forlorn and friendless in strange big cities, the refugees were thrust upon the inadequate mercies of communities already overburdened with their own wants. Warsaw in 1941 sheltered some 130,000 refugees, nearly one third of the ghetto population. Some lived on the streets, their very appearance shocking the passers-by.[48]

Most refugees were housed in unused school buildings or other facilities never intended to be dormitories. The sheer numbers in these placements broke down the plumbing systems and, consequently, the possibilities of personal hygiene and public sanitation. In January 1942 a welfare report summarized the state of the refugees in the Warsaw ghetto: 'Hunger, sickness, and want are their constant companions, and death is the only visitor in their homes.'[49] The statistics of refugee mortality were staggering. They died in their bunks, expiring in nakedness and friendlessness. They died begging in the streets, their last entreaties frozen on their lips, their bodies lining the streets of the Warsaw ghetto. The tricycle-propelled hearses of the undertakers could not keep up with the accumulation of corpses. Covered with newspapers, stiff in the snow, they awaited Mottel Pinkert, the ghetto's chief undertaker, the true 'king of corpses'.

'More and more often at social gatherings we talk about life after death,' wrote Halina Szwambaum from the Warsaw ghetto in June 1942. It was necessary to be prepared, she felt, 'for the day when we shall have to admit that we have been defeated and must be gathered to Abraham's bosom'.

In the ghettos death had become a ubiquitous intimate. Its ubiquity and its intimacy heightened the value of life. The preservation of life stood at the very centre of Jewish tradition: 'Ye shall therefore keep My statutes and Mine ordinances, which if a man do, he shall live by them.' The text was interpreted to mean: '*Live* by them, and not die by them.' During the Hadrianic persecutions, when Jewish martyrdom reached such high proportions as to imperil the survival of the Jews in Palestine, the preservation of life was deemed so important that the rabbis at Lydda ruled that only with regard to three fundamental laws – those prohibiting idolatry, unchastity and murder – should death be chosen over transgression.

The teachings of the religious tradition were incorporated in the folk wisdom: 'A Jew lives with hope.' 'While there's life, there's hope.' 'Even when the slaughtering knife is at your throat, don't lose hope.' 'As long as you draw breath, don't lose hope,' or 'don't think of the grave.' The religious teachings and the folk wisdom, permeating every ghetto in Eastern Europe, supplied the antidote to depression and despair. Everywhere the phrases 'hold on' and 'hold out' epitomized the value of life and survival. In Vilna a popular ghetto song exhorted:

> Moshe, hold on,
> Keep hold of yourself,
> Remember we must get out . . .
>
> Moshe, hold on; hold on, Moshe –
> It isn't very long,
> The hour soon will toll . . .[50]

The ration card represented access to life. The Warsaw ghetto idiot used to admonish passers-by: 'Don't give up your ration card.' 'Don't register your ration card with Pinkert.' Beggars used to sing a ditty:

> I'm not giving up my ration card,
> Better times are coming.[51]

The *rebbe* of Żelechów, counselling his followers to go into hiding, was alleged to have said: 'Every Jew who survives openly sanctifies God.' Each Jewish survivor, he declared, is a hero resisting the Nazis because he refuses to extinguish his precious life.[52] Rabbi Isaac Nissenbaum in the Warsaw ghetto was reported to have said:

> Now is the time for the sanctification of life [*kiddush ha-hayim*] and not for the Sanctification of the Name [*kiddush ha-shem*] through death. Once when our enemies demanded our soul, the Jew martyred his body for *kiddush ha-shem*. Today when the enemy demands the body, it is the Jew's obligation to defend himself, to preserve his life.[53]

The only gladdening aspect of the ghetto, one communal leader noted, was that 'Jews cling so tenaciously to life, fight so stubbornly for life'. As evidence he adduced 'the trifling number of suicides in the ghetto', which he regarded as a 'ray of hope that the Jewish masses in the ghetto will come through everything, survive this hell and live to see better times'.[54] In Lodz the daily statistics of death indicated a higher suicide rate among the assimilated German and Czech Jews than among the Polish Jews. The head of the Warsaw Judenrat's Statistical Office reported, with some astonishment, that the number of suicides in 1940–42 was just 65 per cent of the number in 1939.[55] Ringelblum attributed the low suicide rate to the exhortations against despair by communal leaders. Shakhne Zagan, leader of the Left Labour Zionists, Ringelblum's own party, for example, appropriated the motto that the Bratslaver *hasidim* in the ghetto had scrawled on the walls of their prayer house: 'For the sake of Heaven, Jews, don't despair!'[56]

That summons to optimism, grounded in Judaism's eternal messianic hope, was shared by believer and non-believer. Salvation would come from one source or another. In the Chełm ghetto the Jews sang a Yiddish song, patterned on the Psalms, praying for salvation:

> *O Look from heaven and behold,**
> Look down from the skies and see!
> *For we have become as a derision,*
> *A derision among the nations . . .*
>
> Therefore we plead with You ever:
> Now help us, Guardian of Israel,
> Now take notice of our tears,
> For still do we cry aloud, 'Hear O Israel.'
> O, take notice, Guardian of this nation.
> Show all the peoples that You are our God,
> We have indeed none other, just You alone,
> Whose Name is One.[57]

In the Lodz ghetto, a *hasid* counselled against despair 'because salvation from God appears in an instant'. In the ghetto of Stolin, the *rebbe* exhorted his followers: 'Don't despair, rally yourselves, fellow Jews, and trust in God.'[58]

In Bialystok, however, hope of deliverance was pinned on the Red Army:

> Alas, how bitter are the times,
> But deliverance is on its way;
> It's not so far away.
> The Red Army will come to free us,
> It's not so far away.[59]

The 'Partisans' Hymn', which first became popular in the Vilna ghetto, epitomized the ultimate secular charge against despair: '*Zog nit keyn mol as du geyst dem letstn veg*' – 'Never say you walk the final road.'

Religious people turned to superstition and fantasy to buttress their hopes. They searched for concealed meanings in words and texts, looking for indications of the war's end and the Messiah's coming.

---

*Italicized lines were in the original biblical Hebrew.

The numerical value of the letters for the year 1942, for instance, equalled that for the word 'Sabbath', and thus an omen for the good. A new body of hasidic tales was fashioned in the style of the traditional legends, foretelling deliverance. One story told in the Warsaw ghetto recounted the adventures of two early hasidic *rebbes*, Rabbi Elimelekh (d. 1786) and his brother, Rabbi Zusya (d. 1800). They wanted to return a favour to a man who had done them a good turn in their wanderings. His request was that they tell him when the Messiah would come. Both brothers pondered a while and then replied that great wars would be waged in 1915 and 1942, in both of which the Jews would suffer greatly. In one of these wars, the *rebbes* prophesied, the Jews would be delivered.[60]

Political prophecy was a more substantial ghetto staple. In Warsaw, new words were put to an old tune:

> Listen here, Haman you,
> Jews will live to settle scores.
> You will get your comeuppance.
> Jews have lived and will endure.
> But Haman, you will go to hell.[61]

In Vilna, a popular song urged:

> Let's be joyous and tell our jokes,
> We'll hold a wake when Hitler chokes.[62]

Political jokes reflected the indomitability of the ghetto spirit and became the weapon of the powerless. Humour transformed the reality of power relations, its fantasy permitting the Jew to triumph over his persecutor. The joke afforded relief from the oppression of inferiority and from the tension of anxiety. Late in 1941, when the German army began to suffer reverses on the Russian front, anti-German jokes enlivened the ghettos:

'What's the difference between the sun and Hitler?'
'The sun goes down in the West and Hitler in the East.'

'What's new?'
'Didn't you hear? They are confiscating chairs from the Jews.'
'What happened?'
'Hitler got tired of standing outside Moscow and Leningrad.'

Hitler appealed to the smugglers in the Warsaw ghetto to help him get half a million German soldiers into Moscow. They agreed, but in their own special way – piece by piece, heads, hands, feet, each section separately, little by little.

When furs were confiscated from the Jews in the winter of 1941–2, jokes and jingles coursed through the ghetto:

> Against the Moscow frost and Moscow cold
> He's trying to save himself with Jewish furs and gold.

After the United States entered the war, a rhyming jingle showed a new constellation of anti-Hitler allies:

> Hitler won't be able to cope
> With the English fleet
> And with the Russian sleet,
> With American dollars
> And Jewish smugglers.[63]

Like the inhabitants of Camus's plague city, the ghetto Jews realized that they had no choice but to come to terms with the days ahead in their prison house. That realization was no mere passive reconciliation with their lot. On the contrary, they enlisted their whole historic experience in trying to transform their environment. The commandment to preserve life had generated a strategy of accommodation, a tactic of adaptability, which centuries of powerlessness under oppressors had fashioned into a serviceable tradition. 'Be pliable like a reed, not rigid like a cedar,' the Talmud says. Prohibited from pursuing certain trades and occupations, Jews learned to survive in the interstices of the forbidden. Like grass growing in the clefts of rock, Jews found means of livelihood in the crevices of the economy, in marginal areas overlooked or neglected by hostile authorities. In the ghettos that tradition of accommodation stood them in good stead. Necessity bred innovativeness. There, within limits far more stringent than any past tyrant had ever imposed, the Jews exercised their ingenuity, manufacturing goods for sale, marketing them inside the ghetto, smuggling them outside, producing and preparing food, making something out of nothing.

Powerlessness had also taught Jews other strategies of survival. Lacking weapons and military organization, they learned to use tricks of intelligence and manipulation to prevail against their presecutors. They learned not only to invent, but to circumvent; not only to obey, but to evade; not only to submit, but to outwit. Their tradition of defiance was devious rather than direct, employing nerve instead of force. When the Germans demanded electrical appliances or furs, Jews in a silent boycott destroyed what they had or gave them to Polish acquaintances. Ghetto Jews evaded forced labour, in many ghettos even setting up cooperative security systems within buildings to warn against imminent seizures. *En masse*, Jews disobeyed German decrees. In every ghetto hundreds were constantly being arrested for one transgression or another – violating curfew, not wearing arm bands, smuggling, leaving the ghetto illegally.[64] Not even the severe penalties discouraged them.

The solidarity of the family provided the biological basis for the preservation of life and for Jewish continuity. Parental respect, filial obedience, obligations of kinship, sanctity of the home – these were the elements in family life that gave security and stability to the individual. In times of stress, the family became the Jewish stronghold, the source of comfort and moral strength. In the ghettos family relationships deepened and broadened. Familial responsibility extended beyond the nuclear family to embrace grandparents, aunts and uncles, married brothers and sisters. Families that had been separated became reunited, preferring to share crowded ghetto lodgings with each other rather than with strangers. They shared not only housing and food, but hopes and plans. The young and able-bodied worked for the old and feeble. When the father was seized for forced labour, the onus of providing for the family fell on the mother. Parents and children divided responsibilities for maintaining the household, apportioning tasks as the hardships of the occasion demanded, no longer in accordance with fixed familial roles. When mothers worked, older children assumed household chores, queuing up for rations, cooking, cleaning. Younger children were sometimes taken along to workshops, where mothers could watch out for them and provide them with a bowlful of hot soup at midday. In the poorest families, with fewest resources, the children themselves undertook the perilous task of smuggling to feed the household.[65]

Some families, to be sure, became demoralized. Hunger drove some children or parents to steal food from each other. Some couples quarrelled over property and belongings, their disputes coming under the jurisdiction of ghetto courts. But these were the exceptions. Though tensions and anxieties multiplied, devotion and mutual responsibility within the family kept pace. The stabilizing effect of the family showed up in the statistics. Divorce ceased, but all ghettos recorded a rash of marriages.[66] Marriages were sometimes the hurried decisions of young people who felt they had little time left; in some cases parents withdrew earlier objections to the match; sometimes marriages were conveniences for sharing cramped ghetto space or gaining the protection of labour cards. Widows and widowers married more frequently in the ghettos than in pre-war days. The ghetto heightened emotional needs. At the very time when hunger and disease decreased sexual potency and desire, tenderness and affection supplanted passion.

On seeing two pregnant women in the Warsaw ghetto, an unknown diarist noted: 'If in today's dark and pitiless times a Jewish woman can gather enough courage to bring a new Jewish being into the world and rear him, this is great heroism and daring ... At least symbolically these nameless Jewish heroines do not allow the total extinction of the Jews and of Jewry.'[67]

The Jewish community was, of course, the extended Jewish family. In the ghettos most Jews felt a strong sense of Jewish identity, of belonging, of readiness to share Jewish fate. The proverb 'What will befall all Jews, will befall each Jew' assumed new relevance. In the Lodz ghetto, German Jewish children presented a Hanukkah programme in their school auditorium:

Hunger, cold and conflicts were forgotten. Shoemakers and tailors, physicians, lawyers and pharmacists, all at once, we were one big family. That could not have happened in Berlin ... but here, behind the barbed wire, something existed that united us all – our Jewishness. When they sang together, they forgot their suffering and misery; they were still alive and in song they praised God, who many times before had performed miracles. When they sang about the little lamp whose oil for one day lasted eight, the singers regained their courage and hope.[68]

At a *seder* in the Vilna ghetto, Kalmanovich recounted an anecdote. A child in a ghetto school learned, for the first time, the story of Jacob and Esau. He suddenly called out: 'Teacher, we are the descendants of Jacob and they the descendants of Esau. Isn't that so? It's good that way. For I really want to belong to Jacob and not to Esau.' Reflecting on the anecdote and its lesson for Jewish identity, Kalmanovich concluded that people, in the freedom of their imagination, could choose their own identity. That child chose freely to be a Jew.[69]

Even in the harsh realities of ghetto life, most Jews accepted their fate as Jews. The possibility of hiding out among non-Jews created problems rather than solutions. Living on false Polish identity papers outside the ghetto, wrote a woman in Vilna,

. . . seems to me like treason against my own people. Here, in the worst, most awful moments, I am after all among my own. Never have I felt myself so strongly a Jew, never was I so united with my brothers as now. Intellectually I admit that hiding out among 'Aryans' is perhaps the best, perhaps the only solution. Emotionally, I consider it desertion.[70]

At bottom, Jews shared a deep faith in their ultimate survival and in the preservation of the Jewish people. Early in the war Chaim Kaplan observed: 'Our existence as a people will not be destroyed. Individuals will be destroyed, but the Jewish community will live on.'

11 The Official Community: From Kehilla to Judenrat

Upon entering the towns and cities of Poland in 1939 and of Russian-held territory in 1941, the German invaders ordered Jewish communal leaders to establish Jewish councils, *Judenräte*, in accordance with Heydrich's instructions of 21 September 1939.[1] Everywhere these Judenräte were formed out of the remnants of the pre-war *kehillot*, the legally incorporated religious communities. These, like all political and communal structures, had been disrupted and shattered by the invasion, the bombardments and shellings, the mass flights and evacuations and, above all, by German terror. Only fragments remained of the institutions that had once regulated the country's political and social life.

In Warsaw, where the population held out longest against the Germans, a Jewish citizens' committee to replace the defunct kehilla was formed on 11 September to obtain help for the Jews from the make-shift municipality. The five-man committee, composed of Zionists and heads of the merchants' and artisans' associations, was legitimated by the city's president who, on 23 September, appointed as the committee's head Adam Czerniaków, a former vice-chairman of the pre-war government-appointed kehilla.[2] (In December 1936 the Polish government dissolved the democratically elected Warsaw kehilla for acting 'beyond its competence' – that is, for opposing the government's anti-Jewish policies – and appointed a commissioner and an advisory council, which all parties except the Aguda boycotted. Only a few of the originally elected councilmen continued to serve.)

When the Russians occupied eastern Poland and the Baltic countries, they arrested and subsequently murdered many Jewish communal leaders whom they regarded as anti-Soviet. When those territories were incorporated into the USSR, the Jewish community as a corporate entity ceased to exist. Jewish political parties went underground while Jewish service organizations – schools, hospitals, orphanages, libraries – were taken over and operated by the government.

The Judenräte emerged from the diminished and deficient pool of men who had once led and administered the now lapsed communal institutions. Frank's decree of 28 November 1939, ordering the establishment of Judenräte, provided that communities with up to 10,000 inhabitants were to have a twelve-member council, larger communities a twenty-four-member council. In practice, however, the SS validated councils of varying size. To run the thousand or so Judenräte formed in the Generalgouvernement and the Eastern occupied territories, no fewer than 10,000 men, and probably many more, had to be co-opted. Most had served in pre-war times as board or staff members of local kehillot, social-welfare agencies, professional associations, schools, cultural and religious organizations. The majority had been active in the various Jewish parties, some having beeen elected to kehillot or city councils on their party lists.

Many men active in communal service had reached their positions through the conventional avenues of access in the traditional community: family prestige, wealth, Jewish learning, and dedication to the community through financial generosity and good works. In addition, during the inter-war period, new channels for communal activity had opened up by way of the political parties and professionalization of the social services. As a group, these communal activists were overwhelmingly middle class and professional, but included a growing segment of working-class people whom the political parties had elevated. Whether they had held paid or honorary positions, they were men of decency and integrity, imbued with the tradition of service to the community. 'Do not withdraw from the community,' the Talmud teaches. To be sure, some were tempted by the rewards of prestige and honour, but most regarded communal service as an obligation and responsibility. As a class, they were designated by the Yiddish term '*klal-tuers*' (literally, 'community practitioners'). Today, somewhat indiscriminately, we call them all communal leaders. The problems to which they had addressed themselves in the past were mainly philanthropic and administrative. Few were leaders in the sense that they commanded a voluntary fellowship, a status achieved in the traditional community only by charismatic rabbis or illustrious Talmudic scholars. In the modern East European Jewish community such leadership was exercised only by the authoritative heads of the Jewish parties, a handful of men authentically dynamic and creative.

The German summons to form a Judenrat aroused deep misgivings and created imponderable dilemmas. Though the Germans declared that the Judenrat would have to carry out their orders, most Jews – leaders and masses alike – believed that the Judenrat would operate as a kehilla under a new set of ground rules. Many believed that the Jewish community required some kind of intermediary body to represent its interests *vis-à-vis* the occupying authorities, to plead and negotiate on its behalf. (In somewhat the same way, the German Jews had been motivated to create the Reichsvertretung in 1933.) Without such an institution to serve as spokesman for them, they felt that the Jews would fare worse under direct German control or – an equally dismal prospect – under the governance of Poles, Balts or Ukrainians. When danger threatened, a Jewish body could – like the advocate of the Jews in pre-modern times, the *shtadlan* – intercede on their behalf, exercising tried and true methods to ward off that danger.

Other communal leaders were less confident, fearing that the Judenrat would have neither autonomy nor options, that it would become merely an instrument of German oppression. People were troubled, too, even in those early days of the occupation, that as members of Judenräte, they would become demoralized by the terror of their taskmasters. In the first days and weeks of German occupation, all had experienced that terror and witnessed the atrocities perpetrated by the Germans.[3]

Those who agreed to serve on the Judenräte did so with qualms and forebodings. Most who agreed to serve were prompted by Talmudical precepts, by *noblesse oblige*, a sense of responsibility that they could not or would not repudiate. In nearly every community, the German order to form a Judenrat was discussed and debated by the former communal leaders. In Lublin, in autumn 1939, kehilla members were outspoken about their apprehension towards dealing with the Germans. Having been elected to serve the kehilla in peacetime, some held that they had no mandate to serve in such uncertain times. Others argued that failure to accept their responsibility would expose the Jews to total lawlessness. If we reject our responsibility, they asked, whom will the Germans appoint in our stead? Finally, the argument of obligation to the Jewish community prevailed and the decision was taken to participate.[4]

In Vilna, a consultation of fifty-seven communal leaders was called on 4 July 1941, the very day the Germans ordered the Judenrat to be formed. At the meeting, chaired by the aged Dr Gershon Gershuni, one of Vilna's most prestigious communal leaders, the atmosphere was heavy with dread. Gershuni was categorical: a Judenrat had to be formed, and whoever was selected had to accept the responsibility. He included himself, weeping at his words, and many wept with him. There were few volunteers, and it was decided that those chosen to serve must accept, considering themselves martyrs.[5]

In a small town near Vilna, the rabbi assembled the Jews in the prayer house to select members for a Judenrat in compliance with the German order. Since no one was willing to assume the responsibility, the candidates were chosen by lot.[6]

Every community had to make its decision swiftly, under German pressure. There was neither time nor opportunity for outside consultation, since communication and transportation were completely disrupted. Local branches of nationwide parties or organizations could not apply to headquarters for guidance and had to determine their own policy. Eventually a general pattern emerged, though it showed some local variation. Members of the middle-class parties – General Zionists, Mizrachi, Revisionists and Aguda – and the several professional associations of merchants and artisans assented to participation in the Judenräte as board or staff members, though their parties did not actually sanction such participation. In Warsaw, as Chaim Kaplan noted, divided views prevailed among his Zionist friends.

The left-wing parties, Right and Left Labour Zionists and Bundists, generally opposed participation on political/ideological grounds. Distrusting the centrist and rightist organizations, convinced that these would not protect the interests of Jewish workers and of the Jewish poor, the leftists preferred to stand aside. Furthermore, they wanted to keep their political hands clean from the taint of dealings with the Germans. There were occasional exceptions. In Piotrków, for example, where Bundists had held leading positions in the pre-war kehilla, they continued in the early occupation period to hold those posts in the Judenrat.[7]

The reluctance on the part of communal leaders to participate in the

Judenrat was universal. In some instances, when no candidates could be prevailed upon to accept, the Germans themselves made random appointments. In the absence of legitimate communal leaders, a few unscrupulous individuals who had never served the community volunteered their services to the Germans.[8]

The two ambiguous cases involve Mordecai Chaim Rumkowski of Lodz and Moses Merin of Sosnowiec. Both later became strutting dictators in their wretched ghetto realms, megalomaniacs in the grip of rescue fantasies. Rumkowski, a childless widower and director of an orphanage, had been elected to the Lodz kehilla on the Zionist ticket. In 1937, when the Polish government took over the kehilla and put it under the control of the Aguda, the other parties instructed their members to resign. But Rumkowski, hungry for the prestige of office, stubbornly retained his seat, despite expulsion from his party. When the Germans burst into the kehilla offices in October 1939 and asked for the *Älteste*, Rumkowski, then sixty-three years old, responded, thinking they meant 'oldest', not 'Eldest'. Another story has it that on learning that the Germans were trying to locate kehilla officers, Rumkowski voluntarily reported and offered his services.[9] Neither version can be substantiated.

When the Germans entered Sosnowiec in 1939, they arrested a sizeable group of Jews, humiliating and beating them. In response to a German officer's inquiry about who among them were kehilla officials, Merin came forward, though the kehilla chairman, also present, did not. Merin, then in his late thirties, had been elected on the Revisionist ticket to the kehilla.[10] Whether he volunteered simply to escape further punishment, whether he calculated on improving his own situation or whether he already dreamed of 'power' no one knows.

The apprehensions about participating in the Judenräte were fulfilled to an extent never foreseen by even the most pessimistic of communal leaders. From the start, every order the Germans issued was enforced with relentless terror. Within days, or at the most, weeks, hundreds of Judenrat members were taken hostage, arrested, dispatched to labour camps, shot or hanged. Hundreds of others needed no further inducement to flee for their lives.

In Będzin, the Germans levied a contribution on the Judenrat of 5 kilogrammes of gold and 20 kilogrammes of silver, taking 120 hostages as surety. Until the Judenrat delivered the contribution, the hostages were beaten and tortured. Thereafter, the Judenrat members fled, and no one in Będzin could be induced to hold office.[11] In Lwów, soon after taking office, the chairman of the Judenrat was arrested and subsequently killed for refusing to deliver several thousand Jews, ostensibly for forced labour.

In Częstochowa, within a short time, the Judenrat, originally composed mostly of former kehilla members, lost ten of them, including three rabbis, for sabotaging German orders. They were replaced by persons who had no previous record of communal service.[12] In October 1939 Rumkowski, officially named the Eldest of the Jews in Lodz, invited thirty leading members of various Jewish communal, philanthropic and political organizations to form a consultative council. On 7 November the Gestapo arrested most of them, killing them then or later in concentration camps in Germany. A second advisory council was formed in February 1940, consisting of third-raters with no communal experience or responsibility.[13]

In Vilna, on 26 July 1941, the Germans demanded a contribution of 5 million rubles, 2 million to be paid the following morning. Otherwise Judenrat members would be shot. The news spread swiftly throughout town, and the Jews spontaneously began to raise the money. Men gave watches, women rings. By morning, 667,000 rubles, half a kilogramme of gold and some 200 watches had been collected, far short of the German quota. The Germans kept their word: two Judenrat members were shot. On 2 September, a day of mass seizures, arrests and killings, SS men entered the Judenrat offices and arrested sixteen of the remaining twenty-two members. They were never seen again. That Judenrat was dissolved and a new one reconstituted, consisting of the six survivors plus new members chosen by the Germans.[14]

In Warsaw, within three months of the formation of the Judenrat, seven of its original twenty-four members fled abroad. On 26 January 1940 Czerniaków recorded that he had been summoned to the German police and ordered to pay 100,000 zlotys the next day. Otherwise 100 Jews would be shot. 'Confronted with all this, I turnéd to the SS asking that I be relieved of my office, for in these abnormal circumstances I cannot lead the kehilla. They said, in response, that they would not recommend such a step.' In a few cases Judenrat members resigned without penalty, but more often the Gestapo demanded custody of such persons.[15]

German terror coerced Jewish compliance. Council members who resisted German orders, even by temporization, were removed by terror, in a continuing process of deadly attrition. Their successors, alien to the tradition of Jewish communal service, learned from that experience the wisdom of compliance. Even where original members of original Judenräte continued to hold office and where their own persons were not threatened with death, the duress that the Germans exercised over the entire Jewish population was sufficient to ensure the Judenrat's submission to German orders.

From its inception the Judenrat was looked upon as a reincarnation of the kehilla. Czerniaków's first draft of 13 October 1939 for organizing the Warsaw Judenrat was just a rehash of conventional kehilla departments: chancellery, welfare, rabbinate, education, cemetery, tax department, accounting, vital statistics. The kehilla's primary obligation had been to maintain the community's religious institutions (the rabbinate, *kashrut* and ritual slaughter, ritual baths, prayer houses). Social welfare concerns – care of the poor, the orphaned, the aged – came next, and then support of Jewish schools, maintenance of a cemetery and providing for Jewish burial, and administration of the Jewish hospital.[16]

In performing these functions, the kehilla had operated as a *Gemeinschaft* institution, serving the personal, religious and communal needs of the solidary Jewish group, enhancing its cohesion, strengthening its morale, securing its survival. But the kehilla was an anomalous institution. Throughout its history in Tsarist Russia, it served also as an instrument of the state, obligated to carry out the régime's policies within the Jewish community, even though these policies were frequently oppressive and specifically anti-Jewish: excessive and punitive taxation, an iniquitous system of military conscription intended to effect conversion, harsh efforts to compel 'modernization' of Judaism by forbidding traditional garb, and interference with traditional modes of Jewish education.[17] Traces of the kehilla's duality persisted in independent Poland, where the semi-fascist government meddled intrusively in kehilla affairs. Under German occupation that duality became even more distorted in the Judenrat, as its primary *Gemeinschaft* functions were curtailed.

The Judenrat underwent an even more significant metamorphosis.

With ghettoization and the isolation of the Jews from the rest of society, the Judenrat had to assume functions normally associated with a municipality. New departments were created to provide housing, water and utilities, police, fire protection, a judiciary system of sorts, food production and distribution, fuel distribution, transportation, postal services, public health and sanitation, factory production and employment. The Judenrat was thus transformed into a formal *Gesellschaft* institution, providing general services on an impersonal basis. Its *Gemeinschaft* functions continued to shrink, with the notable exception of social-welfare services.

The dichotomization of Judenrat functions and roles evolved under contradictory pressures of German demands on the one hand, communal interests on the other. Agents of the oppressors, the Judenräte nevertheless regarded themselves as comforters of the oppressed. In their brief, wretched existence, they tried to reconcile their irreconcilable tasks.

To begin with, each Judenrat tried to make some order out of the chaos engulfing its community. The first task was to feed the hungry and heal the sick. At least half the income of the Judenräte, often much more, was spent on welfare and medical needs. In every community public kitchens were organized under Judenrat auspices. Some ghettos set up supplementary food-ration depots for children; others had 'tea houses', which provided hot boiled water by the glass, pitcher or barrel. The Jundenräte maintained hospitals, clinics, first-aid stations, dental clinics, pharmacies, inoculation centres, public baths, barber shops, disinfection stations and public-health inspection teams. They supported homes for the orphans and the aged, shelters for the homeless, and they gave cash assistance to the refugees. They sent supplementary food rations, clothing and fuel to the labour camps where the Jews of their community were dragooned. For children they provided day-care homes, residential centres, remedial services.[18]

The needs were immense, their resources circumscribed. Judenrat officials, pleading as advocates of the Jews, submitted memoranda to the German authorities, supplicated, humbled themselves. They appealed for more food to feed their people, more space for the ghetto, more medicines and medical facilities. They petitioned for decrease in the forced-labour contingents, for release of hostages, for news about prisoners held incommunicado. They pleaded for a halt to harassments and violence, for redress of grievances. Hazarding S S reprisals, they exploited every available channel of authority – German military and civilian, Polish, Balt, Ukrainian – in the hope of extracting supplies or concessions, playing off one bureaucracy against another in the confused and conflicting jurisdictions.

Occasionally the petitions succeeded. Sometimes the Germans yielded a street or two to enlarge the ghetto. Sometimes they lowered their original assessments against the ghetto, as in Bialystok, settling for 6 kilogrammes of gold instead of 25 and for half of their demand for 5 million roubles.[19] But usually they remained intractable. On 26 January 1940 Czerniaków was summoned by Orpo, the German regular police, and told that because a Volksdeutsch had been beaten, the Judenrat had to pay 100,000 zlotys the next day. Otherwise 100 Jews would be shot. Czerniaków appealed to the Gestapo to be released from the payment. They refused. He then tried to obtain a concession by asking to pay in instalments. Again they refused. To salvage something, he asked to be relieved of supplying workers for snow removal. They remained implacable.

Flattery was applied to soften the Germans, but gifts and money were considered more effective. Bribery had long been a way of life in Eastern Europe, going back to Tsarist times, when it was built into the structure of the state bureaucracy. Among Jews bribery was used as leverage to obtain relief from persecution. An official who did not take a bribe used to be called a *roshe*, a villain. Ecclesiastes' cynicism that 'money answereth all things' became the hope for many Judenräte. Some Judenräte maintained standing stocks of furniture, tableware, jewellery and textiles to be available for emergencies. Bribes sometimes accomplished Jewish objectives: prisoners were sometimes released, hostages sometimes ransomed, forced labourers sometimes returned, harsh punishment sometimes mitigated, even death sentences sometimes commuted. But more often than not the insatiable maw of the German occupation swallowed the proffered gifts with few perceptible benefits to the Jewish population.[20]

In Warsaw, shortly after the occupation, random abductions by the Germans of large numbers of Jews for forced labour made venturing out on the street a perilous gamble. The fear of being dragooned aggravated the numerous other hardships and uncertainties of daily life. In an attempt to rule out at least one factor contributing to the chaos,

Artur Zygelboym, the most radical member of Warsaw's first Judenrat, proposed that the Judenrat organize a labour pool from which a specific number of workers requisitioned by the Germans could be supplied. This sort of rational regulation of forced-labour recruitment would, it was anticipated, enable the Jewish populace to move about more freely, assured that they would not be waylaid and kidnapped if they went out for bread or to work. The Gestapo agreed to the proposal and asked for a daily contingent of 2,000 workers. But the seizures did not cease. In response to the Judenrat's protests, the Gestapo replied that other German agencies were culpable. Nevertheless, the Gestapo now insisted on a labour quota as its prerogative.[21]

As the agency through which the Germans obtained forced labourers, every Judenrat set up a labour registry. To avoid a stint of forced labour, people paid to purchase substitutes. In time, procedures for buying exemptions became bureaucratized. The Judenrat used to collect fixed fees for exemptions for given time periods; that income was used partly to pay token wages to the forced labourers (the Germans paid nothing) and partly to replenish the Judenrat's ravaged treasury. In Lublin, for instance, in May 1940, nearly 3,000 people paid sums ranging from 15 to over 50 zlotys for labour substitutes. In the first year of the occupation, the Lublin Judenrat collected almost half a million zlotys from these payments.[22]

The burden of forced labour consequently was borne disproportionately by the poor, though they benefited from the exemption fees, which were used to finance welfare programmes. When the Jewish populace began to resist the labour draft, having learned the cost of forced labour to health and even life, the Judenrat began to seize people forcibly. The situation had a historical precedent. In the days of Tsar Nicholas I, the Jewish community was required to supply very large numbers of Jewish youngsters as recruits for a twenty-five-year term in the Russian army. To make up the required quota, the kehilla, through its agents, used to kidnap orphans or children of the poor. That parallel with Tsarist times was not lost on the ghetto population.[23] On 26 April 1941 Ringelblum commented that 'the melancholy tradition of kidnapping' that the Judenrat had revived was 'like a projection of a picture out of the tragic past'. More and more Jews who could not pay for exemptions refused to report for forced-labour duty. In Częstochowa, for example, when the Germans demanded a large contingent of labourers from the Judenrat, the Jewish police had to round up people forcibly. They managed to get eighty-two persons, detaining them overnight in a prayer house, but at night all but six succeeded in escaping.[24]

To provide the labour contingents demanded by the Germans, the Judenrat became increasingly coercive, for unless workers were forthcoming, the Judenrat and often the entire ghetto were threatened with worse consequences. In Bialystok, for instance, in September 1942, when the Judenrat failed to produce 200 women workers requisitioned by the German Labour Office, Sipo (the German security police) took over, ordering all the ghetto unemployed to assemble in one spot the next morning. The fear that they would be deported or murdered prompted compliance, and 200 workers came forward. Supplying forced labourers quickly ceased to be a means for the rational regulation of a labour pool as first conceived by Zygelboym, but became only another means of appeasing the Germans. In the Judenrat's view, then, Jews who evaded forced-labour duty, who hid from the police summoning them, were not merely transgressing the rules that governed the ghetto, they were jeopardizing what little tranquillity may have prevailed in the ghetto at that time and perhaps even imperilling the ghetto's existence. Thus the Jewish populace and the Judenrat, each acting out of discordant interests and considerations, found themselves on a strategical collision course. The consensus that exists in a normal society concerning desirable and undesirable goals and standards had evaporated.

The most successful strategy the Judenräte devised was to use, or try to use, Jewish productivity to ensure Jewish existence. The entire economic structure that had supported the Jewish population had collapsed. Jewish stores and businesses, workshops and factories, goods and supplies had been damaged in the bombings, then looted and robbed, and finally expropriated. Ghettoization was the final blow, cutting off most economic ties with the non-Jewish population. The idea of ghetto industry, under the aegis of the Judenrat, as a means of restoring economic viability was first advanced by Rumkowski in Lodz. On 5 April 1940, shortly before the Lodz ghetto was sealed off, Rumkowski made a bid to the top German civil administrator: 'I have forty thousand working hands in the ghetto.

This is my gold mine.'[25] He offered to produce finished goods for the Germans, if they would provide the raw materials. His strategy was twofold. First, his plan would provide work and income for the ghetto population and thus bring about a measure of economic self-sufficiency. Second, he hoped to make the Jews invaluable to the occupiers through the rational exploitation of their labour, resourcefulness and enterprise. A similar strategy was independently conceived in 1941 by Ephraim Barash, head of the Judenrat in the Bialystok ghetto.

Elsewhere, the idea of ghetto industry originated out of the needs of the ghetto itself and of its inhabitants. Cooperatives in traditional Jewish trades were set up by Judenräte in Lwów, Cracow, Radom, Siedlce, for example, often in conjunction with remnant trade-union groups or with ORT, the agency for vocational training and rehabilitation: in men's and women's clothing, shoes, hats, carpentry, brushes, bakeries. (Bread baking became a key industry in all ghettos.) The *hasidim* of Aleksandrów who had made their way to Warsaw brought their expertness in hosiery manufacture and in 1941, with the help of the Judenrat and of ORT, established a hosiery plant in Warsaw.[26] Scrap collection and production of articles from scrap furnished work for many Warsaw shops. These undertakings, selling inside and outside the ghetto, legally and illegally, provided a bare livelihood for thousands of ghetto inhabitants.[27] Some Judenräte, Vilna most notably, operated workshops to produce for the ghetto itself (food, vitamins, detergents, chemicals) and to provide it with needed services (laundry, disinfection, repair).

Bialystok, with about 40,000 Jews, had over twenty operating factories that produced a wide variety of finished goods, mostly for German military consumption. Lodz, with over 160,000 Jews, had at its peak 117 factories, workshops and warehouses producing for the Germans. In 1941 the industrial production of the Lodz ghetto brought in over 16 million Reichsmarks, paid out by the Germans mostly for slave wages, the balance as payment for the goods at non-competitive rates. The value of the Warsaw ghetto's official export of industrial production during the first six months of 1942 was nearly 50 million zlotys. The illegal export, finished goods smuggled outside the ghetto and sold clandestinely, was estimated to be far higher.[28]

Ghetto industry brought some money to the ghetto and hence to the Judenräte. Their basic income was derived from taxation, and they taxed whatever they could: wages and earnings, even living quarters. There was a community tax, regular and emergency, a ration-card tax, a hospital tax, a sanitation tax, a labour-registry tax, a welfare tax, a cemetery tax. Special taxes were sometimes levied on the well-to-do, especially when the Judenräte required large sums to meet the extortionate German demands. Assessments were made by Judenrat committees, often in co-operation with representatives of professional groups and of tenement committees.[29]

Taxation, like forced labour, put the ghetto population in direct conflict with the Judenrat, for people resisted paying taxes. The Judenrat, dependent on tax moneys to support basic welfare services or to ransom the ghetto from some German threat, was compelled to enforce collection of taxes and even to apply sanctions against tax delinquents. The Jewish police, officially designated Ordnungsdienst (order service), was the Judenrat's instrument of enforcement. As a ghetto institution, the uniformed Jewish police exemplified the dynamics of degeneration that the Germans set in motion.

The Jewish police was an institution improvised by the Germans when they locked the Jews into ghettos. Initially police functions were to regulate the flow of pedestrian and vehicular traffic inside the ghettos and to maintain law and order. Like its parent organization, the Judenrat, the Jewish police came to serve dual and incompatible purposes: to protect the Jewish community while it was required to enforce German orders. Unlike the men who constituted the original Judenräte, most police recruits were not motivated by a sense of communal responsibility. Those who enrolled did so of their own volition and for their own advantage. The requirements for the police force were few: young, able-bodied men were wanted, preferably with military training. Few recruits had a record of communal service, in part because of their relative youthfulness. The only Jewish political party from which a sizable proportion of police was drawn was the Zionist Revisionists, perhaps because they put a high value on military training and militarism. For the most part, the left-wing parties interdicted their members from joining the police.

Some police chiefs and men were outsiders to the communities that they served, refugees or evacuees who found favour with the Germans, by whom they were appointed. Some were apostates. In Warsaw, the first police chief was Józef Andrzej Szeryński, formerly a colonel in the Polish police, a Catholic convert, reputedly an anti-Semite. He undoubtedly recruited police from his circle of apostate friends. (The Warsaw ghetto had a large population of converts to Catholicism, who were regarded as Jews under German racial law. They worshipped in two Catholic churches within ghetto limits.) On 18 March 1941 Ringelblum noted that a hundred apostates served in the police in prominent positions. One of them, he added, was heard in church to shout 'Down with the Jews'.

To be sure, many ghettos had police chiefs and men who were kind-hearted and community-minded. In Vilna and Kovno, as well as many small towns, the records indicate that such men played a substantial role, at least for a time, in the police. But they, too, like the Judenrat officials, were coerced by German terror into compliance. Charged with enforcing the isolation of the ghetto, the Jewish police at ghetto gates had to check people entering and leaving, examine their identity papers and permits, and search their persons and belongings for contraband. They were supervised by Polish guards and armed German police to ensure that they performed their tasks correctly and with appropriate strictness. Once a Jewish woman brought into the Warsaw ghetto a sack of potatoes, which a German guard on duty confiscated. According to Ringelblum's account, on 17 April 1941 a Jewish policeman asked the German to return the potatoes to the poor woman. To punish him for his audacity, the German guard knocked the policeman down, bayoneted him and then shot him.

Another means the Germans used to control the Jewish police was by directly operating a collateral Jewish police apparatus in some large communities, which by-passed the Judenrat and offered more material inducement than did the Ordnungsdienst. The Germans encouraged members of the pre-war Jewish underworld to set up informer and police agencies to do the dirtier work the Jewish police cavilled at. Such groups existed in Lodz, Kovno, Lublin and Warsaw. The largest operated in Warsaw, with a formidable German name: Überwachungsstelle zur Bekämpfung des Schleichenhandels und der Preiswucherei im jüdischen Wohnbezirk (Control office to Combat Black-Marketing and Profiteering in the Jewish Residential District). Familiarly nicknamed by the Jews 'the Thirteenth', from its location at 13 Leszno Street, it was headed by Abraham Ganzweich, a Polish Jew who had lived in Vienna before the war and may have then become entangled with the Gestapo. An independent police force of about 300, elaborately uniformed, the Thirteenth served primarily as an intelligence agency for the Gestapo, though it also engaged in social-welfare activities to win public legitimacy. Formally dissolved by the Germans in the spring of 1942, about 200 of its staff were absorbed – at German insistence – by the Jewish police.[30]

Before long, German terror set in motion a process of negative selection among the Jewish police, eliminating the soft and irreproachable, leaving those who, with a corroded instinct for self-preservation, were or had become callous and ruthless, tenacious in their will to perform the duties imposed on them.[31] Those duties – ferreting out forced-labour dodgers, calling up recalcitrant taxpayers, seizing smugglers and confiscating their illicit potatoes or onions – stiffened the resistance of the ghetto inhabitants, intent on their own self-preservation. That resistance spurred the police to greater efforts to perform their duty and to intemperate use of billy clubs, bludgeons or rubber hoses. Having lost legitimacy in the eyes of the ghetto, the Jewish police could assert their authority only through force. Instead of being the protectors of the ghetto populace, they had become their assailants and adversaries.

The transformation from kehilla to Judenrat, from *Gemeinschaft* to *Gesellschaft* institution, demanded skills, expertness, and experience previously not in plentiful supply in the East European Jewish community. Jews in Poland had, for the most part, been excluded from the civil-service apparatus and therefore lacked experience in municipal administration. To be sure, the centuries-long experience of administering kehillot stood the Jews in good stead, but it could not satisfy the new needs. Consequently, many outsiders came to fill important posts in the Judenräte. In Warsaw key positions were given to apostates because many had had distinguished careers in public service. German Jews filled some slots in the Lodz Judenrat.

In Vilna, which had belonged to Poland before 1939 but had then become the capital of Soviet Lithuania, remaining nominally Lithuanian under the Germans, Lithuanian-speaking Jews from Kovno who knew their way around the Lithuanian bureaucracy took over responsible posts in the Judenrat. The most dramatic instance is that of Jacob Gens, a Revisionist from Kovno, formerly an officer in the Lithuanian army. He was first appointed police chief and then, with German support, usurped authority in the ghetto before the end of 1941. On 10 July 1942 the SS appointed Gens officially chief of the ghetto, dissolving the Judenrat for incompetence and dilatoriness.[32] The presence of outsiders, aliens by choice or geography, further eroded the Judenrat's *Gemeinschaft* character and reinforced the growing estrangement between it and the populace.

As the scope of their functions increased, the Judenräte enlarged their staffs to hypertrophy. Lodz maintained the largest apparatus, with nearly 13,000 people, about one eighth of the ghetto population in August 1942. At its peak, the Warsaw Judenrat employed 6,000 persons, in contrast to the pre-war kehilla's staff of 530. The Vilna Judenrat as of September 1942 employed over 1,500 people, then nearly 15 per cent of its decimated population. In Lwów the Judenrat staff numbered about 4,000, nearly 5 per cent of the Jewish population. The Bialystok Judenrat had 2,200 persons on its payroll, three times as many as necessary, by admission of Barash himself.[33] The very massiveness of the bureaucracy began to affect the spirit and character of the institution. The communal motivations and social impulses of the original Judenrat boards were often submerged in the administration of complex tasks performed by an unwieldy bureaucracy, in part inexperienced, in part alienated, all terrorized.

The Judenräte grew to behemoth proportions not only because their expanded and additional functions demanded more personnel, but also because the pressures of nepotism, favouritism and patronage were irresistible. Employment in the Judenräte entailed advantages: higher pay, supplementary food rations, official exemption from forced-labour duty, more security than was available to the general population. Naturally, Judenrat officials used their positions to place their relatives on staff and payroll. Family connections became a route to security, a literal lifeline. Influence, knowing the right people, pull – or as it was referred to all through Europe, protection, *protektsye* – was the only way to get a good berth. 'Vitamin P' was the most sought-after commodity to improve oneself. A person assigned to heavy-duty forced labour would habitually complain that he lacked Vitamin P.[34]

The use of influence was rampant everywhere, even in ghettos with a highly respected leadership. A member of the Kovno Judenrat once addressed a memorandum to its chairman, Dr Elhanon Elkes, deploring widespread 'protectionism'. Elkes, in complete agreement, promptly issued an order to Judenrat personnel, forbidding the resort to nepotism and favouritism and setting up a control commission to enforce that order. Nonetheless, that evening Dr Elkes himself wrote a letter of recommendation for a distant relative, 'a poor and helpless woman', who had applied to him for help.[35]

Favouritism in the Judenräte was widespread, but not always unethical or venal. (Barash in Bialystok, at a meeting on 11 October 1942, warned against favouritism, admitting that even he was guilty of practising it.) Most Judenräte became sanctuaries for the community's intellectuals, its scholars, rabbis, writers, its creative stock. The Records and Archives Department of Warsaw's Judenrat was a refuge for Polish Jewry's outstanding historian, Meir Bałaban. Also Dr Edmund Stein, Semitist and rector of the prestigious Institute for Judaistic Studies, was employed by the Warsaw Judenrat. In Lodz, historians, scholars and writers were sheltered in the Judenrat's Statistical Office and Archives. In Vilna Gens readily agreed to a proposal made by communal leaders that Vilna's surviving intellectuals be put on the Judenrat's staff to ensure them some livelihood and security. In Częstochowa teachers exclusively constituted the Judenrat's street-cleaning brigade, work considered unexacting. Performed in the morning hours, this assignment gave teachers free afternoons to give private lessons, in the absence of official schools.[36]

The Judenrat bureaucracy had at its disposal a substantial part of the ghetto's resources: the distribution of food, the allocation of living quarters, the assignment of forced-labour duty. In a society that was all penalty and no amenity, abuses and malpractice in performing these functions multiplied. Hunger broke down traditional canons of morality; distress eroded ethical standards. People capitalized on the advantages of their positions. Those with access to the ghetto's food supply – warehouse workers, distributors, retailers, bakers, public-kitchen employees – took what could be taken. The stealing ranged from pilfering a loaf of bread or a sack of potatoes to large-scale thievery for profitable re-sale on the black market. To the hungry populace it always seemed that corrupt politicians and demoralized bureaucrats were stealing food from the mouths of starving children, a persistent conviction in all cultures in times of disaster, but not always demonstrable. Yet, even in Lodz, where the hunger was great and the stealing prodigious, the proper distribution of the full food supply would not have appreciably alleviated the ghetto's famine. The tragic dilemma, as Ringelblum noted on 30 May 1942, was that the Germans simply did not allocate enough food to keep everyone alive.

Judenrat employees encountered another temptation: bribery. Any Judenrat employee who could provide an amenity – extra food or better housing – or an exemption from special taxes or forced-labour service was likely to be offered a bribe. Many refused to take bribes, yet even those who accepted were not always rascals, but good family men for whom the bribe might make the difference between their family's bare subsistence in the comfortless ghetto world and sufficiency.

The most corruptible and corrupted of the ghetto functionaries were the police. As in all societies, the police became corrupted by the populace. A bribe might win exemption from forced labour; a small present given *sub rosa* to a policeman might obviate paying a large sum in taxes to the Judenrat. The right kind of bribe could guarantee the success of a smuggling operation or release a member of the family from ghetto detention. Perhaps the police who took bribes and gave favours in return were more humane than the incorruptible ones, who carried out orders punctiliously. Still, the police thrived on the hardships of the ghetto, each new adversity providing new opportunities for bribes and payoffs.

Every Judenrat tried to counteract these demoralizing and disintegrative tendencies within its staff. Disciplinary or 'control' commissions were established that attempted to establish codes and standards for proper behaviour. In Warsaw, according to Ringelblum, 700 policemen out of a force of 1,700 faced disciplinary trials. In Bialystok, Barash carried out a massive purge of the police in June 1942, because, as he put it, they promoted lawlessness rather than security in the ghetto.[37]

In Lublin, in the summer of 1942, the Judenrat adopted a set of by-laws governing newly created control and disciplinary commissions. The Control Commission was to supervise the Judenrat's functionaries. The Disciplinary Commission was to investigate complaints of violations of office, to fix penalties, and to allow for appeals. The Lublin approach was rigidly legalistic:

§1. Members of the Judenrat, employees of the Judenrat, including members of the Ordnungsdienst, who fail to live up to their positions through any act, evasion or negligence, and also by their conduct at work or away from it, demean the authority, seriousness or trust of their position, shall be held responsible and incur disciplinary action.

§3b. A felony in the line of duty is a violation of official duty that brings injury both to the interests of the service and to the interests of the individual, or to the interests and reputation of the Council or its institutions. A felony in the line of duty includes a number of misdemeanours or frequent recurrence of misdemeanours in the line of duty that give rise to especially grave consequences.[38]

From the beginning, the Jews regarded the Judenrat as a legitimate successor to the kehilla, and in according it their social validation, treated it with the same mixture of grudging consent and sardonic contempt that had been reserved for the traditional kehilla. As it became increasingly apparent that the Germans permitted the Judenräte neither latitude nor autonomy, the Jews relinquished their consent and sanction. Though they could exercise no political action to remove the Judenräte, the populace's disapproval was seen in the general reluctance to obey Judenrat orders, in the evasion of obligations imposed by the Judenrat and the expressions of contempt for the Judenrat heard in all ghettos from rich and poor, from intellectuals and masses.

The most common epithet everywhere for the Judenrat was *Judenverrat*, 'betrayal of the Jews', 'Jewish fraud' for 'Jewish board'. A popular couplet ran through the Warsaw ghetto:

> When the chairmen is a nitwit,
> The whole kehilla is a shit.[39]

A jingle heard all over Warsaw, which even Czerniaków himself knew, went:

Prexy Czerniaków, the fat pot,
Gets his chicken soup hot.
How so? Just dough!
Money is a dandy thing.

Madam Czerniaków is sure to get her hair done
She takes her tea with sugar and bun.
How so? Just dough!
Money is a dandy thing.

A riddle: 'What is the difference between Czerniaków and Rumkowski?' The answer: 'No difference. Both stink.'

Chaim Kaplan, on 27 October 1940, characterized Czerniaków as a 'nincompoop among nincompoops' and his advisers as 'musclemen'. On 23 May 1942 Kaplan was more caustic: 'After the Nazi leech comes the Judenrat leech . . . There is no end to the tales of its mischief and abominations.'

'The Judenrat lived loathsomely and still more loathsomely did it die,' noted Kruk in his diary on 22 December 1941, commemorating the time when Gens had gained control over the ghetto administration. Soon after, the Vilna ghetto Jews used to refer derisively to Gens as 'King Jacob the First'. A JDC report from Lodz on 24 September 1940 declared that the tragic situation of the Jews was paradoxically, aggravated by 'a certain Mr Rumkowski', who was 'despised and hated by every inhabitant of the ghetto'.

Mordecai Tenenbaum, commandant of the Jewish resistance organization in Bialystok, once noted that Barash was 'a decent man'. He went on to say: 'That is a great compliment for a chairman of a Judenrat. I know three such decent men: Engineer Czerniaków, Dr Brawer [of Grodno], and Barash is the third.'[40]

Eventually the authority of the Judenrat came to rest exclusively on the naked coercive power of the Germans, the only wielders of power in the ghettos. The authority that the Germans delegated to the Judenräte was often divided among board members; complete responsibility for the operations of each department was lodged with its head. The Judenrat chairman generally co-ordinated the work of the departments, settling jurisdictional disputes and arbitrating personal and departmental conflicts. Such decentralized operations characterized the Judenräte in Warsaw, Lublin, Cracow, Lwów and

Kovno, to name some of the largest cities. Interpersonal relations of the board members varied. In Kovno, for instance, most Judenrat officers coexisted in mutual respect. On the Lublin Judenrat, in contrast, quarrels, rivalries, distrust and tension marked the relationships. In none of these Judenräte did any dynamic or creative leaders emerge.

Four Judenräte were marked by strong, even dictatorial, leadership, with authority centralized in the hands of one man – Rumkowski in Lodz, Merin in Sosnowiec and Upper East Silesia, Gens in Vilna and Barash in Bialystok. They were the policy and decision makers in their ghettos, the strategical thinkers on the ghetto's possibilities for survival. All, without doubt, by holding these posts of leadership, satisfied personal ambitions. Barash alone, by virtue of his past experience as head of the pre-war Bialystok community, elicited wide respect from his colleagues and from the Jewish community at large.* He did not manifest the craving for office and the trappings of office that characterized Rumkowski, Merin and Gens; nor did he have their crude megalomania.[41]

Rumkowski, the most original of the four, ruled Lodz by force of personality, tenacity of purpose, organizational intelligence and political shrewdness, even outwitting the SS in its attempt to displace him. His presence and authority were felt everywhere in the ghetto. Every initiative on the part of political parties or individuals that he approved of, he appropriated and made officially his own. Whatever he disapproved of withered and died. He was mocked and despised, yet there was no one in all Lodz to unseat him.

No legitimate social order functioned in the ghettos of Eastern Europe. As the Judenräte, increasingly coerced by German terror, ceased to be regarded as authentic spokesmen for the Jews in the ghettos, countervailing organizations came into being to challenge the Judenräte's authority. Some eventually formed an alternative community, others a counter-community.

---

*Barash and Bialystok Jewry for a brief while profited from the fact that Bialystok was the capital of the General Commissariat Bialystok, a separate administrative entity under Erich Koch, Gauleiter for East Prussia, who actively disliked Himmler and his racial resettlement policies.

Like the kehilla before it, the Judenrat was only one institution in the complex web of associations that knit the East European Jews together. Despite the attempts by the Germans to impose a state of barbarism upon them, the Jews persisted in maintaining or in re-creating their organized society and their culture. The milieu in which the Germans confined them was that state of war or condition of insecurity which Hobbes epitomized: 'No arts; no letters; no society; and which is worst of all, continual fear, and danger of violent death; and the life of man, solitary, poor, nasty, brutish and short.' Nevertheless, in nearly all the ghettos, the Jews conspired against the Germans to provide themselves with arts, letters and society – above all, with the protection of community against man's solitariness and brutishness. Never was human life suspended.

The criss-crossing mesh of institutions enveloped the ghetto. Some like the *bes-medresh* (prayer house) and the *heder* (religious school), were rooted in traditional society. Others, like social-welfare organizations, cultural associations and ideological movements, grew out of modern, urban Jewish life. Unlike the Judenrat and the kehilla before it, these multitudinous organizations were autonomous and voluntary, existing on the basis of the free and uncoerced will of their constituents.

In the ghetto, just as in pre-war normal society, these institutions composed four functional groupings: social welfare/communal; religious/congregational; educational/cultural; political/defence. In pre-war Jewish society, the functional religious and political groupings had served as parallel or countervailing channels of authority to the kehilla. In ghetto society, the welfare, religious, educational and cultural groupings emerged as the Judenrat's rivals or underground components. Some of the political groupings eventually formed an adversary community.

Besides their functional purposes, the voluntary Jewish organizations fulfilled more fundamental, if less tangible, Jewish needs, creating community, enhancing group solidarity and social cohesion, reinforcing belongingness and self-esteem. Membership in an organization extended the periphery of family and kinship circles and entitled one to whatever resources the group could muster and whatever security it could provide. Above all, the organization upheld morale and combated the depression and despair to which solitary individuals succumbed when confronted with the insurmountable difficulties of ghetto existence.

The dislocations of war gave rise to a new network of autonomous Jewish self-help associations. They grew out of Warsaw's civil-defence tenement committees, Obrona Przeciwlotnicza (OPL; anti-aircraft defence), whose original functions during the German invasion were to oversee black-out practices, provide civilian shelter, organize fire protection and fire-fighting and render first aid. In the larger tenements in Jewish neighbourhoods, improvised health, welfare and food-distribution centres were organized for the bombed-out and the refugees. Hundreds of meals, prepared by housewives in the building, were provided out of funds collected from tenants. At the start, the tenement committees operated independently, but they soon came under the aegis of a Coordinating Commission, formed on 14 September 1939, on the initiative of the JDC, with the participation of the leading Jewish welfare organizations of pre-war Poland – TOZ (Towarzystwo Ochrony Zdrowia – Society for the Preservation of Health), and CENTOS (Centrala Towarzystwa Opieki nad Sierotami – National Society for the Care of Orphans). The Co-ordinating Commission became affiliated with the Polish city-wide self-help committee.[1]

These self-help units continued their activities after the fall of Warsaw and into the German occupation. In January 1940, when the Germans ordered the Polish group to sever its relations with the Co-ordinating Commission, the Jewish group became an independent body, calling itself Żydowska Samopomoc Społeczna (ŻSS; Jewish Communal Self-Help).[2] Accredited under the Generalgouvernement's department of Interior, in the division of Bevölkerungswesen und Fürsorge, with by-laws approved on 29 May 1940, the ŻSS – and parallel Polish and Ukrainian agencies – operated throughout the Generalgouvernement in all fields of social welfare, authorized to unite existing welfare agencies and to make contact, through the German Red Cross, with foreign organizations providing money and supplies.

All through German-occupied Poland ŻSS branches came into being, many already operating spontaneously as skeletons of the pre-war service agencies. Within a year, the ŻSS had 118 branches, thirty-eight in large cities. By the beginning of 1942, it had 412 branches. ŻSS personnel was recruited from the recognized social-service agencies and other communal institutions. Its founder and head was Michal Weichert (1890–1967), a man of many talents, trained in law, the theatre and literature. A teacher in a Jewish gymnasium in Warsaw, he served as legal adviser to the JDC and ORT, and enjoyed a career as journalist, actor and director before the war. In mid-1942 the Germans dissolved the ŻSS, but later reconstituted it as the Jüdische Unterstützungsstelle (JUS; Jewish Relief Office). Technically still under the interior Department's jurisdiction, JUS in fact fell under SS control. The Jewish underground thereafter regarded JUS in the same light as the Judenräte. (After the war, Weichert was tried in Poland on charges of collaboration, but was exonerated. He spent the last years of his life in Israel.)

ŻSS's basic strategy was to rescue what could be rescued. Once, early on, the German officer who headed the Bevölkerungswesen und Fürsorge division asked Weichert: 'Don't you realize that you are on a sinking ship?'

'I know,' Weichert replied, 'but I think that one must rescue people even from a sinking ship.'

Since the ŻSS was accredited to the German civil administration, it had access to supplementary supplies of food, clothing and medicine that were not available to the Judenräte. Quantities were small, to be sure, but in the economy of scarcity prevailing in the ghettos, even small amounts extracted from the Germans were beyond price. The very fact that the ŻSS received supplies from the Germans heightened the contrast in the Jewish public mind between the Judenrat and the ŻSS. As one ŻSS official put it, it appeared that the Judenräte took from the Jews to give to the Germans, whereas the ŻSS took from the Germans to give to the Jews.[3]

ŻSS funding came largely from the JDC, which spent about $1 million a year in Poland until America's entry into the war on 7 December 1941 halted the legal transfer of funds. Some moneys were obtained by voluntary donations, fund-raising drives, theatre and concert benefits. (In one community, the local ŻSS raised a substantial sum in October 1941 by selling the opportunity to bless the *etrog* in the celebration of Succot.) ŻSS funding came also from the Judenräte, some of which subcontracted part or most of their welfare programmes to the ŻSS.

The ŻSS network for the most part engaged in supplementary relief, providing supplies and assistance in operating public-kitchen and supplementary food stations for children and the sick. In Warsaw alone, there were 145 public kitchens and forty-five children's kitchens, serving 135,000 meals daily. ŻSS branches distributed clothing, gave cash relief. Obtaining and dispensing pharmaceutical supplies were two of its major achievements. The ŻSS focused much effort on child-care activities. About one fourth of the 1·6 million Jews in the Generalgouvernement were children, on whom, as one CENTOS official put it, 'all our hopes rest, our future, our survival'. In Warsaw alone, 75 per cent of the 100,000 children under fifteen were estimated to require some form of welfare.[4] According to a ŻSS report for July–October 1941, there were then in the Generalgouvernement twenty-six residential centres with 2,734 children; sixty-one children's corners with 9,565 children; 122 public kitchens and nutrition centres serving over 47,000 children; two infant-care institutions with 1,725 babies; and fifteen day-care centres for 6,413 children. Of the thirty orphanages and boarding institutions that CENTOS operated under the ŻSS, the most renowned was Warsaw's Dom Sierot (Orphans Home), under the direction of Dr Janusz Korczak, pediatrician and pedagogue extraordinary.[5]

Relations between ŻSS branches and Judenräte were in some instances close and cordial, but more often marked by tension and friction. The ŻSS on occasion tried to draw the Judenräte into its network, with a view to giving the Judenräte German contacts independent of the SS. The top ŻSS officers, whose headquarters were located in Cracow, arranged a conference there on 27–8 March

1940, at which a delegation of the Warsaw Judenrat met with the head of the Bevölkerungswesen und Fürsorge division. But the attempted strategy of providing the Judenräte with greater manoeuvrability failed simply because the SS declared all other German agencies out of bounds for the Judenräte.

At an annual regional ŻSS conference held in Chełm on 25–6 January 1942 the subject of relations between the Judenräte and the ŻSS unexpectedly surfaced in the discussions. The participants included top members of the regional ŻSS, local ŻSS delegates, local Judenräte delegates, and physicians attached to public-health departments of both ŻSS and Judenräte.[6] The agenda dealt with such matters as epidemic control, public sanitation, child care, relief for new arrivals, food supply and financing. Tensions between the self-help agencies and the Judenräte emerged out of the hidden agenda, when a delegate from the Chełm ŻSS remarked on the antagonism characterizing those relationships. Such antagonism, he observed, harmed the interests of the populace. As a model of sincere cooperation, he pointed to Chełm, where the Judenrat provided a permanent monthly subsidy for the ŻSS. In closing the meeting, the delegate from ŻSS headquarters asked the Judenräte to support the ŻSS: 'I call for understanding, help, collaboration,' he said, 'for you are both institutions of the Jewish population and you must complement each other.'

In Warsaw, relations were impaired by friction. There the ŻSS branch, called Żydowskie Towarzystwo Opieki Społecznej (ŻTOS; Jewish Society for Social Welfare), was in a continual state of opposition to the Judenrat. ŻTOS differed from most ŻSS branches by virtue of its position of national hegemony. Not only did it comprise most of the original personnel of the Coordinating Commission from which the ŻSS developed, but it collaborated closely with the remnants of the pre-war national welfare institutions: TOZ, CENTOS, ORT, Toporol, and Centrala Kass Bezprocentowych (CEKABE; Clearing House of Free Loan Associations). When the Germans later forbade their independent existence, CENTOS became the child-welfare department of ŻTOS, and TOZ its public-health and sanitation department.

ŻTOS developed into a mammoth organization, rivalling the Judenrat in scope of programme and size of staff. It operated departments for refugee care, public kitchens and food distribution, housing, clothing, health, youth, art and theatre, and journalism. ŻTOS also helped religious institutions, even though many observant Jews operated their own welfare agencies: kitchens for their refugee communities and for their students in clandestine *yeshivot*. (A committee called Ezrat Harabanim [aid to rabbis] helped rabbis and Talmudic scholars, especially by ransoming them from forced-labour duty.)[7] At its peak, ŻTOS employed about 3,000 persons, most of them with a record of Jewish communal service. As in the Judenräte, favouritism and patronage inflated the staff with communal élites and party veterans.

In its first year, ŻTOS aided nearly 35,000 families, over 113,000 persons, then about 30 per cent of Warsaw's Jewish population. With the ceaseless influx of refugees, another 15,000 were added to ŻTOS welfare rolls within three months. Refugees accounted for about one third of all welfare recipients. They themselves formed a unique self-help network within ŻTOS. Some sixty *landsmanshaftn*, associations of fellow townsmen, representing localities from which the Jews had been expelled, constituted a central committee of refugees whose members were usually former Judenrat officials of the dissolved communities. Thus the refugees themselves assumed the tasks of aiding their own and representing their cause in the councils of both ŻTOS and Judenrat.[8]

The most pivotal institution within ŻTOS was the network of tenement committees, whose like existed in no other ghetto. Having sprouted originally as civil-defence committees, they were assiduously cultivated by Emanuel Ringelblum in his role as head of ŻTOS's Sekcja Pracy Społecznej (SPS; Section for Communal Work). Intending to use these *ad hoc* tenement committees at first as a source of financial support for ŻTOS, Ringelblum assigned the task of organizing them into one centralized network to former staff members of Keren Kayemet (Jewish National Fund), the major fund-raising organization for Palestine. Since most tenement committees restricted their welfare activities to their own buildings and tenants, the SPS organizers undertook to widen their commitments. Though the tenement-committee activities remained confined to their own buildings, they were eventually drawn into a community-wide programme of welfare and charity.[9]

Up to April 1940, 778 tenement committees had been organized. By September 1940, just a month before the Jews were forced into the ghetto, the number had grown to 2,000, with a committee membership of about 10,000. (Committees had three, five or seven members, depending on the number of tenants in the building.) With ghettoization, the committees had to be reorganized, adding to their roster new tenants who before then had lived outside the limits of the ghetto. In January 1942, 1,108 tenement committees operated in six precincts in the Warsaw ghetto, with committee membership estimated at 7,500.

All tenants paid dues, the sum determined at a public meeting. Well-to-do tenants were assessed according to their means. Campaigns for funds and materials were constantly under way: clothing and furniture collections; entertainments, concerts and dances to raise money: benefits of every variety from low vaudeville to high culture. Some people gave voluntary donations; some offered loans. Mary Berg noted on 4 April 1941 that in her building a special kettle of soup was cooked every Friday for the children's hospital. She also mentioned the popular 'spoon' campaigns, for which tenants were asked to contribute a spoonful of flour or sugar towards a general collection. Even the poor participated in helping others still poorer. Those who had nothing to give offered their labour.

Accredited to ŻTOS, the tenement committees were the only licit grassroots organization in the ghetto. They were permitted to hold meetings and to conduct their business openly. Each was a microcosm of community, involving young and old in its operations, as donors or receivers. Women prepared food for the needy; the well helped the sick. Young people, especially activists in the Zionist and Bundist movements, provided the manpower for the committee's daily tasks and special activities: caring for the children in *ad hoc* nurseries, kindergartens and makeshift classrooms, making the rounds for the collections, selling tickets, organizing entertainments, warning the tenants about the arrival of police or SS. A protective bulwark for their tenants, these committees became, as Ringelblum put it, the forge of opposition to the Judenrat.

Observant Jews in the pre-war community accounted for half, perhaps even more, of East European Jewry – the Soviet Union excepted. Even though secularity was becoming the dominant mode, the norms and values of traditional Judaism still shaped the behaviour of the whole Jewish population. The observance of Judaism had permeated all public aspects of Jewish life. Keeping the Sabbath as a day of rest and abstaining from forbidden foods were observances adhered to by nearly the entire Jewish community. Judaism was practised in thousands of formal and informal groups: synagogues, houses of prayer and houses of study, *yeshivot* and *hedarim*, ritual baths and ritual-slaughter abattoirs, religious courts, congregational bodies, women's organizations, publishing houses and presses. The political spokesman for this profusion of institutions was the Aguda.

The Germans, denying that Jews were a religious group, had rendered the entire public existence of the observant community illegal. Not only were observant Jews singled out for German sport and persecution, not only were most synagogues destroyed or desecrated, but all functions pertaining to the observance of Judaism were outlawed: public and/or private worship, religious study and religious teaching, *shehita*. The entire enterprise of traditional Judaism was forced underground. To be sure, some Aguda leaders were on the boards or staffs of the Judenräte; some were connected with ŻSS and ŻTOS. In Warsaw, for instance, Rabbi Samson Stockhammer functioned in all three communal structures: in the Judenrat he represented the Rabbinical Council, which operated clandestinely; in the ŻTOS he represented the observant community with regard to its welfare needs; perhaps most important, he headed the underground organization of the religious community. Zisha Friedman, too, a pre-war Aguda leader, worked in the Warsaw Judenrat, in ŻTOS, and in the underground.[10] Actually, most leaders of the religious community functioned clandestinely.

All through Poland Jews prayed in secret. On 12 August 1940, on the eve of Tisha B'Av, the fast-day commemorating the destruction of the Temple, Chaim Kaplan noted: 'Public prayer in these dangerous times is a forbidden act. Anyone caught in this crime is doomed to severe punishment. If you will, it is even sabotage and anyone engaging in sabotage is subject to execution.' But Jews prayed in thousands of secret *minyanim*, some 600 in Warsaw alone. They preyed in cellars, attics, back rooms, behind drawn blinds with men on guard. In Cracow, services were held in two prayer houses thanks to the co-operation of Jewish policemen who worshipped there and who warned the congregation when German police were to be expected.

In Lodz, public prayer was permitted in 1940. In Riga the Jews who had been deported from Germany were allowed to conduct public services, but the native Jews were prohibited. In Kovno and Vilna, public services were tolerated. On 4 March 1941 Frank issued a decree affecting the Generalgouvernement, permitting religious services to be held in private homes, synagogues and prayer houses in observance of the Sabbath, the High Holy Days and the three major festivals of Passover, Shevuot and Succot. In practice, however, since German officials arbitrarily forbade worship or subjected the assembled Jews to humiliation and terror, most Jews continued to pray in seclusion.

Prayer took on new solemnity and urgency, with special petitionary prayers augmenting the regular service. In the Kovno ghetto it became customary after the morning and afternoon prayers to recite Psalms 130 ('Out of the depths have I called Thee, O Lord') and 142 ('With my voice I cry unto the Lord'). Also the petitionary and penitential prayers of the *Tahanun*, reserved normally for Mondays, Thursdays and fast-days, used to be recited daily. Composed for the most part during the Crusades, these prayers now expressed a tragic immediacy. They were uttered to the accompaniment of weeping and lamentation, especially at the '*Shomer Yisrael*': 'O Guardian of Israel, guard the remnant of Israel, and suffer not Israel to perish.' Everywhere the rabbis called to penitence and prayer, since Jewish tradition regards these as indispensable for the redemption of all Israel.[11]

The calamitous march of events shook many pious Jews from their traditional moorings. Some rebelled. In one Warsaw congregation, the news that the Jews would be confined in a ghetto arrived just as the cantor was about to start *Neilah*, the closing service of Yom Kippur, when Jews pray importunately for salvation before the heavenly gates of mercy are closed. At once the cantor halted the service, saying that there was no point in praying when the gates of mercy were already locked. That was apparently no isolated incident, for Hillel Zeitlin (1872–1942), journalist, writer, philosopher, one of religious Jewry's charismatic leaders, admitted in 1941: 'Characteristic is the rebellion

against God, against Heaven, which is noticeable among many religious Jews who no longer wish to declare God's Judgement right.'[12]
A less severe judgement of the ghetto's religious moods was rendered
at the same time by an unidentified communal leader:

The truly pious have become even more pious, for they understand
and see God's Hand in everything. The unbelievers, in contrast, have become even more unbelieving. The vacillating, however, have taken to
rebelling against God, conducting war against Him, spiting Heaven.
These are the seemingly pious Jews who have suddenly begun eating
pork and lard.[13]

Most observance of *kashrut* lapsed except among the exceptionally
devout. Not only was *shehita* forbidden, but any sort of meat was
seldom to be had in the ghettos. In the Vilna ghetto, four *shohatim* used
to join up covertly with forced-labour brigades working outside the
ghetto. With their ritual slaughtering knives concealed on their persons, they had clandestine contacts where they could slaughter poultry
according to ritual. Then they risked getting back into the ghetto
with their *kosher* contraband. In the Lodz ghetto only horsemeat was
obtainable. Most observant Jews, driven by hunger, ate it, though it
was not a permitted food. On 23 February 1941, during the great
hunger, the rabbis in the Lodz ghetto ruled under the authority of the
doctrine of *pikuakh nefesh* (saving an endangered life) that the consumption of non-*kosher* meat was permitted for pregnant women and
persons in poor health.

In the Kovno ghetto the only food Jews in forced-labour brigades
received for the whole day was soup made with horsemeat. Devout
Jews abstained from eating it, but at least one rabbi ruled permissively
for the sake of *pikuakh nefesh*. An observant Jew in the Warsaw ghetto
once tried to explain to the director of a public kitchen that his heart-
ache at transgressing *kashrut* would impair his health far more than the
loss to his organism of a few grammes of non-*kosher* food. For most
observant Jews the suspension of *kashrut* was no easy accommodation.
A sense of guilt and self-denigration pursued those who yielded to the
demands of their hunger. For every mouthful of ritually impure food
they consumed, devout Jews vowed that in the future, when they
would once again be free to follow the Law as commanded by God,
they would make up for their present transgressions.[14]

Observing *kashrut* during Passover was a formidable undertaking. The Germans grudgingly gave permission to bake *matzot*, but never in sufficient supply. In most ghettos pious Jews baked *matzot* illegally. One kilogramme of *matzo* cost as much as 6 kilogrammes of bread in Vilna in 1943; yet, noted Herman Kruk, no household was without *matzo*. In Lodz in 1941 the ten-day ration allowed 2½ kilogrammes of *matzo*, whereas the bread ration was more generous. Some households, seeking to accommodate the observance of Passover to the prevailing hunger, compromised and took both bread and *matzo* rations. Beet juice, sweetened with saccharin, substituted for the *seder*'s sacramental wine. 'The only thing we had aplenty', commented one Jew, 'was bitter herbs – not on the table, but in our hearts.'

Like *kashrut*, the Sabbath was nearly impossible to observe. In Lodz, Warsaw, Vilna and Kovno, the Sabbath was a permitted day of rest for brief periods or in certain communal institutions, but for the most part the Germans, with deliberate sadism, forced the Jews to work on Saturdays and the High Holy Days. When the Germans first entered Lodz, they compelled the rabbis to issue a ruling permitting Jewish shops to stay open on the Sabbath and Jewish festivals.[15] In Vilna the rabbis permitted Jews to work on the Sabbath, Yom Kippur and other festivals for the sake of *pikuakh nefesh*. But they counselled Jews not to work if their lives would not be endangered by such a refusal. In the Kovno ghetto, pious Jews sought assignment to labour brigades that did not work on the Sabbath, even though that entailed forfeiting extra food rations or a chance for less strenuous or unpleasant work.[16]

After the Germans had forbidden ritual baths (*mikvaot*), rabbis in the Vilna ghetto ruled against performing weddings, since the brides could not take the prescribed bath. In Lodz, however, the rabbis gave permission, because weddings were often for the sake of *pikuakh nefesh*, when a woman without a work permit married a man who had one and was thus exempted from deportation. In Warsaw the ritual baths were sealed and boarded up, but occasionally were used secretly. In 1940 a hasidic *rebbe* decided that he and his followers must immerse themselves in the ritual bath before Yom Kippur. Negotiations were conducted with the *mikva*'s owner and it was agreed that at 5.00 a.m., when curfew ended, the *mikva* would be made accessible for one hour through a secret entry. The expedition, wrote a participant, 'summons up for us a living picture of our ancestors in Spain during the

Inquisition . . . They surely never imagined that their descendants 400 years later would find themselves in a far worse situation . . . and would re-enact the same procedures that they themselves had experienced.'[17]

Hundreds of secret *yeshivot* and houses of study came into being in the Generalgouvernement and the occupied eastern territories. Warsaw's pre-war *yeshiva* population of 5,000 was greatly diminished by death and flight. Some boys abandoned religious study because they had to go to work, others because they succumbed to disbelief. In the Warsaw ghetto, some 200 *yeshiva* students 'learned' in at least eleven *yeshivot*. Most *yeshiva* students had no legal existence in the ghettos, since they were not registered with the Judenrat, and so were relieved of the onus of forced labour. But that meant that they had no ration cards. Some well-to-do families supplied them with food in quantity, as did some welfare agencies. Students took turns begging on the streets or soliciting food and money among people of means. A *yeshiva* student, found murdered in the Vilna ghetto in June 1942, had probably been buying food illicitly for the *yeshiva* from underworld persons with illegal stocks and may have inadvertently witnessed criminal dealings. Some people in the observant community did not approve of the clandestine *yeshivot* for they felt that the students were separating themselves from the community and evading their responsibilities. But others believed, according to a venerable Jewish tradition, that by studying the Torah these *yeshiva* students were performing the most urgent and efficacious function of any in the ghettos to ensure the salvation of the Jews.[18]

When the Germans entered Poland, they closed down the Jewish schools and requisitioned their property. They further ordered the public schools to exclude all Jewish pupils. The Germans intended to deprive Jewish children of education, but they underestimated the place of education in the system of Jewish values. 'And thou shalt teach them the statutes and the laws and shalt show them the way wherein they must walk.' The survival of Jews and Judaism depended on the uninterrupted transmittal of the tradition from generation to generation. Within a half-year after the German invasion some 180 underground *hedarim* and Talmud Torahs, with about 2,000 pupils, functioned in Warsaw. In Kovno, Vilna, Lublin, Lodz and Cracow thousands of children received traditional instruction in Judaism privately or in secret schools.

General education, too, was a major commitment of the modern secular Jew, as the vehicle for upward mobility and achievement. Faced with the unprecedented wholesale proscription by the Germans of the entire Jewish educational enterprise, the pedagogic apparatus of the Jewish community rallied to thwart and outwit the Germans. All over Poland underground schools came into being. In Warsaw, with some 40,000 Jewish children between seven and fourteen, hundreds of informal classes of about ten children each were organized, each group called a *komplet*, the Polish word to describe pupils studying together outside a formal classroom. These *komplety*, set up in public kitchens and private homes, were operated by CENTOS and the pre-war Jewish school organizations, and were staffed by the teachers of the pre-war schools. Meanwhile, in each community, the teachers, principals and school administrators were pressing the Judenräte to get permission from the Germans to operate schools legally. (The ŻSS, too, intervened on behalf of the schools.)

In Warsaw, representatives of the diverse Jewish school networks, ranging from the traditionalist to the Zionist Hebraist and socialist Yiddishist, along with representatives of the Jewish teachers in the pre-war Polish public schools, jointly formed a coordinating committee, despite their past competitiveness. This committee constituted the major pressure group exerting influence on the Judenrat for the legal re-establishment of the schools. Their status reinforced their cause. Eventually, when the Germans granted permission to reopen the schools, this coordinating committee assumed the responsibility for the educational curricula. It continued to represent and protect its professional interests *vis-à-vis* the Judenrat. The *komplety* that each organization operated became the nuclei of the official schools.[19]

Clandestine *komplety* flourished all over Poland. In Lublin, where about 100 teachers staffed such groups, one *komplet* met in a basement shoemaker's shop, behind a makeshift partition. When a warning was given that Germans were about, the classroom disappeared. Books and papers were hidden, the partition removed, the children dispersed and the teacher, one shoe off, became the shoemaker's customer.[20]

Chaim Kaplan, a long-time Hebrew teacher who organized *komplety* in his own home, described in his diary on 15 February 1941 the conditions of Jewish education under German barbarism:

Jewish children learn in secret. In back rooms, on long benches near a table, little schoolchildren sit and learn what it's like to be Marranos ... In time of danger the children learn to hide their books. Jewish children are clever – when they set off to acquire forbidden learning, they hide their books and notebooks between their trousers and their stomachs, then button their jackets and coats.

The *komplety* attracted a relatively small proportion of the whole Jewish school-age population, but the pupils, especially those on the secondary level, responded with great seriousness to instruction. (Two underground Hebrew secondary schools functioned in the Warsaw ghetto.) 'In pre-war times we had never witnessed such studiousness as the pupils demonstrated in these *komplety*,' wrote one teacher. 'They went after their studies with zest, wanting to finish in one year a course of two or more years. No more dilly-dallying, no more excuses. They asked the teachers for more work.'[21]

On 31 August 1940 Frank finally issued a decree giving the Judenräte in the Generalgouvernement the responsibility to provide elementary and vocational schools for the Jewish population. The Judenräte were also to train and prepare teachers.[22] Secondary and higher education were forbidden. But the decree was arbitrarily applied. German authorities in Warsaw, for instance, refused permission to open Jewish schools on the pretext that typhus would spread. In April 1941 permission was finally given, on a highly restrictive basis; the schools did not begin to operate legally until October 1941.

In Lodz and Vilna the school systems operated under the aegis of the Judenrat, with a standard curriculum and Yiddish as the official language of instruction. (Polish was often the *de facto* language of instruction.) In the Lodz ghetto the schools existed barely two years, from May 1940 until 1942, and at their peak enrolled about 10,000 children in forty-five schools. The Vilna ghetto maintained several elementary schools and a secondary school, with an enrolment of 2,000. Separate religious schools were operated under Orthodox auspices in both Lodz and Vilna.

In Warsaw six schools were opened in October 1941. Enrolments continued to increase. At the end of the school year, in June 1942, there were nineteen schools with nearly 7,000 children. Most schools had four grades; some had five grades. The language of instruction was Yiddish, Hebrew or Polish, though the last was officially forbidden. The curriculum included reading, writing, arithmetic, botany, Bible and Judaism, arts and crafts, and physical education. The Germans forbade the Jewish schools to teach history and geography, but Jewish history and the geography of Palestine were taught. Textbooks were seldom available and, if they were, hardly appropriate to the realities of the ghetto.

The secondary-school curriculum in Vilna included Yiddish, Hebrew, Jewish and general history, geography, biology, physics, mathematics, Latin, German (forbidden by the Germans) and drawing.[23]

Vocational courses in Warsaw alone attracted nearly 4,000 students in the period from September 1940 to May 1941.[24] The trades for which training was offered in all cities – Warsaw, Kovno, Vilna, Lodz, Bialystok – included locksmithing, auto mechanics, electromechanics, optical tooling, turning and carpentry, drafting, dyeing, besides the familiar Jewish trades. In Warsaw and Kovno, vocational courses, besides giving the ghetto residents a chance to learn a trade that would give them some security, also provided a cover for forbidden higher education in some fields – nursing, pharmacy, chemistry, even some medical training, though, as Dr Milejkowski pointed out, high quality could not be expected from such an undertaking.

Like the Jewish schools in Germany after 1933, the ghetto schools, legal or underground, formed a sub-community of love and dedication that provided the ghetto children with shelter, physical warmth, medical and sanitary care, food and emotional security. The ghetto schools erected walls against ghetto harshness and ugliness, and became tiny oases of joy and creativity in the bleak ghettos. Saturday 17 October 1942, Yitzhok Rudashevski noted was a boring day because there was no school: 'I think to myself: what would be the case if we did not go to school, to the club, did not read books. We would die of dejection inside the ghetto walls.'

The ghetto schools imparted a sense of Jewish identity, and by concentrating on Jewish subjects of study, reinforced Jewish solidarity. The world of Jewish culture and tradition helped to sustain them. The children learned to play, to sing, dance and act. The schools themselves became bracing cultural centres for the whole ghetto. Dramatic, choral and musical performances by schoolchildren, which proved particularly popular, were produced to raise funds for social-welfare programmes, particularly on behalf of CENTOS. The sight and sound of the assembled children, neatly dressed, reciting poetry or singing songs in their appealingly childish voices, heartened the ghetto populace. These children, guarantors of survival beyond the ghetto, engendered high morale. In the summer of 1941 the Hebraist schools in Warsaw presented a dramatized version of Yitzhak Lamdan's classic narrative poem, 'Masada'. One could see, wrote the headmaster of a Hebrew school, not just the Masada of the past, but the resurrection of Masada's spirit in the Warsaw ghetto.[25]

In Vilna the literary circle of high-school students, under the direction of the young Yiddish poet Abram Sutzkever, prepared an exhibition and a public festival to commemorate Yehoash, Yiddish poet and translator of the Bible into Yiddish. The materials for the exhibition were smuggled into the ghetto from the Yiddish Scientific Institute (YIVO), where Zelig Kalmanovich, Sutzkever and a task force of intellectuals worked, sorting the library of this famous research institute for the Germans. The Yehoash exhibition, which opened on 14 March 1943, young Rudashevski noted, was exceptionally beautiful. Visitors forgot that they were in a gloomy ghetto. The festival itself, wrote Rudashevski, was produced in a grand manner, in a mood of exaltation. On 6 April 1943 Sutzkever completed a poem, 'Yehoash', about the undertaking:

> Death itself shrinks before this beauty,
> And drives back again
> His grimy smoking cauldron.[26]

Like bread and potatoes, education and culture sustained life in the ghetto. The ghetto's tastes in recreation ranged from low to high culture. Even before the ghetto, the conditions of curfew mothered new forms of recreation. Since people were forbidden to be out on the streets from 7.00 p.m. until 5.00 the following morning, those who lived in the same building or in adjoining buildings with a common courtyard used to visit one another, passing the long evening and night as best they could. Close friends often came to spend the night.

Card playing, always a popular Jewish pastime, became still more popular. (Later, card players used to contribute a portion of the kitty to the local tenement committee.) One party of well-to-do card players devised the idea of a spot of entertainment as a break in the long-run card game. On 8 November 1939 they invited a popular Warsaw singing comedian to entertain them, having raised a large enough sum for his fee. They even set up a cloakroom and a refreshment bar. The idea spread to other buildings: the demand for entertainers grew so rapidly that impresarios could make a living by handling artists' bookings and fees.[27] Entertainers were in demand also in the mushrooming cafés and restaurants that catered to the ghetto *arrivistes* and underworld. The demand, in fact, surpassed the supply: amateurs were soon competing with professionals. The entertainment in private homes, cafés and soon also in public kitchens consisted of variety acts, comic patter, song-and-dance routines, farce or satire on ghetto bureaucracy, and buffoonish or melodramatic one-acters. However poor the talent and trashy the content, this improvised entertainment heightened ghetto morale simply by releasing the audiences for a brief span from their day-to-day anxieties and transporting them into a more cheerful existence of pre-war normality, even if tawdry or vulgar. For thousands of ghetto residents this entertainment was probably the first theatrical performance they had ever attended.

Warsaw's communal leaders, deploring the low culture of this burgeoning entertainment industry, organized in September 1940 a committee within ŻTOS whose dual function was to raise the cultural level of theatrical productions and to organize the nearly 500 actors, musicians, dancers and artists in the ghetto, helping them find employment. ŻTOS thus obtained a percentage of the gate receipts for its welfare programmes. In the first year of its existence the ŻTOS entertainment committee put on 1,814 programmes, which yielded 12,500 zlotys in fees for the artists, over 30,000 zlotys for ŻTOS, apart from the funds that went directly to TOZ, CENTOS and other institutions.

Eventually five theatres operated in the Warsaw ghetto, two performing in Yiddish and three in Polish, sometimes presenting serious drama but more often comedies and revues. Theatres operated also in

Lodz and Vilna. (In Vilna a large segment of the ghetto populace disapproved. Their slogan was: 'A graveyard is no place for entertainment.')

In December 1940 a clandestine organization was formed by Warsaw's Yiddishist élite to raise cultural standards and also to elevate the
status of Yiddish. The presence of the converts in the ghetto was adduced as a cause for the apparent escalating preference for Polish and
the abandonment of Yiddish. Called Yidishe kultur-organizatsye
(YIKOR; Yiddish Cultural Organization), the new group engaged in
propaganda on behalf of Yiddish, demanding that the Judenrat use
Yiddish officially, in addition to Polish and German. A pilot programme to use Yiddish all the time was set up by one tenement committee. The tenement committees generally became the operational
centres for YIKOR activities. Nearly 100 public meetings commemorating the Yiddish literary classicists Mendele, Peretz and Sholom
Aleichem were held in the larger buildings. YIKOR also set up
series of well-attended scholarly lectures and courses in Yiddish.[28]

Tekumah (revival), a Hebraist cultural organization, was formed as
an ideological counterforce to YIKOR, though no real animosity
between the two groups existed. Tekumah served the interests of the
Zionists and Hebraists. One of its most impressive programmes
celebrated Judah Halevi, twelfth-century Hebrew poet and philosopher of Spain, some of whose poems were read by Jacques Lewy, the
Yiddish actor and friend of Kafka. The main speaker, one of Tekumah's most active lecturers, was Dr Edmund Stein, rabbi, historian
and outstanding Semitologist, president of Warsaw's Institute of
Judaic Studies. Stein himself tried to maintain the highest levels of
scholarship in the ghetto. He lectured in a ghetto cellar for former
students of the institute on Socrates, Aristotle, Maimonides and
Saadia Gaon.[29]

The large ghettos had music too. Warsaw, Lodz, Vilna and Kovno
had orchestras. The Lodz ghetto symphony orchestra consisted of
twenty-five professional players and ten amateurs. The Kovno ghetto
orchestra also had thirty-five players. (Strings, naturally, dominated.)
Performances were given at least once a week, sometimes more frequently. Forbidden to play German music, Jewish musicians concentrated on Mendelssohn, Meyerbeer, Halévy, Offenbach and the
wide range of Yiddish and Hebrew art songs and folksongs. In Vilna,

where the Germans seemed less interested in the ghetto repertoire, a largely amateur orchestra at one concert performed Beethoven's Leonore Overture No. 3, Chopin's piano concerto in E minor and Tchaikovsky's Fifth Symphony. The Kovno ghetto had a mandolin orchestra, the Warsaw ghetto several string quartets. Most ghettos had adult choral groups, some affiliated with the political movements, and children's choruses, organized in the schools.

The Kovno ghetto concert hall was in the renowned *yeshiva* of Slobodka, whose buildings the Germans had sequestered in 1941, used for shooting stray dogs, and then abandoned. The ghetto police and workers cleaned the premises and converted it into a small concert hall. The first concert was held in August 1942, and as the orchestra's first strains wafted through the halls, players and listeners alike wept. Their tragic plight had not affected their ability to produce music.[30]

A Viennese journalist, deported to Lodz, described the audience at concerts in the House of Culture, Rumkowski's gift to the ghetto. They have, he noted, their favourite composers and favourite numbers. They respond to *Il Trovatore, Pagliacci, Rigoletto, Madama Butterfly* with smiling recognition and after the concert hum the melodies. 'In this respect the ghetto audience is not at all different from the frequenters of European concert houses.'[31]

In Warsaw, after the Germans shut down institutional libraries and bookstores, underground libraries came into existence, with books circulated by courier librarians. Halina Szwambaum was one: 'In the mornings, until 1 p.m., I am the "lady from the library", since people come to see me; between 1 p.m. and 9 p.m., I am the "girl from the library", since I run around town.' Running around town meant going 'to different apartments, up and down many flight of stairs, with a heavy briefcase'.

In Częstochowa, where the Jewish Labour Bund had maintained a communal library of 20,000 volumes, the whole collection was secretly transferred in two days to a private home. That collection then became a secret library, serving more than 1,000 readers.[32]

In Lodz only one library was permitted to operate officially, with some 7,500 books and 4,000 subscribers. Several small circulating libraries functioned illicitly for a while. The German Jews maintained their own libraries; several political parties operated clandestine circulating libraries.

In the Vilna ghetto the Mefitse haskalah library was operated as the ghetto library by the Judenrat's Culture Department. Augmented by ownerless private collections, it had nearly 100,000 books and a peak membership in August 1942 of nearly 4,000 subscribers, almost a third of the ghetto population. The library circulated books (13,500 during March 1943), maintained a reading room (an average of 206 readers daily during March 1943) and also collected ghetto archival and folklore materials.³³ On 13 December 1942 the library celebrated the circulation of the hundred-thousandth book with a programme of speeches and music. Herman Kruk, the library's director, delivered a paper on ghetto reading and readers. Kalmanovich noted, no doubt from Kruk's statistics displayed in charts and diagrams on the platform, that 70·4 per cent of the books read were Polish, 17·6 per cent Yiddish, 2 per cent Hebrew, the rest Russian and other languages.³⁴

Besides the vast demand for narcotic literature – detective and adventure stories – fiction was most widely read. The most popular Polish novelists were Bolesław Prus, Henryk Sienkiewicz, Stefan Żeromski, Andrzej Strug and Eliza Orzeszkowa. The most widely read Yiddish writers were Y. L. Peretz and Sholem Asch; among Russian writers, Boris Pilniak, Ilya Ehrenburg, Maxim Gorki and Mark Aldanov. The German Jews were more likely to read history and philosophy, but they read also Heine, Lion Feuchtwanger and Emil Ludwig.³⁵ Observant Jews, too unlearned to study Talmud, turned to popular devotional literature. Lodz book dealers did a thriving business in such books, which, because of their sacred character, could not be used as waste. One of the most popular works in all ghettos was *En Yaakov*, a sixteenth-century collection of the haggadic material from the Talmud, systematically classified, which by the late nineteenth century had gone through some thirty editions. Another was *Hok le-yisroel*, a compendium of extracts from the Bible, Talmud, Zohar and other sacred works, arranged for daily reading and study, also popular among the unlearned.³⁶

The serious Jewish reader, Ringelblum noted on 25 June 1942, was fascinated by war writings: 'People particularly enjoy descriptions of the year 1918 and the downfall of the Germans.' The ghetto Jews read about Napoleon, delighting in accounts of the march on Moscow. For the same reason, Ringelblum remarked, Tolstoy's *War and Peace* was enormously popular in the ghetto. 'In a word, being unable to take revenge on the enemy in reality, we are seeking it in fantasy, in literature.'

Well-to-do women who borrowed books from the Vilna ghetto library devoured endless series of sentimental Russian novels. Schoolchildren requested Jules Verne's *Around the World in Eighty Days* and Mark Twain's *The Prince and the Pauper* in Yiddish translations. Working people, who used the library in the evening, members of Zionist youth organizations and refugees from Warsaw read novels with social content – for instance, Upton Sinclair and Theodore Dreiser, Ignazio Silone's *Bread and Wine*, Feuchtwanger's *The Jewish Wars*. Extremely popular was Franz Werfel's *Forty Days of Musa Dagh*, the novel about the annihilation of the Armenians by the Turks, which Werfel wrote in 1932.[37]

Reading was not only narcotic and escape, but also a discipline of mind, an attempt to retain the habits of a civilized existence. Reading about past wars and catastrophes involving other peoples and nations universalized the Jewish experience and transcended the misery within the ghetto walls.

At Emmanuel Ringelblum's initiative and under his direction, a secret Jewish archive was established under the code name 'Oneg Shabbat' (Pleasures of the Sabbath). Its purpose, as Ringelblum described it in his letter of 20 May 1944, was to gather 'materials and documents relating to the martyrology of the Jews in Poland'.[38] A large staff worked systematically to this end, stimulating the production of diaries, chronicles, all sorts of descriptive and analytic writings on every phase of Jewish life under German occupation – political, religious, economic, cultural. Photographs, posters, announcements, official reports, ghetto wit and humour, statistics – all became valuable documentation for Oneg Shabbat.*

In Lodz, Vilna and Bialystok, too, groups of writers, intellectuals and communal leaders gathered and prepared materials to document the Jewish experience under German rule. The idea of preserving a record for history and posterity inspired hundreds, perhaps thousands, of Jews in the ghettos of Eastern Europe to keep diaries or accounts of

---

*Much of the assembled material was buried in crates in the ghetto and uncovered after the war. Originals of the exhumed materials are in the Żydowski Instytut Historyczny in Warsaw; Yad Vashem in Jerusalem has copies of a great many. Some material is also at the YIVO Archives in New York.

their beleaguered existence. The diary became an expression of the will to live, the vehicle through which posthumousness, a modest form of immortality, would be conferred on them.

In his essay on the ghetto, Kalmanovich referred to the ghetto's social, educational and cultural institutions as 'the clear victory of spirit over matter'. For the time that the ghetto Jews managed to cling to familiar cultural terrain, they triumphed over the Germans. The strategy of the communal leadership in the functional welfare, religious, educational and cultural groupings was to hold back the tide of barbarism and create islands of civilization, normality and decency. Operating under terror, amid hunger and disease, they succeeded in helping those they reached to retain and enrich their humanity.

13 The Counter-community:
The Political Underground

'Real politics', Disraeli wrote, 'are the possession and distribution of power.' By that token the Jews in pre-war Eastern Europe seldom engaged in real politics, for political power was not theirs to exercise or bestow. Jewish politics were both symbolic and visionary, with morality and messianism substituting for political and economic power. A minority fragmented by internal social, economic and religious differences, the Jews through their political parties sought to win not power for themselves, but legitimacy as citizens of the states in which they lived. These parties fought for the equality and the rights denied to Jews, and through that political struggle instilled self-esteem in the Jew and inculcated respect for the Jew in the mind of the non-Jew. The Jewish parties defended the rights of Jews to work, to study, to pursue their own national culture, to be secure against defamation and violence. Jewish politics thus became more a matter of honour and dignity than the possession or distribution of power.

These Jewish parties, from the Aguda on the right to the Bund on the left, were not just political parties competing for office and political power. They were also ideological movements, seeking adherents and believers. In the style of the political/ideological movements of Central Europe, the Jewish parties maintained dense networks of institutions and services that provided for the members' needs and interests from cradle to grave – kindergartens, schools, youth groups, women's associations, charitable and loan societies, cultural groups, medical care and burial services. They published daily newspapers, periodicals and books.

The German and Soviet invasions of Poland and the Baltic countries in 1939 shattered this complex political establishment. Jewish political leadership became even more disabled than communal leadership. Veteran party leaders fled the oncoming Germans. Nazi and Communist police alike searched out Jewish party leaders, arrested them and then killed them. The most notable instances under the Soviets were the arrest and murder of the two Bundist leaders Henryk Erlich and Viktor Alter.[1] In German-occupied Poland, the Gestapo, armed with lists of Socialist councilmen and deputies, rounded up dozens of political activists, sometimes incarcerating them in concentration camps, more often killing them right off.[2]

Flight, arrest and murder depleted Jewish political leadership from the start of the occupation, leaving the parties for the most part in the hands of second- and third-echelon activists. In the absence of party veterans, of mature and experienced leaders, young people in the parties began to move forward and make their presence felt. In a short time the conflict between youth and age in the Jewish parties would become critical.

The political parties were outlawed. The parapolitical institutions and personnel of all parties provided the infrastructure for the ghetto's alternative community, the re-fashioned functional groupings in welfare, religious observance, education and culture, which operated in the shadow of legality. Since the parties could exist only clandestinely, the two great parties of pre-war Polish Jewry, the Aguda and the General Zionists, as well as small parties like the Mizrachi, Folkists and Revisionists, disintegrated as political entities. The Aguda leaders and masses, whose habitual pre-war strategy had been political compliance in exchange for the unhindered observance of Judaism, now became engaged in a mass sacrificial endeavour to observe Judaism and to maintain the functional religious groups in the Jewish community. Their party apparatus totally collapsed.

As for the General Zionists, many of their ranking leaders were in the Judenräte, while their activists helped to sustain the functional educational and cultural groups. The substantial number of General Zionists in the Judenräte militated against their maintaining the party as an underground movement. For one thing, their energies were exhausted in the daily burdens of office. For another, they could never have reconciled the contradictory loyalties that such an arrangement would have demanded. In the Generalgouvernement, the presence of the General Zionist movement in the Jewish political underground was upheld almost single-handedly by Menahem Kirschenbaum, a member of the party's pre-war central committee, who in the Warsaw ghetto held a top post in ŻTOS and operated from that vantage point.[3]

Only the left-wing parties and the socialist Zionist youth movements succeeded in maintaining their primary political character and in transforming their pre-war apparatus – or its remnants – into functioning underground organizations. The largest of these was the Jewish Labour Bund, which in the 1930s had emerged as the major political Jewish organization on the municipal level and which controlled most of the Jewish trade unions. The Jewish section of the Communist party had been second in numerical strength before 1939, having commanded a substantial segment of Jewish support, controlling several trade unions and active fractions of some others. The Ribbentrop–Molotov agreements of August 1939 sharply diminished the party's following, but after Germany invaded Russia in June 1941, Communist activity was revived under Soviet instructions. In early 1942 the Polska Partia Robotnicza (PPR; Polish Workers' party), the Communist party in a new guise, made its appearance in the General-gouvernement. Smaller and weaker than the Communists were the Labour Zionists, split into left and right wings. The larger party, the Left Labour Zionists, had fractions in several unions, though not controlling any. The Right Labour Zionists constituted the smallest of the left parties, their influence concentrated in Upper East Silesia.

The socialist Zionist youth movements included Dror, associated with the Labour Zionists; Hashomer Hatzair, whose pro-Sovietism brought it ideologically close to the Left Labour Zionists; Hehalutz, federation of Zionist pioneering (*halutz*) organizations; Gordonia, associated with Hitachdut, a Labour Zionist affiliate. Other *halutz* organizations were eventually accommodated within the leftist *halutz* sphere.

Despite sharp political differences with one another, these parties and organizations shared traits that gave them the viability for underground operation that the other parties lacked. They all had long cultivated attitudes and habits of challenge, defiance and resistance to political authority. Under Poland's reactionary régime, they had learned how to cope with censorship and suppression and how to survive politically in opposition. The experience would serve them well. Furthermore, in normal times the movement's ideology provided its members with profound satisfaction and confidence, for the party ideology postulated a world view that promised to solve all problems and bring an end to suffering and injustice. Under German occupation, party ideology was to become a gospel of salvation, the promise of survival. For the hard-core membership, the party insiders, the *aktiv*, as they were called, the movement was all, the surrogate for family and kinship. The left parties generated a mystique of fraternity that lifted each individual out of his narrow confines and linked him to a universal community of brotherhood. The secular messianic vision of the left – 'We have been naught, we shall be all' – continued to inspire its adherents, even in the bleakness of the ghetto, with the radiant promise of the future.

Most parties maintained a visible, half-legal organizational identity in the web of public kitchens, whose management in Warsaw, Lodz and elsewhere was often assigned by the ŻSS or Judenrat, according to party key.[4] These party kitchens, some located on their former premises, functioned as meeting places where members shared food, information and companionship. There the organization persisted, as movement rather than as party, for people did not congregate for instrumental purposes, but were propelled by their emotional attachment to the movement, by their ties to the past and their traditions, by their convictions about the luminous truth of the movement and its goals.

Though an estimated 2,000 members of *halutz* groups in Poland had fled to Vilna in the autumn of 1939, a few thousand still remained in the Generalgouvernement. Most managed to retain their *kibbutzim*, the training farms where they used to prepare for *aliya* to Palestine. *Kibbutzim* operated in the suburbs of Warsaw, in Zagłębia, in Kielce, Lublin, Radom, Hrubieszów and Częstochowa. With Rumkowski's cooperation, some twenty *kibbutzim* were established in Lodz, with nearly 1,000 members. In the *kibbutzim* the young Zionists engaged in agricultural work and Zionist self-education. The members of the *kibbutzim* were on the way to becoming élitists, having distanced themselves from the teeming ghettos and the masses of Jews. But by late 1941, when the Germans had ordered some *kibbutzim* closed, and when Rumkowski and Merin, viewing the *kibbutzim* suspiciously, had withdrawn financial assistance, the Zionist youth returned to the ghettos. There they confronted a vacuum in Zionist politics, for except for the Left Labour Zionist movement in Warsaw and Częstochowa and the Zionist public kitchens, no substantial political Zionist underground existed.[5] In a short time, the Zionist youth filled that vacuum.

The only underground political organization of significance soon after the German occupation was the Bund, with its centre in Warsaw. Even during the siege of Warsaw, the Bund continued to issue its daily newspaper, setting and printing it by hand, after the destruction of the city's gas works. To serve those made homeless by the bombings and the incoming refugees, the Bund opened public kitchens.[6] Early in the German occupation, the Bund began to shape its underground activities. A relief commission was formed to operate the public kitchens and to distribute relief. Soon fourteen party kitchens and canteens – four just for children – were functioning. A Socialist Red Cross was set up to care for the sick, obtain pharmaceutical supplies, help persons in the forced-labour camps, and provide hide-outs for party leaders wanted by the Germans. A trade-union commission was assigned to organize clandestine cells of fives or tens, by trade, drawn from the most reliable members of the pre-war unions. A political commission undertook to reorganize the party and its youth division Tsukunft, in underground cells, with tight security provisions. A new party council and central committee were also put together.[7]

The Bund re-activated its pre-war militia, which before the war had consisted of some 300–400 men, schooled in the arts of defence, with a tiny arms arsenal at their command. The party militia had been formed in 1920, but its origins went back to the Bundist armed self-defence in Tsarist Russia that arose after the Kishenev pogrom of 1903. The Bund militia in inter-war Poland, like similar defence units of political parties in Central Europe, was intended to protect party meetings from attack and disruption by opposition parties. As the major militia among the Jewish parties (the Left Labour Zionists also had a defence unit), the Bund militia functioned also as a pan-Jewish defence group in Poland against anti-Semitic violence and hooliganism.[8] The Tsukunft, too, maintained a defence arm, called Tsukunft-shturem. Reorganized in the ghetto, under stringent security, it started out in February 1941 with about thirty-five members in seven cells.[9]

The first task of the parties and youth organizations was survival. 'Even in those days', wrote a Dror member about his movement in the first months of German occupation in Vilna, 'one of the most important tasks was to procure bread for the hungry.' Wherever the JDC operated, its branches gave subsidies to the parties and to the *halutz* youth for their welfare activities. (Funds also came from the respective party headquarters abroad through underground channels, though these did not always prove dependable.) The ŻSS too provided significant welfare assistance and cover for political organizational activities. In Warsaw Ringelblum's key position in ŻTOS ensured posts for the Left Labour Zionists, to whose executive he belonged, and the use of various ŻTOS facilities to cloak party undertakings. In Cracow Aaron Liebeskind, leader of the Akiva *halutz* movement, was put in charge of the ŻSS's department of agricultural training so that he could travel in that capacity throughout the Generalgouvernement, ostensibly visiting the *kibbutzim* on official business.

In some ghettos – Bialystok, Kovno, Piotrków – one party or another enjoyed the support of the Judenräte, receiving both welfare aid and protection.

The parties first took care of their own, as a family looks after its members. Each party safeguarded its own constituency, its activists and loyal supporters. Its education and cultural apparatus continued to function in semi-legal fashion. Warsaw was the locus for the parties' central committees, the stronghold of party operations. But throughout former Poland, now the Generalgouvernement and Ostland, were dozens of local and regional party branches, *kibbutzim* and kindred organizations with which contact had to be renewed, which needed financial support, political guidance and moral encouragement. Outlawed as corporate bodies, their people forbidden to travel, to use the telephone, their post censored even if delivered, the parties devised a system of communication that depended exclusively on human intrepidity. Trusted party members, whose appearance and accents enabled them to pass as Poles, travelled across German-occupied Poland and Lithuania with forged papers, risking their lives to deliver news, money, organizational instructions, copies of the underground press to the communities they visited, and to bring back information. (The parties sometimes used couriers of the Polish underground movement.) They also operated, on a very limited scale, for a short time, underground railways that helped members escape from Poland. The Bund had a network of about thirty couriers. Among the couriers of the *halutz* organizations were a group of young women whose exploits became legendary. 'They are a theme', Ringelblum noted, 'that calls for the pen of a great writer.'

Having provided for their own members, the parties then extended the periphery of their concern, to the limit that their resources permitted, moving from the private sphere, as it were, into the public. In the first two years of the war, the parties saw their function in the community at large primarily in terms of building and sustaining morale. Early in 1941 the Bund's Central Committee in the Warsaw ghetto sent a report to its New York organization, describing its functions as it then perceived them:

1. To strengthen the power of resistance and endurance of the Jewish masses in the face of the unheard-of terrible persecutions without parallel in human history ...
2. To inform the Jewish populace about the resistance and struggle against the occupant beyond the borders of the Jewish ghettos both in Poland and in all occupied countries.
3. To implant the firm conviction that though the Jewish masses may be persecuted, the majority will nevertheless survive and live to see the conclusive defeat of the enemy.[10]

That hopefulness and that will to live permeated all the political groupings, despite their ideological differences. The Bundists looked to the Western Allies to defeat the Germans, whereas the Communists and the leftist Zionists looked to the Soviet Union. (England's policy in Palestine had alienated most Zionists; their distrust of England as mandatory power extended also to England as wartime ally.) All the leftist ideologies envisaged the defeat of the Germans, followed by revolutionary upheavals that would bring a new social order. In the first years of the German occupation, party people, habituated to the extravagant flow of rhetoric, often described the atrocities that the Germans committed against the Jews as 'annihilation' and 'destruction'. But in fact no Jewish party, before early 1942, took political cognizance of Nazism as waging war specifically against the Jewish people. Thus, at a clandestine meeting in Warsaw in May 1940, the Bund's Central Committee adopted a policy statement setting forth their political hopes and expectations:

Poland is our homeland, where we are entitled to equal citizenship rights, where our future lies ... Any other solutions offered, under present conditions, by Zionist or other Jewish groups, are wrong and utopian, as they always were. Together with the Polish working masses struggling underground, the Jewish people of Poland see no other means of survival, but the defeat of Hitlerism and the reconstruction of a free, independent and Socialist Poland.[11]

On 1 May 1941 Dror issued a proclamation that avowed once more the movement's dual loyalty to Palestine and socialism and which held out the hope of the inevitable realization of a socialist Palestine:

The struggle with the Hitlerite conqueror has temporarily separated us from Eretz Israel, but just as there is no power in the world that can separate us from the struggle for a socialist world. thus nothing can separate us from the land of our ultimate hope. The building of Eretz Israel is undeniably connected with the collapse of capitalism; a socialist Eretz Israel will rise or fall with the success or failure of socialism.[12]

At the end of December 1943, a representative of the Left Labour Zionists, taking part in a clandestine meeting of the underground Polish Communist front, Krajowa Rada Narodowa (People's Home Council), spoke of victory with the political certitude of her party:

In the struggle for a new world of labour and of social justice, we are not isolated. The working masses of the whole world with the heroic Red Army in the vanguard, are with us. Our struggle is their struggle; their victory shall be our victory. There can be no return to the past, no turning back to the past reactionary and fascist governments. The working masses, the invincible forces of progress and true democracy will prevail in this historic struggle.[13]

Maintaining the traditions of the movement became a conspiratorial activity, yet served to uphold morale. May Day 1940 in Lodz fell on the day the Jews were enclosed within the ghetto. That day Bundist activists visited as many members as they could locate, reminding them of May Day, distributing little red-ribbon boutonnières, and passing the word: 'Hold on and hold out.' In January 1942 Dror proclaimed a fund-raising campaign in the Warsaw ghetto on behalf of the Jewish National Fund to be conducted according to Zionist tradition on the fifteenth day of Shevat, the New Year for Trees, the time for collections to aid Palestine's re-forestation programme.

Party ideology remained binding and the commitment of its adherents remained insusceptible to change even in the drastically altered conditions in which the Jews now lived. Just as before the war, each party continued to believe that it was the sole repository of political truth, that it held the key to a noble future. Any ideological deviation or political concession was regarded as a betrayal of principle. In conformity to the pre-war pattern, some parties worked together on some undertakings, but these were mainly pragmatic ventures. A pan-Zionist interest prevailed, for instance, with regard to the *halutz* youth movements. On the left, Bundists and Left Labour Zionists jointly organized several strikes and demonstrations, as they had occasionally done before the war. But party sovereignty persisted along with ideological divisiveness. In a report of 16 March 1942, sent abroad, the Bund gave its version of the political disharmony in the ghettos:

The Bund's and the Tsukunft's competitors show no concern for the fate of the land where they live. The Left Labour Zionists and the youngsters of the Hehalutz are prepared to relinquish their patrimony to the neighbour to the East [the USSR]. In addition, in their periodical writings, they dream of leaving for Palestine. They minimize the importance of the Allies for the future of their friends and our people. They tie their only hope to the USSR. The remaining former competitors [Aguda] passively await salvation.[14]

The Bund historically held the Marxist view of society in class conflict, its class-conscious bias denying the validity of national/ethnic group consciousness. Thus, according to the Bund, the Jewish working class had more in common with the Polish working class than with the Jewish bourgeoisie. While the Right Labour Zionists upheld Jewish group consciousness over class consciousness, at least until a Jewish state could be established, the Left Labour Zionists took the Marxist position. Thus the ingrained Marxist view of class conflict in the leftist Jewish parties undermined the concept of a common Jewish political interest.

The vehicle best suited to uphold party morale and to propagate the party's views was the underground press. It was also the channel that gave the parties access to the larger society not only as spokesman for their particular ideologies, but as advocate for the oppressed ghetto in its struggle for survival. Every party published, though every publication was illegal. The mere transmission of news was forbidden. The penalty for possession of a radio was death. All printing equipment – typesetting machines and presses – had been immediately confiscated by the Germans when they invaded Poland, and by October 1939 all publishing came under German control. Only the Judenräte were permitted to retain some small printing apparatus.*
Under these circumstances, the mere dissemination of news – war news, political developments, diplomatic affairs, simple chronicles of events inside Warsaw, inside Poland, in Europe or worldwide – became a political function, a form of political opposition to German tyranny. In Lodz an underground inter-party group of about a dozen people maintained an underground radio listening post for five years. Their dissemination of foreign-broadcast news acted as a massive antidote to ghetto apathy.

Some 100 or more illegal bulletins and newspapers were issued in the ghettos of the Generalgouvernement and in Ostland. Nearly half were published in Warsaw alone and eventually distributed in the provinces by couriers.[15] Usually crudely duplicated from typewritten texts, they consisted, on an average, of some eight to twelve pages stapled together, in an edition of a few hundred. According to a questionnaire distributed among members of the Tsukunft, as Henoch Rus noted in his record book on 9 March 1941, the *Yugnt-shtime*, monthly organ of the Tsukunft, had some 3,000–4,000 readers for its edition of 300. Other papers too averaged ten or more readers per copy.

In September 1939 the Warsaw Bundists had foresightedly removed two mimeograph machines from their headquarters and

---

*In 1941 *Gazeta Żydowska* began to be published in Cracow as an official 'Jewish' periodical. Issued bi-weekly, ostensibly under the supervision of the Abteilung für Volksaufklärung und Propaganda (Department for Public Enlightenment and Propaganda) but actually under Gestapo control, *Gazeta Żydowska* printed German news bulletins, decrees affecting Jews, official information about the activities of the Judenräte and neutral filler material.

hidden them. These, plus some initial supplies of stencils, ink and paper, constituted their underground printing establishment. Replacing the supplies became increasingly difficult. If a copy of an underground paper fell into German hands, the make of paper or printing ink could, if traced, expose the whole operation. Publishers of underground papers had to keep ahead of the Gestapo. In at least one instance, the Bund's counter-intelligence saved the party press from falling into German hands. The machines and the paper were removed overnight. The next day, when the Gestapo arrived, they found a vacant apartment.[16] For purposes of security, underground publishers kept changing their papers' names, thus hoping to throw the Germans off the track. Illegal publications were sometimes backdated to pre-war times to bedevil the Germans.

Security in issuing the paper, distributing it, even in reading it, became literally a matter of life or death. Instructions in the techniques of distributing the underground press were detailed in *Yugnt-shtime* of December 1940:

1. Who can be a reader? Not everyone can and not everyone should receive the *Yugnt-shtime*. He should be someone who is *known well* and is *reliable*. He should not be a shilly-shallier, nor a blabbermouth, nor a scatterbrain. It is foolishness and a crime to distribute the paper indiscriminately.

2. *Don't inquire!* Only you and the person who gives you the paper know from whom you get the paper. *No one else.* But you do not know from whom your distributor gets the paper. You should not know and should not ask.

3. *No substitutes!* No one should take your place in receiving or distributing the paper. You must do it yourself, alone. You are the one who is trusted.

4. *Don't make notes!* You must not make any notes, especially not addresses. Remember that if you must write something down, do it in code. Destroy your notes afterwards.

5. *A clean apartment!* Don't procrastinate. If you receive the paper today, distribute it today. Don't let it accumulate in your place.

6. *Keep quiet!* About organizational work, the less said the better. Many are curious, among them those who are paid for their curiosity. If you happen to know more about the organization's work than others, keep quiet, because through your blabbing you can betray the movement. If you happen to know the names of leaders, keep quiet, never

mention any name, for your blabbing can betray someone. This applies not only to the leaders of your organization, but to all underground workers. Don't talk in the street or in public institutions about the work, the illegal press. Remember, blabbing is a crime with regard to the movement.[17]

The instructions were practical and realistic. A month or two after they were issued, a seventeen-year-old Tsukunft activist was caught by the Gestapo with some issues of a party publication. He was imprisoned in Warsaw's dreaded Pawiak prison, where the Germans tortured him to make him reveal the names of the paper's editors. He died without mentioning a single name.[18]

All the underground papers devoted most of their space to military and political news about the war. The news was gathered from BBC broadcasts in many languages from London and also from Russian or underground stations in occupied countries. The Jewish underground parties thus managed to penetrate the wall of censorship erected by the Germans. The news that the underground press circulated in the ghettos helped to keep the Jews informed about major developments on the fronts and in political circles. The anti-Nazi editorials of the underground press articulated the hatred for the Germans that the silenced populace felt. All news about Allied victories and German defeats – scarce, to be sure, in the first years of the war – buttressed by editorial predictions of the ultimate defeat of the Germans, sustained the ghetto Jews and nourished their will to live. 'The only thing that fortifies and encourages us to endure the dreadful tortures', wrote an unknown author in *Yugnt-shtime* in April 1941, 'is the powerful belief that in the conflagration of the war fascism in all its forms will be destroyed forever.' The Left Labour Zionist youth organ, *Yugntruf*, in March 1942, was confident that a new world would be born out of present suffering, in which 'the persecuted and tortured will enjoy the life of a free people rooted in the soil of its homeland, Eretz Israel'. A world without hope, says one of Malraux's characters, is suffocating.

In a vigorous campaign against apathy and depression, *Dror*, the movement's underground newspaper, addressed a series of letters to its readers: 'At times you think that things have come to their end, that you are no longer capable of doing anything. You are mistaken if you think so. Do not let apathy and despair overpower you, or even influence you. Harness yourself to hard, intensive work, work as hard as you can.'[19] The *Yugnt-shtime* exhorted its readers:

The very expression of apathy indicates submission to the enemy, which can cause our collapse morally and root out of our hearts the hatred for the invader. It can destroy the will to fight within us, it can undermine our resolution . . . Our young people must walk head erect, despite the storms which threaten to destroy us.[20]

In March 1941, on the seventieth anniversary of the Paris Commune, Tsukunft issued a booklet *Di parizer komune*, whose essays and poems extolled the revolutionary commune and its leaders. An epigraph taken from Victor Hugo, 'In the grave is the corpse,/The idea lives,' suggested the immortality of the revolutionary idea. The comparison between the Warsaw ghetto and the Paris Commune was unmistakable.[21]

In the summer of 1940, *Dror* published a 114-page mimeographed booklet *Payn un gvure* (*Suffering and Heroism*), a literary and historical potpourri on Jewish martyrdom and resistance during the Crusades, the Chmielnitski massacres of 1648–9 and the Ukrainian pogroms of 1917–20. The introduction pleaded that its readers not abandon their faith in Western civilization and European culture because of Nazi barbarism, arguing that Nazism was a transitory phenomenon, a nightmare in mankind's history, induced by the profound social and economic contradictions of the political order. Therefore 'we can conquer our own depression and not lose hope for a better future'. The authors took pride in their tradition: 'We are an old cultural people with a rich spiritual heritage from which we draw amply. We cannot and will not succumb, for we have survived similar hardships countless times in our 3,000-year-old history.'[22]

The underground press enlarged and fed the animosities of the populace against the Judenräte and the police. Accusations of thievery, corruption and bribery were levelled against the food, fuel and housing departments of the Warsaw Judenrat time and again. The rhetoric flowed in abundance, though proof for the charges was scanty. That may not have mattered in the ghetto court of public opinion. The underground press, particularly the Bund's, presented itself as the defender of the poor against the Judenrat, which was depicted as the agent of the rich and influential. On 1 February 1942 a page-one editorial '"Führer" Mania in the Warsaw Ghetto', in the Bund's *Veker*, denounced the Judenrat in sweeping generalities for nepotism and exploitation of the populace. An editorial in the same issue asked rhetorically 'What Has Happened to the Bread?', suggesting that the cut in the bread ration, which affected the poor and hungry, actually benefited the privileged.

In April 1941 the *Yugnt-shtime* attacked the Warsaw Judenrat in its role as kehilla successor:

An especially sad chapter is the role of the kehilla. The Jewish folk masses always had a negative attitude towards this institution, and nowadays especially . . . Taxes are levied equally on everyone; instead of taxing [just] the rich and the propertied, also the poor and unemployed are taxed.

The *Veker* of 8 February 1942 pursued the same line in its editorial 'The Masses Pay – The Rich Rule'. *Jutrzenka*, issued by Gordonia in the Warsaw ghetto, on 14 March 1942 charged the Judenrat with being 'a tool in the hands of the Germans, traitors who will get their well-merited punishment'. Every underground paper attacked the Jewish police, condemning them as 'shameless blackmailers' and 'thieves' who thrived on the misery of the poor, hard-working, decent populace.

The underground press intensified the popular hostility towards the Judenräte and the police, actively encouraging resistance to official orders. On 23 May 1942 *Dos fraye vort*, Bundist weekly succeeding the *Veker*, printed a news item to the effect that the German Labour Office in Warsaw was making night raids to ferret out skilled workers. The article advised: 'Workers, hide and don't let yourselves be caught.' Those unfortunate enough to 'fall into the enemies' hands' were advised that 'the slogan of the working class in all occupied lands is: *Work badly and slowly*'.

The parties and their press stimulated and organized sabotage in the ghetto factories. In the Lodz ghetto and elsewhere, 'P.P', standing for *pracujcie powoli*, 'work slowly', became an underground code. Mysterious fires were a constant plague in the factories. Production was not only slowed down, but undermined deliberately. In Będzin, the Jewish underground even inserted revolutionary leaflets in clothing destined for German soldiers. Sabotage by the Jews working for the Germans was an important part of the programme of the underground organizations. In Baranowicze, a team of Jews assigned to repair German trains on a local line was instructed to work slowly. The trains used to cross a wooded area controlled by Russian partisans, who usually managed to inflict some damage on the locomotives. The repair work was sabotaged so that seven of the nine locomotives on the line were always disabled.[23] Ghettos located along or near the perimeter of partisan operations, Vilna and Kovno, for instance, were usually extensively involved in systematic sabotage operations directed from the outside.

The most outspoken call to disobedience by the underground press came early in July 1942, after the Germans had shot 110 Warsaw ghetto Jews – ninety men, ten women and ten policemen – in reprisal for the increasing disobedience by the Jewish population to police regulations and for insubordination by the police in carrying out regulations. The 110 victims were taken at random from persons then being held in Pawiak prison on minor charges. An announcement explaining the shootings as an act of reprisal was issued over the signature of Heinz Auerswald, Warsaw ghetto commissar. The underground press responded with savage contempt. *Yedies*, a Hehalutz newspaper, asserted that the Jews would continue to disobey the Germans orders: 'We will continue to evade every one of these cruel laws; we will continue to disobey all these draconic regulations'.[24] On 5 July 1942 *Shturem*, the Bundist weekly under another new name, ran a lead editorial, 'Honour to the Fallen'. It was the most explicit call to disobedience that had appeared in the underground press:

Let us not lament the victims, not weep, not wring our hands. They fell as soldiers at their posts. They were murdered because we Jews are a stiff-necked people, because we do not wish to expire 'loyally' under the bloody German yoke, because we constantly break all regulations and laws which the cynical hangmen promulgate against us. The chief hangman Auerswald has announced in his placards that he murdered 110 Jews in reprisal for our rebelliousness, for our resistance to the Germans. The hangman may be sure that from now on we will disobey his Hitlerite laws still more. We do not fear the even greater punishment with which he threatens us. We have nothing more to lose – we can win everything.

Auerswald's placard is the badge of honour of the struggling Jewish masses in the Warsaw ghetto.[25]

Overt opposition was inhibited by German terror, and the meager record testifies not to passivity, but to a healthy recognition by the Jewish parties of the real deployment of power in the ghettos. Self-discipline and the submission of the individual to the collective were the habitual posture prescribed for members of revolutionary organizations. Under German occupation, that posture became mandatory, for the relationship between discretion and valour was as the ratio of life to death. Civil disobedience as a strategy of political opposition can succeed only with a government ruled by conscience. In 1938, after Kristallnacht, when Gandhi advised the Jews in Germany to employ *Satyagraha*, the Indian version of passive resistance, he disclosed his inability to distinguish between English and German political morality. The Jews in Poland, with sharper political perceptions, made no such miscalculation.

In the first years of the occupation, the Jewish parties essayed several tests of strength. The first came at the end of March 1940 in Warsaw. Youthful Polish hooligans had charged Jewish neighbourhoods, with cries of 'Kill the Jews' and 'We want a Poland without Jews.' They stormed Jewish stores and even homes, robbing, looting and beating up the Jews. The Germans stood by, observing and photographing. An emergency meeting of the Bund *aktiv* was called. In normal times, the Bund would have sent out its party and trade-union militia to fight off the pogromists, but now, under German occupation, the stakes had changed. The question that confronted the meeting hinged on the likelihood that the Germans would intervene and declare all the Jews collectively responsible for any act of resistance undertaken by the Bund. Consequently, the Jewish community would suffer worse from German reprisals than from Polish pogroms. Nevertheless, the Bund decided to fight back. Self-discipline was invoked: the militia would use only iron pipes and brass knuckles, forgoing knives and firearms to minimize the risk of killing a Pole and calling forth German retaliation.

The next day the pogromists encountered Jewish resistance. Fighting took place in different parts of town. Ambulances were called to carry off wounded pogromists. Ringelblum even heard that a Pole had been killed. At evening curfew the fighting halted to be renewed the following morning. That day, at last, the Polish police were ordered to halt the fighting.[26] The anticipated German reprisals did not materialize.

Other Jewish parties had opposed the Bund's action. Most Jews feared that worse would come from such audacious Jewish acts of resistance in those circumstances. While the underground movement and the Jewish populace were clearly at one when the parties vented contempt and hatred upon the Germans or the Judenräte in their press, functioning expressively, the divergence between party and mass was evident when the party engaged in overt acts, functioning instrumentally, purposefully. Although the parties could claim to speak for the people by articulating their feelings, they could not always claim to act for them, simply because terror repressed the will to resist.

On some occasions, when hunger and misery grew intolerable, the parties carried out demonstrations and strikes with substantial popular support. To be sure, spontaneity sparked some demonstrations, yet only the underlying party organization could provide the structure and formulate the goals for such actions. In Lodz the Bund, the Left Labour Zionists and the Jewish Communists, working together on an *ad hoc* basis, succeeded in engaging in their activities some of the more political-minded workers of the pre-war, massive trade-union movement. In the autumn of 1940 the three parties jointly convened a conference of some 130 factory delegates. The party leaders also used to meet with Rumkowski, representing the factory workers and defending their interests *vis-à-vis* the Judenrat. The ghetto was little more than six months old in January 1941, when hunger prevailed over terror and a series of demonstrations and strikes erupted. Workers demanded more food, an increase in the rations, higher wages and even the rights of organization and representation. Rumkowski demanded unconditionally that the party leaders call off the strikes, which had broken out first among the cabinet-makers and then spread to the tailors and textile workers. Party and union leaders refused to accede to Rumkowski's demands, while he stubbornly withheld any concessions. Within a week the strikes collapsed, because some workers, unable to bear the hunger of their children, returned to the factories. In that encounter the parties could not sway Rumkowski, who, for his part, regarded the strikes as a threat to his authority. In that test of strength he demonstrated that he could subdue the ghetto without resorting to German force.[27] But unrest persisted throughout the ghetto. Children, organized by the Bund's juvenile organization SKIF, picketed in front of Rumkowski's home, shouting, 'Rumkowski, you are our misfortune.' So pervasive was the ferment within the ghetto that even the *hasidim*, the most passive element in the population, sent Rumkowski an ultimatum on 29 January 1941 to the effect that if their people did not get more bread and potatoes, they would organize a demonstration. For the next ten days they threatened to parade publicly with Torah scrolls to petition Rumkowski. The demonstration apparently never came off, probably because Rumkowski had summoned the rabbis and counter-threatened a bloody end to a demonstration with Torah scrolls. He reminded the rabbis that he himself had put up a fight with the Germans to keep the Torah scrolls.

In Bialystok about 100 wagoners called a strike at the end of April 1942 against a mandatory registration of horses ordered by the Germans.[28] The action was probably spurred by the underground parties. The most spectacular demonstration occurred in the Częstochowa ghetto, where the Labour Zionists had established a labour council, whose function was to mediate between the 5,000 workers in the ghetto and the Judenrat. Driven by hunger and anger, 1,000 exhausted and emaciated workers convened in the labour council's public kitchen in December 1941 to hear their union leaders call on the Judenrat for increased bread rations and higher wages. One speaker, carried away by his cascading rhetoric, unexpectedly called for a protest demonstration against the Judenrat. The workers, impelled by passion, streamed down the street, swarmed into the Judenrat building, breaking down doors, smashing furniture, wrecking typewriters, assaulting the staff. Their violence communicated the anger they felt because of the hunger their families had to endure, and they demanded what was due to them as human beings. Order was finally restored by the labour council itself; a delegation was then selected from the workers to join the council executive in negotiating with the Judenrat. Finally, after hours of negotiations, during which the strikers barricaded the building, the Judenrat acceded to their demands.[29]

But German terror soon subdued both mass membership and party leadership with regard to overt acts like demonstrations and strikes. Not only did the populace fear the deadly German reprisals, but the parties dreaded decimation of their leadership and ranks. The Germans were always, from the first days of the occupation, on the look-out for Jewish political leaders and activists. They recruited paid agents from the Jewish underworld to help uncover party people and party hide-outs. Survival became a question of security. The very existence of the party was at stake. Quite early, the Bund instituted a solemn oath for its members, demanding 'loyalty unto death', a promise never to betray the organization. Each party suffered severe losses, as its activists were discovered. In 1941, in Lublin, a Bundist who had been distributing anti-Nazi literature was caught by the Germans and publicly hanged.

Couriers were often apprehended, causing the collapse of an entire chain of contact or, even more seriously, jeopardizing a whole underground network. In May or June 1941 a Polish courier travelling on behalf of the Bund's central committee was arrested in Piotrków by the Gestapo. The documents found on her pointed to the party's organizations in a string of cities. Gestapo agents intensified their search for party activists in these places, one of which was Częstochowa. In mid-July a Bundist named Motek Kushnir, who headed the TOZ in Częstochowa, was warned minutes before the Germans arrived. He managed to escape from his office, but the Gestapo then seized five TOZ staff members and Kushnir's mother and brother, threatening to shoot them all if he did not turn himself in. The Bund's local committee decided, however, that Kushnir should remain in hiding for the time being. The Judenrat, which the Germans had involved, then warned the Bundists that the hostages would be shot. The party committee reconvened, debating whether they had the right or responsibility to decide about the life and death of other people. Kushnir, with the concurrence of the majority, decided to turn himself in. The party promised to do everything possible to release him. For weeks Kushnir was tortured by the Gestapo, but finally released at the end of September after the party succeeded in bribing a Gestapo agent with 35,000 zlotys and expensive goods to boot.[30]

The Germans continued their relentless hunt of party activists throughout the Generalgouvernement, driving the parties still deeper underground and forcing them to relinquish public activities. In the spring of 1942 the Germans carried out mass arrests and killings of groups of Jews in many ghettos (according to Ringelblum's information, in Cracow, Tarnów, Częstochowa, Radom, Kielce, Ostrowiec).

These particular actions seemed directed against political activists, though the pattern was not consistent. In Warsaw, late on Friday night, 17 April, and long into the next morning, some fifty Jews were seized in their homes by the Gestapo and shot on the street. That night became known as 'Bloody Friday'. Most of those rounded up were printers and persons associated with the underground press. The rumour was spread in the ghetto that the slaughter had not been arbitrary, that the Germans were after persons involved in 'politics' and in publishing illegal newspapers. Indeed, Czerniaków had summoned a Bundist leader to inform him that the Gestapo had indicated that these killings – 'executions' was the term used – would continue as long as the underground press did. Czerniaków asked him to have the Bund desist from further publication, but the Bundist refused. His party later upheld his position.[31]

The murmurs in the ghetto grew louder and more voluble, spread probably by the Gestapo agents and picked up by a fearful populace, to the effect that the Socialists, the politicals, were causing the troubles in the ghetto. On 30 April 1942 an editorial in the Bundist *Veker*, 'The Bloody Night', addressed itself to the killings and to the rumours:

Then let the dogs be silent who dare to bark on the graves of those who fell during the bloody Friday night in Warsaw. Let them not dishonour the peace of the martyrs. Let them not try to argue that it was the Socialists who brought on the misfortune. That Friday night in the Warsaw ghetto was only one *small* link in the *great* chain of the bestial murders of the Jews by Hitler.

The editorial then proceeded to analyse the recent course of events in the light of new insights. The Jewish political underground had come to see that the German atrocities against the Jews were not merely the destructive fall-out of a fascist war against the capitalist order, but were part of a deliberate design to annihilate the Jews.

Like a tornado the Einsatzgruppen swept through the Jewish settlements of Eastern Europe in the summer of 1941, destroying age-old communities in cyclonic upheaval. The German invasion found the Russians unprepared militarily and the civilian population disoriented and demoralized. Exploiting the superstitious anti-Semitic prejudices of the Lithuanians, Balts and Ukrainians and activating their accumulated hatred for the Soviets, the Germans harnessed the violent energies of these willing collaborators to round up and kill the Jews. In Vilna and Kovno the Lithuanians roamed the streets, capturing Jewish males, hauling them away, purportedly for work. In Lwów the Germans and Ukrainians, in house-to-house hunts for Jews, shot them randomly on the spot. Belatedly avenging the assassination – by a Jew back in 1926 – of Semyon Petlura, notorious anti-Semite and Ukrainian national hero, the Ukrainians staged mammoth pogroms, slaughtering thousands and carrying off other thousands of Jews to Einsatzgruppen headquarters.[1] Within hours or days, those Jews who had been taken away were machine-gunned *en masse* at some remote desolate area. The disaster was epic:

> There was everywhere terrible grief,
> Everywhere panic, and death in full many a form.

Jewish communal leaders appealed to the German military to halt the local pogromists and urged local Baltic or Ukrainian officials to restrain their people. Thousands of Jews besieged the quarters of German and local authorities to obtain the release of husbands, fathers, sons, brothers, to learn of their whereabouts, to send them food. To support their entreaties, the Jews offered gifts and bribes. Driven by anxiety, many Jews responded in panic and hysteria, in constant action and reaction. Others, with less psychic energy, succumbed to depression and apathy, paralysed by fear. Still others, whose husbands or sons disappeared into the violent void, refused to believe that their men had been killed. In response to the strains and anxiety, they indulged in the comfort of wishful beliefs, convinced that husbands or sons had been taken away for work in some distant place, that surely they would return hale and whole after the war's end.

The wild spate of violence ebbed after a month. The Germans began to organize more systematic and disciplined programmes of murder. In Kovno, for instance, in mid-August 1941, the Germans demanded from the Judenrat 500 educated young men. When the Judenrat asked why these were wanted, they were told that the intellectuals would be assigned to classifying government archives and hence would be spared the heavy labour soon to be come obligatory for all Jews. On that understanding, the Judenrat prepared a list. Volunteers, too, offered their services. In all, 534 young educated Jews were taken away and never seen again. Similar ruses were practised in other cities in a deliberate plan to destroy the community's élite.

The German military, having taken over existing industrial enterprises, began operating them to meet the needs of the German war effort. Airfields for supply and military purposes had to be enlarged and new ones constructed. The German army had to be supplied and its equipment kept in repair. Civil occupation facilities and military ones for the continuing campaign against Russia had to be erected. Each Jewish worker in these installations, factories and workshops was issued an identity document, a *Schein*. Usually a white or coloured card, identifying its holder as a skilled worker, it promised security from arbitrary seizure and deadly violence. Its aura of immunity transformed it into a symbol of life. Underlying the emotional significance that the Jews attached to the work card was the reasoned conclusion that, in order to wage war successfully, the Germans would have to make rational use of available manpower. Hence the Jews who provided the labour and the skills that the Germans needed would thus be assured of life. This conviction spurred Jews to seek work, registering with the Judenrat's labour office as skilled workers.

On 15 September 1941, just a month after the Kovno Jews had been enclosed in a ghetto, the Germans sealed off the ghetto. Working parties assigned to outside labour were not permitted to leave. The next day the Germans delivered 5,000 cards to the Judenrat, with orders that they were to be distributed to skilled workers. Signed by SS-Hauptsturmführer Jordan, specialist for Jewish affairs in the German administration of Kovno, these cards became known in the ghetto as 'Jordan permits'. Nearly 30,000 Jews then lived in the Kovno ghetto, some 6,000 to 7,000 having already been murdered by units of Einsatzgruppe A. The cards were entrusted to the Judenrat's labour office, whose officials, jointly with representatives of the various trades, began the distribution according to their registry. Several hours later, after many cards had been issued, a German official at an industrial enterprise telephoned to the Judenrat to make sure that 'his' Jewish workers would receive what he described as their *Lebensscheins* – life permits. Instantly what had seemed to be mere administrative procedure turned into ultimate judgement as to who would live and, in consequence of the German decision, who would die.[2]

The Judenrat officers called an emergency meeting to confront the situation. What should they do? Among the proposals put forward was one to return all the cards to the Germans with a statement that the Judenrat could not and would not distribute them. Someone even suggested burning the cards. Since the whole Jewish community of Kovno appeared to be doomed, it was wrong to save one sixth, just for the Germans to exploit them for German ends. 'If we must die, let us all die together.' Meanwhile, word about the significance of the Jordan permits spread rapidly. Panic swept the ghetto. A mob of thousands of Jews – mostly workers – swarmed to the Judenrat, broke in, searching for the cards, smashing doors, breaking furniture, shouting, 'The cards belong to us.' They seized the remaining cards, after Judenrat staff and Jewish policemen had already grabbed many for themselves.

All that night the Lithuanian police guarding the ghetto kept shooting, stirring even greater terror and panic among the trapped Jews. In the morning manned machine-guns surrounded the ghetto. Armed Germans and Lithuanians ordered all the Jews in the small ghetto to assemble in the public square, lined up by families, in columns. A selection began and the holders of the Jordan permits were separated from the others. All at once a Gestapo official drove into the ghetto with a written message for the SS officer in charge of the selection.

Upon reading it, he ordered his men back to their barracks. The Jews fled into their homes. Inexplicably the *Aktion** was called off.

Two days later, the Germans ordered the Kovno Judenrat to supply 1,000 men daily for heavy work at the airfield. The workers were available, for now everyone knew that work meant life. On 26 September, German police surrounded part of the ghetto, and on the ground that Jews had shot a German policeman, removed about 1,000 people – the old, the sick and women whose husbands had disappeared during the first sweep of the Einsatz squads. They were all shot at the Ninth Fort, part of a massive fortress system built by the Tsars outside Kovno. The next week rumours were spread in town about a leprosy epidemic in the ghetto. A municipal medical commission came to investigate, finding nothing. Nevertheless, on 4 October the Germans once more surrounded the small ghetto. All persons with work documents, who were employed in specified enterprises or at the airport, were permitted to leave. All the others were taken to the Ninth Fort. The hospital was set afire, its patients and medical staff burned alive.

The ghetto lived in unbearable tension and constant mourning for the dead. After the seizure of many women without male support, convenience marriages became common. Anxiety enveloped the ghetto like a shroud. Rumours spread wildly; people were willing to believe anything, good or bad. They were tormented by the thought of recurring disaster, but no one could tell where, when, how or even whether it would strike again. It was like living on a high-angle fault whose contractions and tensions set off a series of earthquakes. Everyone anticipated catastrophe.

On 24 October SS officers toured the ghetto, pausing for a while at a large square called Democrats Place. The next day, one of those officers, SS-Hauptscharführer Rauke, RSHA specialist in Jewish affairs, came to the Judenrat, politely explaining that the ghetto had great tasks to fulfil for the Wehrmacht. The SS, for its part, would undertake to provide the required food rations for persons engaged in heavy labour and their families, but it could not provide such rations for Jews unable to perform heavy work. These would have to be

*Aktion, meaning 'activity' or 'process', is one of those indeterminate German words used by the Nazis to refer to a killing procedure.

moved to the small ghetto. The Germans themselves would make the selection. Rauke then handed to the Judenrat chairman notices to be posted the next day, 26 October, to the effect that on Tuesday 28 October at 6.00 a.m., the entire ghetto population would have to assemble for a mass roll-call at Democrats Place. Anyone found at home thereafter would be shot.

Once again the Judenrat convened in emergency session. In the light of recent events, they had little doubt about the eventual fate of the non-working Jewish population. They decided first to check and verify Rauke's statements, seeking corroboration. The next day, learning nothing from several sources, they managed to secure a confidential meeting of their top officers with Rauke. Dr Elkes, head of the Judenrat, suggested to him that if it was a matter of ensuring bigger food rations for the heavy workers, surely that distribution could be best entrusted to the Judenrat. Otherwise, what was the real purpose of this proposed roll-call?

Rauke acted surprised that the Judenrat was worried by this order, for, he assured them, it was only a matter of administrative expediency. The Germans had thought of giving the Judenrat this responsibility, but knowing that Jews stick together, the Germans were afraid that the Judenrat would distribute the rations equally to all. Consequently, Rauke explained, since their economic interests were involved, the Germans preferred to handle the matter their way. Nothing further could be elicited from him. The Judenrat officers' report to the board did not ease their disquiet. Late into the evening they discussed the possible consequences if they refused to carry out the order. Would it be regarded as sabotage and thus bring even greater disaster to the ghetto? They reached a dead end in their thinking, unable to make a decision. At 11.00 p.m. they agreed to ask Kovno's Chief Rabbi, Abraham Dov Shapiro, to issue a ruling on the basis of Halacha, Jewish law.

Weakened by age and illness, shaken by the events of the recent past, Rabbi Shapiro was agitated even more by the problem put to him. He asked for time to study the Talmudic and rabbinic sources that addressed themselves to related problems. Sustained by valerian, he pored over the texts all night. Late the following morning, he ruled: if a community of Jews is threatened by persecution, and some may be saved by a specific action, then the leaders of the community have to muster the courage and the responsibility to rescue whomsoever may be rescued. The notices should therefore be posted.

28 October dawned cold and overcast, as if, wrote an observer, the sun was ashamed to show its face. The 26,400 Jews of the Kovno ghetto assembled by families as ordered, dazed and dulled by fear. Instructed by the police, they walked as if in a funeral cortège, past Rauke, who, by a flick of his finger, indicated who was to go right, who left, who was to live, who was to die. Small families and young people were directed rightwards, large families and older people leftwards. The procession lasted all day. Nearly 10,000 people were segregated and sent for the night into the desolate small ghetto. The next day they were marched out in columns to the Ninth Fort and shot. A few days later Jordan informed the Judenrat that the *Aktionen* were over, but that the Jews were expected to work in accordance with German orders and requirements.

The ghetto remained a place of mourning without consolation, without joy or laughter, even without tears. Drained of feeling, the survivors were psychically numbed. Fear alone thrived, embracing the whole ghetto. The Deuteronomic text (28: 66–7) expressed the daily reality:

And thy life shall hang in doubt before thee; and thou shalt fear night and day, and shalt have no assurance of thy life. In the morning thou shalt say: 'Would it were even!' and at even thou shalt say: 'Would it were morning!' for the fear of thy heart which thou shalt fear, and for the sight of thine eyes which thou shalt see.[3]

Throughout the Diaspora, Halacha had guided Jews not only in ritual matters, but in all social, economic, political and moral issues. In modern times, despite secularism's erosion of its authority, Halacha continued to retain its full validity for observant Jews in all aspects of their lives. It remained also a frame of reference even for non-observant Jews at times when they confronted difficult and complex moral issues affecting the whole Jewish community. When the communal leaders of Kovno were faced with a problem involving the life and death of thousands of Jews, it was not unexpected that they sought the guidance of Halacha, hoping for ancient wisdom and ethical precepts to instruct them.

No Jewish community had ever before faced a comparable threat of annihilation. In their history the Jews had been subjected to the slaughter of many, enslavement, abduction of women or children, dire economic and religious sanctions. Those persecutions, reflecting the tensions between a hostile non-Jewish ruler and a local Jewish community, provided certain models in rabbinic teaching for the traditionally correct Jewish response. In the Talmud the basic case involved Joshua ben Levi, a third-century rabbi in Lydda, who had given refuge to a political fugitive. When the Roman authorities threatened to destroy Lydda and all its inhabitants, the rabbi presumably convinced the fugitive to surrender to the authorities. Thus Lydda and its people were saved.

Subsequent rabbinic tradition is both ambiguous and divided about Joshua ben Levi's role. The surrender to the authorities of a named individual wanted for a specific crime was generally permitted, whereas the surrender of an unspecified victim was forbidden, even if the whole community should perish as a consequence. Differences in rabbinic opinion even within these limits usually reflected contemporary political conditions. In times when the Jewish community was threatened with severe presecution, the rabbis, ruling leniently, approved of Joshua ben Levi's behaviour and elaborated arguments to justify it. In times when persecution eased, the reasoning hardened.[4] Nearly a thousand years after Joshua ben Levi, Maimonides, addressing himself to this problem, wrote:

If heathens said to Israelites, 'Surrender one of your number to us, that we may put him to death, otherwise, we will put all of you to death,' they should all suffer death rather than surrender a single Israelite to them. But if they specified an individual, saying 'Surrender that particular person to us, or else we will put all of you to death,' they may give him up, provided that he was guilty of a capital crime ... If the individual specified has not incurred capital punishment, they should all suffer death rather than surrender a single Israelite to them.[5]

In many ghettos the rabbis wrestled with the Maimonides ruling, some accepting his authority, others citing variant readings of the text and different cases. Kovno's Chief Rabbi, Shapiro, was one of the few rabbis who rejected the Maimonides position, though he left no record of the legal precedents on which he based his decision. His conclusion – approving surrender of a part if thereby the rest could be saved – was shared by men who themselves knew little of the Jewish tradition. In Vilna, for example, during the *Aktion* of late October 1941, when Gens himself, as head of the Jewish police, directed the Jews to right or left, to life or death, the rabbis sent a delegation to tell him that he was contravening Jewish law. To support their position, they cited Maimonides. Gens, who knew little, if anything, of Jewish law, responded that it was justifiable to surrender a part if the others would thereby be saved.[6]

In Vilna over 20,000 of the 60,000 Jews vanished or were killed outright from the time the Einsatzgruppen entered the city until the Jews were enclosed in Vilna's ghetto on 6 September 1941. The mass shootings took place at Ponary, ten kilometres from town, inaccessible because the Germans restricted all civilian movement. For weeks no one in Vilna knew of the death pits at Ponary. Efforts to get news from non-Jews brought rumours and reports that a ghetto existed at Ponary, that Jews were seen working there. A few persons who survived the mass shootings returned to Vilna early in September, wounded, bloody, shocked and disoriented, with tales so harrowing that they were literally incredible. Doctors at a ghetto hospital thought that these patients were demented, their minds unhinged by personal problems.[7] Illusion was nourished by apprehension, for all the Jews were pervaded by the sense that disaster could strike momentarily, like a river cresting at flood-tide.

Once the Jews were shut up within the walls of Vilna's large and small ghettos, more systematic seizures and killings began. Armed German and Lithuanian police would surround the ghetto, removing hundreds or thousands at a time. By mid-September another 10,000 Jews had vanished.[8] As in Kovno, Lwów, and elsewhere, the work card, the *Schein*, became the sole guarantee of security, the admission ticket to life. The *Schein* was the instrument with which the Germans screened the Jews, winnowing the 'productive' from the 'non-productive'.

Late in the day of Yom Kippur, 1 October 1941, the ghetto suddenly swarmed with German storm troops. Lithuanian militia drove thousands of Jews from their homes on the pretext that their identity cards had to be re-stamped at the ghetto gates. In the rapidly falling darkness, the Jews were herded through the narrow streets of old Vilna, the Jerusalem of Lithuania. It was an eerie, surrealistic procession, with thousands of Jews holding candles to light their way in the blacked-out town. Men, women and children, clutching each other for comfort and assurance, shuffled along, some dazed and apathetic, others pushing and shoving, trying to break through the cordon of Jewish police and escape into the night. At the gate, some 3,000 were taken away to Ponary. Thousands more were rounded up and spirited away in the next few days. Thereafter it became clear to all that Ponary meant death.

The Germans then undertook a new method of eliminating the Jews in mass. They gave the Judenrat 3,000 yellow permits to be distributed to persons engaged in production essential to the German war effort. Some 400 of these cards were allocated to employees of the Judenrat and other ghetto institutions. Each yellow-permit holder was entitled to protect his family, which, under German ground rules, was limited to husband, wife and two children under sixteen.

In accordance with German war-economy priorities, quotas of workers entitled to yellow permits were assigned to each authorized factory and workshop. Upon the instructions of the German factory director, the Judenrat issued permits to those workers. A panic to register in the factories seized the ghetto. Jewish factory managers, with access to German directors, were besieged for *protektsye*. Jews gave gifts and bribes to be entered on a factory roster. Political activists exploited connections and prestige to save their leading members. The Judenrat's labour office, it was said, yielded to party pressure and also succumbed to bribery. The yellow permit became the most desirable of all possessions. 'As precious as a yellow permit' became a new Yiddish coinage.

How the Judenrat managed the distribution of the 400 yellow permits is unclear. Judenrat staff and members of the Jewish police received yellow permits. The German authorities apparently assigned quotas for various categories of ghetto employees: teachers in the ghetto schools, doctors, nurses, orderlies, public-kitchen staffs, sanitation workers and the like. It is impossible to reconstruct on what general principles or by what expediencies the final allocation of permits was made. Ten permits were assigned for teachers, among whom the Communists were the single dominant group. They consequently exerted pressure to get permits for their people. The Germans had assigned only a few permits to ghetto medical personnel. A doctor in the Vilna ghetto, who years earlier had gone to medical school with a

German who was now – coincidentally – the municipality's top medical officer, managed to wring from him a few more permits for medical personnel. Still, there were more doctors than yellow permits. A committee, consisting at least of two doctors and perhaps some members of the Judenrat, sat in session, deciding who among the candidates would get the yellow passport to life.[9]

The dilemmas about whom to save by means of the yellow permits did not cease with their distribution. Then came the problem of the three additional family members. Every yellow-permit holder tried to save those closest to him. Family bonds were the most fundamental and decisive factor in the choice. Yet never did the family undergo a more disintegrative experience. The yellow-permit holder who wanted to save his parents, his wife and children, his brothers and sisters, had to choose among them. In most cases, the decisions favoured, as they would in modern Western societies, the nuclear family – wife and children – over parents, siblings, nieces and nephews. If the yellow-permit holder was unmarried, widowed or childless, he entered the next closest members of his family as wife or children, in whatever capacity would pass the German criterion. Nephews were entered as sons, fathers as husbands, wives as children, mothers as wives.

The Judenrat's labour office made sure that every holder of a yellow permit registered three family members to whom he was entitled. People without family were given fictive husbands, wives and children. Names were changed; identity documents were re-issued to conform to the individual's new status. The Judenrat canvassed the whole ghetto population to make certain that fully 12,000 persons would be covered, that no opportunity for life would be wastefully squandered. Nevertheless, in mid-October 1941, the Vilna ghetto held about 22,500 Jews, about 10,000 more than the permits could cover.

Those without yellow permits who could not get them officially, who could not buy authentic or even forged ones, tried other means of saving themselves or members of their families. Jews with non-Jewish friends tried to hide out with them, at least for the few days during which an *Aktion* was expected to take place. Peasants in outlying areas could sometimes be prevailed upon, for large sums, to hide children or elderly parents. Here and there individual Jews managed to obtain false papers, enabling them to pass as Christians and live outside the ghetto. But most people without yellow permits began to make hiding places or to buy places in already prepared hide-outs for themselves or those whom they could not otherwise protect. Hide-outs became a ghetto fever, an obsession, the cyclone cellars to protect against the German disaster. Hide-outs were located in attics and cellars, behind blind walls. Some held only one person; some held dozens. The hide-out in which young Rudashevski stayed was concealed in the two upper stories of a three-story ghetto warehouse. entered through a hole in the wall of the adjoining apartment house: 'The hole is blocked ingeniously by a kitchen cupboard. One wall of the cupboard serves at the same time as a little gate for the hole. The hole is barricaded by stones.' Bringing bare necessities and a pillow, an imprisoned mass of people bedded down in the inhospitable asylum for the night.

The first major *Aktion* of the yellow permits took place on 24 October after the permit holders and their dependants were ordered to leave the ghetto for their places of work. The remaining Jews were routed from their homes, the Lithuanian police scouring the buildings to uncover hide-outs. 'We are like animals surrounded by the hunter,' wrote Rudashevski.

I feel the enemy under the boards I stand on . . . They pound, tear, break . . . Suddenly, somewhere upstairs, a baby starts crying . . . We are lost. A desperate attempt to shove sugar into the baby's mouth doesn't help. They stop its mouth with pillows. Its mother weeps. In wild terror people demand that the baby be strangled. The baby's wails grow louder; the Lithuanians pound more heavily against the walls.

The Lithuanians did not discover that hide-out, but elsewhere in the ghetto they found some 5,000 Jews to send to Ponary. A few days later, another 2,500 Jews were dragged off from the small ghetto.

On 2 November, while on night duty at a ghetto first-aid station, a doctor was called out on an emergency. The patient was a Jewish policeman whose legs had become paralysed and whose speech impaired. The doctor asked what had happened to him. Another policeman, taking the doctor aside, told him that the Jewish police had just been notified that a three-day *Aktion* was to begin at dawn, that yellow-permit holders and their families would be sent to their places of work, and the remaining Jews would be rounded up for Ponary. Under S S supervision, the Jewish police would have to search out the

concealed Jews, blow up their hide-outs. As soon as the Jewish policeman heard these instructions, he had toppled over and became paralysed.[10] Most Jewish police, however, terrorized by the fear of death –
their own and their family's – obeyed German orders. They hunted
Jews down, uncovering their hide-outs, handing them over to the
Lithuanians and Germans. A new expression was coined in the Vilna
ghetto: 'You can trust me, I'm not a ghetto policeman.'

In those months of violence, the Vilna ghetto's police chief, Jacob
Gens, supplanted the Judenrat as the ghetto's real head. During the
selections, he himself checked the papers of the ghetto Jews as they
passed before him, three blue cards to one yellow card. In October he
participated in the *Aktion* that removed about 150 old and paralysed
Jews from the ghetto and in two *Aktionen* in December that delivered
over 150 Jewish 'criminals' to Ponary. Months later, at a public
meeting Gens exculpated himself: 'I, Gens, lead you to death, and I,
Gens, want to save Jews from death. I, Gens, order hide-outs to be
blown up, and I, Gens, try to get certificates, work and benefits for
the ghetto. I render the account of Jewish blood and not the account of
Jewish honour.' He went on: 'When they ask me for a thousand
Jews, I hand them over; for if we Jews will not give on our own, the
Germans will come and take them by force. Then they will take not
one thousand, but thousands. Thousands and the whole ghetto will be
at their mercy. With hundreds, I save a thousand. With the thousands
that I hand over, I save ten thousand.' Finally, he attempted to vindicate himself before the bar of Jewish history and the verdict of future
generations: 'I will say: I did everything in order to save as many
Jews as possible . . . to usher them into freedom. To ensure that at
least a remnant of Jews survive, I myself had to lead Jews to death;
and in order to have people emerge with a clean conscience, I had to
befoul myself and act without conscience.'[11]

The last of a series of small *Aktionen* took place on 21 December
1941. The next day the ghetto Jews awoke from fitful sleep to habitual
daylight anxiety. But the Germans did not return again. The volcano
ceased for a while its deadly eruptions. The Vilna ghetto, its population now about 12,500, entered a period of stability that was to last
until April 1943. The survivors gathered up the remnant threads of
their lives. Out of the wreckage of their institutions they began to rebuild the community. The normality that they reconstructed was ex-

ternal, part bulwark against the nightmares of the past, a grotesque ordinariness to combat memory. For the ghetto was haunted by 47,000 spectres. Each survivor was burdened by an intolerable weight of guilt feelings, created by the circumstances of the yellow permits. Everyone who survived felt that his life had cost someone else's, a response common to survivors of all kinds of disasters. In Vilna the mathematics of survival were so simple and stark that self-reproach was the most common denominator.

The killing began in the Wartheland as it began to wind down in the Eastern territories. In the farming settlement at Heidemühle, comprising sixteen villages near Turek, the Germans in late September 1941 concentrated above 5,000 Jews from six near-by towns. The displaced peasants were removed to adjacent villages. A Judenrat was organized and the Jews were set to lumbering in the woods, sowing and ploughing the fields. But premonitions of disaster soon began to pervade the Jewish community. On 4 November the Judenrat head convened the community's rabbis, informing them that the German district chief had ordered him to supply a list of all the Jews, each one to be designated as 'fit' or 'unfit', according to his capacity for work. Children under twelve and adults over sixty-five were to be designated as 'unfit'. The Judenrat head turned to the rabbis for guidance. The rabbis responded as to a community disaster, fasting, praying and pondering the problem. On 6 November they ruled that 'the law of the land is the law', even if an evil law. The list should, therefore, be submitted as ordered, but every Jew was to have the right to know which category he was assigned to.

The list began to be prepared. People used *protektsye* to get the records changed, to have one's children entered as older than they were, one's parents as younger. Bribery worked also on the German district officials; changes were constantly being made in the list. Panic intensified as the sense of imminent disaster overtook the community. The rabbis declared Mondays and Thursdays public fast-days; Jews recited psalms all day long, hoping to force God's intercession. The Judenrat head sent his parents away to another community, and others followed his example. Many Jews fled to other towns; some hid among the Polish peasants.

On 8 December 1941, at 2.00 a.m., hundreds of SS troops surrounded the settlement. In a house-to-house search, they routed the Jews from their beds and herded them all into one village. At 6.00 a.m. the Jews were marched out to a field, lined up, men and women separately. At 8.00 three German officers arrived and ordered the head of the Jewish police to read the names of the 'unfit' from the official list. No one responded as he began the roll-call. Those Jews had already fled. The silence hung heavy in the air. Then the German officer ordered the lines of men to file past, while another German officer directed the Jews to the right or left. About 1,100 Jews were sent left-wards and marched off. In the next few days the Judenrat managed, through bribery and intercession, to rescue 400 of them. The rest were sent to Chełmno on 13 and 14 December 1941, just five days after its gas vans had begun to operate.[12]

On 16 December 1941, the German authorities told Rumkowski that 20,000 Jews would have to leave the Lodz ghetto. In his first public announcement on the subject four days later. Rumkowski said he had succeeded in reducing the number by half and had convinced the Germans to permit him to decide, 'on the basis of internal autonomy', who was to leave the ghetto. Those to be transferred, he said, would probably be sent to small towns in the Generalgouvernement where the food shortage was less severe.[13]

To plan and organize the evacuation, Rumkowski right away called a conference of leading officials in his ghetto administration. Subsequently a Resettlement Commission was established, consisting of the head of the office of vital statistics, who was also in charge of new arrivals in the ghetto; commandant of the Jewish police; chairman of courts; commandant of the prison; head of the office of investigations; and director of penal administration. These men, under Rumkowski's imperious command, decided that the contingent of 10,000 deportees would consist of two categories: about 2,000 recent arrivals, expelled from Włocławek and surrounding towns – only the old among them were to be exempted because of the hardships of deportation – and the rest to be taken from persons convicted of misdemeanours or felonies and sentenced, a category designated as 'undesirables'. The families of these persons were to be included among the evacuees. To avoid sub-jectivity and personal involvement, it was said, the lists would be compiled on the basis of the official records of the courts administration, investigations office, prison and penal administration.

That announcement on 20 December 1941 transformed the misery in the ghetto, a time of bitter cold and savage hunger, into terror. Cold and hunger had already turned thousands of law-abiding ghetto residents into 'undesirables', because they had stolen wood for fuel or potato peelings for food. 'Criminals' were now those who had been sentenced for violating black-out regulations. People felt like trapped animals, unable to extricate themselves. Though the deportation procedure provided an opportunity for appeal, in practice only those with *protektsye* from Rumkowski or his associates managed to be exempted. People who did not report for evacuation within three days were cut off from food, since the supply depots were instructed not to issue them rations. The deportees were allowed to take with them personal possessions. Their ghetto paper money, with Rumkowski's picture on the bills, was exchanged for German Reichsmarks.[14]

The deportations got under way in mid-January 1942, when the first contingent of 1,292 poor and ragged men, women and children was sent off. On 17 January Rumkowski made a speech, vindicating himself:

Now, when we are deporting 10,000 people from the ghetto, I cannot pass over this tragic subject in silence. Unfortunately, in this respect, I received a ruthless order, an order which I had to carry out in order to prevent its being carried out by others. Within the framework of my possibilities ... I have tried to mitigate the severity of the decree. I have settled the matter so that *I assigned for deportation that portion which was for the ghetto a suppurating abscess*. So the list included the ousted operators of the underworld, scum and all sorts of persons harmful to the ghetto.[15]

The deportations lasted until 29 January 1942. But Rumkowski's success in satisfying the Germans with 10,000 Jews had been illusory. On 22 February the deportations were resumed. For the next forty days nearly 1,000 Jews were daily deported to an unknown destination. After the Resettlement Commission ran out of 'criminals' and 'sentenced' undesirables, they tackled the records of the welfare recipients. About 80 per cent of the 160,000 ghetto residents were then receiving assistance. To save their activists, the leaders of the political parties submitted the names of their people to the director of the Judenrat's welfare department, who then oblitered them from the welfare rolls. In a parallel effort, the director of the Judenrat's labour office placed party activists in factory jobs.[16]

The hierarchical ranking of categories for deportation – underworld elements, prostitutes, criminals, welfare recipients, non-working people – must have originated with the Germans, because everywhere it prevailed. In Bialystok in September 1941, when the Germans ordered the Judenrat to expel 4,500 'unproductive' Jews to Prużana, Barash ordered lists to be compiled along the same lines. In Radom in 1940, when the Judenrat was compelled to reduce the ghetto population by one third, lists were compiled first of 'harmful' elements and then of 'unproductive' ones.

Work became the fundamental principle justifying the Lodz ghetto's existence. Speaking on 2 March 1942, after the category of deportable 'criminals' had been exhausted, Rumkowski said 'Wholly innocent people have begun to be deported because *a new principle was introduced: that only those people who work can remain in the ghetto*! On the other hand, those who don't yet have or have not gotten work *must leave the ghetto*. The order must be carried out, there is no choice.'[17]

From 22 February to 2 April 1942, over 34,000 men and women were deported. 2 April was the first day of Passover, and pious Jews in this constellation a good omen. But the halt in the deportations, in April as in January, was no cessation, but only a pause. Later in April, Rumkowski issued orders requiring the unemployed, ten years old and up, to submit to examinations by a team of German doctors. Yet those orders were not pursued. Instead, Rumkowski announced at the end of April that starting on 4 May 1942 the Jews from Germany, Luxembourg, Vienna and Prague would be deported, except for the employed among them and the holders of the Iron Cross or other First World War decorations. Hitherto, those Jews as a group had been exempt from the deportations. A Czech Jew, himself an insider in the ghetto bureaucracy, speculated on Rumkowski's motives:

Though in principle no distinction was made, the psychologist must after all understand: The compatriot is the true brother; the newcomer – a step-brother. He does not even understand the language of the ghetto ... If only the natives would have to be deported, the Chairman would have had to turn to his productive elements ... Who can blame a good father when he tries with all his might to spare his beloved child?[18]

From 4 May to 15 May 1942, 10,161 Central European Jews left Lodz in 12 transports. Even those eligible for exemption volunteered to leave, for the half year they had spent in the ghetto, in hunger, cold and abject misery, had deprived them of the will to live. They left almost readily, convinced that wherever they went, they would not be worse off than in the Lodz ghetto.[19]

Where did they think they were going? At first, because their ghetto money was being changed into Reichsmarks, the deportees thought they were going to work in Germany. Others speculated that their destination was the Generalgouvernement. People even heard rumours that the deportees had arrived in Warsaw. But the Lodz ghetto was so tightly sealed, a quarantined Jewish island in a hostile German milieu (substantial segments of native Poles had been displaced), that no news about Chełmno or Auschwitz seeped in. No one knew anything about the fate of the 55,000 deported Jews.[20]

In the summer of 1942 about 10,000 young, able-bodied Jews were brought into the Lodz ghetto from towns and villages in the Wartheland that were being emptied of Jews. A survivor from Brzeziny brought to a Lodz Bundist a postcard which he had received from the rabbi of Grabów. The rabbi wrote that he had spoken with three Jews who had escaped from Chełmno and told him what occurred there. That was the first news in Lodz of the death camps. The Bundists undertook to pass the information on to Rumkowski, with the advice that perhaps in the future he would bribe the Germans instead of obeying their orders. But Rumkowski, it was reported, when shown the postcard, said he had already had this information for some time. Zionists and Bundists alike decided that the news about Chełmno must be transmitted to their party headquarters in Warsaw. Couriers were sent out.[21]

All through the summer, rumours about a resumption of the deportations coursed through the Lodz ghetto, reaching a crescendo of anxiety in early September. The rumours were not groundless: the

Germans were now demanding the sick, children under ten and adults over sixty-five. Rumkowski reactivated his Resettlement Commission to prepare the lists. Sensitive to the horror of the undertaking, he tried to involve the communal and political leaders as his accomplices. He called a meeting of representatives of the political parties, informing them that Hans Biebow, German administrator of the Lodz ghetto, had threatened that if the full contingent of 10,000 children under ten were not provided, the whole ghetto would be deported. Biebow had, however, allowed Rumkowski a certain number of exemptions. He offered these to the party leaders in exchange for their cooperation. They, in turn, said that they would have to consult their committees. Rumkowski gave them until the following morning. That night the Bundists convened a meeting of twenty-one leading members, sixteen of whom were parents of small children. All but one, a mother, voted to reject Rumkowski's offer.[22]

But some were found in the ghetto who would round up other people's children to save their own. Besides the Jewish police, also members of the fire brigade and the so-called 'White Guard' – teamsters of the food-supply department, so nicknamed because of their flour-coated smocks – volunteered to round up the old, the sick and the children in return for their own family's immunity. From 5 September to 12 September, an embargo (*Sperre*) was ordered on all movement in the Lodz ghetto. For the first day the streets were under the dominion of the Jewish police and their helpers, but thereafter the Germans took over, dissatisfied with the ineffectiveness of the Jewish police. The seizure of the old, the sick and the children beggared fantasy.[23] Andromache's grief was ten thousand times multiplied in Lodz:

> O Greeks, you have found out ways to torture
> that are not Greek.
> A little child, all innocent of wrong –
> You wish to kill him.

The Trojan women had their Jewish counterparts:

> As a bird cries over her young,
> Women weep for husbands, for children,
> For the old, too, who gave them birth.

The first news of Chełmno had reached Warsaw long before the couriers from Lodz. At the end of 1941 or early 1942, two escaped Jews from Chełmno came to Warsaw, with an agonized account of the annihilation camp where Jews were being gassed to death. In ŻTOS offices, where they told their story, the listening communal leaders thought that these young men must have undergone such desolating experiences that they had become deranged. The ŻTOS staff actually recorded their report, but withheld distribution because of its implausibility, not wishing further to agitate the inhabitants of the Warsaw ghetto, whose existence was wretched enough without such tales.[24]

Meanwhile, news from Ostland was arriving in Warsaw. At the end of October 1941, a non-Jewish courier undertook a mission on behalf of Hehalutz in Warsaw to make contact with the movement in Bialystok, Vilna and Lithuania. He brought back to Warsaw in mid-November the first news of the mass killings. At the end of December 1941 and early in January 1942, five couriers, members of Hashomer Hatzair and Hehalutz, arrived one by one in Warsaw from Bialystok and Vilna. They had come for money and arms to organize a resistance movement in their ghettos. In January they told a meeting of communal and underground political leaders that more than 50,000 unsuspecting Jews had been taken away to death at Ponary. Those mass killings in Vilna, they were convinced, marked the start of the liquidation of all Polish Jewry. Consequently, they argued, preparations for active defence should begin right away. The older communal leaders did not agree. Some believed that the German killings in the Ostland were in reprisal for Jewish collaboration with the Soviets. Others declared that the Germans would never dare to undertake mass killing on such a scale in Warsaw, in the very heart of Europe.[25] Nothing much came of the meeting, though the young people got some money.

On 25 January 1942 the *Veker*, the Bundist underground paper, reported a new wave of deportations under way in the Wartheland. 10,000 Jews had been sent out from Lodz, selected by 'King' Rumkowski himself. 'Where the deportees are sent is not known.' In Kalisz, the article continued, where once more than 15,000 Jews lived, only 1,000 skilled workers remained: 'The rumours are that the deportees are being killed.' On 1 February 1942 the *Veker* published its first report about the mass gassings: 'From Kolo, Izbica, Dąbie, Kłodawa come dreadful reports about the brutal annihilation by the crazed Hitlerites of the remaining scant Jewish settlements. The Jews are expelled and put to death in a murderous way. They are confined and killed with gas.'

The next week the *Veker* already knew the destination of the trains packed with Jews: Chełmno, eleven kilometres from Koło and Dąbie. 'There they are crammed in, half-naked (men in shorts, women in shifts), in hermetically sealed autos. In these autos they are poisoned with gases. Jews who refused to enter the autos were prodded with electrified bayonets.'

These reports appeared on the third or last pages of a four-page paper, as if the editors themselves had misgivings about their authenticity, or regarded them as inapplicable to Warsaw and the General-gouvernement. News about the progress of the war and stories about Judenrat corruption pre-empted the first pages. In fact, just a week after the last report on Chełmno, an editorial in the *Veker* on 15 February decried rumours coursing the Warsaw ghetto that 150,000 Jews would be deported: 'It is simply a crime to spread these rumours. The nerves of the Jewish populace are strained enough. By spreading these unfounded rumours, people are just doing the work of the Hitlerites – they are psychologically undermining the Jewish masses.'

Authentic reports and exaggerated rumours alike brought on generalized feelings of panic and hysteria. In the face of an unparalleled threat to all Jews, at once mysterious and incredible, the underground movement responded ambiguously. To maintain morale and contain panic it had to discount the reports, which were indeed hard to believe, but in order to mobilize its followers and also the general populace towards some eventual action to counter the threat to the Jews, it was obligated to identify and locate the danger confronting the community. The *Veker*'s next issue, 23 February 1942, brought new details, now on the second page, about the killing procedure at Chełmno: 'The "execution" lasts fifteen minutes, accompanied by the roar of the motor which is set in operation to drown out the screams and groans of the tortured, defenceless victims . . .'

The leftist Zionists, especially the *halutz* youth organizations, had meanwhile begun to think of active defence. To discuss such possibilities Hehalutz convened a meeting in mid-March 1942 of seven persons – two each from the Left Labour Zionists, the Right Labour Zionists and the Bund, and one from Hehalutz.[26] Three of the participants, representing each of the parties, were over forty, party leaders of standing. The rest were younger in years and political experience. Yitzhak Zuckerman of Hehalutz analysed the mass killings in Ostland and the Wartheland as the first step in the eventual annihilation of the Polish Jews. He proposed that a Jewish combat organization be established and arms procured.

Both Right and Left Labour Zionists were prepared to accept these proposals, but the Bundists disagreed.[27] The Bund's senior representative did not think that the Jews were the sole target of the Germans; the Poles too had suffered severe blows, their élite had been murdered, thousands had been incarcerated in labour camps. Furthermore, he held that the groups there assembled were too small, too weak and altogether uninfluential – inside the ghetto and outside – to undertake any successful counter-action on their own. Determination of the ghetto's fate was far beyond the capacity or competence of the ghetto itself and depended on the Allied powers. Besides, Jewish resistance would be feasible and effective only in concert with Polish resistance. The creation of a joint Jewish combat organization seemed premature. For the time being, he declared, each organization should maintain or set up its own combat units, as the Bund had already done.

Nothing came of those deliberations. At about this time, at the initiative of Jewish PPR members in the ghetto, a short-lived organization called the Anti-Fascist Bloc came into being.[28] Its constituent members, besides the PPR, were the Left and Right Labour Zionists and the Zionist youth organizations – Hehalutz, Hashomer Hatzair, Dror. Though they had no arms at all, the bloc members began to form combat units of fives, within each one's organization. When two PPR activists were arrested by the Gestapo and murdered in June, the whole apparatus of the PPR collapsed. The Bund meanwhile continued to train its own militia; in January 1942 the Tsukunft began to rebuild its youth militia, Tsukunftshturem. On 12 April the Tsukunft *aktiv* convened a meeting to discuss the organization of defence.[29]

In April the news about the first mass killings in the General-gouvernement reached Warsaw. An underground paper *Mitteylungen*, issued early in April in the Warsaw ghetto, carried a lead article about the deportations from Lublin, 'The Jewish Population Under the Sign of Physical Annihilation':

> According to reliable information the Jews of Lublin and of the other towns in the Lublin district are being sent to the camp at Bełżec ... It is said ... that the Jews at Bełżec are being killed the same way as at Chełmno, that is, poisoned by gas.[30]

In the Generalgouvernement the mass killings began in Lublin. Around midnight on 16 March 1942, without any prior warning, the German authorities delivered to the Lublin Judenrat's board orders to the effect that only those Jews with work permits stamped by the Security Police (Sipo) could remain with their families in Lublin. (The Judenrat had had no knowledge of this stamping procedure, which had been done at the factories.) Starting at noon on 17 March, Jews with Sipo stamps would have to move from Ghetto A to Ghetto B, with their possessions. The Jews to be evacuated – 1,400 daily, the orders specified – were to assemble at designated places, taking with them fifteen kilogrammes of possessions, money and valuables. The Judenrat was ordered to transfer food supplies from Ghetto A to Ghetto B, to take care of various technical matters, and to provide immediate burial of the dead in the ghetto. The Jewish police were, according to these orders, put at the permanent disposition of the Judenrat, unless needed for other purposes by the Germans.[31]

Stunned and defeated, the Judenrat officers did as ordered. Only bribery offered itself as the one possibility of averting or ameliorating the disaster. Despite a difference of opinion among the Judenrat board as to the efficacy of bribery, two members undertook the task. They collected gold and jewels in large quantities, some obtained forcibly from recalcitrant Jews. The two Judenrat officials brought that royal ransom to the Gestapo. Both were arrested and never seen again.

The evacuation went on as planned. On 19 March a Judenrat official reported to ŻSS headquarters in Cracow: 'There is no official news. The evacuees are apparently being sent to Bełżec, district of Zamość. I have not been able to have this confirmed.' He did not know the nature of the facilities at Bełżec.

Two weeks later, on 31 March, the Germans ordered a special meeting of the Judenrat convened, at which four SS officers were present and six Jews invited by the SS. The senior SS officer announced that the Sipo work permit was now invalid, that henceforth only holders of a J-identity card – 'J' for 'Jude' – could remain in Lublin. All the others would be deported. Furthermore, any person with a J-identity card who protected and concealed any Jew without one would be subject to deportation. The Judenrat roster would be cut from twenty-four to twelve members, but would include only six of those presently in office. Six new members had been appointed by the SS and had already been brought to the meeting. In a further stratagem of deceit, the SS officer assured the Judenrat chairman and his deputy, both to be deported, that they would, 'by virtue of experience in this area', assume 'administrative functions in the Judenrat and ŻSS in their new residence'.

On 9 May after 30,000 Jews had been deported and only 4,000 remained in Lublin, the newly elevated Judenrat chairman wrote to ŻSS headquarters that he was holding 10,000 zlotys to be transferred to the evacuees. Complaining about his inability to get any information on their whereabouts from official German sources, he added: 'After all, now that the evacuation has been completed, nobody can be interested in preventing people from sending parcels of food or clothing to members of their families who had been sent away without anything.'

In Lwów, deportations got under way early in March. Unlike Lublin, where the Germans decided unilaterally who was to go and who to stay, the Lwów Judenrat officials had to participate in a German-dominated commission that determined priorities – anti-socials, welfare recipients, unemployed – and procedures for the resettlement, ostensibly to Polesie. The Jewish police was assigned to round up the Jews to be evacuated. Thousands of Jews, trying to escape the dragnet, hid in attics, cellars, makeshift retreats. (Some Jews managed to stay in hiding for months, with the thought of revenge sustaining them. 'Despite everything', wrote a woman in her diary after six months in a hide-out, 'I still believe in God and I ceaselessly invoke the God of Vengeance!') After three days, the German police and Ukrainians took over, dissatisfied with the meagre accomplishments of the Jewish police. By 1 April 1942, when this *Aktion* had ended, over 15,000 Jews had been sent to Bełżec. It was months before anyone in Lwów realized that those Jews had not been resettled in villages in the East.[32]

In May the Germans began deporting the Jews from Upper East Silesia, where Moses Merin ruled a network of Judenräte, including those of the twin cities of Sosnowiec and Będzin. The Judenrat sent notices to selected Jews instructing them to appear within a few days for resettlement, with up to ten kilogrammes of personal belongings. The notice assured that no one would be harmed. About 1,000 people turned up of their own will. Shortly thereafter the Germans asked for another transport, and the Judenrat once again appealed for volunteers. This time no one came. Merin then convened the rabbis and communal leaders in his jurisdiction to ask for their guidance.

The Gestapo, Merin told the meeting, wanted to deport 10,000 Jews, but he had convinced them of the usefulness of the Jews and the Gestapo lowered their demand to 5,000. This figure, too, Merin hoped, could be reduced. He himself held that the Jews themselves should carry out the Gestapo's orders, because they could then select whom to expel – first, informers, thieves, undesirables; then, the insane, the sick and defective children. (The ranking had, no doubt, been the German proposal.) If the Germans themselves carried out the deportation, Merin argued, they might well send out the community's leading citizens. Merin's attempted blackmail to involve the communal leaders was transparent. That was a tactic that Rumkowski and Gens also attempted, but Merin had no more success than either of them. Most rabbis held that Merin's position contravened Jewish law, that no Jew had the right to deprive another of life. One rabbi only, a notorious sycophant, used Jewish law to legitimate Merin, by declaring the German order as the lesser of two evils. Months later, Merin, eager to justify himself in the eyes of the community, claimed that he had saved some Jews instead of losing all: 'Nobody will deny that, as a general, I have won a great victory. If I have lost only 25 per cent, when I could have lost all, who can want better results?'[33]

All through the spring of 1942 fact and rumour about the mysterious and terrifying mass deportations in the Wartheland and the General-gouvernement filtered into Warsaw. Every ghetto Jew must have heard something, even if he did not listen to the forbidden radio or read the illegal underground press. Many Jews in the Warsaw ghetto had encountered Jews who had escaped from the death camps and heard their tales of horror. The ghetto lived on the precipice of disaster. Any untoward event increased tension and anxiety, provoking near-panic.[34]

On 29 April 1942 Adam Czerniaków, head of Warsaw's Judenrat, noted in his diary that Auerswald, Warsaw ghetto commissar, had asked for population statistics by streets and buildings. That same day, another German official asked for ten maps of the ghetto. Czerniaków wondered whether a new decree, further delimiting the ghetto area, would be issued. On 4 May he noted that the *Transferstelle*, the German agency regulating the ghetto's economic affairs, had demanded a list of all workers in the ghetto, including also communal officials. 'It occurs to me', he remarked, 'that this must be related to the deportation of unproductive elements from Warsaw.'

Rumours of an imminent deportation began to sweep the ghetto. The most reliable information originated from the despised and feared Jewish Gestapo agents, who spoke of 60,000 or 70,000 Jews, perhaps more, to be deported. The shooting of the 110 imprisoned Jews at the beginning of July aggravated the unrest in the ghetto. On 18 July, Czerniaków noted, the ghetto was filled 'with dire forebodings' and, on the next day, 'with unimaginable panic'. The arrival of forty freight cars at a railway siding was seen as hard evidence of impending doom. Czerniaków's headaches grew worse; he began to canvass the German officials for information. They denied that anything at all untoward was under way. On 20 July the Sipo officer assured him that the rumours were 'rubbish' and 'nonsense'.

Before noon on 21 July 1942 Sipo men arrived at the Judenrat, rounded up the officials on hand, confining them in Czerniaków's office. Sipo asked for a list of the others. Soon some forty or more Judenrat officers and staff were arrested and taken away as hostages. Czerniaków was ordered to stay, but the S S set out to locate his wife and she too became a hostage.

At 7.30 the following morning, the small ghetto was surrounded by a detachment of special police. At 10.00 a.m., S S-Sturmbannführer Hans Höfle, whose title was resettlement commissioner for the Warsaw ghetto, appeared with his men at the Judenrat. They ordered the Jews to disconnect the telephone. Then they gave the Judenrat formal typed instructions for the deportations.[35] All Warsaw Jews, regardless of age and sex, were to be resettled in the East, except for those employed by German enterprises, Judenrat staff, Jewish police and Jewish hospital personnel, and their families. Those to be deported could take with them fifteen kilogrammes of personal property, valuables and provisions for three days. The resettlement was to start within the hour.

The instructions further specified that the Judenrat was to be responsible for delivering 6,000 Jews daily to the place of assembly. For this purpose the 1,000-man Jewish police force was to be used. The Judenrat would be held responsible for protecting and inventorying property left behind, for maintaining the required level of productivity in the German enterprises, for promptly burying the dead. The Jewish population was to be informed that anyone leaving the ghetto without authorization would be shot, that any Jew committing an act intended to evade or interfere with resettlement measures would be shot, and that all Jews found in Warsaw at the conclusion of the resettlement who did not belong to the exempt categories would be shot. The instructions closed with the warning that if the Judenrat did not comply 100 per cent, 'an appropriate number of hostages, who will meanwhile have been taken, will be shot in each instance'.

Czerniaków tried to salvage something, fighting a rearguard action. He asked for exemptions to be extended also to ŻSS employees, sanitation workers, and similar categories. Höfle agreed and a supplementary order was issued to that effect, equating those groups with the Judenrat. Czerniaków asked also for the release of several hostages. 'The most tragic problem' he raised affected the children in the institutions. His diary entry expressed hope that he might accomplish something.

That afternoon, Jacob Leikin, the new head of the Jewish police, told Czerniaków that glass had been thrown at a police car. Should that recur, the Judenrat hostages would be shot. Later, Höfle informed Czerniaków that his wife was free for the time being, but if anything should go wrong with the evacuation, 'she would be the first to be shot as a hostage'.

The next morning, 23 July 1942, Czerniaków continued his bargaining with Höfle's subordinate. He won a few exemptions: vocational-school students and husbands of working women. As for the orphans, he was told to take that up with Höfle himself. But

Höfle would not be moved and Czerniaków, unable to save the children, reached his breaking point. He took the cyanide tablet that he had long kept ready for that intolerable occasion, leaving two suicide notes, one to his wife and one to his colleagues: 'I am powerless. My heart trembles in sorrow and compassion. I can no longer bear all this. My act will prove to everyone what is the right thing to do.'[36]

Chaim Kaplan, who had mocked and excoriated Czerniaków in his lifetime, now eulogized him: 'He perpetuated his name by his death more than by his life.'[37]

The man who succeeded Czerniaków was nothing more than a faceless tool of the Germans.

The day the deportations began, the ghetto's communal and underground political leaders convened an emergency conference at ŻTOS headquarters.[38] The twenty-odd participants included top ŻTOS and JDC officials, spokesmen of the Aguda, General Zionists, Right and Left Labour Zionists, Bund, PPR, Hashomer Hatzair and Hehalutz. How were they to confront the new situation? Three points of view emerged. The majority, whose views were expressed by Zisha Friedman of the Aguda and Dr Ignacy Schipper (eminent Jewish historian and lifelong Labour Zionist), opposed resistance on the ground that German reprisals would wipe out the entire ghetto, whereas, according to available information, after some 50,000 to 70,000 were deported, the situation would then become stabilized. A political antagonist summarized their arguments:

The conferees were impressed by what Zisha Friedman and Schipper said. Zisha Friedman believes in faith. 'I believe in God and in a miracle. God will not let His people Israel be destroyed. We must wait and a miracle will occur. Fighting the Germans is senseless. The Germans can finish us off in numbered days as in Lublin. Things as they are can continue a long time. And a miracle will happen. My friends, you who look to the Allies, why are you in despair? You believe that the Allies will win. Or don't you believe that the Allies will bring you freedom? Those of you who look to the revolution and the Soviet Union believe that capitalism is at its end and that only the Red Army will bring you freedom. Then believe in your Red Army. My dear friends, endurance and faith, and then we will have freedom!'

Schipper did not approve of defence. Defence means destroying the entire Warsaw ghetto!!! 'I believe that we can manage to save the core of the Warsaw ghetto. This is a war and every people must make sacrifices. We too must make sacrifices to save the core of our people. Were I convinced that we would not succeed in saving the core of our people, I would have concluded otherwise.'[39]

The leftist and *halutz* youth regarded the deportations as the beginning of the end of the Warsaw ghetto. The Jewish population, they argued, must be roused to resistance against the Germans. The Bund called for passive resistance; the populace should be urged to refuse to obey the Jewish police, to resist leaving voluntarily. The conferees reached no decision, except to meet again.

That day or the next the leftist groups – the members of the defunct Anti-Fascist Bloc and the Bund – agreed to form a united labour committee that would call the Jewish populace to passive resistance against the Jewish police. The committee would also monitor the course of the deportations so as to call for active resistance at the appropriate time. But the accelerating pace of the deportations and the crescendo of terror broke down communication among the six organizations; coordinated action was beyond possibility. Even to cross a street became a perilous undertaking while the SS ruled the ghetto. Each party strove to stay alive, to keep its own members alive and together, and if there was a glimmer of possibility, to engage in some activity – even communication. The Bund operated an underground workshop that produced counterfeit work permits, legitimating its members as employees of the Judenrat, ŻTOS, and other communal institutions whose personnel were exempt from deportations. They also issued leaflets calling on the Jews not to go voluntarily to the place of assembly. The resettlement, the leaflets said, was a snare and delusion, part of the continuing annihilation of the Jews throughout Poland.

On 28 July Hehalutz, at a meeting of its constituents – Hashomer Hatzair, Dror and Akiva – decided to create a Jewish combat organization. Several activists were delegated to make contact with the Polish underground on the 'Aryan' side of Warsaw to obtain arms for the ghetto. The whole arsenal of the new combat force then consisted of one gun. They did for their members what the Bund was doing for its, forging work identity papers. They too issued a leaflet declaring that resettlement meant death, that men should hide their wives and children and should themselves resist German orders.

Hehalutz also decided to take action against the Jewish police and issued a death sentence against Józef Szeryński, whom they mistakenly believed still to be police chief. (Szeryński had been arrested in May 1942 by the Gestapo for stealing furs confiscated the previous winter from the ghetto Jews. He was released from arrest to assist in the deportations in a subordinate capacity.)

The same day, 28 July, eight members of the Left Labour Zionist committee met. The head of the party, Shakhne Zagan, reported that 'two SS officers had given their word of honour to the Judenrat that not one deported Jew had been killed; they are all sent to work'. Work permits were the chief subject on the agenda. ŻTOS, it was reported, was legitimating several thousand additional people, and the Judenrat itself had 'promised to legalize several hundred communal leaders by assigning them to its offices'. But finally the meeting decided that legalizing party members in the workshops and factories would be more secure than ŻTOS or the Judenrat.

The resettlement began at the prisons and the refugee centres. No one in the ghetto could believe that those wasted and devitalized creatures could really be resettled in the East at hard work. In the absence of familiar cues to provide guidance in the uncertainty and confusion of these unprecedented events, anxiety and apprehension among the Jews intensified. To disarm the ghetto's panic, the Germans on 24 July 1942 directed the Judenrat to issue a notice: 'In view of the false information circulating in the Jewish quarter in Warsaw in connection with the resettlement, the Judenrat in Warsaw has been empowered by the authorities to announce that the resettlement of the non-productive population in the Jewish quarter actually will take place in the Eastern territories.'[40]

Thereafter, rounding up the required contingent of 6,000 Jews daily became routinized. SS formations patrolled the ghetto, shooting at random. A Jewish police formation, commanded by Sipo officers, blocked off all entrances and exits of designated buildings. The tenants were ordered down to the street for a check of documents. The Jewish police, meanwhile, scoured the apartments to uncover Jews in hiding. On the street a Sipo officer examined the documents, releasing persons with valid work permits. The others were loaded onto trucks and taken to the *Umschlagplatz*, the staging area. It consisted of two squares at the extreme northern boundary of the ghetto, adjoining a railway siding. On one square stood the Jewish Hospital, whose personnel and patients had been transferred elsewhere in the ghetto, and which now had become an improvised barracks for thousands of Jews awaiting deportation, the old and the young, the rich and the poor, the apathetic and the hysterical, crowded together in the summer heat without adequate sanitary facilities, water or medical aid.

When enough Jews had been assembled to load the trains, they were herded through an inspection team of two or more SS officers at the entry to the second square. A few hundred fit-looking men were separated and sent to transit labour camps. The rest, under the brutal goad of the Jewish police, were pushed into the waiting freight cars.

The diligence with which the Jewish police performed their work was generated by fear and dilated into viciousness. Every policeman's family – wife, children and parents – had been exempted from deportation, but that exemption depended on slavish obedience to German authority. One policeman, trying to wrest a child from its father, responded to the father's plea: 'What makes you think I'm human? Maybe I'm a wild beast. I have a wife and three children. If I don't deliver my five heads by 5.00 p.m., they'll take my children. Don't you see, I'm fighting for the life of my own kids?'[41]

Still the Jewish police – or some among them – were better than Germans or Ukrainians, because they could be bribed. For money or jewels they closed an official eye to Jews in hiding. For kingly ransoms they rescued people from the Umschlagplatz and took the risk of escorting them, with ostensible police protection, out of the danger zone.

The ghetto, though driven by fear of impending death or disaster, responded to the round-ups with the logic of the situation. Everyone wanted to be 'productive'. Like trapped creatures, the Jews scurried back and forth to find a niche to safeguard themselves and their families. Possession of machines or tools – especially a sewing machine – became a lifeline. Long before 8.00 in the morning, when the round-ups began, the Jews were besieging the shops and factories that promised safety.

Every regulative communal structure in the ghetto had collapsed.

For the first time in its venerable history, Warsaw Jewry was without communal resources for maintaining or building morale, without communal leadership.[42] Only nuclear clusters of the political parties remained, isolated fragments of the welfare and religious communities. Apart from the handful of leaflets that the Bund and Hehalutz had managed to distribute, communication had completely broken down in the ghetto. The only source of news came from the German orders issued through the discredited, disorganized and demoralized Judenrat. Rumours gripped the ghetto, displacing each other with lightning rapidity. People said: Only the poorest and the unemployed would be taken; the deportation would last just a few days; as soon as 50,000 or so were deported, the ghetto would resume its old existence.

At the very start of the deportations, the stores closed down and the transaction of normal business halted. Formations of Ukrainian, Lithuanian and Latvian auxiliary police surrounding the ghetto prevented the habitual illegal smuggling of food and barred the entry of Poles to buy and barter from the Jews. The scarcity sent food prices soaring far beyond ghetto inflation. A kilogramme of bread, which in 1940 had cost 4 zlotys and 14 zlotys in May 1942, now cost 45 zlotys. A kilogramme of potatoes cost 15 zlotys, a tenfold increase after 1941. Hunger became a daily concomitant of terror.

The Germans took advantage of the hunger. They announced that beginning on 29 July, for a period of three days, persons who reported voluntarily for resettlement would receive free three kilogrammes of bread and one kilogramme of marmalade. Hunger drove thousands to the Umschlagplatz. Confronted with the hopelessness of their situation, unable to find work, unable to feed themselves or their children, fearful of the next day, these Jews accepted voluntary resettlement and the gift of bread as their solution. No left-wing leaflets warning that resettlement meant death carried weight against the rising hunger and spreading despair. Besides, many Jews regarded voluntary resettlement as a means of keeping the family together. Thousands calculated that it was better for their family to stay together in a new adversity than to be torn asunder in anguish or die of hunger.

The German ruse succeeded so well that the period of voluntary resettlement was extended twice. Now, too, relatives began to get postcards and letters from those deported, purportedly sent from Bialystok, Pinsk, Brześć – even from as far away as Smolensk. Actually written under duress at Treblinka, the messages were the same: the new places were satisfactory, they had work, the children had schools, they urged their relatives to join them. Those letters nourished the illusions that the Warsaw ghetto Jews spun about the fate of the deported. (The same thing happened in all the ghettos.) The wish to live, the inability to believe in one's own imminent death, the universal human faith in one's own immunity to disaster – all these factors conspired to make the Jews believe that resettlement, not death, was the fact. 'At bottom,' wrote Freud, 'nobody believes in his own death.' Not gullibility, or suggestibility, but universal human optimism encouraged them to believe in the deceptions that the Germans perpetrated. In the process of repressing and denying the overpowering threat that confronted them, perceptual distortion and skewed interpretation based on wishful thinking managed to reconcile the illogic and inconsistencies of their fears and hopes. Without accurate information, without corrective feedback from authoritative sources on the course of events, their isolation helped give credence to their distorted and distorting evaluation of their predicament. This mechanism of denial, this arming oneself against disquieting facts, was not pathological, but, as psychologists point out, a tool of adaptation, a means of coping with an intolerable situation in the absence of any possibility for defensive action. The alternative was despair, the quiet stunned reaction of the defeated.[43]

Every individual attempt to stand up to the Germans ended in death. The Jews who refused to budge when ordered, who spat at the German, who cursed him, who slapped his face, threw stones or reached for a stick was shot on the spot. Thousands of such individual acts of resistance became nothing more than induced suicide. They left scarcely a record, except in the German statistics – more than 5,000 shot to death – and a few poignant memories.

In August the Germans changed their techniques in rounding up Jews. Distrustful now of the Jewish police, the Germans demoted them, using increased numbers of Ukrainian, Lithuanian and Latvian auxiliary police. Large SS formations, the so-called Vernichtungs-kommando (Annihilation Squad), buttressed by machine guns, took over. Their procedure was to rout the Jews out of the block-aded buildings – soon whole streets were blockaded – and herd them to the Umschlagplatz. In the first half of August, the small ghetto was liquidated, including its workshops and all its children's institu-tions, boarding homes and orphanages.

A first-aid unit, run by the Judenrat, had been installed at the Umschlagplatz. A small place – two rooms with beds for the sick – it became a centre of clandestine rescue activity. It was operated by Nahum Remba, a General Zionist long active in the kehilla and then Judenrat personnel secretary, aided by several nurses, known at the Umschlagplatz as the Rescue Brigade. Wearing a medic's coat, Remba used to scour the Umschlagplatz for persons to rescue – rabbis, communal leaders. They were taken into the first-aid station, held there until they could be returned safely to the ghetto. Remba saved hundreds of Jews, until the Germans and the Jewish police chief began to suspect him.[44]

When Janusz Korczak and the children of his orphanage came to the Umschlagplatz, Remba tried to save them too. As for Korczak, he long had been ready for death. When the Germans came that hot August morning and blockaded the orphange, the 200 children stood ready, washed and scrubbed from head to toe, dressed in clean clothes, each child holding a little bag with bread and a flask of water. They marched to the Umschlagplatz, Korczak at the head of the procession, hatless, his broken, bent body the orphans' bulwark, his nurses bring-ing up the rear. With armed German and Ukrainian police lining the streets, hurrying them forward, the children marched on. No one cried; no one tried to run away.[45]

Word of their coming had already preceded them to the Umschlag-platz. Remba settled the children back near a protecting wall, hoping to postpone their departutre and perhaps so to rescue them. He urged Korczak to accompany him to the Judenrat to intervene in their behalf, but Korczak refused, not wishing to leave the children alone. (In the 1930s, he once explained to friends why he would not settle in Pales-tine: 'If I left, I would never forgive myself. I detest desertion.') That day the trains were filling slowly and the order went out to load the children. 'I will never forget that procession,' wrote Remba. In contrast to the apathetic huddled masses who were herded into the freight cars, 'all the children were lined up four in a row. Korczak at the head, eyes forward, holding a child with each hand, led the procession.' Remba could not control himself, weeping for Jewish helplessness.[46]

German bestiality increased until 'the Jews came to fear the Germans more than death'. Pious Jews marched to the Umschlagplatz and into the waiting trains wrapped in their prayer shawls, reciting prayers and psalms, oblivious of the violence. *Kiddush ha-shem*, martyrdom for the glorification and sanctification of God, once more re-asserted its place in Jewish tradition. For believing Jews the conviction that their sacrifice was required as a testimony to Almighty God was more comforting than the supposition that He had abandoned them altogether. To be sure, God's design was concealed from them, but they would remain steadfast in their faith. Morale was sustained by rabbis and pious Jews who, by their own resolute and exalted stance, provided a model of how Jews should encounter death. On the Umschlagplatz that August an elderly pious Jew exhorted the despondent masses, sunk in the misery and squalor of their surroundings: 'Jews, don't despair! Don't you realize that we are going to meet the Messiah? If I had some liquor, I'd drink a toast.'[47]

In the second half of August 1942, the Germans invalidated the old work permits, now requiring them to bear a Sipo stamp. The locale of round-ups shifted from tenements to workshops. Dozens of productive enterprises that had been a sanctuary for Jewish workers were liquidated and thousands of skilled workers were carried off in a torrent of violence to the Umschlagplatz, regardless of German economic priorities. Even family dependants of workers with Sipo permits were no longer exempt from resettlement. By 27 August, when the round-ups halted for a brief respite, some 200,000 Warsaw ghetto Jews had been deported. The demographic structure of the ghetto was transformed. The family was disappearing. The age parameters of the ghetto were skewed: the old and the children were being erased from the statistics.

At that very time the young people in the fragmented underground parties – their veteran leaders were either killed or in hiding on the 'Ayran' side – attempted to exercise some autonomy of action. The *halutz* groups set fire to abandoned ghetto buildings, and on 20 August one of their members made an attempt on Szeryński's life, but succeeded only in wounding him. The next day the *halutz* groups received, through the instrumentality of the PPR outside the ghetto, five guns and eight grenades. Then the *halutzim* ventured an unsuccessful attack on Germans and Ukrainians entering the ghetto. Two small parties of young people who had been sent into the woods to organize partisan units perished. On 3 September, in two separate incidents, two leading members of their underground were arrested. The first arrest made it mandatory to transfer the tiny cache of weapons. But that venture too failed: the courier was caught; the arms were confiscated. Every attempt at resistance had ended in death or failure.

In mid-August the Bund, wanting to find out where the Jews were being transported, to verify rumours of death camps and to counteract the deceptive postcards, sent out a courier to learn the destination of the trains. A tall, blond, handsome man, the stereotypic 'Aryan', Zalman Friedrich made contact with a Polish Socialist railway worker who knew the direction taken by the deportation trains. Friedrich reached Sokołów, where he learned that the Germans had constructed a new spur track to the village of Treblinka. The villagers knew of a large camp where dreadful things occurred, but little more. In Sokołów Friedrich met a bleeding and bruised escapee from Treblinka, who described in detail its killing installations and procedures. Friedrich made his way back to Warsaw with his news, but by the time he arrived the Germans had returned to the ghetto in full fury.[48]

On 5 September the Germans issued an announcement that all Jews in the Warsaw ghetto, without exception, were to report the following morning for registration purposes, with food for two days and drinking utensils, within an area of seven square blocks located between the Umschlagplatz and Pawiak prison. Whoever did not comply would be shot. That whole day 'passed with the oppressive sense of imminent death', wrote a Jewish teacher and scholar, now factory worker. 'I would like to die in peace and with the awareness that it must be so . . . I think there is no possibility of extricating ourselves from the clutches of the wild beast and we are only prolonging our death agony.'[49]

The Germans called the *Aktion* an *Einkesselung*, 'encirclement'. The Jews Yiddishized the word to *kesl*, 'cauldron'. That roped-off area, surrounded by armed police, was indeed a cauldron, its human mass seething and churning, evoking the image of Dante's Second Circle, where the blast of hell 'never rests from whirling . . . forever beating and hurling'. The encirclement lasted one week, with nearly 10,000 Jews deported every day. It ended on 12 September 1942, Rosh Hashana 5703. The *kesl* was a place of anguish and terror, violence and resistance. Thousands still managed to summon the energy and the will to live. In that week alone the German statistics recorded that 2,648 Jews were shot to death. But stupor and fatalism, a state of emotional catalepsy, induced thousands of others to surrender passively to German orders.

The ghetto was cut down to four tiny isolated enclaves, separated from one another. The surviving Jews lived at their factories or in hiding. Jewish home life had been extinguished, the Jewish family obliterated. Of the more than 350,000 Jews in the Warsaw ghetto on 22 July 1942, no more than 45,000 or so remained, about 60 per cent between the ages of twenty and thirty-nine.[50] German and Ukrainian armed police patrolled the ghetto, shooting Jews on sight. The streets were strewn with dead Jewish bodies. On Yom Kippur the Germans carried out one more round-up, perhaps only for sadistic gratification. Over 2,000 Jews were taken that day, including some 600 Jewish policemen.

Emerging from the ashes of the Warsaw ghetto, a new issue of a Bundist underground paper entitled *Oyf der vakh* (*On Guard*) appeared on 20 September. Its lead article, 'The Annihilation of Warsaw Jews', warned the Jews: 'Be on guard! Don't let yourselves be destroyed like sheep! Better to die with honour than to be gassed in Treblinka!' Friedrich's report about Treblinka followed. In closing, it exhorted the survivors:

Today every Jew should know the fate of those resettled. The same fate awaits the remaining few left in Warsaw. The conclusion then is: Don't let yourself be caught! Hide, don't let yourself be taken away, run away, don't be fooled by registrations, selections, numbers and roll calls! Jews, help one another! Take care of the children! Help the illegals! The dishonourable traitors and helpers – the Jewish police – should be boycotted! Don't believe them, beware of them. Stand up against them!

We are all soldiers on a terrible front!

We must survive so that we can demand a reckoning for the tortured brothers and sisters, children and parents who were killed by the murderer's hand on the battlefield for freedom and humanity![51]

The report came too late for the 300,000 Warsaw Jews already deported. But it heralded the resistance to come.

15 'For Your Freedom and Ours'

'They were free. Their last links with everyday life were broken,' wrote Gusta Dawidsohn, Akiva activist, in her diary, describing the *halutz* youth in Cracow after the deportations of June and October 1942, which took some 12,000 of the last 17,000 Jews in the ghetto. They 'suddenly felt free to plunge into the maelstrom of underground work; it was a feeling of freedom which sprouted out of the rubble of shattered family life'.[1]

In all the ghettos of the Generalgouvernement and the other occupied lands in Eastern Europe, in the wake of the great wave of killings or deportations, the youth of the Jewish political movements began to organize armed resistance to the Germans. Deprived of family, they had gained freedom and autonomy. Without families, they no longer had the care and anxiety for baby brothers, younger sisters, ageing parents, no more the need to support or protect them. The possible consequences of rash acts held less terror now that the ghetto was no longer peopled by their families, now that the sense of familial responsibility no longer inhibited them.

The knowledge of the death camps and the sense of death's inevitability accelerated their resort to armed resistance. 'One way or another', wrote Hersh Berlinski, 'lies death.' Despair over Jewish powerless and revengefulness against the Germans had converted them to a new outlook. The political hopes and aspirations that had nourished the young people's will to live and which had provided both foundation and framework for their clandestine educational and cultural activities in the ghettos had been shattered by the realization that the Germans meant to destroy all Jews. In Bialystok, Mordecai Tenenbaum, Hehalutz activist and organizer of the Zionist youth underground, who called himself 'the apostle of death', asked the Zionist youth at a meeting on 19 February 1943, whether there was any historic significance in any given person's remaining alive after the liquidation of three and a half million Polish Jews.[2] Mordecai Aniele-wicz, Hashomer Hatzair activist and eventually head of the Jewish combat organization in Warsaw, told Ringelblum of his deep regret that he and his comrades had 'wasted' three years in educational and cultural work. Instead they should have learned how to use arms and schooled themselves in a spirit of revenge.[3]

The young people in the Zionist and Bundist movements, reared in the ideals of secular modernity, rejected the traditionalist values and modes of behaviour that had sustained Diaspora existence for centuries. Contemptuous of the long tradition of Jewish accommodation, they sought ways – whether nationalist or socialist – to combat Jewish powerlessness. Like most modernists, they were fired by the medieval virtues of Christian chivalry that prescribed the defence of honour by arms. To modern secularists the Jewish tradition of martyrdom, *kiddush ha-shem*, was the epitome of the Diaspora fate against which they rebelled. To them, non-believers, martyrdom did not mean bearing witness to God, but merely signified Jewish helplessness, passivity in the face of destruction. The biblical passage in the liturgy that expressed readiness for martyrdom,

> Nay, but for Thy sake are we killed all the day;
> We are accounted as sheep for the slaughter [Ps. 44:23]

embodied values and an ideal that they repudiated.

The only question facing the Jews, Aniélewicz told Ringelblum, was how to choose to die: 'either like sheep for the slaughter or like men of honour'. Among the Zionist youth in the resistance movement, 'like sheep for the slaughter' became an epithet of ignominy, divorced from its original meaning of martyrdom as a meaningful option. These young Zionists, in their statements and proclamations, echoed the feelings of anger against Jewish passivity that Chaim Nachman Bialik had voiced in his poem *Be'ir ha-hareygah* (*The City of Slaughter*), written after the Kishenev pogrom of 1903 :

> Let them raise a fist against Me and demand revenge for their humiliation,
> The humiliation of all generations from their first to last,
> And let them break asunder with their fist the heavens and My throne.

Then, at the turn of the century, the emergent Bundist and Labour Zionist movements, in response to the pogroms erupting in the Tsarist empire, had forged a new instrument to protect the Jews, the *zelbshuts* (self-defence). Recruiting the robust and tough elements among Jews – carters, wagoners, teamsters, abattoir workers, even horse thieves – armed with knives, axes, poles, brass knuckles, clubs, switches and thongs, the socialist Jews served notice on pogromists and indifferentists alike that the Jews would no longer be unresistant victims. They concluded what Machiavelli had long ago argued, that 'among other evils which being unarmed brings you, it causes you to be despised'.

The idea of self-defence had never been extinguished in the ghettos, but everyone – the young as well as the experienced – had realized in the earliest ghetto days that the SS was not comparable to a horde of drunken peasants or even a company of Cossack horsemen and that axes and knives, clubs and switches were no match for the war apparatus that the Germans commanded. Besides, everyone in the ghetto knew that even a limited armed action on a specific target would incur German reprisals whose cost to the ghetto in human life would surpass any benefit. But when it became clear to the underground that no option but death existed, the idea of resistance took on another aspect, becoming an affective undertaking rather than an instrumental one. Scarcely any of the young people seriously believed that resistance could save the remaining Jews in the ghetto, but all believed that by defying the Germans with whatever armed strength they could muster, they would redeem the honour of the Jews.

Resistance was thus not defence in the sense that the *zelbshuts* had been. It was instead an act of desperation, whose Jewish paradigm was the suicidal stand of the Zealots at Masada against Rome's imperial legions. Masada had been incorporated into modern Zionist myth under the influence of Yitzhak Lamdan's epic poem: 'We have one treasure left – the daring after despair.' Since hope for survival had been abandoned, one must die gloriously. Fatalism and the surrender to death haunted many young people in the ghettos. 'We are going on the road to death, remember that,' said Aaron Liebeskind, Akiva activist in Cracow. 'Whoever desires still to live should not search for life here among us. We are at the end.'[4]

One objective that joined all members of all parties in the underground was the passion for revenge on the Germans. Hatred for the Germans consumed them. The Zionist youth in Vilna issued an appeal: 'Convey your hatred of the foe in every place and at every moment!' On 1 March 1943 a member of a Dror kibbutz in Bialystok wrote a letter to comrades in Palestine (which was never posted), describing the production of hand grenades by the underground organization: 'We'll kill our slaughterers; they will have to fall together with us.' Above all, she admonished her overseas comrades: 'We call you to vengeance, revenge without remorse or mercy ... Vengeance! This is our challenge to you, who have not suffered in Hitler's hell. This you are duty-bound to fulfil. Our scattered bones will not rest in peace, the scattered ashes of the crematoria will not lie still, until you have avenged us.'[5]

As the young people plunged into the ramifications and implications of the idea of resistance, they began to define its objectives in more concrete terms than the rhetoric of despair or revenge allowed. In all ghettos, two lines of thought emerged. One view held that honour and vengeance demanded a last stand in the ghetto, a symbolic defence of the ghetto before its final liquidation by the Germans. The other view held that since no practical use could come of a defence in the ghetto, which was unsuitable terrain anyway for guerrilla warfare, Jewish resisters could make better use of their meagre forces by joining up with the Russian partisans in the woods. That debate between the two points of view would continue in many ghettos until the very end.

The first resistance organization was set up in Vilna. It was sparked by a meeting on 1 January 1942 of about 150 young Zionists, who heard Abba Kovner, Hashomer Hatzair activist and poet, read a proclamation calling for self-defence: 'Let's not allow ourselves to be led like sheep to the slaughter.' It breathed with the resonance of Bialik in its condemnation of Jewish passivity and appealed to the youth of Vilna to redeem Jewish dignity and avenge the murder of Jews.[6] Within a short time thereafter, Hashomer Hatzair, Hanoar Hazioni (General Zionist youth), Revisionists, Bundists and Communists formed the Fareynikte partizaner organizatsye (FPO; United Partisans Organization.)[7]

In Warsaw, the halutz groups set about re-activating their combat organization in the relative quiet that followed the *kesl*. At a meeting early in October 1942 with the Left Labour Zionists to discuss formation of a defence organization, two halutz youth leaders – Anielewicz and Zuckerman – launched a bitter attack on the Jewish political parties. The conflict between the youth groups and the Left Labour Zionist party focused specifically on whether the proposed combat organization should have a dual executive apparatus – political and military – or just military. The spokesmen of the youth organizations feared that a political apparatus, controlled by veteran party leaders, would inhibit freedom of military action. The parties, they argued, had done nothing in the days before the present calamity but talk. 'The parties have no right to dictate to us. Except for their youth organizations, they won't do anything; they will only obstruct.'[8]

The Left Labour Zionists responded with the argument that the political parties, and not the youth organizations, had earned the confidence of the Jewish masses. Even if the parties had made mistakes in the past, they would still be the ones to determine the shape of Jewish society in the future. 'Don't think, comrades, that just because you have two broken revolvers, you can be hoity-toity and take no account of anyone else.' The Left Labour Zionists favoured two apparatuses, for 'every armed undertaking in the ghetto must be weighed and measured; we dare not permit any reckless acts that might bring about a premature liquidation of the Warsaw ghetto'. Even if all the Jews were to expire in the ghetto, the party still carried an obligation for its acts to the Jews throughout the world and its fraternal parties abroad. 'We do not want to be maligned in our graves for reckless acts committed here.' The Left Labour Zionist insistence that the political parties oversee the combat organization finally prevailed. The organization was called Żydowska Organizacja Bojowa (ŻOB; Jewish Combat Organization).

When the young people in the ghettos began to form their combat organizations, few gave thought to the political and social requisites of an effective resistance movement: active support by an allied government from the outside and assistance in – or, at the very least, passive approval of – its activities by the indigenous population within the area of operations. Wherever these conditions were absent, Jewish resistance organizations foundered. Despite their courage and readiness for self-sacrifice, the young people by themselves were unable to win the confidence of the Polish underground government, of the Soviet partisan operation, and even of the Jewish populace in the ghettos.

For in those desperate times even more than in normal times, trust and confidence reposed in men and organizations whose past record of accomplishment had demonstrated their responsibility, integrity and ability to lead.

In Warsaw, the Polish capital and centre of all Polish underground organizations, some of the established Jewish parties continued to maintain a Jewish political presence despite the decimation of their ranks. A handful of surviving veteran leaders of the central committees of the Bund, General Zionists and both Right and Left Labour Zionists, living on the 'Aryan' side under false identities, carried on. They had the responsibility to sustain their parties and to render whatever assistance could be given to the beleaguered Jews in the territory that had made up Poland. Even more important was their function of maintaining contact with the outside world – with the Polish underground in the country, with the Polish government-in-exile and with the Jewish representatives in the Polish National Council in London, with their fraternal parties in Palestine and the United States, and with Jewish listening posts in Switzerland and Turkey. Since early 1942 the Polish National Council in London had two Jewish members – Ignacy Schwarzbart, a General Zionist, and Artur Zygelboym, the Bundist who had fled Warsaw late in 1939.[9] (Zygelboym took his life in London on 12 May 1943, at the age of forty-eight.)*

The presence in Warsaw of acknowledged political leaders of Polish Jewry played a decisive role in the development of the resistance movement. One reason the *halutz* youth submitted to the political supervision of the adult parties was their realization that alone they could not succeed. They had been advised by friends in the pre-war Polish scout movement, now associated with the underground Polish Home Army, that to get weapons from the Home Army they would need not merely the backing, but the full instrumentality of a representative Jewish political body of weight and stature.

*His farewell letter read:
'I cannot be silent. I cannot live while the remnants of the Jewish population of Poland, of whom I am a representative, are perishing. My friends in the Warsaw ghetto died with weapons in their hands in the last heroic battle. It was not my destiny to die together with them but I belong to them and in their mass graves.

By my death I wish to make my final protest against the passivity with which the world is looking on and permitting the extermination of the Jewish people.'

Confronted with the need for such political representation, the *de facto* combat organization then coopted, besides the Left Labour Zionists, also the General and Right Labour Zionists. These parties, together with the youth groups (Hehalutz, Hashomer Hatzair, Dror), constituted the Żydowski Komitet Narodowy (ŻKN; Jewish National Committee), which was to serve as the political arm of the combat organization. Adolf Berman, a veteran Left Labour Zionist, living on the 'Aryan' side, became the authorized ŻKN representative to deal with the Polish civilian underground and Israel Chaim Vilner, a Hashomer Hatzair activist, was designated as ŻOB representative to the Polish military underground. The youth organizations also delegated some of their people throughout Poland to set up resistance groups in Bialystok, Będzin, Cracow and Częstochowa.

Negotiations were conducted also with the Revisionists, who agreed to join both the ŻNK and ŻOB, though their membership was short-lived. They failed to maintain security among their members, and a more serious charge levelled against them was their unilateral contacts with right-wing Polish military groups outside the ghetto. They refused to share the weapons they had obtained and tried to bully their way to ŻOB leadership.[10] They later formed their own organization, Żydowski Związek Wojskowy (ŻZW; Jewish Military Union).

Negotiations with the Bund were more complex. The Bund, ready to join ŻOB, nevertheless insisted on maintaining its political autonomy and independence. In mid-October the Bund proposed as a solution to the organizational dilemma the formation of a coordinating committee, consisting of the Bund and the ŻKN, which would serve as the vehicle for overall political and communal representation. On 20 October, general agreement was reached and the Żydowski Komitet Koordynacyjny (ŻKK; Jewish Coordinating Committee) was formed.[11] The ŻKK was to represent the Bund only in matters affecting Warsaw; with regard to the rest of Poland, the Bund retained its autonomy. (In May 1943, after the Warsaw ghetto rising, the Bund agreed to extend coordination over all Poland.) An understanding was also reached that political issues – presumably those of a general nature affecting Poland – would be handled independently by each party and excluded from coordination.[12] Negotiations with the Jewish Communists were protracted because they required instruc-

tions from the Warsaw Committee PPR, which eventually authorized participation in ŻOB and the ŻKK in matters limited to Warsaw alone.[13]

Within a few weeks formal by-laws for the ŻKK and ŻOB were
drawn up, describing the purposes of the ŻKK as the defence of the
ghetto in the event of a further effort by the Germans to deport the remaining Jews and the protection of the Jews in the ghetto from 'the
hirelings and flunkies of the occupant'. (On 29 October ŻOB carried
out its first successful 'execution', killing Jacob Leikin, chief of the
Jewish police.) The ŻKK was to supervise ŻOB and set its policies.
ŻOB's basic combat units were to consist of six members each and a
commander, organized according to places of work, and by parties or
organizations. Every member of a combat unit was to be armed, the
definition of arms extended to include 'axes, knives, brass knuckles,
caustic substances, incendiary materials and others'.[14]

At the time the ŻKK was being formed, Jan Karski, the liaison
officer between the underground in Poland and the Polish government-in-exile, met with Leon Feiner, Bund leader on the 'Aryan'
side, and with an unidentified Zionist leader. Karski wanted to get
information about the fate of the Jews, which he would bring to the
Polish and Allied governments. At one point in their conversation,
the Zionist said to him: 'We are not going to die in slow torment, but
fighting. We will declare war on Germany – the most hopeless declaration of war that has ever been made.' Feiner, confirming these
words, added: 'We are organizing a defence of the ghetto, not because we think it can be defended, but to let the world see the hopelessness of our battle – as a demonstration and a reproach.'[15]

The defence of the ghetto as the objective of Jewish resistance sym-
bolized the isolation of the Jews in Eastern Europe. Resistance movements everywhere – maquis, guerrillas, partisans – were regarded as
auxiliaries of the conventional armed forces on the battlefield, whose
objective, within the limits of their capabilities, was to help the Allies
and hinder the Germans. As irregular forces, they were to stage small-
scale attacks on isolated or unprotected German installations, carry
out diversions, disrupt communications, sabotage military facilities
and, if circumstances allowed, gather intelligence. Merely to enu-
merate these tasks is to demonstrate the disability of the Jews in the
ghettos to perform them. Nevertheless, with regard to home-front

operations, no substantial difference between the Jewish and European resistance movements existed. Both conducted activities to bolster morale, issuing underground papers and proclamations to provide information about Allied progress, and both condemned and executed spies and traitors in their midst.

No resistance movement in Europe was self-sufficient. None had substantial indigenous resources of arms or *matériel*. Nor could any resistance group operate independently to any advantage. To be useful militarily or politically, every resistance activity had to be fitted into an overall Allied strategy and synchronized into an overall Allied schedule. In the first years of the war, Great Britain was the sole support of all resistance movements in Europe, establishing for that purpose the Special Operations Executive, SOE. Until late 1942, when Russia regained the initiative on the Eastern front and reorganized the partisan movement on an expanded scale, London was the headquarters of the European resistance movement, where the governments-in-exile of the occupied countries served as liaisons to the British, pleading on behalf of their underground forces for military and financial assistance.[16]

A resistance organization, to receive aid, had to have the political backing of its government-in-exile and be able to render useful, if minor, military services to the Allies. The Soviet Union, for example, began in 1943 to back only such indigenous Communist resistance movements in the several East European countries as would provide it with post-war political footholds there. In Poland, the Home Army (Armja Krajowa), directed by the Polish government-in-exile and by its plenipotentiary (Delegatura) in Warsaw, was authorized to receive SOE assistance through a system of clandestine landings or drops. In all, nearly 500 flights provided the Home Army with some 600 tons of equipment – one third of its total arms supply – and 40 million zlotys. The Soviet Union, for its part, through the PPR supported the People's Army (Armja Ludowa) with funds and *matériel*, on the calculation that it would establish the Communist presence in post-war Poland.

The surviving Polish Jews, imprisoned in ghettos and SS labour camps, did not fit into any conventional framework that would entitle them to aid from either Allied or Soviet channels. The Jewish resistance organizations in the ghettos had no access to areas where they could perform useful military tasks. Furthermore, their decimation rendered their post-war political importance or influence negligible.

The anomalous Jewish situation and unique objectives of Jewish resistance complicated the fundamental question of arms supply, without which resistance was mere rhetoric. ŻOB and the ŻKK applied for arms to the Home Army, which referred the appeal to the Delegatura, which in turn, solicited the decision of London headquarters. The question was not just military, but political, and it was exacerbated by pandemic Polish anti-Semitism. In mid-November 1942, the Delegatura finally responded to the ŻOB request by expressing readiness to provide some arms if the resistance organizations would take a loyalty oath that in the event of war between Poland and the Soviet Union, they would not use those arms on the side of the Red Army. The ŻOB constituents gave their word, and at the end of November or at the very beginning of December, the Home Army delivered ten guns to ŻOB.[17]

On 2 December 1942 Henryk Wolinski, in charge of Jewish affairs for the Home Army's Chief Command, met with the two representatives of the ŻKK, Feiner of the Bund and Vilner for the ŻKN, who presented him with the by-laws of the coordinating committee. The political question as to the overall representation of the Jews in Warsaw was now clarified. The ŻKK representatives requested a larger supply of arms than the ten pieces already received, which, they said, did 'not suffice to organize an armed resistance or any other action of a collective and non-individual character'. They also wanted help in organizing the purchase of arms on the 'Aryan' side and securing the services of instructors in military training. Most Jews who had been trained in the Polish army and could have served as instructors, they explained, were now with the Jewish police and hence untrustworthy. Wolinski forwarded a memorandum of this meeting and of the ŻKK requests to London with a lukewarm recommendation.[18] On the same application, General Stefan Rowecki, commander-in-chief of the Home Army, sent a splenetic and distrustful radio message to the Polish High Command in London on 4 January 1943:

Too late Jews of various groupings, also Communists, appeal to us for arms, just as if we had full arsenals. As a trial I gave them a few pistols. I am not sure that they will use the weapons altogether. More weapons I will not give because as you know we don't have them ourselves. We are awaiting a delivery. Inform us what connections our Jews have with London.[19]

The information relayed from London apparently proved satisfactory, because at the end of January – after ŻOB's armed challenge to the Germans in the Warsaw ghetto on 18–22 January 1943 – the Home Army delivered to ŻOB forty-nine revolvers, fifty grenades and a quantity of explosives. That delivery, along with the ten guns received earlier, eventually made up about 10 per cent of ŻOB's arsenal.[20]

The rest of their arms ŻOB – like combat organizations in other ghettos – bought at exorbitant cost and great peril from Poles and smuggled them into the ghetto. (In Galicia, where Italian soldiers were stationed, Jews used to buy arms from them.) Funds came from the political parties, which, through the Delegatura, received money from their fraternal parties abroad, from whatever resources still remained with the JDC, and – as the resistance movement gained in authority – from the Judenräte and their institutions. Barash, for instance, not only subsidized the resistance movement in Bialystok, but also sent money to Warsaw. Dr Elkes in Kovno, with the support of several other members of the Judenrat, financed the purchase of arms for the local resistance organization and provided facilities for manufacturing grenades and explosives. In Warsaw the ŻKK set up a citizens' committee of JDC and party leaders who raised funds from private people with resources and who also demanded, and received contributions from the Judenrat amounting to nearly one million zlotys.

ŻOB and the individual parties assigned couriers to the dangerous business of buying, testing and smuggling arms. Both the ghetto and the 'Aryan' city swarmed with police, blackmailers, informers, spies and Gestapo agents looking for victims. Every courier was exposed to dangers and risks that tested to the utmost his and her ingenuity, daring and courage.[21]

In each ghetto, organizing resistance presented a *congeries* of dilemmas even more complex and tangled than arms procurement.[22] Matters that on the surface appeared to be merely practical or technical – where to fight and when to fight – were actually a matter of life and death for the ghetto, however amputated it was at that stage. Decisions on such questions could not responsibly be taken without consulting the ghetto's legitimate leadership, whether it was the Judenrat, the alternative communal leadership or the political underground.

As long as the ghetto leadership held that a possibility of survival for the ghetto existed – because the Red Army was approaching or because the ghetto worked efficiently for the German war economy – it could not support a policy of resistance. That was the case of the Lodz ghetto, where nearly 90,000 Jews remained after the deportations of the children, the old and the sick in September 1942. All through 1943, when nearly all ghettos in the Generalgouvernement and in Ostland were being liquidated, the Lodz ghetto seemed almost an island of serenity in a sea of blood. Its residents, working in the industrial enterprises that appeared to justify their existence, hoped that they would live to see the defeat of the Germans.

No armed resistance movement existed in Lodz. No contact was possible between Jews in the ghetto and Poles outside. The Bundists were cut off from contact with Polish Socialists; the Jewish Communists were isolated from their parent PPR. The ghetto was enveloped in political void. Its total imprisonment, which rendered futile the smuggling even of contraband food, turned the idea of smuggling arms into total fantasy. The Lodz ghetto remained without guns, without weapons, without military resources.

The only strategy the underground parties evolved was to protect their people until the moment of liberation. In February 1944, for instance, when the Germans asked for 1,500 able-bodied, skilled artisans to be sent to Częstochowa, all party leaders – Bundists, Communists, General Zionists and Left Labour Zionists – instructed and exhorted their party activists to resist any effort to make them leave the Lodz ghetto. The parties even undertook to hide some of their people from seizure. Since those in hiding forfeited their food rations, the Bund exacted from its working members a contribution of bread and soup, a sacrificial offering in a time of hunger.

On 6 June 1944 news of D-Day, the Allied invasion of Normandy, stirred the Lodz ghetto to public embraces and tears of joy. No work was done in the factories that day, as the Jews calculated their chances of survival. But their bright hopes began to dim at the end of June, when the Germans ordered a three-week period of deportations, with 2,000 Jews scheduled for weekly departure. Neither Rumkowski nor the parties saw this action as the start of the ghetto's liquidation. The parties still held to their policy of protecting their members and managed to get them exemptions. At that time, an inter-party conference discussed the possibility of the ghetto's liquidation and the question of active resistance. But without political contacts and without arms, talk of resistance was mere quixotism.

The deportations began in earnest on 3 August 1944, after Rumkowski announced that the entire ghetto of Lodz, its workers and its industrial enterprises, were to be transferred elsewhere. The removal procedure was scheduled by factories, and the workers were instructed when to report at a railway siding. Few obeyed. The parties were advocating passive resistance, non-compliance. Despite Rumkowski's pleas and Hans Biebow's threats, only hundreds instead of thousands came forward. Nor could the Jewish police dislodge them from their hide-outs. Once again, as in the September 1942 *Aktion*, armed German formations intervened to accomplish what the Jewish police failed to do. Even so, for days on end, the Germans could not round up enough Jews to fill the trains. By the end of August the Germans finally depopulated the Lodz ghetto.

Several hundred Jews still remained in hiding. Among them was Dr Daniel Weisskopf, who had operated a clandestine radio-listening service and engaged in other underground activities. On 6 November 1944 the bunker in which he and others were hiding was uncovered by an informer. Biebow himself was called to the scene. Weisskopf, a powerful man, attacked both the informer and Biebow, bloodying both. When he was about to strangle Biebow, a German policeman shot him. Weisskopf's last words were 'Germans, your end is near.'[23]

In ghettos where the Judenrat leadership was convinced that there was no chance for survival, cooperation with the resistance movement was likely. Some communal leaders took an intermediate position of giving the resistance organization moral and financial support. without subscribing to its outlook and programme. One form of compromise between the ghetto and the resistance movement was the option in Eastern areas for the Jewish youth to join the Soviet partisan movement. That way they diminished the ghetto's jeopardy through disengagement while they, for their part, joined an irregular army to fight the Germans. The drawbacks were, however, not inconsiderable. The first thing the partisan – Jew or Gentile – learned, if he lived long enough, was that in defence of the Soviet Union no human cost was too high. Jews who joined the partisans suffered additional disabilities. For the most part city-dwellers, they were unfamiliar with life in the open. Some, after years of ghetto deprivation, lacked the physical stamina to sustain the hardships of nature. Few could read maps or repair guns. Dependent on the support of the local peasant population among whom they operated, they were exposed to rampant anti-Semitism and the danger of being turned over to the Germans. Even worse was the anti-Semitism that they encountered from the partisans themselves.[24]

Nevertheless, for those whose primary loyalty was to the Soviet Union, joining the partisans was the only viable option and the only cause worth dying for. For Jewish resisters without an organizational base in the ghetto and without ties to ghetto leadership, serving the PPR or the Soviet apparatus in whatever tasks were assigned to them was a desirable option, for it gave them opportunities to fight or kill Germans. In Cracow, for example, a small group of Zionist youths, isolated from the ghetto community, accepted the leadership of the PPR and under their orders carried out various strikes against German targets (setting fires, stealing weapons and uniforms from German military and police). On 22 December 1942, on PPR assignment, the Zionist resisters blew up two cafés in the heart of Cracow that were frequented by German officers, killing at least twenty, perhaps as many as fifty. The only reverberations in the ghetto from their daring act were the SS searches and threats. That same night about forty resisters were arrested. By February 1943 all members of the PPR and the Zionist combat units were arrested or killed. A month later the ghetto was liquidated without any attempt at an organized defence.[25]

In eastern Poland, where the Soviet partisan movement had by 1943 grown to considerable size and strength, joining the partisans offered the ghetto Jews, in addition to the opportunity of fighting Germans, also at least an even chance of survival under conditions of personal autonomy. In contrast, staying in the ghetto to fight at its ultimate liquidation meant certain death. Nevertheless, for those committed to the defence of the ghetto, to a last stand together with the remaining Jews, joining the partisans was viewed as betrayal, or at the least abandonment, of principle and community.

In Baranowicze these two outlooks collided in near-disaster. There the local combat organization had opted to fight in defence of the ghetto. But in a surprise action about forty members of the group, nearly all refugees from other towns and without ties or loyalty to the Jews of Baranowicze, seized the bunker in which the combat organization's arsenal was cached, planning to make off into the woods with the weapons. A tense confrontation prevented the flight, and only sheer accident saved the rebellious ringleader from being shot.[26]

In the Kovno ghetto a remarkable balance was struck between the Judenrat and the underground despite their divergent views on resistance. In September 1943 the ghetto came under the exclusive control of SS-Obersturmführer Wilhelm Goecke, whose task was to turn the ghetto into a labour concentration camp prior to its ultimate liquidation. Then the question of whether, when, and how the ghetto should defend itself became urgent. A resistance organization had been in the making for some time, but between late 1941 and early autumn 1943 the youth in the Zionist underground had engaged mainly in cultural and educational activities. The Communists in the ghetto, trailed by the Hashomer Hatzair, were in contact with the Lithuanian Communist underground, making plans to form partisan bands. Goecke's arrival spurred the underground to decisiveness.

The Zionist combat organization, deeply tied to the ghetto by virtue of family and friends, at first rejected the plan to join the partisans. They favoured making a last stand in the ghetto despite the contempt the Communists exhibited for notions of 'dying with honour'. But in coming to terms with the Judenrat's view of the ghetto's possibilities, the Zionists changed their plans. In the autumn of 1943, the Judenrat leaders, especially Dr Elkes, hoped that the ghetto could hold out for a few more months. The allies had landed in Italy and were fighting their way north; the Russians held the initiative on the Eastern front and were driving the Germans west. Given these military advantages, which might in weeks or months cause the Germans to retreat from Kovno, the Judenrat leaders believed that nothing should be done to jeopardize the ghetto and provoke the Germans to bring it to a premature end. As for the aspiring resisters, the Judenrat felt that their best chance for survival was to join the partisans. To that end, the top officers of the Judenrat, using the resources of ghetto institutions, provided the underground with money for arms, equipped them with supplies and encouraged them with moral support.

The youth, for their part, accepting the conclusion that the ghetto was an unfavourable terrain for armed defence and that an armed rising against the Germans could not be imposed on a civilian population that was unprepared and unwilling to fight, proposed instead a large-scale programme to construct underground bunkers in which the ghetto Jews could hide at the time of the next *Aktion*. In the event that the Germans uncovered the bunkers, which would be armed, the Jews could defend themselves.

Bunkers were indeed constructed. At a subsequent *Aktion*, a few thousand Jews were deported, but the bunkers were not uncovered and the ghetto offered no fight. Thereafter, general agreement prevailed that the wisest course was to send the young people to the partisans, despite the total disaster that had befallen several earlier parties in the woods. The leaders of the Judenrat equipped and outfitted some 300 young people to leave the ghetto, hoping that they would have at least an even chance to survive.[27] The support that the Judenrat leaders of Kovno gave the youthful resisters derived not so much from agreement with their instrumental goals as from paternal solicitude and a sense that the young people, as their heirs and successors, must be saved for the future.

When the Germans came to liquidate the Kovno ghetto early in July 1944, the ghetto gave no resistance. Instead, a dramatic confrontation took place between Dr Elkes and Goecke. Elkes told Goecke that he knew what the fate of the Kovno Jews would be – the same fate that had befallen all the Jews of Europe. Nothing, he said, would remain hidden from history. Offering Goecke a chance to redeem himself, Elkes asked him to save the ghetto. The Jews, he promised, would know how to reward him after the war. Goecke rejected the proposal on his honour as an SS officer.[28]

For the most part, ghetto Jews regarded the young people who planned and plotted armed resistance as irresponsible hotheads who would bring disaster upon the whole ghetto. Scepticism and contempt marked their attitude towards the handful of inexperienced boys and girls who ventured to fight the Germans. In some ghettos the populace responded with unvarnished fear and hatred to the would-be resisters, seeing them as foolish fanatics or even raving lunatics.[29] In Radoszkowice, a town in the district of Vilna with about 1,200 Jews, the ghetto populace warned the newly formed underground that unless the plans for resistance were abandoned, they would denounce them to the Germans. Observant Jews even assembled in the prayer house to excommunicate the ten members of the resistance who intended to join partisans in the woods.

In the Kobryń ghetto, when the young people began to contact the partisans, their parents, as well as Judenrat officials, advised them instead to safeguard the ghetto's existence by working in the ghetto enterprises. In the Chmielnik ghetto, the influential Jews of the community supported the Judenrat in efforts to persuade the members of the underground of their irresponsibility and to warn them of the misfortune that they could bring upon the ghetto.[30] For the most part, caution and prudence guided the ghetto populace with regard to the danger of German reprisals. On this matter, in contrast to others, a general consensus existed between them and the Judenrat.

Tension between the Vilna ghetto population and the resistance movement brought the ghetto to the verge of civil strife. In late spring 1943, the FPO, whose strongest constituents had become the Communists and the Revisionists, in a strategy of expediency made contact with ghetto chief Gens. Aware that the Russians might soon rout the Germans from Vilna, Gens welcomed the opportunity for friends on the other side. After secret meetings between Gens and the FPO at which the defence of the ghetto was discussed, Gens in various small ways helped FPO members to procure and cache arms and to train in their use.[31] At the same time, through his habitual chicanery, he worked to undermine the FPO. Realizing the threat, the FPO adopted a policy decision that in case the ghetto authorities tried to harm it or any of its leaders, it would mobilize all its units for self-defence. That decision provoked deep opposition within the Bund, an FPO constituent, whose leaders held that any armed combat within the ghetto – except for the defence of the ghetto – would be an intolerable provocation.[32]

On 26 June the first test of strength between the FPO and Gens took place. Gens had ordered the arrest of Joseph Glazman, his former deputy, now FPO vice-commandant, one of the most popular figures in the Vilna ghetto. Arrested by the Jewish police, Glazman, handcuffed and chained, was being taken to a labour camp. Suddenly an armed FPO unit materialized near the ghetto gate, stopped the police vehicle, and freed Glazman. The dashing rescue of a ghetto hero, accomplished without gunfire or injury, was so widely admired in the ghetto that Gens did not dare to punish the FPO. Instead he negotiated with them, asking them to help save his prestige in the ghetto by having Glazman report voluntarily to the labour camp for one week. To avoid further confrontations, the FPO agreed, after receiving assurances about Glazman's safety.[33]

About a week later, in early July, the Gestapo learned from two arrested Lithuanian Communists about the existence of a Communist leader named Wittenberg in the Vilna ghetto. Itzik Wittenberg was the FPO commandant. Forewarned, he went into hiding. Several days later, Gens informed the FPO that he had bribed the Gestapo to forget about Wittenberg. On 15 July Wittenberg agreed to attend a meeting of the FPO staff with Gens. Around midnight, when the meeting with five top FPO staff members began, two Lithuanian policemen came in search of Wittenberg. Abba Kovner said no one by that name was present, but Gens pointed Wittenberg out and the Lithuanians led him away. On the street an FPO unit on alert attacked the Lithuanians, allowing Wittenberg to escape into the night and return to his hide-out.

The next morning the Gestapo demanded Wittenberg from Gens. To coerce the FPO, Gens told them the Germans had issued an ultimatum to destroy the whole ghetto if Wittenberg did not turn himself in. Gens then mobilized some 400 toughs and ruffians, armed with sticks and bludgeons, to look for Wittenberg. The FPO, convinced that the end of the ghetto was at hand, issued the password for mobilization, opened its arsenal and began to distribute arms to its members.

Addressing his thugs in front of the Judenrat building and the crowds that had swelled the street, Gens told them that the whole ghetto was imperilled just because of one person, and he referred to the FPO as the 'snot-noses with their popguns'. Panic swept the ghetto and the fear of imminent disaster made the ghetto populace turn their backs on the FPO. The sympathy generated by Glazman's release had dissipated.

The FPO was given a two-hour deadline to yield Wittenberg. The pressure from communal leaders weighed heavily on them. Confronted with the real possibility of having to fight the Jews in the ghetto, they could not decide what to do. (One FPO member proposed collective suicide as a solution.) The decision was made by Wittenberg's own party. The Communists in the ghetto demanded that the FPO surrender him and save the ghetto from civil strife. The FPO submitted and its staff went to search for Wittenberg, but the police found him first, disguised as a woman, trying to escape. He surrendered quietly and was taken to Gens's headquarters, where a Gestapo car had been waiting since early morning. The next day Wittenberg was dead.[34]

The FPO, under Gens's terror, began to flee to the partisans, but after the first escaping parties were caught in the woods by the Gestapo and slaughtered, the exodus halted. On 1 September 1943, when the Germans and the Estonian police entered the Vilna ghetto, the shrunken FPO, taken by surprise, tried to mobilize for defence, but half the units could not reach their arsenal and others simply fled. Some resisters waited at their pre-selected bit of ghetto terrain for the Germans to arrive, but no armed encounter of significance took place. The FPO did not impede the Germans in their work of rounding up some 8,000 Jews – about two thirds of the ghetto – for deportation. That FPO failure convinced the members that their most prudent course could be to leave the remnant ghetto. Within days about 200 young people succeeded in joining the partisans in the woods.[35]

In Bialystok Barash showed the same parental solicitude for the youthful resistance movement that Elkes demonstrated in Kovno. Indeed, the relations between Barash and Mordecai Tenenbaum, head of the combat organization, were mutually warm and trustful. Barash supported the resistance in Bialystok – and Warsaw as well – with funds, supplies and secure locations for their clandestine operations, such as the manufacture of explosives and grenades. He shared information with Tenenbaum and advised him about how to extend the political base of the combat organization.[36]

After the initial wave of Einsatzgruppe killings in the summer of 1941 subsided, Bialystok was spared the subsequent killings and deportations that amputated the other ghettos in the East. In the autumn of 1941 the population of the Bialystok ghetto stood at about 40,000 and remained at that figure until February 1943. Barash believed that Bialystok's productivity for the Wehrmacht guaranteed its continued existence, and he was confident that, in a contest with the SS, the Wehrmacht would defend the ghetto. Tenenbaum, less confident of the Germans, nevertheless yielded to Barash's evaluation of the ghetto's situation.

In late January 1943, when the combat organization was still in its formative stage, Barash was informed that the Germans planned an *Aktion* in Bialystok. On 31 January 1943, at a clandestine meeting of various underground party leaders with Barash and another Judenrat official, Tenenbaum asked for clarification on the underground's 'limits of patience'. For how long was resistance to be withheld and for what price? How many victims, he asked, would be sacrificed before a counter-attack could be launched? The answer was that as long as a majority of the Bialystok Jews remained untouched, no armed resistance should be offered, lest it provoke greater catastrophe.

On the morning of 4 February, Barash confided to Tenenbaum that the Germans had promised to take no more than three transports each of 2,100 Jews according to lists of the unemployed prepared by the Judenrat. That evening, a few hours before the scheduled round-ups, Tenenbaum told his resistance organization: 'We will sacrifice 6,300 Jews in order to save the 35,000 remaining.' He had accepted Barash's view that the ghetto had a chance to survive: the Russians were now advancing and the situation at the front might bring a swift and radical change to the ghetto's fortunes. The round-ups lasted a few days; about 9,000 Jews were taken. (The Jewish police, refusing to cooperate, had gone into hiding. The Germans themselves went from house to house, routing out Jews from bunkers.) Some days later, Tenenbaum told the members of Dror: 'We are responsible for the lack of action. Those who come after us will judge us, to praise or condemn. We refrained from acting not out of weakness, but out of a sense of responsibility for 10 per cent of Polish Jews.'[37]

The working ghetto population believed Barash and trusted his assurances that productivity would ensure their survival. The deportations of the unemployed frightened them less than the shooting of a German policeman by a forty-year-old ghetto Jew, Abraham Melamed. In immediate reprisal the Germans shot 120 Jews on the street, even though they had ironclad work permits. Melamed had escaped. The Germans threatened to destroy the whole ghetto if he did not surrender. The Jewish police offered a reward of 10,000 Reichsmarks. Three days later, Melamed turned himself in 'to save the ghetto'. In the factories, Tenenbaum noted on 7 February, was 'joy'. Though Melamed was not a member of the combat organization, the populace in Bialystok responded to his act of vengeance the same way the Vilna Jews did to the FPO and Wittenberg.

At the very time the *Aktion* was taking place, Tenenbaum was undergoing a profound personal transformation that may later have affected and impeded the operations of the combat organization. He began to sink into a state of melancholy and suicidal depression that differed markedly from the political despair and thirst for revenge that characterized the young people in the resistance movement. At the end of January 1943, Zvi Mersik, his closest friend in Bialystok, died of typhus. A few days later, on 3 February, Tenenbaum learned from an issue of *Głos Warszawy*, an underground PPR paper, about the armed resistance in January in the Warsaw ghetto and of the high losses among the Jewish combatants. He assumed that his dearest friends in the *halutz* movement were killed. Meanwhile, he had not heard for over three weeks from his dearly beloved, Tema Schneiderman, a Dror activist and intrepid courier. He had had word that she had arrived in Warsaw early in January, bringing 80,000 rubles from Barash for ŻOB, but no news thereafter. (Tema had in fact been killed in the Warsaw fighting that January.) On that same 3 February, overwhelmed by his losses, Tenenbaum confided to his diary his wish to die, even in the face of his obligation to organize the resistance: 'I do not want to wait. I cannot. Cyanide. Quick and simple . . . The dead Mersik is with me. Also in life, yes, to be or not to be. The eternal question. Eternal death.'

The young people in the *halutz* movement were not, however, dedicated to death, even though many were committed to a last stand in the ghetto. Some clung to the possibility of survival by joining the partisans in the woods. On 27 February 1943 the Dror activists discussed their options. Defence of the ghetto had its advocates: 'One thing remains for us. To organize the collective act of resistance in the ghetto, at any cost, to regard the ghetto as our Musa Dagh, to record a proud chapter of Jewish Bialystok and of our movement.' The counter-view had its proponents: 'It is more important to remain alive than to kill five Germans. In a counter-action, everyone without doubt will die. On the other hand, in the woods 40 to 50 per cent of our people will be saved. That will be our honour and that will be our history.' Tenenbaum summed up the discussion: 'We will do everything to get out as many people as possible to partisan combat in the woods. Every one of us who will be in the ghetto during the action must respond with the first Jew taken.'[38] (He himself, as he noted in his diary after a similar discussion with another youth group, was 'wandering after Tema's shadow'.)

A short while later, the combat organization split over this issue, the Communists and part of Hashomer Hatzair opting to join the partisans; the other Zionists, Revisionists and the Bund choosing to make the last stand in the ghetto.

The plan for resistance that Tenenbaum appeared to have formulated early in 1943 remained in effect. Whenever the Germans should come, combat units located at the factories were to start the counter-attack, rallying the workers to join them in setting fire to the installations and revenging themselves on the Germans. Leaflets were prepared in advance to explain to the populace that 'resettlement' meant death in Treblinka. A proclamation drafted by Tenenbaum in mid-January exhorted: 'Do not go to your death of your own free will! Fight for your lives to your last breath! We have nothing left but our honour – we can lose nothing else!'

In July rumours spread that the liquidation of the Bialystok ghetto was imminent. German commissions visited the ghetto, no doubt to decide about its life or death. Even Barash began to lose confidence, but nonetheless the Judenrat continued to encourage the populace about the possibility of survival. Then, without warning, at 2.00 a.m. on Monday 16 August 1943 Gestapo forces surrounded the ghetto. An hour later several hundred fully armed SS troops entered the ghetto, occupying the sites of the factories and Judenrat headquarters. They informed Barash that the entire ghetto population, together with the factory equipment, would be evacuated to Lublin. By 5.00 a.m. notices were posted, instructing the Jews to assemble by 9.00 in a specified area with some personal belongings.

The combat organization was caught unprepared, not on the alert in the factories, but at home in bed. Once mobilized, the young people tried to rally the panicked Jews on the streets with speeches, with leaflets, shouting that resettlement meant death in Treblinka, calling on them to refuse to be evacuated. But to no avail. The ghetto populace streamed past them to the staging area, heedless of their appeals. The young people then set fire to the ghetto enclosures on the side leading into the woods, hoping thereby to create openings through which the Jews could flee. But once again the people did not respond. The 31,000 Jews of the Bialystok ghetto were sent to Treblinka and Majdanek.

The ghetto houses near the flaming enclosures began to burn. The Germans opened fire and the youthful combatants now returned fire. The terrain of their battle was a segment of the narrow, cramped ghetto streets, with low buildings that gave no cover and no vantage point for attack. To assault the Jewish resisters with their paltry weapons and home-made grenades, the Germans brought in tanks and the full equipment of a modern army. Yet the young people continued to fight in their isolation. Some managed to hold out, in hit-and-run attacks from bunkers, until 20 August. Then some managed to escape to the woods. The partisans tried to rescue Tenenbaum, but he refused to leave the ghetto. His last words were said to be: 'Jews, we have no arms. Grab sticks, set fire to the houses!'[39]

Everywhere the Germans employed lies, surprise and stealth to liquidate the ghettos. Sudden encirclements at night or at dawn prevented organized combat groups from mobilizing and co-ordinating their units. In some place the precipitous confrontation generated spontaneous resistance, sparked by hate and the desire for revenge.[40] In a labour camp at Łuck, for instance, when the Germans came to liquidate the carpentry enterprise on 12 December 1942, they were greeted with gunfire. For over half a day the barricaded

Jews succeeded in holding off the Germans despite German grenades tossed into the workshop. Finally the Germans resorted to setting fire to the whole building. In the adjoining buildings, in an act of collective suicide, over fifty Jews hung themselves rather than surrender.[41]

In Marcinkonis, a town with 370 Jews in the Grodno district, the Jewish police warned the Judenrat late at night on 1 November 1942 that the ghetto was being surrounded by an armed force. In the morning the Germans ordered the Judenrat to instruct all the Jews to pack their belongings to be resettled for work elsewhere. A small intrepid group tried to attack the German commissar in charge of the deportation, but when they could not get close enough to him, the head of the Judenrat shouted a warning: 'Jews, if you want to live, run where you can. The game is up.' Panic and pandemonium broke out, many Jews bare-handedly attacking the Germans. At the end, 105 Jews were shot to death. Others flew into the woods. There was no one left to 'resettle'.[42]

In Tuczyn, a town with some 2,000 native Jews and a few hundred refugees from other towns, about twenty-seven kilometres from Równe, the end came on 23 September 1942, when the Germans ordered all Jews to assemble at the ghetto gate the next morning. Two young men began to agitate the ghetto populace to disobey. Hundreds of Jews assembled spontaneously in the prayer house. Young people continued to exhort: 'Resist!' 'Don't go voluntarily!' 'Don't you know that the mass pits are dug already?' Then someone shouted: 'Set fire!' everyone began to bring paraffin, in pitchers, kettles, jugs, cups and glassware, from the ghetto, from the workshops that had employed them. That evening the Jews began to destroy their possessions lest they fall into German hands. As night fell, the fires began to glow, first here, then there. All at once the whole ghetto was aflame. The Germans and Ukrainians surrounding the ghetto, caught unawares, began shooting into the flames. In that confusion, about 2,000 Jews managed to break through the ghetto enclosures, fleeing from the burning ghetto into the woods.[43]

Only in the Warsaw ghetto did Jewish resistance attain its objectives. After the *kesl* of September 1942 and the derailment of organized community activity, leadership passed from the Judenrat and the alternative community into the hands of the political and military underground – the ŻKK and ŻOB. Warsaw was unlike the Bialystok and Kovno ghettos, where the Judenräte retained the people's confidence until the very end and kept open channels of communication to inform and encourage the ghetto; it was also unlike Lublin and Cracow, where the deportations and the Judenräte's collapse left the survivors leaderless, adrift in a sea of chaos and fear. In the Warsaw ghetto the ŻKK and ŻOB filled the seat of leadership vacated by the impotent Judenrat and became figures of authority in the ghetto, providing the surviving 50,000 Jews with information and direction, with cues for coping with unfamiliar situations, and with hope and morale, feeding the desire for revenge.

The mimeograph machine and the gun became the tools of leadership, the means by which the ŻKK and ŻOB established their legitimacy. ŻOB's leaflets furnished the ghetto Jews with an interpretation of the events they were witness to, explaining and uncovering German duplicity and trickery. They helped the populace to evolve a unified response to their predicament, as defined by ŻOB. ŻOB's guns executed Jewish traitors and Gestapo agents, thus enforcing its authority in the ghetto and demonstrating unequivocally that it had become the ghetto's defender against its internal and external enemies.

After the *kesl* thousands of Jews had gone underground, living illegally in the interstices of the ghetto segments, in hide-outs and bunkers devised, with ingenuity and diversity, to conceal dozens and even hundreds of people for months on end. Some hide-outs were equipped with electricity and radios. Some had running water provided by cunningly concealed piping; others had direct access to deep wells. Food stocks for weeks, even months, were laid in. Entrances were inventively camouflaged. Concealed doorways, blocked with sandbags or garbage or a piece of furniture, led to attics, cellars and secret rooms. In constructing the bunkers, the Jews carved out passageways from one apartment to another, from attic to attic, from cellar to cellar. The ghetto soon became an enormous underground network of honeycombs connected by hundreds of invisible arteries, its inhabitants able to move about a square block without going outdoors.[44] Knowing that thousands of Jews eluded them, the Germans fabricated new lies to entice them out into the open. In late November 1942, the Germans declared that the Um-schlagplatz had been liquidated and offered amnesty to the 'illegals', holding out the offer of food and employment as bait. German factory directors promised visions of a good life. The Judenrat was asked to plan a six-month work programme.

To these blandishments and lies ŻOB responded vigorously, exposing the duplicity. A ŻOB leaflet issued on 4 December 1942 explained that the Germans aimed to destroy all the Jews by carrying out their annihilation in stages. The chief German tactic was the lie: 'Let us therefore bravely look the truth straight in the face.' The leaflet, taking up one by one each German assurance to the Jews of life and security, demonstrated German deceit and chicanery from the experience of the past: 'Jews, citizens of the Warsaw ghetto, be on the alert, do not believe a single word or act of the SS bandits.' Excoriating the Jewish agents and traitors in the ghetto, ŻOB called on the Jews to help one another, to show solidarity, and to prepare to defend themselves: 'Remember that also you – the civilian Jewish population – are at the front in the fight for freedom and humanity.'[45]

In the first half of January ŻOB issued an appeal to the ghetto populace not to believe the latest arrival of letters allegedly written by Jews deported from Warsaw, now supposedly in labour camps near Pinsk and Bobruisk. 'Jewish masses, don't believe these stories. They are spread by Jews in the service of the Gestapo.' This latest deceit, the leaflet warned, was just to facilitate the next deportation. The hour is approaching, ŻOB declared, when you must be prepared to resist. 'No Jew should go to the trains. People who don't have the possibility of active opposition should offer passive resistance. That means they should hide.'[46]

The first test came on 18 January 1943, when German troops, in a surprise move, surrounded the Warsaw ghetto. Neither the ŻKK nor ŻOB had any advance warning of the Aktion, nor did they have information about its planned size or scope. Fighting erupted spontaneously on the part of five ŻOB units, all isolated from one another and unable to communicate, but responding uniformly to the German threat to seize Jews for deportation. The ŻOB fighters killed or wounded about fifty Germans and seized some of their weapons, but their own losses were extensive. Nevertheless, after three days, the Germans halted the deportations, having taken a relatively small number of Jews. ŻOB's determined fighting and the abrupt departure of the Germans electrified the ghetto. The events confirmed the hopes: armed resistance could turn back the Germans. ŻOB popularity reached a new high. Bakers baked bread for them; leather workers fashioned holsters for their weapons. Even the smugglers and black marketeers supplied them with food and drink.

More than bread, ŻOB needed money – to buy arms to equip the combat groups. ŻOB began to 'levy' taxes on the still well-to-do Jews in the ghetto, carrying out its threat to arrest recalcitrants. (ŻOB maintained its own 'prison', where it held 'tax-dodgers' and suspected Gestapo agents.) The Judenrat itself responded to ŻOB's appeals and contributed about a million zlotys. In true revolutionary tradition, ŻOB members also carried out bank expropriations. Two such acts took place in February 1943, one on the Judenrat treasury, yielding 70,000 zlotys, and the other on the ghetto bank, which brought in 100,000 zlotys.[47]

February 1943 was also a month for cleaning out Jewish Gestapo agents. In that month alone five of 'the meanest scoundrels of society' were shot. A ŻOB leaflet issued on 3 March 1943 listed them by name, the dates of their execution and the specific nature of their crimes. Warning that ŻOB had a complete list of others still working for the Germans, the leaflet added that 'unless they immediately cease their contemptible actions, they will all be shot!'[48]

The ŻKK, meanwhile, reorganized ŻOB after the January losses. Units of tens replaced the original fives or sixes. Organized by party, each unit consisted of at least eight men and no more than two women, with at least half of the members required to have their own guns. In all, twenty-two combat units were formed. Half were associated with Hehalutz, and of these, five were Dror units, four Hashomer Hatzair and one each Akiva and Gordonia. The Bund and PPR each had four units; the Right and Left Labour Zionists and the General Zionist youth each had one unit. After the January defence, ŻOB was besieged by eager applicants. There was no shortage of volunteers, only of arms. The Bund had a strict recruitment policy, maintaining, as it had in earlier times, tight security precautions, screening each applicant closely, rejecting many. The Bundists in ŻOB also rigorously adhered to regulations with regard to arms, turning away volunteers whose only weapons were sticks and stones.[49]

Morale in ŻOB was high. Few ŻOB members thought they were fighting to preserve their lives, yet none yielded to depression. Becoming a combatant, wrote a member, meant leaving behind the scramble for one's wretched existence, the sense of being pursued like an animal by the Germans. Joining ŻOB meant regaining one's humanity and sense of self-esteem. Belongingness enhanced morale. Responsibility for one's acts, for one's future no longer rested on the individual alone, but on the group. Every group had a leader to whom each member looked for guidance and authority. Responsibility for carrying out the group's aims was shared; personal and private interests were submerged and subordinated to the goals of the group. The interplay between leader and follower, between individual and group, forged new bonds and loyalties, which in turn strengthened and reinforced each individual member's morale and courage.[50]

After the abortive *Aktion* of 18 January, the Jewish leaders were convinced that the Germans were preparing for the final liquidation of the Polish Jews. On 21 January 1943 ŻKN, using Delegatura facilities, sent a radio message via the Polish government-in-exile in London to Jewish leaders in New York:

We notify you of the greatest crime of all times, about the murder of millions of Jews in Poland. Poised at the brink of the annihilation of the still surviving Jews, we ask you:
  1. Revenge against the Germans
  2. Force the Hitlerites to halt the murders
  3. Fight for our lives and our honour
  4. Contact the neutral countries
  5. Rescue 10,000 children through exchange
  6. 500,000 dollars for purposes of aid.
Brothers – the remaining Jews in Poland live with the awareness that in the most terrible days of our history you did not come to our aid. Respond, at least in the last days of our life.[51]

On 7 February the underground Bund leaders sent a radio message to Zygelboym in the Polish parliament-in-exile in London:

In January the Germans began to liquidate the Warsaw ghetto. A few dozen Germans were thereby killed. Several hundred Jews were killed on the spot . . . After three days the *Aktion* was halted. 6,000 were taken away. The liquidation is occurring throughout Poland. In mid-February they are to liquidate the Warsaw ghetto. Alert the whole world. Appeal to the Pope for official intervention and to the Allies to declare German war prisoners as hostages. We suffer terribly. The surviving 200,000 await annihilation. Only you can save us. The responsibility with regard to history will rest on you.[52]

In February the owners of the German industrial enterprises began to campaign among their workers to register for voluntary evacuation. At public meetings of workers, the German industrialists painted an incredibly idyllic Jewish future: 'a paradisiac existence in beautiful bucolic surroundings, a life rich in magnificent amusements in leisure hours and days'.[53] To give authenticity to the campaign, the SS remained behind the scenes, while Walter C. Többens, the owner of the largest ghetto enterprise, employing about 8,000 Jews, was officially put in charge of 'resettlement'. In March the first factories began to be liquidated. The night before the evacuation, a ŻOB unit ignited the Hallmann factory, where 1,000 Jews had worked, destroying the raw materials and machinery packed for shipment. The next day only twenty-five workers showed up for voluntary removal. None of the 3,500 workers in the brush shops turned up for the scheduled evacuation. At the Schultz shops a ŻOB unit freed sixty Jews kept prisoners by the Germans. Increasingly ŻOB was seen by the ghetto Jews as their defender.

On 14 March ŻOB issued another proclamation calling on the Jews to resist the Germans, emphasizing that 'voluntary resettlement' meant only the inevitable annihilation of the ghetto.[54] The leaflet was so effective in reinforcing the resistance of the workers that Többens was forced to reply. On 20 March he issued a leaflet, denying that any harm had come to the Jewish workers who were previously resettled. He tried to discredit ŻOB: 'The ŻOB command cannot help you; they offer only empty promises.' Többens even proposed a conference with ŻOB on the subject of 'resettlement'. The lack of success in effecting a voluntary evacuation prompted the Germans, who were then not ready to show force, to induce the Judenrat to invite ŻOB to a meeting, but that invitation, too, was rejected with contempt. The Judenrat chairman was said then to have told the Germans: 'I have no power in the ghetto. Another authority rules here.'[55]

The sense of urgency in the ghetto increased. Early in April both the Bund and the ŻKN dispatched another round of urgent radio appeals to London, Geneva, New York and Jerusalem. 'Storm heaven and earth,' they cried, asking once again to alert the world to the annihilation of the Jews and swiftly to aid the survivors with money and to rescue them through exchange.[56]

At 2.00 a.m. on Monday 19 April 1943 armed German, Lettish and Ukrainian patrols began to be deployed around the Warsaw ghetto. A half-hour later ŻOB received information about the German troop movements. By daylight ŻOB's units were mobilized. Nine units were located in the central ghetto, eight in the area of the Többens-Schultz workshops and five in the area of the brush works. (Later, units of the Revisionist ŻZW participated in the fighting, as did also 'wild' units, so nicknamed because they were unaffiliated.)

At 6.00 a.m. a contingent of 2,000 heavily armed SS troops entered the central ghetto, with tanks, rapid-fire guns and three trailers loaded with ammunition.[57] The ŻOB units were ready to confront them. The civilian ghetto populace was underground, hiding in their bunkers. ŻOB attacked the entering German columns. With incendiary bottles mass-produced in a secret ŻOB laboratory, they blew up German tanks and German troops. Shooting flared up in several areas. ŻOB units prevented German relief troops from entering the ghetto. By 5.00 p.m. the Germans, surprised and shocked by Jewish reistance, withdrew from the ghetto, having lost some 200 dead and wounded.

'We were happy and laughing,' said a ŻOB combatant. 'When we threw our grenades and saw German blood on the streets of Warsaw, which had been flooded with so much Jewish blood and tears, a great joy possessed us.' Everyone knew that the Germans would return, that the Germans would ultimately defeat ŻOB, that the Jews would soon be annihilated; yet after that day's fighting in the ghetto, people embraced and kissed each other.[58]

That 19 April marked the celebration of the first *seder* ushering in the festival of Passover. One of the combatants, searching for flashlight batteries, came into a rabbi's apartment where a *seder* was in progress.

The room looked as if it had been struck by a pogrom. Only the wine goblets on the table suggested the festive occasion. The reading of the Haggada was punctuated by gunfire and shell-bursts. The assembled Jews wept when the rabbi intoned: 'Pour out Thy wrath upon the heathen nations that do not acknowledge Thee and upon the king-doms that do not call upon Thy name; for they have devoured Jacob and laid waste his dwelling place.'

Early the next day, 20 April, the Germans, using the Judenrat as intermediary, issued an ultimatum to ŻOB, demanding that they lay down their arms by 10.00 a.m. But Lettish Waffen-SS rein-forcements entering the ghetto were received with grenades and explosives. An electric mine killed about 100 Germans of a 300-man force. Corpses began to pile up in the streets. In the late afternoon the Germans brought in tanks and field artillery. Occupying several roofs, they set up heavy machine-guns. Two Higher Police and SS officers appeared, again demanding that ŻOB units lay down their arms. If not, the entire area would be bombed. Once again, ŻOB's reply came from its guns. That very day, the Germans appealed to the ghetto Jews in hiding to volunteer for evacuation with the Többens and Schultz shops. But no one came forward.

The Germans began setting fire to ghetto buildings. ŻOB countered by igniting the warehouses of the Werterfassung, the agency in charge of expropriated Jewish property. Pillars of smoke began to rise over the ghetto. The Germans cut off the supply of electricity, gas and water from the ghetto streets.

ŻOB fighters remained exultant, their morale high. On one roof they flew the red-and-white Polish flag alongside the Jewish blue-and-white banner. On another roof a ŻOB banner proclaimed: 'We shall fight to the last.' (PPR members, impelled by other loyalties, abandoned their units after two or three days of combat. Some managed to escape from the ghetto.)

On Wednesday 21 April the Germans relied more on tanks, howitzers and massive anti-aircraft artillery. The ŻOB fighters shifted from offensive to defensive tactics. Increasingly the Germans resorted to fire, against which ŻOB had no weapons. Columns of smoke were visible for miles around Warsaw. The flames in the ghetto threatened to engulf all Warsaw.

By Thursday 22 April the ghetto was enveloped in dense smoke. To dislodge the tens of thousands of Jews hidden in bunkers and underground shelters, the Germans brought in flame-throwers. With listening devices and police dogs they hunted down the Jews. Emerging from their smoke-filled burning hide-outs, the Jews, hands held over their heads, were marched to the Umschlagplatz. There the Ukrainians, beating and bullying them, loaded them on the waiting freight trains.[59]

The ghetto was a roaring sea of fire. ŻOB fighters regrouped their forces and began rescuing the Jews in the shelters, where thousands were being burned alive. People were seen silhouetted in the window frames of blazing buildings, sheathed in flames, like living torches.

On Friday 23 April the fighting shifted northwards in the ghetto. Többens, having dismantled his plant, was transporting it to Ponia-towa and succeeded in taking with him some 2,000 out of an estimated 8,000 workers. Fighting continued on the terrain of the brush works On that day, Mordecai Anielewicz, ŻOB commandant, sent a letter to his friend Zuckerman, then on the 'Aryan' side: 'It is now quite clear to me that what took place exceeded all expectations.' He asked Zuckerman to get rifles, hand grenades, machine-guns, and explosives. Sooner or later, he believed, everyone would die. Still, he wrote, 'the last wish of my life has been fulfilled. Jewish self-defence has become a fact. Jewish resistance and revenge have become realities.'

That same day, the fifth day of the defence of Warsaw, ŻOB addressed a proclamation to the Polish population of Warsaw:

Let it be known that every threshold in the ghetto has been and will continue to be a fortress, that we may all perish in this struggle, but we will not surrender; that, like you, we breathe with desire for revenge for all the crimes of our common foe.

Summoning up the remembrance of past Polish participation in struggles for freedom and liberation, the proclamation echoed the historic words of Poland's fight against tyranny everywhere: 'A battle is being waged for your freedom as well as ours.'[60]

From that day on, ŻOB fighters shifted to tactics of guerrilla warfare, leaving their bunkers at night to conduct hit-and-run assaults on German formations, to foray for weapons, and to spy out the situation. The sounds of gunfire and of grenade and mine explosions were deafening. Fires raged night and day.

No one had hoped to hold out that long. The ŻOB units, augmented by the Revisionists and the unaffiliated groups, all poorly equipped, numbered about 1,000 combatants. According to the Home Army estimates, the Germans had some 5,000 men and officers, massively equipped.[61]

Fighting became sporadic and isolated, in consequence of superior German fire-power and dwindling Jewish ammunition supplies. The raging fires also limited access to the ghetto areas. ŻOB forces became splintered and crippled. Meanwhile the Germans continued to dismantle their more valuable plants for removal. On 29 April fighting continued at the Schultz factory, where ŻOB units and Jewish workers tried to halt the transfer of equipment.

There was almost no terrain left to fight on. The intense heat of the conflagrations had turned the pavement into a sticky pulp of tar. Food reserves had gone up in flames. The wells, so laboriously dug in the bunkers, were filled with rubble. All around, wrote a ghetto combatant, 'the roar of the fire, the noise of falling walls. Outside the ghetto it was spring, but here a holocaust reigned.'[62]

On 8 May the Germans surrounded the hide-out of ŻOB headquarters. The civilians in the bunker surrendered, but the ŻOB fighters entrenched themselves, ready to fight the Germans. Instead, the Germans stopped up all the entrances and sent gas into the bunker. Over 100 fighters were inside. One of them called out, 'Let's not fall into their hands alive!' They began to kill themselves and each other, in a scene that must have rivalled the mass suicide at Masada. Mordecai Anielewicz was among them. On 10 May about seventy-five ŻOB survivors made their way through the slime of Warsaw's sewers to escape, with the help of comrades on the 'Aryan' side. The Warsaw ghetto became one huge cemetery.

In the Generalgouvernement the only Jews still surviving legally were those in the closed labour camps (for example, Płaszów near Cracow; Janów in Lwów; Skarzysko near Radom; Piotrków; Częstochowa). Other camps, including Trawniki and Poniatowa, where Többens and Schultz had been transferred, were liquidated by

November 1943. There were also about 10,000 Jews in the forests, some trying to survive on their own in nature's hostile milieu, others attached to partisan groups, all hunted and driven. (In the Baltic, too, there were some 15,000 to 20,000 Jews in the woods.) About 30,000 Jews lived as 'Aryans' in the cities – half in Warsaw – disguised, on false papers, exposed to denunciation and extortion by Polish blackmailers. Finally, about 20,000 Polish Jews were assembled in Vittel and Bergen-Belsen, in special camps for 'foreigners' – Jews who, with money, influence or by virtue of élite communal status, had acquired Paraguayan or other citizenship and who were hoaxed into believing that they were being held for exchange.

The ŻKK tried to bring aid and comfort to as many of these Jews as they could reach through their own underground channels and couriers and, to a lesser extent, through the help of the Rada Pomocy Żydom (RPŻ; Council for Aid to Jews), a joint Polish-Jewish organization that had come into existence at the end of 1942 with the meagre financial assistance of the Delegatura.[63] In a report sent by the ŻKN to Zionist leaders abroad, the underground leaders described the conditions under which they lived and worked: 'We go about in disguises. We feel like tightrope aerialists performing over an abyss. Night and day we hover between life and death. Every day we work is a miracle. But we do not cease.'[64]

Every day the number of surviving Jews dwindled. In the cities, Polish police, blackmailers, spies, Gestapo agents and Security Police hunted down Jews, especially Jewish leaders. In the forest, unfriendly peasants and anti-Semitic Polish, Ukrainian or Russian partisans found it easier to destroy Jews than Germans. As for the labour camps and the camps at Vittel and Bergen-Belsen, the Germans liquidated them in rapid order. There were no Jewish communities anymore, no synagogues, no Jewish schools, no Jewish life to sustain. Blood-soaked debris of Yiddish and Hebrew books at the banks of the Vistula were all that remained of the thousand-year-old civilization of Jews in Poland.

'Our tasks now', Leon Feiner wrote in his report of 15 November 1943, 'come down to this: at least to keep alive the remnants who have survived ... so there will be some reserve for the future and witnesses to this crime.'

16 Jewish Behaviour in Crisis and Extremity

Conventional wisdom tells us that the history of the past provides guidance for the strategy of the future, but Edmund Burke was closer to the truth when he wrote that 'you can never plan the future by the past'. The long Jewish past of persecution and disaster offered little that was instructive or relevant in the confrontation with the Final Solution. The Final Solution was a new phenomenon in human history.

Human perception is bound by the known and the familiar. To comprehend the strange and unfamiliar, the human mind proceeds from the reality of experience towards cognition by applying reason, logic and analogy. People view the present and try to discern the outlines of the future through the prism of the past. The Jews, in their earliest encounters with the anti-Jewish policies of Hitler's Germany, saw their situation as a retroversion of their history, but in their ultimate encounter with the Final Solution historical experience and even ideology failed them as explanation.

The responses of the Jewish community were determined not only by the experiences of the past considered in the light of existing knowledge, but also by the dominant values of Jewish tradition and culture and by a modal national character and personality.[1] National character reflects the enduring formative influences of a people's culture and history. Through the processes of socialization during which the values of the group and patterns of behaviour common to all its members are transmitted by family and peers, each individual's uniqueness is modified and seasoned by national characteristics.

Despite the recurrent cycles of disaster that marked their history, the Jews have been committed to a fundamental and abiding optimism grounded in the teachings of Judaism. All creation, Genesis declares, is good. Whatever God does, the tradition teaches, is for good. *Gam zu letova* – 'This, too, is for the best' – which the Tanna Nahum of Gimzo used to say on any distressing occasion, was embodied in the folk wisdom, an expression of optimistic assent and acceptance of God's will.

The tradition teaches that the whole world depends on justice, that good is rewarded and evil punished. The universe is orderly and rational. Whatever exists and is done serves God's purpose and has meaning, though that meaning and purpose are not always revealed to men. In modern times, the liberal, progressive, radical and nationalist ideologies that supplanted or supplemented traditional Judaism incorporated into their secular and sometimes explicitly irreligious doctrines the traditional Jewish optimistic view of man's goodness and of the eventual triumph of justice in a society of order and rationality.

The prime value that the Jews attached to life itself and to Jewish survival generated an activist tradition that influenced the behaviour of the individual and the organized community. The pervasiveness of activism among Jews, especially in defence of their rights and their existence, derived from the exceptional responsibility that traditional Judaism places on every individual Jew. The obligations to preserve Judaism and the Jewish people have rested not on monarchs or prime ministers, nor on high priests, prophets or rabbis, but on each Jewish man and each Jewish woman.

The tradition taught that everything must be done to remove any stumbling block that endangers life. The man who allows a broken ladder to stand in his house violates a precept of Jewish law. All through their history, in the observance of this precept, the Jews invoked the strategy of activism, using not one but all options open to them to save themselves from impending danger. Though they prayed to God, begging for His mercy and succour, they did not passively await deliverance. They applied for protection from one power against the assault of another; they sought refuge in temporary flight or undertook the hazards of permanent emigration. They made every effort to ransom hostages, to offer bribes and gifts to the oppressors. During the Crusades, the medieval pogroms and the Ukrainian massacres of 1648-9, the Jews within walled or fortified communities defended themselves against their assailants.[2]

The religious tradition prescribed patterns of behaviour in conformity with ultimate values, but it was itself affected by the political condition of the Jews. The Talmud began to develop in the first traumatic period of Jewish powerlessness, after the destruction of the Second Temple. The rabbis addressed themselves not just to timeless pieties, but by indirection also to the political realities confronting them so as to evolve an appropriate posture and *modus vivendi* that would ensure Jewish survival. 'Belong ever to the persecuted rather than to the persecutors,' the Talmud taught. 'God loves the persecuted and hates the persecutors.' To compensate for lost national autonomy, the religious tradition elevated powerlessness into a positive Jewish value. It fostered submissiveness and cautioned against rash rebellion: 'The Holy Spirit says, "I adjure you that if the earthly kingdom decrees persecutions, you shall not rebel in all that it decrees against you, but you shall keep the king's command."' (That advice suggests comparison with, for instance, the prudential policies of the French resistance movement during the Second World War, which regarded the price of active resistance to the Germans as too high in terms of human life and suffering.)

To facilitate their survival in powerlessness and to lessen the impact of humiliation and suffering, the Jews made virtues of self-discipline, prudence, moderation, forgoing present gratification for eventual benefit. They learned to practise nonviolent means of resistance and to find ways of circumventing discrimination and deflecting persecution.

The European Jews discerned three stages in the historical situation that confronted them after the National Socialists came to power. The first stage, disemancipation, corresponded with the first six years of the German dictatorship and ended with Kristallnacht. Jews saw that period as a reversion to the pre-Emancipation era, when the modern nation-state was emerging and Jews were poised at the brink of modernity.

The second stage, that of the ghetto and yellow star, coincided with the German conquest and occupation of most European nations and with the establishment of German hegemony over nearly all the others. The Jews saw that period as a fearful retrogression to the darkest days of the Middle Ages, when they were the pariahs of society at the nadir of powerlessness.

The third stage, annihilation, unfolded with the mass killings by the Einsatzgruppen in the second half of 1941 and continued until the end of the war with the operation of the death camps. That period struck the Jews like a cataclysm of unparalleled proportions, a natural disaster without historical precedent or rational meaning.

With these perceptions of their situation, the Jews, leaders and masses, evaluated German goals and intentions with regard to them. Their evaluations defined the choice of available strategies to cope with changed circumstances. Like people anywhere, they resorted to policies and tactics whose usefulness and effectiveness had been demonstrated by historical experience. Strategies were evaluated as to costs and benefits, the possible gains of one course of action weighed against its probable losses and in relation to available alternatives. Policy was always two-pronged: directed internally to strengthen the community and bolster its morale: directed outwardly, in dealings with the oppressor, to alleviate hardships and nullify persecutions.

Jewish communal leaders were confronted with imponderable tasks and unprecedented responsibility under German rule. In this time of crisis followed by extremity, they acted in accordance with their perceptions and evaluations and to the extent of their opportunities. During their lifetime they were judged for good or evil by their contemporaries on the basis of their successes and failures. After their demise, they – their acts as well as their persons – are still judged before the bar of history.

Responsibility means accountability or answerability for one's actions and their consequences. Historical responsibility is defined as an individual's answerability for committing or failing to commit acts that would have affected the outcome of any given situation.[3] A person charged with historical responsibility must have, besides the will and the capability to exercise it, also the opportunity to do or prevent something from being done that would have changed the course of events. Opportunity is determined by external circumstances and resources. The philosophers speak of the ' "can" of opportunity', which is explained this way: 'To have the opportunity to do something requires only that one be in a situation such that if, roughly speaking, one wanted to do it, it would be reasonable to expect that one would be successful in doing it if one were able to do it.'[4]

In the first stage, most Jews and Jewish leaders in Germany foresaw their disemancipation at the hands of the National Socialist dictatorship The severity of their pessimism was, however, mitigated by the unanimous Jewish view, shared by many liberal non-Jews, that the National Socialists could not long retain power. Jewish leadership first responded to disemancipation by conducting a policy of resistance in the posture of accommodation. After a century of struggle for equality, marked by cycles of advance and retreat, most Jews in Germany were not prepared to yield their rights without active effort to retain them. The general strategy was for the Jews to try to hold on and hold out, while their leaders, through official negotiations, backstairs bargaining and petition, sought to protect the achievements of the Emancipation and the rights of the Jews to *Dasein*.

The community geared itself for emergency, re-tooling existing institutions for expanded, or altogether new, tasks. For the most part, unity on pragmatic goals was attained. In times of crisis people rally for the common good, and Jews perhaps even more so. In Jewish tradition, communal unity has a near-transcendental value, for according to one passage in the Talmud the Second Temple was destroyed because of the baseless hatred of one Jew for another. The striving for unity later manifested itself in all Jewish communities under German occupation and duress.

Internal Jewish communal policy was directed towards building morale and organizing self-help. Despite the relentless vigilance of the National Socialists, Jewish leaders nevertheless found means of communicating with the rank-and-file community, providing cues and direction, counsel and encouragement. The external policy, the attempt to shore up the Jewish legal and economic position, was the first to fail. Without friends or allies, in a sea of torrential hostility, the Jews were deprived of resources and lacked opportunities to halt the course of disemancipation that the German dictatorship had set in motion. (Even the once influential Social Democratic party and the once massive German labour movement were completely powerless to defeat or deflect the Nazis.)

In the first years of the National Socialist régime the Jews demonstrated their defiance of the dictatorship by insisting on their rights, but by the last months of 1935 most Jews regarded the continued existence of a viable Jewish community in Germany as no more than a quixotic vision. Germany's foreign-policy successes indicated that National Socialism could no longer be regarded as a transient pheno-

menon in German history. The Nuremberg Laws had sealed disemancipation and presaged further, as yet unadumbrated, degradation.
Re-evaluating their situation, the Jews evolved a new strategy, to
which all but the most stubborn adhered – the orderly dissolution of
the Jewish community in Germany by a programme of systematic
emigration.

Kristallnacht and its consequences undid that Jewish strategy too.
As Germany's anti-Jewish programme entered a new phase of accelerated violence, an intensified sense of urgency entered Jewish
evaluations of the deteriorating situation. The possibility of formu-
lating communal policy on the basis of a limited range of available
alternatives no longer existed. The knife was at the throat; Jewish
leaders no longer had options. Thenceforth their strategy was shaped
by German coercion.

In the post-war years, men who had held leading positions in the
Jewish community in Germany expressed remorse for their under-
estimation of the threat that National Socialism posed to Jewish
existence, for their unrealistic optimism, for their failure to foresee
the outlines of the Final Solution. They blamed themselves for not
having urged early and total emigration and for the consequent loss of
thousands of lives. That self-recrimination bespeaks a refined sense of
guilt rather than an assessment of historical responsibility. It does not
take into account the ' "can" of opportunity'. Had Hitler died or
been assassinated in any of those years, had the English or French
challenged Germany's violation of international treaties, then in the
end Jewish policy would have been successful. With such alternatives,
any call for the dismantling of the Jewish community in Germany
would have appeared cowardly and hysterical.

The historical success or failure of any policy is measured by the
actual outcome of events, but that success or failure is not determined
by prescience or wisdom, by right or wrong. The course of history,
of victory and defeat, is circumscribed by the fortuitous confluence of
resources and opportunity.

The second stage in the Jewish situation came with the German
invasion of Poland in September 1939. It first appeared that the policy
of disemancipation that the Germans instituted right away was now
coupled with a policy of permanent pogrom. In Eastern Europe,

where most Jews had experienced war, pogroms and famine in their lifetime, where want and deprivation had been Jewish familiars, the Jews, trained by the habitude of suffering, viewed German oppression in a historic perspective. Recurrent persecution was their portion. Nevertheless, with God's help, they would, as they had done before in their history, survive. Traditional Jewish optimism tempered the grim reality of German rule by the universal expectation of a short-lived German occupation and a rapid German military defeat. A world ruled by National Socialist Germany was inconceivable to the Jews, whether they looked to God, the Red Army or the Allies for succour.

Within a few months, however, as the Germans began to separate the Jews physically from the rest of the population, to identify them with Star of David arm bands, and to isolate them in ghettos, the Jews saw their situation as a reversion to the darkness of the Middle Ages and they came to a new evaluation of German policy. The Germans, they concluded, were engaged in no random game of terror and persecution, but had embarked on a systematic programme to wipe them out through hunger and sickness, exploitation of their labour and plunder of their property. Everywhere Jewish leadership rallied to resist this German policy: to combat hunger and disease, to prevent the physical extinction of the Jews. The idea of holding on and holding out became the fundamental Jewish policy. In Germany, holding on and holding out had applied to the legal and political rights of the Jews. In the East European ghettos, holding on and holding out meant the struggle for physical survival.

Every strategy that had availed them in past times of stress was tried. Though the continued state of war and the brute force of German rule prevented movement and emigration, huge masses of Jews in the early period of the occupation attempted flight, inside Poland and out. Everywhere Jews resorted to *shtadlanut* – intercession, petition, attempted bargaining – with German officials, indigenous functionaries, church leaders and underground political authorities. Everywhere Jews used money and valuables to elicit favours or obtain remissions, to ransom their captives.

Against the devouring rapacity of the Germans, Jewish material re-sources, even when augmented by aid from American Jews, were piteously insufficient. Intangible spiritual resources were less vulnerable and more enduring – above all, communal solidarity. Everywhere, despite divisions by class and ideology, despite the conflict of generations between traditionalism and modernity, despite the cleavages between the nationalists and the universalists, every Jewish sub-community rallied to help the Jews survive. The single goal that animated all Jewish leaders – whether they were in the official community, the alternative community or the counter-community, and despite the differences in their functions, outlooks and policies – was to keep the Jews alive, to sustain them physically and morally.

The Jewish masses too rallied with energy, inventiveness and optimism to face each cheerless day.* To be sure, thousands among millions of Jews succumbed to demoralization. There were those who, for the recompense of food, security, pleasure or the illusion of authority, stole from or betrayed fellow Jews. But the overwhelming majority brought decency and fraternal solicitude to the ghetto. The traits of national character and the values that their culture had fashioned stood the Jews in the ghettos in good stead. They preserved their humanity by trying to carry on the daily routine of normal existence in a time of crisis – protecting the family, educating the children, feeding the hungry, caring for the sick, satisfying intellectual and cultural needs. 'It is a great deal', says Camus, 'to face destruction while cherishing the idea of a higher civilization.'

The objectives of Jewish leaders and masses were congruent, though they differed, sometimes bitterly, invoking denunciation and recrimination, over the tactics and strategy to attain their common objectives. The Judenräte often missed opportunities and wasted resources, sometimes because of inexperience and inefficiency in operating large administrations under stressful conditions, sometimes because of the infiltration of corrupt and dishonest people into the ghetto bureaucracy. In many ghettos German terror so overwhelmed the Judenräte that their officials lost the ability for independent thought and became fearful of any initiative that might alleviate the ghetto's misery. Then there were a handful of leaders who, because of defects in personality –

---

*The will to live of Jews in the ghettos contrasted dramatically with the passivity and total resignation that characterized the Russian prisoners of war. Even ghetto Jews who encountered them at forced labour and who often risked their lives to give them bread were appalled at the transformation of human beings into wraiths of wretchedness.[5]

unrealized ambitions, vanity – were convinced that only their judgements and strategies were correct and would succeed while those of their critics were wrong and would fail.

For all their weaknesses, failings and wrongdoings, these men – Rumkowski, Merin, Gens – were no traitors. The Jews had no Quislings, Lavals or Vlasovs, no leaders who shared common goals and aspirations with the Germans.[6] The accusation that some Jewish leaders 'cooperated' or 'collaborated' with the Germans arises out of distortions of the historical record. Cooperation and collaboration with the Germans were policies voluntarily undertaken by leaders of nations that retained all or part of their independence and autonomy. In the ghettos of Poland, where German rule was total, where Hans Frank reigned as king, where Himmler's SS kept order and where the German army operated the economy, Germany did not ask for or get either cooperation or collaboration. SS force and terror extracted compliance from the Jews and aimed to bring them to a state of unresisting submissiveness. Unlike Quisling, Laval and Vlasov, no Jew – not even an underworld blackguard who sold information to the Gestapo – ever awaited German victory. No Jew ever hoped for a New Order in Europe. The officials of the Judenräte were coerced by German terror to submit and comply. To say that they 'cooperated' or 'collaborated' with the Germans is semantic confusion and historical misrepresentation.[7]

Could the course of events in the ghettos have been changed had there been fewer missed opportunities and wasted resources? In some ghettos, notably Lodz and Warsaw, more help – within the limits of the available means – might have been rendered to ease the misery of the poorest and most friendless. But the Germans never permitted the ghetto sufficient means to satisfy hunger and cure disease. Even if the ghetto bureaucracies had been more efficient, they could not have halted the course of events that the Germans actuated, simply because the Judenräte lacked the resources and opportunities necessary to thwart German plans. At a time when all Europe lay prostrate under German dominion, the Jews imprisoned within the ghettos had the least opportunity of any people or nation to determine their fate.

The third and final stage of the Jewish situation came with the deportations from the ghettos. The Jews realized that they now confronted even severer threats to their existence than before, though they had neither knowledge nor premonition of death. What they perceived was a major disruption of the wretched existence they had managed to maintain until then. The German strategy everywhere to facilitate the transportation of the Jews to the death camps consisted of lies and deception. The fundamental lie was that the Jews were being resettled for work in the Occupied Eastern Territories, that diligent and industrious Jews would continue to live unharmed in the ghetto.

Reluctant to uproot themselves from the familiar distress of the ghetto, most Jews believed that the future for those deported held nothing more than new hardships in strange and forlorn places. No Jewish official knew otherwise when the deportations began, for none was ever privy to German plans. No Judenrat official ever volunteered to deport Jews from the ghettos, even when they were deceived by German assurances. Everywhere the deportations were conducted under duress, even though Rumkowski and Merin appeared to take the responsibility upon themselves.

After information filtered into the ghetto about the mass shootings in the outdoors, about the operations of mobile death vans, about gassing installations in desolate camps, the first response everywhere was disbelief grounded in shock. Even the wanton and unconstrained killings and cruelties committed by the Germans had not prepared the Jews to grasp the facts of systematic mass murder.

Locked within their ghettos, under strict surveillance and unreined terror, the Jews had no opportunities of verifying the information that came to them, except by asking the Germans, who, unfailingly and unblinkingly, continued to lie. The Jews then tried to assess the possible authenticity of the reports in the light of experience and logic. The horror of an enterprise that would deliberately destroy human beings who were innocent of any wrongdoing was inconceivable. The senselessness of the undertaking further undermined the acceptance of the information. The Jews provided the German war industry with skilled labour, a precious wartime commodity. The wilful destruction of so valuable an asset was as inconceivable on rational grounds as systematic mass murder was on experiential or moral grounds. These evaluations were for the most part shared at all levels of Jewish leadership and by the masses as well. The information about the death camps was rejected all over Europe, not only by the Jews, who, as the first targets and victims, would be expected to disbelieve most because the news threatened them most. In the Netherlands, for instance, members of the Dutch resistance responded to the news – first relayed by Kurt Gerstein – with such utter incredulity that they failed to act on the information in any way, not even warning the Jews.[8]

During the first months of the deportations, in the absence of reliable evidence that deportation meant death, Judenrat officials did not communicate to the community at large their disquiet and anxiety, fearful of spreading panic and undermining morale. That dilemma was described by Leo Baeck, writing about his experiences in Theresienstadt in 1943. A camp inmate told Baeck, in the strictest confidence that a friend who had escaped from Auschwitz had secretly visited him in the middle of the night. At Auschwitz, the friend said, the Jews were gassed to death, except for those assigned to slave labour. 'So it was not just a rumour,' Baeck commented, 'or as I had hoped, the illusion of a diseased imagination.' He pondered his responsibility as to whether he should inform the Judenrat, of which he was an honorary member. 'Living in the expectation of death by gassing would only be the harder,' he reasoned. Furthermore, in an exercise of denial, he thought that death was not certain for all, since some people were selected for slave labour. Perhaps not all transports were sent to Auschwitz. 'So', he concluded, 'I came to the grave decision to tell no one.'[9]

Some Jewish leaders, like millions of the people who looked to them for leadership, could not assimilate the information about the death camps. For them, in Yeats's words, things fell apart, the centre could not hold. Their psychological solution lay in the denial of the information, in the shocked retreat from reality or in suicide. The paralysis of despair overtook many.

Would an alert, if issued, have changed the outcome of the deportations? Would it have saved lives? In Warsaw, the first warnings of the underground that resettlement meant death were unheeded by the ghetto populace. Without evidential corroboration and with non-compliance as the only alternative course of action, the populace rejected the warning, adapting to their situation by repressing and denying the information. Later, when the ghetto Jews in Warsaw and Lodz acted on warnings by hiding *en masse*, by passive resistance, the

Germans managed to dislodge them from their hiding places in a relatively short time. (Whether the Jews were killed resisting deportation in the ghetto in full public view of non-Jews or in Treblinka or Auschwitz in relative privacy was, for the Germans, at bottom only a matter of public relations.) Even when Jewish leaders informed the community, the course of the Final Solution was not halted, but just retarded for a brief historic moment. In the small ghettos of eastern Poland and White Russia, where official leaders, often in concert with underground leaders, warned the ghetto of imminent liquidation, some Jews had opportunities to flee into the woods. But survival was a possibility only for the young and fit, those with the physical stamina and armed equipment that was their admission ticket to the partisans. It was unrealistic to expect that unarmed urban civilians could survive in the woods. Even the Gypsies, a people whose familiar milieu is the open country, were unable to elude the Germans in the very forests that they believed would be their refuge.[10]

Did Judenrat officials have opportunities or resources to prevent the Germans from carrying out the deportations? Were alternative courses of action available to them? In the light of our knowledge that Hitler and his government would not permit rational considerations of maximal self-interest in the conduct of the war to interfere with the execution of the Final Solution, such questions about Jewish opportunities and resources to halt the Final Solution appear absurd.

Some Judenräte had no options at all, being simply confronted with accomplished facts of deportations that the Germans themselves organized and carried out. In other ghettos, however, Judenrat officials could be said to have had, in theory, a limited range of alternatives to unresisting compliance, even though in practice every alternative ended in death. In principle, their options were: non-compliance, attempted nullification of deportation and attempted reduction of the size and scope of deportations in exchange for peaceable compliance.

Non-compliance, in the circumstances of the ghetto, meant either suicide or outright refusal to obey on the part of the Judenrat official. Refusal inevitably entailed being shot on the spot or immediate deportation. Suicide, not a characteristically Jewish response, was more common, because the man who took his life chose not to endanger the hostages taken by the Germans to assure Judenrat compliance. Confronted with Judenrat non-compliance, the Germans, at small cost, intensified the terror. They appointed a handful of demoralized Jews to carry out their orders and brought into the ghetto greater numbers of SS troops and Ukrainian and Baltic auxiliary police.

Some Judenräte attempted to nullify the deportations through the age-old strategy of bribery, but those who delivered the ransom disappeared forever, without deflecting the Germans from their course. In Kovno, when the Germans were already losing the war, even the offer of post-war protection did not dissuade the SS officer from completing the deportations. The strategy of rescue-through-work, pursued relentlessly by both Rumkowski and Barash, appeared to offer the greatest possibility of success. Their objectives were, so to speak, congruent with the temporary interests of the German army, which they were outfitting and supplying and which, consequently, tried to prolong the existence of the ghettos. But if the Wehrmacht could not prevail against the Führer and the SS, how reasonable is the expectation that the Judenrat could have succeeded?

As German terror and the lack of Jewish opportunity rendered each strategy ineffectual and futile, the only course left open to the Judenräte was the strategy of desperation, to save what could be saved, bargaining with the Devil. The Germans, to coerce the Judenräte, threatened to destroy the whole ghetto in case of non-compliance or even temporization. Ocassionally proffering the carrot to temper the terror of the stick, the Germans lyingly assured the Judenräte that once the *Aktion* in question was completed, the ghetto survivors would be spared further affliction.

Could the history of human society or law provide any guidance in such extremity? In desperation some Jewish officials turned to Halacha for an answer, but no legal code could provide any moral or practical guidance for this ultimate dilemma.

Plain sense dictates that in a disaster one rescues as many as can be rescued. The lifeboat cannot hold all the passengers of the sinking ship, and the captain decides who shall be saved. In the ghettos the habitual rules of precedence for saving people from disaster in predictable situations proved inappropriate. In preparing the list for the first deportation from Lodz, Rumkowski, believing that the Jews were being resettled for work, exempted the old among the group slated for deportation, on the grounds that the transfer would be too strenuous for them. But in situations when the Jews themselves suspected that the deportations meant death, the old volunteered so as to spare the young, regarding themselves as the most expendable sacrifice that the community could make.[11]

The terminal decision to try to save some by yielding up others was humanly inevitable in circumstances without choice or opportunity. German Communists incarcerated in Buchenwald, for instance, confronted precisely the same dilemma in precisely the same way. On 7 April 1945, as Allied forces were approaching Buchenwald, the SS commandant told the camp Eldest that unless the camp itself supplied 3,000 men within half an hour, the SS would use full force to assemble the next transport. Either eventuality, it was known, would mean the deaths of camp inmates, since the SS was erasing all evidence of the camp's existence. The underground Communist camp committee that represented the internal camp government, wishing to prevent the premature liquidation of the whole camp by adopting a stance of non-compliance, chose the lesser evil, taking upon itself the responsibility of selecting thousands of inmates whom they knew the Germans would destroy, while protecting others.[12]

That strange psychic process that afflicts the survivors of disaster, natural or man-made, with feelings of guilt, 'existential guilt', just because they have survived and others have not, afflicted also the Jews who remained in the ghettos after the mass killings and the deportations. Even Judenrat officials, whose rescue strategy exposed them to the bitter accusations of the ghetto population, continuously and publicly rationalized their conduct not only to repudiate the charges, but to still their own nagging guilt feelings. The powerlessness of the Jews in their encounter with the Final Solution heightened their sense of guiltiness, for their own tradition placed upon each Jew the obligation for his own life and for the survival of the community. Zelig Kalmanovich spoke for all when he wrote in his diary of the imponderable dilemmas confronting the Jews in those days: 'All are guilty, or perhaps more truly, all are innocent and holy.'

Appendixes

Appendix A   The Fate of the Jews
in Hitler's Europe: By Country

The following pages present a capsule account of the fate of the Jews in the European countries involved in the Second World War. The countries are grouped regionally, the presentation beginning with Western Europe and, continuing eastwards. The account of each country contains three sections: a brief description of the country's wartime status, a condensed characterization of the country's pre-war Jewish population and, finally, a compressed chronology of the course of the Final Solution in that country.

Throughout Europe the fate of the Jews hinged first of all on each country's wartime status *vis-à-vis* Germany. Wherever German rule was total and supreme, the Jews were consigned to annihilation. In 'Greater Germany' (Germany and Austria), in the Protectorate of Bohemia and Moravia, in occupied Poland, Russia and in the Baltic countries, the Jews came directly under the jurisdiction of the SS. Their fate was determined.

In the other countries of Europe – allied to Germany, so-called neutrals and those which, though invaded and occupied by the Germans, nevertheless retained some autonomy – the fate of the Jews depended on each country's commitment to civic equality and on its historical treatment of its Jewish population. Variations from country to country as to the fate of the Jews derived partly from differences in the degree of autonomy permitted by the Germans. German civil administration in the Netherlands and Norway, for example, was more rigorous than German military rule in Belgium.

Wherever indigenous political authority continued to exist, it buffered the Jews from the Germans. In some countries even indigenous political authorities who lacked a basic commitment to equal rights and who were traditionally anti-Semitic could at times be influenced by moral or religious appeals (Slovakia), persuaded by bribes (Rumania) or intimidated by threats of eventual punishment (Hungary) to protect the Jews from the long reach of the Germans. Some states, Vichy France and Bulgaria, for instance, were prepared to stand up to the Germans in order to protect their Jewish nationals, though ready to sacrifice foreign Jews within their jurisdiction.

Sometimes other factors contributed to the rescue of, or failure to rescue, Jews. The German occupation of Europe had turned the continent into a vast geographical trap from which few Jews could escape. For some Jews neutral Sweden's proximity to both Norway and Denmark was a providential geographic circumstance. The small size of a Jewish population also affected the feasibility of rescue or concealment, as in Italy and Denmark. But those factors were merely circumstantial. Denmark's dramatic rescue of its Jews and the overwhelming co-operation that the Italians gave their Jewish compatriots cannot be attributed merely to geography or population size, though these factors helped the undertakings to succeed, but are rather the consequence of the repudiation of anti-Semitism and the commitment to unconditional equality.

The Jews of Europe were socially and culturally diverse, some so acculturated that they had more in common with their fellow nationals than with Jews in other countries. Others remained separate from the non-Jewish population and separatist in their devotion to Jewish tradition. Ultimately the degree of acculturation proved to be without saliency in determining Jewish fate. The separatist Jews of Bulgaria were saved, while the acculturated Jews of Germany were not.

Still less salient to the outcome of the Final Solution was the role of the three Christian religions of Europe: Roman Catholicism, which regards itself as the universal church; Protestantism, primarily the Lutheran, Evangelical and Calvinist churches; and the Orthodox Church, which dominates south-eastern Europe. All yielded primacy to national politics in the countries in which they were located, subordinating the teachings of Christ to the national political tradition.

In Austria the Catholic bishops welcomed the Anschluss as enthusiastically as all Austrians. In Italy, in contrast, the Catholic hierarchy behaved like the Italians whose national aspirations had been kindled by the French Revolution and the libertarian tradition of the Risorgimento. In France the Catholic hierarchy was divided, as all the French were, either defending or attacking the French Revolution, torn between a republican egalitarian tradition and Bourbonism, still in conflict over Dreyfus.

In Bulgaria the Orthodox Church spoke up for the Jews, perhaps because secular political groups spoke up for the Jews. In Greece, however, the Orthodox Church was silent. As for the Protestant churches, their behaviour conformed to the country in which they functioned. In

Germany the Lutheran church abandoned Christian principles in subservience to the racial state. In the Netherlands the Calvinist church demonstrated its rigid conservatism by passivity and indifference to the situation of the Jews. In Denmark the extraordinary politial defence of the Jews that the bishops of the Danish Evangelical Lutheran church demonstrated under German occupation reflected the Danish political ethos more than Christian doctrine.

At bottom, the success of the Final Solution throughout Europe depended on Germany's opportunities and resources to carry it out, that is, whether or not Germany had uncontested and supreme control of a country or territory. Elsewhere, the Final Solution was conditional upon a political tradition that held that all men were equal, that human life was valuable and that the Jews were human beings entitled to life.

WESTERN EUROPE

FRANCE

On 3 September 1939 France declared war on Germany. After eight months of inaction (the 'phony war'), France was invaded from the north by Germany on 17 May 1940. On 10 June Italy declared war on France and invaded from the south. Paris was evacuated on 13 June. Three days later, Marshal Henri-Philippe Pétain took over as head of the French government; the next day he asked the Germans for an armistice. The armistice, signed at Compiègne on 22 June 1940, provided that French forces be disarmed and that three fifths of France be surrendered to German control. One day later, General Charles de Gaulle, head of the French National Committee in London, pledged continued French resistance against Germany. Britain severed ties with the Pétain régime. On 24 June France concluded an armistice with Italy, without yielding any significant concessions.

German-occupied France was divided into three different jurisdictions. Northern France, the area around Lille, was assigned to the military governor of Belgium. Alsace and Lorraine were treated as quasi-incorporated areas in the German Reich, each province governed by a Gauleiter. The rest of the occupied zone was ruled by a succession of military governors (General von Bockelberg, General Otto von Stülpnagel, General Heinrich von Stülpnagel).

A French government was established in unoccupied France on 2 July 1940, at Vichy, and a week later the parliament gave Marshal Pétain the power to establish an authoritarian régime, with Pierre Laval as vice-premier. That régime completely repudiated the Declaration of the Rights of Man. On 15 May 1941 Pétain broadcast a pledge of coopera-tion with Germany. The question as to how much collaboration the French should offer the Germans divided the Vichy government. After the resignation of Admiral Darlan and his supporters in April 1942, ad-vocates for minimal cooperation, Pierre Laval, the advocate of total collaborationism, became the virtual head of the French state. In response to German demands, compulsory labour for all men eighteen to sixty-five years old and unmarried women twenty to thirty-four was in-stituted.

On 8 November 1942 the Allies landed 110,000 men on the North African coast. Within three days, the Germans occupied Vichy France. Italy occupied eight departments, including Alpes-Maritimes and the area between Nice and Grenoble, which came under German occupa-tion the following year after Mussolini's overthrow. In response to harsher conditions of German rule and intensified German terror, French resistance began to increase.

Allied forces landed on the coast of Normandy on 6 June 1944. Other Allied landings took place on the French Mediterranean coast on 15 August 1944. German forces in Paris capitulated on 23–4 August, and French forces liberated the city. The administration of France was handed over to de Gaulle.

Jews in Pre-war France

Of a population of 45 million, the 350,000 Jews who resided in France just before the invasion were less than 1 per cent. Of these, only some 150,000 were native-born. About 50,000 were refugees from Germany, Austria and Czechoslovakia; some 25,000 had just fled from Belgium and Holland. The other foreign-born Jews were largely from Eastern Europe, having come to France during the 1920s and 1930s. The Jewish population was concentrated in Paris, Alsace-Lorraine, and eastern and northern departments.

The native-born French Jews were largely middle class, engaged in the professions, business and commerce. The foreign-born were pre-dominantly workers and small businessmen. The ready-to-wear cloth-ing industry was largely Jewish. The Jewish working class was highly politicized and unionized.

Native- and foreign-born Jews were also differentiated socially. Native-born Jews were highly acculturated, associated with the Jewish community through the consistorial system, their Judaism expressed in lukewarm religious observance. Foreign-born Jews remained largely unacculturated, having transplanted from Eastern Europe their Jewish political affiliations (Bundists, Labour Zionists, Communists) and, for the most part, retaining the use of Yiddish. Distance rather than tension characterized the relationship between both Jewish communities.

Despite the considerable rise of anti-Semitism, native and German-imported, Jewish citizens enjoyed full civic equality and Jewish new-comers were well received. Léon Blum, head of the French Socialist party, had served as Premier of France.

Jews in Wartime France

In the wake of the German invasion, France's rapid collapse and the armistice, large numbers of Jews fled south. Relatively few Jews had lived in what became the unoccupied zone, but by mid-1940, 195,000 Jews lived there, of whom it was believed 145,000 were native-born, 20,000 East European Jews and 30,000 Jewish refugees from Germany and Austria. The Jews in Alsace-Lorraine began to be expelled upon German occupation, and by November 1940 those still there were ordered out, their property confiscated. They themselves were dumped in the unoccupied zone. In occupied France some 120,000 Jews remained in Paris and in smaller communities in Nancy, Bordeaux, Bayonne and also in new communities formed in Charente by Jews evacuated from Lorraine.

In the Unoccupied Zone: On 27 August 1940 the Vichy government annulled a decree of 21 April 1939 that punished slander and libel 'towards a group of people who belong by origin to a particular race or a particular religion', thus providing a 'legal' basis for its subsequent anti-Jewish legislation. On 3 October 1940 a major anti-Jewish statute was enacted that defined as Jews those persons who belonged to the Jewish religion or had more than two Jewish grandparents. It prohibited Jews from holding most public offices, banned them from the judiciary, teaching, the military, banking, real estate and the media, and limited their presence in the professions.

A decree of 4 October 1940 authorized the internment of foreign Jews. Consequently, about 25,000 Jewish refugees from Germany and Austria, including some 7,500 German Jews whom the Germans had driven from Baden and the Palatinate into unoccupied France were interned at Gurs (later also at other camps). These internees were soon thereafter forced into labour brigades, and large numbers of them died of hunger, cold and disease.

On 20 March 1941 a law was enacted creating a General Commissariat for Jewish Affairs, whose function was to implement existing decisions with regard to Jews, propose further legislation as needed, supervise the liquidation of Jewish property where 'legally' prescribed in accordance with the needs of the national economy, and take all police measures with regard to the Jews. Xavier Vallat, long-time anti-Semite, was appointed Commissioner (replaced in June 1942 by Darquier de Pellepoix). On 2 June 1941 a statute basing itself on measures enacted by the Germans in the occupied zone replaced the statute of October 1940. It defined the status of Jews more rigidly and set in motion the expropriation and 'Aryanization' of Jewish property. A census of Jews and Jewish property was also decreed. The law of 22 July 1941 gave the General Commissioner wide powers in the process of expropriating Jewish property and business.

A decree enacted on 29 November 1941 established the Union Générale des Israélites de France (UGIF), whose officially stated purpose was to provide representation for all Jews *vis-à-vis* the state authorities, especially with regard to relief and social welfare. All existing Jewish organizations, excepting religious associations, were ordered dissolved and their property turned over to UGIF. Its board was to be administered by eighteen French-born Jews, nine in each zone, and to be under the authority of the General Commissariat for Jewish Affairs.

In the Occupied Zone: Jews in the occupied zone were subject to both the decrees of the German military government and the decrees of Vichy to the extent that the latter did not contravene the former. Responsibility for Jewish matters was lodged with the Foreign Office staff and the SS. Otto Abetz, German ambassador to Vichy, with two assistants in charge of Jewish affairs, was attached to the staff of the military governor, whose authority and manpower he needed to implement his orders. The SS, technically attached to Abetz, eventually took over responsibility for the anti-Jewish programme. Obergruppenführer Karl-Albrecht Oberg supervised a series of 'experts' on Jewish affairs, including Eichmann's assistant, Hauptsturmführer Theodor Dannecker.

On 27 September 1940 the Germans issued an ordinance that defined the status of Jews in racial terms, forbidding those who fled to return to the occupied zone, ordering a census of all Jews to be completed by 20 October 1940 and requiring public identification of Jewish businesses. On 18 October 1940 all Jewish enterprises had to be registered; their expropriation and 'Aryanization' followed. The French bureaucracy was used to implement these ordinances. On 26 April 1941 Jews were forbidden to engage in a wide variety of occupations, and their employment in positions in contact with the public was forbidden.

Under Dannecker's direction, Paris police compiled a card index of Jews in Paris, by name, street, occupation and nationality. In May and August 1941, the round-ups of Jews began: in the first round-up 3,200 Jews, mostly Polish, were sent to camps at Pithiviers and Beaune la Rolande; in the second, 4,300 Jews, including 1,300 French natives, were sent to Drancy, which was to serve as the chief transit camp for Auschwitz. On 12 December 1941, 1,000 French Jewish lawyers and doctors were rounded up to be held for deportation to the East, as reprisal for an unsuccessful assassination attempt on a German airforce officer.

Decrees prescribing curfew, yellow-star arm bands and badges began to be issued in February 1942, while plans for deportation took shape. On 28 March 1942 the first deportation train left Drancy for Auschwitz. In Paris on 16-17 July 12,884 non-French Jews, including women and children, were rounded up. Those without families were sent to Drancy. The remaining 9,000, including 4,000 children, were penned up in the vast sports stadium Vélodrome d'Hiver, where they spent a week in horrible conditions before being shipped off to Auschwitz. (Only thirty adults returned alive after the war; no child survived.)

Meanwhile the Germans were demanding that Laval hand over all foreign Jews in the unoccupied zone for deportation and that concerted action be taken in both zones against all Jews, French or foreign-born. On 2 July 1942 the Council of Ministers at Vichy decided, with Pétain's approval, to make a distinction in their zone between French and foreign Jews. French Jews would remain under the sovereignty and protection of the French government. In August 1942, 15,000 foreign Jews interned in camps in the unoccupied zone were handed over to the Germans for deportation. After 11 November 1942, when the Germans occupied all of France, they began to round up Jews in Marseilles. Many Jews then fled to the Italian occupation zone in south-eastern France, where they remained in safety until September 1943, when the Germans also occupied that area (see Italy, p. 440). In the area of Nice, more than 5,000 Jews, hunted down for over five months, were deported.

In the last months of the war, in addition to the deportations, mass executions also diminished the Jewish population. The accelerating activity of the resistance movement drove the Germans to ever severer reprisals, and Jews – mostly internees – were singled out as hostages and victims. Hundreds of Jews were executed under such circumstances.

In February 1944 Mercier du Paty de Clam, on the advice of a cousin highly placed in the underground, accepted the post of Commissioner General of Jewish Affairs, having been persuaded that the Commissariat was a good listening post and that he could do good by disorganizing its administration. In this he succeeded to a great extent and was consequently replaced on 1 June 1944.

On 24 August, right after the liberation of Paris, Drancy was liberated. The number of Jews who were deported, executed by the Germans, or who perished in internment camps is estimated at 90,000, most of them foreign-born.

BELGIUM

On 10 May 1940 Germany, which had in 1937 guaranteed Belgium's neutrality, invaded that country without warning. On 27-8 May, on the order of King Leopold III, the Belgian army capitulated. The royal family remained in residence, but the Belgian Cabinet formed a government-in-exile in London and continued to wage war against Germany.

Belgium was put under German military occupation and was ruled by a military governor, General Alexander von Falkenhausen. (The Belgian districts of Eupen, Malmédy and Moresnet were incorporated into the Reich by decree on 18 May 1940.) The actual administration of the country continued to be exercised largely by the Belgian civil service acting under the secretaries-general (heads of government departments), most of whom became compliant accessories of German policy. Also the Rexists, the native Belgian fascist movement, collaborated actively with the Germans. The overwhelming majority of the population, especially the French-speaking Walloons, had no Nazi sympathies and displayed considerable solidarity with the Jews. Resistance and sabotage increased to such an extent that the Germans sought to establish tighter control over the Belgian population. In July 1944 the German military government was changed to a civilian administration under a Reich Commissioner and the post combined the authority of the Wehrmacht and the Higher SS and Police.

Early in September 1944, British and American troops, with the support of a Belgian underground army, liberated Brussels and most of Belgium. In December 1944 the Germans counter-attacked, swept into the Ardennes region and succeeded in penetrating deep into Belgium. After a series of costly counter-attacks (Battle of the Bulge), the Allied forces destroyed and routed the Germans on 16 January 1945.

The Jews in Pre-war Belgium

Before the German invasion, about 90,000 Jews lived in Belgium, 1 per cent of the total population. Of these, 15,000 were refugees from Germany and most of the others were themselves immigrants, predominantly from Eastern Europe, or children of such immigrants. Most Jews lived in Antwerp (55,000) and Brussels (30,000), with the rest in Charleroi, Liège and Ghent.

About three fourths of the gainfully occupied were self-employed; the rest were workers. They were well represented in the clothing industry, small businesses and retail trade. The diamond trade in Antwerp was largely in Jewish hands. The production of fine leather goods was also a Jewish specialty.

Jewish communal and cultural life was a combination of the French consistorial system and the East European mode. The Jews in Brussels were on the whole an acculturated group. Antwerp was a centre of both Orthodoxy and Yiddish secular culture. Besides two day schools that enjoyed government subsidy, many afternoon Jewish schools were operated there under Orthodox and secular auspices.

Despite their relatively recent arrival in Belgium, Jews were well received. In 1938 the Belgian government had allocated a grant of 6 million francs towards the relief of German Jewish refugees. In elections that year the Rexists and other fascist and semi-fascist groups were spectacularly rejected at the polls.

The Jews in Wartime Belgium

In October 1940, six months after German occupation, anti-Jewish policies began to be promulgated. On 23 October 1940 *shehita* was abolished. A decree issued on 28 October 1940 defined Jews according to German racial standards and ordered their registration. Another decree on that date excluded Jews from public service, schools, law, the press and other media. Jewish businesses were required to be registered. The registration, completed later, showed 42,000 Jews in Belgium, only a few thousand of them native-born. Well over 20,000 were in hiding, and an estimated 25,000 Jews had fled to France, from which most were subsequently deported.

Economic measures against Jews and their property were enacted on 31 May 1941, setting in motion the 'Aryanization' of Jewish property and the rapid impoverishment of the Jews. In July 1941 the Jews had to declare their real-estate holdings; orders were issued forbidding banks to accept deposits from Jews; 7,600 Jewish firms still in existence were ordered closed. By mid-1942, Jewish property was completely 'Aryanized'.

The process of isolating the Jews began in the autumn of 1941, when Jews became subject to curfew, were forbidden to travel outside the major cities where they were concentrated, and were prohibited from using the parks or strolling in the streets of Antwerp. As of 31 December 1941 Jewish children were excluded from the public schools. In the spring of 1942 decrees issued in Antwerp compelled Jews into forced-labour brigades for 'Organisation Todt'. On 6 June 1942 Jews were forced to wear the Star of David arm bands.

On 25 November 1941 the Germans ordered the organization of a Judenrat. A Jewish committee had meanwhile been organized, headed by Dr Salomon Ullmann, head of Jewish chaplains in the Belgian army. This *ad hoc* body became the Association des Juifs en Belgique (AJB), to which all Jews were subject. Its initial tasks were to provide social services and organize the education of Jewish children, but it soon was forced to transmit German orders. A Jewish underground organization, Comité de Défense des Juifs, affiliated with the Belgian resistance movement, was active and tried to counteract the AJB.

Early in 1942 deportations began. Queen Elizabeth and Cardinal van Roey had asked protection for the few thousand Jews of Belgian nationality. Falkenhausen agreed to exempt them, but the promise was not fully kept. About 1,000 Jews of Belgian nationality were actually deported. According to German records, 25,437 Jews were deported to Auschwitz via the transit camp at Malines from mid-1942 to mid-1944. Several thousand were sent to Lodz and deported from there. Considerable numbers of Jews died in Belgium of hunger, disease or over-work in labour and transit camps or as victims of random shootings and terror. In sum, about 40,000 of the 65,000 Jews who had remained in Belgium perished. At liberation, about 20,000 Jews were found in Belgium, 6,000 of them German and Austrian refugees, 8,000 Polish Jews, the rest Belgian and Dutch nationals.

LUXEMBOURG

The Grand Duchy of Luxembourg, a 1,000-square-mile triangle bordering on Belgium, France and Germany, with a population of 300,000, was invaded, in violation of its neutrality, by Germany on 9–10 May 1940. Grand Duchess Charlotte and the Cabinet fled, establishing a government-in-exile in London. The German military occupation was succeeded in August 1940 by a Chief of Civil Administration, Gustav Simon, head of the adjoining Gau of Koblenz-Trier. Two years later he announced that Luxembourg, as a 'Germanic' state, would be incorporated into the Reich and, to drive the lesson home, he issued an order for military conscription. The ensuing general strike in the capital city was suppressed with severity, and its many participants were deported.

In September 1944 Allied armies liberated Luxembourg.

Jews in Pre-war Luxembourg

In 1935 about 3,000 Jews lived in Luxembourg, 1 per cent of the total population. It was an ancient Jewish community that had been reconstituted in 1791 after the French Revolution. About two thirds of the Jews lived in the capital, the remainder in smaller cities. Additionally, 1,500 German Jews had found refuge in the country. The Luxembourgian Jews enjoyed complete equality and prosperity. The Jewish community was organized in the consistorial system, with Robert Serebrenik as Chief Rabbi.

Jews in Wartime Luxembourg

When the Germans invaded Luxembourg, over 1,000 Jews fled or were evacuated by French troops. With the German occupation, the local Volksdeutsche emerged to take active part in anti-Jewish persecutions. On 5 September 1940 the major body of anti-Jewish legislation was issued. Jews were ghettoized in communal quarters, compelled to wear arm bands, assigned to forced labour and expropriated. A policy of expulsion and deportation was put into effect early, since Luxembourg was to be incorporated into the Reich. Under the leadership of Rabbi Serebrenik and the Consistory, about 2,500 Jews were evacuated, through illegal channels, to unoccupied France and Portugal in the period between 8 August 1940 and 15 October 1941. Thereafter the possibility of voluntary departure ceased to exist. From October 1941 to April 1943 approximately 800 Jews were deported to Lodz, Auschwitz and Theresienstadt.

After liberation, about 400 Jews were found to have survived in Luxembourg.

THE NETHERLANDS

On 10 May 1940 the Germans invaded the Netherlands without warning. Dutch resistance crumbled, and Rotterdam surrendered on 13 May. Several hours later, its entire centre was wantonly destroyed by

German air bombardment. The government, headed by Queen Wilhelmina, fled to London, where it continued to exist in exile. On 14 May the Netherlands capitulated to the Germans.

The Netherlands, slated for eventual incorporation into the Reich as a 'Germanic' state, was governed by a civilian German administrator, a Reich Commissioner, the Austrian Artur Seyss-Inquart, appointed on 18 May 1940. He suspended the Dutch parliament and Council of State, subordinating the Dutch civil service, under the secretaries-general, to his rule. Important posts were assigned to Dutch Nazis, who became prominent in the country's governance.

On 25 February 1941 a general strike broke out in Amsterdam, Hilversum and Zaandam, paralysing transport and industry. The strike was brutally suppressed in three days by the German army, and martial law was imposed. The Dutch population was heavily fined, and the Germans succeeded in stifling further overt resistance in the Netherlands during the occupation.

In September 1944 Allied airborne forces attempted only partially successful landings at Arnhem and Eindhoven, liberating part of southern Holland, while the Germans continued to retain the rest of Holland. Starvation and German terror, including the vengeful bombing of Rotterdam and Amsterdam, were the lot of the Dutch until 6 May 1945, when the country was liberated by the Allies and Queen Wilhelmina returned to her throne.

Jews in Pre-war Netherlands

Just before the German invasion, 140,000 Jews lived in Holland, 110,000 of them Dutch and 30,000 refugees from Germany and Austria. Nearly 60 per cent, 80,000 Jews, lived in Amsterdam alone.

About half the Dutch Jews were engaged in trade and commerce, many in second-hand and street trade. 10 per cent were in the diamond industry, 20 per cent in other manufacturing, 5 per cent in the professions. Jews played a significant role in the political and cultural life of the country.

The 5,000 Dutch Sephardic Jews were organized in a union of two communities, one with 4,500 members in Amsterdam and the others in The Hague. The largest Ashkenazic communities were in Amsterdam, The Hague and Rotterdam. Both Sephardic and Ashkenazic groups maintained, besides their synagogues, religious schools and charitable organizations that provided a variety of social services, especially valuable for the refugees. Over twenty Jewish newspapers and periodicals, nearly all in the Dutch language, were published.

The Dutch Jews enjoyed full civic equality, and many of their religious and welfare institutions received government subventions. Although most Dutch Jews, especially the middle classes and professionals, were highly acculturated, Jewish communal and cultural life managed to survive, despite the low birth rate and the high intermarriage rate.

Jews in Wartime Netherlands

The first anti-Jewish decree, enacted on 31 August 1940, abolished *shehita*. A decree of 22 October 1940 required the registration of a wide range of business enterprises, owned or operated wholly or in part by Jews or in which Jews had financial interests, Jews being defined in racial terms. Other anti-Jewish decrees, along the German pattern, followed. On 10 January 1941 a decree ordered all Jews to register within a set period with local branches of the Census Office: failure to do so was punishable with five years' imprisonment and/or confiscation of property. The statistics, submitted by the Census Office on 27 August 1941, showed 160,820 registrations, 140,552 of them Jews, 14,549 'half-Jews' and 5,719 'quarter-Jews'.

On 12 February 1941 the Joodsche Raad (Jewish Council) was formed under duress amid a series of violent incidents between Jews and Dutch Nazis, occurring mostly in Amsterdam's old Jewish section. Hans Rauter, Higher SS and Police Leader, Seyss-Inquart's Commissioner for Security and Police, sealed off the area, summoned several of Amsterdam's Jewish leaders and demanded the formation of a Jewish Council, which would be required to preserve order in the Jewish quarter.

A week later, in south Amsterdam, a more prosperous section where one fourth of Amsterdam's Jews lived, another violent incident occurred between a German police patrol and Jews. A few days thereafter, the Germans seized 400 Jews, twenty to thirty-five years old, who were eventually deported to Mauthausen. The seizure and deportation were among the factors that led to the general strike on 25 February 1941. (The SS then threatened the Jews with further reprisals unless the strike was called off.)

On 12 March 1941 the Germans began the process of 'Aryanizing' Jewish property, and a decree of 21 May 1942 authorized complete expropriation, except for items like wedding rings and gold teeth.

The Germans placed all Jewish organizations under the authority of the Joodsche Raad on 18 March 1941. Decrees were then issued prohibiting Jews from travelling, dismissing them from the civil service, cultural posts and the stock exchange, barring them from public parks. On 29 August 1941 Jewish children were barred from public schools and vocational schools.

In the spring of 1941 a Zentralstelle für jüdische Auswanderung (Central Office for Jewish Emigration), under SS-Hauptsturmführer Ferdinand aus der Funten, was charged with rounding up the Jews and deporting them. The Joodsche Raad was made subordinate to the Zentralstelle.

In January 1942 forced-labour camps for Jews were set up. Meanwhile the Dutch Jews began to be concentrated in Amsterdam. On 29 April 1942 the identifying Jewish star was introduced. Jews were further restricted in their occupational activities. Curfew was introduced.

In July 1942, deportations began, continuing until September 1943. Two transit camps, Westerbork and Vught, were set up where Jews were concentrated until schedules permitted their entrainment to Auschwitz. On 29 September 1943, in the last major round-up, about 5,000 Jews, including the heads of the Joodsche Raad, were deported via Westerbork. Only small protected categories of Jews still remained, including diamond workers and Jewish partners in mixed marriages. Most of these were deported early in 1944.

Some 110,000 Jews were deported to Auschwitz, Sobibór and, in smaller numbers, to other camps. About 5,000 survived the death camps. 75 per cent of Dutch Jewry perished.

ITALY

Though politically and ideologically close to Germany, Italy decided, at the start of the war, to maintain her neutrality, but on 10 June 1940 Italy declared war both on Great Britain and on collapsing France, which it invaded from the south. On 27 September 1940 Italy, Germany and Japan concluded a three-power pact, Italy thus becoming a full partner in Germany's war. On 28 October 1940, Italy attacked Greece, but, unable to oust British forces, required military help from Germany. In April 1941, Italy occupied the largest, but least populated, part of Greece and also littoral Yugoslavia. On 22 June 1941 Italy joined Germany in declaring war on Russia, and Italian forces joined the invasion. On 11 December 1941 Italy declared war on the United States. After the Allied invasion of North Africa, Italy joined Germany on 11 November 1942 in occupying the hitherto unoccupied zone of France. Italy took over eight departments in south-eastern France, including Nice.

As the tide of war turned against Germany and with the Allied invasion of Sicily on 10 July 1943, Italy underwent internal upheaval. The Fascist Grand Council and King Victor Emmanuel forced Mussolini to resign. A new government was established under Marshal Pietro Badoglio on 25 July 1943; three days later he dissolved the Fascist party and put Mussolini under arrest. On 3 September 1943, the Allies invaded southern Italy, and on 8 September the Badoglio government surrendered to them. The Germans, however, were prepared for these manoeuvres: they rescued Mussolini and proclaimed him the head of a newly established National Fascist government, later known as the Italian Social Republic. With great dispatch the Germans occupied all of Italy as far south as Rome, as well as all Italian-held territory in south-eastern France, littoral Yugoslavia and Greece. Mussolini's neo-Fascist government notwithstanding, rule of Italy remained in the hands of the German military governor, Gruppenführer Otto Wächter, and two German plenipotentiaries, Rudolf Rahn of the Foreign Office and Obergruppenführer Karl Wolff, general of the Waffen-SS.

In February 1944 the Allies returned part of southern Italy to Italian jurisdiction. Fighting moved north. The allies landed on the Italian coast south of Rome in June 1944, and by mid-August, with the capture of Florence, they controlled Italy as far north as a line running from Livorno to Ancona, but until the very end of the war the industrial north remained in German hands.

On 28 April 1945 Mussolini was captured and shot while trying to escape. Early in May the Germans in Italy capitulated.

Jews in Pre-war Italy

In 1938 some 57,000 Jews lived in Italy, about one tenth of 1 per cent of the Italian population. About 10,000 were refugees from Germany and Austria. Most Jews lived in large cities: Rome (13,700), Milan (8,000), Trieste (5,000), Turin (3,700), Florence (2,800), Genoa (2,700), Venice (2,000), Livorno (1,750) and Ancona (1,000).

An old Jewish community, the Italian Jews since Emancipation had been fully accepted socially and economically into Italian society. Jews were predominantly middle and upper middle class, engaged in trade and commerce, with more than one quarter of the gainfully employed in the professions. Pockets of Jewish poverty remained, especially in the old ghetto of Rome, where several thousand Jews continued to live in slums, eking out a living from street trade and sometimes beggary.

The observance of Judaism, except among the poor, was in decline; the rate of intermarriage on the rise. (In the 1930s, 30 per cent of the

Jews who married wed non-Jews.) The major cities had synagogues and other institutions that provided basic or minimal services in terms of ritual and Jewish education. Zionism existed as a cultural influence rather than a political movement.

Anti-Semitism was not a serious threat to the Italian Jews, even during the early years of the Fascist régime. Three laws, passed in the period from October 1930 to November 1931, provided for the reorganization of the Jewish community under a new civil code that strengthened its status and influence. The individual Jewish communities were to provide for the ritual and educational needs of the community through an annual registration fee. All communities were represented in the Unione delle Comunità Israelitiche Italiane.

After Hitler's accession to power, Italy became a place of refuge for German, and later Austrian, Jews. By 1938 over 10,000 Jewish refugees were in Italy. Under increasing pressure from Hitler, Mussolini acceded to the views of those in his government who felt that Italy should move closer to Germany. Though Nazi anti-Semitism was not to the Italian taste, a series of anti-Jewish laws was enacted in November 1938 that defined the Jews though not entirely on a racial basis, and excluded them from civil service, army service, Fascist party membership and ownership of enterprises employing large numbers of Italians. All naturalizations obtained after 1 January 1919 were nullified and all foreign and denaturalized Jews were ordered to leave Italy by March 1939. (By late 1941 more than 7,000 Jews, most of them denaturalized Italians, had emigrated.) A decree of 29 June 1939 restricted Jewish professionals to practise only among Jewish clients and patients. Marriages between Jews and Italians were forbidden. Limitations were put on property ownership, especially agricultural land. This legislation impoverished the once prosperous Jewish community. Over 10 per cent emigrated; another 10 per cent apostatized.

Jews in Wartime Italy

Whatever hardships the Italian Jews had to undergo from the end of 1938 on, their situation was enviable in contrast to those Jews who lived under direct German occupation. The Italians remained unresponsive to German demands to deport Jews. In Italy proper and in all areas occupied by Italy, the Jews remained safe from deportation, though they were subject to harsh legislation and deprivation. When the Germans occupied Italy, only about 40,000 Jews still remained.

With the German occupation in September 1943, Jews became subject to deportation. The first action took place in October 1943 in Rome, where the Germans managed to round up over 1,000 of the 8,000 Roman Jews and deport them to Auschwitz. Most of the other Jews of Rome had fled or gone into hiding.

The Italian puppet régime issued a police order on 30 November 1943 stipulating that all Jews should be sent to concentration camps and their property confiscated for the state. Up north Jews fled and went into hiding, but the Italian police, in their hunt for Jews, managed to send more than 7,000 to camps at Fossoli di Carpi (near Modena) and Bolzano, which served as assembly centres for deportation to Auschwitz and Birkenau. Many Jews were incarcerated in Italian prisons, the most notorious being San Vittorio in Milan, where torture and murder were common.

About 8,000 Italian Jews were annihilated.

NORTHERN EUROPE

NORWAY

Norway sought to maintain neutrality when war broke out, but on 8–9 April 1940 Germany invaded Norway with sea- and airborne forces. The Norwegians offered resistance and were reinforced by Anglo-French forces that had managed to land on the Norwegian coast, but by 30 April superior German forces had crushed all resistance. King Haakon VII and his Cabinet escaped to London, forming a government-in-exile.

Norway became a Reich Commissariat under the rule of Josef Terboven, who was directly responsible to Hitler. On 25 September 1940 Terboven declared the King dethroned, the government abolished and all political parties dissolved except the pro-Nazi Nasjonal Samling (National Unity party), headed by former Norwegian Minister of War Vidkun Quisling. On 1 February 1942 Terboven rewarded Quisling for his services to Germany by appointing him Minister-President. Within the week Quisling abolished the Norwegian constitution and made himself dictator. Norway's long border with Sweden, which offered avenues of escape, and an active resistance movement, strengthened from London, helped to mitigate the hardships of German occupation and Quisling rule.

In May 1945 the Germans surrendered in Norway. Quisling was arrested, tried, sentenced to death in September and executed 24 October 1945.

Jews in Pre-war Norway

In a population of nearly 3 million, about 1,800 Jews lived in Norway, of whom 300 were refugees from Central Europe. Over 1,000 Jews lived in Oslo and about 300 in Trondheim. The Jews were integrated in all aspects of Norwegian life. The low estate of anti-Semitism is evident in the fact that in 1936 Quisling's Nasjonal Samling vote dropped from 2·23 per cent to 1·83 per cent of the total vote.

Jews in Wartime Norway

Even before Reich Commissar Terboven had decreed the expropriation of the Jews, Quisling's storm troopers began a campaign of terror against them, seizing their businesses for personal profit. No specific anti-Jewish legislation along German lines was enacted, but anti-Jewish policies were carried out within the framework of Terboven's enactments. In July 1941 all commercial establishments were told to submit lists of their employees, indicating their religion. In November an inventory of Jewish-owned real estate was requested from the provincial governors. In June 1942, Jewish businesses were placed under the control of commissioners.

Beginning on 1 March 1942, passports and identity cards had to be marked 'Jew'. The chief of the Norwegian State Secretariat, Fugelsand, the intermediary between the German authorities and the Nasjonal Samling, was put in charge of a 'racial department' to implement the anti-Jewish orders. Jews were interned in labour camps set up in northern Norway. In September 1942 extensive round-ups of Jews began.

On 23 October 1942 a Quisling frontier guard was assassinated. Two of the assassins were identified as Jews. This served as a pretext for Quisling to order the confiscation of all property owned by Jews in Norway. In addition, a further hunt for Jews got under way. Where heads of families could not be found, women and children were taken as hostages. At least half the Norwegian Jews were interned or imprisoned. In November one boatload of victims was sent by sea from Oslo to Stettin. In February 1943 another boatload of Jews, who had been interned in concentration camps, sailed. In all, about 800 Jews were deported, most to Auschwitz, a smaller number to slave-labour camps in Germany. Only twenty-three of the deported Jews survived.

Some 900 Jews, about half the Jewish population, managed to evade arrest and internment. With the help of the Norwegian resistance movement they fled over the border to Sweden. Norway became emptied of Jews.

DENMARK

On 9 April 1940 Germany invaded neutral Denmark. Cecil von Renthe-Fink, German minister in Copenhagen, in demanding Denmark's capitulation without resistance, declared officially that Germany had no intention, then or in the future, of encroaching on Denmark's territorial integrity or political independence. Denmark accepted German occupation.

King Christian X remained on the throne and the Danish army, navy and police remained undisturbed. A government appointed by the King and responsible to parliament continued to function, and parliament continued to exercise its legislative functions. In June 1940, Erik Scavenius known for his pro-German sympathies, was appointed Foreign Minister and exercised considerable influence over ailing Prime Minister Thorvald Stauning. (After Stauning's death, Scavenius became Prime Minister in November 1942.) Notwithstanding various political concessions to the Germans, the Danes continued to maintain a democratic parliamentary government and an independent policy.

In autumn 1942 Hitler changed his policy towards Denmark, intending to incorporate it into Germany. Leading German personnel in Denmark were changed; career diplomat Renthe-Fink was replaced by SS-Obergruppenführer Karl Werner Best, acting as Reich Plenipotentiary. The new Wehrmacht commanding general planned to disband the Danish army and establish military rule in Denmark.

The Danes stiffened against German demands, and even Scavenius opposed German efforts to take over rule of Denmark. Sabotage and resistance within the country increased and reached their climax in August 1943. The German army then entered Copenhagen, disarmed the Danish army, imprisoned the King and declared the Danish government dissolved. A state of emergency and martial law were declared. Though the emergency was officially lifted on 6 October 1943, in effect conditions remained the same, with Danish sabotage and resistance intensifying against the Germans. In July 1944, with news of the attempted assassination on Hitler, general strikes swept Denmark. Until liberation, in May 1945, the Danes remained in a veritable state of war against the occupying Germans.

Jews in Pre-war Denmark

About 8,000 Jews, 0·2 per cent of the total population, lived in Denmark at the time of the German occupation. Some 6,500 were Danish Jews (including 1,300 offspring of mixed marriages), consisting of old

Danish families and also of East European Jews who had settled in Denmark before and after the First World War. About 1,500 were recent refugees from Germany, Austria and Czechoslovakia. The old Jewish families had been thoroughly integrated into Danish social, political and economic life. The later settlers brought with them Zionist and Jewish cultural concerns that helped to revivify Jewish communal life in Denmark. Anti-Semitism, despite extensive imports from Germany, was limited to small, extremist groups.

Jews in Wartime Denmark

Despite efforts by Himmler and other top Germans to convince the Danes that the Jews were an alien element, Jews remained under the protection of the Danish government. No anti-Jewish legislation was enacted and no Jewish property was expropriated. No Jews were ousted from government posts.

After Denmark came under martial law, Best tried to deport the Danish Jews. His plans, confided to a German shipping industrialist, were reported on 28 September to Danish Social Democratic leaders. The Germans had scheduled the round-up of the Jews for 1 October 1943, but in an extraordinary operation involving the whole Danish people and the agreement of the Swedish government, nearly all Danish Jews were hidden and then ferried across to Sweden, where they remained in safety until the end of the war. The Germans managed to round up some 400 Jews, whom they sent to Theresienstadt.

The internment of the Danish Jews in Theresienstadt agitated the Danish government, which repeatedly requested permission to inspect the camp. In June 1944 such permission was granted, and the visit was made by delegates of the Danish Red Cross. As a consequence of persistent Danish interest in the deported Jews, none was sent to Auschwitz. At the end of the war, fifty-one had died in Theresienstadt of natural causes.

FINLAND

When war broke out, Finland announced its neutrality, but on 30 November 1939, Finland was invaded by the Soviet Union. When the Soviet–Finnish war was concluded in March 1940, Finland had to yield territory and make other political concessions to Russia. On 22 June 1941 Finland joined Germany in attacking the Soviet Union. Finland provided a base of operations for the Germans, but was never actually occupied by the Germans, except in the northern regions.

There were 2,000 Jews in Finland. In a visit to Helsinki in July 1942,

Himmler attempted to induce the Finns to deport the Jews, but Finnish Foreign Minister Rolf Witting refused to give the matter any consideration.

In September 1944, Finland capitulated to Russia and then had to fight the Germans to force them to evacuate Finland.

CENTRAL EUROPE

GERMANY AND AUSTRIA

Jews in Pre-war Germany

When the Nazis seized power in 1933, 500,000 Jews, or about 1 per cent of the population, lived in Germany. Subjected to terror and an accelerating process of discrimination, isolation and expropriation, conducted under guise of legality, nearly 150,000 Jews, 30 per cent of the 1933 population, emigrated by November 1938.

The pogrom of 10 November 1938 (Kristallnacht), and the subsequent German policy of forced emigration hastened the exit of another 150,000 Jews. The outbreak of war severely limited the availability of transportation and in effect halted further departures.

With the enactment of the Tenth Decree Supplementing the Reich Citizenship Law on 4 July 1939, the Germans set up the Reichsvereinigung der Juden in Deutschland, subject to the authority of the Gestapo and replacing all autonomous Jewish communal organizations.

Jews in Pre-war Austria

At the time of the Anschluss, 12 March 1938, 185,000 Jews lived in Austria, 170,000 in Vienna alone. In August 1938, responsibility for Jewish emigration was charged to the Zentralstelle für die jüdische Auswanderung, operated by the Gestapo. Under the pressure of terror, some 120,000 Jews left Austria by the time war broke out. Another 6,000 left by the end of 1939. Nearly all remaining Jews in Austria were concentrated in Vienna, where the Israelitische Kultusgemeinde remained the only Jewish organization. The provincial Jewish communities ceased to exist.

Jews in the Wartime Greater Reich (Germany and Austria)

In 1940 the Germans began to deport Jews into the Generalgouvernement of Poland, also evicting some 7,500 Jews from Baden and the Palatinate, whom they dumped into France. On 1 September 1941 a police decree was issued compelling all Jews over six years of age to wear an identifying Star of David. In October 1941 general deportations began to major ghettos in the territory of Poland (Lodz, Warsaw, Lublin) and also as far east as Riga and Minsk. Over 40,000 Reich Jews, regarded as 'privileged' deportees, were sent to Theresienstadt. At the end of 1942, the Kultusgemeinde in Vienna was dissolved and a Council of Elders set up in its place. By that time, 150,000 Jews had been deported from the Greater Reich.

Early in 1943, 20,000 more Jews were deported, including the munitions workers in Berlin who until then had been protected. In May 1943 Berlin was declared free of Jews. On 10 June 1943 the Reichsvereinigung was dissolved, its members having been deported, and on 1 July 1943, under the thirteenth Decree Supplementing the Reich Citizenship Law, any Jews still in the Reich were to be denied protection of the courts and were to be surrendered to Gestapo jurisdiction.

When the war ended, the 28,000 Jews surviving in Germany and in Austria were, for the most part, Jews only by National Socialist racial standards.

CZECHOSLOVAKIA   THE PROTECTORATE OF BOHEMIA AND MORAVIA

On 13 March 1939, having decided to take the two western provinces of Bohemia and Moravia, Hitler summoned two Slovak nationalist and pro-German leaders, Father Jozef Tiso and Ferdinand Durcansky, and told them to proclaim Slovak independence or suffer occupation. The next day the provincial diet in Bratislava voted to secede from Czechoslovakia and form a separate state, a decision that the Germans used to justify their invasion of Czechoslovakia on 15 March. By afternoon, the Germans concluded the occupation without encountering resistance. The provinces of Bohemia and Moravia were declared a Protectorate, a joint, autonomous part of the Reich, whose German inhabitants would become Reich citizens, while the Czech inhabitants were designated as Protectorate nationals. The former Czech head of state, given the title of State President, was responsible to a Reich Protector, who was the factual ruler of the country. To this post of Reich Protector Hitler appointed Konstantin von Neurath, a career diplomat and a former German Foreign Minister, who took over his duties on 16 April 1939.

The Czech army was demobilized; its arms and ammunition were seized by the Germans. Through policies of political harshness and economic exploitation, the Germans established themselves as masters, but political and economic unrest continued to disturb the country. Blaming Neurath, Hitler in late September 1941 appointed as Deputy Protector Reinhard Heydrich, chief of the Reich Security Main Office, who immediately introduced rule by terror and succeeded in breaking Czech resistance.

On 27 May 1942 Heydrich's car was bombed and he was severely injured, dying of his wounds on 4 June. The assassination had been planned and directed by the Czech government-in-exile in cooperation with the British Special Operations Executive, an agency for underground warfare, in the hope of re-animating Czech resistance. The brutal reprisals that the Germans exacted – the destruction of the village of Lidice and all its male inhabitants – stilled futher Czech opposition.

On 5 May 1945 Czech resisters unsuccessfully tried to oust the Germans. On 11 May the Russians entered Prague.

Jews in Pre-war Bohemia and Moravia

About 118,000 Jews lived in the provinces of Bohemia and Moravia, amounting to one third of all Czech Jews. Half the gainfully occupied were engaged in trade and commerce, 20 per cent were in industry and handicrafts, about 10 per cent in the professions. In the Czechoslovak republic, Jews enjoyed full civic and religious freedom. There had always been some anti-Semitism, though no violence. The Jewish religious community maintained a modest network of religious and educational institutions. Zionism attracted a substantial interest.

About 26,000 Jews emigrated between 15 March 1939 and the outbreak of the war, leaving some 90,000 Jews in the Protectorate.

Jews in Wartime Bohemia and Moravia

On 21 June 1939 the Reich Protector issued a comprehensive decree placing Jews under German jurisdiction, defining the status of Jews in accordance with German legislation and setting in motion the isolation of Jews and the expropriation of their property. A Zentralstelle für die jüdische Auswanderung was established by decree on 5 March 1940, similar to the one in Vienna and, like it, subordinate to the one in Berlin. Run by the Gestapo, it was given complete authority over the Jewish community, using the Kultusgemeinde of Prague as its channel for transmitting orders. All subsequent anti-Jewish legislation enacted in the Protectorate conformed to German laws. All new Reich legislation (for example, the introduction of the identifying yellow Star of David in September 1941) was applicable to the Protectorate.

In October 1939 the first deportations of Czech Jews to Poland took place. In the autumn of 1941 the Germans established a central ghetto for Protectorate Jews at Theresienstadt (Terezin), formerly a Czech garrison town. This ghetto was to serve two functions, that of a 'model' camp to which privileged categories of Reich Jews would be sent and also as a transit camp from which to deport Czech Jews to the death camps in Poland. In 1942 alone, about 55,000 Jews from the Protectorate were sent to Theresienstadt, and most were later deported to Auschwitz and other death camps.

About 10,000 Jews from Bohemia and Moravia survived.

SLOVAKIA

In March 1939 Slovakia was declared an independent state, with Father Jozef Tiso, a Catholic priest, as Prime Minister, and with the Hlinka People's party, a right-wing Catholic nationalist group, as the only legal party. Slovakia had to adhere to the German–Italian–Japanese axis, to provide rail and road access for the Germans to the east, and, after the German attack on Russia, also to provide fighting troops. In October 1939 Tiso was elected President; pro-Nazi Voytech Tuka became Prime Minister; Sano Mach, head of the Hlinka Guard, became Minister of the Interior, and Ferdinand Durcansky, Foreign Minister.

For the first two years of the war, Slovakia enjoyed significant benefits from its new status, such as increased trade and help in industrial development, but after the German defeat at Stalingrad and the turning of the tide of the war, Slovak sentiment among both government and people became noticeably less pro-German. At the beginning of 1944, when the Soviet army stood at the frontiers of Ruthenia, young Slovaks began to be more responsive to the appeals for resistance issued by the Czech government-in-exile. Soldiers in the Slovak army began to desert to join resistance groups in the mountains. Popular opposition grew. Open fighting broke out in August 1944. Tiso then proclaimed martial law and total mobilization. The Slovak uprising gave the Germans the pretext they needed to occupy the country. Serious fighting between the Slovak partisans and the Germans continued through October, when the Germans succeeded in crushing the resistance. The Russian advance through Slovakia began in January 1945, but it was not before April 1945 that Slovakia was liberated from German occupation.

Jews in Pre-war Slovakia

In 1938 about 135,000 Jews lived in Slovakia, of whom 40,000 lived in the territory ceded to Hungary (Ruthenia and Subcarpathia). About

5,000 emigrated voluntarily before the war, leaving about 90,000 Jews, 3 per cent of the population. Slovakia was poorer and far less industrialized than the historic Czech crown provinces of Bohemia and Moravia, and so were its Jews. They were engaged mostly in retail trade and handicrafts, servicing the peasantry.

The small segment of well-to-do Jews spoke Hungarian and were assimilated, maintaining religious congregations of a somewhat lukewarm character. Most other Jews were highly traditional, among whom Hasidic *rebbes* enjoyed huge followings.

During the life of the Czechoslovak Republic, Jews enjoyed full civic and religious rights, even though anti-Semitism, particularly among the predominantly peasant population, was widespread.

Jews in Wartime Slovakia

In April 1939 the new Slovak state began to enact anti-Jewish legislation, defining the status of a Jew along religious rather than racial lines (Slovakia was a Catholic country, ruled by a priest and a Catholic party). In rapid succession came a series of decrees excluding and restricting Jews in various professions and occupations. Anti-Semitic violence on the part of the Hlinka Guard accompanied the administrative anti-Semitism.

In August 1940 SS-Hauptsturmführer Dieter Wisliceny, Eichmann's representative from the Reich Security Main Office, arrived in Bratislava as an adviser on Jewish affairs. The Hlinka Guard and the Freiwillige Schutzstaffel (Slovak volunteers in the SS) were reorganized on the model of the SS and given the responsibility of carrying out anti-Jewish measures.

On 26 September 1940 a new decree established the Ústredna Židov (Centre of Jews) as the only authority permitted to represent the Jews, responsible to the Central Economy Office (under the Minister of the Interior) and obliged to transmit its instructions to the Jews.

On 9 September 1941 the Slovak government promulgated a major body of anti-Jewish legislation, containing 270 articles, re-defining the Jews as a racial group, requiring them to wear the identifying yellow Star of David, making them liable to forced labour and evicting them from specified towns and districts.

Plans for deportation began late in 1941; in March 1942 five assembly points for deportees were set up, and despite intensive efforts on the part of Jewish communal leaders to halt them, deportations continued unabated from March to August 1942. By then, only 25,000 Jews remained in Slovakia. Three more transports left in September and October. Some 58,000 Jews 75 per cent of Slovak Jews, had been deported, mostly to Auschwitz.

Futher deportations were put off, partly through the intervention of the Catholic church and partly through a strategy of bribery and promises of financial profit that the Jewish leaders used in negotiations with Slovaks and with Wisliceny himself.

After the Slovak national uprising in 1944, the SS took 19,000 prisoners of whom 5,000 were Jews. Under the subsequent German occupation, 13,500 more Jews were deported. No more than 5,000 Slovakian Jews remained in the country in hiding or on Aryan papers. About 10,000 of those deported in 1944 survived and returned to Slovakia.

HUNGARY

Hungary's policies before and during the war can best be understood in the light of her revanchist goals. In November 1938 Hungary joined Germany in the dismemberment of Czechoslovakia, annexing some Slovakian districts and a part of Subcarpathian Ruthenia. In March 1939, when Slovakia declared itself an independent state, Hungary occupied the rest of Ruthenia. In August 1940 Hungary received northern Transylvania from Rumania under the Vienna Award. As repayment, Hungary joined the Tripartite Pact on 20 November 1940. In April 1941 Hungary occupied the Bačka basin in north-eastern Yugoslavia.

On 22 June 1941 Hungarian forces joined the Germans in invading Russia, though Hungarian military participation was less than wholehearted, with Regent Nicholas Horthy resisting German demands for Hungary's general mobilization. In March 1942 Horthy replaced Hungary's pro-German Prime Minister Laszlo Bardossy with Miklos Kallay, who sought to disentangle Hungary from the war. Hungarian losses on the Russian front and Hungary's preoccupation with her traditional enemy, Rumania, accelerated Hungarian troop withdrawals from the front, to the extent permitted by Germany.

In early 1943, Hungary appeared, in Hitler's eyes, to be acting more like a neutral than a German ally. Consequently, in April 1943 Hitler summoned Horthy to his headquarters in Klessheim Castle near Salzburg and criticized him for Kallay's policies, both as to Hungary's obligations to Germany and as to the need to eliminate Hungary's Jews. Kallay, however, continued his policies and on August 1943 broadcast a peace speech, following the overthrow of Mussolini in Italy, Hungary's traditional ally.

In March 1944, with the war going badly for Germany, Hitler again summoned Horthy and members of his cabinet to Klessheim (Kallay refused to join them). Hitler confronted Horthy with what he regarded as Hungary's treachery, declaring that Germany had to occupy Hungary. Horthy was held incommunicado for a day; when he returned home on 19 March, the German occupation of Hungary had been completed. On 22 March a new Hungarian government was formed under Prime Minister General Dome Sztojay, formerly the Hungarian minister in Berlin. The real rulers in Hungary thenceforth were the SS and Reich Plenipotentiary Edmund Veesenmayer. All political parties and trade unions, with their press, were suppressed. The Sztojay government could not, however, maintain itself because of overt opposition from the right – the Hungarian National Socialists and the Fascist Arrow Cross, under Ferenc Szalasi. Rumania's surrender to Russia in August 1944 and the stunning defeat of the Germans at that time by Russian and Rumanian forces shook Hungary. Sztojay resigned on 30 August; Horthy replaced him with General Geza Lakatos, in an effort to restore more Hungarian autonomy. In October 1944, Russian forces crossed into Hungary. The Budapest radio announced that Horthy was asking the Russians for an armistice. The German SS under Veesenmayer reacted swiftly on 16 October by kidnapping Horthy's son and holding him under threats. They thereby forced Horthy to appoint Arrow Cross Chief Szalasi as Prime Minister. Szalasi cancelled the armistice, but the Hungarian commander-in-chief and his chief of staff went over to the Russians. By November 1944 the Russians had overrun two thirds of Hungary and had reached Budapest's outskirts. Budapest remained under Russian siege until February 1945, though the Hungarians had signed an armistice a month earlier. Finally, by 4 April 1945, no more Germans remained in Hungary.

Jews in Pre-war Hungary

In 1930, 445,000 Jews lived in Hungary, about 5 per cent of the population. Half lived in Budapest, where they made up 20 per cent of the population, and in two other large cities. The rest of the Jewish population was dispersed; there were twenty-four communities with about 1,000 Jews each and 180 with fewer than 1,000 Jews each.

In a country with a landed aristocracy and a large peasantry, the Jews were distinctively middle class. Of gainfully employed Jews, 38 per cent were self-employed businessmen in industry (including small craftsmen), commerce and banking, and also professionals; 28 per cent were salaried (white-collar employees mainly in commerce, banking and industry); and 33 per cent were wage earners (workers), though predominantly in commercial enterprises.

Most Jews in Budapest were highly acculturated, in contrast to the Jews in the small towns where Orthodoxy prevailed. There were three national religious Jewish communities: the Neologs (somewhat similar to reform Jews), the Orthodox, and a smaller organization called 'Status Quo Ante Jewish Communities', who stood somewhere between them. Intermarriage and baptismal rates were quite high; in 1938 there were 35,000 baptized Jews in Hungary. Conversions, the declining birth rate, and continuing emigration as a consequence of Hungary's anti-Semitic policies reduced the size of the Jewish population in Hungary, estimated at about 400,000 in 1939.

Hungarian Jews had been emancipated in 1867, but resentment on the part of the non-Jewish population – because of the territorial losses after the First World War, chaotic economic conditions and the abortive Communist dictatorship of Bela Kun – were vented on the Jews. Horthy came to power as a blaze of pogroms raged in Hungary, particularly in the provinces. The violence was followed by various administrative measures eliminating most Jews from public service and restricting their admission into universities. From 1924 to 1933, under the conservative régime of Count Stephen Bethlen as Prime Minister, the situation of the Jews somewhat stabilized, but in the mid-1930s, under the impact of National Socialism in Germany and its Hungarian admirers, anti-Semitism intensified.

On 24 May 1938, a month after Hitler's annexation of Austria, the Hungarian parliament, in an effort to appease Hitler and prevent seizure of power by the Hungarian Nazis, enacted its first anti-Jewish law, prepared by the Horthy government, despite the bitter opposition of the Smallholders and Socialist parties and Bethlen's conservative followers. The law limited employment of Jews in private business firms to 20 per cent. A year later, a more far-reaching anti-Jewish law was passed, defining the status of Jews, barring them from leading positions in the media, prohibiting the issuance of new trade licences to them or the renewal of old ones. The law also barred further admission of Jews to the professions until their share fell to below 6 per cent. It authorized the government to expropriate, with compensation, Jewish landed property. Jews could no longer acquire Hungarian citizenship by naturalization, marriage or adoption. Voting rights of non-native Jews or those whose forebears were not permanently resident before 1868 were cancelled.

Jews in Wartime Hungary

After Munich and the Vienna Awards, Hungary added another 250,000 to its Jewish population of 400,000: 75,000 Jews in former Slovakian territory, 25,000 in the Bačka basin of Yugoslavia and 150,000 in Transylvania for a total of 650,000 Jews in Greater Hungary. There were, besides, some 100,000 Christians, who were regarded as 'racial' Jews and subject to anti-Jewish laws. (In August 1941 a more stringent law was enacted, defining who was a Jew.)

In August 1941 the Hungarian government rounded up some 17,000 stateless Jews in its annexed Ruthenian territory and pushed them over the border to Kamenets-Podolsk in the German-held Ukraine, but the Germans complained that the Jews disrupted their military communications. After the Hungarians drew off several thousand to be used as slave labourers, the German Einsatzkommandos massacred the remaining 11,000. Several thousand Yugoslav Jews in Bačka were also massacred by the Hungarian occupying forces at Novi Sad.

No further deportations took place, and when the Kallay government took over in March 1942 Jews were subject only to tightening employment restrictions, forced-labour conscription, and more extensive expropriations. Some 16,000 Jews from Austria, Slovakia and Poland even found refuge in Hungary and were not handed over to the Germans. At the end of 1942, Kallay rejected German demands to introduce yellow badges for Jews and deport them to Poland. In May 1943 Kallay, in a public speech, rejected 'resettlement' of the Jews as a 'final solution', so long as the Germans were giving no satisfactory answer about where the Jews were being resettled.

The virtual German occupation of Hungary in March 1944 and the installation of the pro-German Sztojay government drastically transformed the situation of the Hungarian Jews. On 19 March, the very day of the German take-over, Eichmann himself came to Budapest with a battery of SS officers in charge of Jewish affairs. Eichmann ordered the Jewish community leaders to appear for a conference the next day, when they were told to establish a Judenrat, which would have to carry out German orders. Meanwhile, on 29 March new anti-Jewish legislation was enacted, forcing Jews entirely out of the professions, ordering the registration of their property and arranging for its almost instant expropriation. The yellow star was introduced, and the Jews were concentrated in designated places.

To carry out the deportations of the Jews, Eichmann divided Hungary into six zones: Zone I, Carpathians; II, Transylvania; III, northern

Hungary; IV, southern Hungary east of the Danube; V, Transdanubia, including the suburbs of Budapest: VI, Budapest proper.

With the participation of a Sondereinsatzkommando (special-duty commando) that Eichmann had brought from Mauthausen and with the help of the Hungarian police, the Germans began to round up the Jews, concentrating them within the designated zones and deporting them in rapid order. By 7 June Zones I and II had been cleared of nearly 290,000 Jews. By 30 June over 92,000 Jews had been deported from zones III and IV. By 7 July over 437,000 Jews, including some 50,000 from Budapest, had been deported to Auschwitz.

Meanwhile, the Jewish relief committee in Budapest, following up earlier initiatives of Slovakian Jews, began negotiations with SS-Hauptsturmführer Dieter Wisliceny about ransoming the remaining Hungarian Jews from deportation. On behalf of the Jewish relief committee, Joel Brand was sent to Turkey to contact the Allies about the possibilities of exchanging goods for Jewish lives. Negotiations were protracted and complex, but Eichmann never halted the deportation trains. Finally, nothing substantial developed in the rescue of the Jews, except for one trainload of Hungarian Jews who were saved.

In July 1944, after news about the Hungarian deportations had been sent abroad, various high-level interventions on behalf of the Jews began to dismay the Hungarians. Horthy ordered the deportations halted. When the pro-German government was toppled in August, the new Prime Minister Lakatos then asked the Germans to remove Eichmann's Sondereinsatzkommando. Some anti-Jewish restrictions began to be lifted, but after the German *coup* in October 1944, with Arrow Cross leader Szalasi as Prime Minister, the Jews again fell into German hands for deportation. By 26 October some 35,000 Jewish men and women had been rounded up, but since Auschwitz was then being liquidated, these Jews were to be used as slave labourers. The exigencies of war rendered railway transportation impossible, and so the Germans marched off 27,000 Jews on a terrible trek of over 100 miles to Austria. But Szalasi soon stopped these marches because of the high death rate.

Some 160,000 Jews remained in Budapest, subject to terror and murder at the hands of the Arrow Cross, suffering cold, hunger and disease in their ghetto-like quarters, under the rain of Russian bombardment. About 20,000 died that winter. On 14 February 1945 the Russians took Budapest.

Over 450,000 Jews, 70 per cent of the Jews of Greater Hungary, were deported, were murdered or died under German occupation. Within the boundaries of lesser (pre-1938) Hungary, about half the Jews were annihilated. Some 144,000 survived in Budapest, including 50,000 'racial' Jews, and about 50,000 to 60,000 survived in the provinces.

SOUTH-EASTERN EUROPE

RUMANIA

When war broke out, Rumania was under Carol II's dictatorial government. In 1938, threatened by the spectacular rise to power of the Nazi-like Iron Guard, which he himself had earlier encouraged, Carol had dissolved all parties and concentrated power in his own hands. His domestic policies aimed to check the expanding power of the Iron Guard, and in foreign affairs he tried to keep Rumania neutral between the Allies and the Axis, though leaning closer to the Axis. The collapse of Poland and then of France led Carol to sever his Anglo-French ties on 1 July 1940 and proclaim a reorientation of Rumania's foreign policy as a 'neutral ally' of the Axis. Three days earlier, the Soviet Union, having occupied half of pre-war Poland, demanded the cession of northern Bucovina and all of Bessarabia, to which Rumania, on Germany's advice, promptly acceded. Then, to satisfy the revanchist ambitions of its neighbours, Rumania was forced by Germany and Italy to cede the northern part of Transylvania to Hungary as part of the Vienna Awards of 30 August 1940. A week later, Rumania ceded southern Dobruja to Bulgaria.

Carol's policies having brought humiliation to Rumania, the Iron Guard accused him of treachery, and he was deposed in a bloodless *coup* in September 1940 by a military group under General Ion Antonescu, long associated with the Iron Guard. Carol was exiled; his son, Michael I, became king, with Antonescu as *conducator* (leader) of Rumania. All political parties and movements except the Iron Guard were outlawed. Some 120,000 German troops entered Rumania as a 'military advisory mission', to 'protect' Rumania's oil-fields, and in November Rumania joined the Axis.

The Antonescu coalition was torn by violent conflict between the army and the Iron Guard. After a bloody clash between them in January 1941 in Bucharest, in which the Iron Guard carried out a terrible massacre of the Jews and its other 'enemies', the army won complete control of the country, which was then ruled by a military dictatorship under Antonescu. Rumanian armed forces joined German forces and participated in the invasion of Russia in June 1941. Rumanian army units and Rumanian police also took part in Einsatzgruppe D. To compensate for its other territorial losses, Rumania recaptured Bucovina and Bessarabia from the Soviet Union and took also a portion of the south-western Ukraine.

So long as the progress of the war favoured Germany and its allies, the Rumanians supported it, but when the tide turned, particularly with the heavy casualties suffered by the Rumanian army in the Battle of Stalingrad, Antonescu faced considerable domestic opposition. In April 1944 the Red Army recaptured Bucovina, Bessarabia, and Odessa; in August the Russians entered Moldavia, in rump Rumania. On 23 August 1944 Michael arrested Antonescu, took over the government, and surrendered to the Russians.

The Jews in Pre-war Rumania

The Jewish population of pre-war Rumania was 757,000, with the largest concentrations in Bessarabia, Moldavia, Walachia, Crishana-Maramuresh, Bucovina and Transylvania. (In August 1940 some 150,000 Jews in Transylvania came under Hungarian rule, as a consequence of the Vienna Awards). Though Jews made up 4 per cent of the Rumanian population, they formed 25 to 35 per cent of the urban populations in Moldavia, Bessarabia and Bucovina. Two thirds of the Jews lived in urban centres, the rest in villages.

Over 40 per cent of the Jewish labour force were engaged in industry and crafts, another 40 per cent in trade and commerce, and 3 per cent were in the professions and civil service.

Rumania never lived up to its obligations undertaken after the First World War to recognize all Jews living in its territory as Rumanian nationals, and it intensified its attacks on the rights of Jews in the inter-bellum period. In 1938 a special decree, 'Revision of Citizenship', stripped a substantial number of Rumanian Jews of their citizenship. Severe economic discrimination and violent anti-Semitism terrorized the Jewish population.

Assimilation was strong among Jews in the provinces of the Old Kingdom of Rumania, especially Walachia, but among the denser communities in Bucovina and Bessarabia, Jews were culturally separatist, with Yiddish as the predominant language and flourishing movements for Jewish cultural autonomy and Zionism. The Federation of the Unions of Jewish Communities, consisting of religious and provincial bodies, was the central Jewish organization, with the authority to tax its constituents.

Jews in Wartime Rumania

In August 1940, under Carol, the government enacted an anti-Jewish statute, based on the Italian model, which for the most part codified existing legislation. Jews were expelled from the cultural life of the country and from all government service, including the army. They were not permitted to be on the boards of commercial or industrial corporations and were prohibited from buying immovable property without the consent of the government. In October 1940, under Antonescu's coalition régime, anti-Jewish legislation was enacted providing for the 'Rumanianization' of Jewish property. A month later, a similar law affecting Jewish industrial and agricultural property was enacted. Subsequent decrees expelled Jews from all gainful employment. Jews were made liable for forced labour, without pay, instead of military service. Radu Lecca, Commissar for Jewish Questions in Antonescu's government, handled the problems of ghettoization and deportation, while economic despoliation of the Jews was in the jurisdiction of the Labour Minister.

This administrative anti-Semitism was, from the start, accompanied by pogroms and violence. In January 1941, during the fighting between the Iron Guard and Antonescu's army supporters, a massacre took place in Bucharest, in which about 170 Jews were murdered in an especially abhorrent manner.

With the invasion of the Soviet Union and the recapture of northern Bucovina and Bessarabia, unbridled plunder and murder of Jews were authorized by the Rumanian army's high command. The first major wartime pogroms occurred in Iaşi in June 1941, organized by special Rumanian troops assigned to rounding up, deporting and murdering Jews. Thereafter, thousands of Jews were packed in cattle cars on the pretext that they were signalling to Russian planes, and shipped off without food or water, to no particular destination. Those who did not die of suffocation were shot. About 8,000 died. In and around Czernowitz (Cernauti) and Storojinetz, 12,000 Jews were killed; in Bessarabia, over 200,000. Rumanian army units working with Einsatzgruppe D in southern Russia dismayed the Germans with their passion for killing and their disregard for disposal of the corpses.

In August 1941 the Rumanians began to expel Bessarabian Jews across the Dniester, in territory under German military occupation. The Germans resisted having this area become a dumping ground for unwanted Jews, but then agreed that Transnistria, the area between the Dniester and the Bug rivers, could serve as a reservation for Rumanian

Jews. By mid-November 1941 over 120,000 Jews had been deported there, and by late 1942, according to a conservative estimate, some 200,000 Rumanian Jews had been shipped to Transnistria, nearly two thirds of whom had already died of hunger and epidemics. By September 1943, only some 50,000 Rumanian Jews remained alive in Transnistria, along with 25,000 to 30,000 Russian Jews, native inhabitants of that area.

On 16 December 1941 the government dissolved the Federation of the Unions of the Jewish Communities, setting up instead, in Bucharest, the Centre for Rumanian Jews (Centrala Evreilor din Romania), as the 'sole body authorized to represent the interests of the Jewish community of Rumania'. Its functions were to fulfil government demands on the Jewish community, fund the still existing network of Jewish elementary and high schools, and aid the needy, including those in Transnistria. Dr W. Filderman, for many years chairman of the Federation and indefatigable in his efforts on behalf of Rumanian Jews, was shunted aside and replaced by two government-appointed officials.

Early in the summer of 1942 Eichmann's representative, SS Hauptsturmführer Gustav Richter, operating out of the German legation in Bucharest, reached an understanding with the Rumanian government regarding the deportation of the Rumanian Jews to Lublin, but the Rumanians changed their minds a few months later. Lecca, having been snubbed by the SS while in Berlin, became less cooperative. Dr Filderman, meanwhile, though no longer officially head of the Jewish community, submitted several urgent memoranda to the Minister of the Interior, pointing out that though Hungary had not deported its Jews, it had actually profited from its alliance with Germany by receiving Rumanian territory. Other interventions, by Jews and non-Jews, against deporting the Jews finally led to Rumania's definite repudiation of the plan. Nevertheless, Rumania continued to oppress the remaining Jewish population by labour exploitation and expropriation.

At the end of 1942, Antonescu informed the Germans that instead of deporting the Jews to Poland, he would allow them to buy their way out and emigrate to Palestine. In 1943 negotiations began between Rumanian Jewish leaders and the government about the possibilities of emigration via Bulgaria and Turkey to Palestine and regarding improvement of conditions in Transnistria. Nothing significant emerged from the emigration scheme, but during 1942 substantial relief provided by Jewish groups helped to improve the lot of the survivors in Transnistria. German military reversals also influenced Antonescu's decision. In December 1943 the first group of Jews returned to Rumania from

Transnistria, and early in 1944 about 1,500 Jewish orphans were repatriated from there. Between April 1944, when the Russians recaptured Bucovina, Bessarabia and Odessa, and late August, when Rumania surrendered, the situation of the surviving Jews in Rumania remained precarious. It turned out, however, that the Germans, in retreat through Rumania, no longer had the means to continue rounding up the Jews.

In Transnistria only some 50,000 survived out of the 300,000 Bessarabian and Bucovinian Jews. Some 50,000 had been deported to Siberia during the first Russian occupation, and their fate is not known. Most of the others were in the path of Einsatzgruppe D. Except for the 8,000 to 10,000 Jews murdered at Iași in 1941 and other thousands killed in pogroms, about 300,000 Jews in Rumania survived, most of them in Old Rumania proper.

BULGARIA

When war broke out in September 1939, Bulgaria remained neutral. Bulgaria's only interest in the war was the possibility it offered to attain its revanchist goals: the return of territory from Rumania, Greece and Yugoslavia that it had been forced to cede after the First World War. In June 1940, when the Soviet Union demanded from Rumania northern Bucovina and Bessarabia, Bulgaria also pressed its claim for the return of Dobruja, some 3,000 square miles in south-east Rumania. Acceding to Germany's advice, Rumania yielded the territory on 7 September 1940.

In March 1941, when Germany needed passage through Bulgaria to come to Italy's aid in Greece, Bulgaria joined the Axis and demanded, in return for Germany's right of passage, a restoration of its 'historic frontiers', by the annexation of western Thrace from Greece and Serbian Macedonia from Yugoslavia.

Though some German troops remained stationed in Bulgaria, Germany never actively intervened in its internal administration. Bulgaria declared war on the United States on 13 December 1941, in accordance with its membership in the Axis, but never declared war on the Soviet Union. Bulgarian troops moved beyond the borders of Old Bulgaria only into those areas of Yugoslavia and Greece that became part of Greater Bulgaria. On 5 September 1944 the Soviet Union declared war on Bulgaria, and three days later Bulgaria asked for an armistice. On 8 September the Soviet armies moved into Bulgaria, which then declared war on Germany.

The Jews in Pre-war Bulgaria

About 50,000 Jews lived in Old Bulgaria, less than 1 per cent in a total population of over 6 million. An urban group, 55 per cent of Bulgarian Jews lived in Sofia, where they constituted 9 per cent of the population. The majority were largely self-employed in commerce and trade. Those in manufacturing and crafts were engaged in the traditional Jewish occupations of tailoring, shoe-making, brush-making tin-smithing. About 15 per cent of the gainfully employed Jews were in the professions or civil service.

The Jewish community enjoyed complete civic and political equality, first guaranteed under the Congress of Berlin in 1878. The constitution of Trnovo of 1879 provided religious freedom and full equality for all citizens. Under a law of 1880 the synagogue was recognized as the local unit of the Jewish religious community; the Chief Rabbi, recognized by the state as the head of Bulgarian Jewry and authorized to represent it in relations with the government, was paid by the state. The Central Consistory served as an advisory body. Early in the twentieth century, however, as a consequence of a process of secularization and demo-cratization, the Zionists gained control of the local communities and subordinated the Rabbi to the Central Consistory in national matters. Out of special taxes the Jews maintained an extensive network of religious, communal and educational institutions (including courts to settle religious and family disputes). Economically and politically integrated in the life of the country, the Jews nevertheless remained communally and culturally segregated, and the majority of Jewish children attended Jewish schools.

While anti-Semitism had erupted violently occasionally in Turkish times, from the start of the twentieth century until the rise of Nazism in Germany, Jews enjoyed a period of tranquillity and physical security in Bulgaria, relatively free of discrimination. With the expansion of German economic and political influence in the Balkans, an anti-Semitic movement began to take shape in the 1930s. Students returning from German universities and White Russian émigrés spread anti-Semitic propaganda in Bulgaria, yet their effect was limited. In 1937 a Jewish journalist succeeded in gathering statements against anti-Semitism from sixty influential Bulgarian notables, including sixteen former premiers and Cabinet members.

The Jews in Wartime Bulgaria

With the appointment in February 1940 of Bogdan Filov as Premier,

Bulgarian policy shifted in a pro-German direction. The Jews became the first victims. In July 1940 the government announced its intention to introduce anti-Jewish legislation and officially forewarned the representatives of the Jewish communities. The Law for the Protection of the Nation, passed by the Sobranie (parliament) on 24 December 1940, and its first implementing executive order, published on 17 February 1941, defined persons of Jewish origin as any person with at least one Jewish parent. It differed from the German definition in that it exempted certain converts from the racial definition. Consequently, mixed marriages increased sharply in 1940, most doubtless convenience marriages, and hundreds of 'mercy baptisms' were performed. Also exempted from the legislation were Jews who had been war volunteers, war invalids or decorated war veterans.

The law restricted Jewish rights and social relations, along the lines of German anti-Jewish legislation. Jews had to be registered, had to use Jewish first names, were forbidden to have Bulgarian-sounding names. Barred from military service, they had to serve instead in labour squads in the army. The government could exclude them from certain types of employment, expel them from certain towns or confine them in others. Jews could not own or rent real estate or houses in rural communities and had to sell such property within a year. All other property had to be registered with the government. Legislative additions and revisions continued to be issued through 1942, affecting also some 14,000 Jews in Greater Bulgaria – 8,000 Macedonian Jews in the territory wrested from Yugoslavia and 6,000 in annexed Thrace. These Jews were not given Bulgarian citizenship, but were subject to the disabilities of the Bulgarian Jews.

A special tax on Jewish-held property was enacted in July 1941. Jews were then also subject to curfew; telephones and radios were removed from their homes and offices.

In June 1942, at the initiative of the Minister of the Interior, Peter Gabrovski, the Sobranie was asked to delegate to the Cabinet the authority to 'solve the Jewish question'. Gabrovski's consultant, Alexander Belev, a German-trained lawyer, proposed to 'solve the question' by expelling all Jews from Bulgaria and confiscating their property. Over the outspoken protests of a minority, the Sobranie voted blanket authorization to the Cabinet. On 28 August 1942 a Commissariat for Jewish Affairs was established in the Ministry of the Interior, and on 3 September Belev was appointed its head. This agency in charge of Jewish affairs was the link with the German officials in charge of carrying out the Final Solution in Bulgaria. That month

Bulgarian Foreign Minister Ivan Vladimir Popov concluded a secret agreement with German Ambassador Beckerle, surrendering to German jurisdiction those Bulgarian citizens who were Jewish and residing in German-occupied countries.

The Star of David was introduced in September 1943. Orders were issued to expel unemployed Jews from the cities, to confiscate Jewish property and to assign Jews to special quarters in Sofia. Encouraged by these developments, the SS began to press to deport the Jews from Bulgaria, and in January 1943 SS-Obersturmführer Theodor Dannecker, Eichmann's assistant, arrived in Sofia to begin concrete negotiations to this end. In February 1943 an oral agreement was reached between Dannecker and Belev to the effect that 20,000 Jews, mostly from the newly annexed territories, would be deported in March, and that the Jews should first be concentrated in temporary camps near railway stations and allowed to carry enough food and clothing for ten to fifteen days. On 3 February Belev telegraphed all local representatives of the Commissariat for Jewish Affairs to draw up lists of Jews in their areas by family, sex, age and occupation and clearly showing the addresses. On 22 February 1943 the agreement between Belev and Dannecker was signed, and preparations to deport the Jews were begun even before the Cabinet confirmed the agreement on 2 March. The Thracian and Macedonian Jews began to be rounded up, and instructions were issued to prepare deporting Jews from Bulgaria proper.

On 6 March news leaked out in Kyustendil, a town some fifty miles from Sofia, that a camp was to be set up near by for the Jews who would be deported by the Germans 'to the East'. The Kyustendil Jewish community notified the Jewish Consistory in Sofia and also the town's leading citizens, including Dimiter Peshev, a deputy and vice-president of the Sobranie. On 9 March Peshev and his friends went to Gabrovski, who, under personal threat from them, the same day countermanded the deportation orders affecting the Jews of Old Bulgaria, but the deportation of the Macedonian and Thracian Jews remained in force. A total of 11,384 of these Jews were sent to Treblinka and other death camps.

Peshev's protests and opposition succeeded in halting the deportation of the Bulgarian Jews, though as a consequence he himself was dismissed as vice-president. The Germans continued to exert pressure to deport the Jews, but the counter-pressure of Bulgarian opinion, especially of the Bulgarian Orthodox Church, restrained the government from compliance. King Boris, too, was opposed to deporting any but 'Communist elements'.

In May 1943 King Boris ordered the resettlement of the Sofia Jews in provincial towns, despite protests by Jews and Bulgarians. That dispersal appeared to be Boris's acceptance of an alternative to the German proposal to deport the Jews to Poland.

Boris died on 28 August 1943; the changing face of the war and the Allied invasion of Italy shook up Bulgaria. A new Cabinet formed in September under Dobri Boshilov, though pro-German, tried to establish a more independent stance for Bulgaria. Gabrovski and Belev were dropped from the Cabinet, and a more liberal attitude towards the Jews was taken. The Jews were allowed to return to Sofia from time to time to take care of their affairs. In response to German pressure for deportations, the Bulgarians responded that German insistence on deportation would make the government less favourably inclined to Germany. In the summer of 1944 Nikolas Balabanov, Bulgarian minister in Istanbul, was engaged in negotiations with Ira Hirschmann of the United States War Refugee Board (WRB) regarding the evacuation of Jews to Palestine via Turkey. In August 1944 Balabanov wrote to the WRB that the Bulgarian government regretted its anti-Jewish measures and would abolish them 'at an opportune moment'. On 24 August the Commissariat for Jewish Affairs was abolished, and the Jews were free to engage in any occupation. On 29 August the Cabinet voted to abolish all anti-Jewish legislation; the decree was published on 5 September 1944, three days before the Soviet army entered Bulgaria. The 50,000 Bulgarian Jews were spared.

YUGOSLAVIA

When war broke out Yugoslavia, under the regency of Prince Paul, had remained neutral, but on 25 March 1941 it joined the Axis. The next day Paul was overthrown in a bloodless *coup*, and the new government announced that Yugoslavia would remain neutral, though in fact it was anti-German. On 27 March Hitler, outraged at the *coup* issued a directive calling for the invasion of Yugoslavia. That invasion began on 6 April, when German forces, along with their Italian, Bulgarian and Hungarian allies, entered Yugoslavia. The government capitulated on 17 April, though guerrilla forces continued their resistance.

Yugoslavia was partitioned. Serbian Macedonia was ceded by the Germans to Bulgaria. Bačka, the north-eastern basin between the Danube and the Tisza, was annexed by Hungary. The Italians occupied most of the Dalmatian coast and the islands. Old Serbia, with Belgrade as its capital, came under German military rule, with a local puppet government established in August 1941. Virtual rule of the country was in the hands of the German Chief of the Administrative Staff at the Military Commander Headquarters, State Councillor Harald Turner.

Croatia declared its independence on 10 April 1941, and a puppet government was established in Zagreb, under Ante Pavelić, leader of the Ustachi, a Croat nationalist terrorist organization. Notwithstanding this 'independence', Italian forces remained in part of Croatian territory and German troops occupied all important Croatian towns outside the Italian zone.

Ustachi terror and brutality alienated many Croats from support of the Pavelić régime, and the partisans, particularly those under the leadership of Josip Broz, called Tito, made considerable gains among the population, in Serbia as well. Pavelić's influence continued to decline as that of the partisans grew, though severe tensions existed between different partisan organizations. German reprisals against the partisans were extremely harsh.

By early 1944 the partisan movement, supplied by both the British and the Russians, was gaining ground. In September 1944 the Germans began to retreat; on 20 October 1944 Russian troops and Yugoslav partisans ousted the Germans from Belgrade. In Croatia Pavelić managed to hold on with his desperate Ustachi remnants until 4 May 1945, when the last German troops left.

Jews in Pre-war Yugoslavia

Some 76,000 Jews, 0·4 per cent of the total population, lived in Yugoslavia before the German occupation. About 25,000 were Sephardic Jews, whose ancestors had come from Spain in the fifteenth and sixteenth centuries. About 51,000 were Ashkenazim, most of whose forebears had come in the eighteenth and nineteenth centuries from Central Europe, primarily the Hapsburg Empire. The Sephardim were organized in thirty-seven religious communities, the Ashkenazim in seventy-seven.

In a country where 75 per cent of the population was engaged in agriculture, the Jews formed a middle-class element that was concentrated in retail trade, commerce, industry and handicrafts. The Jews in Serbia and Croatia were on the whole well-to-do, while those in the other provinces were poorer.

Besides their well-organized religious communities (114 in 103 places), which enjoyed government recognition and support, the Yugoslav Jews maintained welfare, educational and cultural institutions and conducted a variety of Zionist activities. The religious communities were the focal point of Jewish social life.

Jews enjoyed full civic and religious rights in Yugoslavia. Anti-Semitism had had no tradition in Serbia, but during the 1930s it began to seep in from Croatia, which had long been virulently anti-Semitic. German influence and Yugoslavia's pro-German policies intensified the anti-Semitic climate. The one Jew in the Yugoslav Senate was expelled in 1938, and the Prime Minister asked the Regent to appoint a non-Jew in his stead. In October 1940 two anti-Jewish laws were adopted, one limiting the access of Jews to secondary and higher education, the other halting the issuance of licences for Jewish businesses and restricting the renewal of others. Though not widely enforced by local authorities, no serious opposition was offered to their enactment.

Jews in Wartime Yugoslavia

Serbia: Of the 12,000 Jews in Old Serbia, over 8,000 lived in Belgrade, where, within a week of occupation, the Germans began to register them and introduce the identifying Star of David badge. In May 1941 the Jews were ordered into forced-labour brigades. On 31 May the military commander issued anti-Jewish regulations defining Jews, ordering the registration of their property and removing them from the economic life of the country. 'Aryanization' of Jewish property began in July.

Anti-Jewish violence on the part of the German troops and *Volksdeutsche* was widespread, particularly in Banat, from which the Jews were expelled and brought to Belgrade. In August 1941 the German army carried out a mass internment of adult male Jews, setting up one camp on the outskirts of Belgrade, another at Niš (for Jews in eastern and southern Serbia), and a third at Šabac. Since the death camps were not yet ready, the Germans undertook to shoot the interned Jews *en masse* and by mid-November had murdered about 5,000 male Jews. In December they interned women and children and then shot them too. The few hundred surviving Jews in hiding were hunted down by Serbian collaborators and turned over to the Germans. By mid-1942 the Germans in Serbia had succeeded in 'solving the Jewish question'.

Croatia: Over 30,000 Jews lived in Croatia, 10,000 of them in Bosnia and Herzegovina. Standard anti-Jewish legislation was introduced right after Pavelić's government was set up, defining the status of Jews, requiring the registration of Jewish property, ordering identifying badges for Jews and Jewish businesses. Jews were also ordered to pay heavy levies. Forced labour was introduced within the month. Under a decree of 26 June 1941 and one of 23 November 1941, mass arrests and internments of Jews were ordered.

By October 1941 most Jews in Croatia, Bosnia and Herzegovina were engaged in forced labour, languishing in camps or had already been shot. In August 1942 some 9,000 Jews were deported, most of them to Auschwitz. Smaller groups were deported in 1943 and 1944, including many who had found refuge in the Italian zone, which had, after September 1943, come under German control.

Jewish losses for all of Yugoslavia are estimated at about 60,000.

GREECE

Greece remained neutral when war broke out. In October 1940 Italy attacked Greece, but with British reinforcements that had landed in Crete, the Greeks managed to force the Italians back into Albania. The Germans then began mustering troops to help the Italians. Though the Greeks permitted a British expeditionary force to land in March 1941, superior German forces invading in April broke Greek resistance. The British were evacuated; King George II and his government fled. Italy occupied most of Greek territory, while the Germans occupied Macedonia and eastern Thrace. Bulgaria, having provided land transit for German troops into Greece, was rewarded with western Thrace. In May 1941 the Germans invaded Crete and drove the British out.

The Germans installed a puppet Prime Minister in Athens whose jurisdiction included both the German and Italian zones. Germany itself maintained a military government in Greece, with Max Merten, counsellor to the military governor, in charge of civilian affairs. Conditions of famine intensified resistance in Greece; the Greek resistance movement received support from both the English and the Russians. Greek collaborationists were unable to win popular support and despite the severe reprisals by the occupying forces against the guerrillas, opposition continued. From 1943 on, economic and administrative life in Greece was seriously disrupted by sabotage and resistance activities.

In September 1943, after the Badoglio government in Italy surrendered to the invading Allied forces, German troops occupied Italian-held Greece and extended their military rule over all of Greece. In October 1944, British troops, having landed in Greece, worked with the Greek resistance movement to drive out the retreating Germans. Under Russian pressure, Bulgaria relinquished Thracian Greece.

Jews in Pre-war Greece

The Jewish population in pre-war Greece was close to 76,000, 0·9 per cent of the total population. In Salonika, the most eminent Sephardic settlement in Europe, dating back to the fifteenth century, the 55,000 Jews made up over 20 per cent of the city's population. The Jews, merchants and craftsmen in a land of peasants and soldiers, had once made Salonika a great city of trade, commerce and industry. The Salonikan Jewish community in the late 1930s still retained most of its unique economic functions in trade, commerce and industry, though it was no longer as prosperous as it once had been.

Under a statute of 1920, Greek Jews were organized in twenty-four religious communities, maintaining religious and educational institutions (Salonika had forty synagogues, named after once-famous Jewish communities of Spain). They supported their own social-welfare institutions. Two daily newspapers were published in Ladino.

During the period of stormy strife of the Greek republic (1924–35), overt anti-Semitism – propaganda and violence – became commonplace. The restoration of the monarchy and the subsequent dictatorship under Metaxas (1936–41), with its heavy censorship and control, suppressed popular political agitation, including anti-Semitism.

Nearly 13,000 Jews fought in the Greek army at the time of the German invasion.

Jews in Wartime Greece

After suppressing the Ladino newspapers and confiscating the Jewish community's financial assets and records, the Germans appointed Saby Saltiel, a former communal official, as President of Jews in Salonika. Jews were evicted from their homes, humiliated, arrested and taken as hostages. No formal legislation was enacted until July 1942, when Jews were made liable for forced labour; about 10,000 were rounded up for forced-labour battalions. The terrible conditions in malaria-infested swamps, which caused high mortality among the internees (12 per cent), prompted the Jewish community to offer to exempt the Jews for ransom. After lengthy negotiations, Merten agreed to accept 2·5 billion drachmas (then about $100,000). At the same time, Jewish property and Jewish businesses were being despoiled and confiscated.

In December 1942 the Germans appointed Rabbi Zvi Koretz head of the Jewish community. In February 1943, Dieter Wisliceny, Eichmann's deputy, arrived in Salonika to set in motion the machinery for deportation. The Jews were ordered to wear Star of David badges and to move into ghettos, which were in fact segregated areas. They were subjected to a wide variety of other restrictions.

Deportations began in March 1943 from Salonika and Thrace; at the same time the Bulgarians were assisting the Germans in deporting the Greek Jews from the territory they had annexed. By mid-May some 45,000 Jews from Salonika had been deported.

At the end of September 1943, when all of Greece came under German military rule, SS General Jürgen Stroop took over the SS command in Athens. On 3 October 1943 he issued a general anti-Jewish regulation, defining the Jews and ordering them to register. Jews who did not report to the Germans within five days would be shot, and any Greek providing shelter to Jews would be shot without trial. Early in 1944 the deportations of Jews from Athens began and the Germans began to round up the Jews on the islands of Corfu, Crete, Rhodes and elsewhere.

Over 60,000 Greek Jews were annihilated, most having been deported to Auschwitz.

EASTERN EUROPE

POLAND

The Second World War began on 1 September 1939, when Germany invaded Poland. German forces, estimated at 1·7 million men, highly mechanized and motorized with superior air power, easily overwhelmed the outnumbered and inadequately equipped Polish forces. On 17 September Russia, with whom Germany had concluded a non-aggression pact on 23 August 1939, sent her troops into Poland from the east, and on 19 September the German and Russian armies met near Brest Litovsk. On 27 September, after destructive bombing, Warsaw surrendered and Polish military opposition crumbled. The next day Germany and Russia divided Poland.

The Russians occupied over 77,000 square miles of eastern Poland, with a population of over 13 million. Germany gained an area of 73,000 square miles, with a population of 22 million. Germany annexed Danzig outright and also incorporated into the Greater Reich 32,000 square miles of territory between East Prussia and Silesia. The western portion was divided into two districts (Gauen): Danzig–West Prussia (under Gauleiter Albert Foster) and Warthe (under Gauleiter Arthur Greiser). The remaining 39,000 square miles were designated as Generalgouvernement of Poland, and placed under German civil administration, with Hans Frank as Governor General, appointed on 8 November 1939, and headquarters in Cracow. The Generalgouvernement was divided into four districts, each with its own governor (Cracow, Lublin, Radom, Warsaw), and categorized as 'Nebenland', adjunct of the Reich.

The Germans, determined to carry out their racial policies, began massive deportations of Jews and Poles from the incorporated territories. Thousands of Poles were executed, other thousands were sent to Germany as slave labourers, still others were pushed into the General-gouvernement. In the Generalgouvernement Poles were allowed the barest forms of local self-government, with only the town and village communes in the hands of Polish officials, but real authority was lodged with the German *Kreishauptmann*, the principal district official. The Polish police apparatus remained intact, but was subordinated to German police authority. Certain Polish civil courts were allowed to continue. All other governmental and public functions were taken over by the Germans, from agriculture and industry through education and the press. Though the civil administration under Governor Frank supposedly exercised absolute power, the German army controlled war production in the Generalgouvernement, and the SS and police exercised a wide variety of functions related to racial policy, war production, finances and security. The Germans ruthlessly exploited Poland's economic resources, from raw materials to corporation securities.

The German invasion of the Soviet Union on 22 June 1941 brought Russian-occupied Poland under German rule. The Polish district of Łomża and part of Grodno, between East Prussia to the north and the Generalgouvernement to the south – designated as Generalkommissariat Bialystok, with Bialystok as its headquarters city – became a quasi-incorporated district of the Reich, attached to East Prussia. North-eastern Poland, along with the Baltic countries and White Russia, was included in the Reichskommissariat Ostland (see the Soviet Union, p. 474). East central Poland, the district of Volhynia, became part of the Reichskommissariat Ukraine. Galicia in southeastern Poland became the fifth district of the Generalgouvernement (Lwów).

The Polish government-in-exile, formed in Paris on 30 September 1939 and eventually transferred to London, maintained close contact with underground Polish patriotic groups, including the clandestine Polish Home Army. Polish prisoners of war in the Soviet Union were allowed to form a corps under General Władysław Anders to fight with the Allies.

In July 1944 Soviet troops entered eastern Poland and a provisional

Polish government was established. The following month, as the Red Army neared Warsaw, Polish underground forces, led by General Tadeusz Bor and under the control of the Polish government-in-exile, rose against the German occupation forces. The Red Army, on the far side of the Vistula, failed to come to their support, and after bitter fighting the uprising was suppressed by the Germans on 2 October 1944. The last German forces were finally expelled from Poland early in 1945. The Poles suffered great losses during the fighting and bombardments in 1939 and then in 1944. Some 2·5 million Poles were sent to Germany as forced labourers.

Jews in Pre-war Poland

About 3·3 million Jews lived in Poland before the outbreak of the war' nearly 10 per cent of the total Polish population. More than three fourths of the Polish Jews lived in cities and towns, constituting 27 per cent of Poland's urban population. About 40 per cent were engaged in industry and handicrafts, over a third in trade and commerce, about 6 per cent in the professions. The clothing industry was largely in Jewish hands. The worldwide economic depression in the 1920s and 1930s and the active anti-Semitic policies of the Polish government combined to keep the economic level of the Jewish community low. Except for a thin stratum of wealthy and upper-middle-class Jews, the preponderant majority were lower-middle-class workers, small businessmen, and a proletariat, employed or unemployed.

The republic of Poland had come into being in 1919, after its representatives had signed a treaty with the Allied powers, promising to guarantee the civil and political equality of its minorities, to safeguard their rights as citizens and, in addition, to extend to all minorities the right to establish their own educational, religious, charitable and social institutions. From the start these guarantees were never fully implemented, and in 1934 they were completely renounced. Pogroms marked the inauguration of Poland's independence and were a recurring phenomenon in the twenty years of independent Poland. Universities and professional schools introduced a *numerus clauses* system for Jews. The government's growing control of economic life was accompanied by discriminatory regulations and restrictive practices that succeeded in impoverishing the Jewish community. The rise of Nazism in Germany and, following Marshal Piłsudski's death in 1935, Poland's accelerating fascist course brought near-disaster to the Jewish community. A torrent of anti-Semitic legislation, brutal pogroms and an official government policy of 'evacuating' the Jews from Poland overwhelmed them. In

1938 laws were enacted withdrawing Polish citizenship from Jews resident abroad.

Despite the increasingly hostile atmosphere, the Polish Jews managed to maintain a vital community, with a vast network of religious, educational, philanthropic, social and cultural institutions, without comparison elsewhere in Europe. Besides kehillot, which served the community's religious, welfare and educational needs, Polish Jews were also organized in a range of political parties. These parties put up candidates, whenever democratic elections were conducted, for the Sejm (parliament), city councils and the kehillot. With the increasing impoverishment of the Jewish community, Jewish voters shifted their support in municipal and kehilla elections in the late 1930s from the Zionist parties, which had enjoyed a majority or plurality of votes, to the Bund, which in the elections of 1938 and 1939 won an outright majority in many large cities.

Jews in Wartime Poland

With the German occupation, the Jews became isolated from the Poles. In accordance with Heydrich's instructions of 21 September 1939 to the leaders of the Einsatzgruppen, the Jews were expelled from most of the territories to be incorporated, except for Lodz. In the Generalgouvernement, Jews were expelled from small towns and villages and were forced to make their way to the large cities where they were being concentrated. (About 300,000 Jews fled into Soviet-occupied Poland.) In these larger cities, the Germans ordered the Jews to set up Jewish councils (Judenräte) to govern the Jewish communities in accordance with German instructions. A series of ordinances streamed from Governor Frank whose purpose was to isolate the Jews from the Poles and subject them to special treatment. Jews were required to wear identifying arm bands; they were subject to seizure for forced labour in camps and other German installations being constructed. They were forbidden access to certain sections of the city; they were allotted smaller food rations than the Polish population. They were subject to arbitrary terror and violence; most synagogues were destroyed; thousands of Jews were killed at random. This first period of German occupation lasted about six months.

The next period was ghettoization. The first major ghetto in which Jews were enclosed was in Lodz, on 1 May 1940. Jews were sealed within the Warsaw ghetto in November 1940. By April 1941 most Jews in the Generalgouvernement were ghettoized. After Galicia was taken by the Germans in July 1941, Jews there were subjected to the same process, and by the end of the year ghettoization was completed. During this period Jews endured hunger, disease and impressment into forced-labour brigades. It is estimated that at least half a million Jews died as a result of this policy of annihilation from 'natural causes' and of random terror.

The third stage in German anti-Jewish policy began at the end of 1941, when the death camps became operational. In December the deportation from the Wartheland to Chełmno began. In March the Jews of Lublin began to be deported to Bełżec. From July to September 1942 over 300,000 Jews were deported from Warsaw to Treblinka. Only those engaged in what German military authorities designated as essential war production were exempt from deportation. Himmler, however, ordered all Jewish workers to be replaced with Poles and all ghettos to be destroyed by the end of 1942. The process took somewhat longer. In March 1943 the Cracow ghetto was liquidated. In April the Germans undertook to liquidate the Warsaw ghetto and encountered armed resistance from the Jews. In mid-May the Warsaw ghetto was liquidated. The Lwów ghetto was liquidated in June 1943. The Lodz ghetto lasted longest – until August 1944, when the last 70,000 Jewish workers were deported.

Some Jews remained in slave-labour installations and in hiding. Some took part in the Warsaw uprising under General Bor of August 1944.

When the war ended, some 50,000 to 70,000 Polish Jews were found to have survived – in Poland, in the Polish army and in camps in Germany. About 180,000 or so were repatriated from the Soviet Union. 3 million Polish Jews had been killed.

SOVIET UNION (INCLUDING LATVIA, LITHUANIA, ESTONIA)

On 28 September 1939, when Germany and Russia divided Poland, Russia also concluded pacts with Latvia, Lithuania and Estonia, obtaining from them rights to military bases. Russia ceded Vilna, which had been part of Poland, to Lithuania, whose historic capital it had been.

On 28 June 1940 Russia occupied Bessarabia and north Bucovina, which Rumania had ceded to it under pressure. In July 1940 the three Baltic states were incorporated into the Soviet Union as individual republics and occupied by Russia. Russia's harsh policy and the deportations of large numbers of the population whom Soviet leaders regarded as political opponents intensified popular hostility to Russian occupation and rule. Consequently, in most areas from the Baltic north to the Ukrainian south, which the Germans occupied following the invasion on 22 June 1941, they were generally well received by the local populations.

Through 1941 and 1942 the Germans advanced eastwards to Leningrad (under siege from August 1941 to January 1943) in the north, Moscow, in a line south to Voronezh following the Don River to Stalingrad, and then towards the Black Sea. While the eastern portion of this territory remained a military area and subject to military administration, the western sector of German-held Russian territory, including that part of Poland earlier occupied by Russia, came under German civilian administration. Hitler appointed Alfred Rosenberg to be Reich Minister for the Occupied Eastern Territories. The Baltic countries and White Russia were incorporated into a Reich Commissariat for the Ostland, with Heinrich Lohse as Reich Commissioner, and each of the units (Latvia, Lithuania, Estonia, White Russia) with its own commissioner. To the south was the Reich Commissariat for the Ukraine, reaching as far north as Brest Litovsk and south to the Black Sea, with Erich Koch as Reich Commissioner. Jurisdictional and bureaucratic conflict in both commissariats was frequent, for besides the rivalry between Rosenberg and the two Reich Commissioners, control was variously vested in the Wehrmacht, the SS, with Göring as Plenipotentiary for the Four Year Plan, or Sauckel as Plenipotentiary for Labour Recruitment.

The Baltic countries, whose populations the Germans regarded as racially assimilable, were given a limited degree of autonomy, in contrast to the Ukraine, which was under tight German rule because its people were regarded as racially inferior. Ukrainian nationalists, disappointed by the failure of the Germans to recognize their separatist aspirations, became less enthusiastic about cooperating with the German occupation. The partisan movement, growing in both Ostland and the Ukraine, was reorganized in a military hierarchy commanded from Moscow by Red Army officers.

In January 1943, when the siege of Leningrad was lifted, the Red Army began its counter-attack, which despite reverses and heavy losses, continued to force the Germans back. By late 1944 the Germans had retreated from Russian territory.

The Jews in Pre-war USSR and Baltic Countries

USSR: According to the 1939 census, there were over 3 million Jews in the Soviet Union, about one half in the Ukraine, nearly a million in Russia proper (RSFSR), 375,000 in White Russia, with the balance in the Asiatic USSR. A relatively small number (20,000) lived in the so-called Jewish autonomous region of Biro-Bidzhan.

More than 70 per cent of Soviet Jews were wage earners (industrial workers) or salaried (white-collar and professional employees of the state or state enterprises). A substantial proportion had higher education.

After the Bolshevik Revolution, the traditional religious and communal organizations of the Jewish community were suppressed, as were also the modern Jewish national movements, Zionist and Bundist. The only form of Jewish culture permitted to the Jews was a Yiddish version of Bolshevik culture. Until the mid-1930s Yiddish schools and the publication of Yiddish books, periodicals and newspapers were permitted, but during the Great Purge these institutions were liqudated.

Jews enjoyed equal civic status in the Soviet Union, but popular anti-Semitism continued to exist, especially in the Ukraine.

Lithuania: Some 155,000 Jews made up 8 per cent of the Lithuanian population. Less than half the gainfully occupied Jews were engaged in retail trade and commerce, about 40 per cent were in industry and handicraft, 10 per cent in farming, 9 per cent in the professions.

Though Lithuania had, under the terms of the Paris peace treaty granting it sovereignty, obligated itself to guarantee civic, religious and cultural rights to its minorities, it failed to live up to this commitment. The Jews, nevertheless, maintained a rich and varied communal life, supporting internationally renowned *yeshivot* as well as excellent Yiddish and Hebrew secular school systems, and a diversified press. A range of Jewish political parties defended Jewish interests in the Lithuanian parliament, in the municipalities and in public.

Jews suffered discrimination in higher education and in employment in various professions. The rise in nationalistic feeling, engendered by Lithuanian sovereignty, and the urbanization of part of the population led to intensified anti-Semitism against Jews in business and industry.

Latvia: The more than 93,000 Jews in Latvia were less than 5 per cent of the total population. On the whole somewhat more prosperous than the Lithuanian Jews, Latvian Jews played an important role in expanding Latvia's industry. They were engaged in the production of textiles, paper, leather, tobacco and matches, flour and yeast, and in the importation of crude oil and coal. A small proportion were in banking and in the professions.

Because of the cross-cultural influences in Latvia, many Jews identified with German or Russian culture. Over 50 per cent of the Jewish schoolchildren were enrolled in schools with Russian as the language of instruction, 13 per cent were in German-language schools, over 30 per cent in Yiddish or Hebrew schools, while only 3 per cent attended Lettish-language schools. Jewish political parties, from the Aguda to the Bund, with Zionist and middle-class parties in the centre, represented Jewish group interests in the Latvian assembly. They could accomplish little, however, in the face of the accelerating fascist trend of the country during the 1930s, the suppression of parliamentary government and the abolition of school autonomy in 1934. Anti-Semitism was rampant in the streets and in economic life.

Estonia: There were only about 5,000 Jews in Estonia, less than a half of 1 per cent of the population. About half lived in the capital city of Tallinn (Reval). They were engaged in trade and industry, with about 10 per cent in the professions. Jewish religious and educational institutions existed in a considerable variety, considering the small Jewish population. Anti-Semitism was negligible.

Jews in Wartime USSR

After the Soviet occupation of eastern Poland, about 300,000 Jews fled from Nazi-held Poland eastwards. During the period of Soviet occupation of the Baltic countries, about 10,000 politically suspect Jews (along with non-Jews) were deported to slave-labour camps in Siberia and elsewhere deep in Russia. Thousands of Polish Jews who refused to give up their Polish citizenship were also sent to forced-labour camps.

With the German invasion of Russia on 22 June 1941 a few thousand young Jews in the Baltic countries joined the Red Army and another few thousand managed to flee into Russia. Most Jews in the Baltics, White Russia, the Ukraine, Bessarabia and the Crimea were caught by the German invasion, which advanced too rapidly to permit large-scale flight or systematic evacuation.

Hard upon the invading German army came the Einsatzgruppen, rounding up Jews, murdering thousands upon thousands in mass shootings at execution pits. As the Einsatzgruppen advanced, the German civilian administration moved in and set up ghettos for the remaining population in the larger Jewish cities (Vilna, Kovno, Shavli, Riga, Dvinsk, Minsk, Mohilev, Zhitomir, Berdichev) and ordered Judenräte to be organized. In some places, where massacres proceeded so rapidly, ghettos were no longer needed. In Kiev in September 1941, for instance, over 33,000 Jews were shot in two days at a ravine in outlying Babi Yar. By the end of October 1941, German statistics showed that a quarter of a million Jews had been slaughtered in the Baltic and White Russia. The Baltic and Ukrainian populations collaborated voluntarily with the Germans in murdering the Jews.

During intermittent periods between mass killings, Jews in the ghettos were exploited for slave labour and subjected to hunger and disease. In the summer of 1943 the Germans began to liquidate the surviving remnants of the ghettos (Bialystok in August; Minsk, Lida, Vilna in September; Riga in November). The ghettos in Kovno and Shavli existed until July 1944.

In most ghettos some form of resistance was organized and numbers of Jews managed to escape to join the partisan movement.

Jewish losses were well over 1 million, perhaps as high as 1·3 million. In the Baltic, about 90 per cent of the Jews were killed. Losses in Russia proper were about 100,000. In White Russia about 66 per cent and in the Ukraine about 60 per cent of the Jews were annihilated.

Appendix B   The Final Solution
in Figures

No one can establish with certitude the exact number of Jews murdered in the course of the Final Solution. The first estimate, made at the Nuremberg trials in 1945, of 5·7 million Jews killed has been shown by subsequent censuses and statistical analyses to have been remarkably accurate. The data of the 1959 census in the Soviet Union confirm the staggering Jewish losses during the Second World War.

The Jewish population figures for each country in the following table are estimates of the population within the country's borders at the time the Final Solution began to be carried out.

Estimated Number of Jews Killed in the Final Solution

Country	Estimated pre-Final Solution Population	Estimated Jewish Population Annihilated	
		Number	*Per cent*
Poland	3,300,000	3,000,000	90
Baltic countries	253,000	228,000	90
Germany/Austria	240,000	210,000	90
Protectorate	90,000	80,000	89
Slovakia	90,000	75,000	83
Greece	70,000	54,000	77
The Netherlands	140,000	105,000	75
Hungary	650,000	450,000	70
SSR White Russia	375,000	245,000	65
SSR Ukraine*	1,500,000	900,000	60
Belgium	65,000	40,000	60
Yugoslavia	43,000	26,000	60
Rumania	600,000	300,000	50
Norway	1,800	900	50
France	350,000	90,000	26
Bulgaria	64,000	14,000	22
Italy	40,000	8,000	20
Luxembourg	5,000	1,000	20
Russia (RSFSR)*	975,000	107,000	11
Denmark	8,000	—	—
Finland	2,000	—	—
Total	8,861,800	5,933,900	67

*The Germans did not occupy all the territory of this republic.

Notes

The following abbreviations have been used:

AJC-RC	American Jewish Committee, Records Center
AJDC-A	American Joint Distribution Committee, Archives
AJYB	*American Jewish Year Book*
Blfg	*Bleter far geshikhte*
BŻIH	*Biuletyn Żydowskiego Instytutu Historycznego*
DGFP	*Documents on German Foreign Policy*
IMT	International Military Tribunal, Nuremberg
JLB-A	Jewish Labour Bund, Archives
JSS	*Jewish Social Studies*
LBI-A	Leo Baeck Institute, Archives
LBI, *YB*	Leo Baeck Institute, *Year Book*
NCA	*Nazi Conspiracy and Aggression*
TMWC	*Trial of the Major War Criminals*
TWC	*Trials of War Criminals*
VfZ	*Vierteljahrshefte für Zeitgeschichte*
Y-A	YIVO Institute for Jewish Research, Archives
YiAn	*Yivo Annual of Jewish Social Science*
Yibl	*Yivo-Bleter*
YVS	*Yad Vashem Studies*

I. THE JEWS IN HITLER'S MENTAL WORLD

1. All quotations from *Mein Kampf* are from Ralph Manheim's translation (Houghton Mifflin). Because of the extensive use of this book and also of Hitler's *Secret Book*, no page references have been given. Italics in quotations from *Mein Kampf* are in the original.

2. Heiden, *Der Fuehrer*, p. 34.

3. Heiden, *Der Fuehrer*, p. 190.

4. Friedrich P. Reck-Malleczewen, *Diary of a Man in Despair*, p. 27.

5. For Hitler's early life, I have relied heavily on F. Bradley Smith's splendid study, *Adolf Hitler: His Family, Childhood and Youth*.

6. Wilfried Daim, *Der Mann, der Hitler die Ideen Gab*, passim; William A. Jenks, *Vienna and the Young Hitler*, passim.

7. Text in Ernst Deuerlein, 'Hitlers Eintritt in die Politik und die Reichswehr', *VfZ* 7 (1959): 203–5. Subsequent quotations from Hitler's early speeches are taken from the documents published here.

8. Reginald H. Phelps, 'Hitlers "Grundlegende" Rede über den Antisemitismus', *VfZ* 16 (1968): 390–420. The introduction contains an excellent analysis of the sources in conventional German anti-Semitism from which Hitler derived his ideas.

9. Reginald H. Phelps, 'Hitler als Parteiredner im Jahre 1920', *VfZ* 11 (1963): 277–8.

10. Rauschning, *Hitler Speaks*, p. 238.

11. Adolf Hitler, 'My Political Testament', *NCA*, 6, Doc. 3569-PS, pp. 258–63.

2. ANTI-SEMITISM IN MODERN GERMANY

1. For background on Germany I am indebted to the brilliant work by the late Klaus Epstein, *The Genesis of German Conservatism*.

2. Cited in George G. Iggers, *The German Conception of History: The National Tradition of Historical Thought from Herder to the Present* (Middletown, Conn., 1968), p. 41.

3. Johann Gottlieb Fichte, *Reden an die deutsche Nation* (Berlin, 1808), p. 488.

4. Mosse, *The Crisis of German Ideology*, p. 4.

5. Quoted in Kohn, *The Mind of Modern Germany*, p. 88.

6. Quoted in Adler, *The Jews in Germany*, p. 41.

7. Quoted in Ernest Hamburger, 'One Hundred Years of Emancipation', in *LBI, YB* 14, p. 11.

8. For more on the anti-Christian aspect of anti-Semitism, see Uriel Tal, *Religious and Anti-religious Roots of Modern Anti-Semitism*.

9. Quoted in Stern, *The Politics of Cultural Despair*, p. 61.

10. Quoted in the German original in Alex Bein, 'Modern Anti-Semitism and Its Effect on the Jewish Question', *YVS* 3 (1959): 14.

11. Hamburger, 'One Hundred Years of Emancipation', p. 15.

12. Massing, *Rehearsal for Destruction*, pp. 278–87.

13. Heinrich von Treitschke, 'Unsere Aussichten', in Boehlich, ed., *Der Berliner Antisemitismusstreit*, p. 113.

14. Text published in Reventlow, *Judas Kampf und Niederlage in Deutschland*, pp. 342–4; an English translation in Dawidowicz, *Holocaust Reader*.

15. Quoted in Leschnitzer, *The Magic Background of Modern Anti-Semitism*, p. 219.

16. Nahum N. Glatzer, *Leopold Zunz: Jude-Deutscher-Europäer* (Tübingen, 1964), p. 470. Dr Fred Grubel called this letter to my attention.

17. Massing, *Rehearsal for Destruction*, pp. 300–305.

18. Quoted in Stern, *The Politics of Cultural Despair*, p. 91.

19. Mosse, *The Crisis of German Ideology*, p. 144.

20. Mosse, *The Crisis of German Ideology*, p. 268.

21. Quoted in Cohn, *Warrant for Genocide*, p. 136.

22. cf. Peter Gay, *Weimar Culture*, especially Chapter 3.

3. PHASE ONE: ANTI-JEWISH LEGISLATION, 1933–5

1. Quoted in Martin Broszat, 'The Concentration Camps: 1933–1945', in Buchheim et al., *Anatomy of the SS State*, p. 405.

2. Joseph Goebbels, *My Part in Germany's Fight* (London, 1935), pp. 269–70.

3. Ernst Herzfeld, 'Meine Letzten Jahre in Deutschland, 1933–1938', LBI-A, Memoir Collection, p. 4.

4. AJC-RC, 'Jews in Germany, 1933'.

5. Allen, *The Nazi Seizure of Power*, pp. 210–11.

6. *Dokumente der deutschen Politik und Geschichte*, 4: 147–8.

7. *DGFP*, Series C, 1, Doc. No. 141, pp. 253–5.

8. Pfundtner, ed., *Dr. Wilhelm Frick und sein Ministerium*, pp. 180–81.

9. Heiden, *Der Fuehrer*, pp. 403–4, 407.

10. Fryman [Class], *Wenn ich der Kaiser wär'*, p. 76.

11. Bracher, Sauer, Schulz, *Die nationalsozialistische Machtergreifung*, p. 280.

12. Schleunes, *The Twisted Road to Auschwitz*, p. 70. Originally a doctoral dissertation, this study attempts to trace the evolution of Nazi Germany's anti-Jewish policies up to 1938. Schleunes found much interesting archival material, but failed to place it in any intelligible framework. His only reference to *Mein Kampf* is to dismiss it as an inadequate 'reflection' of German–Jewish relations.

13. Nicolai, *Die rassengesetzliche Staatslehre*, p. 51.

14. Nicolai, *Rasse und Recht*, p. 5.

15. All laws are cited from Hoche, ed., *Die Gesetzgebung Adolf Hitlers*. For an English translation of selected laws, see Dawidowicz, *Holocaust Reader*.

16. cf. Salo W. Baron, 'The Impact of the Revolution of 1848 on Jewish Emancipation', *JSS* 11 (1949): 210.

17. Gottfried zur Beek, *Die Geheimnisse der Weisen von Zion*, p. 236.

18. Fryman, *Wenn ich der Kaiser wär'*, pp. 75–6.

19. *DGFP*, Series C, 4:568–70.

20. Kommission zur Erforschung . . . , *Dokumente zur Geschichte der Frankfurter Juden 1933–1945*, pp. 216–17.

21. 'The Racists' Decalogue', in Massing, *Rehearsal for Destruction*, pp. 306–7.

22. *AJYB* 36:174.

23. Kommission zur Erforschung . . . , *Dokumente zur Geschichte der Frankfurter Juden 1933–1945*, pp. 217–18.

24. cf. Bernhard Lösener, 'Das Reichsministerium des Innern und die Judengesetzgebung', *VfZ* 9 (1961).

25. Stuckart and Globke, *Kommentare zur deutschen Rassengesetzgebung*, 1:12–13.

26. Domarus, *Hitler: Reden und Proklamationen*, 1:537.

4. THE SS: INSTRUMENT OF THE FINAL SOLUTION

1. Quoted in Höhne, *The Order of the Death's Head*, p. 327.

2. Buchheim, 'The SS – Instrument of Domination', *Anatomy of the SS State*, pp. 139–40.

3. Smith, *Heinrich Himmler*, pp. 72–6, 91–2, 121–4, 141–8. The passages that follow in the text are drawn from this excellent study of the young Himmler.

4. Höhne, *The Order of the Death's Head*, p. 59.

5. See Larry V. Thompson, '*Lebensborn* and the Eugenics Policy of the Reichsführer-SS', *Central European History* 4 (1971): 54–77.

6. Martin Broszat, 'The Concentration Camps: 1933–1945', in Buchheim et al., *Anatomy of the SS State*, p. 402. The following pages in the text are based on this study.

7. Aronson, *Reinhard Heydrich und die Frühgeschichte von Gestapo und SD*, is the best source for biographical data on Heydrich. I have drawn from this excellent book for the material on Heydrich and also for the early history of the SD.

8. Höhne, *The Order of the Death's Head*, pp. 170 ff. The following section of the text is based largely on this well-documented journalistic account of the SS and on the scholarly study by Buchheim, cited in note 2.

9. Domarus, *Hitler: Reden und Proklamationen*, 1:624–5.

10. 'Report of SS-Oberscharführer Schröder on the Status of Pro-

jects in II-112', 28 August 1936, in Aronson, *Reinhard Heydrich*, pp. 327–8.

11. Aronson, *Reinhard Heydrich*, pp. 174–7.

12. The text is published in Hans Mommsen, 'Der nationalsozialistische Polizeistaat und die Judenverfolgung vor 1938', *VfZ* 10 (1962): 77–8.

13. Arthur Prinz, 'The Role of the Gestapo in Obstructing and Promoting Jewish Emigration', *YVS* 2 (1958): 205–8.

14. DGFP, Series C, 1:661–2, 732–6. See also Ernst Marcus, 'The German Foreign Office and the Palestine Question in the Period 1933–1939', *YVS* 2 (1958): 179–204.

15. R. Melka, 'Nazi Germany and the Palestine Question', *Middle Eastern Studies* 5 (1969): 221.

16. Quoted in Hans Lamm, 'Uber die innere und äussere Entwicklung des deutschen Judentums im Dritten Reich', p. 47.

17. Quoted in Schleunes, *The Twisted Road to Auschwitz*, pp. 177–8, from a document in the Himmler records at the National Archives. Unfortunately Schleunes has not indicated in which SS division the report was prepared.

18. Mommsen, 'Der nationalsozialistische Polizeistaat', pp. 78–9.

19. Schleunes, *The Twisted Road to Auschwitz*, p. 193. The directive has not been identified as to departmental origin, city or jurisdiction and lacks the exact date.

20. Schleunes, *The Twisted Road to Auschwitz*, p. 194.

21. Melka, 'Nazi Germany and the Palestine Question', p. 222.

22. Melka, 'Nazi Germany and the Palestine Question', pp. 222–3.

23. Interview with Dr Max Gruenewald, New York, 1 February 1973.

24. See note 10.

25. *TMWC*, 29, Doc. 1992 [A]-PS, pp. 206–34.

26. Himmler, *Die Schutzstaffel als antibolschewistische Kampforganisation*, p. 29.

5. FOREIGN POLICY, RACE AND WAR

1. Quoted in Heiden, *Der Fuehrer*, p. 415.

2. Rauschning, *The Voice of Destruction*, p. 6.

3. G. Weinberg, 'National Socialist Organization and Foreign Policy Aims in 1927', *Journal of Modern History* 36 (1964): 434.

4. Mitscherlich and Mielke, *Doctors of Infamy*, p. 91.

5. Helmut Krausnick, 'Judenverfolgung', in Buchheim et al., *Anatomie des SS-Staates*, 2:325. This passage was egregiously mistranslated in the English version. The mistake has, unfortunately, been perpetuated in Bracher, *The German Dictatorship* (p. 336), and in the article 'Ghetto' in the *Encyclopedia Judaica*.

6. Bernhard Lösener, 'Das Reichsministerium des Innern und die Judengesetzgebung', *VfZ* 9 (1961): 281.

7. *DGFP*, Series C, 5:853–62.

8. Rauschning, *The Voice of Destruction*, p. 28.

9. Text in Kotze and Krausnick, *Es spricht der Führer*, pp. 147–8.

10. Domarus, *Hitler: Reden und Proklamationen*, 1:727–8.

11. *NCA*, 3, Doc. 386-PS, pp. 295–305; Domarus, *Hitler*, 1:748–56.

12. Quoted in Schleunes, *The Twisted Road to Auschwitz*, p. 219.

13. Quoted in Genschel, *Die Verdrängung der Juden aus der Wirtschaft im Dritten Reich*, p. 150.

14. Hoche, ed., *Die Gesetzgebung Adolf Hitler*, 27:323. For an English translation, see Dawidowicz, *Holocaust Reader*.

15. *DGFP*, Series D, 1:900–901.

16. Fromm, *Blood and Banquets*, p. 274.

17. Martin Broszat, 'The Concentration Camps: 1933–1945', in Buchheim et al.; *Anatomy of the SS State*, pp. 453–5.

18. Gordon, *Hitler and the Beer Hall Putsch*, pp. 266–7.

19. Arthur Prinz, 'The Role of the Gestapo in Obstructing and Promoting Jewish Emigration', *YVS* 2 (1958): 211.

20. Kochan, *Pogrom: 10 November 1938*, p. 34.

21. Graml, *Der 9. November 1938: 'Reichskristallnacht'*, pp. 17–22.

22. Kochan, *Pogrom*, p. 51.

23. *TMWC*, 32, Doc. 3063-PS, pp. 20–29.

24. *TMWC*, 31, Doc. 3051-PS, pp. 515–19.

25. *TMWC*, 28, Doc. 1816-PS, pp. 499–540; also *NCA* 4:425–57.

26. Kommission zur Erforschung . . . , *Dokumente zur Geschichte der Frankfurter Juden 1933–1945*, pp. 196–8.

27. *NCA*, 3, Doc. 841-PS, 606–8.

28. Text in Genschel, *Die Verdrängung der Juden*, p. 300; also IMT Docs. 1662-PS and 2875-PS (identical texts).

29. Genschel, *Die Verdrängung der Juden*, p. 299; also IMT Doc. 1412-PS. For an English translation, see Dawidowicz, *Holocaust Reader*.

30. *TMWC*, 32, Doc. 3575-PS, 411–15.

31. *Dokumente zur Geschichte der Frankfurter Juden*, p. 198.

32. Hoche, *Gesetzgebung*, 32:69–72.

33. Shaul Esh, 'The Establishment of the "Reichsvereinigung der Juden in Deutschland" and its Main Activities', *YVS* 7 (1968): 19–38.

34. *DGFP*, Series D, 5:933–6.

35. Quoted in Krausnick, 'The Persecution of the Jews', in Buchheim et al., *Anatomy of the SS State*, p. 44.

36. Domarus, *Hitler*, 2:1058.

6. PHASE TWO: FROM INTERNAL WAR TO WORLD WAR

1. Goerlitz, *History of the German General Staff 1657–1945*, p. 345.

2. Sontag and Beddie, *Nazi–Soviet Relations: 1939–1941*, pp. 1–2.

3. Churchill, *The Gathering Storm*, p. 370.

4. *DGFP*, Series D, 6, No. 433, pp. 574–80.

5. Halder, *Kriegstagebuch 1939–1942*, 1:38.

6. Domarus, *Hitler: Reden und Proklamationen*, 2:1315.

7. Domarus, *Hitler*, in order, pp. 1663, 1828–9, 1920, 1937.

8. *DGFP*, Series D, 8:164–7.

9. Broszat, *Nationalsozialistische Polenpolitik 1939–1945*, p. 22; *TMWC*, 26, Doc. 864-PS, 377–83.

10. *TMWC*, 20:211–19.

11. Quoted in Messerschmidt, *Die Wehrmacht im NS-Staat*, p. 354.

12. Minutes, dated 21 September 1939, of Heydrich's staff meeting, Berlin, 19 September 1939; copy from the Institut für Zeitgeschichte.

13. Halder, *Kriegstagebuch*, 1:79.

14. Minutes, dated 27 September 1939, of Heydrich staff conference with Einsatzgruppen chiefs, 21 September 1939. Copy from the Institut für Zeitgeschichte; express letter of Heydrich to chiefs of Einsatzgruppen regarding the 'Jewish question in the occupied territory', 21 September 1939 (IMT Doc. 3363-PS), full German text in *Yibl* (1947), pp. 163–8; English text in Dawidowicz, *Holocaust Reader*. The army was informed of these plans on 20 September; see Halder, *Kriegstagebuch*, 1:81–2.

15. Arendt, *Eichmann in Jerusalem*, pp. 77–8.

16. Shaul Esh, 'Tachnit-av lehakikat hanazim neged hayehudim', *Ha'aretz*, 1 April 1963, p. 7.

17. The most thorough discussion and analysis of the so-called Lublin reservation is Philip Friedman, 'The Lublin Reservation and the Madagascar Plan', *YiAn*, Vol. 8.

18. H. Kr., 'Denkschrift Himmlers über die Behandlung der Fremdvölkischen im Osten', *VfZ* 5 (1957): 197.

19. I. Trunk, 'Shtudye tsu der geshikhte fun yidn in varteland', *Blfg* 2 (1949): 81.

20. IMT Doc. 864-PS (see note 9, above). Keitel briefed his generals on this conference. Cf. Halder, *Kriegstagebuch*, 1:107.

21. Goerlitz, *History of the German General Staff 1657–1945*, pp. 380, 385.

22. Görlitz, ed., *The Memoirs of Field-Marshal Keitel*, p. 137.

23. *TMWC*, 26, Doc. 447-PS, pp. 53–8; English text in Dawidowicz, *Holocaust Reader*.

24. Warlimont, *Inside Hitler's Headquarters 1939–1945*, pp. 150–52, 608.

25. Görlitz, ed., *Memoirs of Keitel*, p. 136.

26. Hoess, *Commandant of Auschwitz*, pp. 125–6, 231–2.

27. Halder, *Kriegstagebuch*, 2:336–7.

28. Keitel, in Görlitz, ed., *Memoirs of Keitel*, p. 136.

29. IMT Doc. C-050, in Jacobsen, 'Kommissarbefehl ...', in Buchheim et al., *Anatomie des SS-Staates*, 2:216–18.

30. Jacobsen, 'Kommissarbefehl ...', 2:225–7; IMT Doc. NOKW 1076.

31. IMT Doc NOKW 1692, in Jacobsen, 'Kommissarbefehl ...', 2:223.

32. IMT Doc. 878-PS, in Jacobsen, 'Kommissarbefehl ...', 2:250; *NCA* 3:636.

33. *TMWC*, 35, Doc. D-411, pp. 81–5; English text in Dawidowicz, *Holocaust Reader*.

34. Höhne, *The Order of the Death's Head*, p. 358.

35. *TMWC*, 38, Doc. L-180, pp. 670–717; *TMWC*, 30, IMT Doc. 2271-PS, p. 73.

36. The fullest sources regarding the operations of the Einsatzgruppen in Russia are *TWC*, 4, Case No. 9, *Einsatzgruppen Case*; Hilberg, *The Destruction of the European Jews*; Reitlinger, *The Final Solution*.

37. Affidavit by Otto Ohlendorf, 5 November 1945, *NCA*, 5, Doc. 2620-PS, p. 342.

38. Jäger report, Einsatzkommando No. 3, Kovno, 1 December 1941, in Hilberg, *Documents of Destruction*, pp. 56–7. Photostat of the original document, held by the USSR, in the Institut für Zeitgeschichte, Munich.

39. Y-A, 'Raport Bundu w sprawie prześladowań Żydów', May 1942; for an English translation, see Dawidowicz, *Holocaust Reader*.

7. THE ANNIHILATION CAMPS: KINGDOM OF DEATH

1. Höss testimony, *TMWC* 2:398, 416. See also his autobiography, *Commandant of Auschwitz*, pp. 160, 205.

2. Ohlendorf's testimony, *TMWC* 4: 318; also his testimony in *Einsatzgruppen Case*, p. 251.

3. Letter to Gottlob Berger, 28 July 1942 (NO–626), in Heiber, ed., *Reichsführer!*, p. 134. Similar admissions appear in *The Memoirs of Doctor Felix Kersten* (New York, 1947), pp. 174–5, 234. See also the affidavits by Konrad Morgen, 13 July and 19 July, SS–65, SS–67, *TMWC* 42:551–65, quoting Reich Physician-SS Dr Ernst Robert Grawitz to the effect that Hitler had given Himmler the order and the responsibility to destroy the Jews.

4. *TMWC*, 26, Doc. 710-PS, pp. 266–7; English text in Dawidowicz, *Holocaust Reader*.

5. Klaus Dörner, 'Nationalsozialismus und Lebensvernichtung', *VfZ* 15 (1967): 140. I have relied heavily on this splendid study about bio-racial killing.

6. *TWC*, Case No. 1, *The Medical Case*, 1, Doc. 630-PS, p. 848.

7. *TWC*, Case No. 1, *The Medical Case*, 1, testimony of Victor Brack, pp. 843–4.

8. *TWC*, Case No. 1, *The Medical Case*, 1, p. 877.

9. *TWC*, Case No. 1, *The Medical Case*, 1, Himmler to Brack, 19 December 1940 (Doc. No–018), p. 856; letter dated 13 August 1941, from the Bishop of Limburg to the Minister of Justice (Doc. 615-PS), pp. 845–7.

10. Helmut Krausnick, 'The Persecution of the Jews', in Buchheim et al., *Anatomy of the SS State*, p. 97. See also *TWC*, *The Medical Case*, 1, Doc. NO–205, pp. 721–2. Brack, in a letter to Himmler, 23 June 1942, advocating mass sterilization of two to three million Jews still fit to work, wrote:

'On the instructions of Reichsleiter Bouhler I placed some of my men – already some time ago – at the disposal of Brigadeführer Globocnik to execute his special mission. On his renewed request I have now transferred additional personnel. On this occasion, Brigadeführer Globocnik stated his opinion that the whole Jewish action should be completed as quickly as possible so that one would not get caught in the middle of it one day if some difficulties should necessitate a halt of the action.'

11. Höss, *Commandant of Auschwitz*, p. 262.

12. Henkys, *Die nationalsozialistischen Gewaltverbrechen*, pp. 64, 95, 245, 246.

492 Notes to pp. 175–86

13. Mitscherlich and Mielke, *Doctors of Infamy*, p. 114.

14. *TWC*, *The Medical Case*, 1, Docs. NO-365 and NO-997, pp. 870–71, 887–8, draft letters from Rosenberg's Ministry for the Occupied Eastern Territories, October 1941.

15. Höss, *Commandant of Auschwitz*, p. 163.

16. Affidavit of Karl Rudolf Werner Braune, *TWC* 4:215.

17. Minutes of the Wannsee Conference IMT Doc. NG-2586-G, *TWC*, Case No. 11, *Ministries Case*; German original published in full in Kempner, *Eichmann und Komplizen*, pp. 133–47; English text in Dawidowicz, *Holocaust Reader*.

18. Seabury, *The Wilhelmstrasse*, pp. 126, 128–9.

19. Himmler to Krüger, 19 July 1942, NO-5574; English text in Dawidowicz, *Holocaust Reader*.

20. Piotrowski, ed., *Hans Frank's Diary*, pp. 256–7.

21. Krausnick, 'The Persecution of the Jews', p. 104; Berenstein et al., *Eksterminacja Żydów*, No. 157, p. 297; Eichmann trial document 1253, Ganzenmüller to Wolf [*sic*], 28 July 1942.

22. Quoted in Hilberg, *The Destruction of the European Jews*, p. 314.

23. IMT Doc. NO-2405; Berenstein et al., *Eksterminacja Żydów*, p. 320.

24. *NCA*, 8, Dieter Wisliceny, Affidavit C, 29 November 1945, pp. 612–13. For more, see correspondence of Edmund Veesenmayer, Reich Plenipotentiary in Hungary, with Eichmann et al., on the need for railway cars, in Randolph Braham, ed., *The Destruction of Hungarian Jewry*, 1:346–51, 367–71.

25. For more on how these racial policies in the occupied Eastern areas were applied and their cost in military terms, see the impressive work by Dallin, *German Rule in Russia*; also Koehl, *RKFDV*. Two interesting documents are IMT Doc. 2220-PS, a memorandum by HSSPF Lieutenant General Krüger, 12 April 1943 on failures in the administration policy of the Generalgouvernement, *NCA* 4:855–60; and IMT Doc. 054-PS, a memorandum of 7 October 1942 on the mistreatment of Ukrainian workers in Germany and the impact on the occupied population, *NCA* 3:90–99.

26. Helmut Heiber, 'Der Generalplan Ost', *VfZ* 6 (1958): 291–2.

27. *TMWC*, 38, Doc. L-180, p. 986.

28. *TMWC*, 30, Doc. 2271-PS, p. 76.

29. *TMWC*, 32, Doc. 3663-PS, pp. 435–6; English text in Dawidowicz, *Holocaust Reader*.

30. Lageberichte, Distrikt Galizien, 29 August 1942, in Philip Friedman, 'Hurban yehude Ivov betkufat 1941–1944', in N. M. Gelber,

ed., *Lvov: Entziklopedya shel galuyot* (Jerusalem 1956), pp. 745–6.

31. M. Shatner, 'Khurbn pshemishl', in Menczer, ed., *Przemyśl Memorial Book* (Sefer *Pshemishl*), p. 512.

32. Cf. A. Eisenbach, 'Di felkeroysrotung-politik fun daytshn imperyalizm...', *Blfg* 3 (July–December 1950): 44–6.

33. Quoted in Krausnick, 'The Persecution of the Jews', p. 107; in the German edition, 2:424–5.

34. Krausnick, 'The Persecution of the Jews', pp. 108–10; in German edition, 2:426–8; the English translation is neither accurate nor complete. For a full English version, see Dawidowicz, *Holocaust Reader*.

35. Doc. NO-1611, Himmler to Pohl, Krüger, Globocnik; English text in Dawidowicz, *Holocaust Reader*.

36. Doc. NOKW-134, National Archives.

37. National Archives, T-77, Roll 620, Wi/ID1.26; Roll 621, Wi/ID1.13; MA 285, pp. 2927–8.

38. For documents relating to Operation Reinhard, see Schnabel, *Macht ohne Moral*, pp. 441–57. See also *TMWC*, 34, Doc. 4024-PS, pp. 58–92.

39. Deposition of Kurt Gerstein, *Le Monde juif*, 19, January–March 1964; English text in Dawidowicz, *Holocaust Reader*.

40. Quoted in Naumann, *Auschwitz*, pp. 177–8.

41. *TMWC*, 29, Doc. 1919-PS, pp. 110–73; excerpts in English translation in Dawidowicz, *Holocaust Reader*.

8. A RETROSPECTIVE VIEW

1. E. Deuerlein, 'Hitlers Eintritt in die Politik...', *VfZ* 7 (1959): p. 199.

2. The Reichswehr reports of Hitler's speeches were published by Deuerlein, 'Hitlers Eintritt'; the Bavarian police reports were published by Reginold H. Phelps, 'Hitler als Parteiredner', *VfZ*, Vol. II (1963).

3. Deuerlein, 'Hitlers Eintritt', p. 212; Phelps, 'Hitler als Parteiredner', p. 301. Deuerlein's document dates the meeting 29 April 1920; Phelps has corrected this.

4. Baynes, ed., *The Speeches of Adolf Hitler*, 1:14.

5. Ludecke, *I Knew Hitler*, p. 72.

6. Gordon, *Hitler and the Beer Hall Putsch*, pp. 265–307.

7. Bayerisches Hauptstaatsarchiv München, Abt. II, Geheimes Staatsarchiv, MA 103 476, pp. 1169–79. I am indebted to Professor

Harold J. Gordon, Jr, for his helpfulness in providing the documentation that enabled me to obtain a copy of the constitution. Paragraph 14 (p. 1173) provided for the expropriation of the Jews; Paragraph 14a expropriated those 'who profited from the distress of the German people during the war', a fine legal category; Paragraph 15 provided the death penalty for evasion of expropriation; Paragraph 16 (p. 1174) provided for the round-up of persons and the establishment of concentration camps.

8. Quoted in Heiden, *Der Fuehrer*, p. 118.

9. Professor Jäckel, in his incisive book, *Hitler's Weltanschauung*, argues that Hitler first advocated the physical liquidation of the Jews in *Mein Kampf*. One piece of evidence that he adduces in support of his view is a statement that Hitler made in an interview while in Landsberg, to the effect that his past methods in fighting the Jews had been too soft and 'that in the future the most severe methods of fighting will have to be used' (p. 57). Actually Hitler had always stressed the need for the most ruthless methods in confronting the enemy. If indeed he meant anything specific at this time, he may have been referring to tactics rather than goals.

10. Kotze and Krausnick, *Es spricht der Führer*, p. 154.

11. *DGFP*, Series D, 6:580.

12. Domarus, ed., *Hitler: Reden und Proklamationen*, 1:537.

13. *DGFP*, Series C, 5:855.

14. Blumental et al., *Dokumenty i Materiały*, 3:31.

15. *TMWC* 29:415.

16. Blumental et al., *Dokumenty i Materiały*, 3:192; text in *Biuletyn Głownej Komisji Badania Zbrodni Niemieckich (Hitlerowskich) w Polsce*, Warsaw, Vol. 13, Document 28, pp. 27F–29F.

17. Cf. Deuerlein, 'Hitlers Eintritt'; and Phelps, 'Hitler als Parteiredner', pp. 274–330.

18. Abel, *The Nazi Movement: Why Hitler Came to Power*, pp. 155–6. This book is primarily an analysis of 600 autobiographies written by members of the NSDAP in 1934.

19. For a pentrating psychoanalytic study, see Ernst Simmel, 'Anti-Semitism and Mass Psychopathology', in his *Anti-Semitism: A Social Disease* (New York, 1946). Also suggestive is Martin Wangh, 'National Socialism and the Genocide of the Jews', *International Journal of Psycho-Analysis* 45 (1964): 386–95. A pioneering study of the psychological origins of the National Socialist movement is Peter Loewenberg, 'The Psychohistorical Origins of the Nazi Youth Cohort', *American Historical Review* 76 (December, 1971): 1457–1502.

20. For more on the relationship between witchcraft and modern anti-Semitism, see Leschnitzer, *The Magic Background of Modern Anti-Semitism*, and Joshua Trachtenberg, *The Devil and the Jews* (Cleveland and New York, 1961). For perspective on National Socialist anti-Semitism in the light of medieval millenarians, see Norman Cohn, *The Pursuit of the Millennium* (New York, 1961).

21. Ernst Hiemer, *Der Giftpilz* (Nuremberg, 1938).

22. Curzio Malaparte, *Kaputt* (New York, 1946), p. 91.

23. Trevor-Roper, ed., *Hitler's War Directives*, p. 212.

24. Quoted in Buchheim, 'Command and Compliance', *Anatomy of the SS State*, p. 338.

9. BETWEEN FREEDOM AND GHETTO: THE JEWS IN GERMANY, 1933–8

1. The sources differ as to the occasion; some refer to a meeting of the Gemeinden, 13 April 1933; others cite the first meeting of the Reichsvertretung in September 1933.

2. The authority on Jewish defence during the Weimar Republic is Arnold Paucker, whose study 'Der jüdische Abwehrkampf', in Mosse and Paucker, eds., *Entscheidungsjahr 1932*, pp. 405–99, was later expanded into a book, *Der jüdische Abwehrkampf in den letzten Jahren der Weimarer Republik* (Hamburg, 1968). See also his 'Jewish Defence Against Nazism in the Weimar Republic', *The Wiener Library Bulletin* 26 (1972): 21–31.

3. Esra Bennathan, 'Die demographische und wirtschaftliche Struktur der Juden', in Mosse and Paucker, *Entscheidungsjahr 1932*, pp. 87–131.

4. Hilde Ottenheimer, 'The Disappearance of Jewish Communities in Germany, 1900–1938', *JSS* 3 (1941): 191.

5. *AJYB*, 39:336–7; 36:158–60; Zvi Asaria, *Die Juden in Köln* (Cologne, 1959), p. 332.

6. Werner Rosenstock, 'Exodus 1933–1939', LBI, *YB* 1 (1956): 373–90.

7. Bruno Weil, *Der Weg der deutschen Juden* (Berlin, 1935); English translation quoted from AJC Office Report, 21 February 1935, AJC-RC, 'Jews in Germany 1935'.

8. Heinz Kellermann, 'Ende der Emanzipation?', *Der Morgen* 9 (August, 1933): 173–7.

9. Messerschmidt, *Die Wehrmacht im NS-Staat*, p. 45; Leo Lowen-

stein, 'Die Linie des Reichsbundes jüdischer Frontsoldaten', in *Wille und Weg des deutschen Judentums*, pp. 7–11.

10. Quoted in Wolfgang Hamburger, 'The Reactions of Reform Jews to the Nazi Rule', in Strauss and Grossmann, *Gegenwart im Rückblick*, pp. 154, 160–62.

11. Heinrich Stern, 'Die inneren Voraussetzungen für Hilfe und Aufbau in deutschen Judentum', *Der Morgen* 9 (August 1933): 165–72.

12. Hans Joachim Schoeps, 'Der Deutsche Vortrupp – der Ort geschichtlicher Besinnung', in *Wille und Weg*, p. 55; Schoeps, 'Wir gehen einen deutschen Weg', *C-V Zeitung*, 13 July 1933, p. 275; Schoeps, *Die letzten dreissig Jahre*, p. 101.

13. *Jüdische Rundschau*, 4 April 1933; quoted from the English translation by Harry Zohn in Nahum N. Glatzer, *The Dynamics of Emancipation* (Boston, 1965), pp. 104–8; also in Dawidowicz, *Holocaust Reader*.

14. *3 Jahre Zionistische Bewegung*, passim.

15. 'Eine Erklärung der deutschen Rabbiner', *Gemeindeblatt der Synagogen-Gemeinde zu Köln a/Rh.*, 31 March 1933, reproduced in Asaria, *Die Juden in Köln*, p. 329.

16. Leo Baeck, 'Das Judentum in der Gegenwart', *Der Morgen* 8 (1933): 237–40.

17. Martin Buber, *Die Stunde und die Erkenntnis: Reden und Aufsätze*, especially 'Das Erste' and 'Erkenntnis tut Not'.

18. Ernst Simon, 'Von Palestina nach Deutschland: Eindrücke und Besinnung einer jüdischen Reise', *Der Morgen* 10 (1934): 115; Joachim Prinz, 'A Rabbi under the Hitler Regime', in Strauss and Grossmann, *Gegenwart im Rückblick*, pp. 231–8; Max Gruenewald, 'Education and Culture of the German Jews under Nazi Rule', *Jewish Review* 5 (1948): 81.

19. Willy Mainz, in Ball-Kaduri, *Das Leben der Juden in Deutschland im Jahre 1933*, pp. 133–4; Isi Jacob Eisner, 'Reminiscences of the Berlin Rabbinical Seminary', LBI, *YB* 12 (1967): 46–7; Michael L. Munk, 'Austrittsbewegung und Berliner Adass Jisroel-Gemeinde 1869–1939', in Strauss and Grossman, *Gegenwart im Rückblick*, pp. 146–7; Yehiel Jacob Weinberg, *Seride Esh* (Jerusalem, 1961), pp. 3–7; conversation with Dr Alexander Altmann, 8 February 1973; interview with Josef Kalter, 5 February 1973.

20. Ernst Simon, 'Jewish Adult Education in Nazi Germany as Spiritual Resistance', LBI, *YB* 1 (1956): 92.

21. Herbert Freeden, 'A Jewish Theatre under the Swastika', LBI, *YB* 1 (1956): 142–62.

22. Ball-Kaduri, *Das Leben der Juden*, p. 34.

23. Dr [Julius] Blau, *Zur Geschichte der Reichsvertretung* (Frankfurt/M, December 1937), typescript, LBI-A; Max Gruenewald, 'The Beginning of the "Reichsvertretung"', LBI, *YB* 1 (1956): 51–67; Hugo Hahn, 'Die Gründung der Reichsvertretung', in Tramer, *In zwei Welten*, pp. 97–105; Kurt Lowenstein, 'Die innerjüdische Reaktion auf die Krise der deutschen Demokratie', in Mosse and Paucker, *Entscheidungsjahr 1932*, pp. 401–3; *AJYB* 34 (1932–3): 58–9; K. Y. Ball-Kaduri, 'The National Representation of Jews in Germany', *YVS* 2 (1959): 159–78; Ernst Herzfeld, 'Meine letzten Jahre in Deutschland, 1933–1938', LBI-A, Memoir Collection.

24. Friedrich Brodnitz, 'Zentralausschuss der deutschen Juden für Hilfe und Aurbau', *Der Morgen* 8 (1933): 276–9; the JDC Archives contain a wealth of correspondence and reports of the Zentralausschuss and also a complete file of its newsletter, *Informationsblätter*.

25. AJDC-A, 'Germany: General and Emergency, 1933': 'Bemerkungen zu einem wirtschaftlichen Verhandlungsprogramm', proposed by Dr Werner Senator, 15 August 1933 (3 pp.); 'Entwurf von Thesen betr. Wirtschaftsfragen der deutschen Juden', attached; Werner Senator, on letterhead of Jewish Agency for Palestine, Jerusalem, 1 October 1933, to J. C. Hyman, AJDC, New York (3 pp.).

26. These minutes (7 typescript pp.), as well as related documents of less substantive interest, are in the Martin Buber Archives (Ms. Var. 350), at the Jewish National and University Library, Jerusalem.

27. At the second meeting of the Homburg Circle; see note 26.

28. *AJYB* 36:179, 182, *Informationsblätter*, March–April 1936, p. 25.

29. Otto Hirsch, 'Die Reichsvertretung der deutschen Juden', *Der Morgen* 9 (1934): 437–9.

30. Notes by Julius Brodnitz, in Ernst Herzfeld, 'Meine letzten Jahre', pp. 17–18.

31. Published as an announcement of the Reichsvertretung, *Jüdische Rundschau*, 3 November 1933.

32. Franz Meyer, 'Bemerkungen zu den "Zwei Denkschriften"', in Tramer, *In zwei Welten*, pp. 114–27, gives the complete text of the document (pp. 120–23). For an English translation, see Dawidowicz, *Holocaust Reader*. Apart from attributing its authorship to Georg Landauer, a ZVfD leader, Meyer does not give any information about the document, except to say that it was given to him in the strictest confidence.

33. Nathan Feinberg, 'Jewish Political Activities against the Nazi Régime', in Conference on Manifestations of Jewish Resistance, *Jewish*

Resistance During the Holocaust: Proceedings, pp. 74–93; see also Oscar I. Janowsky and Melvin M. Fagen, *International Aspects of German Racial Policies* (New York, 1937).

34. *AJYB* 36:175; interview with Dr Friedrich Brodnitz, 27 February 1973; the text of the memorandum is published in Franz Meyer, 'Bemerkungen', in Tramer, *In zwei Welten*, pp. 124–7; for an English translation, see Dawidowicz, *Holocaust Reader*.

35. See note 25.

36. A. Szanto, 'Economic Aid in the Nazi Era', LBI, *YB* 4 (1959): 208–19; Rudolph Stahl, 'Vocational Retraining of Jews in Nazi Germany 1933–1938', *JSS* 1 (1939): 169–94.

37. *Sonderbeilage zur Jüdisch-liberale Zeitung*, No. 35/36; LBI-A, 'Reichsvertretung', AR-C.A. 103, 31/221. Ernst Herzfeld, in 'Meine letzten Jahre', characterized the protest as quixotic.

38. Richard Fuchs, 'The "Hochschule für die Wissenschaft des Judentums" in the Period of Nazi Rule', LBI, *YB* 12 (1967): 3–31.

39. cf. Colodner, *Jewish Education in Germany under the Nazis*, passim.

40. Buber, *Die Stunde und die Erkenntnis*, pp. 128–30; an English translation in Dawidowicz, *Holocaust Reader*.

41. Fritz Friedlander, 'Trials and Tribulations of Jewish Education in Nazi Germany', LBI, *YB* 3 (1958): 191–2.

42. 'Jüdische Erwachsenenbildung', in Buber, *Die Stunde und die Erkenntnis*, pp. 111–12; an English translation in Dawidowicz, *Holocaust Reader*.

43. Ernst Simon, 'Jewish Adult Education', passim.

44. Georg Lubinsky, quoted in Ball-Kaduri, 'The National Representation of Jews in Germany', *YVS* 2 (1959): 174.

45. Rosenstock, 'Exodus 1933–1939'.

46. Ball-Kaduri, *Vor der Katastrophe*, p. 42.

47. Translation of a memo by officers of the Hilfsverein der deutschen Juden, Berlin, April 1934, to Dr B. Kahn, AJDC-A, 'Germany: General and Emergency: Emigration 1933–1937'.

48. cf. 'Die Agudas Jisroel und die Auswanderung', *Der Israelit*, 18 November 1937.

49. Central Bureau for the Settlement of German Jews (JAFP), *Report to the XIXth Zionist Congress and to the IVth Council of the Jewish Agency in Lucerne*, London, July 1935, pp. 6, 21.

50. Landauer, *Der Zionismus im Wandel*, pp. 13–46 and passim.

51. Yisrael Gutman, in Conference on Manifestations of Jewish Resistance, *Jewish Resistance*, p. 115.

52. The text of the memorandum is published in S. Adler-Rudel, 'The Evian Conference on the Refugee Question', LBI, *YB* 13 (1968): 261–71.

53. Ball-Kaduri, *Vor der Katastrophe*, pp. 41–2; Kurt R. Grossman, 'Deutsche Juden auf der Linken', in Strauss and Grossman, *Gegenwart im Rückblick*, pp. 86–105. Grossman published the full text of Tucholsky's letter of 5 December 1935. For more on Tucholsky, see Poor, *Kurt Tucholsky and the Ordeal of Germany*, esp. pp. 221–3.

54. 'Confidential Notes of a Brief Visit to Berlin by Dr Selig Brodetsky, August 29–September 2, 1934 '(3 pp.), AJC-RC, 'Germany, Jews, 1934'.

55. Genschel, *Die Verdrängung der Juden aus der Wirtschaft im Dritten Reich*, p. 263; Reichsvertretung der Juden in Deutschland, *Arbeitsbericht für das Jahr 1938* (processed), AJDC-A.

56. *Arbeitsbericht des Zentralausschusses für Hilfe und Aufbau bei der Reichsvertretung der Juden in Deutschland für das Jahr 1936* (processed), p. 163.

57. *3 Jahre Zionistische Bewegung*, pp. 31, 43–4.

58. Ernst Herzfeld, 'Meine letzten Jahre', p. 30.

59. 'Das Programm der Reichsvertretung', *C-V Zeitung*, 26 September 1935; an English translation in Dawidowicz, *Holocaust Reader*.

60. Jüdischer Central-Verein, *Aufgaben/Satzung/Organisation*, Berlin, [1935]; an English translation in Dawidowicz, *Holocaust Reader*.

61. This practice was inaugurated by Rabbi Max Gruenewald in Mannheim.

62. Leo Baeck, 'A People Stands Before Its God', in Boehm, ed., *We Survived* (Santa Barbara, Cal., 1966), pp. 285–6.

63. cf. Ludwig Misch, 'Memoirs', LBI-A.

64. Most of this narrative is found in Freeden, *Jüdisches Theater in Nazi-deutschland*, pp. 58–65; also, interviews with Dr Friedrich Brodnitz, 27 February 1973, and Dr Max Gruenewald, 1 February 1973; Kurt Jacob Ball-Kaduri, 'Leo Baeck and Contemporary History', *YVS* 6 (1967): 121–9; Max Gruenewald, 'About the Reichsvertretung der deutschen Juden', in YIVO Colloquium, *Imposed Jewish Governing Bodies under Nazi Rule*, pp. 42–54; *AJYB* 38:324–5, and 40:203; *Mitteilungsblatt der Hitachduth Olej Germania*, October, I, and December, I, 1937.

65. 'Erwerbt die Beitragskarte für Hilfe und Aufbau', *Informationsblätter*, 22 May 1933; confidential informal statement on the JDC budget for European Jewish relief in 1937, presented by Dr Bernard Kahn, 3 December 1936 (12 pp.), AJDC-A, 'Germany: General and Emerg-

ency'; *Arbeitsbericht des Zentralausschusses für Hilfe und Aufbau . . . 1936*, p. 13; Kurt Alexander, 'Die Reichsvertretung der deutschen Juden', in Reichmann, ed., *Festschrift zum 80. Geburtstag von Rabbiner Dr. Leo Baeck*, p. 80; *AJYB* 38:325.

66. *AJYB* 40:204.

10. DEATH AND LIFE IN THE EAST EUROPEAN GHETTOS

1. Yad Washem, *Blackbook of Localities Whose Jewish Population Was Exterminated by the Nazis*, p. xi and passim.

2. Zygelboym, *Zygelboym-bukh*, pp. 107–15; Julien Bryan, *Siege* (New York, 1940), p. 36.

3. Y-A, 'Di arbet fun der dzhoynttsentrale in poyln far di 13 milk-homekhadoshim (september 1939–oktober 1940)', pp. 3–4.

4. Blumenthal, *Aleksander*, passim.

5. 'Der onheyb', *Zygelboym-bukh*, pp. 116–17.

6. 'Report of Mr. [H.] Szoszkies [Shoshkes] on the Situation in Warsaw', in 'Report on Mr. Szoszkies' Visit to JDC Office, Paris, December 5, 1939', AJDC-A, 'Poland: General and Emergency: Pogroms 1940.'

7. Central Commission . . . , *German Crimes in Poland*, Vol. 1, is the best single source for this documentation. Also, all memorial books of Jewish communities contain descriptions of similar crimes. For documentation on Polish participation, see E. Ringelblum, 'Stosunki polsko-żydowskie w czasie II wojny światowej,' *BŻIH* 28 (October–December 1958): 3–37.

8. Herman Kruk, *Togbukh fun vilner geto*, p. 55. Kruk was a member of the Bund in Warsaw, who had fled to Vilna at the outbreak of the war and remained there until his death in a slave-labour camp in Estonia in September 1944.

9. Brenner, *Vidershtand un umkum in tshenstokhover geto*, pp. 8–9.

10. Baler, ed., *Pinkes Kovel*, p. 84.

11. Moritz Goldstein, 'German Jewry's Dilemma before 1914', LBI, *YB* 2 (1957): 240.

12. Huberband, *Kiddush ha-shem*, pp. 84–7.

13. English translations of some of Frank's ordinances in Dawidowicz, *Holocaust Reader*.

14. *Zygelboym-bukh*, pp. 142–50.

15. Chaim A. Kaplan, *Scroll of Agony*, p. 195. Kaplan was a Hebrew educator and writer. He was deported from Warsaw in 1942.

16. Jacob Nochimovski, 'Meditsinishe unterzukhungen baym arbetsamt fun kovner geto', *Fun letstn khurbn* 10 (December 1948): 28–37.

17. Mordecai Lenski, 'Problems of Disease in the Warsaw Ghetto', *YVS* 3:283–93.

18. 'Fun undzer lider-zamlung', *Fun letstn khurbn* 7 (May 1948): 95–6.

19. Accounts of this meeting and its immediate consequences, varying in minor details, are in Mendelsohn, *The Polish Jews Behind the Nazi Ghetto Walls.* pp. 6–7; *Zygelboym-bukh*, pp. 125–36; 'Report of Mr. [H.] Szoszkies' (note 6); Shoshkes, *Bleter fun a getotog-bukh*, pp. 11–20.

20. Philip Friedman, 'The Jewish Ghettos of the Nazi Era', *JSS*, Vol. 16, 1954, passim.

21. Ringelblum, *Notes from the Warsaw Ghetto*, p. 82.

22. Zelig Kalmanovich, 'Der gayst fun geto', *Yibl* 30 (1947): 169–72.

23. Rudashevski, *The Diary of the Vilna Ghetto*, p. 32.

24. Ruta Sakowska, 'Łączność pocztowa warszawskiego getta', *BŻIH* 45/46 (January–June 1963): 94–109.

25. Kaczerginski, ed., *Dos gezang fun vilner geto*, p. 19.

26. Extract from the diary of Dr Lazar Epstein, *Yad Vashem News* 3 (1971): 15.

27. Halina Szwambaum, 'Four Letters from the Warsaw Ghetto', *Commentary* 31 (1961): 491.

28. Alexandra Solowiejczyk, 'Dray fertl yor unter di daytshn in vilne', *Yibl* 30 (1947): 59–93. The paraphrased passage is on p. 89.

29. Quoted in Isaiah Trunk, *Lodzher geto*, p. 149.

30. Trunk, *Lodzher geto*, p. 337; Dąbrowska and Dobroszycki, *Kronika getta łódzkiego*, 1:11–12, 72–3.

31. Czerniaków, *Yoman geto varsha*, p. 254; excerpts in English translation in Dawidowicz, *Holocaust Reader*.

32. *NCA*, 3, Doc. 1189-PS, p. 833.

33. Berg, *Warsaw Ghetto: A Diary*, p. 53.

34. Based on entries in the Chaim Kaplan and Ringelblum diaries.

35. Dąbrowska and Dobroszycki, *Kronika*, 1:563–4.

36. Yehuda Elber, 'Erev shabes in a varshever hoyf (fun mayn getotogbukh)', *Di goldene keyt* 74 (1971): 142.

37. S. Glube, 'Maykholim in lodzh', *Fun letstn khurbn* 9 (September 1948): 78–81.

38. A. Rosen, [reply to a questionnaire], *Blfg* 1 (August–December 1948): 195–200.

39. 'The Little Smuggler', translated from the Polish original of Hen-

rkya Lazawert; the complete poem in English in Dawidowicz, *Holocaust Reader*.

40. Smuggling in the Warsaw ghetto was best described by Opoczynski, *Reportazhn fun varshever geto*, pp. 62–74; an English translation in Dawidowicz, *Holocaust Reader*. See also Goldstein, *The Stars Bear Witness*, pp. 76–8; Abraham M. Karmi, 'The Jewish Cemetery in Occupied Warsaw', *Yad Vashem Bulletin* 16 (February 1965): 42–7.

41. Apfelbaum, ed., *Maladie de famine: recherches cliniques sur la famine exécutées dans le ghetto de Varsovie en 1942*, pp. 10–11.

42. The best single source that describes this demoralized society in Warsaw is Jonas Turkow, *Azoy is es geven*, pp. 133–78, 195–246, and passim; see also Ringelblum, *Ksovim*, passim.

43. 'Ankete vegn farbroykh in varshever geto', *Blfg* 2 (January–December 1949): 273–89; P. Tykocinski, 'Voluvke', *Blfg* 1 (August–December 1948): 203–10; Dworzecki, *Yerushelayim delite in kamf un unkum*, pp. 156–7; Samuel Gringauz, 'The Ghetto As an Experiment of Social Organization (Three Years of Kovno Ghetto)', *JSS* 11 (1949): 13.

44. Isaiah Trunk, 'Mayrev-eyropeishe yidn in di mizrekh-eyropeishe getos', *Di goldene keyt* 15 (1953): 80–102; Dąbrowska and Dobroszycki, *Kronika*, 1:517–20; Kaufmann, *Die Vernichtung der Juden Lettlands*, passim.

45. Apfelbaum, *Madalie de famine*, pp. 112–13. See also Falstein, *The Martyrdom of Jewish Physicians in Poland*, pp. 190–92, 200–295.

46. Lenski, 'Problems of Disease', pp. 288–90; Isaiah Trunk, 'Epidemics and Mortality in the Warsaw Ghetto, 1939–1942', *YiAn* 8:82–122.

47. Calculated from the data in Trunk, *Lodzher geto*, pp. 222–3.

48. Ruta Pups-Sakowska, 'Opieka nad uchodźcami i przesiedleńcami żydowskimi w Warszawie w latach okupacji hitlerowskiej', *BŻIH* 65/66 (1968): 73–104.

49. Y-A, Wasser Collection, 'January [1942[Report of the Refugee "Town" Dzika and Niska'; English translation in Dawidowicz, *Holocaust Reader*.

50. Dworzecki, *Yerushelayim delite*, pp. 295–458 and passim. See also Dworzecki, 'The Day-to-Day Stand of the Jews', in Conference on the Manifestations of Jewish Resistance, *Jewish Resistance*, pp. 152–81.

51. Y-A, Wasser Collection, 'Folklore'.

52. Unger, *Sefer kedoshim*, p. 181. This book, like most accounts of religious life during the Holocaust, is unreliable as a documentary source. Many such works are little more than contemporary exercises in myth-making or hagiography. The efforts to reconstruct conversations long

after the event should be regarded with great scepticism. This literature is on the whole shoddy. See Hersh Wasser on Hillel Seidman, *Blfg* 1 (January–March 1948): 186–97.

53. Eck, *Hatoim bedarke hamavet*, p. 36.

54. A. Einhorn [reply to a questionnaire], *Blfg* 1 (April–June 1948): 121.

55. Seidman, *Togbukh fun varshever geto*, p. 149.

56. Ringelblum, *Ksovim fun geto*, 2:117.

57. Bakalchuk-Felin, ed., *Yizkorbukh Khelem*, pp. 589–90.

58. Peter Schindler, 'Responses of Hassidic Leaders and Hassidim During the Holocaust . . .', pp. 90, 163.

59. Y-A, Wasser Collection, 'Folk Songs'. For an English translation of the whole poem, see Dawidowicz, *Holocaust Reader*.

60. Y-A, Wasser Collection, 'Folklore' (9 pp.). MS, titled 'Hosofe tsu: Remozim fun geule'.

61. N. Blumenthal, 'Verter un vertlekh fun der khurbn-tkufe', *Yidishe shprakh* 22 (1962): 30.

62. Kaczerginski, ed., *Lider fun getos un lagern*, p. 324.

63. Y-A, Wasser Collection, 'Folklore', apparently collected by S. Lehman, late 1941.

64. Y-A Sutzkever-Kaczerginski Collection, No. 305, Statistisher Amt in vilner geto; politsey-amt, 'Tetikeyt fun di politsey-revirn far dem ershtn halbn yor 1942'.

65. Mark Dvorjetski [Dworzecki], 'Adjustment of Detainees to Camp and Ghetto Life', *YVS* 5 (1963): 193–220, and 'Der mentsh in tehom', *Di goldene keyt* 74 (1971): 73–82; Gringauz, 'The Ghetto As an Experiment', *JSS* 11 (1949): 17; interview with Isaac Orenstein, 10 May 1973; Rudashevski, *Diary of the Vilna Ghetto*, passim.

66. cf. Huberband, *Kiddush hashem*, pp. 92–3.

67. Y-A, Wasser Collection, No. 32–6, handwritten ms., pp. 3–27, entries 27 June 10 July 1942.

68. LBI-A, Memoir Collection, Ruth Alton (Tauber), 'Litzmannstadt (Lodz Ghetto)'.

69. Zelig Kalmanovich, 'A togbukh in vilner gheto', *Yibl* 35 (1951): 60–61. For excerpts in English translation, see Dawidowicz, *Holocaust Reader*.

70. Solowiejczyk, 'Dray fertl yor', *Yibl* 30 (1947): 77. cf. Henia Karmel-Wolfe, *The Baders of Jacob Street* (Lippincott, 1970), in which her heroine, Halina Bader, returns 'home' to the Cracow ghetto, rather than live disguised as an 'Aryan'.

II. THE OFFICIAL COMMUNITY: FROM KEHILLA TO JUDENRAT

1. cf. Isaiah Trunk, *Judenrat*, a comprehensive study of the Judenräte in Eastern Europe. I have relied heavily on its extensive documentation.

2. 'Report of Mr. [H.] Szoszkies [Shoshkes] on the Situation in Warsaw', in 'Report on Mr. Szoszkies' Visit to JDC Office, Paris, December 5, 1939', AJDC-A, Poland: General and Emergency: Pogroms 1940; Shmaryahu Ellenberg, 'My Meetings with Adam Cherniakow', *Yad Vashem Bulletin* 16 (February 1965): 50–54; A. Hartglass, 'How Did Cherniakov Become Head of the Warsaw Judenrat?' *Yad Vashem Bulletin* 15 (August 1964): 4–7; Czerniaków, *Yoman geto varsha*, pp. 2–6. It appears that Czerniaków extracted that appointment on his own, without the consent of the other committee members.

3. A summary of the arguments pro and con participating in the Judenrat is in Gar, *Umkum fun der yidisher kovne*, pp. 288–94.

4. Blumenthal, *Teudot migeto lublin*, p. 40.

5. Herman Kruk, *Togbukh fun vilner geto*, pp. 8–12.

6. Trunk, *Judenrat*, p. 19.

7. Dworzecki, *Yerushelayim delite*, pp. 41–2; Kruk, *Togbukh*, pp. 169–70; Celemenski, *Mitn farshnitenem folk*, pp. 76–7, 100–104.

8. Trunk, *Judenrat*, p. 16.

9. Jasni, *Di geshikhte fun yidn in lodzh*, passim; Solomon F. Bloom, 'Dictator of the Lodz Ghetto', *Commentary* 7 (1949): 111–12; Jacob Nirenberg, 'Di geshikhte fun lodzher geto', in Jewish Labour Bund, *In di yorn fun yidishn khurbn*, pp. 235–6.

10. Trunk, *Judenrat*, pp. 25–6; Philip Friedman, 'Two "Saviors" Who Failed', *Commentary* 26 (1958): 479–91.

11. David Liwer, 'Khurbn Bendin', in Stein, ed., *Pinkes Bendin*, p. 186.

12. Brenner, *Vidershtand un umkum in tshenstokhover geto*, p. 15.

13. Trunk, *Lodzher geto*, pp. 30–31, 63, 362.

14. Kruk, *Togbukh*, pp. 46–8, 69; Dworzecki, *Yerushelayim delite*, pp. 44, 71.

15. Trunk, *Judenrat*, pp. 318–19.

16. For more on the inter-war kehilla in Poland, see Jacob Lestchinsky, 'Economic Aspects of Jewish Community Organization in Independent Poland', *JSS* 9 (1947): 319–37; and Ruta Sakowska, 'Z dziejów gminy żydowskiej w Warszawie 1918–1939', *Studia Warszawskie*, Vol. 14, 1973.

17. cf. Isaac Levitats, *The Jewish Community in Russia, 1772–1844* (New York, 1943).

18. Trunk, *Judenrat*, pp. 115–42; see also M. Merin to JDC, 24 February 1941, AJDC-A, and Y-A, report of the Department of Social Welfare, Vilna Ghetto Judenrat, April 1945, both in English translation in Dawidowicz, *Holocaust Reader*.

19. Blumenthal, *Darko shel yudenrat*, p. 67; excerpts in English translation in Dawidowicz, *Holocaust Reader*.

20. Trunk, *Judenrat*, pp. 388–400.

21. Zygelboym, *Zygelboym-bukh*, pp. 142–50.

22. Blumenthal, *Teudot migeto lublin*, pp. 164–5, 207–9, and passim. For excerpts in English translation, see Dawidowicz, *Holocaust Reader*.

23. cf. Celemenski, *Mitn farshnitenem folk*, p. 75.

24. Brenner, *Vidershtand un umkum*, p. 32.

25. Trunk, *Judenrat*, p. 401, and *Lodzher geto*, p. 437.

26. Peretz Opoczynski, 'Di shopn', *Blfg* 7 (October–December 1954): 89.

27. E. Ringelblum, 'Stosunki polskożydowskie w czasie II wojny światowej', *BŻIH*, 28 (October–December 1958): 3–37.

28. Trunk, *Lodzher geto*, pp. 50, 87–8, and *Judenrat*, pp. 76–90. See also J. Winkler, 'Dos geto kemft kegn virtshaftlekher farknekhtung', *Blfg* 1 (August–December 1948): 3–40.

29. Trunk, *Judenrat*, pp. 237–47.

30. Abraham Rosenberg. 'Dos "draytsentl" (a tsushtayer tsum problem fun kolaboratsionizm in varshever geto)', *Blfg* 5 (January–June 1952): 187–225, and 5 (July–September 1952): 116–48.

31. For more on the police, see Trunk, *Judenrat*, pp. 474–527, 586–7; William Glicksman, 'Daily Record Sheet of the Jewish Police (District I) in the Czestochowa Ghetto (1941–1942)', *YVS* 6:331–57.

32. Kruk, *Togbukh*, pp. 74–5, 304–5.

33. Trunk, *Judenrat*, pp. 50–53.

34. I. Kaplan, *Dos folks-moyl in natsi-klem*, pp. 34–5.

35. Samuel Gringauz, 'The Ghetto as an Experiment of Jewish Social Organization (Three Years of Kovno Ghetto)', *JSS* 11 (1949): 10.

36. Eck, *Hatoim bedarke hamavet*, p. 83.

37. Blumenthal, *Darko shel yudenrat*, pp. 195–201.

38. Blumenthal, *Teudot migeto lublin*, pp. 365–8; the complete text in English, see Dawidowicz, *Holocaust Reader*.

39. Y-A, Wasser Collection, 'Folklore II'.

40. Neustadt, *Khurbn un oyfshtand fun di yidn in varshe*, 2:357–8.

41. For portraits of Rumkowski, see Tabaksblatt, *Khurbn lodzh*, pp. 27–9, 164–71; Solomon F. Bloom, 'Dictator of the Lodz Ghetto', *Commentary* 7 (1949): 111–12; Saul Bellow, *Mr. Sammler's Planet* (New York, 1970), pp. 230–33. For portraits of Gens and Merin, see Philip Friedman, 'Two "Saviors" Who Failed', *Commentary* 26 (1958): 479–91.

12. THE ALTERNATIVE COMMUNITY

1. Ruta Sakowska, 'Komitety domowe w getcie warszawskim', *BŻIH* 61 (January–March 1967): 59–86.

2. I have drawn heavily for information on the *ŻSS*, in all its mutations, from Michal Weichert, *Yidishe aleynhilf*, and Sakowska, 'Komitety domowe'.

3. Quoted in Trunk, *Judenrat*, p. 339.

4. A. Berman, 'O losie dzieci z zakładów opiekuńczych w getcie warszawskim', *BŻIH* 28 (October–December 1958): 65–78.

5. L. Bursztyn, 'Odezwy Janusza Korczaka z lat okupacji', *BŻIH* 45/46 (1963): 262–6. For an English translation of three of these documents, see Dawidowicz, *Holocaust Reader*. For Korczak's biography and writings, see *Selected Works of Janusz Korczak*, and Olczak, *Mister Doctor: The Life of Janusz Korczak*. Of exceptional insight and beauty is Aaron Zeitlin's poem in prose, 'Yanush Kortshaks letster gang', in *Vayterdike lider fun khurbn un lider fun gloybn un Yanush Kortshaks letster gang* (New York, 1970).

6. Minutes of the conference translated into Yiddish from the Polish original, in Bakalshuk-Felin, ed., *Yizkor-bukh khelem*, pp. 601–19.

7. There is no systematic compilation of data about the participation of rabbis and observant Jews in welfare institutions. See individual biographies in Lewin, *Ele ezkra*. Also of interest is Hersh Wasser's review of Hillel Seidman's *Togbukh fun varshever geto*, in *Blfg* 1 (January–March, 1948), especially pp. 186–8.

8. Jonas Turkow, *Azoy iz es geven*, pp. 61–87; Menachem Linder, 'A yor yisa', *Blfg* 1 (April–June 1948): 3–13; Wasser, review of Seidman's *Togbukh*; Ruta Pups-Sakowska, 'Opieka nad uchodźcami i przesiedleńcami żydowskimi w Warszawie w latach okupacji hitlerowskiej', *BŻIH* 65/66 (1968): 80–83.

9. Eck, *Hatoim bedarke hamavet*, pp. 20–27; Sakowska, 'Komitety domowe . . .', *BŻIH* 61 (1967): 64–6; Chaim Kaplan, *Scroll of Agony*, pp.

227–9, 259; Peretz Opoczynski, 'Di tragedye fun a hoyz-komitet', *Blfg* 14 (1961): 171–9.

10. Neustadt, *Khurbn un oyfshtand fun di yidn in varshe*, 2:688–9, 598–9.

11. Trunk, *Judenrat*, pp. 187–96; Dworzecki, *Yerushelayim delite in kamf un umkum*, pp. 288–92; Y-A, Vilna Archives, No. 577a; Oshry, *Khurbn lite*, pp. 104–8.

12. Hillel Zeitlin, [response to a questionnaire], *Blfg* 1 (April–June 1948): 111–14. For an English translation, see Dawidowicz, *Holocaust Reader*.

13. [Response to a questionnaire], *Blfg* 1 (August–December 1948): 201–2.

14. Trunk, *Lodzher geto*, p. 455; for an English translation, see Dawidowicz, *Holocaust Reader*; Oshry, *Khurbn lite*, p. 143; Rachel Auerbach, 'Bagegenishn mit Pole Elster', in *Dray – Ondenbukh*, p. 57.

15. Mentioned in *Min hametzar*, literary supplement in *Hamispar*, underground Hebrew newspaper issued irregularly in Lodz, No. 1, 8 July 1941; the entire issue, along with other fragments, published in *Dappim leheker hashoa vehamered*, Part 1, pp. 115–39.

16. Rabbi Elhanon Person, 'Dos religyeze lebn in kovner geto', *Fun letstn khurbn* 9 (September 1948): 44.

17. Y-A, Wasser Collection, [Huberband], 'Der marsh in mikve arayn'. For more on ritual baths, see Huberband, *Kiddush ha-shem*, pp. 88–92.

18. Huberband, *Kiddush ha-shem*, pp. 75–114; Person, 'Dos religyeze lebn', p. 44.

19. Ruta Sakowska, 'O szkolnictwie i tajnym nauczaniu w getcie warszawskim', *BŻIH* 55 (July–September 1965): 57–84.

20. Nahman Korn, 'Dertsiyungproblemen un kinder-elnt in geto: zikhroynes', in Litvin and Lerman, eds., *Dos bukh fun lublin*, pp. 503–8.

21. Anna Natanblut, 'Di shuln in varshever geto', *Yibl* 30 (1947): 173–87.

22. 'Verordnung über das jüdische Schulwesen im Generalgouvernement', *Verordnungsblatt für das Generalgouvernement*, 1, No. 51 (September 11, 1940): 258.

23. Rudashevski, *The Diary of the Vilna Ghetto*, pp. 117, 135.

24. Esther Goldhar-Mark, 'Dos yidishe fakh- un hekhere shulvezn in varshe in der tsayt fun der daytsher okupatsye', *Blfg* 2 (1949): 175–206.

25. Zylberberg, *A Warsaw Diary*, pp. 34–5.

26. Rudashevski, *Diary*, pp. 134–5; Sutzkever, *Lider fun geto*, pp. 24–5.

27. Turkow, *Azoy iz es geven*, pp. 195–6. Turkow provides the fullest account of entertainment and cultural activities in the Warsaw ghetto, pp. 195–246.

28. Y-A, Wasser Collection, 'Yidishe kultur-organizatsye – yikor'; Emanuel Ringelblum, 'Cultural Work of the Jewish Underground in Poland', report written Warsaw, 20 May 1944, *Newsletter of the YIVO* 5 (November 1944): 1, 6–8; Turkow, *Azoy iz es geven*, pp. 247–55; Ringelblum, *Ksovim fun geto*, 2: 164–8.

29. Eck, *Hatoim bedarke hamavet*, pp. 40–41; Neustadt, *Khurbn un oyfshtand*, pp. 309, 692–3.

30. J. Gurevich, 'Kovner geto-orkester,' *Fun letstn khurbn* 9 (September 1948): 52–8.

31. Oscar Rosenfeld, 'Konzert im Kulturhaus', in Trunk, *Lodzher geto*, pp. 447–50.

32. M. Kushnir, in Jewish Labour Bund, *In di yorn fun yidishn khurbn*, p. 308.

33. Y-A, Sutzkever-Kaczerginsky Collection, 'Report of the Culture Department for March 1943'. English translation in Dawidowicz, *Holocaust Reader*.

34. References to the library celebration are found in the diaries of Kalmanovich, Kruk, and Rudashevski, all entered 13 December 1942; a parallel set of statistics for the last three months of 1941 appears in Kruk, *Togbukh*, p. 131.

35. Trunk, *Lodzher geto*, p. 401.

36. 'Lomdim ve-korim', *Min hametzar*, in *Dappim*, p. 130.

37. Dina Abramovich, 'Vilner geto-biblyotek', in Sudarsky et al., eds., *Lite*, pp. 1671–8.

38. For more on Oneg Shabbat, see Ringelblum, *Ksovim fun geto*, 2: 76–102.

13. THE COUNTER-COMMUNITY: THE POLITICAL UNDERGROUND

1. cf. Lucy S. Dawidowicz, 'Two of Stalin's Victims', *Commentary* 12 (December 1951): 614–16.

2. A straightforward account of political activity in the ghettos can be found in Isaiah Trunk, 'Dos politishe lebn in di getos', in his *Geshtaltn un gesheyenishn*, pp. 132–72.

3. Neustadt, *Khurbn un oyfshtand fun di yidn in varshe*, 2: 634–5.

4. Rachel Auerbach, 'Bagegenishn mit Pole Elster', in *Dray – Odenbukh*, p. 54; Tabaksblatt, *Khurbn lodzh*, pp. 90–99.

5. Cf. Israel Gutman, 'Youth Movements in the Underground and the Ghetto Revolts', in Conference on Manifestations of Jewish Resistance, *Jewish Resistance*, pp. 260–84. For more on the activities of Zionist youth, see Tenenbaum-Tamaroff, *Dappim min hadleka*, pp. 112–26; 'Korespondentsya pnimit', *Dappim leheker hashoa vehamered*, 1: 148–56; Bronia Klibanski, 'The Underground Archives of the Bialystok Ghetto Founded by Mersik and Tenenbaum', *YVS* 2 (1958): 295–329.

6. Zygelboym, *Zygelboym-bukh*, pp. 107–15; Goldstein, *The Stars Bear Witness*, pp. 31–2.

7. Goldstein, *The Stars Bear Witness*, pp. 42–55; Jewish Labour Bund, *In di yorn fun yidishn khurbn*, pp. 329–39.

8. A fascinating account of this aspect of Bund history that also illuminates a whole chapter of Jewish social history is Bernard Goldstein, *20 yor in varshever bund 1919–1939* (New York, 1960).

9. JLB-A, record book kept by Henoch Rus, activist in Tsukunft, January 1941–June 1942. I am grateful to Mr Hillel Kempinski for making this document available to me.

10. Only portions of this document were published in 'A briv fun varshe', *Undzer tsayt*, July 1941, pp. 10–13. No date was given; the report was probably written at the end of 1940 or early 1941.

11. Quoted in *The Ghetto Speaks* (American Representation of the Bund), No. 1, 1 August 1942.

12. Quoted in J. Kermish, 'The Land of Israel in the Life of the Ghetto As Reflected in the Illegal Warsaw Ghetto Press', *YVS* 5: 112–13.

13. 'Deklaratsye funem farband fun yidishe arbeter geleyent durkh Pola Elster . . .', in *Dray*, pp. 110–11.

14. 'List Bundu', 16 March 1942, Y-A from original in the archives of Studium Polski Podziemnej, London; an English translation in Dawidowicz, *Holocaust Reader*. Party rivalries have done great disservice to the historical record. Every party tried to magnify its role and belittle that of its opponents during the occupation and long after. Ringelblum, for instance, a highly partisan Left Labour Zionist, has fewer than a dozen references to the Bund, mostly negative comments about a few individuals. Politics was Ringelblum's life, colouring his whole account of Jewish life in the ghetto, despite his historical commitment.

15. No satisfactory work on the underground press has yet been

done. Very inadequate is Joseph Kermish, 'On the Underground Press in the Warsaw Ghetto', *YVS* I (1957): 85–123; a listing of the Bundist underground press appears in H. Kempinski, 'Di untererdishe prese fun "Bund" in varshever geto', *Undzer tsayt*, March 1949, pp. 28–30.

16. Goldstein, *The Stars Bear Witness*, pp. 44–5, 88–9.

17. JLB-A, *Yugnt-shtime*, No. 3, December 1940.

18. Celemenski, *Mitn farshnitenem folk*, pp. 69–70.

19. Quoted in Joseph Kermish, 'The Land of Israel ...', *YVS* 5 (1963): 125.

20. Quoted in Joseph Kermish, 'On the Underground Press in the Warsaw Ghetto', *YVS* I (1957): 103–5.

21. Abrasha Blum, ed., *Di parizer komune: zamlbukh* (Warsaw, 1948).

22. *Payn un gvure in dem yidishn over in likht fun der kegnvart*, Munich, 1947. Reprinted from the mimeographed original published in 1940.

23. E. Lidowski, 'Vidershtand-organizatsye', in *Baranovitsh: sefer zikaron*, pp. 472–3.

24. Chaim Kaplan, *Scroll of Agony*, pp. 306–7; Czerniaków, *Yoman geto varsha*, pp. 315–16; Kermish, 'On the Underground Press', *YVS* I: 110–11.

25. Copies of much of the Bundist press are in the Franz Kursky Archives of the Jewish Labour Bund in New York, which also has a few issues of other party papers. No copy of Auerswald's placard, referred to in the cited editorial, appears to be extant.

26. Goldstein, *The Stars Bear Witness*, pp. 51–3; Ringelblum, *Ksovim fun geto*, 1: 105–6. Chaim Kaplan, *Scroll of Agony*, pp. 134–5, describes the pogroms, but apparently did not hear of the Jewish counter-attack. Ringelblum reports also that when pogromists attempted to attack the Judenrat building, members of the labour brigades drove them off (p. 107).

27. Tabaksblatt, *Khurbn lodzh*, pp. 100–101; Jacob Nirenberg, 'Di geshikhte fun lodzher geto', in Jewish Labour Bund, *In di yorn fun yidishn khurbn*, pp. 227–30; Frank, *Togbukh fun lodzher geto*, pp. 24–9; 'Podziemne życie polityczne w getcie łódzkim (1940–1944)', *BŻIH*, No. 54, 1965, passim.

28. Trunk, *Judenrat*, p. 532.

29. Zvi Rosenwein, 'Der hungershtrayk in tshenstokhover geto', in Singer, ed., *Tshenstokhov*, pp. 47–51.

30. Brenner, *Vidershtand un umkum in tshenstokhover geto*, pp. 60–63; M. Kushnir, 'Di tetikeyt fun "Bund" in der tsayt fun der hitleristisher

okupatsye in tshenstokhov', in Jewish Labour Bund, *In di yorn*, pp. 306–15.

31. Goldstein, *The Stars Bear Witness*, pp. 103–4; cf. Ringelblum, *Ksovim fun geto*, 1:354.

14. WHO SHALL LIVE, WHO SHALL DIE

1. On Vilna, see Tzippora Birman's letter, 1 March 1943, 'Appendix One', to Bronia Klibanski, 'The Underground Archives of the Bialystok Ghetto Founded by Mersik and Tenenbaum', *YVS*, Vol. 2, especially pp. 308–9. On Kovno, see Samuel Gringauz, 'Khurbn kovno', *Fun letstn khurbn*, No. 7, May 1948, especially pp. 10–15. On Lwów, see Rubinsztajnowa, 'Pamiętnik ze Lwowa', *BŻIH*, No. 61, January–March 1967, especially pp. 89–91.

2. This incident and also those that follow in the text are recounted in different variations by Gringauz, 'Khurbn kovno' and Jacob Goldberg, 'Bletlekh fun kovner eltestnrat', both in *Fun letstn khurbn*, No. 7, May 1948; Garfunkel, *Kovno hayehudit behurbana*; Gar, *Umkum fun der yidisher kovne*.

3. Garfunkel, *Kovno*, pp. 74–9. See also Braun and Levin, *Toledoteha shel mahteret*, pp. 45–8.

4. See David Daube, *Collaboration With Tyranny in Rabbinic Law* (London, 1965), a brilliant and elegant elucidation of this question. I have very roughly summarized a few points of Dr Daube's learned and sophisticated work.

5. Maimonides, *Mishneh Torah: The Book of Knowledge*, trans. Moses Hyamson (Jerusalem, 1965), Chapter 5, Precepts, p. 40b.

6. Dworzecki, *Yerushelayim delite in kamf un umkum*, p. 294.

7. cf. Balberyszski, *Shtarker fun ayzn*, pp. 207–8; Dworzecki, *Yerushelayim delite*, pp. 53–5.

8. For a contemporary statistical record, see Kruk, *Togbukh fun vilner geto*, pp. 258–61.

9. Very little has been written on the distribution of yellow permits. Unfortunately the entries in Kruk's diary from 2 October to 21 December 1941, consisting of some 100 manuscript pages, are missing. Kalmanovich made no entries during this period. Mr Shlomo Kovarsky, a survivor of the Vilna ghetto and an active member of its resistance movement, provided some information that helped me reconstruct the procedure. See also Dworzecki, *Yerushelayim delite*, p. 102; Balberyszski, *Shtarker fun ayzn*.

10. Dworzecki, *Yerushelayim delite*, pp. 108–9.

11. Dworzecki, p. 308. Dworzecki presents the Gens text as if it were verbatim, though it is clearly a reconstruction from memory. No such talk by Gens is mentioned by either Kruk or Kalmanovich, nor do they refer to that specific occasion mentioned by Dworzecki. Kalmanovich, in his diary entry of 25 October 1941, cites a talk by Gens in a similar vein. Justifying himself and the Vilna ghetto police for carrying out an *Aktion* in a near-by town, Gens said: 'To be sure, our hands are stained with the blood of our brethren, but we had to take upon ourselves this dreadful task. We are clean before the bar of history.'

12. S. Glube, 'Di din-toyre', *Fun letstn khurbn* 6 (August 1947): 44–7.

13. Dąbrowska and Dobroszycki, 'Biuletyn z 20 grudnia 1941 (sobota)', *Kronika getta łódzkiego*, pp. 323–9.

14. J. Nirenberg, in Jewish Labour Bund, *In di yorn fun yidishn khurbn*, pp. 253–7.

15. Dąbrowska and Dobroszycki, 'Biuletyn Nr. 7, za okres od 14 do 31 stycznia 1942', *Kronika*, p. 398. Italics in original.

16. Tabaksblatt, *Khurbn lodzh*, p. 103.

17. Dąbrowska and Dobroszycki. *Kronika*, p. 440. Italics in original.

18. Quoted in Trunk, *Lodzher geto*, pp. 258–9.

19. Trunk, *Lodzher geto*, pp. 260–61.

20. Dąbrowska and Dobroszycki, 'Biuletyn Nr. 9: za miesiąc luty 1942', *Kronika*, pp. 402–3; Barbara Beatus, 'O genezie rozwoju i działalności Lewicy Związkowej w getcie łódzkim', *BŻIH* 54 (April–June 1965): 49.

21. Nirenberg, in Jewish Labour Bund, *In di yorn fun yidishn umkum*, pp. 260–62; Tabaksblatt, *Khurbn lodzh*, pp. 103–4.

22. Y-A Mordecai Goldstein, oral interview, transcript (7 pp.). Cf. also Nirenberg, in Jewish Labour Bund, *In di yorn fun yidishn khurbn*.

23. A lengthy journalistic contemporary account of these September deportations is Y-A, Joseph Zelkowicz, 'In yene koshmarne teg', 74-page typescript. Extracts in English in Dawidowicz, *Holocaust Reader*.

24. Jonas Turkow, *Azoy iz es geven*, p. 257.

25. Y-A, 'Powstanie i rozwój Ż.O.B.', report written in Warsaw, March 1944, and sent through underground channels to London, May 1944. Its author, or major author, is Yitzhak Zuckerman (orig. Cukierman), a member of the high command of Żydowska Organi-

zacja Bojowa – ŻOB. For an English translation, see Dawidowicz, *Holocaust Reader*. This conference with the couriers from Vilna and Bialystok is mentioned also by one of the surviving couriers, Chayke Grossman, in her memoirs, *Anshe hamahteret*. Mordecai Tenenbaum, who came to Warsaw in January 1942 and remained there until October, in his letter to his comrades in Palestine, written in Bialystok, April 1943 (*Dappim min hadleka*, pp. 127–8), refers to a meeting in April. What appears to have remained in his memory was a combination of the March meeting and one held on 22 July 1942.

26. Three reports of that March 1942 conference exist. One is Zuckerman's 'Powstanie i rozwój Ż.O.B' cited above. The second is Hersh Berlinski's memoirs, published in *Dray*, pp. 154–87, written late 1943 into 1944. Discrepancies exist between both texts as to dates, persons involved and minor matters. A third report by Elihu Gutkowski is very brief and in part indecipherable. The original is in the archives of kibbutz Lohamei hagetaot.

27. It is extremely difficult to reconstruct the views of Mauricy Orzech, the Bund's senior representative, since they have come down to us only in the reports of his political opponents – Zuckerman, Berlinski, Tenenbaum, Grossman. See also Neustadt, *Khurbn un oyfshtand fun di yidn in varshe*, pp. 132–3, and Cukierman [Zuckerman], 'Powstanie żdyowskie', *Nasze Słowo* 3 (19 April 1948): 5–10.

28. According to Zuckerman, the Anti-Fascist Bloc was formed at the initiative of the Left Labour Zionists. Ber Mark, *Blfg* 4 (January 1941): 64, attributes its founding to the PPR.

29. JLD-A, Hennoch Rus record book, 'Protocol No. 1, January 8, 1942; Protocol No. 9, April 12, 1942'.

30. Y-A, Wasser Collection, 60.7. The issue is dated 1942 and numbered '1'. The latest date mentioned in the text is 27 March 1942.

31. N. Blumenthal, *Teudot migeto lublin*, passim: T. Brustin-Bernstein, Ida Rappaport-Glickstein, and Hertz Goldberg, in Litvin and Lerman, *Dos bukh fun lublin*, pp. 363–4, 396, and 484–5, respectively.

32. Rubinsztajnowa, 'Pamiętnik ze Lwowa', *BŻIH*, No. 61, January–March 1967; Philip Friedman, 'Hurban yehude lvov bitkufat 1941–1944', in N. M. Gelber, ed., *Lvov: Entziklopedya shel galuyot* (Jerusalem, 1956), passim.

33. David Liwer, 'Khurbn Bendin', in Stein, ed., *Pinkes Bendin*, pp. 188–9; Trunk, *Judenrat*, pp. 422–3, 425–6. A widely used source for Merin speeches and conversations is Pawel Wiederman, *Płowa Bestia* (Munich, 1948). Employed in the Judenrat, Wiederman was a

keen observer. His memoirs, however, record alleged conversations verbatim at which he was not present, and whose contents he could not possibly have known. At best his evidence is hearsay; it is probably highly coloured.

34. cf. Abraham Lewin, 'Funem geto-togbukh', *Blfg* 5 (October–December 1952): 22–68.

35. The text of Höfle's order to the Warsaw Judenrat is published in Berenstein, Eisenbach, and Rutkowski, eds., *Eksterminacja Żydów*, pp. 300–302; an English translation in Dawidowicz, *Holocaust Reader*.

36. Joseph Kermish, 'Introduction', in Adam Czerniaków, *Yoman geto varsha*, p. xix.

37. Suicide under such circumstances occurred elsewhere. cf. Jacob Frum, 'Lomzher geto un ir sof', in Sabotka, ed., *Lomzhe: Ir oyfkum un untergang*, pp. 286–9.

38. This account of the meeting of 22 July 1942, and of subsequent underground activities is based on a variety of reports, which, though somewhat inconsistent and contradictory, furnish an outline of the events. The sources are 'Powstanie i rozwój Ż.O.B.' (see note 25); Hersh Berlinski, memoirs in *Dray*, pp. 154–87; A. Berman, 'O ruchu oporu w getcie warszawskim (Refleksje)', *BŻIH* 29 (January–March 1957): 40–57; Y-A, report by Leon Feiner (Berezowski), 31 August 1942, to Arthur Zygelboym, Bundist representative in the Polish National Council in London; Goldstein, *Finf yor in varshever geto*, pp. 245–50.

39. Berlinski, in *Dray*, pp. 159–60.

40. Much of this account of the deportation from Warsaw is based on an underground report sent by the *Żydowski Komitet Narodowy* from the Warsaw ghetto, 15 November 1942, to Jewish organizations in Jerusalem, London, and New York. Many official documents were appended. An English translation was issued in mineographed form by the World Jewish Congress, *Extermination of Polish Jewry: Reports Based on Official Documents*. A Yiddish translation of most of the document is in Neustadt, *Khurbn un oyfshtand fun di yidn in varshe*, pp. 78–96. A compelling description of the deportations is also in Turkow, *Azoy iz es geven*, pp. 282–394.

41. Donat, *The Holocaust Kingdom*, pp. 80–81.

42. In *Eichmann in Jerusalem*, Arendt writes: '... if the Jewish people had really been unorganized and leaderless, there would have been chaos and plenty of misery, but the total number of victims would hardly have been between four and a half and six million people' (p. 125). This extraordinary argument on behalf of chaos derives from

total ignorance of the historical evidence. The Germans managed with amazing facility to deport over a quarter of a million Jews from the Warsaw ghetto at this time precisely because the Jews of Warsaw were 'unorganized and leaderless'.

43. The small body of scientific literature on human response to disaster sheds light on Jewish behaviour during the deportations. Robert Jay Lifton, *Death in Life: Survivors of Hiroshima* (New York, 1967), is suggestive, especially for his concept of 'psychic closing off'. Other works I have found instructive include Harold Basowitz et al., *Anxiety and Stress: An Interdisciplinary Study of a Life Situation* (New York, 1955); Herman Feifel, ed., *The Meaning of Death* (New York, 1965); William H. Form and Charles P. Loomis, 'The Persistence and Emergence of Social Cultural Systems in Disasters', *American Sociological Review* 21 (April 1956): 180–85; George H. Grosser et al., eds., *The Threat of Impending Disaster: Contribution to the Psychology of Stress* (Cambridge, Mass., 1964); Bradford B. Hudson, 'Anxiety in Response to the Unfamiliar', *Journal of Social Issues* 10 (1954): 53–60; F. P. Kilpatrick, 'Problems of Perception in Extreme Situations', *Human Organization* 16 (1957): 20–22; Henry Krystal, ed., *Massive Psychic Trauma* (New York, 1968); Eugene E. Levitt, *The Psychology of Anxiety* (New York, 1967); Richard S. Lazarus, *Psychological Stress and the Coping Process* (New York, 1966); Joost A. M. Meerloo, *Patterns of Panic* (New York, 1950); New York Academy of Medicine, *Panic and Morale: Conference Transactions* (New York, 1958); Neil J. Smelser, *Theory of Collective Behavior* (New York, 1965); Martha Wolfenstein, *Disaster: A Psychological Essay* (Glencoe, Ill., 1957).

44. Turkow, *Azoy iz es geven*, pp. 298–302.

45. [Yehoshua Perle], 'Khurbn varshe', *Blfg* 4 (July–September 1951): 119–21.

46. This only surviving fragment of Remba's memoirs is recorded by Ringelblum, *Ksovim fun geto*, 2: 213–14.

47. Seidman, *Togbukh fun varshever geto*, p. 77. Such attitudes and incidents were recorded all over Eastern Europe. See especially *Zeszyty oświęcimskie, II: Rękopisy członków sonderkommando* (1971), pp. 108–15, a description by a Jew who worked in an Auschwitz Sonderkommando. He mentions that pious Jews from Poland and Hungary drank toasts with brandy brought specially for the occasion, danced and sang before entering the gas chambers, because they were going to meet the Messiah.

48. Goldstein, *The Stars Bear Witness*, pp. 117–18. No source indicates when Friedrich set out. My reconstruction conforms with the

surmises of Vladka Meed and Chana Fryshdorf, survivors of the Bundist underground with whom I talked.

49. Abraham Lewin, 'Tog-bukh fun varshever geto', *Blfg* 7 (April 1954): 76.

50. [Author unknown], 'Struktura demograficzna ludności żydowskiej pozostałej w Warszawie', *BŻIH* 37 (January–March 1961): 98–105.

51. JLB-A, *Oyf der vakh*, September 20, 1942. Friedrich's report was subsequently published in *Undzer tsayt*, September 1952, pp. 32–5.

15. 'FOR YOUR FREEDOM AND OURS'

1. Dawidsohn-Draengerowa, *Pamiętnik Justyny*, pp. 86–7. Excerpts in an English translation in Dawidowicz, *Holocaust Reader*. For an account of Jews in Cracow during the German occupation, see Dora Agatshtein Dormond, in Bauminger et al., *Sefer Kroke*, pp. 389–401.

2. Tenenbaum-Tamaroff, *Dappim min hadleka*, p. 91.

3. Ringelblum, *Ksovim fun geto*, 2: 147–9.

4. Dawidsohn-Draengerowa, *Pamiętnik Justyny*, p. 101.

5. Tzippora Birman's letter, 'Appendix One', to Bronia Klibanski, 'The Underground Archives of the Bialystok Ghetto Founded by Mersik and Tenenbaum', *YVS*, 2: 322–4.

6. Y-A, Sutzkever-Kaczerginsky Collection, 'Lomir zikh nisht lozn firn vi shof tsu der shkhite!' (5 pp. typescript), dated 'Vilna, in the ghetto, 1/1/1942'. An English translation in Dawidowicz, *Holocaust Reader*. Cf. Abba Kovner, 'Di letste oyfn moyer', *Di goldene keyt*, Vol. 46, 1963.

7. Y.A, Sutzkever-Kaczerginsky Collection, Nisl Reznik, 'Geshikhte fun F.P.O.', 12 March 1944 (typescript, 11 pp.).

8. The only source for this discussion is Berlinski's memoirs, in *Dray*, pp. 169–71.

9. For more on the Polish government-in-exile and its origins, see Karski, *Story of a Secret State*, especially pp. 124–34.

10. Yitzhak Zuckerman, in a 5-page typed Yiddish letter, 31 December 1972, in response to a series of questions I put to him about the organization of, and political relationships within, ŻOB; later cited as Zuckerman, 'Tshuves'.

11. Edelman, *The Ghetto Fights*, p. 28. This memoir is, on the whole, unreliable for dates. Nevertheless, Zuckerman ('Tshuves') also puts the date of the establishment of the ŻKK at the end of October 1942.

12. Y-A, Report B, 'Sprawozdanie za czas od 1 Lipca 1943r. Do 15 list. 1943r', Warsaw, 15 November 1943, from Berezowski [Leon Feiner], for the Central Committee of the Bund in Poland, to Dr Emanuel Scherer, its representative in London. Dr Feiner cites a section of the ŻKK by-laws that does not appear in the version that has survived (see note 14). In his report, which included an explanation of the function of the ŻKK, Feiner wrote: '"Political issues", so states Paragraph 2 of the Coordinating Commission's by-laws, "being settled independently by each of the coordinating parties in accordance with their ideology, are excluded from coordination."' It is possible that this paragraph was introduced in a revised ŻKK statute about July 1943.

13. Not all reports mention the participation of the PPR. Two explanations are possible. (1) The ŻKK leaders may have been reluctant to include the PPR in reports that went to or via the Home Army and the Polish government-in-exile, both of which regarded the PPR – quite correctly – as an agent of the Soviet Union and disloyal to them. (2) By late 1943, when the Bund and the ŻKN were sending reports abroad, the PPR no longer played any role in the underground remnant Jewish community.

14. The original text from the Central Archives of the Polish Home Ministry is published as 'Aneks 2' to Bernard Mark, 'Statut Żydowskiej Organizacji Bojowej', *BŻIH* 39 (July–September 1961): 59–60. A full English translation in Dawidowicz, *Holocaust Reader*.

15. Karski, *Story of a Secret State*, pp. 328–9.

16. Michel, *The Shadow War*, pp. 52 ff. Chapters dealing with the military and political organization of West European resistance, especially French resistance, appear reliable. The section on Jewish resistance, however, betrays ignorance of a high order. The material on Polish resistance is sketchy and imprecise.

17. The only source regarding the Delegatura's demand for a loyalty oath is Berlinski. As for the date of the arms delivery, most sources indicate late December, but according to the evidence of Henryk Wolinski's memorandum (see note 18), those ten pieces must have been delivered by 3 December 1942.

18. The original text from the Central Archives of the Polish Home Ministry is published as 'Aneks I' to Bernard Mark, 'Statut Żydowskiej Organizacji Bojowej,' *BŻIH* 39 (July–September 1961): 58–9. A full English translation in Dawidowicz, *Holocaust Reader*.

19. This text is the version received in London, 7 January 1943, and published by Adam Ciołkosz, 'Broń dla getta warszawy,' *Zeszyty*

Historyczne Instytut Literacki (Paris, 1969), p. 22. A variant text, 'Too late Jews of various Communist groupings' etc., appeared in a Yiddish translation in Ber Mark, *Dokumentn un materyaln vegn oyfshtand in varshever geto* (1953). Mark used a copy of the document as transmitted, Ciołkosz a document as received. Whether the discrepancy is based on Mark's honest rendering of the text or whether it is a political falsification, I cannot judge. Neither version establishes General Rowecki as a friend of the Jews.

20. Edelman, *The Ghetto Fights*, p. 31; Y. Zuckerman, 'Di yidishe kamforganizatsye un der poylisher untergrunt', *Payn un gvure* (New York, 1959), p. 32; an English version of Zuckerman's letter to the commander-in-chief of the Home Army, 26 November 1943, requesting aid for ŻOB and recapitulating what aid had been given, appears in *Extermination and Resistance*, pp. 14–19. See also Y. Zuckerman, 'Twenty-Five Years After the Warsaw Ghetto Revolt', in Conference on Manifestations of Jewish Resistance, *Jewish Resistance*, p. 30.

21. The best account of the perils of buying and smuggling arms is Meed, *On Both Sides of the Wall*. See also Klin, *Mitn malekh-hamoves untern orem*.

22. For a somewhat rhetorical presentation of these dilemmas, see Yitzhak Zuckerman (Cukierman), 'Powstanie żydowskie', *Nasze Słowo* 3 (19 April 1948): 6.

23. Trunk, *Lodzher Geto*, pp. 282–308, 327–34, 464–71; Jacob Nirenberg, in Jewish Labour Bund, *In di yorn fun yidishn khurbn*, pp. 281–94.

24. The fairly rich Yiddish and Hebrew literature on Jews among the Soviet partisans deals extensively with the hazards and hardships they encountered and with the anti-Semitism that poisoned most relations. The Russians eventually broke up all the Jewish partisan bands and dispersed their members in non-Jewish groups. The Jewish partisans were beyond the reach of Jewish communal policy as shaped in the ghettos and were, for the most part, prevented by their Soviet superiors from using the partisan organization as an instrument of Jewish vengeance.

25. cf. Neustadt, *Khurbn un oyfshtand fun di yidn in varshe*, pp. 148–9, 423–5, 485–7, 491–4; Aaron Nirenstein, 'Vidershtand fun yidn in kroke unter der hitleristisher okupatsye', *Blfg* 5 (January–June 1952): 226–63.

26. Eliezer Lidowski, 'Vidershtand-organizatsye', in *Baranovitsh: sefer zikaron*, cols. 475–9.

27. Samuel Gringauz, 'Khurbn kovne,' *Fun letstn khurbn* 8 (June 1948): 27–38; Braun and Levin, *Toledoteha shel mahteret*, pp. 73–4, 129–248; Sarah Neshomit, 'Beginnings of the Partisan Movement in the

Kaunas Ghetto', *Extermination and Resistance*, pp. 129–39; Rahi Ben-Eliezer, 'Kamfs-bavegung in kovner geto', *Fun letstn khurbn* 10 (December 1948): 3–15.

28. Garfunkel, *Kovno hayehudit behurbana*, pp. 194–5. The author reconstructed the dialogue between Elkes and Goecke from the report of a communal leader who was present at the confrontation.

29. L. Brenner, *Vidershtand un umkum in tshenstokhover geto*, p. 116.

30. Trunk, *Judenrat*, pp. 457–8.

31. Niusia Dlugi, 'Der Vitenberg-tog in vilner geto', *Yibl* 30 (1947): 192–3.

32. Kruk, *Togbukh fun vilner geto*, pp. 563–4, 569–70, 573–4.

33. Kruk, *Togbukh*, pp. 582–6; Kalmanovich, 'A togbukh in vilner geto', *Yibl* 35 (1951): 56. See also Reznik, 'Geshikhte fun F.P.O.'; Niusia Dlugi, *Yibl* 30 (1947): 194–5.

34. Reznik, 'Geshikhte fun F.P.O.'; S. Kaczerginski, [7th notebook of wartime diary, Yiddish, entry dated 27 July 1943], handwritten ms., Y-A, Sutzkever-Kaczerginski Collection; Brayne As, Shimon Palewski, Zenia Berkon, 'Der Vitenberg-tog in vilner geto', *Yibl* 30 (1947): 200–213. All accounts differ in many details.

35. Reznik, 'Geshikhte fun F.P.O.', pp. 9–11.

36. Tenenbaum's diary, *Dappin min hadleka*, reveals the close relations between Barash and Tenenbaum and their mutual regard.

37. Tenenbaum, *Dappin min hadleka*, pp. 67–8, 81.

38. Minutes of this meeting, found after the war, were first published in Kaczerginski, *Khurbn vilne*, pp. 315–22; an English translation appeared in *Commentary* 8 (February 1949): 105–9. A somewhat altered translation in Dawidowicz, *Holocaust Reader*.

39. For more on the resistance in the Bialystok ghetto, see Reisner, *Der umkum fun bialystoker yidntum*, pp. 162–9; Ber Mark, *Der oyfshtand in bialystoker geto*, passim; Chayke Grossman, *Anshe hamahteret*; Kantorowicz, *Di yidishe vidershtand-bavegung in poyln*, pp. 284–95.

40. cf. Joshua Vermut, 'Mayne iberlebungen', in Meltzer, ed., *Sefer Horodenka*, pp. 296–7.

41. A. Zigelboym-Savitski, 'Der oyfshtand in geto', in Shtrachman, ed., *Sefer Lutsk*, pp. 517–18.

42. Leyb Koniuchowsky, 'Der umkum fun martsinkantser yidn', *Yibl* 37 (1953): 222–4.

43. Mendel Mann, 'Der oyfshtand in tutshiner geto', *Fun letstn khurbn* 9 (September 1948); 59–66.

44. cf. Donat, *The Holocaust Kingdom*, pp. 111–12.

45. Original Yiddish text published in Mark, ed., *Oyfshtand in var-*

shever geto: naye dergentste oyflage un dokumentn-zamlung (1963), pp. 197–200. An English translation in Dawidowicz, *Holocaust Reader*.

46. 'Oyfrufn', *Blfg* 4 (January–March 1951): 83–4.

47. Hersh Berlinski, 'Zikhroynes', *Dray*, pp. 188–91.

48. Text in Bernard Mark, 'Aneks 3: Statut Żydowskiej Organizacji Bojowej', *BŻIH* 39 (July–September 1961): 61–2. An English translation in Dawidowicz, *Holocaust Reader*.

49. Chana Krystal-Fryshdorf, 'Iberlebungen beysn oyfshtand', *Undzer tsayt*, April–May 1949, pp. 17–18; Y. Zuckerman, 'Powstanie i rozwój Ż.O.B.'

50. Chana Krystal-Fryshdorf, 'Iberlebungen in geto-oyfshtand', *Undzer tsayt*, April–May 1958, pp. 22–3.

51. Y-A, coded radio message No. 15, sent from Warsaw on 21 January 1943. The message was addressed to Stephen Wise of the American Jewish Congress, Nahum Goldmann of the World Jewish Congress, and George Backer, then of the AJDC.

52. Y-A, coded radio message No. 59, sent from Warsaw on 7 February 1943, by Leon Feiner (Berezowski) and Mauricy Orzech (Janczyn). The cryptic remarks about the January armed defense were not understood. On 10 February Zygelboym, via radio, asked for further information, which Feiner provided in a later radio message.

53. Zuckerman, 'Powstanie i rozwój Ż.O.B.'

54. The leaflet issued to counteract Többens's appeals was printed on a mimeograph machine brought at great risk from the brush works area of the ghetto. For an account of that transfer and the attempt to return it, see Krystal-Fryshdorf, *Undzer tsayt*, April–May 1949, pp. 19–20.

55. Zuckerman, 'Powstanie i rozwój Ż.O.B.'

56. Y-A, coded radiograms No. 67, sent from Warsaw on 6 April 1943, by ŻKN to the Zionist Executive in London and Jerusalem; No. 67a, sent by David Guzik of the JDC in Warsaw to JDC in New York; No. 67d, to Dr Schwartzbart in London, Dr Silberstein of Vaad Hatzala in Geneva, and M. Neustadt in Tel Aviv, signed by Zionist party leaders in Warsaw; No. 70, submitted on 13 April 1943, by Feiner and dispatched on 17 April 1943, to Zygelboym in London.

57. The following account of the defense of the Warsaw ghetto is based on Zuckerman, 'Powstanie i rozwój Ż.O.B.', ŻOB/ŻKK daily communiqués and situation reports, in 'Getto w Walce', *Przełom*, No.17, 19 April 1948 (excerpts in English in Philip Friedman, *Martyrs and Fighters*, New York, 1954); Y-A, coded radio messages sent by ŻKK to London; reports of individual participants – Sholem Grajek, Simha

Rathauser, Toviah Borzykowski – in Neustadt, *Khurbn un oyfshtand*, pp. 264–92.

58. Zivia Lubetkin Zuckerman, testimony at the Eichmann trial, quoted in Gideon Hausner, *Justice in Jerusalem* (New York, 1966), p. 223.

59. Y-A, Abraham Hersh, eye-witness report.

60. The text of the appeal was written by Samsonowicz, a Bund activist on the 'Aryan' side, on behalf of ŻKK and ŻOB. An English translation in Dawidowicz, *Holocaust Reader*. Cf. Meed, *On Both Sides of the Wall*, p. 183.

61. cf. Stefan Krakowski, 'Stosunek sił w powstaniu w getcie warszawskim', *BŻIII* 62 (1967): 23–41. Stroop's report very likely understated, for professional and ideological reasons, the number of troops involved.

62. Ziviah Lubetkin, 'The Last Days of the Warsaw Ghetto', *Commentary* 3 (May 1947): 401–11.

63. Y-A, Report A, 22 June 1943, and Report B, 15 November 1943, sent by Leon Feiner, on behalf of the Central Committee of the Bund in Poland to the Bund representative in the Polish parliament-in-exile in London. Original in Polish; a Yiddish translation of most of the document in: Jewish Labour Bund, *In di yorn fun yidishn khurbn*. Also, Y-A, 'Sprawozdanie z działalności Rady Pomocy Żydom', 23 October 1943. An English translation is in Władysław Bartoszewski and Sofia Lewin, eds., *Righteous Among the Nations: How Poles Helped the Jews, 1939–1945* (London, 1969), a complacently tendentious and self-serving work.

64. Y-A, report, in the original Polish, of the ŻKN, sent from Warsaw on 24 May 1944, signed by Dr A. Berman [Borowski], Yitzhak Zuckerman [Antek] and three others. An English translation in World Jewish Congress, *Extermination of Polish Jewry: Reports Based on Official Documents*.

16. JEWISH BEHAVIOUR IN CRISIS AND EXTREMITY

1. cf. Rabbi Yehoshua Moshe Aaronson, 'The Story of the House of Bondage in Konin', in *Extermination and Resistance*, pp. 110–16.

2. cf. Jacob Katz, *Exclusiveness and Tolerance: Studies in Jewish-Gentile Relations in Medieval and Modern Times* (Oxford, 1961), especially pp. 86–7; Rabbi Nathan Hanover, *Abyss of Despair (Yeven Metzulah)*, trans. Abraham J. Mesch (New York, 1950).

Raul Hilberg, whose knowledge of Jewish history is not equal to his rashness in generalizing about it, has flawed his otherwise valuable work with uninformed comments and distorted conclusions about Jewish behaviour, especially on pp. 662–9, but also elsewhere (e.g., pp. 145–6, 154–6, 206–8, 315–22, 328–9). His deficiency in Jewish history is especially evident on pp. 145–6, his description of what he presumes were the kehilla's functions.

3. See Robert Stover, 'Responsibility for the Cold War – A Case Study in Historical Responsibility', *History and Theory* 11 (1972): 145–78. This excellent article clarifies and isolates the elements of historical responsibility.

4. Bruce Aune, 'Can', *The Encylopedia of Philosophy*, quoted in Stover, 'Responsibility for the Cold War', p. 153.

5. Abba Kovner, 'The Miracle Born of Despair', in Hashomer Hatzair, *The Massacre of European Jewry*, p 225; Z. Levinbook, 'Umkum fun baranovitsher yidntum', in *Baranovitsh: sefer zikaron*, p. 571; Alexander Dallin, *German Rule in Russia*, p. 427.

6. For more on collaboration, see Robert Aron, *The Vichy Regime 1940–44* (Boston, 1969), passim; Stanley Hoffmann, 'Collaborationism in France during World War II', *The Journal of Modern History* 40 (September 1968): 375–95; John A. Armstrong, 'Collaborationism in World War II: The Integral Nationalist Variant in Eastern Europe', *The Journal of Modern History* 40 (September 1968): 396–410.

7. The most egregious example is Hannah Arendt, *Eichmann in Jerusalem*, in which she flatly states: 'Wherever Jews lived, there were recognized Jewish leaders, and this leadership, almost without exception, cooperated in one way or another, for one reason or another [*sic*], with the Nazis' (p. 125). Miss Arendt's penchant for grand philosophic schemata flourishes on her disdain for historical evidence. One would have expected, nevertheless, that the expert on totalitarian terror in its philosophic aspect would have recognized the phenomenon of totalitarian terror in its historical reality.

8. cf. Louis de Jong, 'The Netherlands and Auschwitz', *YVS* 7:39–55. Jong's conclusive findings about disbelief in and rejection of the information of the death camps and the failure of the Dutch underground to inform the Jewish Council has nevertheless not halted him and others from accusing the leaders of the Jewish Council of 'collaboration' with the Germans.

9. Leo Baeck, 'A People Stands Before Its God', in Boehm, ed., *We Survived*, p. 293.

10. Jan Yoors, *Crossing* (New York, 1971), passim.

11. cf. Z. Kalmanovich, 'A Diary of the Nazi Ghetto in Vilna', *YiAn* 8:33.

12. Benedikt Kautsky, *Teufel und Verdammte* (Zurich, 1946), pp. 292–4.

Sources

It would be impracticable and immodest to attempt to present a full bibliography of the Final Solution and the Holocaust. The general reader interested in pursuing these subjects can obtain useful bibliographies from the Jewish Book Council of America (15 East 26th Street, New York, N.Y. 10010) or from the Anti-Defamation League of B'nai B'rith (315 Lexington Avenue, New York, N.Y. 10016). A magisterial bibliographical work is the Bibliographical Series issued jointly by the Yad Washem Martyrs' and Heroes' Memorial Authority in Jerusalem and the YIVO Institute for Jewish Research in New York. Since the publication in 1960 of the first volume, *Guide to Jewish History Under Nazi Impact*, edited by Jacob Robinson and Philip Friedman, eleven more volumes have appeared: four devoted to writings in Yiddish, five to Hebrew works and one to the Hungarian Jewish catastrophe. The latest volume (1973) is *The Holocaust and After: Sources and Literature in English*, edited by Jacob Robinson with the assistance of Mrs Philip Friedman.

The German documents captured by the Allied armies at the war's end have provided an incomparable historical record, which, with regard to volume and accessibility, has been unique in the annals of scholarship. The very volume of the documents has posed unprecedented problems, for no individual can in his lifetime possibly master these sources. The National Archives and the American Historical Association jointly have published sixty-seven volumes of *Guides to German Records Microfilmed at Alexandria, Va.* For my work I have limited myself mainly to published German documents. The most important series of these publications are:

International Military Tribunal. *Trial of the Major War Criminals Before the International Military Tribunal: Official Text.* 42 vols. Nuremberg, 1947–9. (Blue series)

Nuernberg Military Tribunals. *Trials of War Criminals Before the Nuernberg Military Tribunals Under Control Council Law No. 10.* 15 vols. Washington, D.C., 1949–53. (Green series)

Office of the United States Chief of Counsel for the Prosecution of Axis

Criminality. *Nazi Conspiracy and Aggression*. 11 vols. Washington, D.C., 1946–8. (Red series)

United Nations War Crimes Commission. *Law Reports of Trials of War Criminals*. 15 vols. London, 1947–9.

Documents on German Foreign Policy 1918–1945. Series C, 1933–7, 5 vols.; Series D, 1937–41, 13 vols. Washington, D.C. 1957–67.

Blumenthal, Nachman, Borwicz, Michal, Friedman, Filip, eds. *Dokumenty i Materiały*. 3 vols. Lodz, 1946.

In writing about the Holocaust, I had access to several archival collections; the most important were at the YIVO Institute for Jewish Research, New York. Among these were the Sutzkever-Kaczerginski Collection on the Vilna ghetto; the Wasser Collection, largely, but not exclusively, on the Warsaw ghetto; and the Zonaband Collection on the Lodz ghetto. The Archives of the American Jewish Joint Distribution Committee and the Franz Kursky Archives of the Jewish Labour Bund provided me with extremely valuable documentation. For more circumscribed topics I used unpublished materials at the Zionist Archives, the Leo Baeck Institute, and the Records Center of the American Jewish Committee, all in New York.

The spate of *yizkor* books, unique commemorative collections in Yiddish and/or Hebrew devoted to individual communities, renders the researcher's task even more laborious in separating the documentary wheat from the epitaphic chaff. The flow of memoirs, too, forces the researcher into a rigorous process of selection. I have limited the following list of sources to those published works that I regard as most useful. In the interest of brevity I have listed only a few basic sources for both appendixes. A complete listing of the mass of articles and studies for each country would be disproportionate to the text and too specialized for most readers.

I have excluded all periodical and serial articles from the list of sources, though many appear in the notes. Several periodicals and serials, frequently cited in the notes, should be mentioned here because they are fundamental documentary sources.

American Jewish Year Book, published by the American Jewish Committee, 1899–date.

Biuletyn Żydowskiego Instytutu Historycznego, published quarterly by the Żydowski Instytut Historyczny w Polsce, Warsaw, 1950–date.

Bleter far geshikhte, published quarterly, now irregularly, by the Żydowski Instytut Historyczny w Polsce, Warsaw, 1948–date.

Fun letstn khurbn, published by the Central Historical Commission of the Central Committee of the Liberated Jews in the US Zone, Munich, 10 issues, 1946–8.

Vierteljahrshefte für Zeitgeschichte, published quarterly by the Institut für Zeitgeschichte, Munich, 1953–date.

Yad Washem Studies on the European Jewish Catastrophe and Resistance, published irregularly by the Yad Washem Remembrance Authority, Jerusalem, 1957–date.

Year Book, published by the Leo Baeck, Institute, London, Jerusalem and New York, 1956–date.

YIVO Annual of Jewish Social Science, published by the YIVO Institute for Jewish Research, New York, 1946–date.

Yivo-bleter, published irregularly by the YIVO Institute for Jewish Research, New York, 1931–date.

PART I: THE FINAL SOLUTION

Abel, Theodore. *The Nazi Movement: Why Hitler Came to Power.* New York, 1966.

Allen, William Sheridan. *The Nazi Seizure of Power: The Experience of a Single German Town 1930–1935.* Chicago, 1965.

Arendt, Hannah. *Eichmann in Jerusalem: A Report on the Banality of Evil.* Rev. and enl. ed. New York, 1965.
    The Origins of Totalitarianism. New York, 1958.

Aronson, Shlomo. *Reinhard Heydrich und die Frühgeschichte von Gestapo und SD.* Stuttgart, 1971.

Baynes, Norman H., ed. *The Speeches of Adolf Hitler, April 1922–August 1939.* 2 vols. London, 1942.

Beek, Gottfried zur (Ludwig Müller). *Die Geheimnisse der Weisen von Zion.* 5th ed. Berlin, 1920.

Berenstein, T., Eisenbach, A., Rutkowski, A., eds. *Eksterminacja Żydów na Ziemiach Polskich w Okresie Okupacji Hitlerowskiej: Zbiór Dokumentów.* Warsaw, 1957.

Best, Werner. *Die deutsche Polizei.* Darmstadt, 1941.

Bidess, Michael D. *Father of Racist Ideology: The Social and Political Thought of Count Gobineau,* New York, 1970.
    ed. *Gobineau: Selected Political Writings.* London, 1970.

Blau, Bruno. *Das Ausnahmerecht für die Juden in Deutschland 1933–1945.* 2nd ed. Dusseldorf, 1954.

Boehlich, Walter, ed. *Der Berliner Antisemitismusstreit.* Frankfurt, 1965.

Boelcke, Willi A., ed. *The Secret Conferences of Dr. Goebbels: The Nazi Propaganda War 1939–1943*. New York, 1970.

Bracher, Karl Dietrich. *The German Dictatorship: The Origins, Structure, and Effects of National Socialism*. New York, 1970; Penguin, 1973.

Bracher, Karl Dietrich, Sauer, Wolfgang, and Schulz, Gerhard. *Die nationalsozialistische Machtergreifung*. 2nd ed. Cologne, 1962.

Briffault, Herma, ed. *The Memoirs of Doctor Felix Kersten*. New York, 1947.

Broszat, Martin, *Nationalsozialistische Polenpolitik 1939–1945*. Stuttgart, 1961.

　　ed. *Studien zur Geschichte der Konzentrationslager*. Stuttgart, 1970.

Buchheim, Hans, et al., *Anatomy of the SS State*. New York, 1968. (*Anatomie des SS-Staates*. 2 vols. Olten und Freiburg im Bresigau, 1965.)

Bullock, Alan, *Hitler, A Study in Tyranny*. Rev. ed. New York, 1964; Penguin, 1962.

Cecil, Robert. *The Myth of the Master Race: Alfred Rosenberg and Nazi Ideology*. London, 1972.

Central Commission for Investigation of German Crimes in Poland. *German Crimes in Poland*. 2 vols. Warsaw, 1946–7.

Churchill, Winston. *The Gathering Storm*. New York, 1948.

Cohen, Elie A. *Human Behaviour in the Concentration Camp*. New York, 1953.

Cohn, Norman. *Warrant for Genocide: The Myth of the Jewish World-conspiracy and the Protocols of the Elders of Zion*. New York, 1967.

Council for Protection of Fight and Martyrdom Monuments. *Treblinka*, Warsaw, n.d.

Crankshaw, Edward. *The Gestapo: Instrument of Tyranny*. New York, 1956.

Dahrendorf, Ralf. *Society and Democracy in Germany*. New York, 1967.

Daim, Wilfried, *Der Mann, der Hitler die Ideen gab: Von den religiosen Verirrungen eines Sektierers zum Rassenwahn des Diktators*. Munich, 1958.

Dallin, Alexander. *German Rule in Russia, 1941–1945: A Study of Occupation Policies*. New York, 1957.

Delarue, Jacques. *The Gestapo: A History of Horror*. New York, 1964.

Dicks, Henry V. *Licensed Mass Murder: A Socio-psychological Study of Some SS Killers*. London, 1972.

Dokumente der deutschen Politik und Geschichte. 4 vols. Berlin, n.d.

Domarus, Max, ed. *Hitler: Reden und Proklamationen, 1932–1945*. 2 vols. Würzburg, 1962.

Eisenbach, Artur. *Operation Reinhard: Mass Extermination of the Jewish Population in Poland*. Poznan, 1962.

Epstein, Klaus. *The Genesis of German Conservatism*. Princeton, N.J., 1966.

Fest, Joachim C. *The Face of the Third Reich: Portraits of the Nazi Leadership*. New York, 1970.

Frick, Wilhelm. *Die Nationalsozialisten im Reichstag 1924–1931*. 2nd enl. ed. Munich, 1932.

Frick, Wilhelm, and Gütt, Arthur. *Nordisches Gedankengut im Dritten Reich: Drei Vorträge*. Munich (1936).

Friedländer, Saul. *Kurt Gerstein: The Ambiguity of Good*. New York, 1969.

Fritsch, Theodor. *Handbuch der Judenfrage: Die wichtigsten Tatsachen zur Beurteilung des jüdischen Volkes*. 53rd ed. Leipzig, 1933.

Fromm, Bella. *Blood and Banquets: A Berlin Social Diary*, New York, 1944.

Fryman, Daniel (Class, Heinrich). *Wenn ich der Kaiser wär': Politische Wahrheiten und Notwendigkeiten*. 5th enl. ed. Leipzig, 1914.

Gay, Peter. *Weimar Culture: The Outsider as Insider*. New York, 1968.

Genschel, Helmut. *Die Verdrängung der Juden aus der Wirtschaft im Dritten Reich*. Göttingen, 1966.

Goerlitz, Walter. *History of the German General Staff 1657–1945*. New York, 1953.

Gordon, Harold J., Jr. *Hitler and the Beer Hall Putsch*. Princeton, N.J., 1972.

Görlitz, Walter, ed. *The Memoirs of Field-Marshal Keitel*. New York, 1966.

Graml, Hermann. *Der 9. November 1938: "Reichskristallnacht"*. 3rd ed. Bonn, 1955.

Grossman, W. *Die Hölle von Treblinka*. Moscow, 1946.

Halder, Generaloberst (Franz). *Kreigstagebuch 1939–1942*. Edited by Hans-Adolf Jacobsen. Stuttgart, 1962–4.

Heiber, Helmut, ed. *Reichsführer! . . .: Briefe an und von Himmler*. Stuttgart, 1968.

Heiden, Konrad. *Der Fuehrer: Hitler's Rise to Power*. Boston, 1969.
    A History of National Socialism. New York, 1935.

Henkys, Reinhard. *Die nationalsozialistischen Gewaltverbrechen: Geschichte und Gericht*. Stuttgart, 1964.

Hilberg, Raul. *The Destruction of the European Jews*. Chicago, 1967.
    Documents of Destruction: Germany and Jewry 1933–1945. Chicago, 1971.

Hillgruber, Andreas. *Hitlers Strategie: Politik und Kriegsführung 1940–1941*. Frankfurt, 1965.

Himmler, Heinrich. *Die Schutztaffel als antibolschewistische Kampforganisation*. Munich, 1936.

Hitler, Adolf. *Mein Kampf*. Translated by Ralph Manheim. Boston, 1943.

Hitler's Secret Book. Introduction by Telford Taylor. New York, 1961.

Hitler's Secret Conversations 1941–1944. Introduction by H. R. Trevor-Roper. New York, 1953.

Hoche, Werner, ed. *Die Gesetzgebung Adolf Hitlers*. 33 vols. Berlin, 1933–9.

Hoess, Rudolf. *Commandant of Auschwitz: The Autobiography of Rudolf Hoess*. Cleveland and New York, 1960.

Höhne, Heinz. *The Order of the Death's Head: The Story of Hitler's SS*. New York, 1970.

Die Hölle von Maidanek: Bericht der ausserordentlichen polnisch-sowjetischen Kommission zur Untersuchung der von den Deutschen im Vernichtungslager Maidanek in der Stadt Lublin begangenen Verbrechen. Zurich, 1945.

Hull, David Stewart. *Film in the Third Reich: A Study of the German Cinema 1933–1945*. Berkeley, Cal., 1969.

Jäckel, Eberhard. *Hitler's Weltanschauung: A Blueprint for Power*. Middletown, Conn., 1972.

Jacobsen, Hans-Adolf. *Nationalsozialistische Aussenpolitik 1933–1938*. Frankfurt, 1968.

Jenks, William A. *Vienna and the Young Hitler*, New York, 1960.

Kempner, Robert M. W., *Eichmann und Komplizen*. Zurich, 1961.

Kessel, Joseph. *The Man with the Miraculous Hands*. New York, 1961.

Kochan, Lionel. *Pogrom: 10 November 1938*. London, 1957.

Koehl, Robert. L. *RKFVD: German Resettlement and Population Policy 1939–1945*, Cambridge, Mass., 1957.

Kogon, Eugen. *The Theory and Practice of Hell: The Concentration Camps and the System Behind Them*. New York, [1950].

Kohn, Hans. *The Mind of Germany: The Education of a Nation*. New York, 1960.

Kommission zur Erforschung der Geschichte der Frankfurter Juden. *Dokumente zur Geschichte der Frankfurter Juden 1933–1945*. Frankfurt, 1963.

Kotze, Hildegard von, and Krausnick, Helmut. *Es spricht der Führer*. Gütersloh, 1966.

Kraus, Ota, and Kulka, Erich. *The Death Factory: Documents on Auschwitz*. Oxford and London, 1966.

Lamm, Hans. 'Über die innere und äussere Entwicklung des deutschen Judentums im Dritten Reich'. Doctoral disseration. Erlangen, 1951.

Langer, Walter C. *The Mind of Adolf Hitler: The Secret Wartime Report*. New York, 1972.

Laqueur, Walter. *Russia and Germany: A Century of Conflict*. Boston, 1967.

Lebovics, Herman. *Social Conservatism and the Middle Classes in Germany: 1914–1933*. Princeton, N.J., 1969.

Leschnitzer, Adolf. *The Magic Background of Modern Anti-Semitism: An Analysis of the German-Jewish Relationship*. New York, 1956.

Lochner, Louis P., ed. *The Goebbels Diaries 1942–1943*. New York, 1948.

Ludecke, Kurt. *I Knew Hitler: The Story of a Nazi Who Escaped the Blood Purge*. New York, 1937.

McRandle, James H. *The Track of the Wolf: Essays on National Socialism and Its Leader, Adolf Hitler*. Evanston, Ill., 1965.

Manvell, Roger, and Fraenkel, Heinrich. *Himmler*. New York, 1965.

Maser, Werner. *Hitler's Mein Kampf: An Analysis*. London, 1970.

Massing, Paul W. *Rehearsal for Destruction: A Study of Political Anti-Semitism in Imperial Germany*. New York, 1949.

Meinecke, Friedrich. *The German Catastrophe: Reflections and Recollections*. Boston, 1963.

Messerschmidt, Manfred. *Die Wehrmacht im NS-Staat: Zeit der Indoktrination*. Hamburg, 1969.

Mitscherlich, Alexander, and Mielke, Fred. *Doctors of Infamy: The Story of the Nazi Medical Crimes*. New York, 1949.

Mosse, George L. *The Crisis of German Ideology: Intellectual Origins of the Third Reich*. New York, 1964.

Naumann, Bernd. *Auschwitz: A Report on the Proceedings Against Robert Karl Ludwig Mulka and Others Before the Court at Frankfurt*. London, 1966.

Neumann, Franz. *Behemoth: The Structure and Practice of National Socialism 1933–1944*. New York, 1944.

Neusüss-Hunkel, Ermenhild. *Die SS*. Hanover, 1956.

Nicolai, Helmut. *Die rassengesetzliche Staatslehre: Grundzüge einer nationalsozialistischen Rechtsphilosophie*. Munich, 1932.

　　Rasse und Recht: Vortrag gehalten auf dem deutschen Juristentage des Bundes nationalsozialistischer deutscher Juristen am 2 October 1933 in Leipzig. Berlin, 1933.

Niewyk, Donald L. *Socialist, Anti-Semite, and Jew: German Social*

Democracy Confronts the Problem of Anti-Semitism 1918–1933. Baton Rouge, 1971.

Nolte, Ernst. *The Three Faces of Fascism: Action Française, Italian Fascism, and National Socialism*. New York, 1966.

Norton, Donald Hawley. 'Karl Haushofer and His Influence on Nazi Ideology and German Foreign Policy, 1919–1945'. Doctoral dissertation. Clark University, 1965.

Olden, Rudolf. *Hitler*. Amsterdam, 1935.

O'Neill, Robert J. *The Germany Army and the Nazi Party, 1933–1939*. New York, 1966.

Orlow, Dietrich. *A History of the Nazi Party 1919–1933*. Pittsburgh, Pa., 1969.

Pfundter, Hans, ed. *Dr. Wilhelm Frick und sein Ministerium: Aus Anlass des 60. Geburtstage des Reichs- und preussischen Ministers der Innern, Dr. Wilhelm Frick am 12. März 1937*. Berlin, 1937.

Pinson, Koppel S., ed. *Essays on Antisemitism*. 2nd rev. and enl. ed., New York, 1946.

Piotrowski, Stanislaw, ed. *Hans Frank's Diary*. Warsaw, 1961.

Pulzer, Peter G. J. *The Rise of Political Anti-Semitism in Germany and Austria*. New York, 1964.

Rauschning, Hermann. *Hitler Speaks: A Series of Political Conversations with Adolf Hitler on His Real Aims*. London, 1939.
    The Revolution of Nihilism: Warning to the West. New York, 1939.
    The Voice of Destruction. New York, 1940.

Reck-Malleczewen, Friedrich Percyval. *Diary of a Man in Despair*. New York, 1970.

Reichmann, Eva G. *Hostages of Civilisation: The Social Sources of National Socialist Anti-Semitism*. Boston, 1951.

Reitlinger, Gerald. *The Final Solution: The Attempt to Exterminate The Jews of Europe*. 2nd rev. and enl. ed., New York, 1961.
    The SS: Alibi of a Nation 1922–1945. London, 1956.

Reventlow, Ernst. *Judas Kampf und Niederlage in Deutschland: 150 Jahre Judenfrage*. Berlin, 1937.

Ringer, Fritz K. *The Decline of the German Mandarins: The German Academic Community, 1890–1933*. Cambridge, Mass., 1968.

Robertson, E. M. *Hitler's Pre-War Policy and Military Plans 1933–1939*. New York, 1967.

Rogger, Hans, and Weber, Eugen, eds. *The European Right: A Historical Profile*. Berkeley, Cal., 1965.

Rosenberg, Alfred. *Der Zukunftsweg einer deutschen Aussenpolitik*. Munich, 1927.

Schellenberg, Walter. *The Schellenberg Memoirs*. London, 1957.

Schleunes, Karl A. *The Twisted Road to Auschwitz: Nazi Policy Toward German Jews 1933–1939*. Urbana, Ill., 1970.

Schnabel, Reimund, *Macht ohne Moral: Eine Dokumentation über die SS*. Frankfurt, 1957.

Schubert, Günter. *Anfänge nationalsozialistischer Aussenpolitik*. Cologne, 1963.

Seabury, Paul. *The Wilhelmstrasse: A Study of German Diplomats Under the Nazi Regime*. Berkeley and Los Angeles, Cal., 1954.

Smith, Bradley F. *Adolf Hitler: His Family, Childhood, and Youth*. Stanford, Cal., 1967.
   Heinrich Himmler: A Nazi in the Making 1900–1926. Stanford, Cal., 1971.

Sontag, Raymond James, and Beddie, James Stuart. *Nazi–Soviet Relations: 1939–1941*. New York, 1948.

Stein, George H. *The Waffen SS*. Ithaca, N.Y., 1966.

Sterling, Eleanore. *Judenhass: Die Anfänge des politischen Antisemitismus in Deutschland (1815–1850)*. Frankfurt, 1969. (Rev. ed. of *Er ist wie du*, Munich, 1956).

Stern, Fritz. *The Politics of Cultural Despair: A Study in the Rise of the Germanic Ideology*. Berkeley and Los Angeles, Cal., 1961.

Stuckart, Wilhelm and Globke, Hans. *Kommentare zur deutschen Rassengesetzgebung*. Munich and Berlin, 1936.

Tal, Uriel. *Religious and Anti-religious Roots of Modern Anti-Semitism*. New York, 1971.

Taylor, Telford. *Sword and Swastika: Generals and Nazis in the Third Reich*. New York, 1952.

Trevor-Roper, H. R. *The Last Days of Hitler*. New York, 1947.
   ed. *Hitler's War Directives 1939–1945*. London, 1964.

Warlimont, Walter. *Inside Hitler's Headquarters 1939–1945*. New York, 1964.

Weinberg, Gerhard L. *The Foreign Policy of Hitler's Germany: Diplomatic Revolution in Europe 1933–36*. Chicago, 1971.

Weinryb, Bernard Dov. *Jewish Emancipation Under Attack: Legal Recession Until the Present War*. New York, 1942.

Weizsäcker, Ernst von. *Memoirs of Ernst von Weizsäcker*. London, 1951.

Wheaton, Eliot Barculo. *The Nazi Revolution 1933–1935: Prelude to Calamity*. New York, 1969.

Wormser-Migot, Olga. *Le Système concentrationnaire Nazi (1933–1945)*. Paris, 1968.

PART II: THE HOLOCAUST

Adler, H. G. *The Jews in Germany: From the Enlightenment to National Socialism*. Notre Dame, Ind., 1969.

Adler-Rudel, S. *Ostjuden in Deutschland 1880–1940*. Tübingen, 1959.

Apfelbaum, Emil, ed. *Maladie de famine: recherches cliniques sur la famine exécutées dans le ghetto de Varsovie en 1942*. Warsaw, 1946.

Auerbach, Rachela. *Der yidisher oyfshtand: Varshe 1943*. Warsaw, 1948.

Avtichi, Aryeh, ed. *Rovne: sefer zikaron*. Tel Aviv, 1956.

Bakalchuk-Felin, Melech, ed. *Yizhor-bukh Khelem*. Johannesburg, 1954.

Balberyszski, M. *Shtarker fun ayzn*. Tel Aviv, 1967.

Baler, Bezalel, ed. *Pinkes Kovel*. Buenos Aires, 1951.

Ball-Kaduri, Kurt Jakob. *Das Leben der Juden in Deutschland im Jahre 1933: Ein Zeitbild*. Frankfurt, 1963.

    Vor der Katastrophe: Juden in Deutschland. Tel Aviv, 1967.

Baranovitsh: sefer zikaron. Tel Aviv, 1953.

Bauminger, Aryeh, Bossak, Meir, Gelber, N. M., eds. *Sefer Kroke*. Jerusalem, 1959.

Berg, Mary. *Warsaw Ghetto: A Diary*. New York, 1945.

Bickel, Shlomo, ed. *Pinkes Kolomey: geshikhte, zikhroynes, geshtaltn, khurbn*. New York, 1957.

Blum, Abrasha, ed. *Di parizer komune: zamlbukh dershinen in 1941 in varshever geto*. Warsaw, 1948.

Blumenthal, Nachman, ed. *Aleksander*. Tel Aviv, 1968.

    Darko shel yudenrat: teudot migeto byalistok. Jerusalem, 1962.

    Teudot migeto lublin. Jerusalem, 1967.

Bochner, Mordecai. *Sefer khzhanov: lebn un umkum fun a yidish shtetl*. Munich and Regensburg, 1949.

Borzykowski, Tuvia. *Between Tumbling Walls*. Beit Lohamei Hagetaot, Israel, 1972.

    Tsvishn falndike vent. Warsaw, 1949.

Braun, Zvi A., and Levin, Dov. *Toledoteha shel mahteret: He-Irgun haloham shel yehudei Kovno bemilhamet ha-olam hashinaya*. Jerusalem, 1962.

Brenner, L. *Vidershtand un umkum in tshenstokhover geto*. [Warsaw, 1941.]

Buber, Martin. *Die Stunde und die Erkenntnis: Reden und Aufsätze 1933–1945*. Berlin, 1936.

Celemenski, Jacob. *Mitn farshnitenem folk*. New York, 1963.

Colodner, Solomon. *Jewish Education in Germany Under the Nazis*. New York, 1964.

Conference on Manifestations of Jewish Resistance. *Jewish Resistance During the Holocaust: Proceedings*. Jerusalem, 1971.

Czerniaków, Adam. *Yoman geto varsha: 6.9. 1939–23.7.1942.* Jerusalem. 1968.

Dąbrowska, Danuta, and Dobroszycki, Lucjan. *Kronika getta łódzkiego.* Vol. 1: January 1941–May 1942. Lodz, 1965.

Dappim leheker hashoa vehamered. Part 1. Tel Aviv, 1947.

Dawidsohn-Draengerowa, Gusta. *Pamiętnik Justyny.* Cracow, 1946.

Donat, Alexander. *The Holocaust Kingdom.* New York, 1965.

Dray – Ondenkbukh: Pole Elster, Hersh Berlinski, Eliyohu Erlich. Tel Aviv, 1966.

3 Jahre Zionistische Bewegung in Deutschland. Sonderdruck des Berichtes der Zionistische Vereinigung für Deutschland an den XXV Delegierntag. Berlin, 1936.

Dworzecki, M. *Yerushelayim delite im kamf un umkum.* Paris, 1948.

Eck, Nathan. *Hatoim bedarke hamavet.* Jerusalem, 1960.

Edelman, Marek, *The Ghetto Fights.* New York, 1946.

Extermination and Resistance: Historical Records and Source Material. Vol. 1. Kibbutz Lohamei Haghettaot, Israel. 1958.

Falstein, Louis, ed. *The Martyrdom of Jewish Physicians in Poland.* New York, 1963.

Frank, Shlomo. *Togbukh fun lodzher geto.* Buenos Aires, 1958.

Freeden, Herbert. *Jüdisches Theater in Nazideutschland.* Tübingen, 1964.

Freier, Recha. *Let the Children Come: The Early History of Youth Aliyah.* London, 1961.

Gar, Joseph. *Umkum fun der yidisher kovne.* Munich, 1948.

Garfunkel, L. *Kovno hayehudit behurbana.* Jerusalem, 1959.

Geto in flamen: zamlbukh. New York, 1944.

Goldstein, Bernard. *Finf yor in varshever geto.* New York, 1947.
    The Stars Bear Witness. New York, 1949.

Grossman, Chayke. *Anshe hamahteret.* Israel, 1950.

Grossman, Mendel. *With a Camera in the Ghetto.* Ghetto Fighters' House, Israel, 1970.

Hashomer Hatzair. *The Massacre of European Jewry: An Anthology.* Israel. 1963.

Huberband, Simeon. *Kiddush ha-shem: ktavim miyome hashao.* Tel Aviv, 1969.

Jasni, A. Wolf. *Di geshikhte fun yidn in lodzh: in di yorn fun der daytsher yidn-oysrotung.* 2 vols. Tel Aviv, 1960, 1966.
    ed. *Sefer Klobutsk: Yizkor-bukh fun der farpaynikter klobutsker kehile.* Tel Aviv, 1960.

Jewish Labour Bund. *In di yorn fun yidishn khurbn: di shtim fun unterer-dishn bund.* New York, 1948.

Kaczerginski, S. *Khurbn vilne: Umkum fun di yidn in vilne un vilner gegnt.*
New York, 1947.
    Partizaner geyen! 2nd enl. ed. Bamberg, 1948.
    ed. *Dosgezang fun vilner geto.* Paris, 1947.
    ed. *Lider fun getos un lagern.* New York, 1948.

Kaganovich, Moshe. *Der onteyl fun yidn in der partizaner bavegung in
Sovyet-Rusland.* Rome and New York, 1948.

Kantorowicz, N. *Di yidishe vidershtand-bavegung in poyln beysn 2tn velt-
krig (1941–1945).* New York, 1967.

Kaplan, Chaim A. *Scroll of Agony.* New York, 1964.

Kaplan, Israel. *Dos folks-moyl in natsi-klem: reydenishn in geto un katset.*
Munich, 1949.

Karski, Jan. *Story of a Secret State.* Boston, 1944.

Kaufmann, Max. *Die Vernichtung der Juden Lettlands: Churbn Lettland.*
Munich, 1947.

Klin, David. *Mitn malekh-hamoves untern orem: mayne iberlebenishn in
poyln beys der natsi-okupatsye 1939–1945.* Tel Aviv, 1968.

Korczak, Janusz. *Selected Works.* Warsaw, 1967. (Published for the
National Science Foundation, Washington, D.C. and available from
the US Department of Commerce, Clearinghouse for Federal
Scientific and Technical Information, Springfield, Va. 22151.)

Kruk, Herman, *Togbukh fun vilner geto.* New York, 1961.

Landauer, Georg. *Der Zionismus im Wandel dreier Jahrzehnte.* Edited by
Max Kreutzberger. Tel Aviv, 1957.

Lewin, Isaac, ed. *Ele ezkra.* 7 vols. New York, 1956–1972.

Litai, Chaim Lazar. *Muranowska 7: The Warsaw Ghetto Rising.* Tel Aviv,
1968.

Litvin, M., and Lerman, M., eds. *Dos bukh fun lublin.* Paris, 1952.

Mark, Ber, ed. *Dokumentn un materyaln vegn oyfshtand in varshever geto.*
Warsaw, 1953.
    Khurves dertseyln: dos bukh fun gvure. Lodz, 1947.
    Der oyfshtand in bialystoker geto. Warsaw, 1950.
    Der oyfshtand in varshever geto. Warsaw, 1955.
    *Oyfshtand in varshever geto: naye dergentste oyflage un dokumentn-
zamlung.* Warsaw, 1963.

Meed (Miedzyrzecki), Wladka. *Fun beyde zaytn geto-moyer.* New York,
1948.
    On Both Sides of the Wall: Memoirs from the Warsaw Ghetto. Beit
Lohamei Hagettaot, 1972.

Meltzer, Shimshon, ed. *Sefer Horodenka.* Tel Aviv, 1963.

Menczer, Arie, ed. *Sefer Pshemishl.* Tel Aviv, 1964.

Mendelsohn, S. *The Polish Jews Behind the Nazi Ghetto Walls.* New York, 1942.

Michel; Henri. *The Shadow War: European Resistance 1939–1945.* New York, 1972.

Mosse, George L. *Germans and Jews: The Right, the Left, and the Search for a 'Third Force' in Pre-Nazi Germany.* New York, 1971.

Mosse, Werner E., and Paucker, Arnold, eds. *Entscheidungsjahr 1932: Zur Judenfrage in der Endphase der Weimarer Republik.* 2nd rev. and enl. ed. Tübingen, 1966.

Neustadt, Meilech. *Khurbn un oyfshstand fun di yidn in varshe: Eydesbleter un azkores.* 2 vols. Tel Aviv, 1948.

Olczak, Hanna. *Mister Doctor, The Life of Janusz Korczak.* London, 1965.

Opoczynski, Peretz. *Reportashn fun varshever geto.* Warsaw, 1954.

Oshry, Ephraim. *Khurbn lite.* New York, 1951.
    Sefer divrei Efraim. New York, 1949.
    Sheelot uteshuvot mimaamakim. 3 vols. New York, 1963–8.

Payn un gvure in dem yidishn over in likht fun der kegnvart. Lodz, 1947. (Reprinted from mimeographed original issued in Warsaw, July 1940.)

Perlow, Isaac, ed. *Sefer Radom.* Tel Aviv, 1961.

Poor, Harold L. *Kurt Tucholsky and the Ordeal of Germany 1914–1935.* New York, 1968.

Prinz, Joachim. *Wir Juden.* Berlin, 1934.

Reichmann, Eva, ed. *Festschrift zum 80. Geburtstag von Rabbiner Dr. Leo Baeck am 23. Mai 1953.* London, 1953.

Reisner, Raphael. *Der umkum fun bialystoker yidntum, 1939–1945.* Melbourne, 1948.

Ringelblum, Emanuel. *Ksovim fun geto.* 2 vols. 2nd rev. ed. Warsaw, 1963.
    Notes from the Warsaw Ghetto. New York, 1958.

Rothenberg, I., ed. *Dos yidishe Radom in khurves.* Stuttgart, 1948.

Rousset, David. *The Other Kingdom.* New York, 1947.

Rudashevski, Yitzhok. *The Diary of the Vilna Ghetto: June 1941–April 1943.* Ghetto Fighters' House, Israel [1972.]

Sabotka, H., ed. *Lomzhe: ir oyfkum un unterang.* New York, 1957.

Schindler, Peter. 'Responses of Hassidic Leaders and Hassidim During the Holocaust in Europe, 1939–1945, and a Correlation Between Such Responses and Selected Concepts in Hassidic Thought'. Doctoral dissertation, School of Education, New York University, 1972.

Schoeps, Hans Joachim. *Die letzten dreissig Jahre: Rückblicke.* Stuttgart, 1956.

Seidman, Hillel. *Togbukh fun varshever geto.* Buenos Aires, 1947.

Shoshkes, H. *Bleter fun a geto-tog-bukh.* New York, 1943.

Shtrachman, Nahum, ed. *Sefer Lutsk.* Tel Aviv, 1961.

Simon, Ernst. *Aufbau im Untergang: Jüdische Erwachsenenbildung im nationalsozialistischen Deutschland als geistiger Widerstand.* Tübingen, 1959.

Singer, S. D., ed. *Tshenstokhov.* New York, 1958.

Stein, A. S., ed., *Pinkes Bendin.* Tel Aviv, 1959.

Strauss, Herbert A., and Grossman, Kurt R. *Gegenwart im Rückblick: Festgabe für die jüdische Gemeinde zu Berlin 25 Jahre nach dem Neubeginn.* Heidelberg, 1970.

Sudarsky, Mendel, et al., eds. *Lite.* New York, 1951.

Sutzkever, Abram. *Lider fun geto.* New York, 1946.

Tabaksblatt, Israel. *Khurbn lodzh: 6 yor natsi-gehenem.* Buenos Aires, 1946.

Tenenbaum-Tamaroff, Mordecai. *Dappim min hadleka.* Tel Aviv, 1947.

Tramer, Hans, ed. *In zwei Welten: Siegfried Moses zum Fünfendsiebzigsten Geburtstag.* Tel Aviv, 1962.

Trunk, Isaiah, *Geshtaltn un gesheyenishn.* Buenos Aires, 1962.
    Judenrat: The Jewish Councils in Eastern Europe Under Nazi Occupation. New York, 1972.
    Lodzher geto. New York, 1962.

Turkow, Jonas. *Azoy iz es geven.* Buenos Aires, 1948.

Unger, Menashe. *Sefer kedoshim: rebeyim oyf kiddush-hashem.* New York, 1967.

Varshever geto-oyfshtand: 19ter April 1943–19ter April 1947. Landsberg, 1947.

Weichert, Michal. *Yidishe aleynhilf 1939–1945.* Tel Aviv, 1962.

Wille und Weg des deutschen Judentums. Berlin, 1935.

World Jewish Congress. *Extermination of Polish Jewry: Reports Based on Official Documents.* New York, July–August 1943.

Wulman, L. *In kamf farn gezunt fun yidishn folk (50 yor OSE).* New York, 1968.

Yad Washem. *Blackbook of Localities Whose Jewish Population Was Exterminated by the Nazis.* Jerusalem, 1965.

YIVO Colloquium. *Imposed Jewish Governing Bodies Under Nazi Rule.* New York, 1972.

Zygelboym, Artur Shmuel. *Zygelboym-bukh.* Edited by S. Hertz. New York, 1947.

Zylberberg, Michael. *A Warsaw Diary: 1939–1945.* London, 1969.

APPENDIX A THE FATE OF THE JEWS IN HITLER'S EUROPE: BY COUNTRY

Braham, Randolph. *The Destruction of Hungarian Jewry: A Documentary Account.* 2 vols. New York, 1963.

Centre de Documentation Juive Contemporaine. *Les Juifs en Europe (1939–1945): rapports présentés à la première conférence européenne des commissions historiques et des centres de documentation juifs.* Paris, 1949.

Chary, Frederick B. *The Bulgarian Jews and the Final Solution.* Pittsburgh, Pa., 1972.

Fried, John H. E. *Anti-Jewish Legislation in Europe and North Africa, Imposed or Inspired by National-Socialist Germany.* Nuremberg, 1947. (Mimeographed)

Knout, David. *Contribution à l'histoire de la résistance juive en France 1940–1944.* Paris, 1947.

Levy, Claude, and Tillard, Paul. *Betrayal at the Vel d'Hiv.* New York, 1969.

Meyer, Peter, et al. *The Jews in the Soviet Satellites.* Syracuse, N.Y., 1953.

Molho, Michal, ed. *In Memoriam: Hommage aux victimes juives des Nazis en Grèce.* 2 vols. Salonika, 1948–9.

Poliakov, Leon, and Sabille, Jacques. *Jews Under the Italian Occupation.* Paris, 1955.

Presser, Jacob. *The Destruction of the Dutch Jews.* New York, 1969.

Schwarz, Solomon M. *The Jews in the Soviet Union.* Syracuse, N.Y., 1951.

Toynbee, Arnold Joseph, and Toynbee, Veronica, eds. *Hitler's Europe.* London and New York, 1954.

Warmbrunn, Werner. *The Dutch Under German Occupation 1940–1945.* Stanford, Cal., 1963.

World Jewish Congress. *European Jewry Ten Years After the War: An Account of the Development and Present Status of the Decimated Jewish Communities of Europe.* New York, 1956.

Yahil, Leni. *The Rescue of Danish Jewry.* Philadelphia, 1969.

Index

More About Penguins
and Pelicans